The Celebrated Mary Astell

Women in Culture and Society
A series edited by Catharine R. Stimpson

The Celebrated
Mary Astell

An Early English Feminist

Ruth Perry

The University of Chicago Press

Chicago and London

Ruth Perry is director of women's studies at the Massachusetts Institute of Technology. She is the author of *Women, Letters, and the Novel;* the editor of George Ballard's *Memoirs of Several Ladies of Great Britain Celebrated for Their Skills in the Learned Language, Arts, and Sciences;* and the coeditor of *Mothering the Mind.*

The University of Chicago Press, Chicago 60637
The University of Chicago Press, Ltd., London
© 1986 by The University of Chicago
All rights reserved. Published 1986
Printed in the United States of America

95 94 93 92 91 90 89 88 87 86   54321

Library of Congress Cataloging-in-Publication Data
Perry, Ruth, 1943–
  The celebrated Mary Astell.

  (Women in culture and society)
  Includes index.
    1. Astell, Mary, 1666–1731.   2. Feminists—England—
  Biography.   3. Women's rights—England—History—18th
  century.   I. Title.   II. Series.
  HQ1595.A7P47 1986   305.4'2'0924 [B]   85–28922
  ISBN 0-226-66093-1
  ISBN 0-226-66095-8 (pbk.)

For Taylor

Contents

Illustrations

Foreword

Mary Astell was born in 1666, the daughter of a businessman and civic figure in the city of Newcastle-on-Tyne. In that year, Isaac Newton was developing calculus. Aphra Behn, whom many consider to be the first professional woman writer in English, was deciding to enter the intelligence service of King Charles II in order to earn her living. John Milton was waiting for the publication of *Paradise Lost*.

Mary Astell's life responded to the meaning and influence of these events. She believed in reason, in the mind's ability to comprehend the flux and forms of reality. Moreover, arguably the first systematic feminist theoretician in the West, she staunchly declared that women, too, were preeminently rational. They were, then, deserving of education. Famously, she designed original proposals for institutions that would cultivate women's reason. Yet, like Behn and other ambitious women of her age, she had to struggle against an ideology of gender that, at best, assigned sweet beauty, not supple brains, to Eve and her modest daughters.

Despite the reputation that Astell earned while she was alive, despite the significance of her career, historians have often refused to remember her, even in their footnotes. The last study of Astell appeared in 1916. Symbolically, various editions of the *Oxford Companion to English Literature* fail to mention her. Now, however, Ruth Perry has given Astell a monumental tribute. Combining new archival materials with a vibrant sense of history, Perry solidly proves how much Astell deserved her contemporary reputation; how significant her work was; how perverse historians' judgments have been.

Astell was courageous. Around 1688, a provincial girl, she left Newcastle for London, a tough, raucous, and corrupt urban center. Once there, she coped. She became the first English woman of letters. Among her weapons were intelligence; independence; hard work; fierce principles; and the companionship of other women. Marking her death, in

1731, of breast cancer, was the bravery that pain can stimulate for such warriors as Astell.

Nevertheless, this virtuous, visionary, and brilliant woman is also a problematic figure in and for feminist theory. A strength of Perry's biography is her willingness to confront the limits of Astell's ideological convictions and polemical strategies. Perry explains Astell, but Perry refuses to rationalize away the difficulties Astell embodies. She was a chaste woman. Her celibacy helped her to survive, but her legacy asserted that a rational woman might have to sever mind from body, and then repress the body in order to release the mind.

Astell was also conservative, loyal to her class and to established ecclesiastical and political authorities. She embodied a paradox that has often haunted feminists. Some may be radical about inequities of gender, but accept, and even praise, hierarchy and authority elsewhere. Their counterparts are the revolutionaries who are radical about almost all inequities, but accept, and even praise, gender hierarchies and male authority.

Yet, Astell's conservatism was complicated. If she accepted the political authority of the state, she resisted authority over women in domestic life. She advised women not to marry unless they could find a man into whose hands they could entrust their moral life. In this doubled resistance to the liberal thinkers of her day, whose democratic vision failed to include women, she made the first feminist critique of possessive individualism.

Astell lived to think, to write, to mend and tend and celebrate the mind and its conclusions about God, the state, and human nature. As Perry's biography shows, the life of a mind has drama, pith, adventure. Struggling to permit women's consciousness to flourish, Astell was at odds with a culture she also wished to serve. One wonders who she might have been if she had been born in 1866; if she could have inherited and refined her ideas rather than having to help create them. She might have been the founder or president of an actual women's college, an Emily Davies, or, if American, an M. Carey Thomas. She might have been a philosopher or scholar, a Jane Harrison, or, if American, an Elsie Clews Parsons.

A measure of biography is that it both invites such speculation and satisfies a sterner need for information. Perry's work is a study of a woman at work, an act of homage, and a cautionary tale that more than meets these measures. Austere, ardent, arduous, Mary Astell's life has, at last, found just representation.

CATHARINE R. STIMPSON

Acknowledgments

It is a real sorrow that the scholar whose encouragement and advice most strengthened my purpose and aided my task did not live long enough to read this book. James L. Clifford made me feel from the start that this project was worthy and that it was possible. From him I learned the pleasures of the biographical hunt and the importance of generosity within the scholarly community. Other skilled researchers who gave me direction at crucial points in the project are Terry Belanger, Arthur Cash, Howard Erskine-Hill, Ra Foxton, Isobel Grundy, Robert Halsband, Phyllis Horsley, Joanna Lipking, Sherry O'Donnell, Barbara Schnorrenberg, A. H. Scouton, and Barbara Wheaton. Dolores Hayden taught me to love libraries. Kathryn Crecelius, Irving Kaplan, Edwin McCann, Maurice Sagoff, Susan Staves, and William Youngren supplied me with much-needed information. Margaret Doody, Moira Ferguson, Morris Golden, Christopher Hill, Margaret C. Jacob, and Beatrice Scott were kind enough to read earlier drafts and to give me the benefit of their advice.

I am grateful to His Grace the Duke of Beaufort, Lord Harrowby, and G. H. H. Wheler for putting their family papers at my disposal and for allowing me to print excerpts from them. Librarians and archivists on both sides of the Atlantic have proved consistently helpful and patient: in the Bodleian, the British Library, the archives of the SPCK, and the rare-book collections of Harvard University. In particular I want to acknowledge the assistance of Miss Margaret McCollum and Mrs. J. L. Drury, Assistant Keepers of the Department of Palaeography and Diplomatic at the University of Durham; M. J. Denny and the late R. Mc D. Winder of Hoare's Bank in London; Kenneth Carpenter, past Director of the Kress Library, Harvard University; and Rodney Dennis and Hugh Amory of the Houghton Library, Harvard University. To the more than fifty librarians who answered my request for bibliographical information about their holdings on Mary Astell, I also give my grateful thanks.

MIT's School of Humanities and Social Sciences generously provided financial assistance for this project when it was needed. The Bunting Institute provided a haven and a community during the early stages of the work, 1978–80.

Finally, this book was written and revised over a period of six years without a word processor. I had the good fortune to work with three highly intelligent and competent women who typed three successive drafts; each nurtured the project in her own way: Ruth Spear, Mary Mitchell, Linda Lee.

Editorial Note

I have preserved wherever possible the original spelling and punctuation of the eighteenth-century documents which I cite. However, all dates have been regularized to the new style. Thus, I interpret January, February, or March 1705/6 as 1706.

Some of the letters reproduced in Appendix C were undated. I have placed them among the dated letters according to subject matter, handwriting, or other evidence. But *caveat lector*; the order is conjectural.

The Celebrated Mary Astell

Chapter One
The Rediscovery of a Woman's Voice

Some perhaps will think there's too much of the Woman in it, too much of my particular Manner and Thoughts. It may be so; but as an Affectation of other Peoples ways is generally Ridiculous, so the keeping up to our own Characters is that which best becomes us. And there is this Advantage in it, that is these Papers shall survive me, by speaking Truths which no *Man* wou'd say, they will appear to be genuine and *no Man* will be blam'd for their Imperfections.

Mary Astell, *The Christian Religion As Profess'd By a Daughter of the Church*, 1705

As Mary Astell knew only too well, English literary history was the history of male writers—creating and reacting to a canon of texts which spoke to their experiences as men and to their public positions on terrain they claimed. Of this male monopoly she noted: "Histories are writ by them, they recount each others great Exploits, and have always done so."[1] Even today, despite dozens of "appreciations" of Jane Austen and Mary Wollstonecraft, as well as scores of articles about women writers of the seventeenth and eighteenth centuries—poets, playwrights, novelists, *bas bleus*—literary historians still write about the seventeenth and eighteenth centuries without invoking their names.[2] Long after Robert Halsband and Isobel Grundy have given us Lady Mary Wortley Montagu—her letters, poems, and biography—much literary history of the period still fails to take her seriously. It is the natural response of a female scholar, after watching the figures of eighteenth-century English literary history parade by with hardly a woman among them, after reading the great poets, philosophers, and essayists of that time without ever hearing a female voice, to want to see the shape of a woman worked among these more familiar forms of Augustan culture. One wants to know what the effects of cultural change were on the lives and thinking of women, to understand shifting sensibilities with regard to marriage, work, sexuality, religion, art—shifts related to but not the same as those that occurred in men's thought with the development of a capitalized economy, a rationalistic secular culture, world travel, literacy, and scientific and technological methods in farming, manufacturing, and shipping.

For almost two decades now, scholars have been more self-conscious in their historical studies and reconstructions about the difference that gender makes. One begins to glimpse the difference the Civil War, the Glorious Revolution, the English Enlightenment made to the way women thought about themselves; how their relations to their families were modified by new economic realities; how they, as women, wrote and spoke about the changes that were radically altering the culture in which they lived.[3] The more focused work of excavating women's literary history and women's texts has also flourished. Known women writers of the eighteenth century have been written about and anthologized; new ones have been discovered.[4] The demographic facts of life, and fuller information about literacy and publishing, help to give us a better sense of what eighteenth-century Englishwomen were reading and writing and thinking.[5] Several books have been published recently about the history of feminism in the period.[6]

This study belongs to this new period of scholarship. The stories of the women who were Astell's female contemporaries (Aphra Behn, [Mary] Delariviere Manley, Elizabeth Elstob, Lady Mary Wortley Montagu) form an important context for understanding a woman like Mary Astell.[7] Their struggles with respectability, their attempts to gain public recognition, their irregular domestic arrangements form the context for Mary Astell's life and the constraints upon her as a writer, as much as the intellectual currents of her day, or the political positions of the male contemporaries she addressed. Women of her time were brought up with very different expectations of the social world in which they found themselves than were men. The mythology of, say, Tom Jones, a free-spirited, untrammeled youth setting forth to make his fortune in the big city, was not available to them. Moll Flanders was hardly an acceptable substitute.

Women's lives, more than men's, were defined by their social milieu, which they were relatively powerless to affect except by marriage. What men might call "making their Fortune," Mary Astell remarked dryly, was "with us Women the setting ours to sale, and the dressing forth our selves to purchase a Master; and when we have got one, that which we very improperly term our Business, the Oeconomy of his and our own Vanity and Luxury, or Covetousness, as the humor happens, has all the application of our Minds. . . ."[8]

Biographical narrative must reflect the different forces that shaped a woman's life. Public and private influences on the life must be weighted differently.[9] For example, what if social codes were stricter for women and social location more decisive? What if these things determined a woman's access to various drawing rooms and salons; to the conversation of educated people, and more important, to their libraries; to the advantages of other people's carriages or visits to their country estates? Then a class-conscious context, with its inhabitants and their favors, must be reconstructed to show how they affected a woman's free choice. If she was more dependent upon those in her immediate neighborhood for human contact, because it was dangerous for a single woman to walk out too far abroad, and because the heavy, awkward garments she wore and her insubstantial shoes made walking arduous and exhausting, then the neighborhood and its local inhabitants must be depicted as vividly as the literary establishment which took only passing notice of her.

It does not make sense to develop chronologically the successive stages of a woman's intellectual thought and published works as direct responses to the events of the commonweal (as one might do with a great man), or to chronicle the reception of her work by friends and enemies, or to judge her achievement with the standard measures of worldly success. No woman planned a career as a writer; there was no such concept as a *woman* of letters. Furthermore, success for a woman writer prior to the middle of the nineteenth century is difficult to gauge, since public acclaim generally entailed an unpleasant notoriety, and financial remuneration was considered ill-bred. The extraordinarily high value placed on maidenly modesty and humility complicated immeasurably any woman's psychological stance vis-à-vis the world of public discourse, which in turn complicates the biographer's task of ascribing meaning to writing and publishing. Certainly Mary Astell was divided against herself in this way, her writerly egotism made uneasy and her ambition ambivalent by the conventional expectations of her sex. When she stopped writing for the public in 1709, it may well have been because she felt she had spent enough time in the limelight, and had pressed to the limits a respectable visibility.

The story of a woman writer has a double focus: the effects of public exposure on her private life and the way private concerns of friends and family found expression in works addressed to the public. The biographer cannot separate "The Life" and "The Work" as the standard biographies of men have often done. That will not answer the questions we need answered: How did she come to be a writer in the first place? Who supported her in her eccentric activity? Who did she imagine was her audience? Who *was* her audience? What influence did she exert on her friends and those around her? What was the nature of the connections she formed with other women and men? What was the meaning for her of rejecting conventional social roles? What was her relation to other women who did and who did not write?

Yet at the same time as women's eighteenth-century realities must be taken into account, it is a mistake to conflate public and private meaning just because the writer is a woman, as historians and critics have often done. Lady Mary Chudleigh's diatribe against brutal, domineering husbands is consistently interpreted, for example, as a complaint about her own—although there is no other sign of tyranny at home. Similarly, Mary Astell's most sincere admirer of the next generation, George Ballard, supposed that because she declaimed vociferously against marriage in print, she must have been disappointed in an engagement to a man she wished to marry—although there is not one shred of evidence that this is so.

With that proviso, that a woman's writings are not the same as her life, the elaborations of private life have an important place in the

A studious but not unfashionable woman of 1692. Mary Astell may have looked like this. From Jacques Du Bosc, The Excellent Woman *(1692). By permission of the Houghton Library, Harvard University.*

biography of an eighteenth-century woman. It would be a serious distortion, for instance, not to detail Mary Astell's private friendships in telling the story of her life. Self-consciously identifying herself by gender before any other social categorization, she wrote four of her books expressly for a female audience. Her sense of self was very much bound up in relationships with other women; she both needed and relied upon the community of friends who supported her. She was dependent on these connections in a way no male contemporary, however down on his luck, would have been, because of the economic and social vulnerability of being unmarried.

Indeed, all the important sustaining friendships of Mary Astell's life were with other women. True, her bookseller Rich Wilkin believed in her and thought her an unusual comrade-in-arms; a number of old-fashioned religious scholars like George Hickes, Henry Dodwell, Daniel Waterland, and John Norris admired her. But it was Lady Elizabeth Hastings who sent her a regular quarterly allowance so that she could afford to live in her little house on Swan's Walk in Chelsea. It was her long-time neighbor Lady Catherine Jones to whom she dedicated a number of her books, and with whom she lived for several years at the end of her life. These two women, together with a third friend, Lady Ann Coventry, financed her one serious educational venture of a practical kind. Inspired by Astell's writings, they helped her to start the Chelsea charity school, under the auspices of the Society for the Propagation of Christian Knowledge. These women were simultaneously Astell's patrons and her disciples. Given their strong mutual influences—and the centrality of friendship in Astell's system of values—some sense of these women is necessary as a guide to Mary Astell's sensibility.

Mary Astell first came to my attention as a writer of considerable force, a woman who took her powers seriously and who tried to awaken other women to a recognition of their real value. She wrote with an energy and assurance that seemed several centuries ahead of her time. Hers was the first sustained, mature, self-confident woman's voice after Anna Van Schurman to insist upon her equal rationality—and humanity—with men. A generation earlier, Margaret, duchess of Newcastle, had written intelligently if intermittently about women and education (she has very interesting views about natural philosophy); but her arguments were brief and abrupt. Mary Astell's tracts were fully argued, with an Augustan grace and wit recognizable to anyone familiar with the tones of that era.

She left behind her six books, two long pamphlets, and a volume of letters exchanged with the Reverend John Norris of Bemerton on the subject of the love a Christian owes to God. Her first three books were feminist books written for an audience of women. In the first she discussed the need for women's colleges; in the second she gave women rules to train their minds for rigorous philosophical thought; and in the third she examined the imbalance of power in the marriage relation. After that she wrote closely reasoned polemics upholding the political position of the Tories and the hegemony of the Church of England.[10] With the exception of her spirited defense of women, the attitudes displayed in these works were common enough: a love of order and absolute belief in the Stuart succession, a belief in Cartesian rationalism together with loyalty to the Church of England. She shared with her fellow Londoners excitement about the latest observations of the heavenly bodies, the habits of other cultures, and the party politics of Whig and Tory.

Like most English thinkers of her era, Mary Astell had a passionate interest in political philosophy; she was endlessly involved in debating the rights of the governed and the prerogatives of authority. The writers she took seriously in her own work were, predictably, Hobbes and Locke and Shaftesbury, as well as Defoe and D'Avenant. She devoted hundreds of pages to her responses to their points, carefully noting the page numbers of their works in her own margins.

Indeed, her theorizing about women can be seen as a special case of this interest in the dynamics of political power. That is, her defense of women's rights came not from a general concern with the inequalities of the existing economic or political system, nor from an awareness of stifled human potential among other disenfranchised groups—the poor, the colonized, the enslaved. On the contrary, she never considered these groups at all, and her limitations as a feminist theorist can be traced to this blindness. She used the word "slavery" strictly as a metaphor when bemoaning the plight of women, and did not observe that a number of her acquaintances owned or traded in actual slaves to work British plantations in the Caribbean. The issue of women's rights was rather for her a special case, close to home, for exploring assumptions about the rights of male governors and the obligations of the female governed.

The questions she addressed were central to post–Civil War England, and she used a familiar seventeenth-century political vocabulary to describe the aim of her project: "with an English Spirit and Genius, . . . to retrieve, if possible, the Native Liberty, the Rights and Privileges of the Subject." She framed the issue of men's power over women in the political terms of her day—passive obedience, political tyranny, slavery, and freedom—and located her conclusions about the power relations between the sexes in the context of the obedience a subject owed his king. But, being a woman, she had an oblique angle of vision. As one of the subject people, albeit upholding the ideology of the ruling class, her conclusions about power in the state and the family have an ironic twist, and add a new resonance to the chorus of opinion that we know as the intellectual history of her time.

In many ways, Mary Astell was a representative Augustan, although she was often aware of the contradictions inherent in subscribing, as a woman, to the ideologies of her day. She was spokesperson for the High Church and Tory positions, and her prose could be anthologized as the pattern of rational argument for those positions; her work was indistinguishable in this respect from that of other (male) writers of the Age of Reason, except for occasional references—irate, insinuating, or eloquent—to the moral and intellectual conditions of women's lives. While her trail of references displayed the influences of Plato, Virgil, Marcus Aurelius, Descartes, Arnauld, and Locke, she decried her culture's refusal to educate its women and its crippling prejudices about women's minds. Her feminist polemics reveal her discomfort in trying to appropriate for herself the intellectual forms of her day. In 1705 she wrote: "They allow us Poetry, Plays, and Romances, to Divert us and themselves, and when they would express a particular Esteem for a Woman's Sense, they recommend History; tho' with Submission, History can only serve us for Amusement and a Subject of Discourse. For tho' it may be of Use to the Men who govern Affairs, to know how their Fore-fathers Acted, yet what is this to us, who have nothing to do with such Business?"[11]

Sometimes her conflicting loyalties simply baffled her, as when her sense of the requirements of hierarchy ran athwart her allegiance to the rights of women as individuals. She believed in absolute monarchy and in its replication at the level of the family. But she saw that women were victimized by the institution of marriage and therefore advised them not to marry, while recognizing that were her advice taken seriously, "there's an end to the Human Race."

She never went so far as to advocate that women should come in for their share of governmental power, run businesses, or be ordained for the clergy; but she took seriously her own ambition as a sign of the soul's immortality, and chafed under cultural expectations of female passivity. Already at eighteen she was feeling the pinch, expressed in her poem "Ambition."

I

What's this that with such vigour fills my brest?
   Like the first mover finds no rest,
   And with it's force dos all things draw,
Makes all submit to its imperial Law!
Sure 'tis a spark 'bove what Prometheus stole,
   Kindled by a heav'nly coal,
   Their sophistry I can controul,
Who falsely say that women have no Soul.

II

Vile Greatness! I disdain to bow to thee,
   Thou art below ev'n lowly me,
   I wou'd no Fame, no Titles have,
And no more Land than what will make a grave.
I scorn to weep for Worlds, may I but reign
   And Empire o're my self obtain,
   In Caesars throne I'de not sit down,
Nor wou'd I stoop for Alexanders Crown.

III

Let me obscured be, & never known
   Or pointed at about the Town,
   Short winded Fame shall not transmit
My name, that the next Age may censure it:
If I write sense no matter what they say,
   Whither they call it dull, or pay
   A rev'rence such as Virgil claims,
Their breath's infectious, I have higher aims.

IV

Mean spirited men! that bait at Honour, Praise,
   A wreath of Laurel or of Baies,
   How short's their Immortality!
But Oh a Crown of Glory ne're will die!
This I'me Ambitious of, no pains will spare
   To have a higher Mansion there,
   Where all are Kings, here let me be,
Great O my GOD, Great in Humilitie.

The paradoxes express her ambivalent efforts to make the best of a difficult lot: to turn the tables on fate and make a virtue of necessity. The male military images are poignant choices for a young woman already feeling hampered by her gender. The only acceptable heroism was martyrdom; men might prove themselves by doing, but women could only by believing—and by fervently, if passively, resisting the impinging world. As a woman with extreme opinions, she resolved to accept martyrdom as her lot. "And tho I want a Persecuting Fire/ I'le be at le[a]st a Martyr in desire."

Religious writing had traditionally been an acceptable outlet for women's expressiveness—witness the "commonplace book"—and Astell found this a comfortable frame from within which to ask the questions that interested her most, the questions posed by the new natural philosophy: the nature of thought, intelligence, God, the soul, the definition of a "state of nature," and the nature of proof. Theology was to be as philosophically defensible as mathematics. Christianity was a rational system, with clear and explicable principles. Religion was "far from being *Dark* and *affectedly Mysterious*," she wrote in *The Christian Religion as Profess'd by a Daughter of the Church* (1705). The precision and elegance of mathematical paradox was a good analogy for religious revelation: "No body will call the Mathematicks an obscure and mysterious Science, and yet it proposes Theorems which will appear as Abstruse and Mysterious as any Doctrine in the Gospel, to those who know nothing of that Science, nay even to such as have some smattering in it. Theorems that will pass for direct Nonsense and Impossibilities to an unskilful Person, who yet it's like may have confidence enough in his good understanding to pass his verdict on them; and which even a modest and ingenious Person may look upon as strange and incomprehensible." She gave examples to her less knowledgeable readers. "For wou'd not your Ladiship think I banter'd you, shou'd I affirm, That there are certain Lines which tho' they infinitely approach, yet will never meet? and that there are finite and determinate Spaces equal to infinite? and yet that there are such Lines and such Spaces may be demonstrated."[12]

She knew every rational argument for the existence of God. The world had to start somewhere: "Shew us how and from whence the World had its being," she demanded. "It's Eternity won't now pass upon us; Mathematics as well as divinity have discover'd too many Absurdities in that Supposition. Sir *Isaac Newton*, if your *Reason* is *sublime* enough to Understand him, will Demonstrate this to you, as well as any Divine, and you cannot suspect him of Priestcraft. Your Self-Moving Atoms and their lucky Jumble into such a Beautiful Form as that of the Universe, is yet more ridiculous. Shew us then some New and Better way of Accounting for our own Being, and the Origine of the World, if you reject that of an Infinitely Perfect and Self-Existing Mind."[13]

Newton's laws provided her with another instance of the ordered universe. Gravity was not a property of matter, but a principle of organization: "Mutual Attraction or Gravitation, is one of the most Universal and Uniform Affections of Bodies; but it is not essential to Matter, any more than Motion is, both proceeding from the Will and Power of a Superior Cause . . . and were it once suspended, unless a Miraculous Power interpos'd, there wou'd be no more distinction among Material Beings; all wou'd crumble into Dust, and every single Atom, either remain at rest, or else proceed in strait Lines, according as its Projectile Motion happen'd to be at the withdrawing of mutual Attraction."[14] Even her notion of heaven was a rationalist's notion—a place where all knowledge was complete and perfect, all mysteries finally illuminated. "Poor we that toil in Life's hard drudgeries," she penned as a young woman; "Pick scraps of Knowledge here and there,/ While the blest Souls above do all things know." To be in heaven would be to know everything; learning of an incomplete, partial sort was just one more of the irritations of an earthly, mortal existence.

Astell's learning and her eloquence—as well as her unimpeachable theological positions—made her a celebrated figure at the turn of the century. Although women writers of a generation earlier, such as Katherine Philips, Margaret Cavendish the duchess of Newcastle, and Aphra Behn, had suffered untoward effects from publishing what they wrote,[15] their pioneering efforts modified expectations about female authorship. In Astell's case, her following among certain aristocratic women was probably because of her writing, not in spite of it. Her published work elevated her to their level and gave her a prominence which neither her birth nor her meager fortune could confer.

She did battle for them all in defending the Church of England against the tide of secularization. Astell's positions on these debates are instructive, for she enunciated as clearly as any the stubbornly anachronistic High Tory line. She refused the contemporary skepticism and religious doubt. She was also profoundly antagonistic towards the "egalitarian" drift of her day: the rights of individuals within the state, religious toleration, and class levelling. Rather than questioning authority she strenuously defended it, on historical and theoretical grounds.

Her tracts are clever, conversational, and thorough. Nevertheless, her most significant and lasting contribution to the history of ideas has been her feminism, the by-product of her experiences as a woman in the Age of Reason. *She* would have been surprised to know what posterity has made of her, for she considered herself more a metaphysician than a projector, more a philosopher than a crusader. Her views about women were inextricably bound up with questions about the nature of intelligence and the soul, and the definition of natural government. Although we may read her today for her feminism, she wrote primarily to address these other issues. She herself would have been horrified by the implied radicalism of the label "feminist."

Whoever reads Astell carefully will not find a feminist heroine of the past with whom it is easy to identify. The stamp of her ultraconservative attitudes are impressed on everything she wrote. She struggled in earnest with her very real sense that society had not made adequate provisions for her or for other bright women, and she tried to reconcile that recognition with her equally powerfully held but conflicting belief that it was selfish and antisocial and *dangerous* to challenge the fundamental arrangements of the society to which one was born, a society which had protected and cherished one since birth, and without which one would not have survived.

She was that oddity, a self-made woman. Born a gentlewoman, but without the means of one, she came to London at the end of the seventeenth century with only her eloquence, her ambition, and a few introductions. By the end of her life, her example and her writings had cleared a little space for the intellectual woman in English society. Had she been a man, she would have lived an unexceptional life of the cloth, publishing a volume of sermons every decade, and slowly making her way up the hierarchy of preferments. As it was, she embarked on her studies "ignorant of the Natural Inferiority of our Sex," and remained unpersuaded the rest of her life. As one of the earliest polemicists to write from this stance in the modern age of printing and mass dissemination, her ultimate influence in the history of the English-speaking women's movement is incalculable.

It is perhaps problematic to call Mary Astell a feminist, to read into the past an ideology that could only be located in the present world, with its birth control pills, equal educational opportunities, and other forms of modern enlightenment. Indeed, although Astell's name has been preserved all these years as a very early proponent of women's colleges, one of the reasons that her special contribution has not been given its due is that the vocabulary for registering the novelty of her position has not been available. Even the word "feminist" was not in use until the 1890s. To write of her as a feminist is to create a special version of her—almost to reinvent her—with her collaboration and the aid of historical hindsight. In what, then, does her uniqueness consist? How did her attitudes embody a shift in consciousness, the possibility of a new sensibility? What makes her an obvious precursor in the history of feminism?

She was not the first to advocate women's education—Anna Van Schurman and Bathsua Makin published books on the subject before she did. In 1673 Bathsua Makin wrote: "Were a competent number of Schools erected to Educate Ladyes ingenuously, and how industrious the next Generation would be to wipe off their Reproach." Makin, who was of a practical turn, ran a school. Aware that "Women were formerly Educated in the knowledge of Arts and Tongues, and by their Education, many did rise to great height in Learning," her solution was to maintain unusual standards for her pupils—an interesting experiment in the midst of Restoration frivolity. The specific curriculum she proposed for girls was French and Latin beginning at eight or nine, to be followed by lessons on herbs, shrubs, trees, minerals, metals, and stones; astronomy; geography; arithmetic; and history. She herself had been educated at home, and like so many of the intellectual women of that time had a scholar brother (John Pell, distinguished mathematician and linguist) whose example and companionship offset the general discouragement of her own efforts in this direction. "Meerly to teach Gentlewomen to Frisk and Dance, to Paint their Faces, to curl their Hair, to put on a Whisk, to wear gay clothes, is not truly to adorn but to adulterate their Bodies," wrote Bathsua Makin, recognizing that the attention paid to women's external appearance was somehow at the expense of training them for an inner life.

But Bathsua Makin was married, and did not think of education as a means to create an alternative to marriage. Nor did she believe that the aim of education was to teach women to think more rigorously, as Mary Astell did. She told her readers that she hoped her discourse, *An Essay to Revive the Antient Education of Gentlewomen, in Religion, Manners, Arts & Tongues, with an Answer to the Objections against this Way of Education* (1673), would "be a Weapon in your hands to defend your selves, whilst you endeavour to polish your Souls, that you may glorify God, and answer the end of your Creation, to be meet helps to your Husbands."[16] Astell, of course, emphatically denied that being helpmeets to husbands was the purpose and end of any women's creation.

Anna Van Schurman, the other advocate of women's education with whom Astell is often compared, spent the later part of her life in a stately Dutch mansion with a community of fellow Labadists, members of a Protestant sect somewhat like the Quakers. William Penn traveled there to observe firsthand their life of love and harmony.[17] Men and women called one another "frère" and "soeur," worked hard, lived simple, celibate, ritualistic lives, and shared physical tasks as well as in administrative matters equally.

Van Schurman never married, for her father, as her earliest tutor, had appreciated her extraordinary mind and had exhorted her on his deathbed to forgo marriage. She obeyed his injunction and devoted herself first to art and then to languages and philosophy until she "obtained a considerable place among the learned men of that age." She made her home with her mother, but when the mother died Van Schurman joined the religious community forming around Jean Labadie.

Contemporary with Bathsua Makin, she corresponded with Makin on the subject of women's education, although her book *The Learned Maid or, Whether a Maid may be a Scholar* (1641; translated into English in 1659) was of a very different kind than Makin's discourse. A learned production in Latin with ample quotations from the Greek Bible, it was the work of a rhetorician, and displayed delight in all forms of scholastic discourse. It proved in a rigorous sequence of syllogisms that women *could* profit from education, even if they did not participate in the public affairs of the church or state. The private pleasures of learning were sufficient said Van Schurman; and no one could doubt that she meant it.

In many ways Van Schurman's communal way of life was closer to Astell's concept of a woman's college than Bathsua Makin's improved boarding school, although Astell would not have been comfortable with the democratic mix of classes and sexes in the Labadist community. The economic basis of Van Schurman's community was also very different from that proposed by Astell in *A Serious Proposal to the Ladies*. Labadists all labored in order to be economically self-sufficient; they farmed, brewed beer, baked bread, spun and wove cloth, bound books, manufactured silk, and made opium pills. Mary Astell envisioned her institution as relieving not physical but intellectual hunger, and the women she had in mind for it were the daughters of well-to-do parents for whom the £500 she suggested as an entrance fee would be considerably less than the price of a dowry.

A more important distinction between Astell and these earlier educationalists is that the earlier writers become enmeshed in the question of whether or not women are educable, and whether education will ruin their modesty. Astell, on the other hand, takes the offensive. Instead of defending women's right to an education, she assumes it and carries the argument from there, criticizing the social institutions (schools, marriage) which thwart women's intellectual ambition. Her conviction that social prejudice, rather than anything innate, accounted for *all* failings attributed to women, was a very different message from these others. "Women are from their very Infancy debar'd those Advantages, with the want of which they are afterwards reproached, and nursed up in those Vices which will hereafter be upbraided to them. So partial are Men as to expect Brick where they afford no straw,"[18] she remarked. She recognized that the gender prejudice in her society was oppressive; she was not simply in favor of extending the opportunity for formal learning to more people. She realized that the radical political theories of the seventeenth century had not addressed the inequalities between men and women, and she argued that the female mind and spirit had to be reappropriated by women for their own needs.

By the time Astell came to write, the forceful feminist statements of the French Cartesians Jacques Du Bosc and Poulain de la Barre had also been translated into English.[19] Astell herself, in 1694, may have been inspired to write her first book by the publication two years earlier of a translation of Jacques Du Bosc's *The Excellent Woman*, the avowed purpose of which was "to serve the Honour and Happiness of the Female Sex, who are perhaps the larger Half of Mankind; and who doubtless are, or may be, as Important, at least, as the Other." These thinkers not only argued for women's basic equality with men but for the necessity of developing women's equal gifts. Poulain de la Barre's *De l'égalité des deux sexes* (1673), published in English as *The Woman As Good As The Man* (1677), asserted that since women's sense organs were anatomically the same as men's (and received sense data in the same way), and since women's minds functioned the same as men's, there was no reason that women could not become philosophers—or anything else—if they applied themselves as men did. He explicitly argued that women would make good teachers, lawyers, scholars, diplomats, politicians, and even military leaders—systematically covering every phase of public life from which women had been excluded. He even advocated physical training for women so that childbearing would not incapacitate them when pursuing these professions. But despite Poulain de la Barre's extraordinary insight, he still assumed that the most important goal of every woman's life was to bear and raise children.

Du Bosc and Poulain de la Barre were men, and Frenchmen at that. As a woman, Astell continuously demonstrated a feminist sensibility in expression and imagery as well as in explicit statement. It is there in her metaphors of childbirth, as when she refers to "miscarriages" of conversation, or in her unconscious use of the pronoun "she" rather than "he" when referring in the singular to the generality of humankind.

But other women, it will be urged, stood up for themselves as women, wrote defenses of their sex. Of the generation before Astell's, Aphra Behn, that assured and voluble writer of the 1670s and 1680s, commonly held to be the first woman to earn her own living with the pen, was deeply attuned to the power relations between men and women. She wrote about sexual duelling in her plays and poems, asserting her sense of her own power and sexual independence in images of lust between women or in portraits of impotent men. But Aphra Behn was not philosophically interested in the power relations between men and women. She did not theorize about the politics of gender or connect gender to questions of other kinds of political authority, as Astell tried to do. Neither she nor any of the other writers on the subject who preceded Astell explored the way men systematically tyrannized over women in society.

Ideas are sometimes incipient in a culture for a long time before they find a proper interpreter. When they are finally given voice in some authentic way, we recognize that as a claim akin to discovery, and sometimes even label the idea with the name of the person who first articulated it. Thus we speak of Darwinism, although Darwin did not originate the idea of evolution but derived it from Buffon, Lamarck, and even Lucretius. We refer to certain beliefs about the unconscious mind as Freudian, although a man named Georg Groddeck identified the "id" in *The Book of the It* some years earlier than Freud. The names we give to these ideas testify to the syncretic power and intelligence of their first serious exponents, as well as to their original contributions to the theory or idea. This is the sense in which Mary Astell can be called the first English feminist. She was the first English writer for whom the ideas we call "feminist" were the central focus of sustained analysis, a writer who infused an energy into them which is, to the modern ear, unmistakably feminist in tone and sensibility.

Among the modern historians studying the phenomenon we call "feminism," a consensus about the definition is emerging. Joan Kinnaird, in her excellent article "Mary Astell and The Conservative Contribution To English Feminism," distinguishes among Astell's contemporaries the "feminist," the "learned lady," and the "unconventional woman," and adds that the true feminist is distinguished by her "identification with her sex as a whole and a personal commitment to the advancement of women."[20] Another recent writer on the intellectual origins of seventeenth-century feminism, Hilda Smith, distinguishes the feminists of the period as "individuals who viewed women as a sociological group whose social and political position linked them together more surely than their physical or psychological natures." She adds that they argued specifically against "intellectual restriction and domestic subordination."[21] These definitions have in common the recognition of women as a separate class, quite aside from any other social or economic grouping, and a woman-centered identification with that class. Kinnaird includes a second criterion—the desire to better conditions for women, to champion their cause. Moira Ferguson, in her splendid collection of English feminist polemics, 1578–1799, defines this writing as urging or defending "a pro-woman point of view which includes resistance to patriarchal values, convention, and domination, or a challenge to misogynous ideas."[22] Implicit in these definitions is what some modern feminists call in their rhetorical shorthand a recognition of oppression and a conviction of women's intellectual and moral worth. In the movement that emerged in the 1960s, other properties of feminism often accompanied these fundamental attitudes, such as the celebration of "women's values" or "women's culture," or the view that the subjugation of women is part of a larger picture of social inequity—but these are not essential to a definition of feminism.

Astell, who styled herself "A Lover of her Sex" on the title page of her first book, argued in all these strains. Yet there is more to her feminism than can be encompassed by an abstract definition. When Astell enjoins literate Englishwomen to live up to what is noblest in their natures, in language that is at once sonorous, majestic, and inspiring, one is put in mind of a statesman of whom it could be said "he loved his people." Astell loved women in that way, as a leader, and protested that there was nothing unique about herself, that all women had it in them to do as she had done, to be "extraordinary." She was irritated by the condescension implicit in the public's astonishment at her achievements. "An Ingenious Woman is no Prodigy to be star'd on," she snapped.[23]

She was a crusader for the attitude that we now name "sisterhood"; she urged women to feel as she did, and to support one another. "Let the Men malign one another, if they think fit, and strive to pul down Merit when they cannot equal it," she cried in her Preface to Lady Mary Wortley Montagu's *Turkish Letters*. "[L]et her own Sex at least do her Justice . . . let us freely own the Superiority of this Sublime Genius as I do in the sincerity of my Soul, pleas'd that a *Woman* Triumphs, and proud to follow in her Train."[24] Women, she felt, were well out of the world of aggressive competition, power politics, and senseless violence that men had created. "Have not all the great Actions that have been perform'd in the World been done by them?" she asked. "Have not they founded Empires and over-turn'd them? Do not they make Laws and continually repeal and amend them? Their vast Minds lay Kingdoms wast, no bounds or measures can be prescrib'd to their Desires. War and Peace depend on them, they form Cabals and have the Wisdom and Courage to get over all these Rubs which may lie in the way of their desired Grandeur. What is it they cannot do? They make Worlds and ruin them, form Systems of universal Nature and dispute eternally about them, their Pen gives worth to the most trifling Controversie, nor can a fray be inconsiderable if they have drawn their Swords in't." Women, heretofore, were expected to participate in this mad egotism, to supply the admiration and appreciation for such "manly" activity that men withheld from one another. Astell continued: "It is a Woman's Happiness to hear, admire, and praise them, especially if a little Ill-nature keeps them at any time from bestowing due applauses on each other. And if she aspires no further she is thought to be in her proper Sphere of Action, she is as wise and as good as can be expected from her."[25] Astell asked her female audience to turn aside from this subservient function in the male world with its egoistic emotional forms, and to create alternative societies of their own, mutually supportive circles of women, who, without the envy and malice which characterized men's relation to one another, might help one another to cultivate their understandings of the highest Good, and to act upon those understandings in the world.

Astell's pride in self, her cool assurance, her public appreciation of other women's work, and her suggestions of an alternative female way-of-being-in-the-world, may seem obvious to modern feminists, but they created a sensation in London in the closing years of the seventeenth century. Her writing was extraordinarily effective by any standards. Her fine Augustan style, spare and exact, has aged well because she trimmed her sentences of the usual conventional phrases, epithets, and flourishes; she has the knack of perfectly summing up an argument with a vivid image. One feels in her prose the refreshment of a strong, humorous presence, a woman who, though not writing in order to exhibit her wit, nonetheless enjoys the range of tonalities she has at her command—from a lively, sensible exposition sprinkled with quips and barbed jests, to an elevated and magisterial prose demonstrating terrible and inexorable ironies. It is a tribute to Astell's literary qualities that none of the modern scholars who have written about her can resist quoting her balanced and elegant examples of eighteenth-century wit: "If all Men are born free, how is it that all Women are born Slaves?" or "The Mind is free, nothing but Reason can oblige it, 'tis out of the Reach of the most absolute Tyrant."

Astell did not polish her work; her texts have the charm of a highly intelligent woman's easy flow of spirits. In several places she boasts that her productions have taken but "a few hours" or "an afternoon," as if the paper merely caught the overflow of an always active mind. For this reason, her unpublished writing, her private letters, are not very different from her printed works; they reveal the same lively mind and clarity of thought. They do extend our sense of her human range, however, and show her as an affectionate, argumentative, and sometimes impatient observer of the world around her. Her restless quickness is evident in the way she often dashed off letters that were full of abbreviated words—a private shorthand—without careful recopying, without rewriting.

These textual sources of information have been essential in my attempt to build an imaginative impression of this woman, because few supporting third-person descriptions of her have survived. Fortunately, the literary materials are rich, and the poems and letters span some thirty-six years.

Her poetry is an invaluable textual source in the effort of reconstruction. The manuscript of early verse that has survived was written before she was twenty-two. These poems speak eloquently of the spiritual issues that dominated Astell's life as a young woman. They lament the fruitlessness of fixing her hopes on earthly happiness, and affirm instead her rededication to otherworldly ideals—exchanging her ambition to have fame on earth for a celestial crown of thorns. They speak of her loneliness and isolation. "Long have I liv'd on hope, but will/ A Hope that's always baulk'd continue still?/ Is't not a sign the flood dos still remain/ When my poor Dove comes empty home again?" And they show her willing herself back from the edge of desperation with a promise that the conscious suffering of a Christian is redemptive, seen in the proper way.

> Fondly I thus complain'd, when lo
> A beamling shot from Heav'n upon me shin'd;
> In a right medium did the objects show,
> And my dull thoughts refin'd.

If one refined one's way of thinking about worldly happiness and unhappiness, and put one's present misery in the proper perspective—of training or testing for the eternal happiness of heaven—all became bearable again.

Astell also wrote about the pleasures of solitude, the beauties of nature, and the joys of friendship—the standard poetical subjects for her period. Like many women of the late seventeenth century, she took Cowley's odes as the apotheosis of the poetic art, and imitated his diction and his stanza. Thus, her early verse of the 1680s is more formal and conventional than her prose, and her particular sparkle is almost entirely suppressed.

Only where she writes in the sarcastic, satiric vein she finds so comfortable, about the conceit and untrustworthiness of a designing beau, do we hear the poetic voice of the Mary Astell of *A Serious Proposal to the Ladies* or *Some Reflections Upon Marriage*. Our one surviving example of versifying in this voice is a poem she wrote for Lady Mary Wortley Montagu. Lady Mary—already married—had apparently received some love verses from an importunate suitor, and Astell composed these lines for her to use as a rebuff. One imagines these two ladies at tea, reading and discussing the fellow's poem and intentions, Mary Astell more disapproving than the younger woman, and ghost-writing this reply partly to show her incorrigible friend the proper response to such impertinence.

I

While pretty, powd'red Beaux prefer'd
To sigh, & whine, & versify,
What Mortal does not know their end?
Tis for their own dear selves they Die.

2

Ah! who, think they, can see this Face,
This jaunty Air, this Shape, this Mien,
And not be Charm'd w.th such a Grace?
She must be mine, were she a Queen!

3

Thus Traytors, infamous & base,
Cringe, flatter, keep a mighty pother
Til rais'd to a Confidence & Place:
False is ye Statesman, false ye Lover.

4

Ridiculous in him to claim
Or Gratitude, or Charity,
Who offers under Love's fair Name,
The most outrageous Injury.

5

If we th'improbable suppose,
That wanton hearts can e'er be True,
Who wou'd her Fame & Vertue lose,
Ruin herself to pleasure you?

6
W. Pride to conquer such a Heart,
Y. must e'er it can make its suit,
All honest Sentiments desert,
And sink ye Man into ye Brute?

7
Yo^r Poetry does much improve,
But still yor Morals are ye Same
Remember *Semele* & *Jove*;
Wou'd you once more expose my Name?

8
Threatning's a pretty way to Woo
But your kind Threats deserve my Thanks,
While odious Wishes you pursue,
You change Respect to Insolence.

9
To some fond Girl display yor Art,
My Heart is vow'd away & gone
Nor shall from Honor's Laws depart,
Nor be ye purchase of a Song.

The sarcastic diction, humor, and vocabulary of this "Anti-Song," as she titled it, is so much closer to her unique prose style than her other poetry that it reinforces one's impression that her desire to protect women from the depredations of men was a subject that gave her critical abilities full play. The inhibiting conflict she felt in expressing her thwarted ambition—her perpetual state of feeling exiled or ignored by the world— these are replaced with an object upon which it is safe to turn the full force of her wounded and scornful intelligence.

Other than these textual records, very little evidence of Mary Astell's life remains after all this time. Her name appears in few public records. As a woman she had little or no business in the world of commerce, politics, or law. She was born, she died; she owned a small house for some years; she kept a bank account; she helped to open a charity school in Chelsea: these facts the public listings can supply. But no one picked up and passed along anecdotes about her. Her papers, when they were discovered, were not considered of much interest to anyone, and so they were not saved. When I began this project, only four of her letters had been preserved in the two great libraries of Britain, the

Bodleian at Oxford and the British Museum, and these had been saved because they had been addressed to prominent men of the period: Sir Hans Sloane, John Walker, Henry Dodwell. A remarkable manuscript booklet of her early verse had also been kept because it was dedicated to Archbishop William Sancroft, although no one tried to ascertain who the young lady was who signed herself "M.A." Had she addressed these verses to a woman—as she must have done with much of her writing—they would not have survived at all. In a private estate in Gloucestershire I found forty more letters in an old pocketbook, folded up just as they had been left more than two and a half centuries ago. A few more poems and fragments came to light in the possession of generous individuals in Kent and Staffordshire. These things survived because they were part of the estates of Astell's wealthy friends, whose families could afford to pass on their mansions and muniments entire and unexamined for generation after generation. If Astell had not corresponded with members of these great houses, hardly a scrap of her private writings would be preserved today. When she died, no one saw fit to collect her books and papers. Nor were there any relatives to save her things simply in the spirit of preserving family history. Her brother and his wife and their offspring died long before Astell did. She, of course, never married and had no children. She was the last of her line.

No painting of Mary Astell is known to exist. The only physical description we have of her is in a few sentences from Lady Louisa Stuart, whose grandmother, Lady Mary Wortley Montagu, first met the celebrated Mrs. Astell when she was still a girl and Astell had already passed her fortieth birthday. Taking exception to the adjectives "fair" and "elegant" from a man who had never laid eyes on Mary Astell, Lady Louisa offered instead the family tradition that Mary Astell was

> a very pious, exemplary woman, and a profound scholar, but as far from fair and elegant as any old schoolmaster of her time: in outward form, indeed, rather ill-favored and forbidding, and of a humour to have repulsed the compliment roughly, had it been paid her while she lived. For she regarded such common-place phrases as insults in disguise, impertinently offered by men through a secret persuasion that all women were fools.[26]

The distaste for flattery is accurately reported—one can read it in the "Anti-Song" quoted above—and is a common enough Augustan attitude; Pope and Swift repeatedly satirized the fawning of courtiers, fops, and fools. Certainly Astell disliked the custom of paying elaborate compliments to women, which was tantamount, she said, to "calling them fools to their faces; for what are all the fine Speeches and Submissions that are made, but an abusing them in a well-bred way?"[27]

But the portrait of Astell as intolerably severe is an exaggeration. Her manners were simple and direct, and honest above all; she was active and cheerful. Indeed, she thought it the duty of a Christian to be in good spirits and thought a calm cheerfulness was proof of a properly ordered life. "Neither GOD nor Wise men will like us the better for an affected severity and waspish sourness."[28] Her conversation was supposed to have been extremely diverting. She went into society; she entertained at home. If she was selective about her visiting list, it was because she was jealous of her time. Sometimes during the hectic winter season in London, she escaped to Burwash in Sussex, a little country village where she could read and write in peace and isolation.

She practiced a moderate abstinence in eating and drinking, for reasons of both economy and health. But she was far from thinking that the virtue of these practices was in an improving self-denial. It was a calculated moderation which had in it, rather, an element of "Epicurism" as she put it: "for by living thus," she wrote, "according to Nature, the simplest refreshments and such as are in almost every ones power, have a greater relish than the most study'd delicacies to an indulg'd and disorder'd Appetite, that is always longing after what it has not."[29]

I imagine her as a spritely, well-bred lady in sober, dark clothes, with a touch of haughtiness which came from an extreme consciousness of being born a gentlewoman. This overdeveloped sense of class in Astell was held in due proportion to her relative poverty and her marginality as a single woman without family. She derived much of her psychic strength from the English class system, which she assumed institutionalized the natural order of things. It gave her a sense of entitlement which enabled her to resist the culture's insidious message that she was inferior, and to perceive the pervasive sexism of her society.

In many ways Astell and her wealthy friends—beholden to neither fathers nor husbands—had an enviable freedom which must have made the limitations placed on them as women even more palpable. Accordingly, they might have been expected to perceive the discrepancy between what was denied them as women sooner than their poorer sisters for whom gender prejudice was simply one more degradation. An upperclass woman in a class-bound society was freed, at least, from the belief that all men were her superiors. As Astell puts it in the 1706 Preface to *Some Reflections Upon Marriage*: "For if by the Natural Superiority of their Sex, they mean that every Man is by Nature superior to every Woman . . . the greatest Queen ought not to command but to obey her Footman."[30] Privilege prepares the way for dissatisfaction and revolt, just as the energy for change always comes from those who already have some power. Virginia Woolf's *A Room of One's Own* begins with a comparison of the luncheons of college men—sole poached in cream, partridges and sauces, wine and port—with the dinners of boiled beef and yellowing sprouts at women's colleges. It is hard to imagine a more privileged vantage-point from which to consider the question, and yet it was there, at the pinnacle of success for women—at one of those colleges for which Mary Astell so longed—that Virginia Woolf saw most clearly how far short that success fell from what men were granted.

This study is an attempt to integrate these issues and to tell the story of a particular woman who, shaped by certain social, political, and intellectual forces, both represented her historical era and transcended it. To the scholars of the past who were also interested in Mary Astell, and who did the original excavation, I am grateful. First, there was George Ballard, an amateur historian and ladies' staymaker, whose zeal to recover the histories of England's women scholars and writers led him to collect all the information he could about Mary Astell, starting about five or six years after her death. He was able to speak to people who had known her when she lived, in particular an Anglo-Saxon scholar named Elizabeth Elstob who knew Astell for at least ten years in London. Ballard's fifteen-page sketch of Astell's life, including a listing of her published works, has been the main source of information about her for all subsequent scholars.[31]

It is possible that Astell would have been dismayed that a dressmaker preserved her memory, that she owed her reputation to a lowly tradesman. On the other hand, she would have heartily approved of his project. Indirectly, she may have been responsible for it, since it was Elizabeth Elstob who first interested Ballard in the fact that so many learned women had been ignored by historians and therefore lost to history, and encouraged him in his zeal to collect information about them. Elizabeth Elstob, in turn, had been politicized on this issue by Astell, who wrote in 1705: "since the Men being the Historians, they seldom condescend to record the great and good Actions of Women; and when they take notice of them, 'tis with this wise Remark, That such Women *acted above their Sex.* By which one must suppose they wou'd have their Readers understand, That they were not Women who did those Great Actions, but that they were Men in Petticoats!"[32] Ballard picked up and repeated Astell's *bon mot* about exceptional women being treated like "men in petticoats" in his own book, *Memoirs of Several Ladies* (1752). He also used her hint that a woman may have written *The*

Whole Duty of Man, and made it one of the central examples in his
volume of how women's accomplishments are suppressed in the writing
of history.

Ballard's account of Astell provided the information for the entry
in the nineteenth-century *Dictionary of National Biography*. Until 1916,
when Florence Smith's Columbia University Ph.D. dissertation on Astell was published, no one corrected Ballard's facts or added to the little
store of information about Astell's life. Florence Smith's book was the
first full-length treatment of Astell's ideas. She gave the gist of most of
Astell's published work and outlined Astell's contribution in three areas:
education, religion, and politics. What Smith is less clear about are the
meanings of Astell's positions, given her political context, and how her
attitudes ran with or counter to the prevailing ideologies. Smith obviously admired her subject as a woman of considerable achievement,
but because of her own historical limitations, she did not treat Astell
as a pioneering feminist thinker. Finally, Smith's interest in Astell's
writings was academic, not to say antiquarian, and she made no attempt
to imagine how this woman felt, let alone how she lived in a day-to-
day way. Nevertheless, Smith's *Mary Astell* has been widely admired by
feminist scholars; Virginia Woolf mentions it in *Three Guineas*. Her
book has insured a continuing awareness of Mary Astell in our century,
and for that we are deeply grateful. More recently, Regina Janes and
Joan Kinnaird have remarked on Astell's political conservatism, and
Kinnaird has written brilliantly on the implications of Cartesianism for
the development of feminist thought in Astell and others.[33]

My effort here is to unfold the story of Astell still further, and to
add to the growing store of information about her and her circle of
acquaintances, as well as to explain more of the political and social
context within which the events of her life took place. I have sketched
the ever widening circles of influence that defined Astell's thought,
beginning with her family of origin, her friends, her patrons, her political allies, her enemies, her heroes, her admirers. I have also tried to
imagine a living woman back in these contexts, a woman well aware
of the anomaly that her gender made her, and self-conscious about
being a woman writing in a world of men. In reconstructing Mary
Astell's world, I hope to give new shape to her texts, her motivations,
and to the social and psychological history of women of her day.

Chapter Two

The Coal of Newcastle

To introduce poor Children into the world, and neglect to fence them against the temptations of it, and so leave them expos'd to temporal and eternal Miseries, is a wickedness, for which I want a Name; 'tis beneath Brutality, the Beasts are better natur'd, for they take care of their off-spring, till they are capable of caring for themselves.

Mary Astell, *A Serious Proposal To The Ladies*, 1694

In 1666, the year Mary Astell was born, her family's status as gentry was confirmed and recorded by a heraldic visitation to Northumberland.[1] Her paternal uncle Isaac registered the Astell coat of arms for his brothers and sister, and testified that their Oxford-educated great-grandfather Thomas Astell and his son John Astell had been barristers at Grey's Inn. For generations the Astells had been middle-class professionals: lawyers, preachers, merchants. No blue blood ran in their veins; they owed their pedigree to the exploits of an ancestor during the Hundred Years' War. As Astell humorously explained to one of her wealthy, aristocratic friends, their gentility was due to "my dusty Great Great etc. Unkle Harry, who about four hundred years ago had an Augmentation given him for taking Don Diego Valdera Prisoner."[2]

Her father, Peter Astell, was a coal merchant in Newcastle—no ordinary businessman, for the coal trade there in the seventeenth century was the richest in England. "Coals to Newcastle" came to mean superfluity, as tons of high-quality ore were mined daily from the coalfields in the surrounding countryside and shipped down the river Tyne for ports all over England and half of Europe. Since the late sixteenth century, as England's supply of timber dwindled and coal increasingly became fuel for the nation, the Newcastle industry had boomed. By 1640 ten thousand men were employed in the Newcastle coal trade as hewers and pickers, graders and cart-drivers. Most of the hearths in London burned Newcastle coal. Wood became more and more expensive; only the very rich or those with their own stands of timber could afford the aromatic luxury of wood fires for cooking and for warming rooms. In a very short time the city of Newcastle, whose trickle of business in coal and grindstones had always been thought an odd, local specialty, became the center of a national industry.

The coal merchants of Newcastle, a guild known as the Hostmen, in which Mary Astell's grandfather, father, and uncle Isaac all held the position of clerk, had, since the time of Henry III, the exclusive right to weigh, measure, and vend coals on the Tyne River. In medieval times this had been the least of their duties, for originally theirs had been a guild of hostelers, the official hosts of feudal Newcastle. They lived within the walls of the city and were responsible for overseeing the transactions of visiting merchants. The Hostmen arranged accommodations for such visitors, stabled their horses, provisioned their ships, and advised them about local tradesmen. As part of their responsibilities, the Hostmen also supplied visiting merchants with coal and grindstones, trivial local commodities not claimed by any other established guild.[3]

As wood shortages grew acute and the coal business increasingly lucrative, the Hostmen were carried on the crest of the new industry, many of them making enormous fortunes overnight. Every bit of coal mined in that vicinity passed through their hands, for they were the only tradesmen legally entitled to sell it to outside merchants. They could buy it up at any price they wished, and sell it at huge profit. In time they came to own most of the coal mines as well, by admitting to their company (besides those whose parents or masters were Hostmen) only those who "had Colemynes, or had Coales of theire owne."[4] By the beginning of the seventeenth century the Hostmen either owned outright or held leases to most of the coal mines around Newcastle. Intermarrying with local landowning families, both gentry and nobility, the Hostmen created a hybrid aristocracy in the North, the landed and merchant interests being intertwined there early, as nowhere else.

Lesser members of the company like the Astells, who did not own any mines, worked for company members who did, or became involved in some other aspect of the coal business. Mary Astell's grandfather, William Astell, was bailiff of Wickham manor and clerk to the bailiff of Gateshead manor, two of the richest coal-bearing manors in the county. As bailiff and clerk to a bailiff, he was an agent of the coal owner, hired to keep order and to collect revenues. He weighed, sorted, and delivered the coal from the mines to the keelmen on the river. The Astells also went into shipping, and Peter Astell had a part ownership in four ships when he died in 1678.[5]

The way the Hostmen consolidated and preserved their monopolistic power in the forty years or so during which they rocketed into economic prominence leads modern economic historians to cite the case of the Newcastle coal industry as a paradigmatic instance of the emergence of modern capitalism from the institutions of medieval town-economy.[6] At first the Hostmen's monopoly had been a mere extension of the guild system, which protected each trade by guaranteeing exclusivity to the practitioners. But the subsequent expansion of the coal market to all of England and even parts of Europe upset the balance of medieval economic interrelationships. Outstripping all other guilds in wealth and power, the Hostmen began to dominate the fortunes of Newcastle, and to influence local and national politics in ways which had been unimaginable in earlier times.

Queen Elizabeth's charter of 1600 gave the leadership of the town into the hands of the coal Hostmen, along with the right to perpetuate their power by choosing their legal successors[7], in return for the considerable tax revenues generated by Newcastle coal. The first legally designated leader of the Hostmen was also the first mayor; the forty-two Hostmen named in that first charter included all ten aldermen, five of the councillors, and four of the other officers of the town.[8] The interests of the coal industry and of municipal government were so closely identified that the Hostmen paid their company dues directly into the town coffers. No other guild kept accounts this way, nor did any but the Hostmen pay the expenses for their guild's annual mystery play out of the town treasury.[9] Their civic power gave the Hostmen the legal weapons of fines and imprisonment with which to protect their business; they began to further manipulate the market, to limit output and fix coal prices, and to exclude rather than absorb possible competitors.[10]

The Hostmen were resented both by coal owners outside their guild and by rising entrepreneurs in other fields whose growth their monopolistic practices limited. As the century progressed, these groups whittled away at the Hostmen's prerogatives. Independent "fitters" began to set up in business to transport coal, making arrangements on the sly with independent keelmen. As the old veins were worked out and mining had to be done farther and farther afield, expensive "way leaves" were built by competitors and rented to Hostmen at exorbitant fees; these were wooden tracks fitted to the wheels of a coal wagon, sometimes graded over as much as six miles, permitting a single horse to pull three or four chaldrons of coal down to the wharves. Mine owners were also forced to excavate deeper and deeper, at greater expense to themselves and greater danger to their workers. By the end of the seventeenth century they were building long wooden pipes to insert into the mine shafts to carry air down to the workers.[11]

Enterprising merchants from other guilds who could cover their losses with more immediately profitable lines of business began buying up land, leases, and mines from the increasingly impoverished Hostmen who could no longer afford to work their mines. A new consolidation of coal interests was effected by the end of the seventeenth century, an agglomeration that displaced the older partnership between the ancient landed families—many of them Catholic—and the Hostmen. As Edward Hughes put it: "the notable developments which took place in the coal industry in the first half of the eighteenth century were made not by the privileged members of the powerful Hostman's Company which had monopolized the trade since Queen Elizabeth's day, but, for the most part, by new men starting more or less from scratch."[12] Men who had their fortunes from tallow manufacture or trade in salt consolidated and capitalized the coal industry. These newcomers eroded the economic prerogatives of the Hostmen and at the same time bought up the manors of the old Northumberland aristocracy, displacing both groups simultaneously.[13]

This was the world into which Mary Astell was born. All of her male relatives belonged to this once-powerful guild of merchant rulers; she was also connected on both sides to the older, landed gentry of Northumberland. These antecedents help to explain the fierceness of her class pride and unbending conservative loyalties. Her earliest political education looked back to the past days of glory, when Hostmen and gentry sat together on the Newcastle corporation, when their governance of the town and of the coal trade was undisputed, and when newly exploited coal mines poured forth riches without stint, diffusing prosperity through all of Newcastle. It had been a feudal world overlaid with the luxury of capitalist expansion. While her grandfather was skimming a handsome profit on the exportation of coal, her great-uncle, lord of Bellister manor, was keeping his tenants to their feudal obligations of two days of mowing and shearing, spinning the requisite hanks of yarn, repairing the mill dam, and transporting a load of whatever he chose to Newcastle once a year.[14] But by the end of the seventeenth century the Hostmen no longer controlled the coal industry, and in 1697 Bellister manor was sold to a goldsmith, Alderman Ramsey, and passed out of Mary Astell's family's hands.[15] All her life Mary Astell defended established power and hereditary privilege, with a fervor far more characteristic of a Tory gentleman living on his family estate than of a merchant's daughter living in genteel poverty in London.

The particular place of the Astell family in Newcastle history is also instructive. During the Civil War the Hostmen were royalists. At a time when merchants for the most part chafed under obligations to the sovereign, the Newcastle Hostmen identified solidly with the Stuart monarchy, which supported their monopoly and renewed the charter of their city. They defended the divine right of Charles I against opposition from the Long Parliament, and when in 1642 the lines were drawn and both sides began to arm for civil war, the Newcastle coal men refused to send their coal south to the enemy but set themselves instead to resist the parliamentary forces.

The Newcastle position was a crucial one. The strategists of London knew that neither they nor the rest of the south and east of England could long survive the shortages of coal presaged by the withdrawal of Northumberland. In short order Parliament set about to compel Newcastle's capitulation. This call to arms was issued:

Whereas the greatest part of this kingdom, and more especially the City
of London and most maritime towns are served and furnished with coals
from the town of Newcastle-upon-Tyne and the adjacent parts of Northumberland and the Bishoprick of Durham: which being now kept by
forces consisting of papists and other ill-affected persons under the command of the Earl of Newcastle, the city of London and all the greatest
part of this kingdom are like to suffer very deeply in the want of that
commodity so absolutely necessary to the maintenance and support of
life. . . . It is therefore hoped that there are none that will be backward to
contribute their best assistance towards the reducing of that place in the
recovery whereof all men are interested.[16]

The first round of hostilities only served to confirm the resolution
of the monarchist northerners. Newcastle's fighting force, trained in
border skirmishes with the fierce clans of Scotland, proved too much
for the new parliamentary army, and the first attempts to reduce Newcastle failed. At length the rebels were forced to ally themselves with
Newcastle's traditional enemies, the Scots, who in 1644 invaded and
held the city for them. Mary Astell's maternal grandfather, George
Errington, another member of the Company of Hostmen, distinguished
himself as a hero in the royalist cause during this battle waged in the
streets and alleys of Newcastle. It is recorded that he and a few other
men valiantly defended Newcastle's Pilgrim Street Gate.[17]

When the city fell, Parliament ordered that a committee be formed
to judge and punish the resisting royalists. Delinquent royalists and
suspected papists were to be identified, and their goods and lands seized
in retribution. Worse, they were to pay the expenses of the hated invading Scottish army from the profits of confiscated collieries. But the
committee selected in London for this task of retaliation, to assess and
sequester the estates of delinquents and recusants, was, oddly enough,
made up of prominent men in the Newcastle corporation, Hostmen
and aldermen like John Blakiston, Henry and George Dawson, Thomas
Ledgard, and Thomas Bonner. Clearly they were not expected to wreak
parliamentary vengeance upon their own.

William Astell, Mary Astell's grandfather, had been registered as a
lawyer at Grey's Inn during these negotiations between Newcastle and
the victorious parliamentary forces. He arrived in Newcastle shortly
after the appointment of the local committee to deal with royalists and
recusants. He was not a stranger to the city; his aged mother lived there
and his father had been buried beneath the chancel of St. John's Church
twelve years before, the first of four generations of Astells to be interred

there. His older brother Thomas had long since been vicar of nearby Haltwhistle, and his sister was married to George Blenkinsop of Bellister Castle.

When William Astell returned to Newcastle in 1645, the town corporation paid him £10 because "the said William Astell was at London serviceable to this Town. . . . And that he was att great Charge in bringeing downe his wife and ffamily to this Towne."[18] It is not clear what service William Astell rendered Newcastle in his capacity as a London lawyer, but given his connections in the city and the timing of his return he may well have negotiated for the coal interests, and had some part in easing the reprisals of the Long Parliament against the city for its stubborn noncooperation and ill-advised loyalty to the Stuarts. It is noteworthy that no Astell property was seized after the battle of Newcastle and no Astell paid a fine for resisting the republican cause although, according to his epitaph in St. John's Church, William Astell never swerved from loyalty to the Church of England and to Charles I. That he acted as an intermediary for the coal men in these negotiations is further suggested by the fact that soon after his arrival in Newcastle William Astell's name appeared on the Hostmen's books as their clerk.[19] In time he was also appointed as a minor official in several other capacities: clerk to Newcastle coroners, clerk to the bailiff of Gateside, and bailiff of several other of the richest coalfields in the area. From the start of his residence in Newcastle he was identified with coal interests and his earliest registered employment was to protect their property and police their operations.[20]

The siege and fall of Newcastle seems then not to have really dislodged the traditional leaders from their seats in the city government, despite the claims of historians who trace the declining fortunes of the Newcastle corporation to this defeat, and to it, too, the bitterness among the lesser gentry of the North which flavored the later Jacobite cause.[21] Nonetheless, the reversal in national policies during the 1640s did encourage a rash of local protests against the coal power—as if there were a hope that the new republican forces in Parliament might second a challenge to the royalist coal men.

The leader of the struggle against the corporation was Ralph Gardiner, the most indefatigable troublemaker Newcastle had ever known— filing suits (his father was an unemployed lawyer), petitioning Parliament, and publishing it all in an eloquent volume dedicated to Oliver Cromwell, *England's Grievance Discovered in Relation to the Coal Trade*. Indeed, this book tells us much of what we know about seventeenth-century opposition to the coal monopoly. No figure was more universally hated by the coal community than Ralph Gardiner, who harassed the leading citizens of Newcastle for years. Mary Astell must have grown up on stories about him as the devil incarnate, a bogeyman who scared children, a dangerous enemy to law and order.

Gardiner had his own motives for opposing the law that forbade him to sell his beer to traders on the Tyne, but his serious opposition to the Newcastle corporation commenced with the case of Thomas Cliffe. An Ipswich-trained shipbuilder, Cliffe got into trouble with the corporation when he almost involuntarily overstepped the ancient exclusive right of Newcastle shipwrights to mend all boats sailing up or down the Tyne. With three of his men he rescued a ship foundering in a storm upon the rocks near Tinemouth Castle: the "ship had been quite lost if the said master should have run to Newcastle, to have agreed with the free [i.e. native] carpenters, whose excessive rates and demands, often surmounts the value of the ship in distress, and their tediousness, in coming and going that distance, that often the ships in distress are quite lost."[22] After saving the ship, Cliffe and his men shouldered the dashed hull and carried it to the sands below North Shields, six miles downstream of Newcastle. There, they set about to mend it, despite the existing laws which forbade any but freemen of Newcastle to exercise their trades anywhere on the Tyne down to the sea.

Within a few days, the corporation of Newcastle dispatched armed men to stop the work and imprison the workmen. Cliffe's wife and daughter, who were standing nearby, protested loudly and bitterly when they saw what was happening to their workmen, whereupon the deputized policemen turned their clubs and truncheons upon them. They broke the daughter's arm and beat Ann Cliffe to the ground so badly that she died a few weeks later. Although tried and found guilty, the attackers never were punished, while Thomas Cliffe was sued by the corporation for violating the privileges of the town. Among the company men sitting on that case in 1649 was William Astell, who undoubtedly argued that breaking the town's monopoly on the river was illegal and dangerous both to local and national interest.[23]

Cliffe's suit was never settled. After spending hundreds of pounds in legal fees, he finally fled forever from North Shields: "I dare not go home by reason of their threats to put me where I shall never see sun nor moon more if they light on me."[24] But his cause was taken up by Ralph Gardiner, then a young brewer from Shields who was systematically organizing resistance to the corporation, and who in time collected affidavits from disaffected tradesmen barred from their trades, from independent mine owners and shipowners, from the coal buyers and traders in Newcastle—all of whom were at the mercy of the corporation in one way or another.[25]

Gardiner's book is handsomely done, with expensive engravings and a map of the Tyne River; he must have had the backing of some wealthy people. He shows the tyranny of the mayor and burgesses at Newcastle, their material greed and their cruel lack of fellow feeling. They insisted on their monopoly on the river at the cost of human lives, he claimed, forcing ships to journey up the river in foul weather in accordance with the law, to cast their ballast overboard or to take on provisions, when at Shields they were in greater safety. They callously starved people, he said, by engrossing

> all provisions into their hands, as corn, etc. and have kept it in their corn lofts till so dear, and at such high and excessive rates, that most people could not buy it, and that the people of Northumberland, and county of Durham, being in great want for bread, that many were constrained to let their beasts blood, and made cakes thereof, to eat instead of bread, and in the spring time many of these beasts dyed, being over-blooded.
>
> Other poor people killed their coal-horses for food, some eating dogs, and cats, and starved, many starved to death, sixteen, or seventeen dead, in a hole together; and yet at the same time many hundred bowles of corn cast into the river, being rotten, and mouldy, and eaten with rats, and some of those people boasting, they hoped to see the day a bowle of corns price should buy a silk gown. This was not in the time of war, and the countries might have had plenty, if it had not been engrossed by them.[26]

He charged that the Newcastle burgesses operated a blacklist which prevented their enemies from finding work; they robbed legitimate merchants by pretending that they were in violation of the terms of the monopoly and confiscating their goods. And by insisting that ballast be cast at Newcastle "they have spoiled the river . . . to the great prejudice of the commonwealth; by the obstruction of the river, and endangering of shipping."[27] Gardiner recognized that the coal industry had come to control the economic fortunes of thousands of people in and around Newcastle in a new, impersonal way. Wage labor had replaced older feudal relationships based on customary obligation and personal loyalty. Under the old system, labor had been paid to an overlord, whether in produce or time, as part of a social and political relationship; it was personalized, a proportion of a particular person's capability, and hence elastic or variable. But when Newcastle began to produce on a large scale a commodity not destined for use in the local market, labor was reduced to a single homogeneous standard, and laborers, like their products, began to be seen as interchangeable.

What Gardiner and his associates charged was that with the monopoly on coal came a value shift such that property was protected before human life itself. Even under the old system of privilege, a guild's wealth had consisted in its supply of skilled labor rather than in its valuable property. But in seventeenth-century Newcastle, the power in the hands of the mercantile elite was exercised to build up property, capital, and trade without even the pretense of responsibility for other members of the community.

The corporation of Newcastle felt obliged to put a stop to Gardiner's accusations. They had him arrested. In order to extort a confession they kept him locked up in a tower, where he was "forced to evacuate in the same room he lay and eat his meat."[28] Several writs of habeas corpus served for him vanished unaccountably, nor would his accusers bring his case to trial or allow him visitors or counsel. Eventually Gardiner escaped to London where he carried on his fight from a safer distance. But his firsthand experience of the Newcastle magistrates confirmed his hatred of them more than ever, especially of Dawson and Bonner, "who understande their office no more than a Company of geese, only they can carry a White stafe and sitt where other knowing majors hath done and can sett brancks upon womens heads and gags in their mouths which the law doth not provide."[29]

The "brancks," which Gardiner cites as an example of the official abuse of power, was a distinctive local punishment used to keep in line "chiding and scoulding women." An iron muzzle that fit over the head and face and forced an iron tongue into the mouth, gashing the flesh and causing it to bleed, it was a Newcastle specialty for strong-willed, articulate women. Gardiner obviously considered it barbarous in 1655 (he includes a picture of it in his book),[30] although there is a report of its use in Newcastle as late as 1741.

Heavy-handed, tyrannical Dawson, the man Gardiner accused of using this instrument of medieval torture, was Henry Dawson, a coal man who took turns being mayor of Newcastle with his brother George Dawson and Thomas Bonner.[31] In 1653, the very year that Gardiner broke out of jail and escaped to London, William Astell apprenticed his fifteen-year-old son, Peter Astell, to George Dawson, also a Hostman. From that point on Mary Astell's father appears on the books of the Hostman's Company as a steady employee.[32] One of his early tasks was to help Dawson collect a new tax which the Hostmen decided to levy on all grindstones and rubstones sold in their port. They made three pence on every chaldron of grindstones shipped abroad and eight pence if the ship was owned by a foreigner. The proceeds were to "paie the officers of the Company their yearely stipends" and to "defray such other extraordinarie charges as are incident to this ffraternitie."[33]

Peter Astell probably met his future wife's family in his capacity as a collector for the Hostmen, because his father-in-law-to-be, George Errington, a coal merchant of considerable wealth, was in arrears to the Hostmen for fines over a number of years. Peter Astell must have

A woman in the brancks, a seventeenth-century punishment for scolds. The metal lever forced into her mouth by the muzzle had sharp points on it. From Ralph Gardiner, England's Grievance Discovered *(1655).*

been sent to collect them, and that is how he first met Mary Errington, Mary Astell's mother.

They were married in an Anglican ceremony in St. John's Church in 1665, and the next year their first child was born, the daughter who was to become a signal curiosity of her age. By that time Peter Astell was twenty-nine, already fairly prosperous, with a substantial house on an "opulent" street in Newcastle, just below the western gates of the medieval walls which surrounded the city.[34]

The house Mary Astell grew up in was large, comfortable, and well-furnished. On the first floor there was a hall large enough to take twelve "trimwork" chairs and a long bench with a tufted cushion, two Spanish tables, and various other odds and ends. A sleeping chamber with a fireplace opened off this hall. There was another heated bedroom off a spacious parlor, furnished with eight Russian leather chairs, another Spanish table, shelves, a side table, and so on. Upstairs there was a dormitory with four beds, and a "garett chamber" with two more beds; an assortment of chairs, tables, stools, and chests of drawers was shared between the two rooms. The kitchen was remarkably well-appointed, with many implements, pots and pans, covered dishes, serving trays, bowls, and the like; there was also a fully equipped brewhouse. The Astells must have kept a good table; they laid a fresh cloth every two or three days, and ate off china and pewter. They undoubtedly kept a number of servants to maintain this establishment. There were pictures and maps and tapestries on the wall; mirrors, rugs, and many feather pillows. All the windows were curtained; there were at least five fireplaces; and there was a certain amount of silver plate.[35] This standard of living might have been achieved by a considerable landowning farmer in the South, although in the impoverished North it accompanied a higher social status.

Mary Astell's mother, née Errington, came from one of the old wealthy Catholic families that formed the gentry of Newcastle, and probably brought a respectable dowry with her. Mary Astell was raised in the Church of England, but this close family connection to Catholicism makes explicable her nonchalance about the threat of popery, and her later sympathies with the Jacobites.[36]

Peter Astell and his wife named their baby Mary, both for the mother and for the father's older sister, a maiden aunt named Mary Astell who was living with the family. The little girl was petted and praised, for she was the first child of that generation to be born to her father's family. When she was two, her mother had another baby, this time a boy, named Peter, for the father. In time this brother became an attorney, like his grandfather, with a suite of offices on the best street in town. Another son, William, born when Mary was six years old, lived only a week and was buried beneath the chancel of St. John's a few blocks from the family home.

The Newcastle in which young Mary and Peter grew up was, after London, Bristol, and Norwich, the largest and most prosperous city in England. Indeed to the eyes of the journal writer Celia Fiennes, touring England in 1695, "it most resembles London of any place in England, its buildings Lofty and Large, of brick mostly or stone. The streetes are very broad and handsome and very well pitch'd, many of them wth very ffine Conduits of water in Each allwayes running into a Large stone Cistern for every bodyes use. There is one great streete where in ye Market Crosse, there was one great Conduit with two spouts wch falls into a Large ffountaine paved wth stone which held at Least two or three hodsheads for the inhabitants." She went on to describe some of the particular buildings which dignified Newcastle's streets: the hall for the assizes and sessions for the shire of Northumberland—a large brick building within brick walls standing by the west gates, visible as one entered the city. There was also the large, stone church "wth a very high tower finely Carv'd full of spires and severally devisees in the Carving—all stone." This elegant steeple on St. Nicholas Church, famous throughout England, was the pride and joy of Newcastle; it was designed by Robert Rhodes and later copied by Sir Christopher Wren in the steeple of St. Dunstan's-in-the-East. Its peal of five bells rang through the town on all important occasions. And down by the river was the municipal building with stone pillars on three sides. Its spacious rooms on the second floor were for the mayor, the council, and use by the jury, and there was also "a very large hall for the judges to keep the assizes for the town . . . [which] opens into a Balcony wch Looks out on ye River and ye Key [quay]. . . . There is a ffine Clock on the top just as ye Royal Exchange has. The Key is a very ffine place and Lookes itself Like an Exchange being very broad and soe full of merchants walking to and againe, and it runs off a great Length wth a great many steps down to ye water for the Conveniency of Landing or boateing their goods, and is full of Cellars or ware houses."[37]

Coal lay beneath this mercantile splendor and coal dominated the landscape. From the bustling quay down by the Tyne, one could see three, four, or five hundred sails in a single fleet, carrying coal to London.[38] Everywhere horses and oxen pulled open carts of black, shining coal towards the great river. These myriad conveyances were such a feature of the landscape that in 1696, when James II and Louis XIV of France considered invading England in order to reinstate James II on the throne, they planned to move through Newcastle in order to seize the thousands of carriages and cart-horses which plied their trade around the city, carrying coals from the mines to the Tyne, and to commandeer them for moving supplies and ammunition during their campaign.[39] "This Country all about is full of the Coale," wrote Celia Fiennes, "ye sulpher of it taints y^c air and it smells strongly to strangers—upon a high hill two miles from Newcastle I could see all about the Country wch was full of Coale pitts."[40]

Mary Astell must have grown up taking for granted the omnipotence of the coal trade and the values of the coal merchants as unthinkingly as the permanent acrid smell of coal in the air she breathed. The effect of her family's place in the coal industry and in Newcastle can be seen both in the style and assumptions of her work. The abiding political belief of her adult life was that William's reign was illegitimate, and that the revolutionary settlement of 1689 was a compounding of the terrible mistake of the Civil War. She idealized Charles I as a religious and political martyr and condemned as self-serving and power-mad all who had challenged his proper rule. Her *An Impartial Enquiry into the Causes of Rebellion and Civil War in this Kingdom*, written in 1704, is an endorsement of Lord Clarendon's interpretation of the events leading to the Civil War, the version she had heard from her family. The threat of popery and French domination had been much magnified, she said, by men who would "set whole Nations on fire, only that their own despicable selves may be talk'd of, and that they may warm them at the Flame."[41] *A Fair Way with the Dissenters and Their Patrons* (1704) continued her campaign against political permissiveness. There she argued that since the avowed aim of the dissenters was to substitute for existing officials in church and state those whose ideology agreed better with their own, it was criminal folly for any who supported the present alliance of church and state to allow dissenters to hold office, disseminate their propaganda, or to compete on equal terms with those they sought to replace. The notion of a reasoned consensus was sentimental; politics was a matter of power, and both sides were out to win. War was the real danger, of course; and if the forces of dissent were allowed to gather momentum, war was inevitable.

Astell had seen the violent effects of a polarized political situation on the streets of Newcastle. In 1686, 1687, and 1688, she saw her native city riven with riots, conspiracies, charges and countercharges. It was then that she left for London. A few months afterwards, when William and Mary were crowned, a rioting mob (infiltrated, they said, by rebellious covenanters from over the Scottish border) tore up the fine new bronze statue of James II and threw it into the Tyne.

Without getting ahead of our story, let us note that, from the beginning, her friends and contacts in the capital were from the ranks of disaffected Stuart sympathizers. She snubbed one early acquaintance—the writer Elizabeth Thomas, "Corinna" of Pope's *The Dunciad*—because she was "too much a *Williamite*; I know where she has slighted some of her *best Friends* upon that Account," added an observant gossip.[42]

The idealization of the wronged Stuarts gave Astell an example of highborn tragedy with which to identify, and fused her Christian stoicism with a romantic belief in a doomed political cause. The downwardly mobile fortunes of her family were part of a larger national disaster. Life was difficult and fate unkind, but it was God's severe training for the afterlife; it was good for her immortal soul. She aspired to follow the royal martyr even to heaven, where he surely was: "did Monarchs Know/What 'tis with GOD, & Cheribims to dwell,/With Charles they'd leave their Empires for a Cell."

The class consciousness of Astell's Hostman forebears may also have had some bearing on her view of marriage. Because her father died when she was twelve, she did not have a sufficient dowry for an alliance with a gentleman of her own social standing. She would never have considered marrying beneath her. Indeed, she wrote that no man who really loved a woman higher-born than he, would ever consent to such a match. This combination of circumstances created a situation which prevented her from marrying, or at least liberated her at an early age from the illusions about the institution of matrimony which a more hopeful candidate might have entertained longer.

Finally, her family's once proud position is reflected in how comfortably, without qualification, she held her opinions. The security of belief which resonates in her prose suggests the self-possession of one raised on the side of power, no matter how threatened it might be. She was sure of what was due her, with none of the apologetics or coyness typical of women of her day, self-conscious about their ignorance of politics and trained to be modest and retiring. As a member of the ruling elite in a contested situation, her thought was politicized to an unusual extent.

She always began her arguments, whether about women's education, occasional conformity, or the advisability of marriage, with an insistence on the traditional authority of the Stuart monarchy and the established church of England. Stability was an unarguable good in her mind; doubt was a waste of time and dissent undermined domestic peace and spiritual well-being. The political controversies which had riven Newcastle both before the Restoration and again in 1688 were to her mind destructive and unproductive. The good life was based on obedience to traditional hierarchy; all else followed from that.

Newcastle itself at that time was an odd combination of a social back-water and a commercial success; that too left its mark on Mary Astell's character. South of Presbyterian Scotland and north of cosmopolitan London, Newcastle benefited from the ferment of its international traffic but was spared the licentiousness, the moral sophistication, of Resto-ration London. The busy port saw a great many foreign traders come and go, and there was regular and frequent access to the latest news from London. Nevertheless, the intellectual advantages of this urban life were combined with the securities of sober seventeenth-century pietism and civic traditionalism, a mixture which conferred on Mary Astell her peculiar qualities of mind. In her maturity she identified herself as one of the intelligentsia, able and ready to join in the public controversies about religious toleration and political orthodoxy, yet she preferred her quiet, almost pastoral, life in Chelsea to the theaters and drawing-rooms of central London. Her old-fashioned religious devo-tion, the hours she spent each day in silent meditation and study, were more the practices of a seventeenth-century lady living in rural retire-ment than of an eighteenth-century gentlewoman living in London.

Astell never received a formal education, as she often complained later in life; there were no schools for girls in Newcastle when she was growing up. The Royal Grammar School, begun by Thomas Horsley and incorporated by Elizabeth I in the 1600 charter, one of twenty such free schools in all of England, was for boys only.[43] Its presence both increased literacy among her male contemporaries and made more marked her exclusion from the world of letters.

There was much to see and learn, however, in a busy town like Newcastle. There were public exhibitions, like the operating theater at the Barber Surgeon's Hall, where visitors could range themselves around and watch a dissection or listen to a lecture. When Celia Fiennes visited in 1695, there were "two bodyes that had been anatomized, one the bones were fastend wth wires the other had had the flesh boyled off and so some of ye Ligeament remained and dryed wth it. Over this was another roome in wch was the skin of a man that was taken off after he was dead, and dressed, and so was stuff'd—the body and Limbs. It Look'd and felt like a sort of parchment."[44]

Commerce was lively enough in Newcastle to maintain many small shops comparable in quality to those of London. In less thriving towns a single storefront supplied all commercial needs, but in Newcastle, along Flesh-Market Street or Bigg-Market Street or Groat-Market Street, where once only these staples had been vended (bigg was a kind of grain), there were shops for hardware, linen, woolens, and the newest books from London. Each trade had its own territory: shoemakers and cobblers could be found at Castle Stairs and at the head of the "Side," vendors of milk in Gallowgate and Percy Streets, furniture dealers in the lower half of Pilgrim Street, and the tanners between St. Andrew's Church and the Friars. Booksellers with collections of old books peddled their wares upon the Tyne Bridge.[45] Saturday was marketday, with a great thronging fair stretching through the middle of town. Whole streets were given over to selling corn, hay, cheese, meat, with stands displaying leather, woolens, linen, ribbons, lace, beads, etc. The flesh-market on Saturday was supposed to be the best of its kind in all of England, where a quarter of a lamb sold for two or three pennies.[46]

For all the bustle of foreign trade and urban life, Newcastle still maintained its city traditions and festivals, its local pomp and ceremony. Three times a year regional fairs were held in Newcastle, changing the face of the city for days. Known throughout the North, these fairs were announced to the countryside by the hoisting of flags from the highest buildings and the ringing of the great bell of St. Nicholas. That bell was known as the "thief and reever bell" because all banished persons, whether debtors or thieves, had free run of the city to attend the fair as long as it was in progress.[47]

At the time of the annual assizes, which were also held in Newcastle, there were parades and feasts for the visiting judges. Mary Astell's grandfather, while he lived, had been among the county bailiffs leading the parade to St. Nicholas on Assize Sunday, followed by the sergeants in blue cloaks, cocked hats, and swords, with mace bearers in attendance. After these rattled the carriages of the mayor, town and country sheriffs, judges, aldermen, and others from their official breakfast at the mansion house on the river. When they reached the west door of St. Nicholas, they all swept in to the solemn strains of the great organ, followed by the judges in their robes, trainbearers, marshalls, and cryers, and the press of spectators, who soon filled the old church to overflowing.[48]

Not far from Mary Astell's house was the park, called the Forth, with a bowling green and a tavern, and edged with stately lime trees. The incorporated companies held their annual picnics and meetings here. Every Easter crowds of children bowled their eggs on the green, shrieking with delight when the pace-eggers swooped down with their blackened faces and wooden swords.[49] Here too, twice a year, civic ceremonies were enacted—the mayor, sheriff, and aldermen in their scarlet gowns, ceremonially bearing the symbols of their office, the mace, sword, and cap of maintenance. Astell's parents told her of how her grandfather, William Astell, had played his part in these ceremonies as under-sheriff of Newcastle before she was born.[50]

At Whitsun were church-ales, to raise money for the poor of the parish, with dancing and bowling on the Forth to the piping of town musicians. On May Day eve singers went around chanting the May carol, and by morning a tall maypole always appeared in the town square, while Morris dancers danced through the streets. At Christmastime mummers and carol singers and town musicians provided entertainments in halls and in the city streets. Newcastle was a very musical city. There were many local musicians, and the books of the incorporated companies show frequent payments to musicians and pipers on festive occasions. A visiting circuit judge in 1676 remarked that the entertainment arranged for him by the city was a ride down to Tinemouth Castle on the town barge, accompanied by the eerie strains of four or five drone bagpipes and a trumpeteer.[51]

Astell's pleasure in music had much to feed on in this environment. It was an era when everybody sang, and when part books were set out after dinner as frequently as, in the next century, card tables were arranged to while away an evening. Lutes, virginals, and recorders were commonly played; books of recorder and flageolet instruction were available in the first decade after the Restoration. At least twenty existed by the end of the century.[52]

Election day in Newcastle had special "inversion" elements, when the boys noisily carried about one of their number as a mock mayor while the men elected the new mayor. The schoolboys, Mary Astell's brother among them, were released for the day from their academic exercises to enact their noisy parody of the electoral process. In the Royal Grammar School, where the town burgesses were gathering, desks and books were put away and preparations begun for a feast of roast goose, apples, pears, beef, and bread. The floor was thickly strewn with rushes and sweet-smelling herbs; jugs of wine and ale were passed about freely.

In the seventeenth century, as later, the backdrop for these festivals was endless scenes of women scrubbing, chopping, boiling, baking, roasting—servants and mistresses alike—creating the feasts with which the community celebrated its holidays. Mary Astell's family probably kept two or three servants, but a girl of her class and prospects would have been expected to help with the baking, brewing, washing, mending, and other household chores. Her contemporary, Elizabeth Elstob, the Anglo-Saxon scholar, also raised in Newcastle and of a similar class background, could spin thread and knit her own stockings.[53] Astell and her mother and aunt also baked bread two or three times a week, and there were huge washings, to be done every month or so, of accumulated linen and clothes. At regular intervals the women also disappeared into the brewhouse with its assortment of tubs, hogsheads, copper pans, and kegs to effect the mysteries of beer, ale, and cider-making.[54]

Mary Astell spent many hours of her youth doing fancy needlework, like most Stuart women; it must have been trying for one as impatient and quick as she. Little girls began their stitchery at very young ages, graduating from samplers to raised embroidery or cutwork and lace-making. Astell may have used the skills she learned at these tasks to bind and adorn prized books, as some girls did. For even as a girl she was studious. At an early age she practically knew the Bible by heart, and the Book of Common Prayer as well. Her family owned these books, along with two or three others. She read also in the church library, which had over a hundred volumes and was considered valuable enough in 1677 to be put in the care of a librarian hired at £3 per annum.[55]

By far the most important intellectual influence on Mary Astell was her uncle Ralph, her father's older bachelor brother, who, according to tradition, tutored her when she was young. With no children of his own, it is not surprising that he formed an attachment to the intellectually precocious child. Ralph Astell was the family poet, and the only Astell prior to his celebrated niece to publish his writing. Two of his poems survive: a sixteen-page poem printed as a pamphlet, celebrating the Stuart restoration in 1660, and a memorial to his father, carved in the stone church floor where William Astell was buried. He communicated to Mary Astell a love of language and a belief in its power. The epitaph carved in the floor of St. John's Church displays Ralph Astell's literariness, his feeling for the printed word, and his penchant for metaphor:

> Stay, reader, stay, who would'st but cannot buy
> Choice books come read the churches library
> Which like Sybelline leave here scatter'd flies
> Perus'd alas here by men's feet that lies
> In single sheets, then neatly to be bound,
> By God's own hand, when the last trump shall sound;
> Amongst the rest glance on this marble leaf
> 'Tis Astell's title page. . . .[56]

Even as a young girl she must have read those words on the cold stone slab, this image of the crypt lid as Astell's title page, as if her grandfather were a book and the burial vault an entire library. The leap

of imagination from lives to books and from death to immortality—
sheets "neatly" bound "By God's own hand"—recognizes that printed
texts live longer than men and that the writer who apostrophized visitors
in the church's chancel would be read long after the mortal remains in
the vault turned to dust.

The conception of *Vota Non Bella*, Ralph Astell's long poem wel-
coming Charles II to the throne at the Restoration, written, as it were,
with the voice of Newcastle and printed locally for the occasion, suggests
an even more interesting influence on his young niece, the author-to-
be. The opening stanza presents utterly conventional conceits: the king
is likened to the sun, the church to the rightful mother, whose seamless
vestments are the Anglican liturgy. But Uncle Ralph sounds his own
odd note by identifying himself, the speaker, as a "black Northern lass"
come to pay court to the new king, with "Coale dust-powder" in her
hair and as a beauty patch "a good round Coale:/ This sets me off, and
makes me Penny-fair;/ White Swans are common, but a Black one rare."
All the terms of the poem are from what might be called a female
perspective. The restoration itself he views as a delayed *accouchement*,
the racked country unable to receive any assistance in her travail because
of the evil offices of "the Great Dragon (known by his Red Nose)."

'Twas Treason for to cast a pitying Eye
On her in this her great extremity;
Her throws [throes] grew sharp, her bones seem'd out of joynt,
She faints and swounds, each minute at deaths point. . . .
    Kind *Cheshire* quickly heard her piteous moan,
(Enough to melt an heart hew'd out of stone
Into a fount of Tears) nor does she spare
Her dearest bloud to Usher in the *Heir*.
She *knocks* up *Booth*, who with his Loyall band,
Is ready straight to lend his helping hand:
But whil'st that others doe too tardy rise,
(Wiping the slumber from their half-shut Eyes)
They are surprised, and he forc'd to flie,
And leave poor *Britain* in the Straw to lie.
    And thus she lay! affrighted and forlorn;
No hopes at all a Saviour would be born:
Till Heav'n imploy'd that Noble Instrument,
And from the North St. GEORGE-on-Horse-back sent
T'obstetricate; whose Journey scarce was don,
When she began to Travell with a Son. . . .[57]

There is nothing new in these images of St. George and the dragon, the rescue of a woman in distress, or the image of a woman heavy with child needing a place to birth her baby. But they are grotesque images to use for the thirty-year-old Charles, protected by General George Monck, trying to reclaim the kingdom in which his father had been beheaded. The names of the peers who offered ineffectual (because premature) military assistance to the Stuart cause are feeble props in Ralph Astell's supernatural tale of dragons, avengers, and the miraculous birth which sets the world to rights. The metaphor of childbirth is pursued with peculiar persistence, and the literal images from the quotidian round of neighborhood occurrence intrude strangely in the world of epic events: "Her throws grew sharp, her bones seemed out of joynt," "Help help (*good Neighbors*) with your *quick* supplies. . . . " Interesting choices for an old bachelor, they betray an unusual sympathy for the circumstances of women.

Astell's adolescent verse was much more conventional than that of her uncle. She read avidly—Milton, Spenser, and the "matchless Orinda"— but, as with so many women of her generation, Cowley was her favorite, with his frank, simple language of the heart, his irreproachable subjects, his piety, and his good manners. She admired his heroic loyalty to the Stuarts during the Civil War and the image of his simple life after the Restoration. "Some few Friends and Books, a cheerful heart, and innocent conscience, were his constant Companions," Thomas Sprat had written in the Introduction to the 1668 edition of Cowley's works. "His Poetry indeed he took with him, but he made that an Anchorite, as well as himself: he only dedicated it to the service of his Maker."

Astell copied Cowley's renunciatory and religious themes in youthful "imitations" of the sort he himself had invented: a resonant new form which followed another's meter, diction, and stanza form, while commenting on the meaning of the original. Her poem "Solitude" is such an "imitation," following Cowley's "The Wish," in its direct address and the dream of pastoral retirement. Comparing the city to a giant hive, Cowley had written that one endured sharp stings for the honey of material advantage. "Ah, yet, e're I descend to th' Grave/ May I a *small House*, and a *large Garden* have!/ And a *few Friends*, and *many Books*, both true,/ Both wise, and both delightful too!"

Astell's version portrays a young woman who was at eighteen already more ascetic than her elders, and more severely and exclusively intellectual.

> Now I with gen'rous Cowley see,
> This trifling World & I shall ne're agree.

Nature in business me no share affords,
And I no business find in empty words:
  I dare not all the morning spend
  To dress my body, & not lend
A minuit to my Soul, nor can think fit,
To sell the Jewel for the Cabinet.

With an adolescent lugubriousness, she renounces all pleasure—that of dressing, of fashion, of wit, of romance, of "balls and revelling," of "the modern Muse," and of "idle visits." Her "thinking mind" and "Mournfull Spirit" cannot reconcile trivial satisfactions such as these with the "solid Comfort" of the promised afterlife, a reward which comes only to those who learn to embrace their sorrows on earth. She depicts herself as plain and straightforward, refusing to practice the arts of flattery as she refuses paint for her face.

  My unpolish'd converse Ladies fly,
  'Twill make you dull, I have no railery,
  I cannot learn the fashionable art,
  To laugh at Sin, and censure true desert.

And yet for all the self-righteousness of these remarks, her tone is neither sour nor smug.

  O happy Solitude, may I
  My time with thee, & some good books employ!
  No idle visits rob me of an hour,
  No impertinents those precious drops devour.
    Thus blest, I shall while here below
    Antedate Heav'n. . . .

This is sunny language, written by someone who enjoys her own pursuits, and for whom time is precious.
    Uncle Ralph taught his niece more than a love of *belles lettres*. The philosophical assumptions of the Cambridge Platonists, newly conceived and excitedly discussed in the university when he was matriculating, so dominated Mary Astell's thinking that it is inconceivable that she did not learn these too from the teacher of her youth. First admitted as a pensioner at St. John's College in 1651, Ralph Astell migrated briefly to Emmanuel in 1653 while it was under the sway of Ralph Cudworth, Benjamin Whichcote, and John Worthington. After the publication of *The Leviathan* in 1651, these moral philosophers evolved a position from

which to refute Hobbesian materialism. They argued that the essential nature of the universe was spiritual, and that, as Plato and Plotinus had affirmed, the most important truths about reality had to be divined intellectually. They adopted from these revered classical thinkers a belief in abstract ideas, virtues, and moral values which came from God—of which material instances in everyday life were only poor and imperfect imitations. They asserted that there was an Intelligence in Nature which was spiritual and not simply material. "God ought to be to us the measure of all things, and not man, as men commonly say," they quoted from Plato.[58]

The Platonists never lost sight of God. They broke with Descartes finally, reluctantly, after they had learned from him the power of rationalism, because they rejected his assertions about the mechanistic nature of the universe. As Pascal had pointed out, Descartes was quite willing to dispense with the notion of God: "he had to make Him give a fillip to set the world in motion; beyond this, he has no further need of God."[59] Descartes believed in God-the-creator, necessary as the First Cause in a chain of events, but he did not finally believe in a God immanent in the universe. His dualism was resisted by the Platonists, who believed that all matter was infused with spirit, and that it was impossible to consider the one without the other.

The Platonists believed that the mind could and should be trained to lead one to God. This belief that reason gave one access to God was seen as a threat to the traditional Protestant emphasis on passive availability to faith; it undermined the opposition of the supernatural to the natural and of grace to nature. The Platonists responded by maintaining that reason was God-given, a candle lit by the Lord, as the favorite metaphor from *Proverbs* went. "I oppose not rational to spiritual," asseverated Benjamin Whichcote, refusing the dichotomy that his critics accused him of, "for spiritual is most rational."[60] Their claims for the role of reason in religion were not what Locke claimed in *The Reasonableness of Christianity* (1695) or Toland in *Christianity Not Mysterious* (1696), because they never repudiated the mystery at the heart of Christian faith. The role of reason was to lead the believer up to the mystery of faith and conferral of grace, to show the Christian what reason could not solve, to give him or her "an almost mystical awareness of God at the point where the rational and the spiritual merge."[61]

These ideas infuse all of Astell's formulations about religion, the nature of reality, and the function of thought. Her dismissal of the changes and chances of this mortal life in favor of the eternal—the persistent theme of her moralizing and occasionally self-pitying remarks—is essentially a choice to value abstract ideas over concrete, literal manifestations. Her insistence that the tenets of Christianity could be arrived at logically and that they were reinforced—not subverted—by rigorous philosophical thought was the very cornerstone of Christian Platonism. Her intellectual programs for other women always began with training in abstract thinking so that they might ascertain the moral dimensions of ordinary experience by logical analysis. They had to learn to discount the influence of the appetites and the senses, whose purpose was merely to preserve the body, so as to perceive and be guided by higher imperatives. As Henry More had said, the aim of spirit was not just to liberate itself from matter, but to control it.[62]

Steady, disciplined reason was the only proper instrument for determining truth. It alone could abstract moral truth from the material world, it alone could expose the innate ideas which lay behind one's experience; it alone could lead one to God. The true nature of experience could be ascertained only by considering its relation to the ultimate purpose of human life, which was to contemplate and love God. Therefore, everything was secondary to training and purifying the mind for that purpose: "the Mind being the Man, nothing is truly and properly his Good or Evil, but as it respects his Mind," Mary Astell would later write.[63] Reason was the only ladder to heaven, and the improving and strengthening of it was a religious act.

When this connection between reason and religious faith was later contested by John Locke, Mary Astell entered into the controversy, defending in spirit and in substance ideas that Ralph Cudworth, Benjamin Whichcote, and Henry More had enunciated. Under her uncle's tutelege, she might have read Henry More's *An Antidote against Atheisme, or an Appeal to the Natural Faculties of the Minde of Man, whether there be not a GOD* (1653), or *The Immortality of the Soul, so farre forth as it is demonstrable from the Knowledge of Nature, and the Light of Reason* (1659). John Smith's *Select Discourses*, edited by John Worthington in 1660 (and containing the important essays "The True Way or Method of Attaining to Divine Knowledge," and "The Excellency and Nobleness of True Religion") might also have been among Ralph Astell's possessions, and read young by his precocious niece. The first part of Ralph Cudworth's *The True Intellectual System of the Universe* (1678) was published the year before Ralph Astell died, although the entire text was not available in English until Mary Astell herself was dead. Her ideas about reason and religion have something in common with all of these, but in a manner so obviously hers, so digested and assimilated and without the scholastic paraphernalia of these thinkers, that they were probably transmitted orally, talked through with her preceptor while her attitudes and mental set were being formed.

A northeast view of St. Nicholas Church, Newcastle, where Ralph Astell was curate. From John Baillie, Newcastle upon Tyne *(1801).*

Astell followed these thinkers, too, in her emphasis on right living and loving charity towards all. The Cambridge Platonists made it a tenet of their faith to try to live like Christ. If God's essence was love and charity, if He was the fountainhead of these ethical qualities in the universe, then to live in a pure and godly manner was to demonstrate the existence of these qualities as platonic entities in the world. As Whichcote said: "*A good Mind, and a good Life. All else is about* Religion."[64] This belief in action, in living one's principles, was another part of what alarmed the Calvinists at Emmanuel College, who objected to this emphasis on "outward things." For Astell, who cared about consistency in everything, this unity of thought and action was essential. She would have been pleased by George Ballard's summation of her character. She was a woman, he said, "wholly wrapt up in Philosophical

Metaphysical & Theological & indeed all kinds of Divine Speculations," whose *"Life & Doctrine"* were "exactly conformable unspotted & all of a Piece."[65]

Whether Astell felt her uncle lived up to these ideals or not, Uncle Ralph's life was somewhat less exemplary. For eleven years he was merely the underpaid curate of St. Nicholas Church, never rising higher in the church hierarchy. He apparently drank to ease his disappointments. He was suspended from his duties on December 17, 1677, for fortifying himself when he mounted the pulpit. The church records on this occasion itemize "one pint of sack when Mr. Astell preached 1s. 2d."[66] A new curate was hired in the spring. It is probable that, after this, eleven-year-old Mary saw more of her uncle than ever. It would be interesting to know whether she saw his life as a success or failure, and just how much of the rather desperate Christian resignation of her earlier poems was learned from him. The motif of sorrow on earth is there, of course, in her later prose and in her letters, but it is determined rather than sentimental and even rather cheerful.

She was probably about eight years old when she began to take lessons from her uncle in the weekday quiet of St. Nicholas Church, a short walk from her house. She was lucky to have an educated uncle who believed enough in women's learning to tutor her. In the North, 83 percent of the women could not even sign their own names in the 1660s and 1670s, although by the 1680s and 1690s this measure of illiteracy was down to 72 percent. Astell was not the only little girl being taught to read and write at this time.[67] Still, the common practice would have been to discontinue her lessons as soon as her brother was sent off to the Royal Grammar School. Boys and girls were usually taught the rudiments of reading and writing together at home until the boys began their formal schooling, at which point the girls began their training in domestic skills.

Inside St. Nicholas's heavy door was a vast stone room adorned with richly carved oaken pews and an ancient oak screen covered with beautiful and delicate carved tracery. Memorials etched in the stone walls and columns and the banners and coats of mail and helmets hanging along the center and side aisles, seen in the flickering colors of stained glass, must have conferred on the lessons a sense of hushed and reverential importance.[68] There, in a smaller chamber off the vaulted interior, Uncle Ralph read books of sermons, poems, and histories of England with his young niece.

Astell obviously received from her uncle a sense of vocation in fusing learning and religion—indeed, in conceiving the aims of intellectual life as religious. Her rhetorical style—half lively and persuasive conversation half close doctrinal argument, larded with the elevated phrases of sermons—suggests early familiarity with books of theological argument and histories of religious ideas. But she could not yet imagine how to put together a life out of these interests and skills. She could not take the path her uncle had taken and become ordained for the clergy, although it was a profession that would have provided a forum for her eloquence and controversy for her contentious spirit. She might have been a hero among the Tory churchmen, an articulate ally of Francis Atterbury, rather than a cranky woman with surprisingly well-argued opinions against occasional conformity and toleration. She would have been assured of a stable place in some community—and of a living; she would not have had to depend on the charity of her highborn friends to support her in London. For the coal of Newcastle could no longer provide her with an income as it had her forefathers, and, if she did not marry, Mary Astell would have to invent a new kind of life for herself.

Chapter Three

The Self-Respect of a
Reasoning Creature

For till we are capable of Chusing our own Actions and directing them by some Principle, tho we Move and Speak and do many such like things, we live not the Life of a Rational Creature but only of an Animal.

Mary Astell, *A Serious Proposal To The Ladies Part II*, 1697

Most of, if not all, the Follies and Vices that Women are subject to (for I meddle not with the Men) are owing to our paying too great a deference to other Peoples judgments, and too little to our own, in suffering others to judge for us, when GOD has not only allow'd, but required us to judge for our selves.

Mary Astell, *The Christian Religion As Profess'd By A Daughter of the Church*, 1705

When Astell was twelve years old, her father died. As the death of either parent unmistakably marks the passing of an era for a child of any age, it must have done so for Mary Astell. The change in her life was signalled by the mourning clothes that she and her family wore. They draped black baize in the parlor, the staircase, and the front hall. Her father's body was laid out in a coffin lined with wool; for a few days there was a stream of visitors—friends, neighbors, members of the company of Hostmen—come to pay their respects to the family and to toss a sprig of rosemary or rue into the coffin in a last gesture of farewell. It probably fell to Mary to comfort ten-year-old Peter and to help her mother prepare the biscuits and cold meats, set out the wine and ale for the guests, and purchase and distribute the mourning gifts: rings, gloves, and scarves.[1]

Strangers came into the house to count the linen and plate, and to estimate the worth of the furniture, curtains, hangings. She was abruptly and unpleasantly aware that her mother was worried about money. Her father had not been a wealthy man; what he earned as a petty official was negligible the year before he died. For example, there is a record of a total of £15 18s. 3d. paid him by the Hostmen: £10 for calculating the amount of coal cleared through customs in the preceeding four years, £3 6s. 8d. as his annual wage for his services as clerk to the Hostmen—a position his father and his brother Isaac Astell held before him—and £2 11s. 7d.[2] for collecting the tax on grindstones. But, as a Hostman, he had many opportunities for profitable business both legal and illegal. An active, enterprising man, he was improving on his fortune when he died at forty. A number of people owed him money, he had investments in four different trading vessels, and he was an eighth owner in another business. His assets at his death came to above £500, including the £128 invested in shipping ventures, £170 17s. 6d. collected from his debtors, and £50 on him, so to speak, "in purse and apparell."[3]

The sum of £500 was not an insignificant one at a time when a skilled laborer might support his family on £60 a year. Peter Astell had been a solid citizen, and there was a vast difference between his income and that of the coal workers in Newcastle. A good "hewer," digging coal at the bottom of the stratum with a wedge or mallet, could make at best two shillings eightpence a day; the horse drivers who carried the coal from the hewers to the shaft made a shilling a day; the "overman" who placed workmen and checked the pits for sulphur made ten shillings a week, whether the pits were working or not. Carters, the men who hauled coal or timber from the mines into town, were paid eight pence to a shilling a day, depending on whether they supplied the cart and the horse. A man with a team of horses might make as much as a shilling and a half a day for drawing water. Women made considerably less, when there was work for them at all. The wives and daughters of the coal miners were occasionally hired to wash ore for anywhere from four to ten pence a day.[4]

On the other hand, Peter Astell's £500 was a lesser sum than what numbers of well-born youths lost every year at the London gaming tables. Allowances of wealthy noblemen often ran to several thousands a year. And in this case the money had to stretch a long way, for Mrs. Astell had to raise and educate two young children and to look after "old Mrs. Astell," the children's maiden aunt.

Mary Astell's mother was not destitute of other resources. The Erringtons had been a large and prosperous Newcastle coal family and on her husband's side she was related to the Blenkinsops of Bellister Castle, Northumberland.[5] But the fortunes of these families had been steadily declining with the general decline in the coal industry, and they could not spare a great deal for the widow. In fact, tracing their straitened circumstances into the next generation, one finds Mary Astell's young cousin, Robert Blenkinsop, forced to sell Bellister Castle for £734 in 1697.[6]

Peter Astell's guild, not his family, helped his widow and her two children. The Hostmen took up a collection, and gave Mrs. Astell £2 5s. 6d. as an outright gift and loaned her £21 more, presumably to help defray the funeral expenses while the estate was being settled.[7] And they promised to continue to "old Mrs. Astell," Peter Astell's older sister, the annuity he had earned for so many years as the Hostmen's clerk, an indication that he had been her only means of support.[8] This gratuity, £3 6s. 8d., was spending money—what a lady's maid might have earned at that time, beyond her clothes and room and board. On February 5, 1680, the Hostmen's books record yet another gift to the family: "Md. Astell Herewith this day granted charity by order to the company 40 shillings which summe is paid out of monies granted to the poor as afforesaid."[9]

Uncle Ralph, old and infirm, could not have been much help. He had already been suspended from his post as curate and was another mouth to feed. Nevertheless when the "passing bell" tolled again for her family the following year, this time for Ralph, Mary Astell must have felt his loss keenly because it meant an end to her lessons and the loss of yet another "father," just as she was reaching the age when a young girl begins to contemplate the inevitabilities of her own adulthood—one of which is a husband—and to take special notice of the grown men in her immediate vicinity.

Even at this distance, without special knowledge about the quality of Mary Astell's attachment to her father or to her uncle, one is tempted to speculate that losing these men at this crucial stage of development fixed her affections on the little community of women in which she lived. Certainly it made real to her the possibility of living this way. Three Mary Astells they were, continuing under one roof with her younger brother—her aunt, her mother, and herself. For six years they remained thus, the little family of women, through Mary Astell's adolescence. In 1684, when she was 18, her aunt died.[10]

After three hundred years speculations about motivations may seem pitifully inadequate, but it cannot be wrong to link the fact of this little household with the message of Astell's first tract: that society ought to provide institutional arrangements for communities of women, gardens meant only for Eves, as an option for women who did not wish to marry or who needed a place to live temporarily. Men could not be relied on to keep on living. As she grew into adulthood in a household with other women, knowing that it was unlikely that she would marry, she quite naturally considered such an arrangement a serious alternative to marriage.

Mary Astell's mother never paid back the £21 which the Hostman's Company loaned her at the time of her husband's death, though it was entered as a debt against her every year in their books until 1691, and they undoubtedly dunned her for it.[11] It must have been a humiliation to the family, trying to keep up a social position without the wherewithal to do so. It must also have been difficult to be the object of charity after such prosperous beginnings. Class was all that separated her from the daughters of the uneducated workers of the city, women who washed ore for four pence a day.

Her mother's relatives must have pledged themselves to see to young Peter's professional education. He was probably apprenticed to a local lawyer, for it was too expensive to send him to London to train in proper style at the Middle Temple.[12] Law was a thriving business in Newcastle in 1690, for there were interminable disputes about the rights to mines and way leaves, copyholds, and enclosure. Young Peter Astell also learned to draw up conveyances of property, search for titles, prepare marriage settlements, arrange transfers of tenancy, and the like.[13]

In time he was quite successful and rented chambers on the "Side," the most fashionable street in town. He was able to pay his mother's debt to the Hostmen's Company a few years before she died.

Newcastle held no such prospects for Mary Astell. She was a burden to her family, and neither marriage nor independence seemed possible. At seventeen or eighteen she became extremely depressed and began to write lugubrious poems about her isolation and unhappiness.[14]

> I Love you whom the World calls Enemies
>   You are my Vertues exercise,
>   The usefull Furnace to refine
> My dross, the Oil that maks my Armour shine.[15]

She rededicated herself to a religious life, like a nun without vows. She was welcome, at least, to a heavenly father. "Hark how he calls, come unto me/ All that are laden and opprest," she wrote. "Wipe thy blind eyes dark'ned with tears."

Things did not improve for her. Her aunt died; her brother began his apprenticeship. But she and her mother were still in debt. And she felt keenly the want of work for her mind and soul. A poem at twenty-one, written after Cowley's "The Motto", shows her lively sensibility still freighted with unhappiness, as she struggles with her fate. "What shall I do?" the poem begins, asking the terrible question facing her. Just as quickly came her reply, an assertion of Christian stoicism—her lifelong strategy for dealing with deep disappointment. But as she lists the terms of merely mortal happiness in order to renounce them, one is aware of a longing which her protestations cannot quite erase.

> What shall I do? not to be Rich or Great,
>   Not to be courted and admir'd,
>   With Beauty blest, or Wit inspir'd,
> Alas! these merit not my care and sweat,
>   These cannot my Ambition please,
> My high born Soul shall never stoop to these;
> But something I would be thats truly great
> In 'ts self, and not by vulgar estimate.

She continues on a self-consciously intellectual note. "If th' old Philosophers were in the right," she wrote, "if this low World were always to remain" (if nothing more could be expected beyond this life—no apocalyptic Judgment Day), "who would not then, with all their might/ Study and strive to get themselves a name?" But since fame on earth was as finite as human life itself, it was shortsighted to strive for it when one might gain instead eternal happiness. "But since Fames trumpet has so short a breath,/ Shall we be fond of that wch must submit to Death?"

In any case her sex prohibited such ambition, and so the lesson was more easily learned.

> Nature permits not me the common way,
> By serving Court, or State, to gain
> That so much valu'd trifle, Fame . . .

She was already bitterly aware of the limits on her future. She could join the ranks of those who were blind to the advantages of *this* world, and become a social outcast for her beliefs.

> But O ye bright illustrious few,
> What shall I do to be like some of you?
> Whom this misjudging World dos underprize,
> Yet are most dear in Heav'ns all-righteous eyes!

But even religious martyrdom, taken to its most adventurous extreme, was banned to her because of her sex. But for that, she might have liked to be a missionary.

> How shall I be a Peter or a Paul?
> That to the Turk and Infidel,
> I might the joyfull tydings tell,
> And spare no labour to convert them all:
> But ah my Sex denies me this,
> And Marys Priviledge I cannot wish;
> Yet hark I hear my dearest Saviour say,
> They are more blessed who his Word obey.

The church required her, as a woman, to submit to her fate, and she tried to make the best of it. But the last stanza of this poem is an attempt to revive her religious enthusiasm in the face of repeated discouragements. "Up then my sluggard Soul," she wrote, admonishing herself to keep alive the desire to do good works and serve the Lord.

> Up then my sluggard Soul, Labour and Pray,
> For if with Love enflam'd thou be,
> Thy JESUS will be born in thee,

And by thy ardent Prayers, thou can'st make way,
For their Conversion whom thou may'st not teach,
Yet by a good Example always Preach:
And tho I want a Persecuting Fire,
I'le be at lest a Martyr in desire.

It is a poignant glimpse into the psychology of a bright young woman who despaired about her future but who seems to have found solace in writing, and harnessed the conventions of devotional poetry to pull her up from the slough of despond.

Within a matter of months after writing this poem, Astell apparently determined to go to London to try her luck. Things could not be worse than they already were. It was not exactly clear how she was to live once she ventured forth. She may have hoped there was some family property to track down in London, although it cannot have been much.[16]

If she left intending to support herself as a writer, it was an extremely daring plan for a woman—foolhardy for one not interested in turning out plays or fiction. Aphra Behn had been the only woman thus far to scrape by, writing popular comedies and romances. The great Grub Street establishment was only opening up, where an educated person might barely keep body and soul together by translating, proofreading, cranking out topical essays and pasted-up letters or thinly disguised gossip about famous people. She may have thought she could turn to teaching if worse came to worst, or even be picked up by a wealthy family as a governess. In any case, she fancied herself a writer and an intellectual. She had long had a local reputation for being witty and precocious. London was the great center for culture and learning, for books and philosophy; these things drew her like a magnet.

It took nearly two weeks to get from Newcastle to London, in a stagecoach that bumped over bad roads. Long journeys were dangerous, too, for highwaymen lay in wait all along the routes to London to stop coaches and rob their passengers. It cost £4 10s. to reserve a place in a public coach, with twenty pounds of luggage. A private coach cost £15, as much as a year's lodgings in London.[17] A woman of Mary Astell's class would have generally been expected to travel with at least one maidservant, although it is possible that she did not have the financial margin to support one. Nevertheless, if even £100 of her father's legacy had been set aside for her, it would have been enough to send her and a maid to London, to secure her for a period of at least a year, and to give her a chance to see what a new life might bring. There were family friends who had residences in London—the Pitts, the Bowes—people on whom the twenty-one-year-old Mary Astell might rely to introduce her into society, or to whom she might apply if she needed help.

She must have settled in Chelsea almost from the start, and she remained there the rest of her life. Chelsea was, at that time, a pleasant and thriving little town whose character was changing. Originally settled by wealthy and well-placed people—Sir Thomas More established his family there because it was close enough to town to informally receive Henry VIII and others of the court—during the Restoration it became more populous, even called "village of the palaces" because of the number of great estates built along the Thames. Dr. John King, minister of the Chelsea church in 1694, wrote that during that "late Reign of Diversion" so many barges and pleasure boats had frequented the wide Chelsea beach on the Thames that the area had been known as "Hyde Park on the River."[18] By King's own time—a half-dozen years after Astell settled there—a number of the great houses had been converted to boarding schools for young ladies and gentlemen, and others rented out as lodgings, where respectable rooms might be had more cheaply than in the heart of the great city.

Other contemporaries wrote of Chelsea in the same way, as a choice neighborhood inhabited by wealthy families and respectable young lady boarders:

> The Sweetness of its Air, and Pleasant Situation, has of later Years drawn several Eminent Persons to reside and Build here, and fill'd it with a great Number of Boarders, especially Young Ladies, and it has Flourish'd so extremely for Twenty or Thirty Years last past, that from a small stragling Village, 'tis now become a large Beautiful and Populous Town, having about Three Hundred Houses, and above that Number of Families, some of which are very great, (which is near Nine times its number in the year 1664).
>
> Its Vicinity to London, no doubt, has been no small Cause of its late prodigious Growth, and indeed 'tis not much to be wondered why a Place should so Flourish, where a Man may perfectly enjoy the Pleasures of Country and City together, and when he Pleases in Less than an Hours time either by Water, Coach, or otherwise, to be at the Court, Exchange, or in the midst of his Business. The Walk to Town is very even and very Pleasant . . . [19]

Any of these advantages might have drawn Mary Astell to Chelsea. The lower prices suited her means, the wealth and respectability of the local population suited her conservative attitudes and her social origins. The number of girls' boarding schools made Chelsea a safe enclave for

one in Mary Astell's situation, a neighborhood with an unusual number of young unmarried women in the streets and in the shops. Physically, the area conformed to the geographical configuration she had
just left behind her. There were large open fields not far away that
were like the town moor of Newcastle, where local domesticated live-
stock could graze; and beyond these fields, stretches without human
habitation. Proximity to a great river and such parks as the Apothecary's Garden, the private Ranelagh Gardens, or even St. James Park
on the other side of the bridge into town—these natural features were
like the landscape at Newcastle with the Tyne flowing by and the
shaded Forth to walk in.

It is not clear what Mary Astell had in mind when she went to
Chelsea. Too genteel and intellectually sophisticated to want to enter
demeaning service as a governess or a teacher in a boarding school,
perhaps she hoped to be taken into some great family as a companion.
Perhaps she hoped from the start for the patronage of some highborn
ladies, as did finally happen. That this solution was in her mind one
can see from these lines which she wrote shortly after coming to London.

> I fear not to obtain my ends,
> While GOD and a good Conscience are my Friends;
> Nor need a Patron, if with Heav'n
> I can preserve my reck'nings ev'n.

She is still protesting in her usual Christian paradoxes that she does
not need anything, but she did need a patron, or some source of income.
In *The Christian Religion* she writes: "Getting an Estate indeed is not
a Womans business, and therefore for the most part she is free from
the Solicitude of *laying House to House, and Land to Land,* so uncomely
in a Christian, who is but a *Stranger and Pilgrim upon Earth, who has
no abiding City here.* . . . [But] it were well if we knew how to keep
and use what our Relations have provided for us, and did not put it
out of our own power, into hands that seldom or never dispose of it
as they ought."[20] On the one hand, women were freed from the cor-
rupting necessity to lay up treasure on earth; on the other hand it would
be better if they knew how to preserve what "Relations have provided
for us" and to dispose of their own fortunes, however small, for their
own purposes.

At length, Mary Astell exhausted what little resources she had in
London. Her distant relatives turned a deaf ear. The family friends who
had at first seemed so cordial turned cooler when it became apparent

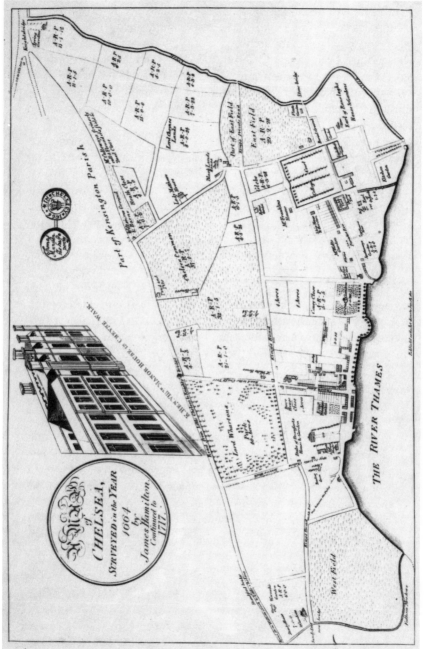

Chelsea as it was when Mary Astell first arrived there. By permission of the Royal Borough of Kensington and Chelsea Libraries and Arts Service.

that this rather unbending young woman actually had no visible means of support. We know that finally, in desperation, she went to Lambeth Palace and asked to see the archbishop of Canterbury, William Sancroft, who had just been released from the Tower, where he and six bishops had been quartered for refusing to endorse James II's Declaration of Indulgence, which they felt undermined the established church. His refusal had seemed to her a glorious gesture, and even perhaps a sign from on high.

Archbishop Sancroft's behavior was exemplary in the ways that mattered to Astell. He had led the bishops and four hundred lesser clergy out of the church after the revolutionary settlement, to give up their positions and preferments, rather than swear allegiance to the House of Orange. He was also known far and wide for his charity, for which both Swift and Dryden eulogized him in verse. Among his papers, in addition to the hundreds of requests for help, there are a number of poems from the recipients of that charity, gratefully acknowledging his kindness.[21]

These pleas for assistance and charity fill a number of large volumes, and among the requests from the year 1688 there is an undated letter in Mary Astell's handwriting, hurriedly written upon a ragged and dirty piece of paper. The speaker identifies herself as a gentlewoman, unable to survive any longer alone in the city.[22]

> My Lord
> I come to y^r grace as an humble petitioner being brought to very great necessaty threw some very unfortunate cercumstances y^t I have Laine under for some time I have pawned all my cloaths & now am brought to my Last Shift yt is to desire ye charity of y^r grace & some others of ye bishops, my Lord I am a gentlewoman & not able to get a liflyhood, & I may say with ye steward in ye gospelle worke I cannot & to beg I am ashamed, but meer necessaty forces me to give yr grace yt trouble hoping yr charity will consider me, for I have heard a very great & good character of w^t charity you have done & do dayly, so yt I hope for y^r pitty upon my unhappy state, & if yr grace please to admit me to speak to you I will give you a very just account of my cercumstances wch is to Long to do in writing so I humbly beg yr admitance to
> > My Lord
> > > yr graces
> > > > most humble & most
> > > > > devoted servant

The *mot* about pawning her clothes and being down to her last shift seems somewhat risqué for Mary Astell, although the verbal play itself is very much her style of wit. It is possible that she did not even consciously register the pun in the stress of the moment. The biblical reference to the parable of the talents is characteristic; it was one of her favorite stories.

Mary Astell's misery in her first year in London is also attested to by verses from "The Complaint," written in the same period. It is an apostrophe to God, in the manner of Donne or Herbert, and speaks of her loneliness, her isolation, and the unfairness of her lot in life. The second stanza almost begins to whine, her need is so great.

> What dost thou mean my GOD, (said I,
> Once in a sad and melancholy fit,)
> Why dost thou so severely try
> Thy Servant, as if yet
> I had not been explor'd sufficiently.
> So much to stretch will break the wire,
> What Gold can always strugle with the fire?
> And Lord what mortal in thy sight can stand,
> If all his ways be too exactly scan'd?
>
> If I ask wealth, it is to be
> Thy Steward only, not to make it mine.
> And when I wou'd have dignitie,
> 'Tis that it might be thine,
> And Vertues light to more advantage shine.
> 'Tis my design when Wit I crave,
> That thou both use and principal shou'd have.
> For well I know that these no blessings be,
> If as from thee they came, so they ascend not up to thee.

But the fourth stanza effects a wonderful transcendence, in which the repetitions, not to say the image of the covenant, hold out hope and a sense of continuity that belie the overt despair of the words.

> But yet methinks 'tis somewhat hard,
> My mind being to the lowest measure fit,
> Content with wages, begs not a reward,
> Thou shou'dst contract it yet,
> And I of necessaries be debar'd.

Long have I liv'd on hope, but will
A Hope that's always baulk'd continue still?
Is't not a sign the flood dos still remain,
When my poor Dove comes empty home again?

Appealing to Archbishop Sancroft was an inspired idea. He helped her with gifts of money and with contacts. "Permit me to say," she wrote when presenting him with a handstitched booklet of her own poems in 1689, "that the Condiscention and Candor, with which your Grace was pleased to receive a poor unknown, who hath no place to fly unto and none that careth for her Soul, when even my Kinsfolk had failed, and my familiar Friends had forgotten me; this my Lord, hath emboldened me to make an humble tender of another offering, which tho but of Goats hair and Badger skins, is the best I have to give, and therefore I hope may not be altogether unacceptable."[23]

We do not know what transpired in their meetings, but she may have communicated to Sancroft her penchant for natural philosophy, her secret ambition to write, despite the required protestations of reluctance to part with her "beloved obscurity." Or Sancroft himself may have considered writing her best hope of survival as a single woman. He may have recognized her intelligence and the clarity and coherence of her views, and directed her towards the conservative publishing establishment. This would explain how she met Rich Wilkin, who published her first book in 1694, and who handled all her work for the next thirty-six years, until his business passed into the hands of a relative, William Parker.[24]

Rich Wilkin was the perfect bookseller for Mary Astell, and her connection with him undoubtedly had something to do with her tenacity and eventual success. Operating from a shop in St. Paul's churchyard whose sign depicted a king's head, Wilkin was a monarchist, a conservative man, and highly respected for his strict probity and polite bearing. "He is a Bookseller of good reputation," ran a contemporary account of him, "and is scrupulous in doing the least injustice; neither was he less accomplished in the art of Obedience whilst he was an Apprentice, than that of Government since he has been a Master. He is devout at Prayers, and reverent and attentive in hearing; and is not only a true Son of the Church, but also a resolute Champion in behalf of the Hierarchy, as well remembering that prophetic apothegm of James I 'No Bishop, No King!' "[25]

Wilkin sympathized with Astell and admired her acuity and style. He may have supported her financially. The fact that they shared a whole range of social attitudes and religious and political opinions was

*William San-
croft, Archbishop
of Canterbury.
By permission of
the National
Portrait Gallery,
London.*

a comfort to Astell, and helped to legitimize her entry into the public world of letters. Wilkin probably commissioned the three political tracts she wrote supporting the Occasional Conformity Bill in 1704, pamphlets which were much appreciated by the Tories, who campaigned for it. For years Astell used his shop as her mailing address. On at least one occasion they worked together in a cause they both believed in: helping John Walker collect cases for his voluminous compilation of the "numbers and sufferings of the Clergy of the Church of England, Heads of Colleges, Fellows, Scholars, etc. who were sequester'd, harass'd, etc. in the late times of the Grand Rebellion."

Wilkin cannot have made much money on Astell's books, although he continued to print and sell them when she was long out of vogue. One can gauge her waning success in later years by the number of copies of her books which stayed on his shelves unsold. When the contents of Richard Wilkin's shop went up for sale on February 7, 1738, there were still ten quires lying around of *A Serious Proposal To The Ladies* in two parts from the 1730 edition. And in 1749, when his successor William Parker died, there were still 548 copies of the last edition of *Some Reflections Upon Marriage* on hand to be auctioned off, and 366 copies of the one and only edition of *The Christian Religion*.[26]

However she expected to get her living, Mary Astell came to London to engage in the life of the mind and to pursue truth: to read, to think, and to discuss ideas with other intellectuals. Thinking about her life and work as a whole, what strikes one about this woman, what marks her as a figure of the Enlightenment, is her unqualified belief in right reason and her faith—both personal and ideological—in the mind. She had a lonely and difficult life, and through it all seems to have found her most continuous and sustained source of pleasure in her own mind. She was never discouraged in her intellectual pursuits by the fact that she was a woman, although she was well aware that learned women "at best have the Fate the Proverb assigns them, Vertue is prais'd and starv'd."[27] Even in her blackest hour in London, she wrote in her poem "Affliction," so long as she could read and think she could find life sweet.

> I find I can both eat and drink
> And sleep and breathe, and move, and read, and think
> The Sun shines on me, flow'rs their odor yeild
> If not in mine yet in my neighbors feild.

The new natural philosophy, originating in such thinkers as Descartes and Bacon, made it possible for Astell to conceive of her nature as essentially intellectual. Descartes had asserted that formal scholastic education was of no special use in apprehending reality or ascertaining how the mind functioned; any serious person might cultivate self-conscious thought, which was marked by logic, clarity, and inner certainty. This radical epistemology put women on a theoretical par with men, despite differences in training and information.[28] Baconian empiricism, too, equalized the starting places of the sexes in the quest for knowledge. A woman as well as a man could imitate the introspective philosophy of Locke, could collect and record natural curiosities, could peer through microscopes and telescopes and describe what she saw there. Science, not yet a profession, was an intellectual hobby in which women of quality might take part, as well as their husbands.

Aphra Behn's translation of Bernard de Fontenelle's *Plurality of Worlds* for the London market is a case in point. In this work a learned narrator-philosopher explains the Copernican universe to an eager Marchioness, who illustrates the popular conception of women as ignorant but capable participants in the "new way of ideas." Herself interested in science, Behn appreciated the fact that this speaker was a woman who, although Fontenelle made her say "a great many very silly things," also occasionally made "observations so learned that the greatest Philosophers in *Europe* could make no better."[29] Fontenelle himself said he introduced the "fair lady" into his work to encourage women to take an interest in these matters. Anyone who could follow the plot of *La Princesse de Clèves* and keep the characters straight, he asserted, could learn about the sun and earth, planets and fixed stars.

Other ideologies, too, made it possible for women in late seventeenth-century England to conceive of themselves as the equals of men. These included the political formulations developed during the Civil War, the interregnum, and the Glorious Revolution—from the antiauthoritarian, communitarian, self-regulatory model of the Quakers and other radical dissenters, to the democratic, representational model invoked by the revolutionary settlement of 1689. The questioning of traditional authority had improved women's status temporarily, as revolutionary situations always do at first.[30] In France, for example, *les précieuses* flourished at a time of political instability; and women participated in the early stages of the French Revolution.[31]

In seventeenth-century England, both Hobbes and Locke had posited the basic equality of all human beings, albeit from very different vantage points. Each also insisted on the contractual basis of government, with a special emphasis on the rights of individuals, which were voluntarily given up in exchange for society's protection of individual life and property. Each in his own way also worked with the analogy to the family and the recognition of parents' rights over children, an analogy which ought implicitly to have empowered grown women.[32]

Mary Astell, as we shall see, rejected both Hobbes and Locke—their ethics and their epistemology—and most emphatically of all their construct of a "state of nature," although she was a divine-rights monarchist to the end.[33] She chose instead the philosophical idealist route to belief in herself and her powers, and her way was charted by French and English idealists who derived ultimately from Descartes.

Poulain de la Barre was probably the first thinker to apply Cartesian skepticism to the question of women, and to discount custom and received wisdom in examining the question afresh. Before his work, arguments about the nature of women's minds and morals were con-

ducted at one remove, like those between Chaucer's "Wyf of Bath" and
her husbands, by instancing and counter-instancing authoritative statements from scripture or classical sources. Long lists of exemplary cases
of learned, brave, or otherwise remarkable women were adduced. Poulain de la Barre, on the other hand, worked out a deductive line of
argument that Astell adapted to her own rather severe Christianity.[34]

Men and women alike had been created by God for the same noble
purposes she reasoned, and they must have been provided with the
same intellectual equipment for those purposes, since God did nothing
in vain. If the ability to think abstractly was what distinguished humans
from other animals, it was as much a woman's purpose in life as a man's
to make use of this God-given faculty. This line of reasoning, spelled
out most clearly in *A Serious Proposal Part II* (1697), is the premise upon
which Astell builds the rational foundation for religious belief in *The
Christian Religion as Profess'd By A Daughter of the Church* (1705). "Nay,
had I been shut up in a den from my Infancy, if Reason had ever
budded, I must have thought *what am I and from whence had I my
being?*"[35]

Poulain de la Barre's writings gave Astell her method of attack and
thus prepared the way for both volumes of *A Serious Proposal*.[36] Although
both she and Poulain de la Barre argued what Pope called "the high
Priori road," tonally they were very different. For one thing, the French
rationalist—a renegade late in life from the priesthood and a convert
to Protestantism—does not justify his approach in religious terms as
Astell does. For another, it is a philosophical issue for him, not a personal
one, and he wrote to convince other thinkers, not to exhort women to
set themselves free.

Added impetus to English feminism came from another French
Cartesian, Jacques Du Bosc, whose *The Excellent Woman* was translated
into English in 1692. This was a series of essays upon such topics as
"reading," "chearful humour," "reputation," "courage," and "birth or
nature and education"—all couched in terms of women's lives. The
preface insists upon the power that women have by virtue of bestowing
or withholding their applause from men and their actions, but argues
that they might do more active good if they were "bred to useful
Knowledge and Vertue." What virtue is learned by the management of
a needle? asked Du Bosc. How inappropriate for young women to
mold wax when they should be molding their minds! "We have reformed
our Nunneries," reads the translation, "the Schools of our Women,
from Popery and Superstition, but not from Pride and Vanity; nor have
made them, as we should do, the Schools of Vertue, and Religion, and
useful Knowlege." The principles of scientific reasoning took less time

and application to master than most women spent in doing complicated embroidery and making tapestries. Du Bosc even speculated that patriarchy and the subordination of women originated in superior male strength combined with the disadvantages and restrictions imposed on women by repeated pregnancies and the demands of child care. All this must have been suggestive to Astell.

Astell's notions about intellectual life, of course, also came from her character—from her own "natural" interest in ideas and the appeal of the abstract. One can see it in her literary preference for those works which were topical or political, for pamphlets or poems which pronounced on the current scene or otherwise laid down rules of taste or morality. She preferred these to works which mimetically constructed fictive scenes of character and event. The elegance of Pope's derisive intelligence delighted her. Of all the great French writers of the seventeenth century, including Racine, Moliere, and Corneille, she found Boileau most congenial—that stylist and critic whose influence on English letters is most felt in Alexander Pope's *Essay on Criticism* (1711). Boileau's satiric wit amused her; his judgments about taste and beauty, right and wrong, interested her.

When she read stories, she chose them from the ancient world— Homer, Thucydides, Virgil—not from her own time. She never read romances, but preferred the didactic verse-narratives of Dryden and Prior. She did not enjoy drama in an age when most educated people thought at least some plays or playwrights worthy of serious attention. In fact, the only play she ever mentions is *The Rehearsal* (1671), a satire written by George Villiers about heroic tragedy in general and Dryden's *Conquest of Granada* (1670) in particular. *The Rehearsal* reads better than it plays, and is more like a critical comment on drama than a dramatic event itself—more a treatise on literary form and standards to exercise the rational mind than a tale to intrigue the imaginative faculty.

Whatever difficulties Astell endured when she came to London, she did not stop reading and thinking about philosophy—or experiencing its consolations. It suited her abstract mind; it satisfied her abstemious and intellectual character. She turned to the work of John Norris, the best-known Platonist of his day (sometimes thought of as the last Cambridge Platonist). She admired him as the thinker who criticized Locke for relegating God to an unimportant role in the way human sensations build into ideas. In reading Norris's *Discourses*, she was struck by a gap in reasoning, and decided to write to him directly about it. Such a thing had honorable precedent, for had not Princess Elizabeth of Bohemia corresponded with the famous M. Descartes about her objections to his work? Lady Conway with Henry More? And Lady Damaris Masham with this very man Norris?[37]

Mary Astell approached him boldly, as an intellectual equal. She had read his work carefully, and wanted to point out the inconsistency she had spotted in the third volume of his *Discourses*. He had argued there, she said, that people ought to love God as the efficient cause of all their pleasure. Astell, who had been living on her own in London for six years by that time, and had suffered privations of the spirit as well as of the body, remarked to Norris that it appeared to her that as God was the efficient cause of *all* sensation—pain as well as pleasure— one was forced to the unhappy conclusion that, given His responsibility for it, pain may in fact do one good. Therefore, one could not love Him merely because He was the cause of all pleasure—as Norris had suggested.

Astell's letter, like everything she wrote, is lively and straightforward. She wastes little time in formalities but, as if leaning forward in her chair with a smile, addresses Norris earnestly about a line of abstract thought that she has been recently considering. She writes as an informed admirer—one who has read all of his work, has conversed with it, has learned from it, and wants to pursue further with that other mind some of her thoughts. She needs, she says, to test the rigor of her thought against someone else's judgment.

"Sir," she wrote, "though some morose Gentlemen wou'd perhaps remit me to the Distaff or the Kitchin, or at least to the Glass and the Needle, the proper Employments as they fancy of a Woman's Life; yet expecting better things from the more Equitable and ingenious Mr. Norris, who is not so narrow-Soul'd as to confine Learning to his own Sex, or to envy it in ours, I presume to beg his Attention a little to the Impertinencies of a Woman's Pen. . . . For though I can't pretend to a Multitude of Books, Variety of Languages, the Advantages of Academical Education or any Helps but what my own Curiosity affords; yet, *Thinking* is a Stock that no Rational Creature can want."

She then went on to exhibit the advantages of this rationality by disputing the reason Norris gave for the love of God. She had read the latest volume of the *Discourses*, she assured him, with the customary pleasure and profit with which she read all his work. She had thought hard about it, and as usual had tried "to raise all the Objections that ever I can to make them undergo the severest Test my Thoughts can put 'em to."[38]

She offered the correction with relish. Uncle Ralph's tutelage had left its mark; philosophical discourse was her favorite form of discourse, and "love of God" and the place of suffering in mortal life were her favorite subjects. Norris, who had no way of knowing this, was astonished by the clarity and force of her argument. He answered with wonder "to see such a Letter from a Woman," adding, "I find you thoroughly comprehend the Argument of my Discourse in that you have pitch'd upon the only material Objection to which it is liable."[39] He then hastened to defend and clarify his line of argument, and, curious to find out what else this extraordinary woman had to say, asked her to spell out for him the rest of her views on religion and the love of God, and the implications of these concepts for human life.

Astell's response was prompt and to the point. A naturally gifted philosopher, she must have been pleased to be in correspondence with this admired thinker, a learned man who had himself already conducted several famous correspondences—including one with Henry More about the "Theory and Regulation of Love" (published in 1688) and another with Damaris Masham, the intellectual daughter of Ralph Cudworth.

Norris had declared in his first work, *An Idea of Happiness* (1683), that the highest happiness and fulfillment was—as Plato had stated—the contemplative love of God. The earliest of Locke's English critics, he objected at once to the limitations of Locke's sensory-based theory of knowledge. In his remarks on Locke's *Essay Concerning Human Understanding* (published in 1690 as an appendix to *Discourses Upon the Beatitudes*), Norris criticized Locke for not exploring the *nature* of ideas and of thought (as opposed to the *origin* of ideas) and for not distinguishing what he called "objective" or absolute truth from contingent phenomena. Furthermore, he pointed out that Locke's theory of the origin of ideas in the senses only holds for ideas of bodies—and does not account for moral or metaphysical ideas such as Order, Truth, Justice, Good, Being, and so on.

Like the earlier Cambridge Platonists, Norris resented the imputation, by those who sought to "explain" Christianity, that religious belief implied the suspension of reason. "[W]e acknowledge the use of reason in religion as well as they, and are as little for a senseless and irrational faith as they can be," he wrote in *An Account of Reason and Faith*, his rebuttal of Locke's *Reasonableness of Christianity* (1695) and Toland's *Christianity not Mysterious* (1696). "[T]hey do ill to insinuate that it is by so many popular declamatory strains upon the reasonableness of religion, and in particular of faith, whereas they do, or should know, that the thing in question between us is not whether there be any use of reason to be made in believing, but only what it is, or wherein the true use of it does consist."[40] As Mary Astell stated it the same year—with a belief that also derived from Whichcote and the Platonists—reason was not contrary to religion, but in most ways irrelevant to it.

But as it is a fault to Believe in matters of Science, where we may expect Demonstration and Evidence, so it is a reproach to our Understanding and a proof of our Disingenuity, to require that sort of Process peculiar to Science, for the Confirmation of such Truths as are not the proper Objects of it. It is as ridiculous as to reject Musick, because we cannot Tast or Smell it, or to deny there is such a thing as Beauty because we do not hear it. He who wou'd See with his Ears and Hear with his Eyes may indeed set up in *Bedlam* for a Man of an extraordinary reach, a Sagacious Person who won't be imposed on, one who must have more Authentick proof than his dull Fore-fathers were content with.[41]

Norris is best known in the history of philosophy for introducing and disseminating Malebranche's attenuated Cartesianism in England. Nicholas Malebranche (1638–1715), whom Norris considered the "Galileo of the intellectual world," insisted on seeing all things directly in God. The objects of thought were not the things of the world that ostensibly presented themselves to view—the carriages, the mud, the people—but abstract ideas enacted through, and suggested by, the carriages, the mud, and the people. Norris's most complete exposition of Malebranche and refutation of Locke can be found in *An Essay Towards the Theory of the Ideal and Intelligible World* (1701). There he argued that the intelligible world existed in the mind of God and preceded the material world. God must have imagined or thought out the world before He could create it. Unlike Locke, Norris maintained that the mind can and does have a relation to "objective" or absolute truth, and that pure forms of ideas are present to the mind before we experience their imperfect manifestations in the material world. Thus, we can conceive of a perfect circle or a perfect square, he reasoned, although we do not find examples of exact geometric forms in the natural world.

Norris acknowledged his debt to Plato, Plotinus, Proclus, and Marsilio Ficino—as well as to contemporary French and English Platonists—for the contrast between the ideal world of essences and eternal truths and the visible world of contingent sensory experience. From Descartes he adopted the dualism of thought and extension, but he modified it with Malebranche's pantheistic explanation that eternal, immutable ideas come from God manifested in nature. In Malebranche's metaphysics, Norris also found the mechanism he needed for explaining how the material world—which is outside the mind—can be perceived, since with Descartes he believed that sensible knowledge is neither certain nor demonstrable. According to Malebranche, the influence of the material world can be explained by God's simultaneous action in the two realms of mind and body. Thus, walking in the country and coming upon a tree, we at once see a particular tree in our path and simultaneously apprehend the idea of a tree. God is the source both of the sensory perception and the idea, although through different channels. At the exact moment that the external body, the tree, makes an impression on our soul, He permits us access to the idea of "treeness" which exists externally in the mind of God in accordance with the laws by which He unites our souls and bodies. Thus if the world disappeared, God could still produce in us sensation. These ideas in Malebranche and in Norris represent an important transition from dualism to idealism, and are an essential philosophical link between Descartes and Berkeley.[42]

Astell and Norris wrote back and forth about the metaphysical properties of the soul, the possibility of higher and lower natures, the relation of the ideal to the material world. Like the earlier generations of Platonists, they both believed that reason was to be used not to prove God, as Descartes had assumed, but to love Him, and their letters explore the properties of that love. Astell fully agreed with Norris that as God was the cause of all thought, sensation, and feeling, one ought to try to love the Creator rather than his creatures, but she was more aware than Norris of the difficulties of managing to do so. On the other hand, she could see that since human beings were finite and imperfect, no mere mortal could ever satisfy the infinite desire of a rational soul. "'Tis true, a Sister Soul may give somewhat better Entertainment to our Love than other Creatures can," she wrote, "but she is not able to fill and content it." God alone was the proper object of infinite love. One had to learn to "tune" one's love "to the right Key" and to find one's way to that rational, becoming, and useful form of love which could be "secured from Disappointment, Jealousy, and all that long Train of Pain and Grief which attends Desire when it moves towards the Creature, [which will] set us above all Difficulties, render our Obedience regular, constant and vigorous, refine and sublimate our Natures, and make us become Angels even whilst we dwell on Earth."[43]

Norris recommended to her the works of Malebranche—particularly *Recherche de la Vérité* (1674), *Méditations Chrétiennes* (1683), and *Traité de Morale* (1684), because he felt that her objections to his own ideas would be overruled by reading the master. He also directed her to read Sylvain Régis, another minor Cartesian who had argued that since God was the only true substance, He was the only true cause. He recounted Malebranche's explanation that if we were permitted a clearer idea of the soul, we would be so ravished by the vision that we would be unable to think of anything else—not even our own bodily needs— and so would perish. Astell replied, "I am exceedingly pleas'd with

M. Malbranch's Account of the Reasons why we have no Idea of our Souls, and wish I could read that ingenious Author in his own Language, or that he spake mine."[44]

Had she read French, she would have been forced to confront Malebranche's assertion that the fibers in women's brains were too soft and delicate for the effort needed to get to the bottom of the most difficult and abstract truths. Their imagination, he wrote, "n'a point assez de force et d'étendue pour en percer le fond." He granted that there were exceptional women who were strong, constant, and rational, but stated that for the most part their minds were better suited "à décider des modes, à juger de la langue, à discerner le bon air et les belles manières" than to philosophy.[45]

Despite her basic agreement with Norris that God is the only efficient cause of all sensation, Astell continued to be uneasy with the way Norris dismissed the world. When their correspondence was to be published, she quickly added a disclaimer to this part of the argument. The problem with deriving all things directly from God was that it offered no explanation for the infinite variety of the world itself, Astell wrote; it "renders a great Part of GOD's Workmanship vain and useless." If the objects of our senses have no "natural Efficiency" in producing sensations, "if there is nothing in their own Nature which qualifies them to be instrumental to the Production of such and such Sensations, but that GOD should so please, what end do they serve? And what then becomes of that acknowledged Truth that GOD does nothing in vain, when such Variety of Objects as our Senses are exercised about are wholly unnecessary?"

One did not have to go far, she assured Norris, to retain the idea of God's preeminent role in human sensation. One could use some such construct as More's "plastick part of the soul" to explain the congruence between object and sensation. And when "this sensible Congruity is wanting as in the Case of Blindness, Deafness or the Palsie Etc. the Soul has no Sensation of Colours, Sounds, Heat and the like." Such an emendation would not change the gist or intent of Norris's argument. One could point to a direct relation between the senses and sensation without giving up a belief in the ultimate causality of God. That money was essential to buy things did not imply that money itself was responsible for the existence of, or the pleasure in, what was bought. With a telling example, she reasoned: "If a bountiful Person gives me Money to provide my self Necessaries, my Gratitude surely is not due to the Money but to the kind Hand that bestowed it, to whom I am as much obliged as if he had gone with me and bought them himself."

Her own reconciling suggestion to the philosophical dilemma of granting God's complete agency but also giving the senses and objects of the world their due, was the formulation that God produces our sensations "*mediately* by his Servant Nature" rather than "immediately by his Almighty Power."[46] Locke's posthumously published "Remarks" on Norris repeated this line of thought: "if the perception of colours and sounds depended on nothing but the presence of the object affording an occasional cause of God Almighty to exhibit to the mind the idea of figures, colours, and sounds; all that nice and curious structure of those organs is wholly in vain."[47]

Norris, as I have said, was so astonished at the philosophical abilities of his interlocutor that he assumed his equally surprised readers would "be tempted to question whether my Correspondent be really a Woman or no, To whom my Answer is, that indeed I did not see her write these Letters, but that I have all the moral and reasonable Assurance that she did write them, and is the true Author of them, that can be had in a thing of this Nature." He mentioned, among the beauties of her prose, "moving Strains of the most natural and powerful Oratory."[48]

Norris need not have been so amazed by Astell's grasp of these ideas and deeply felt presentation of them. They were concepts that had sustained her in difficult times. This was the heart of her feminism, and the groundwork for her feelings of self-worth. Her feminism, as we shall see, was also fed by her highly politicized sense of power relations between governments and constituencies, and by her love of other women; but this belief in the immaterial intellect, which had no gender and was the essential feature of human nature, was the base upon which she built the rest. Because she believed in a firm and immutable truth which all minds were capable of reaching, given time and training, women were equal to men in the only respect that mattered. The miracle of reason itself seemed to bless her logic, for surely that marvelous faculty was a sign of something "too Divine, to have it once imagin'd that it was made for nothing else but to move a portion of Matter 70 or 80 Years."[49]

For, since GOD has given Women as well as Men intelligent Souls, why should they be forbidden to improve them? Since he has not denied us the faculty of Thinking, why shou'd we not (at least in gratitude to him) employ our Thoughts on himself their noblest Object, and not unworthily bestow them on Trifles and Gaities and secular Affairs? Being the Soul was created for the contemplation of Truth, as well as for the fruition of

> Good, is it not as cruel and unjust to exclude Women from the knowledge
> of the one, as well as from the enjoyment of the other?[50]

The empty-headed flirts that Pope and Swift depicted, who curled
their hair, played at cards, gossiped over tea tables, and dandled their
lapdogs, were the result of misdirected ambition and improperly used
intelligence. Although Astell, too, deplored the waste of such an empty
existence, she thought it cruel and willfully shortsighted to ridicule
women's preoccupations without understanding the cause for them and
offering a remedy. Those who consigned women to lifelong ignorance
and frivolity did not understand this function and meaning of reason;
they were too wedded to custom and a materialistic view of things to
recognize the true purpose of human life. Any who accepted women's
inferiority without considering the cosmic purpose of all human intelligence were even blinder than those they condemned to darkness.

> As for those who think so Contemptibly of such a considerable part of
> GOD's Creation, as to suppose that we were made for nothing else but
> to Admire and do them Service, and to make provision for the low concerns
> of an Animal Life, we pity their mistake, and can calmly bear their Scoffs,
> for they do not express so much Contempt of us as they do of our Maker;
> and therefore the reproach of such incompetent Judges is not an Injury
> but an Honor to us.[51]

Mary Astell insisted on the primacy of the intellect, of course,
because it was the key to her confidence that she was meant for better
things than women's frivolous pleasures or domestic labors. That the
mind was to her an instrument for perceiving perfection, that it was
drawn to truth ("Truth is so very attractive, there's such a natural
agreement between our Minds and it"), proved the intellectual purposes
of human life. Indeed the mind made possible the concept of perfection,
which did not exist embodied in the world but only as an abstract idea
in the mind, planted there by God to goad rational beings to "advance
and perfect" their beings.

For her, the mighty thing about human nature was its unwillingness
to accept ignorance. Just as "a rational mind will be employed" and
women turned to plays and romances for lack of anything better, Astell
explained sensibly that "she who has nothing else to value herself upon,
will be proud of her Beauty, or Money and what that can purchase,
and think her self mightily oblig'd to him, who tells her she has those
Perfections which she naturally longs for."[52] She understood the com-
petitions of fashionable life as perversions of the instinct for excellence

with which their Maker had endowed all human beings, and she doubted the protestations of those of her sex who claimed to be satisfied with their allotted roles as ignorant women.

> A being content with Ignorance is really but a Pretence, for the frame of our nature is such that it is impossible we shou'd be so; even those very Pretenders value themselves for some Knowledge or other, tho' it be a trifling or mistaken one. She who makes the most Grimace at a Woman of Sense, who employs all her little skill in endeavoring to render Learning and Ingenuity ridiculous, is yet very desirous to be thought Knowing in Dress, in the Management of an Intreague, in Coquetry or good House-wifry. If then either the Nobleness or Necessity of our Nature unavoidably excites us to a desire of Advancing, shall it be thought a fault to do it by pursuing the best things?[53]

Thus, women needed education as part and parcel of the universal human impulse for excellence, and when she recommended that they withdraw to centers of learning, it was great ambition, not a spirit of retreat, that moved her. Study and meditation, as she understood them, were the natural outcomes of the self-respect of a reasoning creature. They justified one's life and guaranteed a certain sort of independence.

Mary Astell had been looking for a mentor when she wrote to Norris. She wanted the critical response of a rigorous thinker to her ideas, for she had found little formal guidance in her life. "Hitherto I have courted Truth with a kind of Romantick Passion, in Spite of all Difficulties and Discouragements; for knowledge is thought so unnecessary an Accomplishment for a woman, that few will give themselves the Trouble to assist them in the Attainment of it."[54] His correspondence was the greatest advantage that could befall her, she gratefully wrote. "I have brought my unwrought Ore to be refined and made current by the Brightness of your Judgement, and shall reckon it a great Favor if you will give your self the Trouble to point out my Mistakes, it being my Ambition not to seem to be without Fault, but if I can, really to be so."[55]

Norris was far from displeased with her appeal to him. He told her that her love of truth and her genius for it "makes me not only willing to enter into a Correspondence with you, but even to congratulate my self the Opportunity of so uncommon a Happiness."[56] But despite the gallant response, he was not as interested in directing her studies as in discussing his own ideas. Astell asked for advice about how to proceed in her own thinking. "When you think we have sufficiently examined the Subject we are upon," she suggested respectfully, "I desire the Favour of you to furnish me with such a System of Principles as I may relie on, and to give me such Rules as you judge most convenient to initiate a raw Disciple in the Study of Philosophy."⁵⁷ Norris made a gesture in the direction of instruction, and recommended that she read Malebranche and Antoine Arnauld. Incorporated into *A Serious Proposal To The Ladies*, which was written in the year of their correspondence, is an injunction obviously learned from him:

> And since the *French Tongue* is understood by most Ladies, methinks they may much better improve it by the study of Philosophy (as I hear the French Ladies do,) *DesCartes*, *Malebranch*, and others, than by reading idle *Novels* and *Romances*. 'Tis strange we shou'd be so forward to imitate their Fashions and Fopperies, and have no regard to what is truly imitable in them!⁵⁸

But for the most part their correspondence was addressed to the implications of his arguments about the love of God, and the possible flaws in his line of thought—things that interested him more than anything else.

At the end of ten months, Norris felt that enough ground had been covered to make the letters worthy of publication. In the meantime, Astell's first book, *A Serious Proposal*, had achieved some success, and although she was reluctant to grant her permission at first—perhaps the required modesty of convention—she did in the end permit Norris to print privately *Letters Concerning the Love of God* "Between the Author of Proposal to the Ladies and Mr. John Norris." In 1742, the "bluestocking" Mrs. Chapone told George Ballard that Astell's letters with Norris were generally thought to be her most "sublime" work.

Ultimately, one must understand Astell's philosophical stance in the light of her conviction that, as it was impossible to change the material circumstances facing her as a woman, her best hope lay in perfecting the intellectual and spiritual aspects of her character as a hedge against the inevitable disappointments of this life. This basic attitude marks the verse that she wrote long before her contact with Norris. What Norris gave Astell was the formal terminology—the philosophical arsenal—to defend this point of view. His influence can be seen in the difference between the first and second parts of *A Serious Proposal*.

Mary Astell stated in the opening pages of *A Serious Proposal Part II*, that like the original *A Serious Proposal*, it was written to educate other women to see through the empty and demeaning roles they were expected to play in English society. She said she had decided to write it because, although *A Serious Proposal* had been well received, no one had been roused to action to establish such a college as she had suggested. *Part II* moved the locus for change to each individual woman's mind rather than waiting for an institution. The book provided the reader with instruction in philosophical dispute, that she might examine for herself propositions about the purposes of human life—as Astell herself had done in her letters with Norris. In her first book, although she left the particulars up to those who were to govern the college, the purpose of her institution was to acquaint the women who attended "with Judicious Authors, give them opportunity of Retirement and Recollection and put them in a way of Ingenious Conversation, whereby they might enlarge their prospect, rectify their false Ideas, form in their Minds adequate conceptions of the End and Dignity of their Natures, not only have the Name and common Principles of Religion floating in the Heads and sometimes running out at their Mouths, but understand the design and meaning of it . . . and not only to feel Passions, but be able to direct and regulate their Motions; have a true Notion of the Nothingness of Material things and of the reality and substantialness of immaterial. . . ."[59]

A Serious Proposal Part II was a set of more detailed instructions for these same ends, a kind of "how-to-do-it" manual to be used at home, for women too timid to trust their own readings of *Les Principes de la Philosophie de M. Descartes* or Antoine Arnauld's *L'Art de Penser*, but who nevertheless wanted to improve their natural reasoning capacities. For them Astell distilled these works, laying out step-by-step the methods which these seventeenth-century philosophers claimed were necessary to attain truth.

A Serious Proposal Part II was the answer Astell made to her own request for a formal set of rules for thinking—the "System of Principles" she was so eager for; it is probably best understood as a training manual for Norris's brand of Christian Platonism. Certainly it incorporates the notions of those thinkers who had been seminal for Norris. From Norris's letters to Elizabeth Thomas we can deduce something of the intellectual program that he recommended to disciples who presented themselves in this manner: "Madam, Since we are rational Creatures, whose greatest Happiness consists in the perfect Contemplation of Truth and Love of Good, I think it concerns us most to apply our Thoughts to those Things that tend to the Improvement of our Reason." He recommended a study of geometry to "prepare" the mind for contemplation, and a thorough reading of Arnauld's *L'Art de Penser*, Malebranche's *Recherche de la Vérité*, and Descartes' *Méditations* (including instructions for teaching oneself French), to be followed by

More, Allestree, Burnet, and—with great caution and circumspection—
Locke.[60]

Antoine Arnauld's *L'Art de Penser* (1662), a favorite of Norris's, is
well represented in Astell's second *Serious Proposal*. It was an enormously
popular method book for philosophers, outlining the process for scru-
pulously rigorous thought. By 1697 it had gone through six French
editions and three English editions (the earliest in 1674 at the urging
of Locke, with the "recommendation and approbation" of the Royal
Society of London).[61]

Arnauld, a member of the Port Royal School in France, had written
it quickly, on a dare, as a summary of everything anyone needed to
know for clear, logical thinking. Its impulse was practical, pedagogical,
and it soon became the handbook for every philosopher of that century.
It gave Astell the system she was looking for, and at the same time
verified her earlier conviction that a trained mind, because it clarified
human choice, was necessary to secular and religious welfare alike.
Arnauld's association with a famous educational establishment also appealed to her. Originally a convent school for women, since 1223 Port
Royal des Champs had offered its sanctuary to both men and women,
without requiring vows. Blaise Pascal, whom Astell greatly admired,
was only the most famous of the seculars who made use of this retreat.
Before Arnauld died, he desired "that his heart be sent to Port Royal,
which he had always loved, because his mother, six sisters, and five
nieces, all admirably pious and full of the spirit and virtue of the family,
were *religieuses* of that house."[62]

In *L'Art de Penser*, Arnauld had argued that since ideas were merely
the perceptual or cognitive acts of limited and finite selves, they had to
be tested and examined. In discussing the process, he anticipated many
of the questions of the eighteenth-century empiricists about thought—
how ideas arise, the relations between them and the material world,
the degree of certainty of our knowledge—though he did not treat
them as epistemological dilemmas but as preliminary explanations for
his instruction on how to cultivate the mind, which seemed to him the
more useful enterprise. He wrote:

> Nothing is more to be esteemed than aptness in discerning the true from
> the false. Other qualities of mind are of limited use, but precision of thought
> is essential to every aspect and walk of life. To distinguish truth from error
> is difficult not only in the sciences but also in the everyday affairs that men
> engage in and discuss. Men are everywhere confronted with alternative
> routes—some true and others false—and reason must choose between
> them. Who chooses well has a sound mind; who chooses ill, a defective

one. Capacity for discerning the Truth is the most important measure of men's minds.

Our principal task is to train the judgement, rendering it as exact as we can. To this end the greatest part of our studies should be devoted.

We are accustomed to use reason as an instrument for acquiring the sciences, but we ought to use the sciences as an instrument for perfecting the reason: Accuracy of mind is infinitely more important than any speculative knowledge acquired from the truest and most established sciences.[63]

Astell followed this line closely, although she put more emphasis on the responsibility of living a principled life, and the impossibility of doing so without a good understanding.

> . . . everyone who pretends to Reason, who is a Voluntary Agent and therefore Worthy of Praise or Blame, Reward or Punishment, must *Chuse* his Actions and determine his Will to that Choice by some Reasonings or Principles either true or false, and in proportion to these Principles and the Consequences he deduces from them he is to be accounted, if they are Right and Conclusive a Wise Man, if Evil, Rash and Injudicious a Fool. If then it be the property of Rational Creatures, and Essential to their very Natures to Chuse their Actions, and to determine their Wills to that Choice by such Principles and Reasonings as their Understandings are furnish'd with, they who are desirous to be rank'd in that Order of Beings must conduct their Lives by these Measures, begin with their Intellectuals, inform themselves what are the plain and first Principles of Action and Act accordingly.[64]

All terms had to be clarified; one had to separate and distinguish the particular ideas conveyed by each word. "Thus many times our Ideas are thought to be false when the fault is really in our Language," she explained. "We make use of Words without joyning any, or only loose and indeterminate Ideas to them, Prating like Parrots who can Modify Sounds, and Pronounce Syllables."[65] She warned her women readers to pay particular attention to their use of "particles"—what we call conjunctions—for these were the words which gave the connections among ideas. She stressed this because although she did not believe women as generally illiterate as they were assumed to be—and was in fact convinced that they often pretended to spell worse than they knew in order to avoid being called proud, pedantic, or unwomanly—she did think that the misuse of "particles" was a common mistake made by women.[66]

She held with Arnauld that the mind followed a natural form of reasoning (another proof that all were intended to think). The steps in her method, which presumably built upon this natural capacity, were an amalgam of Descartes' *Rules for the Direction of the Mind* and the Port Royal Logic.[67] After setting out these rules—with many qualifications and examples—she demonstrated the method for her uneducated female audience by showing them how to take up systematically two sample questions: first, whether or not there was a God or a Perfect Being, and second, whether or not riches determined happiness.[68]

Astell's overriding concern was to teach other women how to think rigorously, so as to give them the wherewithal to make the important choices of their lives. She wanted to equip them to resist the false logic that attached them to the shallow and dangerous delights of this world, and to give them a taste for the lasting pleasures of the next. She wanted them to learn how to "withdraw" their "Minds from the World, from adhering to the Senses, from the Love of Material Beings, of Pomps and Gaities; for 'tis these that usually Steal away the Heart, that seduce the Mind to such unaccountable Wanderings, and so fill up its Capacity that they leave no room for Truth."[69]

Raised to be playthings or drudges, their lives filled with distraction and frivolity, women stood in special need of disciplined thought, she believed; to clean away false ideas and corrupt values which clogged their minds. "For tho we are acquainted with the Sound of some certain words, e.g. *God, Religion, Pleasure* and *Pain, Honour* and *Dishonour*, and the like," she wrote, "yet having no other *Ideas* but what are convey'd to us by these Trifles we converse with, we frame to ourselves strange & awkward notions of them, conformable only to those *Ideas* sensation has furnish'd us with, which sometimes grow so strong and fixt, that 'tis scarce possible to introduce a new Scheme of Thoughts, and so to disabuse us, especially whilst these Objects are thick about us."[70] Without any other basis for understanding, a woman "who sees her self and others respected in proportion to that Pomp and Bustle they make in the world, will form her Idea of Honour accordingly,"[71] she explained. "When a poor Young Lady is taught to value her self on nothing but her Cloaths, and to think she's very fine when well accoutred. When she hears say that 'tis Wisdom enough for her to know how to dress her self, that she may become amiable in his eyes, to whom it appertains to be knowing and learned; who can blame her if she lay out her industry and Money on such Accomplishments, and sometimes extends it farther than her misinformer desires she should? . . . What tho' she be sometimes told of another World, she has however a more lively perception of this, and may well think, that if her Instructors were in earnest when they tell her of *hereafter*, they would not be so busied and concerned about what happens *here.*"[72]

Although she wanted to turn her readers into metaphysicians, Astell was never especially prescriptive about other kinds of knowledge. "Whoever has a Rational Soul ought surely to employ it about some Truth or other, to procure for it right Ideas, that its Judgments may be true tho its Knowledge be not very extensive."[73] Unlike other educationalists, who assumed a male model for learning, she was not interested in fitting up women to join arcane academic controversies about theological precedent or ancient texts. She simply wanted to make available the life of the mind to others of her sex. The conventions of "scholiasts" were unnecessary, she told her readers. One needed only those languages necessary for access to useful writers and the careful study of a few well-chosen volumes. Mastery of ancient languages and a great range of books was mere pedantry, useful for those who cared more about worldly knowledge than about spiritual equilibrium. Native common sense was sufficient to any controversy. Nothing in the rhetorical rules of disputation was of real use, since "Truth not Victory is what we shou'd contend for in all Disputes." Eloquence, she said, was a matter of clarity rather than rhetorical skill. She had a philosopher's ideal of writing—that it be clear, straightforward, controlled, without "peculiar or Affected Phrases. . . . For Plain and Significant Language is ever best, we have a mistaken Idea of Learning if we think to pretend to't by sending our Reader every minute to the Dictionary."[74]

When Mary Astell's *A Serious Proposal* came out, many thought that Ralph Cudworth's daughter Damaris Masham had written it, as she was the notable contemporary woman to have a clearly reasoned idealist position and a concern for women's education. But although Lady Masham had been a correspondent of Norris's some years earlier, she was now the companion and confidant of John Locke—and less and less in sympathy with the otherworldly views of Astell and Norris.[75] When the Astell-Norris letters were published in 1695, it was she, ironically, who attacked the volume in a critical pamphlet, *Discourse Concerning the Love of God* (1696), and claimed that in perpetuating the Malebranchian theories of love for pure abstract forms, Mr. Norris had abdicated his responsibility for evolving ethical solutions to living in the "real" world.

She also rides hard Mary Astell's modest disclaimer to the *Letters* (about the value of publishing her "crude Rhapsodies" at all) by sneering at the "rhapsodies" which she says substitute for "reason." "Pompous Rhapsodies of the Soul's debasing her self," she mocked, deriding Astell's idealism, "when she descends to set the least part of her Affections upon anything but her Creator . . . are plainly but a complementing God with the contempt of his Works, by which we are most effectually led to Know, Love, and Adore Him."[76]

Astell did not reply immediately to the *Discourse* when it appeared, not thinking it "proper (after some Peoples fashion) to trouble the World with *answers* and *Replies*. . . . The justifying one's own opinions, merely as they are one's own, being in my mind a very poor employment."[77] But nine years later, when Norris was preparing his own response to Locke's criticism of his idealist position, Astell published her own thoughts on the matter in *The Christian Religion as Profess'd By a Daughter of the Church* (1705), directed at Locke, whom she seems to have thought was her critical opponent: "Some Men indeed have writ of Love, as if they knew nothing of it but what they learn from good Eating and the like sensations. And for Reasons to themselves best known, they write *Discourses* to perswade us, that we are under no necessity of taking our Affections off the Creature to place them solely on the Creator."[78]

Her indignation at the insulting phrases of the *Discourse* seems quite fresh after nine years: "This is not the place to take notice," she wrote, "how those who are so severe upon their Neighbors for being wanting (even in Private Letters writ without a design of being Publish'd) in that exactness of *Expression* which ought to be found in *Philosophical Disquisitions*, do themselves confound the notion of Love with the sentiment of Pleasure, by making Love to Consist barely in the act of the Mind towards that which pleases." She objected to that simplified definition of love, "for it is certain we shall be pleas'd with that which pleases whether or no it be commanded. . . . Love in this sense is no more in our power than the motion of our Pulse."[79] The "love" that she was concerned to define, the "love" that she and Norris had written about, was a more abstract movement of the soul towards its true good, a state which could be striven for with the rational mind.

Astell surmised that Lady Masham also had a hand in the *Discourse Concerning the Love of God* because she occasionally refers to the anonymous author as "they" or "them." Nor was she wrong to include both in her target, for Locke had composed his "An Examination of Malebranche's Opinion of Seeing all Things in God" and "Remarks upon some of Mr. Norris' Books" while living with the Masham family at Oates in the winter of 1693, although neither work was published until after his death. He can only have applauded Lady Masham's resolve to attack the Astell-Norris letters when they appeared, discussing and refining the very theories that so disturbed him.

This empiricist critique of Astell helps us to situate her thought in the dominant philosophical discourse of her day. Lady Masham announced it as her intention in the *Discourse* "to show the unserviceableness of an Hypothesis lately recommended to the World for a Ground of Christianity, and Morality," and the "injuriousness of that Hypothesis to True Religion, and Piety." Not that true religion was in any immediate danger, she added, because the exhortation to love all things in God was too "Visionary to be likely to be received by many Intelligent Persons; And too abstruse to be easily entertain'd by those who are altogether unconversant with Scholastic Speculations." Her objection, which was also Locke's, was to the nugatory character of such principles. People are never motivated by pure ideas, she wrote; "not one of the Six hundred Thousand would have marched through the Wilderness, had not *Moses* allow'd them to desire the good things of *Canaan*, but told them they must desire nothing of the Creature."[80] By not attaching desire to anything specific, Masham wrote, we could lead reason off in an "endless Chace after whatever strikes our Imagination with any Pleasing Idea." Astell noted this opposition of "ideas" to "reason" and rewrote the sentence in her refutation nine years later: "Tho' we act suitable to our *Nature and desire things that can be enjoy'd*, and thus go on in the *chace of Pleasing Ideas*, yet we will . . . keep them under the *government and direction of Reason*, which our indulg'd desires shall not at all impair."[81]

Why, asked Astell, was the affirmation of God as "the sole Object of our Love, as Love imports the motion, especially voluntary motion and tendency of the Mind to its true good," such an "*unserviceable*" notion? Where is the hurt of this, she asked, "that our Modern Divines and Philosophers shou'd make such an out-cry against it, as if the Loving GOD in this manner were destructive of all Religion?" Surely it was not any more impractical or unserviceable an idea—and no more counterintuitive—than Mr. Locke's own concept of the secondary qualities of objects, which formed no unimportant link in his epistemological argument. He would have us believe, she said acerbically, that qualities such as color and taste do not inhere in the objects themselves, but that the bulk, figure, and motion of insensible parts have the power to produce such sensations in us. "Every Man's Experience confutes this every Day," she wrote (quoting verbatim the language that the *Discourse* had directed against her nine years earlier). "I will allow them [the charge that it is "unserviceable" to love the Creator rather than the Creature] just so much and no more than they will allow me That *the daily sense and experience of Mankind* disproves what a great Philosopher asserts when he tells us That *Flame* is not *Hot and Light*, nor *Snow White and Cold*, nor *Manna White and Sweet*."[82]

Astell tried in this later work to clarify what she and Norris had meant by "love of God," by showing how one might satisfy hunger and thirst—the most primal material needs of all—and all the while keep one's mind on the Creator rather than the creation.

> Your Spirits fail and you grow faint, you Eat and Drink . . . and why so? not for the mere pleasure of Eating and Drinking, this I may say without a *Rhapsodie*, were below a Rational, much more a Christian, Mind. Tho' 'tis certain you feel Pleasure in it, and you thank GOD for it, since by this easie sensible way, without engaging your self in the troublesome Examination of the state of your Body and the suitableness of the nourishment, you Eat and Drink what will support it. But you do this only to keep your Body in Health that it may be able to serve your Mind, that both may serve their Redeemer, in which service all your Happiness consists.[83]

With Blakean idealism, she talked of love which carried one beyond the "prejudices of sense": "You look thro' the Creature to the Creator as the Author of all your Delight, and thus every morsel gives a double Pleasure, considering the hand that feeds you, or to speak more correctly [i.e., philosophically], the Power of GOD giving you divers modifications."

It was not that she did not understand the objections to her abstract system of values. "There's a difficulty 'tis true in setting our Affections on things above and not on things on the Earth, in being dead to Sense and placing all our Felicity in a Spiritual and Invisible Object." But she thought that it was possible—and better—to retrain the impulses to this way of living, and that it was a successful strategy for her own psychic survival. What neither Locke nor Masham fully credited, not being pious themselves, was that to Astell, religious practice was not a chore to be made more reasonable, or a gamble to be explained. Her Christian Platonism stilled her pointless longings and justified her intellectual, solitary existence. Renunciation could be a source of energy, and her conception of Christian love helped to fill her life. As she put it: "since the Persons we Love are ever in our Thoughts . . . if then we Love GOD He will be ever in our Thoughts with Pleasure. . . . His Worship and our Addresses to Him whether in our Closets or in the Place where his Honour dwelleth, will be the pleasantest not the heaviest part of our Lives."[84]

Mary Astell wrote *The Christian Religion* as her own refutation of Locke. Framing the work as a letter to her lifelong friend and patron, Lady Catherine Jones, about the anonymous *The Ladies Religion* (1697), Astell notes that this volume is in fact little more than an abstract of

Locke's *Reasonableness of Christianity* (1695) and keeps referring sarcastically to the "divine" credited with the authorship on the title page. Throughout her volume, Astell cites *The Ladies Religion* against *Reasonableness of Christianity* and vice versa, and both against *Discourse Concerning the Love of God*. Since she surmised that all three came from the same hand—that is, from Locke—her purpose was to show the internal contradictions of his thought. She was very sorry when "the great Mr. L." died while her book was in press, for she had looked forward to his reactions to her arguments.

The Christian Religion was Astell's philosophical manifesto—"what I think a Woman *ought* to Believe and Practice"—written at the height of her fame. Over four hundred pages of propositions and explanations given in numbered paragraphs, as in Pascal's *Pensées*, the work establishes in its first half the grounds for natural and revealed religion, and the second half spells out the implications for action on the basis of these beliefs—one's duty to God, to one's neighbors or community, and to oneself. The Anglican orthodoxy of this book was such that when it first came out some credited it to Francis Atterbury, then dean of Carlisle, the leading theoretician of the High Church party.

Astell wrote it, as she did her earlier books, for her fellow women, her sisters, to give them a solid basis for belief so that they would not be easily led into skepticism. She intended it as an inoculation against the materialist philosophy of Locke and the fashionable deism of the day. She objected to the instrumental view of religion which dismissed the "mysteries" and retained only what was useful for moral suasion. Locke had written in *Reasonableness of Christianity*, with an interesting choice of metaphor, that the classical philosophers had shown the beauty of virtue: "They set her off so as drew Men's Eyes and approbation to her: But leaving her unendowed, very few were willing to espouse her. . . . But now there being put into the Scales on her side, *An exceeding and immortal weight of Glory* [i.e. Heaven]; *Interest* is come about to her; And Virtue now is visibly the best bargain. . . . Upon this foundation, and upon this only, Morality stands firm."[85] Such a utilitarian ethic reduced the afterlife to a mere trick to keep people in line, rather than an embodiment of transcendent spirituality which the earthbound ought to strive to imitate in life, a spirituality which could transform the minds and hearts of believers in a fundamental way.

"Most Men are so Sensualiz'd, that they take nothing to be Real but what they can Hear and See," wrote Mary Astell. "Others who wou'd seem the most refined, make Sensation the fund of their Ideas, carrying their Contemplations no farther than these, and the Reflections they make upon the operations of their Minds when thus employ'd."[86]

Locke's theory of knowledge was limited to the prosaic and material. Astell was convinced that the highest purpose of human thought was the contemplation of pure ideas, which by virtue of their abstract nature, had the power to draw the mind away from sense, moderate the passions, and focus the distractable mortal mind on an immaterial Good. "Men Speculate what will be of use to Human Life," she remarked with gentle irony, "what will get them a Name in the World, and raise them to the Posts they covet. But the Contemplation of Immaterial Beings and Abstracted Truths, which are the Noblest Objects of the Mind, is look'd on as Chimerical and a sort of Madness; and to study to come up to the pure Morals of the Gospel is in their account Visionary." Rather than spending so much time studying our own natures, she continued, we ought to pay more attention to our relation to God, that is, to our place in the universe and to our obligations to our Maker.

Locke, of course, objected to conceiving of religion as the contemplation of abstract ideas, because he thought it beyond the grasp of "vulgar capacities." In *Reasonableness of Christianity* he had written, "you may as soon hope to have all Day-Labourers and Tradesmen, the Spinsters and Dairy Maids perfect Mathematicians, as to have them perfect in *Ethicks* this way. Hearing plain Commands, is the sure and only course to bring them to Obedience and Practice."[87] He denied the necessity of abstract philosophical thinking for an essential understanding of Christianity. He declared:

> The Writers and Wranglers in Religion . . . dress it up with notions; which they make necessary and fundamental parts of it; As if there were no way into the Church but through the Academy and Lyceum. The greatest part of Mankind have not leisure for Learning and Logick, and superfine distinctions of the Schools. Where the hand is used to the Plough, and the Spade, the head is seldom elevated to sublime Notions, or exercised in mysterious reasonings. 'Tis well if Men of that rank (to say nothing of the other Sex) can comprehend plain propositions, and a short reasoning about things familiar to their Minds, and nearly allied to their daily experience.[88]

To Astell, who, like Whichcote and Cudworth before her, felt that "the Service of GOD is most Reasonable in its self, and indeed most delightful to a Rational Nature," Locke confused the issue by selecting from scripture what he thought prevented people from wrongdoing, but ignoring the positive exhortations to love and charity. "It were to be wished," she replied dryly, "that there were no Controversies, no *Writers and Wranglers in Religion to fill it with niceties and dress it up with Notions*; but that all of us, whether Divines or others, receiv'd the

John Locke.
Portrait by
M. Dahl, c. 1696.
By permission of the
National Portrait
Gallery, London.

Truth [of Scripture] *in Faith and Love, endeavouring to keep the Unity of the Spirit in the bond of Peace.*"[89]

She was also acutely aware that, in his statement, Locke had dismissed women along with workers as incapable of following the reasoning which set up God as the fountainhead of Good, the source of that absolute idea, and which then attempted to communicate with that idea through universal love. She denied that such concepts were mysterious or inaccessible; they were only *"plain Propositions and short Reasonings about things familiar to our Minds, as* need not *amaze* any part of Mankind, no not the *Day Labourer and Tradesmen, the Spinsters and Dairy Maids*, who may very easily *comprehend* what a Woman cou'd write." As usual, she disclaimed any special abilities but used herself as the example that proved the capacities of all women. The author of *The Christian Religion*, she urged her readers, "has not the least Reason to imagine that her Understanding is any better than the rest of her Sex's. All the difference, if there be any, arising only from her Application, her Disinterested and Unprejudic'd Love to Truth, and unwearied pursuit of it, notwithstanding all Discouragements, which is in every Womans Power as well as in hers."⁹⁰

Mary Astell was also extremely sensitive to the political implications of Locke's seemingly neutral religious arguments. She could see why the biblical injunction to universal love did not sit easy with someone of his political stamp. For one thing, it enjoined a person to love his enemies, and for the author of *Two Treatises of Government*, that contradicted what for him was an even more *"Fundamental* law, the law of preservation." According to this law, one could not love a "persecutor." She did not forbear from pointing out that the alternative to a policy involving the sovereignty of the people and their resistance to tyrannical "persecutors" was the High Church doctrine of passive obedience.⁹¹ And could the Bible be wrong? she asked. Surely God would not lay down *"traps or snares to render* us *Miserable,"* nor would He enjoin us to love our enemies against our true interests. Perhaps, she concludes sarcastically, "everything is not True which we find in the *Discourses* of our Modern Authors, who not only refine upon Philosophy, by which they do Service to the World; and upon Politicks, by which they mean to Serve their Party; but even upon Christianity it self, pretending to give us a more *Reasonable* account of it."⁹²

Like the conservative divines of her day, Astell was alarmed by Locke's Socinian tendencies. In *Reasonableness of Christianity*, she charged he did not credit the divinity of Christ, and called "Him no more than an *extraordinary Man*, and *extraordinary Person*."⁹³ In her own book she went to some lengths to prove that Christ was divine, adducing the supernatural manner of his birth, his preaching, and his martyrdom.

She was likewise disturbed that Locke did not argue for an immaterial soul, and attended very closely to those arguments both in the *Essay* and in the *Correspondence with Stillingfleet* which concerned the existence of a spiritual substance separable from matter. In his third letter to Stillingfleet, Locke set forth the possibility of God's superadding to parcels of matter (i.e., to human beings) the property of thought, offered as an alternative to his own materialistic ontogeny of thought in Book IV, iii, 6 of the *Essay*. There he suggested two possible explanations for how material beings came by the property of immaterial thought, neither of which, he said, could be conclusively proved. Either God had arranged a sufficiently complicated set of neurophysiological connections—what Locke called a "suitably organized system of matter"—so that He in fact made it possible for matter to think, or else He had superadded the immaterial power of thought to mere matter. In the latter case, Locke instanced Newton's law of gravity—the fact that matter can attract matter although we do not understand how or why—to show that properties other than the primary ones (solidity, extension, number) can inhere in matter, and that these "superadded properties" do not otherwise interfere with our definition of matter as substance with solidity, extension, number, and so on. He stated that gravity, like thought, could have been superadded to material substance whether or not we understand how. And he added wryly that if one insisted upon denying everything whose manner of origin we cannot understand, it would prove a more dangerous rule to follow, and a much greater threat to religion, than his own so-called skepticism. In fact, the burden of Locke's reply to Stillingfleet was that religion was safe in the wake of *An Essay Concerning Human Understanding*, "that all the great ends of morality and religion are well enough secured barely by the immortality of the soul, without a necessary supposition that the soul is immaterial," and that several of Stillingfleet's arguments had much more problematic consequences, theologically, if one followed them through to their logical conclusions.[94] The difficulty, from Stillingfleet's point of view, was that Locke was unwilling to argue conclusively for superaddition, and insisted that neither of his alternative explanations for the conjunction of thought and matter could be more definitively proved than the other.

Astell pounced upon what she saw as an inconsistency between the argument of superaddition and those parts of the *Essay* (notably Book IV, iii, 29) in which Locke had stated that it was impossible to combine ideas which were opposed in their essences. Matter—body—cannot think, she held; the idea of "thought" is excluded from the essential idea of matter; they are repugnant to one another. To argue that the superaddition of thought to matter was always an arbitrary possibility for an all-powerful God, simply confused the issue. She wrote: "I know that a Triangle is not a Square, and that Body is Not Mind, as the *Child knows that Nurse that feeds it is neither the Cat it plays with, nor the Blackmoor it is afraid of*, and the Child and I come by our Knowledge after the same manner." She then went on to say that we cannot distinguish one idea from another on the basis of what God *may* do, what foreign properties he *may* endow substance with, or else all basis for knowledge is destroyed, and "neither the Child nor Mr. L. himself can say, whether Omnipotency may have not endued the Cat with the Nurse's Faculties."[95]

Finally, Astell ended her discussion by using Locke's argument to Stillingfleet against his own conclusions. She said that to claim the superaddition of thought to matter was tantamount to conceding the separation of these two.

For I do not find that the Arguments of the Great Mr. L. who is at best able to defend the Cause, not those he thought fit to use against so Great and Learned an Adversary as the late Bishop *Stillingfleet*, amount to any more than that God *can* do what we find He *has* done, (viz.) make another Substance besides Body, whose Essential Property, if not its very Essence shall be Thought, and can Unite this Thinking Substance to Body, which is what we call the Union between Soul and Body. For if there is *nothing at all in Matter as Matter that Thinks*, then GOD's *bestowing on some Parcels of Matter* a Power of Thinking, is neither more or less than the making an Arbitrary Union between Body and something that is not Body, whereby this *Composite* has Properties that *Matter as Matter is no way capable of.* So that it is not Body that Thinks, but the Mind that is United to it, Body being still as incapable of Thought as ever it was.[96]

Astell's commentary on Locke is not remarkable as philosophy, although her first critical impulse was to look for inconsistencies, which she generally found. Her conventionally pious reasons for exposing Locke's weak points are no longer interesting to us; her metaphysics has long been out of fashion. Further, she exerted her ingenuity not to break any new ground but to defend the old. Nonetheless she took on the greatest philosopher of her day with admirable savoir faire, in the spirit of questing for truth, and her exposition must be of interest to anyone who reads the philosophy of that period.

Once again Astell's publication drew Lady Masham into print. Four months after Astell's *The Christian Religion* appeared, Masham fired back *her* version of a Christian theology suitable for women. Ostensibly written several years earlier but revived to defend the now-dead Locke, Masham began her *Occasional Thoughts in Reference to a Vertuous or Christian Life* (1705) by extolling the pleasures of rational conversation, lamenting her present solitude, and announcing her intention to develop and write down "such Thoughts as were lately suggested to me by others." She went on, defending many of Locke's ideas about knowledge, government, education, the natural light of reason, the state of nature, etc.—and responding to some of Astell's points in *The Christian Religion*. At the end of her book, she advises women to take the opportunity to educate themselves while educating their children—and she sympathizes with those who have none but infants to talk to all day long. She warns that intellectual women will be mocked and scoffed at in their benighted society, much as Astell might have done. In town, wrote Masham, such a woman will be the "Jest of the *Would-be-Witts*," and in the country her understanding of Christian theology will make people suspect her of heresy "whilst her little Zeal for any Sect or Party would make the Clergy of all sorts give her out for a *Socinian*, or a *Deist*. . . . The Parson of the Parish, for fear of being ask'd hard questions, would be shy of coming near her."[97] Unlike Astell, Masham also objected to the identification of female honor with simple chastity, a virtue she obviously thought was overrated, and noted was not valued in men at all.

All of this was predictable: that Masham's positions would be as sensible and down-to-earth as Astell's were abstract and idealistic, that Masham would focus on life-on-earth while Astell stressed preparation for the hereafter. Like seconds in the duel between Locke's empiricism and Norris's idealism, their exchange is a fascinating reprise of that great debate. Masham found Astell's Neoplatonic idealism as infuriating as Locke found Norris's, and a more suitable target for her scorn. She tried to puncture it with her pragmatism. Each registered deeply the other's barbs. But as Astell demonstrated in *The Christian Religion*, she was the better metaphysician, and within her own premises she maneuvered with ease and agility.

As we shall see in the next chapter, Astell came to prominence with a book which proposed colleges for women. Yet she valued academic work only as it honed the intellect, and she valued the intellect only as it led to faith and understanding in God. Indeed, her significance in the history of feminism is not so much that she favored women's education as that she presented women as rational beings capable of serious thought, in need of refuge from the fashionable world.

To the modern sensibility, her claim for equality on the basis of rationality—"I think, therefore I am as good as anyone else"—seems an unnecessary refinement of a claim based on simple humanity or an absolute political right. Tied to education and to leisure, this is more elitist than a conception of equality based in productivity or in need. Furthermore, to the present action-oriented age, Astell's decision to contemplate abstract Truth rather than to try to change the material conditions of women's lives seems both passive and effete. But she was the inevitable female projection of the English Enlightenment. Her commitment to reason was eminently sensible and it did not lead her into hopeless deadlock with her culture or into fruitless despair. It provided her life with a task, a purpose, and a meaning.

Chapter Four

England's First Feminist
A Serious Proposal to the Ladies

There is a sort of Bravery and Greatness of Soul, which does more truly ennoble us than the highest Title, and it consists in living up to the dignity of our Natures, scorning to do a mean, unbecoming thing; in passing [in]differently thro' Good and Evil Fortune, without being corrupted by the one or deprest by the other. For she that can do so, gives evidence that her Happiness depends not on so mutable a thing as this world; but in a due subserviency to the Almighty, is bottom'd only on her own great Mind. This is the richest Ornament, and renders a Woman glorious in the lowest Fortune.

> Mary Astell, *A Serious Proposal*, 1694

Our earliest historians of feminism placed Mary Astell at the start of a tradition that resurfaced at the end of the eighteenth century in Mary Wollstonecraft, and at the end of the nineteenth century in Charlotte Perkins Gilman.[1] Her first book, *A Serious Proposal*, with its scheme for an all-female college, a "Protestant nunnery," and its insistence on women's right to a life of the mind, created that reputation overnight. It burst upon London in 1694 and was read and talked of from Pall Mall to Grub Street. The ideas were original and compelling and the author a novelty: her tones were the recognizable tones of an elegant society woman. What made her write this book, living alone in Chelsea at twenty-eight, is a matter of speculation. But because her earliest books were her feminist texts, one function they probably had was to establish her right to speak.

Remarks about Astell's book turn up in private correspondence, in journals, and in the books of contemporaries. Her name became a byword for accomplished speech: "had I but the least part of Mrs. Astell's eloquence to persuade you . . . "[2] Young ladies at boarding school and the wives and daughters of tradesmen and shopkeepers read her feminist treatises and argued their points. John Evelyn thought her writing "sublime," and wished "that at the first *Reformation* in the Kingdom, some of those demolished Religious Foundations had been spared both for Men and Women; where single Persons devoutly inclined, might have retired and lived without Reproach or insnaring Vows. . . . And what should still forbid us to promote the same Example, and begin such Foundations, I am to learn more solid Reasons for, than any I confess, as yet I have."[3] Grub Street publisher John Dunton called her "divine Astell" in his autobiographical *Life and Errors* (1705), and promoted *A Serious Proposal* in a number of his publications. A query was printed in the *Athenian Oracle* from a dubious reader asking if he should immediately embark upon the private education of a woman friend of his.

A little tract that I have lately read, very much encourages women to be studious, and contrary to the general opinion of most men, maintains, that they are capable of making as great improvement in it as we are. Now I must confess, I am so far from the author's opinion, judging by that acquaintance I have had with the sex, that I believe it impossible their

natural impertinencies shou'd ever be converted into a solid reasoning; I
am something the more desirous to be determined in this matter, because
I have a particular friend amongst the fair sex, over whom I have some
power, that has a great inclination to begin, if she may ever be able to
make one amongst the learned world. She hopes well of her own side, but
I am unwilling she shou'd engage her self in an affair, that will prove
successless in the end. But we are at last both contented to be determined
by you.[4]

In *The Challenge, Sent by a Young Lady to Sir Thomas . . . or, The Female
Warr* (1697), another Dunton epistolary production, a male writer addresses his female interlocutor thus: "even you have lately had a *serious
proposal* to make a Schism among your Sex, set up *Protestant Nunneries*,
and exclude your selves from the *World*: the surest way I must confess,
to procure you *Husbands*."[5]

Defoe, that cultural magpie, was dazzled by *A Serious Proposal*, and
seized upon its central idea for a section on "An Academy for Women"
in his *Essay Upon Projects* (1697). Steele incorporated over a hundred
pages of it in his *The Ladies Library* (1714), without ever acknowledging
the theft. Ralph Thoresby, the antiquarian, noted the occasion in his
diary when he went to Chelsea to meet "the obliging Mr. Croft, the
minister, who introduced me to the celebrated Mrs. Astell."[6] "Thanks
for the agreeable Entertainment which Mrs. *Astell* has afforded me. I
am pleased with her Project, but do not think it likely to succeed,"
wrote Richard Gwinnett to Elizabeth Thomas.[7]

This must have been when Samuel Richardson, then a young man,
first heard of Astell. Forty years later, his Sir Charles Grandison, that
ideal proponent of bourgeois culture, expounds a "Protestant nunnery"
scheme very much like Astell's to the company after dinner, for two
pages. It has been suggested too, that Astell was the model for his pious
and articulate Clarissa, both because of her eloquence and wit and
because of her ardent religiousness. How fitting that the independent,
passionately rational tones of Mary Astell helped Richardson imagine
the first real heroine of English fiction.[8]

Astell's later scholarly religious tracts undoubtedly appealed more
to divines such as Dr. Waterland, Dr. Charlett, and Dr. Hickes—who
mentioned her to one another as the author of the closely reasoned
tracts they admired for exposing "moderation" in religious matters.[9]
John Walker boasted of her help in his compilation of the indignities
suffered by Anglican clergymen during the interregnum, *The Sufferings
of the Clergy* (1714), and proudly prints his thanks to "the most ingenious
Mrs. Astell."[10] Her name came to be associated with the religious phi-

lanthropists of the SPCK like Robert Nelson, Dr. John Sharp, archbishop of York, and with nonjurors like Hickes, Dodwell, and Archbishop Sancroft. Although her religious and political tracts have much to recommend them, *A Serious Proposal To The Ladies* (1694), her first book, caught everybody's attention from the start. It was a lively polemic about the need to train women intellectually, coupled with a plan for educational residences which would resemble something between a women's college and a convent without vows. "Women's education" was the available vessel into which she poured both her resentments about women's second-class place in society and her rather abstract interest in theories of knowledge. She suggested that unmarried women pool their resources—that is, the dowries of the wealthier members—to support those from the middling ranks of society who had nowhere else to go and no visible means of support. The redeeming social value of the plan was that the college would provide training for virtuous social service—such as teaching or nursing.

It is not hard to understand the popularity of *A Serious Proposal*. It is tart, lively, sensible. Astell really is best when she is partisan and polemical, arguing one position against another—fighting for a cause rather than expounding doctrine. The sentiment is freer in this first book than in later ones, where she begins to imitate the ideological cant of her day. This first tract contains the unguarded responses and opinions of an intelligent woman, without the moves of formal debate, the rhetorical fanfare, the conventional terms she later adopted when positioning herself in the public arena. One feels what a fine conversationalist she must have been; her style sparkles with bons mots. She punctuates for the rhythms of speech, which are choppier and more active than the rhythms of prose. She gives end stops to incomplete phrases and runs sentences together; she uses commas and semicolons in accord with the patterns of breath rather than syntax. The prose reads aloud very well, with a slightly sarcastic, clearheaded, humorous tone. "How can you be content to be in the World like Tulips in a Garden," she demanded of her audience who flowered everywhere in ornamental silks and laces, "to make a fine *shew* and be good for nothing?"

> This is a Matter infinitely more worthy your Debates, than what Colours are most agreeable, or what's the Dress becomes you best? Your *Glass* will not do you half so much service as a serious reflection on your own Minds, which will discover Irregularities more worthy your Correction, and keep you from being either too much elated or depress'd by the representations of the other. 'Twill not be near so advantageous to consult with your Dancing-master as with your own Thoughts, how you may with greatest

exactness tread in the Paths of Vertue, which has certainly the most attractive *Air*, and Wisdom the most graceful and becoming *Mien*: Let these attend you and your Carriage will always be well compos'd, and ev'ry thing you do will :arry its Charm with it."

It is as if Jane Austen were preaching to a church full of women, teasing them, wheedling, explaining, flattering, cajoling. If Austen had given her conservative heroine of *Mansfield Park*, Fanny Price, a freer rein—had let her speak to her heart's content—this is what she would have sounded like.

Were not a Morning more advantageously spent at a Book than at a Looking-Glass, and an Evening in Meditation than in Gaming? Were not Pertinent and Ingenious Discourse more becoming in a visit, than Idle twattle and uncharitable Remarks? than a Nauseous repetition of a set of fine words which no body believes or cares for? And is not the fitting our selves to do Real Services to our Neighbors, a better expression of our Civility than the formal performance of a thousand ridiculous Ceremonies, which every one condemns and yet none has the Courage to break thro?[12]

Astell speaks directly off the page, immediately intimate, while at the same time relishing her phrases. She wrote as if to a group of admiring acquaintances; she was from their ranks, she understood their concerns. Her first line of attack was on the hesitations of her women readers, their internal resistance to taking themselves seriously. She tried to woo them from their usual courses, and exhorted them to do themselves justice, to ignore debasing conceptions, to imagine themselves capable of the highest endeavors. Referring to the way women permitted their attention to be monopolized by men, she wrote, "We value *them* too much and our *selves* too little, if we place any part of our desert in their Opinion, and don't think our selves capable of Nobler Things than the pitiful Conquest of some worthless Heart." "Can we Think and Argue Rationally about a Dress, an Intreague, an Estate? Why then not upon better Subjects?"[13]

She warned against the easy mediocrity which was all that society expected of women. "The first thing I shall advise against is Sloth," she wrote, and a "stupid Indifference to any thing that is excellent." What some called "contentedness," she insisted was "an ungenerous inglorious Laziness. [W]e doze on in a Circle with our Neighbours, and so we get but Company and Idleness enough, we consider not for what we were made ... [D]are to break the enchanted Circle that custom has plac'd us in," she exhorted. "[W]hat is it that stops your flight, that keeps you groveling here below, like *Domitian* catching Flies, when you should be busied in obtaining Empires?"

She encouraged women to fulfill their best selves, to think clearly, and not to be misled by social custom or by current fashion. "[M]ost of, if not all, the Follies and Vices that Women are subject to (for I meddle not with the Men) are owing to our paying too great a deference to other Peoples judgments, and too little to our own." She urged women to get back in touch with their common sense. Indeed, her whole emphasis is very much on what we nowadays call "consciousness-raising." Her excessively italicized prose reads sometimes like emphatic letters from an aunt or an older sister, repetitively and affectionately trying to correct certain habits of mind.[14]

For a number of reasons, Astell's proposal spread quickly through the literate population of London. More copies of this book sold than any of her others, and today there are more extant copies of *A Serious Proposal* than of any other work by Astell. By 1701 five editions had been issued. One reason for this popularity was that the education of women interested the public just then, and had become a subject of contention.

Education for Englishwomen had been seriously in arrears for over a century, since schools and libraries in women's monastic orders had been disbanded during the Reformation. In Spain and Italy, women's scholarship had been integrated into cultural life, and intellectual women were both students and professors at the great universities and were prized by their native cities.[15] England had never had a tradition for women's scholarship, as on the Continent, and there had never been learned orders for women in England. True, there had been abbesses in England, women from powerful families for whom no suitable marriage mate could be found, or who, by virtue of their birth and wealth, chose instead to have intellectual or administrative careers. It had taken Catherine of Aragon, who came from the sophisticated court of her mother, Queen Isabella of Spain, to raise the tone of Henry VIII's court and encourage the European practice of tutoring wealthy girls alongside their brothers. Catherine provided her own daughter Mary with the best tutors and encouraged the writing of several treatises on women's education. The intellectual attainments of her stepdaughter, Elizabeth I, are well-known.[16]

Nevertheless, convents in England had been where good families boarded their daughters, while girls from poorer families attended day school. And when they closed their doors, their lands and property confiscated, gone was the one social institution which had protected—however limitedly—the tradition of women's learning. Catherine of Aragon's notions about educated daughters were banished from England as effectively as her religion; within a few generations it was uncommon for a woman even to be able to read or write her native tongue well. In 1684, Dr. George Hickes noted: "It is shameful, but ordinary, to see Gentlewomen, who have both Wit and Politeness, not able yet to pronounce well what they read. . . . They are still more grossly deficient in Orthography, or in Spelling right, and in the manner of forming or connecting Letters in Writing."[17]

Learned women were rare by Mary Astell's time. Even wealthy girls were not trained to read and write but to embroider and do fancy stitching, to dance the latest dances, sing and perhaps play the flute, and to prepare condiments, jellies, and sweetmeats. In the Hastings family, for instance, George, the eighth earl of Huntingdon, was sent to Wadham College, Oxford, as well as to Foubert's Academy to learn "those exercises befitting a gentleman." He read the Greek New Testament and Juvenal, Latin and English verse, and studied grammar and rhetoric.[18] His sister, a woman of great intelligence and ambition who was later to become one of Mary Astell's friends and patrons, was given only dancing and music lessons in London during the short winter season.[19]

In Astell's neighborhood in Chelsea, where once had lived Sir Thomas More's enlightened household, in which daughters and sons were educated equally, there was Josiah Priest's school, satirized by Thomas D'Urfey's *Love for Money, or The Boarding School* (1691) as an establishment where young female boarders spent their time flirting with lecherous teachers and consuming large quantities of bread and butter. Where once Margaret Roper strolled in the courtyard with Erasmus, discussing Quintilian, the girls in Josiah Priest's Chelsea school imitated the gestures of their dancing master; where once the great Holbein had sketched the remarkable More family, these boarding-school girls now japanned boxes.[20]

One meaning of this change was that gender had become a more important determinant of educational status than social class. While the sons of rich plebeians were being educated at Oxford and Cambridge to fill the ranks of the church, it was becoming more and more commonplace for women who were their social superiors to remain ignorant and illiterate. The universities were open to the male offspring of brewers and haberdashers, but closed to the daughters of the oldest noble families in England.[21] The ideology of class leveling, which had ascendancy during the interregnum; the development of a cash economy, which seriously disadvantaged the landed aristocrats; the new entrepreneurial spirit of individual endeavor and advancement, which took hold in the seventeenth century—all these began to act as a counterweight, in exceptional cases, to the social determinants of class and lineage for men. This possibility of mobility and opportunity for men but not women, as much as anything, stuck in Astell's craw. Increasingly it was possible and seemly for a man to move up in the world—whereas for a woman the obstacle of gender was insurmountable. On every hand she saw men of lower class than herself succeeding as writers, preachers, and scholars, while she had difficulty simply finding a way to feed herself or to buy paper to write on.

Astell's book also addressed another serious contemporary problem, the demographics of the marriage market: there were simply more women than men in London. Not all women could marry, and there was no creditable social solution for those who stayed single. The year that *A Serious Proposal* was published, there were 77 males for every 100 females in London. As Defoe's Moll Flanders put it in 1722: "The market is against our sex just now."

Historians have suggested that this surplus of women was due to men dying in the wars (the War of the League of Augsberg lasted from 1689 to 1697; the War of the Spanish Succession from 1701 to 1713) and to men being more susceptible to disease, in particular to the plague. More men than women also migrated to the colonies. That middle- and upper-class women were increasingly relegated to reproductive labor, only emphasized this demographic imbalance. Professional tradesmen operating within a cash rather than a barter system increasingly fulfilled the economic functions that women had carried out in manors and villages of an earlier time.[22] This inevitably increased the pressure on women to marry men who could support them.

Astell's *A Serious Proposal*, then, can be read as a solution to the economic realities of the particular class of women for whom she wrote. She eloquently describes the dynamics of the marriage market for the unlucky gentlewoman.

> For the poor Lady . . . having spread all her Nets and us'd all her Arts for Conquest, and finding that the Bait fails where she wou'd have it take, and having all this while been so over-careful of her Body, that she had no time to improve her mind, which therefore affords her no safe retreat, now she meets with Disappointment abroad, and growing every day more and more sensible that the respect which us'd to be paid her, decays as fast as her Beauty; quite terrified with the dreadful Name of *Old Maid*, which yet none but Fools will reproach her with, nor any wise Woman be afraid of; to avoid this terrible *Mormo*, and the scoffs that are thrown on superannuated Virgins, she flies to some dishonourable Match as her last, tho'

much mistaken Refuge, to the disgrace of her Family, and her own irreparable Ruin.[23]

She explicitly recommends the financial advantages of her plan to parents who are well-to-do, but who wish to dispose of excess daughters genteelly, without cutting too deeply into their fortunes. Each of the sponsoring members could contribute £500 to the residential school she proposes, an inconsiderable sum for a dowry "as the world goes," but far cheaper than maintaining their single daughters "in the *Port* which Custom makes almost necessary."

A Serious Proposal had an enormous impact on the contemporary women who read it. Such women as Judith Drake, Lady Damaris Masham, Elizabeth Thomas, Lady Mary Chudleigh, Elizabeth Elstob, and Lady Mary Wortley Montagu—these we know of—were encouraged by her book to think of women as a misunderstood and oppressed class of people. Their lives were changed by Astell's texts and by her example; she showed them how to take themselves seriously as thinkers and writers.

Judith Drake was the first imitator; *An Essay in Defense of the Female Sex* (1696), immediately attributed to Astell, was a spirited reply to the common charge that women were frivolous and inconstant.[24] She presented satirical portraits of beaux, poets, coffeehouse politicians, and the like, to show that men could be as fatuous, as "impertinent" as women. She argued from biological design: among animal species, the females were every bit as clever, subtle, and cunning as the males. (Astell, of course, was always quick to deny the importance of "base" animal nature in her discussions of women.) But Drake did not object to the lack of formal schooling for women as Astell did, since women could always read on their own, and since no modest woman wanted to be known as a pedant. She also posed the question of "whether the time an ingenious Gentleman spends in the Company of Women, may justly be said to be misemploy'd or not?"—a question which never would have occurred to Astell, who did not concern herself with what was good or bad for men.[25]

Lady Mary Chudleigh was the Devonshire wife of the second son of a baronet, a poet who acknowledged Astell as her inspiration. In *To Almystrea* (an anagram for Mary Astell), she wrote:

> Your bright Example leaves a Tract Divine,
> She sees a beamy Brightness in each line,
> And with ambitious Warmth aspires,

Attracted by the Glory of your Name,
To follow you in all the lofty Roads of Fame.

Her second stanza is an exalted resolution to live as Astell exhorted her
readers to live, in the pure realm of Platonic ideas:

> To wish for nothing but exchange of Thoughts,
> For intellectual joys
> And Pleasures more refin'd
> Then Earth can give, or Fancy can create.[26]

She echoed Astell's celebration of the mind and rejection of the world
of merely material manifestation. Women were meant to live contemplative lives, and only had to free themselves from custom and fear to
soar in the heady altitudes of philosophical and religious thought. "Let
our vain Sex be fond of glitt'ring Toys,/ Of pompous Titles, and affected
Noise," she wrote in language borrowed from *A Serious Proposal*, "Des-
cant on Faults,/ And in Detraction find/ Delights unknown to a brave
gen'rous Mind,/ While we resolve a nobler Path to tread,/ And from
Tyrannick Custom free."

Lady Chudleigh's great feminist poem is *The Ladies Defence: or, The
Bride-Woman's Counsellor Answer'd* (1701), a dialogue in four voices. She
wrote it to answer Mr. Sprint, a Nonconformist minister who had
preached an infuriating sermon on female weakness and the necessity
for male domination.[27] He delivered his oration at a wedding, and
published it in 1699 under the title *The Bride-Woman's Counsellor*. Lady
Chudleigh prefaced her poetical reply with the remark: "The Knowledge I had of my Inability for so great a Task, made me for a while
stifle my Resentments . . . [b]ut when I found that some Men were so
far from finding fault with his Sermon, that they rather defended it,
and express'd an ill-natur'd sort of Joy to see [women] ridicul'd . . . I
had not the Patience to be Silent any longer."

She composed her irritation into heroic couplets, shaped as a conversation among Sir John Brute, a tyrannical husband: Sir William
Loveall—gallant but naive; a parson who is a caricature of Mr. Sprint;
and pert Melissa, who speaks in Lady Chudleigh's voice, reminding
them all that it is *her* life they are talking about. Astell's influence is
very clear in the give-and-take about education in this poem. Echoing
A Serious Proposal, Melissa says:

> Tis hard we should be by the Men despis'd,
> Yet kept from knowing what wou'd make us priz'd:

Debarr'd from Knowledge, banish'd from the Schools,
And with the utmost Industry bred Fools.
Laugh'd out of Reason, jested out of Sense,
And nothing left but Native Innocence:
Then told we are incapable of Wit,
And only for the meanest Drudgeries fit. . . .

And Sir John Brute growls:

By Heav'n I wish 'twere by the Laws decreed
They never more should be allow'd to Read.
Books are the Bane of States, the Plagues of life,
But both conjoyn'd when studied by a Wife. . . .

Gallant Sir William chimes in, irrelevantly:

Had you the Learning you so much desire,
You, sure, wou'd nothing, but your selves admire:
All our Addresses wou'd be then in vain,
And we no longer in your Hearts shou'd Reign. . . .

The parson agrees with Sir John Brute:

But Women were not for this Province made,
And shou'd not our Prerogative invade. . . .

But Lady Chudleigh gives Melissa the last word with an emphasis that
shows she has thoroughly absorbed Astell's message.

But spite of you, we'll to our selves be kind:
Your Censures slight, your little Tricks despise,
And make it our whole Business to be wise.
The mean low trivial Cares of Life disdain,
And Read and Think, and Think and Read again,
And on our minds bestow the utmost Pain.

Lady Mary Wortley Montagu was only five years old when *A Serious
Proposal* was published, but she read it a few years after and it made a
deep impression on her. Later in life she told her daughter that she had
wanted to be a nun in her early teens.

It was a favorite Scheme of mine when I was fiveteen, and had I then been
mistriss of an Independent fortune, would certainly have executed it and
elected my selfe Lady Abbess. There would you and your 10 children have
been lost for ever.

She recurs to this monastic image elsewhere in her correspondence, and
recommends that her granddaughters live as lay nuns—just as she had
dreamt of doing at fifteen.[28]

By eleven, Lady Mary was already studious. Hiding from her governess, she worked from ten to two and from four to eight in her
father's library with a Latin dictionary and grammar. She wrote verse,
self-conscious about being both a woman and a writer. The preface to
one notebook declares: "1 I am a Woman 2 without any advantages of
Education 3 all these was writ at the age of 14."[29]

Although she never published under her own name, despite Mary
Astell's urging when they came to meet in later years, Lady Mary was
a public figure all her life. Her extemporaneous verse and her witticisms
found their way into the gossip columns of the London newspapers.
Her relation to the literati—Pope, Gay, Arbuthnot, Lord Hervey—and
her witty exchanges with them always made good copy, especially after
Pope's infatuation had curdled to hatred. But it would have been too
déclassé to print, and so although a few poems were published in the
strictest anonymity, her letters were sent to correspondents, and the
prose and poems stayed in notebooks. Some of her remarks and attitudes, of course, were picked up and printed in others' published
anecdotes.

Briefly, in 1737, she embarked upon publishing a fortnightly paper
called *The Nonsense of Common-Sense* (to signal its contrariety to the
leading opposition paper of the day, *Common Sense*). Nine issues were
put out at two- and three-week intervals before publication ceased. She
sounds very much like Mary Astell in number 6, in which she proclaims
herself a friend of the fair sex and "a protector of all the oppressed,"
and defends women's rationality. She kept a printed copy of this single
number, and scribbled on the top of it: "Wrote by me. M.W.M."[30]

Elizabeth Elstob was another younger woman to whom Astell's
assured and forthright defense of women's learning made a real difference. *A Serious Proposal* had fortified her as a young girl, and encouraged
her to pursue her own studies despite the disapproval of the uncle with
whom she lived.[31] Secretly and then openly she imitated her classicist
older brother William Elstob, who had mastered Latin and Greek and
then begun to study Anglo-Saxon while at Queen's College, Oxford.
When he matriculated and obtained a living in London, she joined him

*Self-portrait of
Elizabeth Elstob.
This portrait first
appeared inside the
letter G on page I
of* An English-
Saxon Homily on
the Birth-day of
St. Gregory *(1709).
Reproduced by
courtesy of the
Trustees of the
British Museum.*

there, and shared his house, his intellectual friends, and his scholarly labors. Her first project for publication in these liberated circumstances was a translation of Scudéry's prize-winning *An Essay Upon Glory*, which she advertised as "done into English by a Person of the Same sex" in 1708. Astell had recommended Scudéry in *A Serious Proposal*, and had urged her countrywomen to imitate the French in their intellectual women rather than in their fashions in clothes. Elstob's *A Saxon Homily on the Birthday of St. Gregory* (1709), had an even firmer feminist tone. Dedicated to Queen Anne as the most recent in a long line of distinguished female rulers, it self-consciously and proudly claimed for Elstob herself a place as the first female Anglo-Saxon scholar in history. The spirited defense of women's right to a learned education in the Preface is reminiscent of Astell's tone.

It is likely that Elizabeth Elstob and Mary Astell were acquainted by then, for in addition to their common Newcastle origins, they were virtually the only two respectable, single women living in London who were known for learning and for writing books. That they were linked in the public mind can be seen by Elstob's inclusion in a satiric portrait of Astell in 1709, as "a certain Lady, who is now publishing Two of the choicest Saxon Novels."[32] We know that by 1714 Astell was collecting subscriptions from her wealthy friends for Elstob's Anglo-Saxon grammar. Elstob explicitly designed this English grammar for a female audience, since previous Saxon grammars had been written in Latin, and hence were out of reach of most women. Elstob thought "the original of our Mother Tongue" should be put within the reach of other women, especially since it had given her such pleasure and satisfaction to study it.

Elizabeth Thomas was still another contemporary writer who followed in Astell's footsteps. Her panegyric to "Almystrea" compared Astell to St. Theresa, imitating Norris, who pays her this compliment in the introduction to their letters. She praised Astell as a champion of her sex. "Too long! indeed, has been our Sex decryed/ And ridicul'd by Men's *malignant Pride*," she wrote:

> When you, most generous *Heroine*! stood forth,
> And show'd your Sex's *Aptitude* and *Worth*.
> Were it no more! yet you bright *Maid* alone,
> Might for a World of *Vanity* Atone!
> Redeem the coming Age! and set us free!
> From the false Brand of *Incapacity*.[33]

Approbation was not universal, of course. Susanna Centlivre took a less positive view of Astell in *The Bassett Table* (1705), where she represented her as the abstracted and pedantic Valeria, who is more interested in her microscope and dissections, hilariously enough, than in her suitors. She is teased by a more "normal" female character in the play, who derisively suggests: "you should bestow your fortune on founding a college for the study of philosophy where none but women should be admitted; and to immortalize your name they should be called Valerians, ha ha ha!"

The influence of *A Serious Proposal* continued late into the century. Dr. Johnson followed Astell's model in the choices he ascribed to the two heroines of *Rasselas* (1759), Pekuah and the princess Nekayah, for the best possible ways of life. "Pekuah was never so much charmed with any place as the convent of St. Anthony, and wished only to fill it with pious maidens, and to be made prioress of the order," he wrote. The princess proposed instead "to found a college of learned women, in which she would preside, that, by conversing with the old, and educating the young, she might divide her time between the acquisition and communication of wisdom, and raise up for the next age models of prudence, and patterns of piety."[34]

Sarah Scott, sister to Elizabeth Montagu, "queen" of the blue-stockings, wrote a utopian novel, *A Description of Millenium Hall* (1762), based on Astell's *A Serious Proposal*, in which several world-weary women establish an all-female community on a fine, old country estate, in order to cultivate the rational delights of a studious life and prepare for the hereafter. Explicitly conceived as an alternative to the marriage market and a home for distressed gentlewomen, Sarah Scott's institution was an imaginative fulfillment of Mary Astell's first book.

A Serious Proposal opens with the observation that it is an experimental era, and that people are interested in "profitable adventures"—although what the speaker has in mind concerns something more important than mere money. Be ambitious of the *best* things, she told her audience of women. "Remember, I pray you, the famous Women of former Ages, the *Orindas* of late, and the more Modern *D'acier* and others, and blush to think how much is now, and will hereafter be said of them, when you your selves (as great a Figure as you make) must be buried in silence and forgetfulness!"[35]

She wrote, she said, because she knew women were capable of everything, and she hated to hear them dismissed disrespectfully as weakminded or frivolous. The vices of the fair sex were clearly traceable to lack of education. "Were the men as much neglected, and as little care taken to cultivate and improve them, perhaps they wou'd be so far from surpassing those whom they now despise, that they themselves wou'd sink into the greatest stupidity and brutality."[36]

She wrote as an explainer and defender of her sex, and a participant in the rituals of gender: at the tea table, before the dressing-room glass, adroitly parrying the absurd language of gallantry in the drawing room. She had only scorn for the topsy-turvy values of polite society. Isn't it ridiculous, she asked, for a woman to think herself a greater or better person because she has more money or a "more ingenious Taylor or Milliner than her Neighbor?"[37] As women, we get tricked into making stupid choices and living worthless lives, she warned. "Thus Ignorance and a narrow Education, lay the Foundation of Vice, and imitation and custom rear it up—Custom, that merciless torrent that carries all before."[38]

Astell's style is one of friendly exhortation, personal and warm rather than public or stentorian. Her arguments circle around as she talks her way in and out of a sequence of ideas. Her discourse is not so much like formal exposition as lively and earnest conversation among friends. There are occasional rhetorically elevated moments, which she builds to from homely detail and candid, colloquial observations. She has written down her speaking voice, and we listen in fascination to one who is used to having the floor.

At the center of *A Serious Proposal* is an admonishment to distinguish between disinterested friendship and predatory lust. Astell waxes lyrical about the joys of a happy retreat, where one might dwell securely and exclusively among other women. She imagines in several places the simple but adequate furnishings of her institution, and the common pleasures of the inmates. "In a word, this happy Society will be but one Body, whose Soul is love, animating and informing it, and perpetually breathing forth it self in flames of holy desires after GOD, and acts of Benevolence to each other."[39] It was a vision of community fueled by sublimated desire—the very desire she and Norris agreed was felt for the creature but owed to the Creator. Freer than a Catholic convent—"Ev'ry act of our Religious Votary shall be voluntary and free"—her Protestant nunnery was imagined with the monastic spirit of simple asceticism and obedient ritual, but with the fellowship of other women elevated to an equal importance. Her repeated reprise extols friendship and the blessing of living among friends. Even in heaven, she says, the "happy Souls" "now and then step aside from more general Conversations, to entertain themselves with a peculiar friend."[40]

Without predicting the responses of all men, Astell knew she would be ridiculed by some. Ignore them, she entreated her women readers; and reconsider the choices of your lives. Written not for the population at large but for dissatisfied, thoughtful, sensible women, Astell's work was meant to bring them into the age of reason. Assuming them rational, she explained to them the advantage of living ascetic, intellectual lives. But what startles the modern reader in perusing *A Serious Proposal* is Astell's use of the terms and constructs of the contemporary male discourse about faith, knowledge, and certainty. One is not used to having these concepts trained upon women's problems. The dissonance between form and content reminds one how male the eighteenth-century intellectual world was, and how absent from it were the sounds of women's voices, talking among themselves.

In its historical context, Astell's *A Serious Proposal* can be seen as an important milestone in a developing tradition of women's writing. Since the Restoration in England, women had begun to write and publish in increasing numbers. One early, interesting voice—whom Astell was sure to have known as the duchess of her native Newcastle—was Margaret Cavendish, universally ridiculed in her own day as "mad Madge." Even her contemporary, the intellectual Dorothy Osborne, wrote: "Sure, the poor woman is a little distracted, she could never be so ridiculous else as to venture at writing books."[41] Pepys records how, when Margaret Cavendish asked to visit the Royal Society, it occasioned a great debate among members. There were many who thought it a bad precedent to permit a female in the place. When the appointed day for the visit came, the halls were thronged with people come to gawk at her.[42]

John Evelyn's wife once met the Duchess of Newcastle and thought her a phenomenon worth describing:

> I acknowledge, though I remember her some years since, and have not been a stranger to her fame, I was surprised to find so much extravagancy and vanity in any person not confined within four walls. Her habit particular, fantastical, not unbecoming a good shape, which she may truly boast of. Her face discovers the facility of the sex, in being persuaded it deserves the esteem years forbid, by the infinite care she takes to place her curls and patches. Her mien surpasses the imagination of poets, or the description of a romance heroine's greatness; her gracious bows, seasonable nods, courteous stretching out of her hands, twinkling of her eyes, and various gestures of approbation, show what may be expected from her discourse, which is airy, empty, whimsical, and rambling as her books, aiming at science, difficulties, high notions, terminating commonly in nonsense, oaths, and obscenity. . . .
>
> I found Dr. Charlton with her, complimenting her wit and learning in a high manner; which she took to be so much her due, that she swore if the schools did not banish Aristotle, and read Margaret, Duchess of Newcastle, they did her wrong, and deserved to be utterly abolished. . . . Never did I see a woman so full of herself, so amazingly vain and ambitious. What contrary miracles does this age produce. This lady and Mrs. Philips! The one transported with the shadow of reason, the other possessed of the substance and insensible of her treasure. . . .[43]

But then Mrs. Evelyn did not think it proper for women to write books and publish them, any more than did Dorothy Osborne. Further, "mad Madge" composed in her own idiom, rather than taking her terms from the male discourse of her time. Of her own eclectic and original fancy she wrote: "I took great delight in . . . such fashions as I did invent myself . . . also I did dislike any should follow my Fashions, for I always took delight in a singularity, even in accoutrements of habits."[44]

Margaret Cavendish was married to a man thirty-four years older than she, harmlessly addicted to horsemanship and swordsmanship—"two Arts," wrote his enthusiastic lady, "he hath brought by his studious thoughts, rational experience, and industrious practice, to an absolute perfection."[45] There were no children. He appreciated and encouraged her writing.

One important thing Margaret Cavendish bequeathed to the next generation was an explicit statement of her ambition to be famous, to be remembered after she died. Although Astell never refers to her directly, the desire for fame that will outlast one's lifetime, crops up again and again in *A Serious Proposal*. "I fear my Ambition inclines to vain-glory" wrote the duchess, "for I am very ambitious; yet 'tis neither for Beauty, Wit, Titles, Wealth, or Power, but as they are steps to raise me to Fames Tower, which is to live by remembrance in after-ages."[46] She also, in the course of a remarkable, wide-ranging career, touched on the subject of women's education. Her dedication of *Philosophical and Physical Opinions* (1663) "To The Two Most Famous Universities of England" opened with this splendid sentence:

> Most Famously Learned,—I Here Present to you this Philosophical Work, not that I can hope Wise Schoolmen and Industrious, Laborious Students should Value it for any Worth, but to Receive it without Scorn, for the good Encouragement of our Sex, lest in time we should grow Irrational as Idiots, by the Dejectedness of our Spirits, through the Careless Neglects and Despisements of the Masculine Sex to the Female, thinking it Impossible we should have either Learning or Understanding, Wit or Judgment, as if we had not Rational Souls as well as Men, and we out of a Custom of Dejectedness think so too, which makes us Quit all Industry towards Profitable Knowledge, being employed only in Low and Petty employments which take away not only our Abilities toward Arts, but higher Capacities in Speculations, so as we are become like Worms, that only Live in the Dull Earth of Ignorance, Winding our Selves sometimes out by the Help of some Refreshing Rain of good Education, which seldom is given us, for we are Kept like Birds in Cages, to Hop up and down in our Houses, not Suffer'd to Fly abroad, to see the several Changes of Fortune, and the Various Humours, Ordained and Created by Nature, we must needs want the Understanding and Knowledge, and so consequently Prudence and Invention of Men; Thus by an Opinion, which I hope is but an Erroneous one in Men, we are Shut out of all Power and Authority, by reason we are never Imployed either in Civil or Martial Affairs, our Counsels are Despised, and Laught at, the best of our Actions are Troden down with Scorn, by the Over-weening conceit, Men have of Themselves, and through a Despisement of Us.

The poet Katherine Philips, the "matchless Orinda," was another Englishwoman who had written in the generation before Astell. Not unlike the French *précieuses*, "Orinda's" intellectual and literary interests were bound up in her intensely felt affection for others of her sex. She thought friendship the highest expression of human feeling, and it is for her sweet poetry about friendship that she is justly celebrated. Edmund Gosse claimed that Katherine Philips "invented a new species of literature" in eulogizing her female friends. She was "the first sentimental writer in the English language," he wrote. She imitated the forms of friendship-poetry among men, she explained, because men had heretofore excluded women from "friendship's vast capacity." She meant to show that women as well as men were capable of noble and elevated feeling for one another, and Gosse recognized in her romantic poems to Rosania and Lucasia, and her voluminous correspondence about friendship, the first signs of a new sensibility.

Self-consciously treating women's friendship as a poetic theme of serious stature, Orinda's verse mythologized her relationships with other women, enshrining every step along the way with such titles as "To the truly Noble Mrs. Anne Owen, on my first Approaches" or "To the Excellent Mrs. Owen, upon her receiving the name of Lucasia, and Adoption into our Society, December 28, 1651."[47] Mary Astell admired her enormously, and represented her in several places as a prime example of women's excellent capacity. Universally known and esteemed by the end of the seventeenth century, Orinda was a safe heroine. Abraham Cowley, Lords Orrery and Roscommon, Nicholas Rowe, and William Temple had written respectfully about her as a poet. Eulogies had been unstinting; she was a conventional favorite, a name everyone recognized and accepted. In her unique status as an admired woman writer, one could be proud of her and confident in imitation. A number of phrases from Katherine Philips's ode "Upon Mr. Abraham Cowley's Retirement" for example, are repeated in Astell's imitations of Cowley, in "Ambition," and in "Awake my Lute, daughters of Musick come." As the high priestess of female friendship, "the English Sappho," her poems also validated women's love for others of their own sex. For both reasons, her work had an enormous impact on literate young women of Astell's generation.

By Mary Astell's time, more leisured women than ever before were closet intellectuals. Mrs. Evelyn's daughter, the same age as Mary Astell, read secretly in her own room, voraciously copying out history and theology into a commonplace book, and planning a correspondence with a clergyman whom she asked to be her spiritual mentor—as her astonished parents found out when they went through her things at her untimely death of smallpox at nineteen.[48] So far as anyone can tell, Mary Evelyn had not intended to publish what she wrote—although her loving father did see to it that *Mundus Muliebris* was printed after her death.

Following in the footsteps of the early seventeenth-century educationalists Anna Van Schurman, Bathsua Makin, and Hannah Woolley,[49] a few other women during Astell's lifetime wrote an occasional poetic defense of their sex. Sarah Fyge Egerton replied to Robert Gould's *Love Given O're: or A Satyr Against the Pride, Lust, and Inconstancy, &c. of Women* (1682) with a poem called *The Female Advocate* (1687).[50] An anonymous "Young Lady" published a Pindaric ode called *The Triumph of Female Wit or The Emulation* in 1683, which called forth several responses in verse, in which she decried women's exclusion from the sciences, arts, and letters.

> They let us learn to work to dance or sing
> Or any such like trivial thing,
> Which to their profit may increase or pleasure bring.
> But they refuse to let us know
> What sacred Sciences doth impart
> Or the mysteriousness of Art.
> . . . .
> As if a rational unbounded Mind
> Were only for the sordid'st task of Life design'd.[51]

Taking heart from Aphra Behn's successes, women were also beginning to write for the theater in numbers—among them Mary Pix, [Mary] Delariviere Manley, Susanna Centlivre, and Catherine Trotter Cockburn.[52] Catherine Trotter also wrote philosophy, encouraged by Elizabeth Burnet and her husband Gilbert Burnet, John Norris, and John Locke.[53]

A few poets dared to publish serious nonpolemical verse. The countess of Winchilsea published twice—a long poem called "The Spleen" in 1701, and a collected edition of her work in 1713.[54] Aware that she was trespassing on what had been, traditionally, male territory in writing verse—"an intruder on the rights of men"—she expected no quarter for her crime.

> Did I, my lines intend for publick view,
> How many censures, wou'd their faults persue,
> Some wou'd, because such words they do affect,
> Cry they're insipid, empty, uncorrect.
> And many, have attain'd, dull and untaught
> The name of Witt, only by finding fault. . . .

> Alas! a woman that attempts the pen,
> Such an intruder on the rights of men,
> Such a presumptuous Creature, is esteem'd,
> The fault, can by no vertue be redeem'd.

Her premonition was well-founded, and she became a target for the Scriblerians and the model for Pope's invention, Phoebe Clinket, a presumptuous lady scribbler, self-absorbed, in an ink-stained dress with pens stuck in her hair, so obsessively intent on catching her own least word that she orders her maid to follow around after her with a writing desk strapped to her back so that her mistress can write down any poetical thought the moment it strikes her.[55] If Mary Astell and the countess of Winchilsea knew one another, no clue of the acquaintance remains; but they were both borne along on the same historical current.

Of the women whose reputations inspired her, and to whom Astell was consciously indebted, there were, besides Katherine Philips, two Frenchwomen: Mme de Scudéry, whom her friend Elizabeth Elstob translated, and Mme Dacier, who was herself the translator of Astell's favorite author, Marcus Aurelius.[56] If she could warm to a woman-centered sensibility in Katherine Philips, and delight in the sophisticated wit and repartee of Scudéry, so too did she appreciate the disciplined scholarship and classicism of Mme Dacier, to which she refers her readers on a number of occasions.

The idea of an educational retreat for unmarried women, too, can be found in English letters before Astell's publication, although there is no reason to think she was familiar with these sources. Robert Burton's *Anatomy of Melancholy* suggests that "some time or other, amongst so many rich Bachelors, a benefactor should be found to build a monastical College for old, decayed, deformed or discontented Maids to live in, that have lost their first loves, or otherwise miscarried, or else are willing howsoever to lead a single life."[57] A schoolmaster named Clement Barkdale wrote a seven-page pamphlet on the subject in 1675 called *Letter touching a College of Maids or a Virgin Society* (1675).[58] Obviously interested in women's education, Barkdale was the English translator of Anna Van Schurman's *De Ingenii Muliebris* (1641; trans. 1659). His "letter" explains itself as an elaboration of a design proposed the day before over venison, at an occasion where a half-dozen rich, virtuous young ladies were present. He specifies the number of servants necessary to such an establishment, including a minister to lead prayers several times a day and individual governesses for each student to guide her in a program of private reading and devotion, a design for comfortable and decorous garments, a garden stocked with herbs and medicinal plants as well as beautiful flowers, and a library of "choice Authors of *History*, *Poetry*, and especially of *Practical Divinity* and *Devotion*: Not only *English*, but of Learned, as well as Modern *Language*." His curriculum included music, dancing, needlework, drawing, moral and natural philosophy, and the young ladies were to be encouraged to make "some of the easier Experiments in Natural things."

George Hickes, too, had suggested in a sermon in 1684 that his wealthier parishioners put their money into colleges for women "much like unto those in the Universities, for the Education of young Men, but with some alteration in the Discipline, the Oeconomy, as the nature of such an Institution would require."[59] Hickes personally supported the scholarly activities of a number of women—Elizabeth Elstob, Dorothy Grahme, Susanna Hopton, Catherine Bovey—and recommended Astell's books in the 1707 edition of his translation of Fénelon's *Traité de l'education des filles*.[60] His friend and colleague, Dr. Smalridge, also sold subscriptions for Elstob's Anglo-Saxon productions, and is thought to have supported her for a while when her brother died.[61] Women's education seems to have been a cause favored by High Churchmen of the early eighteenth-century, and such men as Robert Nelson and the leading lights of the SPCK raised funds for girls' charity schools, to spread literacy to the female poor.

Thus it can be seen that most of the elements of Astell's *A Serious Proposal* existed before she wrote, although she reconfigured them and gave them real force. That others had given these sentiments lip service earlier made her insist all the more sharply on their full meaning.[62]

Intellectual, single, poor, and urban, she could not have existed outside of London. She wrote as a representative female, with the emotional realities, activities, and behaviors of other eighteenth-century women. It is this which gives her voice its characteristic feminist emphasis—the lived experience behind the opinions, visible in her images, in the situations she depicted, and in the arguments she used. She was read in her own day, as now, because she was forceful and authentic. She did not mind being who she was; she even liked being a woman—although there is a suicidal streak running through her poems. But she found her society's attitudes towards women intolerable, and she tried to imagine her way out of its double binds.

Chapter Five

The Veil of Chastity

I have heard it generally complain'd of by very good *Protestants*, that Monasteries were Abolish'd instead of being Reform'd: And tho' none that I know of plead for Monasteries, strictly so call'd, in *England*, or for anything else but a reasonable provision for the Education of one half of Mankind, and for a safe retreat so long and no longer than our Circumstances make it requisite.

> Mary Astell, *The Christian Religion As Profess'd by A Daughter of the Church*, 1705

In a garret of her house there lived a maiden lady of seventy in the most retired manner, of whom my landlady gave me this account: that she was a Roman Catholic, had been sent abroad when young and lodged in a nunnery with an intent of becoming a nun; but the country not agreeing with her, she returned to England, where, there being no nunnery, she had vowed to lead the life of a nun as near as might be done in those circumstances.

> Benjamin Franklin, *Autobiography*, 1771

If the intellectual problem for Mary Astell was learning to think incisively enough to identify and follow the path of virtue in every day's moral dilemmas, the practical problem was how to manage a respectable life in London without a fortune, without a husband, and without a paying profession. Where were women to go, how were they to live, if they chose not to marry and if gentlewomen like herself, without means, could not afford to run their own establishments? Few trades were open to women, and all of them compromised respectability to some degree; a genteel woman was simply not expected to earn her daily bread. At the time she wrote *A Serious Proposal* this was a far more pressing concern to Mary Astell than even the question of her intellectual training.

If she had been born in an earlier century, she would have taken orders. Monastic life would have suited her—the regularity and order of it, the company of other women, the high seriousness of purpose. She was deeply religious and ritualistic in her habits. Every day of her life, rain or shine, she walked down to the river and along the embankment to the Chelsea church. She strictly kept all the fasts and vigils of the Church of England. She would have appreciated the asceticism of the convent. As it was, she was uncomfortably aware of the disparity between her own modest style of living and the luxury that surrounded her, a disparity which raised in her unwanted feelings of envy and self-righteousness. She was also conscious that others mocked her severity, called her a prude, and wondered at her abstemiousness.

If her way of life was dictated by economic constraints, these choices were reinforced and rationalized by her focus on Platonic realities which superseded the material world. The style of life she evolved for herself in Chelsea was the familiar enough male pastoral ideal of the *beatus vir*, the "happy man" celebrated by Horace and Virgil.[1] The neoclassical ideal of rural retirement from the corruption and hurry of the city in the eighteenth century was not yet that Rousseauean dream of innocent rustic life, but a sophisticated Roman notion of the civilized being who withdrew to a country villa—with murals on the walls and a fine library—to better enjoy the life of the mind, surrounded by the healing pleasures of nature. The idea was to escape from the mediocrity and corruption of civilization, not from its highest expressions.

Chelsea felt like a country village, but was not far from London. As Bowack wrote of its convenience in 1705: "a Man may perfectly enjoy the Pleasures of Country and City together, and when he Pleases in Less than an Hours time either by Water, Coach, or otherwise, to be at the Court, Exchange, or in the midst of his Business."[2]

In her lodging, habit, and diet, Mary Astell followed what was plain and decent: "what Nature, not Luxury requires . . . such things as are fit and convenient, without occasioning scruple to oneself or giving trouble or offence to others."[3] She was fond of the image of Antoninus returning to his farm after leading a heroic army to victory, to dig and boil turnips for his simple repast. During Lent, the Ember days, the Rogation days, Fridays, and the Vigils, she took only bread and water. But it was a discipline she undertook with cheerful vigor rather than hollow-cheeked denial, for she was a very Anglican in her asceticism and objected to extremity of any sort. To relish privation would have meant an attention to physical sensation beyond what was due it. She appears to have tolerated the substantial material comfort of the aristocratic friends with whom she dined and whom she entertained in her own quarters, without admonishing them to eschew all luxury. Besides, she wrote, "our Lord has taught us, that Mercy is to be prefer'd before Sacrifice; and that Bodily Exercise profiteth but a little, the chief business being to obtain a divine and God-like temper of Mind."[4]

She had not learned her asceticism at home. The Newcastle kitchen had been unusually well stocked and provisioned. Especially when her father was alive, the Astells had kept a very good table. Later in life when she could not afford a cook she was able to prepare a proper meal for her wealthier friends with her own hands.

When she dined by herself, however, it was generally upon bread and cheese and a few "herbs" if they were in season. She took the teachings of the New Testament quite literally and tried to simplify her material needs as much as possible, to loosen her grasp on mortal life and fix her passions elsewhere. Not unlike other devout Anglicans of her day, she saw her own spiritual struggles as a battle against flesh and felt the need for constant vigilance to restrain her appetites and resist the "Objects of Sense."

Everywhere in her writings she emphasizes that material pleasures are merely transitory and that "the Grand Business that Women as well as Men have to do in this World be to prepare for the next."[5] Mortal things were precarious; treasure on earth could be snatched away in an instant by death; it was wasteful to "lavish out the greatest part of our Time and care, on the decoration of a Tenement, in which our Lease is so very Short."[6] The French idealists to whom Norris had introduced her were appealing for this reason as well. Had not Pascal stressed the emptiness of "divertissements" and the necessity for educating the immortal soul? "A man in a dungeon, ignorant whether his sentence be pronounced, and having only one hour to learn in, but this hour enough, if he know that it is pronounced, to obtain its repeal, would act unnaturally in spending that hour, not in ascertaining his sentence, but in playing picquet."[7] *Les messieurs du Port Royal* not only embodied her ideal of rational process and charitable behavior, but a religious asceticism which suited her, with their Jansenist disapproval of pomp and circumstance and their demand for a plainer and less sensuous form of worship.

Astell was drawn to Christian primitivism on the whole, with its emphasis on literal interpretation of scripture, its severe simplicity, communalism, and its reverence for the early church fathers, especially Augustine. She came to admire Fénelon, for example, one of the more famous French Augustinians, who never surrendered his belief in a deeply experienced grace as the basis of faith.[8] Far from rejecting his thought as superstitious popery, she found his brand of Catholicism especially congenial. She also admired him because he suffered for his beliefs, and was "a fool to y.[e] World."

She read his posthumously published letters when they came out, and found much in them to revere. "I have bin reading y[e] late A. Bp. of Cambrays Letters," she writes to a friend,

w.[ch] make me very sick of my own. He has left a Noble Model in y.[s] as in other things, but y[e] World is too much y[e] World to follow it. Good manners, falsely so call'd, & a mean Complaisance to y[e] follys & vices of y[e] Age, has quite banish'd y[t] Noble Simplicity w.[ch] he so admirably describes & w.[ch] is indeed y[e] Ground, & y[e] Perfection of all y[t] is Great, Good & Agreeable. It consists in a perfect disengagem[t] from ourselves, as well as from y[e] World, & a concern to approve ourselves to GOD only. . . . Nothing is so contrary to Divine Simplicity as Worldly Wisdom, w.[ch] wou'd do every thing itself, & trust nothing to GOD, is always admiring it's own Works, & ordering y[m] for it's own Glory. But he y[t] wou'd be Simple, must become a fool to y[e] World, w.[ch] is in reality to be truly Wise. I am affraid y[e] good A. Bp. did not meet wth many Proselytes to this Doctrine in his own Country, nor is it like to be much relish'd here. Men will be Men, y[t] is, Weak, Vain, Inconstant, Unjust, False & Presumptuous. They will follow their own Ways, Inclinations & Customs, & we must be Content, for we cannot new Model y[m].[9]

Fénelon's virtue and intellectual bent, his simplicity, his willingness to be "a fool to y.ᵉ World, w.ᶜʰ is in reality to be truly Wise"—these formulations appealed to Mary Astell, who also advocated "a perfect disengagem.ᵗ from ourselves, as well as from y.ᵉ World." She distinguished this attitude from the zeal of enthusiasm. Fénelon preached losing the self in religious feeling, rather than exalting and parading one's religious effusions. She explained how his quietism, which she admired, went beyond mere "sincerity"—that quality of mind and personality so highly prized among the jaded wits of society. "The Sincere do indeed say nothing but w.ᵗ they Think," she explained, "nor wou'd pass for any thing but w.ᵗ they Are. But they are always studying y.ᵐ.selves, composing their Words & Thoughts, reflecting on y.ᵐ.selves thro fear they have done too little or too much & therefore are not Simple. They are neither easy w.ᵗʰ others nor others w.ᵗʰ y.ᵐ There is nothing free & natural in their Conversation. They are always as it were setting y.ᵐ.selves in the Glass, & are too full of y.ᵐ.selves to be lik'd either by GOD or Man."[10]

Less interested in mortification of the flesh than in "due poise of mind," she uses words like "calm" or "balance" to describe the state of being which must be striven for: a nunlike detachment from things of this world and an intellectual clarity about those of the next. Her asceticism, which was an extension of her rationalism, consisted of a belief in subduing the flesh so as not to interfere with the operations of the mind and spirit. Bodies were a nuisance—"Material Beings with which we're compass'd," as she put it. But properly managed, kept under control and not unduly stimulated, the body could be prevented from interfering with the superior functions of the mind.

> The Animal Spirits must be lessen'd, or rendred more Calm and Manageable; at least they must not be unnaturally and violently mov'd, by such a Diet, or such Passions, Design, and Divertisments as are likely to put 'em in a ferment. Contemplation requires a Governable Body, a sedate and steady Mind, and the Body and the Mind do so reciprocally influence each other, that we can scarce keep the one in tune if the other be out of it.[11]

She was convinced—like the rest of her nation—that the "true and proper Human Nature consists in the exercise of that Dominion which the Soul has over the Body in governing every Passion according to Right Reason." Those swayed by emotional whims or physical desire rather than by "judgment" were, as she put it, "always in extreams: they are either violently good or quite cold and indifferent, a perpetual trouble to themselves & others, by indecent Raptures, or unnecessary

Scruples; there is no Beauty and order in their lives, all is rapid and unaccountable; they are now very furious in such a course, but they cannot well tell why, & anon as violent in the other extream."[12] There was no keeping track of such persons. Very much a woman of her age, Astell found passion irritatingly unaccountable: the truest beauty lay in order.

These attitudes—that worldly pleasure was ultimately unsatisfactory and that one ought to govern one's passions and appetites with right reason—are embedded everywhere in English culture, from Jeremy Taylor's *Holy Living and Holy Dying* (1650) to William Law's *A Serious Call* (1728). They survive in the great ethical poetry of that century, from Pope's *Essay on Man* (1734) to Johnson's *The Vanity of Human Wishes* (1749). What distinguished later seventeenth- and eighteenth-century expressions of these values from earlier versions was the emphasis on the intellectual pleasures of solitude and the delight in studying and cultivating the natural world. To the medieval Christian, nature's satanic power had to be opposed and held in check at all costs. But with the new scientific interest in natural phenomena spurred by Bacon's writings, the attention of a Christian could be plausibly directed to reading the book of nature and understanding the complexities of God's miraculous world. The Neoplatonic assertion that He was immanent in nature in a protoplastic spirit which infused all organic life (a concept Malebranche carried to pantheistic extremes) was entirely compatible with the neoclassical view that contemplation of nature was spiritually and morally beneficial.

As Maren-Sofie Røstvig reminds us, the turning away from the city—locus of ambition, power, lucre, and vice—also had a political meaning in England, dating back to the Civil War, when deposed royalists and ejected Anglicans retired quietly to their country holdings to wait out the strife. Even in the Restoration period, these associations were strong, and the political energy of the squirearchy derived in part from its nostalgic continuity with the "good old days" of rural England, in contradistinction to the era brought in by the new breed of men who dominated the cities, the Puritan middle classes. From Denham's *Cooper Hill* (1642) to Pope's *Windsor Forest* (1713), certain rural landscapes came to be associated with the peace and prosperity of the Stuart reign in opposition to cursed London, the seat of the parliamentarians, and were adopted by royalists as symbolic locations of order and serenity.

Although Puritan theology, too, insisted on the natural world as a means to revelation, it did not carry with it the injunction to a contemplative life. For example, Puritans at Cambridge had always deemed Neoplatonists such as Whichcote and More too intellectual, as if their abstract thought were a substitute for faith. Robinson Crusoe on his lonely island never sat still long enough to contemplate the perfect arrangements of the natural world or to enjoy them. He offered from time to time grateful thanks to the God who had preserved him thus far, but he never attempted to derive from the idea of that God the moral ideas by which to regulate his life.

Røstvig distinguishes at least four strands in the concept of "the happy man" so central to the late seventeenth-century English literary sensibility: the happy husbandman who industriously improves his land; the serene contemplator, who retires to think in the quiet and peace of the country; the hortulan or gardening saint, whose resolve to cultivate his own holier attributes—love, charity, asceticism—is encouraged by communion with the visible order and harmony of nature; and the innocent Epicurean, who seeks recreation in the natural pleasures of the countryside. She traces the association of rural life with perfect happiness in the poems of Platonists such as More, Smith, and especially Norris, in late metaphysical verse by Marvell and Traherne, and in a host of other poems by Herrick, Denham, Waller, Pomfret, and Dryden. But Cowley, she affirms, did the most to popularize these themes, and he gave them their purest expression. His translations of Horace and essays on "Liberty," "Solitude," and "Obscurity" all emphasized the necessity of freeing oneself from others' ideas, from ambition, and from sensual passion.[13]

The prose fiction of the next century romanticized this theme in the cliché of the prosperous, well-run gentleman's estate, from Lord Monodi's estate in Book III of *Gulliver's Travels* to Allworthy's Paradise Hall in *Tom Jones*. By the middle of the eighteenth century, the ostentatious courting of solitude reached such a frenzy that it became fashionable for people all across England to dig out caves and grottoes on their property as special places of contemplation, burrowing ever deeper in their search for true isolation.

Cowley was a great favorite with women of Astell's generation, possibly because these themes adapted so readily to a woman's lot. Indeed, there was a strong tradition of noble women living alone on their country estates in the seventeenth century—a tradition deriving in part from the numbers of women who managed their estates singlehandedly at the time of the Civil War, while their husbands fought or fled.

Such women, according to panegyrical memoirs of them, set aside certain hours every day to chronicle their spiritual progress, to pray, and to excerpt morally edifying passages from their reading. The mythology of this rural piety was codified by Ballard in his 1752 *Memoirs of Several Ladies.*[14] But one can read into such reports of regimen and resolve a form of intellectual retirement for the "beata femina." Lady Warwick kept a diary to remind herself that God's hand was visible in all things and to record what she learned from the events of daily life. She wrote down the religious meaning of all of her experience, finding spiritual instruction in adding sugar to bitter tea, or in the overheard conversations of workmen putting in a gravel walk. She passed two hours every day in meditation, and according to *Rules For a Holy Life* rose each day thanking God for another day to live, read from the Bible, and prayed before going about her worldly duties. Astell's friend, Lady Elizabeth Hastings, living on her Ledstone estate near Leeds, maintained a similar regimen, and called together her household—family, servants, and guests—several times a day for prayer. Lady Warwick's friend Lady Elizabeth Mordaunt kept a spiritual ledger listing on one side those things she had to be thankful for, and on the other those moral failings in herself which needed attention (oversensitivity to the slights of others, self-righteous pleasure in the follies of others, etc.).[15]

In her youthful poems imitating Cowley, Astell adopted the persona of the "serene contemplator." She wrote in the loose and unequal lines of the Pindaric ode so fashionable with women of her generation.[16] She imaged a humble existence spent in her own pursuits, free from "formalities" and "custom"; mistress of her own time, she was neither the target of others' envy nor the slave of her own ambition. She praised the "middle way" as eloquently as Robinson Crusoe's father, at the beginning of that book.

> From my secure and humble seat,
>   I view the ruins of the Great.
> And dare look back on my expired days,
> To my low state there needs no shameful ways.
>   O how uneasy shou'd I be,
>   If tie'd to Custom and formalitie,
> Those necessary evils of the Great,
> Which bind their hands, and manacle their feet.
> Nor Beauty, Parts, nor Portion me expose
> My most beloved Liberty to lose.
> And thanks to Heav'n my time is all my own,
>   I when I please can be alone;
> Nor Company, nor Courtship steal away
>   That treasure they can ne're repay.
>   No Flatterers, no Sycophants,
>   My dwelling haunts,

> Nor am I troubl'd with impertinents.
> Nor busy days, nor sleepless nights infest
> My Quiet mind, nor interrupt my rest.

Such retirement motifs were woven into the very fabric of conservative political and religious ideas of that time, and are as common in the work of women as of men. Much of the poetry written by Katherine Philips, Anne Finch the countess of Winchilsea, and Lady Mary Chudleigh, extoled the pleasures and virtues of rural retirement. This was because all three poets were royalists and sentimental about the land (to which Anne Finch and her husband had been forced to retire by the political necessities of 1688), and also because for literary, "scribbling" women, life in the city meant notoriety, derision, and unwanted attention.

From her upstairs back window in Chelsea, Mary Astell watched many gentlemen farmers visit the Apothecary's Garden, to collect new plant slips to try out on their country estates. Sometimes called the Physic Garden, this three-acre field had been set aside in 1673 for the cultivation and study of exotic plants, brought from all over the world by botanists, travelers, and explorers.[17] Laid out neatly in rows edged with perennial green hedges, there were hundreds of varieties of differently colored medicinal plants from all over the world. Enterprising and progressive landowners were free to acquire cuttings or plants from the garden for their own grounds.[18]

Evelyn described its technological sophistication in 1685:

> I went to Lond: next day to see Mr. Wats, keeper of the Apothecaries Garden of simples at Chelsey: where there is a collection of innumerable rarities of that sort: Particularly, besids many rare annuals the Tree bearing the Jesuits bark, which had done such cures in quartans: & what was very ingenious the subterranean heate, conveyed by a stove under the Conserveatory, which was all Vaulted with brick.[19]

The Physic Garden was a good place for Mary Astell to stroll, with its swept paths and well-tended beds of sweet-smelling herbs. Other suburban delights were also available to her in her neighbors' gardens and in the open fields around Chelsea. When she could afford it later in life, she retreated even further into the country during the winter season, when "y.ᵉ Flys buz most," that "time of Noise & Clutter and consequently of least enjoym.ᵗ to a reasonable Mind."[20]

In this context, it is not difficult to see Astell's proposal for women's colleges as a communal version of the ideal of happy retirement, a practical way of arranging for wealthier women who had the means for it to help less fortunate women to realize the dream too. But when it was translated into a possibility for women, the contemplative life took on an odd militancy, because it undermined the cultural assumption that women were made for men, for marriage, and for reproduction. The *beatus vir* was a bachelor ideal; only rarely did the poet imagine a "quiet wife" in the scene. It was much more radical to propose such a life for groups of maiden women.

Astell was not alone in her observation that women sorely needed schools, but she was unique in seeing that they needed institutions which made another way of life possible. This difference can be seen by comparing the spirit of her proposal to that suggested by Daniel Defoe a few years later. The careers of these two intersected at various points, for they both wrote for a popular audience during the same period, and occasionally they addressed themselves to the same issues.[21] When Defoe picked up Astell's idea of women's colleges for his *Essay upon Projects* (1697), he credited her with having published first, although in his Preface he declared that his ideas were formed "long before the Book call'd *Advice to the Ladies*, was made Publick." At the same time he assured his readers of his "very great Esteem," for that book and also of his "great Opinion of [its author's] Wit."

Mary Astell meant her community of women to be a semipermanent arrangement, a home as well as a school, a complete environment rather than just a service institution. She envisioned it as a place of "Religious Retirement" so that "those who are convinc'd of the emptiness of earthly Enjoyments, who are sick of the vanity of the world, and its impertinencies . . . need not be confin'd to what they justly loath."[22] And it must be remembered that she conceived of such a community because she herself had needed one so desperately when she first came to London. She had herself in mind when she counted among the functions of such a place the protection of "Daughters of Gentlemen who are fallen into decay. . . . For hereby many Souls will be preserv'd from great Dishonours, and put in a comfortable way of subsisting, being either receiv'd into the House if they incline to it, or otherwise dispos'd of." It could be a way station for women hoping to marry eventually. Prudent men, she wrote, would "reckon the endowments they here acquire a sufficient *Dowry*; and that a discreet and vertuous Gentlewoman will make a better Wife than she whose mind is empty tho her Purse be full."[23]

*Daniel Defoe.
From James
Caulfield,* Por-
traits, Mem-
oirs, and
Characters of
Remarkable
Persons, *vol. 1
(1819).*

For Defoe, the ladies' academy was to "differ but little from Publick
Schools, wherein such Ladies as were willing to study, shou'd have all
the advantages of Learning suitable to their Genius."²⁴ He made his
proposal with the same civic ardor that he suggested such measures as
group insurance pools, a system of taxing retailers of manufactures, a
commission for inquiring into bankrupt estates, and other institutional
innovations to make society and its businesses run more smoothly.
Defoe was much more taken up with the practical details for imple-
menting these plans than with any philosophical rationale for them.
True, he was sympathetic to women's deprivation:

> One wou'd wonder indeed how it shou'd happen that Women are con-
> versible at all, since they are only beholding to Natural Parts for all their
> Knowledge. Their Youth is spent to teach them to Stitch and Sow, or
> make Bawbles: They are taught to Read indeed, and perhaps to Write

their Names, or so: and that is the heighth of Woman's Education. . . . The Capacities of Women are supposed to be greater, and their Senses quicker than those of the Men; and what they might be capable of being bred to, is plain from some Instances of Female Wit, which this Age is not without.[25]

But he writes as an administrator rather than as a scholar, and is much more interested than Astell in the practical arrangements of the institution, its rules and regulations. As with the rest of his social inventions, he gives enough practical detail about this one to make it credible. He echoes Astell's phrases and arguments (God would not have furnished women with minds if He had not meant them for use; men are responsible for women's foolishness by preventing their instruction and improvement); but basically he cares little about the social meaning of such an institution.

A school was a problem in social engineering for Defoe. He did not want it used for incarceration—as a place to lock away extraneous or unwanted women. No one should be kept there against her will, he wrote. He even thought ahead to what was to be done with the year's tuition if a young woman withdrew in the middle of the term. He imagined architectural plans which made possible easy surveillance: "The Building shou'd be of Three plain Fronts, without any jettings, or Bearing-Work, that the Eye might at a Glance see from one Coin to the other; the Gardens wall'd in the same Triangular Figure, with a large Moat, and but one Entrance."[26] If a man should try to enter these private precincts "to solicit any woman, though it were to Marry," he would be charged with a felony. (It is worth noting that whenever men imagined such a retreat for women, they invariably thought of it as a target for designing men where the breach was sure to be attempted and which therefore stood in need of protection.)

Mary Astell on the other hand imagined a safe refuge, peaceful and quiet, secure from the harassment which beset women in the world of men. She thought of it as a country retreat such as she loved, one with the "serene & unmingled Delights w.ch Noble Minds enjoy when they get loose from the Town to Converse w.th y.mselves & a few of their own character."[27] Hers was the pastoral ideal of an urban dweller, a blissful recess from the noise and hurry of the world. She did not think through her institutional arrangements as carefully as Defoe. She defended them rather in social and psychological terms, trying to answer in advance the unspoken objections to women's learning then current in the culture, and spelling out the advantages to society of such a school.[28] Learning did not ruin women or make them vain and ridiculous, whatever the wits might think. On the contrary, it was essential for their spiritual welfare that women be provided with education; it was a moral imperative.

While Defoe was calculating that there ought to be one such school in every county and ten to serve London, Astell was explaining why the leisured classes had a social and moral obligation to provide schools for their daughters. Defoe was moving about the pieces of his world like Crusoe arranging his island. Mary Astell was imagining a possible life for herself, a more communal version of the life she was to lead for the next thirty years in Chelsea.

The nunnery of course was the time-honored solution for single gentlewomen that Astell adapted for her *Proposal*. These establishments had never had the bad name in England that they had, say, in France—partly because they never had the same power or wealth in England that they had on the Continent. Even in their fullest flowering there had never been more than about 140 convents in England, most of them quite small. A number of them had had as few as six or seven nuns, while the largest had, perhaps, fifty. The dissolution in England was premature, a result of Henry VIII's willfulness, not of degeneracy in the institution. Although increasingly they had been given over to devotional activity rather than to scholarship—the reading of saints' lives and scripture replacing the study of classical texts, and the observation of canonical hours becoming the single most important aspect of the regimen—they provided at least minimal schooling for poor girls living in their neighborhoods, and for the gentlemen's daughters who boarded in them. Ironically, the monastic establishment also provided women with their only route to worldly power and independence.[29]

By Mary Astell's day it had been a century and a half since the doors of these institutions had been closed, the lead taken down from the roofs and sold with the bells, the plate sent to London to be melted down, inmates turned away, and the buildings left to decay. No general provision was made for these religious women, and the distress of these nuns sent out into a world for which they were ill-suited gives a measure of the difficulty of surviving in a society which increasingly thought women intended solely for wives and mothers. Margaret Vernon, abbess of Little Marlow in Buckinghamshire, afraid that she might starve under the new dispensation, petitioned Thomas Cromwell, whom Henry VIII had placed in charge of the dissolution, to "provide for us that we shall have such honest living that we shall not be driven by necessity either to beg or to fall to other inconvenience."[30] He made her governess to his son; what happened to the rest of the women in her abbey is not known. Some asked permission to live on in their old houses, having nowhere else to go. A number were granted small living stipends—on the order of £5 or £6 a year. The pension rolls show that many of these women died within a few years of dissolution, unable to adjust to their new circumstances.[31]

The closing of the convents meant the end to an alternative refuge for a woman outside of her family circle—a refuge whose lack Richardson dramatically illustrated in *Clarissa*. The particular financial pressures that forced Clarissa out of her home may have been more typical of Richardson's day than of an earlier time, but we find her plight echoed by at least one seventeenth-century girl who found living at home so unbearable that she sought sanctuary in a convent abroad, begging a friend "to informe mee if itt was true that I heard there was a nunery in Holland for those of the Protestant relligion; and . . . upon what conditions they admitted any to there society, because if they were consistent with my relligion I did resolve upon his advertisement immediately to goe over."[32]

In England there was nowhere for a genteel woman to go, nothing for her to do, if she would not—or could not—marry. The dilemma is expressed clearly by the author of *A Protestant Monastery* (1698), who wrote about the advantages of monastic life to men and women alike (citing Astell's *A Serious Proposal*): "How many Families are there so burdened with Daughters, their Parents cannot, either for want of Beauty, or Money, dispose of in Marriage or in any other decent manner provide for?" he wrote. "Yet are they obliged to maintain them according to their Quality; till usually at their Decease, they leave them without Habitation; and many times, scarce a quarter enough to keep them decently. Whereupon, it too often comes to pass, that they are forced to wander about from Lodging to Lodging, or to betake themselves to servile Employments; or, which is worse, are tempted to prostitute their Virtue to gain their Bread."[33]

Astell was certainly aware of the earlier precedent of the nunneries. She called her proposed institution a monastery without vows and envisioned a regimen which mixed devotion and education, with living arrangements which would accommodate both those who wanted to live there permanently and those who needed a more temporary refuge. These latter residents could enroll for the benefit of the discipline and the training and then return to the world as educators and exemplars. Young girls might be boarded there, safe from the temptations and corruptions of the world. Those in need of retreat and protection might find it there in a community of other women.

. . . here Heiresses and Persons of Fortune may be kept secure from the rude attempts of designing Men; And she who has more Money than Discretion, need not curse her Stars for being expos'd a prey to bold importunate and rapacious Vultures. She will not here be inveigled and impos'd on, will neither be bought nor sold, nor be forc'd to marry for her own quiet, when she has no inclination to it, but what the being tir'd out with a restless importunity occasions. Or if she be dispos'd to marry, here she may remain in safety till a convenient Match be offer'd by her Friends, and be freed from the danger of a dishonourable one.[34]

In the end, it was the Catholic tinge to Mary Astell's plan, its similarity to the old nunneries, that prevented it from being put into practice. Fear of France and resentment of James II, fed by continuing stories of Huguenot persecution, had exacerbated anti-Catholic feeling in England to the point where just the hint of papist associations was enough to condemn any project. A great lady who read Astell's *A Serious Proposal*—some say it was Lady Elizabeth Hastings, some say it was Princess Anne herself—had apparently been ready to donate £10,000 to the building of a retreat for intellectual women, but was talked out of it again on the grounds that "it would look like preparing a way for Popish Orders," and that "it would be reputed a *Nunnery*."[35]

Obviously, the papist bugbear never frightened Astell. Although a devout Anglican, she always maintained that deism and atheism were a much greater threat to religion than Catholicism. The idea of monasteries did not seem in the least bit dangerous to her. She had grown up wandering amidst the ruined monasteries and convents of Newcastle, and their tumbledown walls covered with creeping vines had never seemed to her ominous, but rather mournful, lonesome, even romantic.

Newcastle in fact had been an important center of monasticism before the Reformation, and many were the reminders of this earlier way of life on the landscape of Mary Astell's childhood. So hospitable had it been to religious orders that the city had once been known as "Monkchester." "New House," a mansion built out of the ruins of the old Franciscan priory, had still existed in her childhood, standing at the top of what is now Leazes Lane.[36] Charles I had lived there while a captive of the Scots army, before he was returned to London and beheaded. Mary Astell often walked by it as a girl. There were also the visible remains of the buildings which had once housed the Black Friars or Preaching Friars. By Mary Astell's day the ruins were tenanted by old beggar women who had nowhere else to go. As late as 1789 these old buildings stood, reminding passersby of their bygone life.[37]

An order of Carmelites or White Friars had also made their home in Newcastle, and there had been a large nunnery, St. Bartholemew's, whose prioress and last nine nuns finally surrendered their lands and their home to Henry VIII in 1540. The back gate to it, "Nun gate," still stood in Mary Astell's day as a memento of this early refuge for religious women, and the bit of land on the edge of town called the Nun's moor was known to be just a sliver of the rich and extensive farmlands that had once belonged to the nuns from the great convent of St. Bartholemew's.

There were only a few latter-day examples of such voluntary, communal, monastic life. A local philanthropist had endowed a residence "for twelve ancient widows or spinsters" in 1685 in nearby Great Lumley, which Astell may have heard about. It seems unlikely that she would have known of Mary Ward's little community of Catholic women at London in the early part of the seventeenth century.[38] On the other hand Bishop Hacket's account of the remarkable clan at Little Gidding first appeared in 1693, the year before *A Serious Proposal*, and may well have had a direct influence on Astell's book. There he described the Ferrar family, a primitive matriarchy which comprised the entire parish of the little depopulated village, living in a house next door to the church. They were all single persons—including their mother, a widow of eighty—and they devoted their lives to prayer and work.

> Their apparel had Nothing in it of Fashion, but that which was common yet plain: and much of it for Linnen and Woolen spun at home. . . . They gave no Entertainment but to the Poor whom they instructed first, and then relieved, not with Fragments, but with the best they had. . . . Their business was, either they were at Prayer, or work; nothing came between. . . . They had the more leisure for work, because they fasted so much: and their diet at their meals was soon drest . . . besides their daily temperance was such, as they sat not long at them. . . . Their Bread was Coarse, their Drink small and of ill relish to the Tast. . . .

Strangers who visited were asked to read the following message which hung in their parlor:

> He that by report of our Endeavors, will remonstrate that which is more perfect, and seek to make us better, is welcome as an Angel of God. He that by chearful participating, and approbation of that which is good, confirms us in the same, is welcome as a Christian friend. He that in any way goes about to divert, or disturb us in that which is, as it ought to be among Christians (though it be not usual in the World) is a Burthen while

he stays, and shall bear his Judgment whoso he be. He that faults us in absence, for that which in presence he made shew to approve, shall by a double guilt of Flattery and Slander, violate the Bands both of Friendship and Christianity.

> *Subscribed,*
>> Mary Ferrar, Widow, Mother of this Family, aged about Fourscore years: who bids adieu to all Hopes and Fears of this World, and only Desires to Serve God.[39]

All of this would have appealed to Astell—the general asceticism, the cheerfully shouldered burden of continual self-improvement, the turning away from things of this world. But there is this important difference: the community at Little Gidding included men, whereas for Mary Astell part of the charm of her imagined establishment was that only women would be welcome within its walls.

In practically everything she wrote, everywhere she left her mark, Mary Astell reveals how entirely she cast her lot with women. This predisposition was as important to her thought, and to an understanding of the impulse of her writing or the story of her life, as recognizing what she meant by "reason" and "education." The avowed purpose of *A Serious Proposal* was to make "you Ladies" "as perfect and happy as 'tis possible to be in this imperfect state; for I love you too well to endure a spot on your Beauties, if I can by any means remove and wipe it off."[40] She was a self-appointed crusader to save women from the frivolity that co-opted their attention and energies, to salvage their minds for what she considered a higher calling. And if we moderns consider metaphysical speculation upon the properties of an ideal world dubious as a lifetime's work, it does not diminish the scope of Astell's intention, which was nothing less than to rescue her sex from ignorance and sloth and to point the way towards a better life.

It would be misleading, however, to claim that all this energy was purely disinterested social conscience, without a component of what we might call the "personal." In the letters to Norris, for example, one gradually becomes aware that whenever she speaks of earthly love (as opposed to the love of God) she is speaking of loving other women. The objects of her sentences are always female. Indeed she wrote at some length to Norris about these feelings, asking him about how to overcome them—not because she felt any shame for the passion that women called forth from her, but because her intellectual convictions forbade her to love *any* mere sublunary creature, shadows as they were of the Divine.

It was a problem which vexed her mightily, this "strong Propensity to friendly Love" which she could not control. She asked advice of Norris—as one who had thought about the nature of love—on how to control her feelings. She could not help herself from loving God's creatures, though she knew with her mind that since all delight came directly from God, her love was due the Creator rather than His creatures. She struggled against these undisciplined feelings, but she found it exceedingly difficult to abstract the true source of her pleasure from its visible manifestations in the world. She wrote to Norris as to a confessor about her recalcitrant emotions. Try as she would, she could not seem to prevent "an agreeable Movement in my Soul towards her I love." The letter is worth reading closely.

Permit me to add a Word or two more which is of greater Concernment to me because of practical Consideration; you have fully convinced me that GOD is the only proper Object of my Love, and I am sensible 'tis the highest Injustice to him and Unkindness to my self to defraud him of the least Part of my Heart; but I find it more easie to recognize his Right than to secure the Possession. Though I often say in your Pathetic and Divine Words, *No, my fair Delight, I will never be drawn off from the Love of thee by the Charms of any of thy Creatures,* yet alas, *sensible* Beauty does too often press upon my Heart, whilst *intelligible* is disregarded. For having by Nature a strong Propensity to friendly Love, which I have all along encouraged as a good Disposition to Vertue, and do still think it so if it may be kept within the due Bounds of Benevolence. But having likewise thought till you taught me better, that I need not cut off all Desire from the Creature, provided it were in Subordination to, and for the sake of the Creator: I have contracted such a Weakness . . . by voluntary Habit, that it is a very difficult thing for me to love at all without something of Desire. Now I am loath to abandon all Thoughts of Friendship, both because it is one of the brightest Vertues, and because I have the noblest Designs in it. Fain wou'd I rescue my Sex, or at least as many of them as come within my little Sphere, from that Meanness of Spirit into which the Generality of 'em are sunk, perswade them to pretend some higher Excellency than a well-chosen Pettycoat, or a fashionable Commode; and not wholly lay out their Time and Care in the Adornation of their Bodies, but bestow a Part of it at least in the Embellishment of their Minds, since inward Beauty will last when outward is decayed. But though I can say without boasting that none ever loved more generously than I have done, yet perhaps never any met with more ungrateful Returns which I can attribute to nothing so much as the Kindness of my best Friend [God] who saw how apt my Desires were to stray from him. . . . And though I have in some measure rectified this Fault, yet still I find an agreeable Movement in my Soul towards her I love, and a Displeasure and Pain when I meet with Unkindness. . . . Be pleased therefore to oblige me with a Remedy for this Disorder, since what you have already writ has made considerable Progress towards a Cure, but not quite perfected it.[41]

"Oblige me with a Remedy for this Disorder," she wrote Norris, since he had laid it down as one of his religious principles that one must cut off all desire from the "Creature." She found it hard to obey his injunction, having "contracted such a Weakness," probably by "voluntary Habit," that she found it "a very difficult thing for me to love at all without something of Desire." Perhaps as the author of her discomfort and an expert on these matters, he could offer her a palliative, since "what you have already writ has made considerable Progress towards a Cure, but not quite perfected it."

Try to distinguish between the movements of the soul and those of the body, Norris replied. "Thus, because we find Pleasure from the Fire, this is Warrent enough to approach it by a Bodily Movement, but we must not therefore *love* it. . . . By which you may plainly perceive what tis I mean by saying that Creatures may be sought *for* our good, but not loved *as* our Good." Of course he admitted that this advice, as with a great many other duties of a Christian, was "more intelligible than practicable." But, he added, the best way to put into practice this disregard of material objects was "by long and constant Meditation to free our Minds of that early Prejudice that sensible Objects do act upon our Spirits, and are the Causes of our Sensations."[42]

It is affecting to imagine Mary Astell alone in her rooms in Chelsea struggling against that "agreeable Movement in my Soul towards her I love," reshaping the urge into a more benevolent, serviceable, and universal form. Surely the energy of her feminism is here, in the "*sensible* Beauty which does too often press upon my Heart, whilst *intelligible* is disregarded."

She tried to act upon her impulses at their most general level, as a diffused protective love for all women and a desire to improve their characters and their capacities. She sternly dismissed her own painful disappointments in love as the just deserts of self-involved, self-indulgent feeling: "I can attribute to nothing so much as the kindness of my best Friend [God], who saw how apt my Desires were to stray from him, and therefore by these frequent Disappointments would have me learn more Wisdom than to let loose my Heart to that which cannot satisfie." She tried to understand her unhappy episodes of unrequited love as God's attempts to retrain her affections, so to speak, to pry them away from the particular individuals who caught her fancy and fix them on *Him*—the proper object of all such heated feeling. "I thank the Lord that I am Friendless," she had written in one of the poems she gave to Sancroft, renouncing the very thing that mattered most to her in the world. With her usual emphasis on Christian paradox, she tried to believe that her frustration was for the best.

> I thank thee Lord that I am Friendless too,
>   Tho that alas be hard to do!
>   Tho I have wearied Heav'n with Prayers,
>   And fill'd it's bottles with my tears.
> Tho I always propos'd the noblest end,
>   Thy glory in a Friend.
> And never any earthly thing requir'd,
>   But this thats better part divine,
> And for that reason was so much desir'd;
>   Yet humbly I submit,
>   To that most perfect will of thine,
> And thank thee cause thou has denied me it.
>   Thrice blessed be thy Jealousie,
>   Which would not part
> With one smal corner of my heart,
> But has engross'd it all to Thee!

By the time of her correspondence with Norris, she had come to think differently about this and to admit her misery at rejected desire. But she explained in a footnote added later that what she suffered was the pain of a Christian watching a soul go astray, spurning her spiritual assistance: "next to Sorrow for our Sins, our Neighbors refusing to receive the Spiritual Good we wish them, is the justest, greatest, and most lasting Cause of Grief."[43]

The Christian rationale, the moral justification for the importance of friendship, was mutual criticism. Best friends—which Astell invariably thought of as persons of the same sex—could help one another, gently read back one another's faults, and generally aid and abet the interminable self-improvement that Astell thought the will and duty of every Christian. In her ideal college, that earthly Eden, "we shall have opportunity of contracting the purest and noblest Friendship; a Blessing, the purchase of which were richly worth all the world besides! For she who possesses a worthy Person, has certainly obtain'd the richest Treasure!" Nothing there would hinder "two Persons of a sympathizing disposition" "from entering into an holy combination to watch over

each other for Good, to advise, encourage and direct, and to observe
the minutest fault in order to its amendment."[44] It was a species of
chaste marriage as she described it, with more equal power relations
than in traditional unions and without the physical dangers that threatened women in heterosexual intercourse.

She defended Platonic friendship on the grounds that as the truest
manifestation of Christian love, it had the "social force to dilate our
hearts [and] deliver them from that vicious selfishness and the rest of
those *sordid passions*, which express a narrow and illiberal temper, and
are of such pernicious consequence to mankind."[45] She blamed the
"degeneracy of the present Age". upon the "little true Friendship that
is to be found in it," and cited Jeremy Taylor's formulation that friendship is "Charity contracted . . . a kind of revenging our selves on the
narrowness of our Faculties" in which one practiced towards two or
three what one was willing, but not able, to practice towards all. Jeremy
Taylor's essay, published in 1657, had been written in answer to the
question that Katherine Philips, the poet, had asked him: "How far
[is] a dear and perfect friendship . . . authorized by the principles of
CHRISTIANITY?"[46] The question bears a curious resemblance to Astell's appeal to Norris—both women essentially asking for doctrinal
direction on this matter of handling and interpreting their passionate
feelings for other women.

Whether or not Mary Astell was a lesbian is not the most fruitful
way to ask the question that next presents itself. For one thing, intense,
spiritualized friendships with other women were not unusual in that
culture. No one looked askance when Katherine Philips accompanied
her beloved Ann Owen, or "Lucasia," on her honeymoon to Ireland,
leaving her own husband (thirty-seven years her senior) and daughter
to look after themselves. She continued in Ireland for several years, first
living with Lucasia and her husband and then near them. The primary
loyalty existing between Clarissa Harlowe and Anna Howe is a literary
example from the eighteenth century of the same phenomenon. The
fact is that men and women of that day inhabited separate worlds; their
social rounds and domestic activities kept them in the society of their
own sex much of the time. Social intercourse with those of the opposite
sex was strictly regulated before marriage. As a result, there were simply
more same-sex intimacies and ones of greater intensity than we are used
to in our modern world, steeped as it is in post-Freudian heterosexuality.[47]

A growing body of historical literature about nineteenth-century
communities of women identifies an erotic element in those communities, from the undergraduates of Vassar in the 1870s to the settlement
houses of Jane Addams or Lilian Wald at the turn of the century. These

readings resist the assumption that such women were loveless and lonely spinsters, pining away without men. The point of this scholarly literature, aside from the question of which particular physical actions any of these women engaged in, is that many women—both married and single—found in friendships with others of their own sex the emotional support and nurture which kept them going. In her study of political activists at the turn of the century in America, Blanche Wiesen Cook asserts that "frequently the networks of love and support that enable politically and professionally active women to function independently and intensively consist largely of other women."[48] Certainly this was true for Mary Astell, who lived and worked essentially with women, whose friends constituted a family and a career for her; without their love and companionship she could not have survived.

I am sure that Mary Astell never physically acted out a passion with anyone of either sex. Her belief was that the more one denied the urges of the body, the better. Nevertheless, one senses a libidinous energy in her pleas for women, at the same time that she completely dismisses men, writing as if they were a race apart, with completely different tastes and inclinations. Even among those who were her sisters-in-arms, like Lady Mary Wortley Montagu or Judith Drake, her thought is unusual in its prepossession in favor of women and the bitter tone it takes towards men. She considered men as sexual predators in an unequal contest, unprincipled Lovelaces out for what they could get. She warned women not to depend on *their* admiration and not to trust *their* intentions. If women ever really considered how foolish and immoral were most men, she wrote, "They wou'd never be so sottish as to imagine, that he who regards nothing but his own brutish Appetite, shou'd have any real affection for them, nor ever expect Fidelity from one who is unfaithful to GOD and his own Soul. . . . They wou'd not value themselves on account of the Admiration of such incompetent Judges, nor consequently make use of those trifling Arts that are necessary to recommend them to such Admirers."[49]

Outside of the sexual arena she admired certain men: John Norris for one, or religious leaders like Sancroft, Fénelon or Henry Dodwell, who would sooner lose their worldly power and wealth than compromise their conservative principles. But for the most part she felt that men—because of their ruling position in society—were too sensualized, too rooted in the material world, too distracted to pursue Platonic ideals or Christian virtue. She held in particular contempt the "beaux" and "topping sparks of the town" who—unlike unschooled women of the same stamp whom she forgave and tried to teach—ought to know better. She knew these men of fashion found her precepts ridiculous:

"For Vertue her self as bright as she is, can't escape the lash of scurrilous Tongues; the comfort is, whilst they impotently endeavor to throw dirt on her, they are unable to soil her Beauty, and only render themselves the more contemptible. They may therefore if they please, hug themselves in their own dear folly, and enjoy the diversion of their own insipid Jests."[50] She obviously enjoyed leaving the men behind to hug themselves and jest "impotently," while she withdrew to a place where "you may more peaceably enjoy yourselves, and all the innocent pleasures it is able to afford you," as she wrote to her female audience, "and particularly that which is worth all the rest, a noble, Vertuous and Disinterest'd Friendship."

Her imagination painted for her a scene of meditation, rural walks, long involved intellectual discussions, reading and reciting aloud, and musical ensembles of voice, recorders, and virginals. Humans were gregarious, after all. It was not fit that "Creatures capable of and made for Society, shou'd be wholly Independent, or Indifferent to each others Esteem and Commendation." Once they had adjusted to such amiable society, she told her readers, she had no doubt that they would lose their taste for flirtation and for men, leaving behind them those "Follies which in the time of your ignorance pass'd with you under the name of love; altho' there is not in nature two more different things, than *true Love* and that *brutish Passion* which pretends to ape it."[51]

Others before Astell had sung the praises of women's friendship and imagined secular communities of women—although none so practically or earnestly as she. In some ways it was an inevitable fantasy, given how total was male authority in the culture. The notion crops up in Restoration drama, usually with reference to the classical example of Hippolyta and the Amazons, as in Shadwell's *Woman-Captain* (1680) or D'Urfey's *A Common-Wealth of Women* (1685). Margaret Cavendish also wrote several plays on this theme, one called *The Female Academy* (1662) about a "school" where young ladies were "instructed to speak wittily and rationally, and to behave themselves hansomly, and to live virtuously," and another called *The Convent of Pleasure* (1668).

The heroine of *The Convent of Pleasure*, Lady Happy, explains why the perfect retreat for women necessarily excludes men:

> *L. Happy.* Men are the only troublers of Women; for they only cross and oppose their sweet delights, and peaceable life; they cause their pains, but not their pleasures. Wherefore those Women that are poor, and have not means to buy delights, and maintain pleasures, are only fit for Men; for having not means to please themselves, they must serve only to please others; but those Women, where Fortune, Nature, and the gods are joined

to make them happy, were mad to live with Men, who make the Female sex their slaves; but I will not be so inslaved, but will live retired from their Company. Wherefore, in order thereto, I will take so many Noble persons of my own Sex, as my Estate will plentifully maintain, such whose Births are greater than their Fortunes, and are resolv'd to live a single life, and vow Virginity: with these I mean to live incloister'd with all the delights and pleasures that are allowable and lawful; My Cloister shall not be a Cloister of restraint, but a place for freedom, not to vex the Senses but to please them.[52]

With a vast sum of money left to her by her father, Lord Fortunate, Cavendish's heroine is in the enviable position of designing for herself the perfect life. She spares no expense or effort on the most gratifying material conditions: fresh flowers and cool rustling silk in the summer, fires and heavy damasks in the winter. In the larger details, too, Lady Happy orchestrates a life of plenty and ease in a self-sufficient community with her friends, including "Women Physicians, Surgeons, and Apothecaries." They supply their own food out of their forest, streams, and gardens; they hire their own cooks and servants (women, of course).

This picture of highborn women disporting themselves in innocent enjoyment free from the tyranny of men is much like Astell's vision— only rather more luxurious than she thought was good for anyone, and without her intellectual or religious rationale. It seems unlikely that Astell knew Margaret Cavendish's play; it was never acted, and Astell never took much interest in plays, whether between covers or on the stage. But both women were responding to the same cultural pressures with their parallel fantasies, although each highlighted different aspects of the problem.

In one scene, in amateur skits they put on for one another—plays within the play—Margaret Cavendish's characters dramatize the aspects of heterosexual life they were glad to leave behind. They show husbands who drink or gamble, who beat their wives or philander, as well as the trials of continual pregnancies, the deaths of young children, and painful—even fatal—*accouchements*. These skits point up a truth that cannot be ignored in assessing any woman's attitudes toward men in that period, which is simply that sexuality was dangerous; conditions in late seventeenth-century London, when Mary Astell was writing, were extremely unfavorable to the biological female.

A married woman with regular sexual contact had a 10 percent chance of dying in childbed. Furthermore, the high incidence of childhood rickets and abysmal ignorance about its cure meant that many women grew up with abnormally flattened pelvic girdles that narrowed the birth canal and made childbirth an even more difficult ordeal than it was with normally formed bone structures.[53] Marriage was a risk; everyone in Astell's time knew of women who had suffered and died in labor, women who were pregnant more often than they cared to be, women who were wrenched by the early death of child after child. The rate books of Chelsea, where Astell lived, are filled with records of disbursements to pay for one night's firing for some poor woman or another, just delivered of a child or just about to be, and the coach fare to ship her off to some other parish in the morning.

Astell herself thought of sexuality as dangerous and destructive. She wrote a poem on the occasion of the death of Eleanor Bowes, a fifteen-year-old bride married just three months, which strongly conveys her sense that marriage itself was fatal.[54] Her negative emphasis is all the more striking when compared to Lady Mary Wortley Montagu's poem on the same occasion; Lady Mary characterized the brief marriage as "three months of rapture" filled with the "sweets of love." Young Eleanor Bowes was lucky to die before the honeymoon ended, wrote cynical Lady Mary. Sexuality did not worry her as much as the cooling of ardor.

Mary Astell never understood this worldly attitude, or the heterosexual dimension of Lady Mary's character, although she was very drawn to the younger woman. She often lectured Lady Mary about her duties as a Christian and about being more careful of her reputation—but Lady Mary only laughed at her seriousness, and deflected her warnings with a jest. Astell even had a dream about Lady Mary drowning—"Shipwreck" was her word for social ruin—in which she leaped into the raging sea to Lady Mary's aid, whether to save her or to join her is hard to tell. "Give me leave to tell my dream," she wrote to her friend in a chiding strain, "tho my waking, most reasonable & tendrest thoughts, are it seems not worth notice."

> Methought I saw you last night wth agony of Soul, Shipwreckt, struggling for Life wth ye insulting billows indifference. I cry'd, I beg'd, but all in vain y^t they wou'd take a Boat y^t lay by y^m & try to assist you. Not one wou'd run ye least hazard, or so much as spoil their fine clothes in your service. Whereupon I threw myself out of ye window into ye Sea, resolv'd to save . . . you.[55]

For all her sensitivity to the inequality and injustice of the arrangements between men and women, Astell never challenged the sexual double standard. She simply did not think about it.[56] Indeed, her unquestioning prudery comported well with conventional attitudes in her

*Lady Mary
Wortley
Montagu.
Portrait by G.
Kneller, 1715. By
permission of the
Scottish
National
Portrait Gallery.*

culture about relations between the sexes. In *The Christian Religion,* for example, she warns that if a woman were seen too frequently in the company of a man not her husband—and men could be helpful, she maintained, as advisors in worldly affairs or as teachers—her necessary concern for her reputation obliged her to break off the relationship completely at the first whisper of impropriety.[57] There was no excuse for tarnishing one's reputation. All causes of "shipwreck" seemed to her equally avoidable. With the oblivious disapproval of one who does not understand the temptation, she was impatient with women who found themselves in troubled waters.

All her life Astell resisted male attractions with no difficulty. Not only did she never marry, but there is no evidence that she ever entertained any suitors. She explicitly disapproved of beaux as a class—witness the "Anti-Song" she wrote for Lady Mary—and in general distrusted the intentions of men towards women. She fumed at the universal opinion that women needed husbands and really did think that women were, on the whole, better off living with other women. She could not understand why anyone would choose the world of gallantry if she had an alternative.

> You are therefore Ladies, invited into a place, where you shall suffer no other confinement, but to be kept out of the road of sin. . . . You will only quit that Chat of insignificant people, for an ingenious Conversation; the froth of flashy wit for real wisdom; idle tales for instructive discourses. The deceitful Flatteries of those who under the pretence of loving and admiring you, really served their *own* base ends, for the seasonable Reproofs and wholsom Counsels of your hearty well-wishers and affectionate Friends; which will procure you those perfections your feigned lovers pretended you had, and kept you from obtaining. . . . All that is requir'd of you, is only to be as happy as possibly you can, and to make sure of a Felicity that will fill all the capacities of your Souls! . . . Happy Retreat! which will be the introducing you into such a *Paradise* as your Mother *Eve* forfeited, where you shall feast on Pleasures, that do not, like those of the World, disappoint your expectations, pall your Appetites, and by the disgust they give you, put you on the fruitless search after new Delights, which when obtain'd are as empty as the former. . . . Here are no Serpents to deceive you, whilst you entertain yourselves in these delicious Gardens. No Provocations are given in this Amicable Society, but to Love and to good Works. . . .[58]

Here, as in her poem on Mrs. Bowes, she describes female society as a kind of prelapsarian world where piety is as natural as eating or breathing and where *ennui* is unknown. It is a paradise such as that in which "Mother Eve" once lived, a garden without serpents. Thus a girl might live—or feel about her life—before the fall into physiological womanhood and the necessity of facing the problems of adult women—courtship, marriage, pregnancy, *accouchement*, and adultery. Astell describes her community of *religieuses* as a place from an earlier time of innocence and safety—such as she pictured in her poem to young Eleanor Bowes before "the fatal Nuptial Knot was tie'd" and the "cup" "poisoned."

Undoubtedly these attitudes had survival value, and may have accounted in some measure for Astell's popular success. Not even her biting polemic could dispel the saintly aura. She could always gloss her feeling with religious doctrine: "we suffer Passion to lead when it ought to follow," she wrote in *The Christian Religion*. "Wise Men in all Ages have exclaim'd against Prejudices and Prepossessions, and advis'd us to get rid of them, but they have not inform'd us how, nor enabl'd us to do it, Christianity only does this. And it does it by stripping sensible things of their deceitful appearances, and finding us nobler Objects of our Passions than any this World affords."[59] When she wrote to Norris at twenty-seven asking him to help her to be a better Christian, to deal with the "sensible beauty [which] does too often press upon my heart," it was love in her own terms that she was trying to resist. At thirty-one she was still looking to St. Paul as the standard of perfection: "And tho we have not the Ambition to aspire to *St. Paul's* Perfection who was *crucified to the World and the World to him*, a greater Character than that of *Universal Monarch*. . . . Yet sure we can't deny that it is Possible, and very much our Duty, to be more indifferent to the Objects of Sense than most of us are."[60] At forty-eight, reading Pascal, she argued that one had to keep a watch on one's appetites and desires—even when they were "Innocent & Laudable"—lest they become too strong.

> M. Paschal [Pascal], I own, argues so justly ag[t] all attachment, y[t] I begin to think giving a check to our most innocent desires is no little Obligation. It being harder to keep y[e] right measure in w[t] is in itself Innocent & Laudable (this requiring exactness of Judgm[t] Comand of ones Passions & constant Watchfulness) than to avoid great & obvious Faults w[ch] are too glaring to escape our Observation. . . .[61]

These pious attitudes are representative of women of Astell's class, whether the configuration of motives behind them is typical or no. Certainly, Christian stoicism was safer for a woman than a life of sensual indulgence. Also, women were used to seeking meaning beyond the narrow compass of their lives in another existence, which was the reward for cheerfully enduring this one. More than a hundred years later, George Eliot was still playing this tune, as the following extract from a letter illustrates:

> For my part, when I hear of the marrying and giving in marriage that is constantly being transacted, I can only sigh for those who are multiplying earthly ties which, though powerful enough to detach their hearts and thoughts from heaven, are so brittle as to be liable to be snapped asunder at every breeze. . . . I must believe that those are happiest who . . . are considering this life merely a pilgrimage, a scene calling for diligence and watchfulness, not for repose and amusement.[62]

Astell assumed in her readers an impulse to perfection such as she found in herself, similarly thwarted by weakness and temptation from within, and the prejudice against learned women from without. Her projected school had the double aim of correcting the intellectual conditions for women and providing a protective quarantine against the corruption of the world. As she imagined it, her ideal society would have the therapeutic effect of reeducating the appetite for good, realigning moral values and experience.

In that sense, Astell's advocacy of chastity was but a means to an end, a veil for the protective love and ambition she felt for other women. She saw them as primarily rational, independent beings—like herself— and thought that monastic life best promoted these qualities. She believed that a lofty philosophic indifference to the material world was most conducive to religious faith and intellectual pursuit—a state of mind most difficult for a married woman, quick with child year after year and anxiously scanning her living children for signs of illness. Given heterosexual life as it existed in her time, only in communities of other women could she imagine the ideal conditions for meditation and study. There is "no Posterity so desireable as the offspring of our Minds," wrote Astell. She wanted to free other women from the biological imperatives which otherwise dominated their lives and deflected them from what she thought of as their higher purposes. "The whole World is a single Ladys Family," she asserted, "her opportunities of doing good are not lessen's but encreas'd by her being unconfin'd." A woman without children had more time to give to larger philosophical researches or philanthropic chores. "Particular Obligations do not contract her Mind, but her Beneficence moves in the largest Sphere."[63]

Astell believed that those whose social class gave them the leisure to pursue rational ends had a responsibility to make public the fruits of their cogitation. "And if the necessity of the world requires that some Persons shou'd Labour for others, it likewise requires that others shou'd Think for them. Our Powers and Faculties were not given us for nothing, and the only advantage one Woman has above another, is the being allotted to the more noble employment."[64] Her college was not meant to give young women Greek or Latin scholastic training like their brothers at Cambridge or Oxford, but to provide them an opportunity for this "more noble employment"—the chance to think about spiritual matters rather than to pass their lives in childbearing and housekeeping. Its other purpose was to permit them a way of being in community with other women—which, as Astell could see, was the only way to guarantee both autonomy and companionship.

Chapter Six

A Monarch for Life

'Tis better that I endure the Unreasonableness, Injustice, or Oppression of a Parent, a Master, &c. than that the Establish'd Rules of Order and good Government, shou'd be superseded on my account.

> Mary Astell, *The Christian Religion As Profess'd by A Daughter of the Church*, 1705

If the Authority of the Husband so far as it extends, is sacred and inalienable, why not of the Prince? The Domestic Sovereign is without Dispute Elected, and the Stipulations and Contract are mutual, is it not then partial in Men to the last degree, to contend for, and practice that Arbitrary Dominion in their Families, which they abhor and exclaim against in the State? For if Arbitrary Power is evil in it self, and an improper Method of Governing Rational and Free Agents, it ought not to be Practis'd any where; Nor is it less, but rather more mischievous in Families than in Kingdoms, by how much 100000 Tyrants are worse than one.

> Mary Astell, 1706 Preface to *Some Reflections Upon Marriage*

A few blocks from Mary Astell's modest dwelling on Paradise Row lived another independent woman, the beautiful and notorious Hortense Mancini, duchess of Mazarin, in an establishment of a different character. She had moved to Chelsea a few years before Astell came, in what was for her semiretirement after fifteen years in London spent in a whirl of pleasure and gaiety. A personification of the stylish licentiousness of the Restoration court, the duchess had been bred early to this way of life under the tutelage of her uncle, Cardinal Mazarin, in the court of young Louis XIV. Here she first came to know Charles II, in the days of his exile. Later, when she fled to England to escape her mad and tyrannical husband, the former duke of Meilleraye and Mayenne, the newly restored monarch welcomed his old friend with a pension of more than £4,000 a year. This extremely generous allowance supported her large and colorful household, her menagerie of parrots, monkeys, cats, and dogs, the hospitality which drew the brightest wits of Charles's court to drink, dispute, and gamble.[1]

Even under her later retrenchment policies, the duchess's Chelsea house was a scene of luxury, visited by brilliant people, stocked lavishly with fine wines, adorned with priceless possessions. History could not have provided a better foil to studious and sober Astell than this flamboyant duchess with her perfume, silks, headdresses, and laces. The one was a natural ascetic, encouraged by impecunious circumstances to make of her cramped circumstances a virtue. The other was intemperate, impulsive, and lively, raised among the decadent voluptuaries of the French court in luxury everyone took for granted.

"In abstinence few or none ever surpassed her," wrote Astell's first biographer, "she would live like a Hermit, for a considerable time together, upon a crust of bread and water with a little small beer. And at the time of her highest living, (when she was at home) she very rarely eat any dinner till night; and then it was by the strictest rules of temperance. She would say, *Abstinence was her best Physick*. And would frequently observe, *that those who indulged themselves in Eating and Drinking, could not be so well disposed or prepared either for study or the regular and Devout Service of their Creator.*"[2]

While Astell took conscious pride in living like an anchorite ("I had ye Honor of her Grace ye Duchess of Ormond's Company at my Cell last week," she wrote to a friend),[3] the festivities lasted all night at the home of the duchess of Mazarin, a street away. "Play is followed by the most exquisite repasts in the world," reported one of the admiring regulars. "There you will find whatever delicacy is brought from France, and whatever is curious from the Indies. Even the commonest meats have the rarest relishes imparted to them. There is neither a plenty which gives a notion of extravagance, nor a frugality that discovers penury or meanness."[4] So wrote St. Evremond, the aging French aristocrat and philosopher who watched over his adored duchess until the end of her life. When she allowed it, he would visit her, "a little old

Hortense Mancini, the duchess of Mazarin. Engraving 1678 by G. Valck, after a painting by P. Lely. Courtesy Bibliothèque Nationale, Paris.

man in a black coif, carried along Pall Mall in a sedan chair," bringing with him a "pound of butter made in his own dairy, for her breakfast."[5]

Astell lived in Chelsea during the duchess of Mazarin's last years, when the duchess no longer presented such a brave spectacle and the strain of her debts and recurrent illnesses must have been apparent to all. William III, the dour Dutch king, had discontinued the pension that merry Charles had bestowed upon her. Her French husband managed to cut off the allowance given her out of the huge estate she had brought him. Debts piled up, and although her friends evidently took care of many of them, her unpaid poor rate of sixteen shillings, still visible in the Chelsea rate books, testifies to her straitened circumstances. It is said that her guests even went so far as to "leave under their plates the wherewithal to pay for their entertainment."[6] Her health declined in these years as well. After an irregular and somewhat dissolute life, she died at fifty-two.

She had been a well-known figure in London, because of her notorious history, the manner and scale of her Chelsea life, and her famous charm. Interestingly, she was admired by several women writers. Aphra Behn dedicated to her *The History of the Nun: or, The Fair Vow-Breaker* (1689); and [Mary] Delariviere Manley, in her Introduction to *The Adventures of Rivella* (1714), pays tribute to her as the most bewitching woman of her generation: "What youthful Charmer of the Sex ever pleas'd to that Height, as did Madam the Dutchess of *Mazarin*, even to her Death; tho' I am told she was near twice *Rivella's* Age? Were not all Eyes, all Hearts, devoted to her, even to the last?"

When she died in 1699, many took notice of the event. John Evelyn registered it in his diary, adding that "all the world knows her storie."[7] An alert and enterprising bookseller, capitalizing on renewed public interest in the Mazarin case, unearthed and translated the legal briefs of the celebrated lawsuit which her estranged husband, the duke, had instituted against her in order to have her extradited and sent back to France.[8] It was upon reading this scandalous record of contested connubial authority that Mary Astell composed *Some Reflections Upon Marriage* (1700). She claimed to have written it in a single sitting, remarking that an afternoon was not much to throw away upon such a subject.

The Mazarin case interested Astell on many counts. As neighbors, she and the duchess had known one another by sight, as nodding acquaintances, although they moved in different worlds. From others in the neighborhood she had heard the old stories about the duchess's affairs, anecdotes retold and embellished when she died. After seeing the legal briefs, Astell went back to read the duchess's autobiographical *Mémoires D'Hortense et de Marie Mancini* (1676), relishing the details:

the brilliance of the family, the obvious waste of a spirited woman's talents and intelligence. But the arguments about a husband's authority and the submission owed him by his wife—as set forth by M. Hérard, the advocate for the duke of Mazarin—these interested her most of all.

The popular outline of the duchess's story is neatly summarized by John Evelyn.

> Now also died, the famous Dutchesse of Mazarine, in her time the richest Lady in Europ, Niece to the greate Cardinal Mazarine, & married to the Richest subject in Europ, as is said: she was born at Rome, Educated in France, an extraordinary Beauty & Witt, but dissolute, & impatient of Matrimonial restraint, so as to be abandonned by her husband, came into England for shelter, liv'd on a pension given her here, & reported to have hastned her death, by intemperan[t]ly drinking strong spirits &c: She has written her owne Story & Adventures & so had her other Extravagant sister, wife to the noble family *Colona*.[9]

"Matrimonial restraint" hardly gives an adequate idea of the fanatical behavior of the duke of Meilleraye and Mayenne towards his young wife, any more than what Mary Astell was to call "ill education" did justice to what it meant to be raised in the debauchery of the French court. Cardinal Mazarin, guardian to several nieces and nephews, including the future duchess of Mazarin, appears to have treated them with less than parental solicitude, indeed as pawns and diversions. For example, in her *Mémoires* the Duchess tells of the "plaisanterie" her uncle perpetrated on her younger sister to the amusement of the entire court. He accused the six-year-old girl of an "indiscretion" with one of the older men who paid court to her, and claimed that she was pregnant, that her figure was changing. Marie-Anne denied it bitterly, crying that she had never even kissed any but young Louis XIV himself and the count de Guiche. Nevertheless, the Cardinal carried his joke to great lengths, had the little girl's clothing taken in every night to make it appear to her that she was putting on weight, and one morning slipped a newborn baby into bed with her, demanding to know its father. Hortense reports enjoying it all immensely, for she understood what was going on, watching the proceedings from her Olympian vantage of age nine.[10]

The torments which her own life held in store did not begin until a little later, at thirteen, when the duke of Meilleraye and Mayenne was so smitten with her that he swore if he could only marry her he would not care if he breathed his last three months after. Cardinal Mazarin was irritated by this unexpected passion, for he had intended this man as a match for her sister, and he threatened to marry Hortense to his valet. Nevertheless, this man who enjoyed such immense worldly power was afraid of death. He had no children of his own, and there was no one to carry on his name. The duke of Meilleraye and Mayenne was patient, and when the cardinal knew he was about to die, he gave Hortense to the duke on the condition that they take the name of Mazarin.[11]

The duke proved an impossible husband. A religious fanatic, he woke his young wife in the middle of the night to tell her his visions, and he forbade her to nurse the baby on fast days.[12] Sexually obsessed, he mutilated the magnificent statues in the Palais Mazarin and splashed paint on the nudes to make them "decent." He wanted to forbid his farmers to milk cows because it looked so obscene, and once considered sawing off the teeth of his young daughters to make them unattractive and thus to protect them from future sexuality. His jealousy made of Hortense's life a nightmare, for he wanted to prevent her from seeing anyone but himself. He kept her on the move and endangered her health, so she said, by demanding that she travel when very pregnant or just after giving birth. If she enjoyed a place too much, they left it; if she spoke to a servant or seemed to like a maid, he dismissed her; any man who visited more than twice was refused admittance. French-woman that she was, she finally lost patience when she realized that he was running through her money at a great rate, wasting her fortune, impoverishing her children's future, selling off the priceless objects of her inheritance, and even demanding her jewels. According to her account, she saw three millions disappear without making a sound, but finally demanded a separation and division of property.[13]

While her case was being deliberated, Madame Mazarin was packed off to the Abbey de Chelles, where the abbess was her husband's aunt. There were orders to keep Hortense under constant scrutiny. Nevertheless she managed to disrupt the quiet routine with a number of high-spirited pranks. In the end the court decreed that she should return to her husband, and explicitly ordered her to submit to his authority both in and out of the bedroom. At this point she planned and executed her escape. She fled to the court of Charles II, "seeking Relief" as Mary Astell put it, "by such imprudent, not to say scandalous Methods, as the running away in Disguise with a spruce Cavalier."[14]

Astell's considered opinion of the case was that the duchess's behavior was inexcusable—but also that it was understandable. She was disturbed by the dirty linen washed in public, and even more by the inadequate excuses made for Hortense Mancini's affairs of "Gallantry"— for which the "modest and discreet" had "a harder Name." Yet they must be ill-natured indeed, she wrote, who did not pity the duchess's misfortunes at the same time as they condemned her conduct, and who did not regret that "such a Treasure should fall into his hands who was not worthy of it, nor knew how to value and improve it." Who was more to blame, she asked, comparing the Duke of Mazarin to his unfortunate wife, "he whom Nature never qualify'd for great things" or she "who being capable of every thing, must therefore suffer more and be more lamented?"[15] She had been sacrificed to a crazy man who was her inferior in every way, but because she had to obey him, she was wrong to leave him; and she compounded her error by a life of dissipation.

But what neither M. Hérard, the duke's lawyer, nor anyone else writing about the case seemed to have any inkling of, and what Astell was trying to communicate, was how a woman might suffer in an untenable marriage.

> To be yoak'd for Life to a disagreeable Person and Temper; to have Folly and Ignorance tyrannize over Wit and Sense; to be contradicted in every thing one does or says, and bore down not by Reason but Authority; to be denied one's most innocent desires, for no other cause but the Will and Pleasure of an absolute Lord and Master, whose Follies a Woman with all her Prudence cannot hide, and whose Commands she cannot but despise at the same time she obeys them; is a misery none can have a just Idea of, but those who have felt it.[16]

She saw the situation sympathetically, from a woman's point of view, at the same time that she disapproved of Mme Mazarin's manner of life as immoral, wasteful, and purposeless. Better to have turned her time to account in religious meditation, philanthropic works, or philosophic study, Astell thought, for she was "capable of being a great Ornament to her Family and Blessing to the Age she liv'd in." Now she could "only serve (to say no worse) as an unhappy Shipwrack to point out the dangers of an ill Education and unequal Marriage."[17]

Hortense Mancini's case was an extreme one, to be sure, but no less illustrative of the risks a woman ran when she married and put herself entirely in her husband's power. She left "all that is dear to her, her Friends and Family, to espouse his Interests and his Fortune," and make it "her Business and Duty to please him!"[18] Long before Richardson's *Clarissa*, Astell described how limiting, how isolating, how crushing, a bad marriage could be for women. As Clarissa wrote affectingly when she thought she was about to be married against her will to Solmes: "*Marriage* is a very solemn engagement, enough to make a young creature's heart ache with the *best* prospects, when she thinks seriously of it! To be given up to a strange man; to be ingrafted into a strange family; to give up her very name, as a mark of her becoming his absolute and dependent property; to be obliged to prefer this strange man, to father, to mother—to everybody: and his humours to all her own. . . . To go no-whither: to make acquaintance: to give up acquaintance: all at his pleasure, whether she think it reasonable to do so or not."[19]

What made it worse, said Astell, was that most men had only the most exploitative intentions in regard to their wives. Men married for money and were more interested in improving their wives' estates than their understandings. "For pray, what do Men propose to themselves in Marriage? What Qualifications do they look after in a Spouse? What will she bring is the first enquiry? How many Acres? Or how much ready Coin?" Not that she thought these irrelevant considerations, or expected her readers to live on love: "Marriage without a Competency . . . is no very comfortable Condition," she acknowledged.[20] The odds for happiness were no better if men chose for beauty, however, for that too was an unregulated appetite subject to change. In time, she predicted cynically, he would find the same reason for another choice.

How could a man respect his wife, she asked, when most men had "a contemptible Opinion of her and her Sex? When from his own Elevation he looks down on them as void of Understanding, and full of Ignorance and Passion, so that Folly and a Woman are equivalent Terms with him? Can he think there is any Gratitude due to her whose utmost services he exacts as strict Duty? Because she was made to be a Slave to his Will, and has no higher end than to Serve and Obey him!"[21] A man married for reasons that had nothing to do with the good of his spouse and were not calculated to improve her mind or elevate her spirit. Neither did he marry out of motives of admiration, for "no man can endure a Woman of Superior Sense," she warned, or even would treat one civilly "but that he thinks he stands on higher ground."

A man marries because "he wants one to manage his Family, an House-keeper, an upper Servant, one whose Interest it will be not to wrong him, and in whom therefore he can put greater confidence than in any he can hire for Money. One who may breed his Children, taking all the care and trouble of their Education, to preserve his Name and Family. One whose Beauty, Wit, or good Humour and agreeable Conversation, will entertain him at Home when he has been contradicted and disappointed abroad; who will do him that Justice the ill-natur'd World denies him, that is, in any one's Language but his own, sooth his Pride and Flatter his Vanity, by having always so much good Sense as to be on his side, to conclude him in the right, when others are so Ignorant, or so Rude as to deny it. Who will not be Blind to his Merit nor contradict his Will and Pleasure, but make it her Business, her very Ambition to content him. . . . In a Word, one whom he can intirely Govern, and consequently may form her to his will and liking, who must be his for Life, and therefore cannot quit his Service let him treat her how he will."[22] Women who did not face squarely this prevailing state of affairs were likely to end up as unhappily as the duchess of Mazarin.

In truth, Astell opined, women must be by far the stronger sex, psychologically, to be capable of so difficult a duty as submission. Even Cato, "with all his Stoical Principles was not able to bear the sight of a triumphant Conqueror . . . but ran to Death to secure him from it."[23] Yet men expected those they considered ignorant and weak to have the patience "to bear a continual Out-rage and Insolence all the Days" of their lives. A woman must be wise and good and "much above what we suppose the Sex capable of, I fear much greater than e'er a Man can pretend to, who can so constantly conquer her Passions, and divest her self even of Innocent Self-love, as to give up the Cause when she is in the right, and to submit her enlightened Reason, to imperious Dictates of a blind Will, and wild Imagination, even when she clearly perceives the ill Consequences of it, the Imprudence, nay Folly and Madness of such a Conduct."[24]

There was a terrible disparity between this reality and the vanity in which most young women were raised. But Astell went beyond Restoration commonplaces about women's rude awakening after marriage. The trouble was, she said, that women's expectations for themselves stopped short with finding a husband. "What poor Woman is ever taught that she should have a higher Design than to get her a Husband?" cried Mary Astell. "Heaven will fall in of course; and if she make but an Obedient and Dutiful Wife, she cannot miss of it. A Husband indeed is thought by both Sexes so very valuable, that scarce a Man who can keep himself clean and make a bow, but thinks he is good enough to pretend to any Woman, no matter for the Difference of Birth or Fortune, a Husband is such a Wonder-working Name as to make an Equality, or something more, whenever it is pronounc'd."[25]

Too late a woman learned what idol her husband worshiped, which her vanity or perhaps the importunities of her relatives hid from her before: "and now he has got that into his possession, she must make court to him for a little sorry Alimony out of her own Estate."[26] Small wonder if she were shocked and cast down, wrote Astell feelingly. The only help a poor woman had when she recognized her all-too-common fate, continued this moralist, steering her usual course, was not to meditate upon revenge or consolation but to prevail upon her passions and "sit down quietly." She must not seek solace in other admirers, nor allay her grief with diversions, nor use cordials to support her sinking spirits. She must not complain to others of her husband, but must try rather to conceal his faults, only reproaching him "unintentionally" with her own unimpeachable virtue. In the long run, suffering would open her eyes and teach her the difference between truth and appearances, between a solid and an insubstantial good, and prove to her how ephemeral is all earthly pleasure. Truly "affliction . . . [is] the only useful School that Women are ever put to," concluded Astell bitterly.[27]

The duchess of Mazarin had never learned these difficult lessons, and Astell blamed her more for this than for having fled her impossible husband. "A Woman who seeks Consolation under Domestic troubles from the Gaities of a Court, from Gaming and Courtship, from Rambling and odd Adventures, and the Amusements mixt Company affords, may Plaister up the Sore, but will never heal it," Astell wrote sternly. Illicit sexuality was an erosion of principle with more serious consequences for the soul than simple unhappiness. "An ill Husband may deprive a Wife of the comfort and quiet of her Life; may give her occasion of exercising her Virtue, may try her Patience and Fortitude to the utmost, but that's all he can do: 'tis her self only can accomplish her Ruin. Had Madame *Mazarin's* Reserve been what it ought to be, Monsieur *Herard* needed not to have warded off so carefully, the nice Subject of the Lady's Honour, nor her Advocate have strain'd so hard for Colours to excuse such Actions as will hardly bear 'em."[28]

Nowhere in *Some Reflections Upon Marriage* is there the slightest sympathy for the predicament of lovers, or a flicker of acknowledgment of "the biological." She found it as necessary to her argument as to her literal survival, to deny the existence of heterosexual physiological drives. Female activists operating in the public sector—especially before the twentieth century—often banked their heterosexual fires this way, so as to protect themselves from criticism in that quarter. It is how they neutralized their "handicap," so as to compete more equally in a man's world. As Astell saw it, a woman married in order to propagate the species and to promote social order. She sacrificed herself to civic duty; if she was a reasonable creature, sexual preference was besides the point. "A Woman indeed can't properly be said to Choose," she wrote; "all that is allow'd her, is to Refuse or Accept what is offer'd."[29] Choice, attraction, passion, love—"or rather a Blind unreasonable Fondness, which usurps the Name of that noble Passion"—was a kind of temporary insanity which clouded the judgment and could not be trusted to direct a woman to her true interests.

With a disbelief in a female heterosexual urge that today seems overrighteous, Astell assumed that any sexual encounter outside of marriage was to be blamed on duplicitous, predatory men. She did not draw distinctions between men who courted women to marry them and those who simply wanted to seduce them. Their bad reasons were the same: lust fixed on transient physical qualities, acquisitiveness, and ignorance of the spiritual qualities of the other. Either way, the woman stood to lose. "It were endless to reckon up the divers Stratagems Men use to catch their Prey, their different ways of insinuating which vary with Circumstances and the Ladies Temper," she wrote. "Sometimes a Woman is cajol'd, and sometimes Hector'd, she is seduc'd to Love a Man, or aw'd into a Fear of him."[30]

As she got older, Astell's suspicious prudery became more pronounced. In the 1730 edition of *Some Reflections Upon Marriage* she went so far as to quote George Savile, Lord Halifax's *Lady's New Year's Gift* or *Advice To A Daughter* (1688), approving his instructions to his daughter for avoiding heterosexual contact. The seventeenth-century *locus classicus* of patriarchy, this work gives the most controlling set of injunctions that a protective or jealous father could think up. But whereas Halifax compares his daughter to an innocent lamb, dumb and helpless, Astell reminds her readers that the duty of guardians was to educate the defenseless and vulnerable woman rather than simply to tremble for her—to put within her reach the means to discern and resist evil. Keeping her ignorant increased her jeopardy. "A Woman cannot be too watchful, too apprehensive of her danger," wrote Astell, "since Man whose Wisdom and Ingenuity is so much Superior to hers, condescends for his Interest sometimes, and sometimes by way of Diversion, to lay Snares for her. For tho' all Men are *Virtuosi*, Philosophers and Politicians, in comparison of the Ignorant and Illiterate Women, yet they don't pretend to be Saints, and 'tis no great Matter to them if Women who were born to be their Slaves be now and then ruin'd for their Entertainment."[31]

Astell's disapproval of sexuality was not common among sophisticated Londoners of her day. *Some Reflections Upon Marriage* was published the same year that Congreve's *Way of the World* first played, with its laughing concatenation of lovers and cuckolds, its array of clever men and women plotting to enjoy one another's sexual favors, and its complicated cynicism about conventional Christian teachings. "To pass our youth in dull indifference, to refuse the sweets of life because they once must leave us, is as preposterous as to wish to have been born old, because we one day must be old," tossed off the rakish Mrs. Marwood, to the delight of her London audience. "For my part," she added, "my youth may wear and waste, but it shall never rust in my possession."[32]

Astell, who never went to the theater, did not find such sallies amusing. She did not approve of jests about morality and found much of what passed for wit objectionable. Even Steele's relatively pious urbanity in *The Spectator* was too strong for her nice moral sense. Although she read the numbers when they appeared, her covering note sent with a packet of back issues as light reading for a friend in the country, reproduced the following disparagement of Mr. Steele's work, with a small air of triumph: "I heard tother day y^t a Learned Critic is of Opinion y^t Mr Steele's Papers are Injurious to Religion & Virtue, by discoursing of y^m in a ludicrous & superficial manner, representing some of ye vilest Sins as Gallantrys, & rendring y^t ye Obj^t of Raillery only, wch ought to be detested." She assumed that her interlocutor had also observed this deplorable tendency in Mr. Steele: "I make no doubt y^t Yo^r L^{dp} has often observ'd y^t in his highest fits of Piety he talks more like a Man of ye World than a Real Xtian. Two Characters so opposite, y^t he who endeavours to reconcile y^m only spoils y^m both. The Plausible Man having too little of Religion to do his business in ye next world, & too much to succeed in this."[33]

Although Astell was in a moral minority, she was not alone in her implacable, old-fashioned Christian idealism. The licentious spirit of the Restoration court had produced a widespread revulsion in the culture, and while many applauded the lessening of restraints in this age of new freedoms, others, like Astell, saw in it the unravelling of society's moral fabric. This conservative element complained that the youth was tempted by atheism, and that appeals to "natural religion" only led people away from God. Though the reign of Charles II had been dominated by figures of visible sinfulness like the unreconstructed Rochester, the wits of the period following the Glorious Revolution were far more dangerous. Urbane, skeptical, and coolly irreligious, they challenged traditional beliefs and practices under the cover of reason, using the theories of the natural philosophers and the latest reports from travelers about other cultures to promote an undermining moral relativism. One modern historian of the period asserts that although there was nothing new about belief in a moral decline, and "men had for centuries bemoaned the decay and growing dissoluteness of the world," there was in fact some special justification for such lamentation in late seventeenth-century England, when there did rather suddenly appear "a profusion of bad books and bad morals."[34] He adduces the rising crime rate as a sinister counterpoint to the growing toleration of free speech and inquiry. Many besides Astell in this period were alarmed at what looked like a steady deterioration of manners and morals accompanying a growing atheism. Men like Josiah Woodward, who privately printed hundreds of pamphlets declaiming against gaming, swearing, drinking, fornication, and the like, were eager to organize local chapters in their own towns of his Society for the Reformation of Morals.[35]

It is a historical irony that the much deplored Victorian image of woman as a pure, morally superior, self-abnegating "angel in the house" can be traced to just such a late seventeenth-century priggishness as this, derived in part from a reaction to Restoration license, and in part from a pragmatic, protective, feminist stance. Modern feminists have learned from writers such as Virginia Woolf, who struggled against it, to recognize in this role as social guardian of pure ideals a soul-destroying passivity and renunciation of self. And yet, turned on its head, the denial of single women's sexuality might preserve their independence, while self-abnegation was the only plausible philosophy for women who insisted, against reason, upon marrying. Astell's imagination could project no more hopeful vision upon the inevitabilities of married life than this. As she wrote in *Some Reflections Upon Marriage*: "She who marries purely to do Good, to Educate Souls for Heaven, who can be so truly mortify'd as to lay aside her own Will and Desires, to pay such an intire Submission for Life, to one whom she cannot be sure will always deserve it," had to be satisfied with the reward of her own virtue. Such a woman, she continued, "does certainly perform a more Heroic Action than all the famous Masculine Heroes can boast of, she suffers a continual martyrdom to bring Glory to GOD and Benefit to Mankind, which consideration indeed may carry her through all difficulties, I know not what else can."[36]

There seems to be little evidence of private motive for this book on marriage, although 1700 was the year that Astell's only brother married, the last remaining member of her Newcastle family of origin. Perhaps she felt a pang at his freedom of choice, or felt sorry for his wife, and it may have led her to consider the difference in meaning of marriage for men and for women. As it happens, Peter Astell, his young wife, and the two infant sons born to them all perished within a decade: the burial dates in the parish register tell a grim story.[37] These subsequent events would further fuel Astell's feeling that marriage was dangerous, that death followed in its train.

In asserting that a woman, in marrying, tacitly agreed to obey a possibly unworthy authority, Astell seems never to have considered what obedience a woman owed her father, apart from what she thought children of both sexes owed "parents" or "family." It will be remembered

that her own father died when she was twelve. Growing up in a household of women made it possible for her to regard male power as an
unnecessary trespass on the freedom of women—a thought that might
not have occurred to a woman who had grown up subject to the regular
exercise of power by her father or other male relatives. "Only let me
beg to be inform'd," she asked sarcastically, "to whom we poor fatherless
Maids, and Widows who have lost their Masters, owe Subjection? It
can't be to all Men in general, unless all Men were agreed to give the
same Commands; do we then fall as Strays to the first who finds us?"[38]

Some Reflections Upon Marriage, written in the last years of William III's
reign, must also be understood in part as a response to polarizing parties
and contested authority in national politics. Certainly Astell saw questions of connubial authority as continuous with the "larger" questions
of authority in the church and state—issues very much alive to her and
to other Tories of her stamp since the 1688 revolution. Despite the fact
that the Restoration had reinstated monarchy in England, after the
Glorious Revolution no English king would forget that he sat on his
throne at the sufferance of his people. Royal authority had been dealt
a blow from which it never recovered. It was the final act in a forty-
year drama relocating monarchical prerogative in relation to a powerful
middle class and a waning nobility.[39]

The Tory party rallied in opposition to this new balance of power,
and prepared to resist the rising commercial interests. Bolingbroke's
retrospective description in his *Letter to Sir William Windham* (1717),
characterized the party as made up of "the bulk of the landed interest,"
dedicated to upholding the traditions and privileges of the national
church and the constitutional monarchy, and to resisting the interna-
tionalist implications of the 1689 settlement.[40] Linda Colley, Mark Goldie, and J. G. A. Pocock have demonstrated a greater heterogeneity
among Tories in the late Stuart period than has been previously recognized, and their centrality in forming and stabilizing popular ideology
in England at this time.[41] Colley has also made it clear that far from
being disenfranchised by the revolution of 1688–89, Tories combined
successfully with Whig politicians afterwards to exclude Dissenters from
Parliament, and in the last years of Anne's reign, virtually monopolized
state employment.[42]

Astell subscribed to the broadest tenets of Tory conservatism—
leadership in the church and state by a traditional elect, the preservation
of the values of classical humanism, the hierarchical ordering of society—in opposition to the new order of political men who emphasized
rather the protection of individual liberty, personal property, and ex-

panding trade and finance. Mary Astell thought these latter tendencies extremely dangerous. Her philosophical idealism no less than her political leanings dictated a more absolutist stance. An ardent monarchist, she resisted every step of the way the republican impulse of her times. A king embodied the principle of absolute authority, she said; he could not be responsible to the passion and folly of each man in his kingdom. She thought it obvious, as she put it, that 100,000 tyrants were worse than one.

In an era when authority was becoming secularized, Astell clung to the belief that the hierarchy of the Church of England, culminating in a divinely appointed king, conferred the authority of God upon the monarchy.[43] Although those who had once been thought of as divine deputies were increasingly viewed as delegated representatives—chosen by men, not God—she continued to insist that to question the authority of the king was tantamount to questioning the authority of God. One owed obedience to one's monarch as a matter of religious principle, and not merely so long as it was politically or economically expedient, but for life.

This too was her final pronouncement on the dilemma of the duchess of Mazarin. An extraordinary document, *Some Reflections Upon Marriage* simultaneously established a woman's right to direct her own fate, that is, to abstain from matrimony, while at the same time maintaining High Tory principles of political submission, including, should a woman choose to marry, submission to her personal ruler. Astell's starting point in this meditation upon the power relations between the sexes is the monarchy, and the question of what duty a subject owes her king. She begins by granting that if a woman married, she owed her husband the same obedience that a loyal subject owed his king. This was a commonly understood equivalence: legally speaking, husbands were considered their wives' governors, answering for their debts, able to invalidate contracts, responsible for their property. As late as 1726 a woman of Tyburn who killed her husband was punished under the law for treason rather than for murder.[44] As a royalist, Astell accorded to husbands an authority which she denied to men in general. Marriage legitimated a man's power over a woman, and the family, like the monarchy, had to be respected once it was constituted.

Although she was misunderstood in her own day and still is in ours, not only did Mary Astell *not* resist the principle of absolute authority in the family, she even used it as another argument against those men of Whiggish principle who considered it their right to tyrannize at home but who objected to the doctrine of passive obedience in the state because, they said, it encouraged tyranny. "For whatever may be said against Passive-Obedience in another case," wrote Mary Astell acidly, "I suppose there's no Man but likes it very well in this; how much soever Arbitrary Power may be dislik'd on a Throne, not *Milton* himself wou'd cry up Liberty to poor *Female Slaves*, or plead for the Lawfulness of Resisting a Private Tyranny."[45] She stressed the point again when she added the 1706 preface: "Far be it from her [i.e., the author] to stir up Sedition of any sort, none can abhor it more; and she heartily wishes that our Masters wou'd pay their Civil and Ecclesiastical Governors the same Submission, which they themselves exact from their Domestic Subjects."

But, continued Astell, the difference between the state and family was that while one was born into the former, willy-nilly, one could exercise some choice as to the latter. No woman was obliged to marry. Few men had the moral stature to warrant putting one's life into their hands, and a woman of sense was better off staying away from the whole business. "She who Elects a Monarch for Life," wrote Astell, "who gives him an Authority she cannot recall however he misapply it, who puts her Fortune and Person entirely in his Power; nay even the very desires of her Heart according to some learned Casuists, so as that it is not lawful to Will or Desire any thing but what he approves and allows, had need be very sure that she does not make a Fool her Head, nor a Vicious Man her Guide and Pattern, she had best stay till she can meet with one who has the Government of his own Passions, and has duly regulated his own Desires, since he is to have such an absolute Power over hers."[46]

Along with Astell's pride in her own intellectual powers and her loving ambition for other women, this, then, was a third source for her separatism: a simultaneous belief in authority and recognition of its incompatibility with justice in domestic life. She unequivocally believed that a hierarchical system of power was necessary and right in church and in state; but when it came down to it, in private life, she could not abide the tyranny that men exercised over women. So she recommended that women never marry at all, that they never consent to a private despot; for a single woman could enjoy that freedom which was the right of every English subject, so long as she had no master other than the sanctioned leaders of religious and political life. In other words, it was *because* she believed in authority that Astell advised women not to marry. If one married, one was bound to submit to one's husband in all things, and no self-respecting woman need saddle herself with a supererogatory tyrant.

Nobody else was saying these things, one may be sure, and Astell's uncompromising language did not soften the truths she was proclaiming. The book circulated widely. In Astell's native Newcastle, unmarried Nan Chaytor, courted by a beau in "scarlet stockins and a tie wig which was powder'd to a nicety," asked her father to pick up a copy for her in London: "If my dear father would buy me a little book called *Reflections on Marriage* it would be very acceptable . . . it's only stitched together like a play."[47] Wilkin brought out a second edition in 1703, and in 1706 Astell added a long preface for a third printing. Together with *A Serious Proposal Parts I and II*, it was deemed popular enough to warrant yet another edition in 1730, in the last round of sales of Astell's works during her lifetime.

Inevitably, Astell was accused of promulgating subversive ideas, of "blowing the trumpet of rebellion" to half of mankind, and of contradicting scripture. But as she was quick to point out in the 1706 preface to *Some Reflections Upon Marriage*, although she described domestic politics as truthfully as she could, her conclusions were far from seditious. However unjust, patriarchy had to be preserved because it kept the peace. As in a state—the analogy is hers—"unless this Supremacy be fix'd somewhere, there will be a perpetual contention about it, such is the love of Dominion."[48] Thus, in spite of her obvious resentment at the injustice of marriage as it existed, she did not budge an inch from the rigid monarchist stance she maintained on the parallel political question of what action a people had a right to take towards an unjust monarch.

She preached a kind of passive obedience adapted for married home-life, complete with divine right, nonviolent resistance, and martyrdom. But her tones betrayed a Hobbesian cynicism when she described obedience in marriage, whereas there is full conviction in her statements about political authority in the state. The best way to serve one's country, she wrote earnestly in her most serious political tract, was "to cultivate in our minds and in those of our fellow subjects, *a Reverence for Authority. A Readiness to excuse the almost unavoidable Slips of our Governors, and a backwardness in Censuring their Measures, of which indeed Private Persons are not Competant Judges. . . .*"[49] When she applied the same principles to marriage, she could not resist a bitter sarcasm. "A Wife must never dispute with her Husband," she wrote; "his Reasons are now no doubt on't better than hers, whatever they were before. . . . And if she shew any Refractoriness, there are ways enough to humble her; so that by right or wrong the Husband gains his Will. For Covenants betwixt Husband and Wife, like Laws in an Arbitrary Government, are of little Force, the Will of the Sovereign is all in all."[50]

Astell was probably the first person to consider the rights and duties of women as a political question. Susan Okin has indirectly argued Astell's timeliness in this by pointing out that the seventeenth-century idealization of the family as a group united by mutual affection, their interests adequately represented by a loving father, was an ideology which disenfranchised women. It delimited a new private sphere as appropriate and sufficient for women, and at the same time subsumed women's political rights as individuals to the requirements of family, as determined by the husband or the father.[51] Astell was quick to observe this discrepancy between the rights of men in a state and the rights of women in marriage; among the many theories proliferating about the right of individuals to act according to their consciences, none seemed to apply to women. She noted that although there were many rationalizations for the claims of individuals to depose their governors in a state, none were willing to extend this reasoning to permit women like the duchess of Mazarin to rid themselves of odious and immoral husbands.

Mrs. Talbot, later in the century, told George Ballard that if she had read *Some Reflections Upon Marriage* before her own matrimonials, it would have alarmed her extremely and might have even prevented her from taking that step. She added, "I cannot be sufficiently thankfull that in a state so justly represented by her to be for the generality attended with so many mishaps, that I have hitherto been so very fortunate to escape them."[52]

Were there no happy marriages, then? A few, Astell admitted, even a surprising number considering "how imprudently Men engage, the Motives they act by, and the very strange Conduct they observe throughout." But even a happy marriage was not the proper fulfillment of a woman's life. Again and again Astell returns to this point: that women were meant for better things than managing a household or breeding children. They had to learn to aim higher, and not consider a match such a favor. No woman had "reason to be fond of being a Wife, or to reckon it a piece of Preferment when she is taken to be a Man's Upper-Servant."[53] It was just a lowly job, and although one was required to fulfill its attendant duties and responsibilities, one ought not give it one's soul or enlist one's whole heart in its service—particularly as soul and heart were owed elsewhere. The duty a woman was obliged to pay her husband, insisted Astell, was "only a Business by the Bye. Just as it may be any Man's Business and Duty to keep Hogs; he was not Made for this, but if he hires himself out to such an Employment, he ought conscientiously to perform it."[54]

The analogy between getting married and keeping hogs was not lost on Astell's contemporaries. Her friends expected her to frown upon all alliances, even those made under the best possible circumstances. "I want to know w^t Mrs. Astell says to Lady Ann Vaughns resolution," wrote Mary Grevile to her "dearest Aunt," Lady Ann Coventry; "she has chose a handsome Man and one to whom so great a fortune must be infinitely acceptable."[55] Mrs. Astell would undoubtedly have disapproved, handsomeness not being a sufficiently accurate indicator of spiritual stature, which was for her the most important requirement in a husband.

Of course Astell understood the implications of her stand: "if a Wife's case be as it is here represented," she wrote, "it is not good for a Woman to Marry and so there's an end of the Human Race."[56] Marriage, she conceded, was probably the best conceivable arrangement for domestic quiet and for the education of children. Civil duty and the good of society might therefore persuade a responsible woman to enter the bonds of holy matrimony. "It is the Institution of Heaven," she wrote without enthusiasm, "the only Honourable way of continuing Mankind."[57]

This was how Mary Astell came to her formulation that although women were equal to men in every way save their opportunities for self-improvement, a woman had to be prepared to play the role of obedient martyr if she married. "A Woman that is not Mistress of her Passions, that cannot patiently submit even when Reason suffers with her, who does not practice Passive Obedience to the utmost, will never be acceptable to such an absolute Sovereign as a Husband," warned Astell.[58] Only she who undertook the role prepared to endure pain and privation for the greater glory of God, was properly armed against the exigencies of married life. A married woman had need of great reserves of Christian humility, self-denial, and patience. If she could view her circumstances as an opportunity to discipline the mind and purify the soul, to prove her spiritual endurance and to strive for the dignity of patient martyrdom, that was as much as society permitted women in this life anyway.

> A Prospect of Heaven, and that only will cure that Ambition which all Generous Minds are fill'd with; not by taking it away, but by placing it on a right Object. She will discern a time when her Sex shall be no bar to the best Employments, the highest Honor; a time when that distinction, now so much us'd to her Prejudice, shall be no more, but provided she is not wanting to her self, her Soul shall shine as bright as the greatest Heroe's.[59]

Recognizing the heroic dimensions of self-denying martyrdom was Astell's way of valorizing most women's spiritual and emotional strength in a world where gender was a "bar to the best Employments" and "the highest Honour." She knew that she had suffered without having consciously sinned, and her strong sense of justice required a concept such as "martyrdom" to explain this suffering and to justify God's order in the world. Astell was consistently at some pains to prove that spiritual good was at odds with material well-being, and martyrs were proof of her principle that holiness went hand in hand with suffering. The good, the truly religious, were not meant for this world. They followed a beacon different from self-interest, and were guided by the pure Platonic light of philosophic principle. "I am persuaded that the greatest sensible Calamity, no not Death itself, is worthy to be put in the ballance with the very least spiritual advantage," she had written at twenty-seven to Norris, "and I believe on these principles 'twere easie to demonstrate that Martyrdom is the highest Pleasure a rational creature is capable of in this present State, a strange Paradox to the World."[60]

It took character to submit to an unworthy authority for a higher good. "There is not a surer Sign of a noble Mind," she wrote, "than the being able to bear Contempt and an unjust Treatment from ones Superiors evenly and patiently. For inward Worth and real Excellency are the Ground of Superiority, and one Person is not in reality better than another, but as he is more Wise and Good. But this World being a place of Tryal and govern'd by general Laws, just Retributions being reserv'd for hereafter, Respect and Obedience many times become due for Order's sake to those who don't otherwise deserve them."[61] In an imperfect world, one was often required to tender a perfect obedience to an imperfect authority.

Astell's monarchist opinions had been inculcated in her from earliest youth. Uncle Ralph's "Heartie Gratulation" to Charles II in *Vota, Non Bella* gives the family bias. Coal men in Newcastle had always supported their Stuart kings. Even when James II tried to take back the Newcastle charter, to break the free elections and install his own men as sheriff, mayor, and aldermen—even then, the Hostmen of Newcastle remained loyal to him. And when he fled to France in 1688 and William and Mary were brought to the throne, there was such resistance in Newcastle that the local vicar had to be threatened "that his salary will be stopped, unless he pray for king William and queen Mary by name."[62]

Mary Astell had been twenty-two at the time of the Glorious Revolution, when these national changes had polarized her native Newcastle. All her life she maintained that chaos and violence were the inevitable effects of tampering with monarchical succession. The consistent message of her political pamphlets was that factionalism always brought discontent and conspiracy.⁶³ In a state that permitted rebellion, strong and cunning men would inevitably try to usurp power for their own ends, "under the specious Pretences of the People's Rights and Liberties."⁶⁴ This was her conclusion in *An Impartial Enquiry into the Causes of Rebellion and Civil War in This Kingdom*, and she could cite Clarendon's newly published history, chapter and verse, on the details.⁶⁵ Her romanticized treatment of Charles the Martyr in that pamphlet was simultaneously a compliment offered to the new Stuart queen and an extension of the cult which, during the 1690s according to Linda Colley, had sustained Tories "deprived of contact with and the confidence of the current dynasty."⁶⁶

Astell disagreed with Locke's *Two Treatises of Government* on the question of political prerogative, as she disagreed with him on everything else. Whereas he described government as a voluntary association among free men to better preserve their lives, liberties, and property, subject to dissolution and reconstitution should that government not answer their needs, Mary Astell countered: "The people have no Authority over their own Lives, consequently they don't invest such an Authority in their Governours."⁶⁷ Just as she maintained on the question of marriage, Mary Astell held that the laws of God and man required unquestioning obedience to ordained authority at all times. Civil peace and prosperity in a kingdom depended upon this unshakeable rule, for otherwise subjects spent all their energies contending for power— whether seizing it or protecting it—rather than in more productive pursuits.

Rulers, Astell thought, had a duty to "vigorously exert that lawful Authority *GOD* has given them" and to prevent rebels from infecting the minds of their people "with evil Principles and Representations, with Speeches that have double Meanings and equivocal Expressions, *Innuendo's*, and secret Hints and Insinuations."⁶⁸ A free press and a free pulpit produced a factionalized, dissatisfied, rebellious population, she thought, and no sensible government could afford to permit such slander and subversion to go unchecked. She agreed with Swift's Brobdingnagian king who

> knew no reason why those who entertain opinions prejudicial to the public should be obliged to change, or should not be obliged to conceal them. And as it was tyranny in any government to require the first, so it was

weakness not to enforce the second: for a man may be allowed to keep poisons in his closets, but not to vend them about as cordials.[69]

Mary Astell also thought that anonymous political pamphlets ought to be outlawed. Critics of the monarchy or of the established church ought to be forced to acknowledge the views they printed and to be punished accordingly.

This insistence on official orthodoxy might seem an unexpected turn for a woman who placed so much emphasis on right reason, who believed that the mind had a natural affinity for truth and that the universe was governed by Intelligence. Yet Astell agreed with Bolingbroke that although the "good of society may require that no person be deprived of the protection of the government on account of his opinions in religious matters," it did not follow that "men ought to be trusted in any degree with the preservation of the establishment, who must, to be consistent with their principles, endeavor the subversion of what is established."[70]

She believed that authority should be respected, right or wrong, and that even when the behavior of rulers was contrary to the dictates of sense or religion, a loyal subject was bound to accord them at least a "passive obedience." This byword of the conservative Tory position in the reign of William and Mary echoed the language of *The Whole Duty of Man* (1657), the most influential religious manual of the latter half of the seventeenth century: "An obedience we must pay either Active or Passive: The active in the case of all lawful commands . . . [b]ut when he enjoins anything contrary to what God hath commanded . . . [w]e are in that case to obey God rather than man. But even this is a season for the Passive Obedience; we must patiently suffer what the ruler inflicts on us for such a refusal, and not to secure ourselves, or rise up against him. *For who can stretch forth his hand against the Lord's Annointed and be guiltless?*"[71]

"Passive obedience" meant nonrebelliousness in the face of intolerable commands. Anyone who held to this doctrine after the events of 1688 was distinctly High Tory. It was also often accompanied by a belief in "passive resistance," a kind of early nonviolent resistance which had taken the form of refusing to read James's Declaration or, later, of refusing to endorse an oath of loyalty to William and Mary. Such a passive refusal to comply with the demands of government constituted a conservative alternative to the solution offered by Locke and other political thinkers, who claimed that the people had the right to overthrow a government that did not answer their needs. Belief in passive obedience meant that one could resist the government only in nonviolent ways because anything else was a crime against divinely ordained succession and so ultimately a crime against God. As Astell acidly pointed out in another connection, the martyrs of the early church "never contended for it with Weapons in their Hands."[72] Passive obedience implied a total belief in the jurisdictional rights of one's governors, even though one ultimately had to consult one's own conscience on moral questions. It assumed little specific responsibility on the part of the government towards the governed and implied that subjects ought never actively question or resist, let alone contest with violence, the dictates of their rulers. Locke sneered at it as a political solution: "Who would not think it an admirable peace betwixt the mighty and the mean when the lamb without resistance yielded his throat to be torn by the imperious wolf? . . . no doubt Ulysses, who was a prudent man, preached up passive obedience, and exhorted his company to a quiet submission by representing to them of what concernment peace was to mankind, and by showing the inconveniencies which might happen if they should offer to resist Polyphemous, who had now the power over them."[73] Astell would have countered that Polyphemous was far from being a lawfully constituted authority.

The Stuarts, on the other hand, *were* a lawfully constituted authority, and Astell felt it her duty to be as loyal to them as she insisted women be to their husbands once they had sworn the sacred oaths of matrimony. The allegiance to a monarch was for life, and not merely so long as the vicissitudes of party politics dictated. With Anne on the throne, of course, the issue had been moot. But after 1714, Astell's sympathies were with the Jacobites, that remnant which, after the arrival of Hanoverian George, swore loyalty to the true Stuart succession and schemed to put the Pretender back on the throne. She was a Chelsea neighbor and friend of Francis Atterbury, leader of the conservative wing of the Tory clergy and a man embroiled for years in various Jacobite plans. She was also close to the duchess of Ormonde, wife of James Butler, the second duke of Ormonde, a Jacobite hero who organized and financed with his own great wealth an invasion of England from the shores of Spain where he lived in exile.

Ormonde had been impeached along with Bolingbroke and Harley on grounds of high treason in the first purge of Tory ministers upon the death of Queen Anne. His name along with theirs became the rallying cry for the Tory opposition to the new regime, and the cry that rang in the streets after the trial of Robert Harley, Lord Oxford, according to Smollett, was "High-church, Ormonde and Oxford for ever!"[74] Shortly thereafter Ormonde fled the country, knowing he had no chance of being acquitted under Walpole's ministry despite this popular support. He took up residence abroad, where he participated in the planning of all subsequent Jacobite plots to overturn the Hanoverian rule. His wife remained behind to suffer alone whatever further indignities were offered by disapproving neighbors and a suspicious government.

Mary Astell was a loyal friend to this woman in the years that followed, both out of a personal liking for her and a sympathy for her cause. She looked out for the duchess and worried, for instance, about her living so close to the disapproving scrutiny of the Whig minister Walpole, whose house was on the grounds of the Chelsea Royal Hospital. It would be a good deal safer and more restful for the duchess, she thought, to summer at Richmond. She inquired after her well-being when the duchess left town to visit her sister, Lady Ann Coventry, in the country. "I am glad to hear y^t my Lady Duchess of Ormonde enjoys her Health," she wrote, adding sympathetically, "A good Cause & a Good Conscience & y^t Nobleness of Spirit wch her Grace Inherits from so many Heroic Ancestors, render ye Injured abundantly more Great & Happy than those who have ye Power and Injustice to Injure y^m." When the Duchess was in town, she saw her regularly and reported to friends: "Yo^r L^{ap} will be pleas'd to hear her Grace is well, & much Greater & Happier than her Persecutors."[75]

The extent of the duchess of Ormonde's involvement in Jacobite activities leads one to wonder if the sympathetic and spirited Mary Astell also took part in similar undercover activities. The family of Ormonde was too deeply implicated in the Jacobite cause for Astell to have been ignorant of their relation to it. And she, in turn, was too politically minded to have been indifferent to their sentiments on these issues. We know that the duchess of Ormonde took part directly in the negotiations carried on by disaffected Tories in England with those on the Continent. Her name turns up in code, in several of her husband's letters about Jacobite business. Furthermore, she was in direct correspondence with the Pretender himself.[76]

One could easily construct a case for Astell's complicity in these activities. She was certainly sending enough parcels, letters, and packages both to the duchess and to her sister, Lady Ann Coventry, to be passing information. There were regular requests from Lady Ann, for example, to purchase and perfume packets of snuff for her in London, and send them up to the country. And then there were packages with more political contents. On January 6, 1719, for instance, Astell writes: "On Saturday last I sent a Parcel to Marleborough Street according to Yo^r L$^{ap's}$ Order. I am glad to find by y^t Elegant & Xtian Speech in it, wch I suppose you have heard of, y^t there are so many honest Folks at

James Butler, second duke of Ormonde. Portrait by M. Dahl. By permission of the National Portrait Gallery, London.

Hereford, y.ᵗ y.ᵉ good L.ᵈ Coningsby can find but 3 Men to his Mind in y.ᵗ City."⁷⁷ "Honest Folks," she writes, taking obvious satisfaction in Hereford's conservatism. She was apparently providing some kind of clipping service—or forwarding of information—for the Ormonde family. It could have been about the parliamentary debates over occasional conformity which were going on just then. The Occasional Conformity Bill and the Schism Act—Tory bills that had been bitterly fought for the decade before—were under attack, indeed about to be repealed. The debate in Parliament had led to an acrimonious exchange between Lord Coningsby and High Tory champion Francis Atterbury, and Atterbury's *mot* was being repeated everywhere.⁷⁸ But it is also possible that what Mary Astell sent to Marlborough Street had something to do with the expedition that Ormonde was organizing from Spain, about which he kept in regular communication with his duchess.

In addition to these facts, we know that Mary Astell had her own connections in France, which kept her informed of the duke of Ormonde's activities and of events in the Pretender's court in Rome. "I have a Letter from Paris," she wrote to Lady Ann Coventry in March 1720, "w.ᶜʰ says y.ᵉ Duke is very well at Madrid, & in as much Honor & Esteem w.ᵗʰ y.ᵉ New Ministry there as he was w.ᵗʰ y.ᵉ old; And y.ᵗ y.ᵉ Lady at Rome [Queen Clementina] is four moneths gone."⁷⁹ She also seems to have been anxious about the privacy of her mail at a time when the Whig ministry was carefully monitoring all Jacobite correspondence. She was glad to avail herself of the offer of George Pitt, M.P. for Southampton, to send her letters under his cover as a member of Parliament.⁸⁰ And just at the time of the Layer trial, the last big Jacobite roundup in London, when Walpole's regime finally closed in on Francis Atterbury and thwarted the latest plan for an invasion, Astell appears to have sent something suspicious to Lady Ann Coventry, for in her next letter she writes how relieved she was "to hear mine was acceptable & came safe w.ᵗʰout y.ᵉ prying eyes of y.ᵉ Vigilant Ministers."⁸¹ That her sympathies were with the Jacobites, whether or not she was actively participating in their machinations, is also clear from her reactions to the Layer trial.

Christopher Layer's capture was the dramatic centerpiece of Walpole's anti-Jacobite campaign of 1722, and although Layer's so-called conspiracy was hardly worth the publicity it got, it served Walpole's purposes well enough. Layer may have been a charlatan and informer, or he may simply have been a fool—the sort of heedless, self-parading enthusiast who can be found in any movement. The common view was that he was a romantic and hotheaded young man who wanted desperately to be part of a revolutionary upsurge, without the faintest idea

*Christopher Layer,
executed for trea-
son. From James
Caulfield,* Por-
traits, Memoirs
and Characters of
Remarkable Per-
sons, *vol. 2 (1819).*

of how to organize a serious effort. He had traveled to Rome, where he had been received by the Pretender several times, convinced him of his undying fidelity, and managed to extract a promise from the royal couple to stand godparents, by proxy, at the christening-to-be of his own as yet unborn child. Upon returning to England he used this promise to ingratiate himself with various Jacobite peers, and is supposed to have arranged with the duchess of Ormonde to stand in for Queen Clementina as godmother to his newborn child at the christening, and Lord North and Grey to stand in for James II. According to at least one historian, the famous christening actually did take place, in Chelsea, over a china shop, in the lodgings of a Mrs. Fox.[82]

This was all very heady for Mr. Layer, who was soon convinced that he was destined to be lord chancellor in the new regime. He drew up a scheme for capturing the king, the Prince of Wales, other officers of the state, the Bank of England, and the Tower of London. These daring exploits were to be followed by spontaneous uprisings which would expel the Hanoverians and return the Stuarts to the English throne. The newspapers added that "Mr. *Layer* pretended that the late Duke of *Ormond,* General *Dillon,* and others, were to come over and put themselves at the Head of the Rebels." Now the truth was that Ormonde *had* been arming for an invasion several months earlier, although certainly not as part of Layer's grand scheme, but he had abandoned his preparations when it became clear that the plan was impracticable and that the government was mobilized to repel them.[83] It was just this mixture of truth and fancy that infuriated serious Jacobites, for whom the Layer episode was like a bad nightmare.

Layer and his cohorts had set about to implement their plan with extraordinary indiscretion. For example, with no precautions about secrecy, they enlisted in their pay twenty-five sergeants who had lately been discharged from the army. Although only minor figures on the edge of the Jacobite network, they gave Walpole the opportunity he had been waiting for. He had already arrested Atterbury and was delighted to get his hands on Lords Orrery and North and Grey. Perhaps he thought Layer might lead him to other conspirators. In any case he had been looking for a way to consolidate his reputation with George I, and when Layer came along with his hare-brained fantasy of taking over the country, Walpole used him to discredit the Jacobites and win the gratitude of a shocked king and nation. He arrested Layer with great fanfare, and brought him to trial before a crowded courtroom, to make an example of him.

No one, upon reflection, could have considered Layer a real threat. With none of the caution of a serious conspirator, he had been taken in his apartment, in full possession of extremely damaging evidence—bundles of treasonable papers and munitions. Furthermore he had confessed, almost eagerly, to more particulars about the so-called conspiracy than was necessary. Yet his prosecutors seem not to have marked his bungling stupidity, although it outraged Astell and her Jacobite-sympathizing friends.

Astell did not attend the trial, but she followed it closely and wrote several letters reporting what she had heard to Lady Ann Coventry. She obviously considered it news of prime importance and was engrossed in its details.

All yᵉ talk now is about Mʳ Layer's Trial who was found Guilty Thursday morning about 3—for so long yᵉ Trial held. The Witnesses agᵗ him were fully prov'd infamous, no Jury wou'd have taken their evidence, but his own Confession before yᵉ Council, wᶜʰ exactly agreed wᵗ all they swore, did his business. It was indeed more particular than yᵉ Evidence in some things, wᶜʰ one wou'd have thought he cou'd not have mention'd wᵗʰout a design to turn Evidence. For instance, he said L.N. & Grey stood Godfather to his Child representing yᵉ Pretender KNOWINGLY. He had told yᵉ Council much more than his Accusers cou'd urge agt him. As yt he was at Rome, yt he ask'd a Letter of Credit, but yt it was not granted &c. The Scheme found among his Papers he also own'd there. And yet he told his Friends before his Trial yt he had made no Confession yt cou'd hurt him. In a wd a Gentleman of yᵉ Law who stay'd out yᵉ whole Trial & from whom I had this account thinks it as hard to determine, whether there is more Folly, Madness, or Knavery in yt Confession. His Council insisted to have yt Confession brought into Court wch was a point of Law, but yᵉ Judges over-rul'd it; & insted thereof took Mr. De la Fay [Walpole's assistant] and Mr Stanians Oaths. They alleging yt to bring in yᵉ minutes of yᵉ Council book was to discover yᵉ Secrets of yᵉ Governmt, & the names of those he had accus'd. The Declaration from *Lucca* is another matter of Discourse. The Chevalier's Friends disown it; it is in yᵉ hands of none but yᵉ Governmt. There was no Mob, or Rout at yᵉ Burning of it, according to yᵉ Acct yᵉ Sherif gives his Friends, tho yᵉ News Papers make a Lying Story. It seems it denys yt there is any present design on foot. So yt as a Gentleman well observ'd, either the Plot, or yᵉ Declaration is an Impoosture.[84]

Astell apparently agreed with the gentleman-at-law who reported the incident back to her: that the whole thing had a stagey quality whose effect was to make the Jacobites look ridiculous. There was complicity in Layer's elaborate confession, and a blatant disregard for legal process in the prosecutor's management of the case. Layer was obviously saying more than he had to, despite the fact that "the Witnesses agt him were fully prov'd infamous." The entire "plot" was a fantastic and misguided adventure, whether or not any of its participants were in earnest, and the trial itself she took as a cold-blooded, put-up job, a piece of clever propaganda contrived by Walpole to defame the movement and scatter and frighten the Jacobites. Her report of the talk about it is a kind of hasty shorthand, meant for a political familiar who has all the details vividly in her mind too. There is a tacit agreement to trust what the Chevalier's friends might say in preference to Walpole's lies.

At the very least it is clear that Astell was not frightened by the prospect of a Jacobite coup, and was impervious to the hysteria that the Walpole administration was trying to whip up about such a threat. Rather, she feared that it was only the beginning of the government's persecutory campaign against the Jacobites. This suspicion was confirmed in the months that followed, for Walpole and his associates used the Layer conspiracy to "prove" the imminent danger of treason, and so to justify their campaign against all Jacobites and Jacobite sympa-

thizers. A long series of witnesses were examined for evidence of disaffection, and the government made it increasingly uncomfortable for
anyone with nonjuror or Jacobite leanings.[85] In March we find Astell
reporting to Lady Ann that Walpole and his men were still fanning the
flames of publicity about the Layer trial, making sure the details were
widely circulated.

> There are Two Protests about printing Layer Trial, w.[ch] but for y.[m]
> had never appear'd & was printed at 14 Presses in 4 days as y.[e] Bookseller
> owns. There is to my knowlege a very great lie in it, about y.[e] Xtning, but
> it is too long to insert y.[e] story here. . . .[86]

Astell apparently had her own sources of information about the infamous christening, probably the duchess of Ormonde herself. Furthermore, she wrote, she was beginning to feel the heat herself.

> . . . Y.[e] folks in fashion being so ill-natur'd in this Neighborhood, y.[t] I think
> I must quit it, since they will not allow me to go to y.[e] Chappel quietly.
> M.[r] Walpole's worthy Woollen Draper (Robin Mann) now M.[r] Justice of
> Peace, thinking fit to take upon him Ecclesiastical Jurisdiction, & my
> Acquaintance, except y.[e] good Duchess, being affraid of me, convey y.[m]
> selves from me. A persecution I am not concern'd at for my own sake,
> since I shall always account it an honour & happiness to suffer for a good
> Conscience.

We do not know whether Astell was examined in court during the
political probing after the Layer trial, and whether Robert Mann had
any evidence to connect her with the Jacobite conspiracy of 1722. Her
"persecution" at his hands may have consisted simply of irritating visits
to question and detain her.

It is quite possible that the recent reissue of her *Bart'lemy Fair: or,
An Enquiry After Wit* with its new preface was seen as subversive. First
published to refute the anonymous *Letter Concerning Enthusiasm* (1708),
when Shaftesbury claimed the letter among his recently collected *Works*,
she decided that "the Poyson being thus a-new prepar'd and spread
abroad, is it not fit to renew the Antidote?" The purpose of Astell's
tract in 1709, and especially when reissued in 1722, was to moderate
antipapist feeling by showing that deism was a more dangerous threat
to the peace of England than any form of popery. "They who tell us,
that Popery is worse than Atheism, cannot think as they say, unless
they think it better to live without GOD in the World, than without
a good Preferment," she wrote tartly in the 1722 preface. In the context

of the events of 1722, her book could only have been taken as a defense of Jacobitism, and an attack on the latitudinarian supporters of the Hanoverian regime. Nor did she disguise her contempt for Walpole's regime in the new preface: "Our modern Politicians who have no Dependance upon GOD and His Providence, act like themselves, when they lay their Schemes deep and make them black as Hell, and carry them on by wicked Artifices."

Whatever their reasons, Walpole's deputies kept after Mary Astell, as she says herself, in the months following the sensational Layer trial, following her to chapel. By this time the case against her old friend and neighbor Bishop Atterbury was in progress, and he had been taken to the Tower while the charges against him and the plan for his exile were being drawn up. Walpole's campaign of fear and suspicion was succeeding. As a result of Robert Mann's attentions, Astell found herself shunned by less political friends and neighbors, all but the duchess of Ormonde, who was already tarred by the same brush. Life became so unpleasant for her that she finally had to move to new lodgings on Mannor Street. Eventually Lady Catherine Jones, the daughter of the earl of Ranelagh, took her into her house and under her protection, and Walpole's men stopped hounding her.

Mary Astell and her friend Elizabeth Hutcheson, the wife of Ormonde's man of business in London, Archibald Hutcheson, might well have been operating as intermediaries between Ormonde on the Continent and his family in England. It does not seem likely that we will ever know. The authorities who followed and questioned Astell seem not to have had any firmer evidence against her than her long association with nonjurors and conservative Tories, her consistent opposition to Whig principles, and her close friendship with the duchess of Ormonde and the Atterburys. This encounter with the Walpole ministry, however, marked the definitive end of her public career, and after 1722 she wrote nothing more with a political cast.

Having sketched in the continuities between Astell's ideology in the domestic and public spheres, we can now go back and fill in the particulars of her political stands in the reign of good Queen Anne. An active Tory pamphleteer for a few years, she wrote in the service of those causes that seemed to her most central to the welfare of England. An analysis of these causes and her positions in relation to them, will extend what we know of her political and religious beliefs, and her sense of her own agency in the society in which she lived.

Chapter Seven
In the Service of the Lord

About this time, observing the pernicious artifices of the sectaries, she to her lasting honour, courageously and successfully attack'd them on all sides; and engaged the attention of the publick for a considerable time, with her productions; which were of excellent service in countermining the sly designs that were then very artfully carried on, in order to corrupt at present, and to subvert upon any proper opportunity, both church and state.

> George Ballard, "Mary Astell," in *Memoirs of Several Ladies of Great Britain*, 1752

The Men began to stare upon each other, and having silenc'd the Lady with some difficulty, Mr. Styles went on: The Lady has some Reason on her Side . . . the only way to make England Happy, is by Enacting an Anti-Salique Law, entailing the Crown, I mean, upon the Females.

> Mary Astell, "A Prefatory Discourse to Dr. D'Avenant," from *Moderation Truly Stated*, 1704

From 1703 to 1709, Astell was increasingly drawn into party politics and the public debate about political and religious toleration, as it was framed by the Occasional Conformity Bill. In 1704, at the boiling point of the controversy, Astell published three tracts on the subject. In doing so, she was perhaps the first woman not of royal family to enter seriously into mainstream political discourse. In a sense, Astell never decided to "go into" politics, but simply exercised her citizenly prerogatives, without feeling that she was disadvantaged as a woman. She read her contemporaries with interest and concern and responded as persuasively as she could. In these simple acts of participation, she broke ground for others, and created a new role for women to play in public life—neither queen nor royal mistress, but something closer to the roles taken by ordinary men.

The spectacle of a woman entering so boldly into the arena of politics and religion was obviously a novelty in early eighteenth-century England. Jane Barker and Elizabeth Singer Rowe had written political poems; Aphra Behn's plays made topical references; and several women were known to be the authors of religious books—both prophetic tracts and devotional manuals.[1] These last were the natural outgrowth of the commonplace book, which was often written for private purposes, but sometimes published posthumously by grieving families or admirers. In addition, one can find broadsides and an occasional brief pamphlet written by a woman in response to current political issues. Such were the productions of Anne Docwra, Elinor James, [Mary] Delariviere Manley, and a few women printers and booksellers—often widows of guildsmen—who were hard-pressed for current copy.[2] But none argued a party position in detail, as Mary Astell did, taking into account what other pamphleteers had to say and expecting to be read by them.

Elinor James was probably the most prolific woman pamphleteer of the generation before Astell. Beginning in 1681, she wrote numerous pamphlets and broadsides, all signed boldly with her full name, on such subjects as the supremacy of the Church of England and the necessity for an oath of allegiance from Catholics and Dissenters, the ill-advised union with Presbyterian Scotland, or the deliverance of the Tory high flyer, Dr. Sacheverell. Her basic conservative political principles were like Astell's, but Mrs. James was not an intellectual and did not reach for historical precedent or philosophical rationale to justify her attitudes.

She simply announced them whenever she felt that the king or Parliament had need of advice. "I know you will say *I am a Woman, and why should I trouble my self?*" she observed in 1687. But that did not stop her then any more than it had stopped her in the past. "Why was I not always so [i.e., a woman] when I pleaded with the Parliament about the *Right of Succession*, and with *Shaftesbury*, and *Monmouth*, and at Guild-Hall, and elsewhere?"[3]

She was best known for her defense of James's 1687 Declaration of Toleration, in a pamphlet called *A Vindication of the Church of England, in an answer to a Pamphlet entituled, A New Test of the Church of England's Loyalty* (1687).[4] The one extant portrait of her shows her in a red silk dress with this celebrated pamphlet open on the table before her.[5] She also took an interest in many issues of lesser moment: she wrote a broadside to the mayor and aldermen of London complaining about the practice of throwing squibs (fireworks) in the streets, another to the House of Lords to discourage an intended tax on the old East India Company, and another to the printers of London exhorting them to treat their apprentices fairly.[6] This last, a most sensible piece of exposition, written from her own practical experience with apprentices in her husband's guild, demonstrates her native shrewdness to much better advantage than do all her polemics defending the Church of England. "I have been in the element of Printing above forty years, and I have a great love for it," she begins, and then proceeds to give some very practical advice to printers about how to get the best from their apprentices: "when a boy has served half his time, and has gained some experience in his trade, he presently begins to set up for conditions with his master; then he will not work unless he has so much for himself, and liberty to go where he pleases; which if his master denies, he then strives to vex his master, and waste his time and goods."[7]

Elinor James had direct access to the means of production for her writings, as she was married to a printer. [Mary] Delariviere Manley had a similar advantage. A contemporary of Astell's, she wrote fiction à clef with a political bite and collaborated with Swift on some Tory pamphlets;[8] she also lived in a common-law liaison with a printer. For both women these connections facilitated and protected their efforts at political journalism, and somewhat neutralized the practical difficulties of a woman making pronouncements on public events. Of Thomas James, that indefatigable chronicler of Grub Street life John Dunton wrote that he was one of the best London printers in the business, and "something the better known for being Husband to that She-State Politician *Mrs. Elianor* [sic] *James.*"[9] Mrs. Manley's companion was John Barber, a Tory printer who came to be a friend of Swift's and

Harley's and who was eventually elected alderman and even lord mayor of London. When John Barber died, Elinor James's son succeeded him as city printer.

Mary Astell wrote as a celebrity—admired by some, ridiculed as reactionary by others. She too was probably eased into print as a political commentator by her long-standing relation with bookseller Rich Wilkin. He may have commissioned her to write the pamphlets of 1704, both for ideological and business reasons. Pamphlet wars of the early 1700s were lucrative for the booksellers who helped to manage them, and they often tried to maintain customer interest through an exchange or two. These pamphlets appealed to the world in various matters of public policy under discussion in the courts or Parliament, ran from fifteen to fifty pages, and were usually keenly satirical, naming names, caricaturing positions, and taking apart page by page the arguments of fellow con-troversialists. Cheap, usually six pennies apiece, they flooded the book-sellers' stalls in the early part of the century. In the rapidity of the answers and counteranswers, and the attentiveness of their small but active readership, these pamphlets are probably like nothing so much as the exchanges of letters—sometimes among three or four people—that appear today in our political and intellectual journals.

Astell was pressed into service to expose the charges of extremism leveled at the High Church party by those for toleration, charges which were damaging Tory chances with the Occasional Conformity Bill, an important issue, and one which Astell and Wilkin cared about.

Party feeling had polarized sharply in the last years of William III's reign, in anticipation of the complicated question of succession. The acts that had excluded Jacobites and nonjurors from holding public office, following the settlement of 1688, had built up a backlog of re-sentment against the latitudinarian policies of the parliamentary gov-ernment. Those who remained faithful to the Stuart succession and to the doctrine that the monarch was and ought to be the head of the national church, felt victimized by William's regime. Mary Astell's glo-rification of martyrs is part of that mentality.

On the other hand, the religious martyrdom that was continually before the public eye was the case of the Huguenots. For many, their plight illustrated the danger of a narrowly defined national religion and the need for toleration. For those who feared and distrusted French influences, they were living evidence of the cruelty and barbarism of the papists.

To conservative churchmen, arguments for religious toleration sounded like justification for their continued exclusion from political positions in the new regime. In latitudinarian attitudes they saw a dilution of piety, a slackening of moral resolve, and a venal play for power. The business of government was to uphold the authority of the church, thought Astell and her associates, not to represent a broad base of religious interests.

Even before Anne came to the throne in March of 1702, an event which most Tories hailed as a happy turning of the tide, High Churchmen had begun to take the offensive against combined Dissenter and Whig interests. The most inflammatory of these, Dr. Henry Sacheverell, a High Church zealot and a fellow of Magdalen College, delivered excoriating sermons at Oxford and wrote pamphlets such as *The Character of a Low Churchman* (1701) and *On the Association of . . . Moderate Churchmen with Whigs and Fanatics* (1702), which stereotyped and condemned all Dissenters as base opportunists in the most unbending language. Bishop Burnet characterized Sacheverell as "a bold, insolent man, with a very small measure of religion, virtue, learning, or good sense," who "resolved to force himself into popularity and preferment, by the most petulant railings at dissenters and low churchmen, in several sermons and libels."[10] Even allowing for Bishop Burnet's bias, it seems clear now that Sacheverell was a careless and shallow demagogue whose intent was to vilify Dissenters rather than to defend a High Church position rationally.

Sacheverell first raised the contagious cry "The church in danger!" and warned his audience that the time had come to reward her true friends rather than her enemies. Together with the other High Church polemicist, Charles Leslie, a nonjuror, he revived the attitude—which had gone underground with the settlement of 1688—that "passive obedience" and "passive resistance" were the truest forms of patriotic idealism, a position which implied that the so-called Glorious Revolution had been illegal. This same Sacheverell became a cause célèbre later in 1709 when he incensed the moderate ministry (Marlborough, Somers, Godolphin) by preaching a rabidly anti-Dissenter sermon at St. Paul's on "the perils from false brethren." When they moved to impeach him for it, High Church indignation mounted quickly, and there were demonstrations for him on the streets of London. The trial itself became a public drama, as if the fate of the Anglican church hung in the balance. Nearly 100,000 copies of the contested sermon (which Sacheverell sold for £100) were hawked on the streets.[11] Sacheverell's defense speech at his trial was universally attributed to the more politically astute pen of Francis Atterbury.

Charles Leslie, the other High Tory agitator whose rabid views against toleration helped set the tone of party politics in the reign of Queen Anne, also left a trail of pamphlets behind him. He attacked

Burnet and Tillotson for Socinianism in 1694, and the Quakers in *The Snake in the Grass* (1696) and *Satan Disrob'd from his Disguise of Light* (1696). In 1698 he argued against deism in *A Short and Easie Method with the Deists* so successfully that he is supposed to have converted Charles Gildon. At the same time he published a companion piece, *A Short and Easie Method with the Jews* (1698). In these and many other controversial essays on religious matters, he consistently took the extreme High Church position that merely the existence of other religions within the state was potentially dangerous and ought not to be encouraged. His twenty-page tract, *The New Association of those Moderate-CHURCH-MEN with the Modern-Whigs and Fanaticks, to UNDER-MINE and BLOW-UP the present Church and Government*, the title of which deliberately echoed Sacheverell's *On the Association of . . . Moderate Churchmen with Whigs and Fanatics*, argues that those trained and determined to continue in a Dissenting religion must accept their fate as outsiders. "Did the *Primitive Christians* in their *Apologies* to the *Roman Emperors*, complain of their not being admitted into the Senate, or Intrusted with the *Offices of Government . . .*?" he asked. Did they claim a *right* to such employment or think themselves injured when they were not so employed? "No, they were neither *Whigs* nor *Fanaticks*," he answered emphatically.

If Dissenters were true to their principles, Leslie went on, and continued to prefer their own standards and beliefs to those of the Church of England, then they ought not to participate in the affairs of an institution whose inadequacies they must feel keenly, and for whose replacement they could only wish eagerly. Moderate men were also to be feared, he said, meaning those who stood for toleration; for although they themselves might be ashamed "to put their own Hands to pull down the Church," they were determined to "let in the *Whigs* and *Fanatics* upon her, who wou'd do it *Effectually!*" It was all too reminiscent of that dark year 1641, when the Puritans had scattered seditious tracts before them, preparing the way for open revolt. Once again, he warned in 1702, the combined forces of Whigs and Dissenters were "doing all that is in their Power to *expose* all the *True and Faithful Sons* of the *Church of England*, to the *Fury* of the *Mob*, and *Detestation* of *Mankind*; Representing them as *Dogs, Wolves, Serpents*, very *Devils!*"

Mary Astell was sympathetic to these attitudes—the horror of another revolution, the danger of permitting political dissent, and the impossible wish to return to the status quo before the irredeemable mistake of 1688. But although she too sounded the rallying cries of "passive obedience" and "the church in danger," her political arguments were careful and reasoned, and she sought to disassociate herself from

"Mr. L[esle]y, or any other Furious Jacobite whether Clergyman or Layman."

The increased political activity of the "high flyers" was a sign of renewed hopes now that Queen Anne was ascending the throne. It had been fourteen years since there had been a good English Stuart monarch, and it warmed many a Tory heart that that time had come again. Moreover, Anne was known to be sympathetic to the High Church position, had spoken for it, and was herself a conservative Anglican. At the same time, she was well aware of her bipartisan obligations, and her closest advisers—the moderate Godolphin, Marlborough and his wife, Sarah Churchill—were increasingly sympathetic to the Whig position.

If the Tory leanings of this last Stuart queen created a more sympathetic climate for Astell's political opinions than had prevailed since 1688, her mere presence as a ruling woman created a more sympathetic climate for female activism. On the London stage, for example, more new plays written by women were produced during the reign of Queen Anne than at any other time up to the present day.[12] Mary Astell, who at one time had hoped Anne might provide the backing for her "protestant nunnery" proposal, and who had dedicated *A Serious Proposal Part II* to her while she was still Princess of Denmark, wrote optimistically in 1705: "May we not hope that She [the queen] will not do less for Her own Sex than She has already done for the other; but that the next Year of Her Majesties Annals will bear date, from Her Maternal and Royal Care of the most helpless and most neglected part of Her Subjects."[13]

Beyond direct expectations of patronage, Astell was encouraged and heartened by having a monarch who was a woman; it justified her in taking up a staff in the public arena. It is no simple coincidence that the years of Mary Astell's most active participation in public life were the years Queen Anne was on the throne. So women had been encouraged to express themselves during the reign of Elizabeth I, and in the nineteenth century the "woman question" revived when Victoria ascended to power. Throughout her writings, one way or another, Mary Astell exults over the fact of a female sovereign. There was nothing a woman could not do! "Her majesty will give them full Demonstration, that there's nothing either Wise, or Good or Great that is above her Sex."[14] Anne's presence on the throne established the preeminence of class and birth over gender—a corrective for sexism deriving more from feudal culture, in which women of great families had played their parts, than from any seventeenth-century notion of the equal natural rights of persons. If "every Man is by Nature superior of every Woman," wrote

Astell, "it wou'd be a Sin in any Woman to have Dominion over any Man, and the greatest Queen ought not to command but to obey her Footman." Surely "no Municipal Laws can supersede or change the Law of Nature," she added, taking a gratuitous parting shot at those who argued for equality from assumptions about an original "state of nature."[15]

Other than such an occasional indulgence in irony on the subject of women, the tones of Astell's pamphlets are indistinguishable from those of her male contemporaries. In the time-honored tradition of respectable Orinda, she did not put her name on the title page, but called herself variously "a Lover of Her Sex," "the Author of *A Serious Proposal to the Ladies*," "a very Moderate Person and Dutiful Subject to the Queen," "Tom Single" (in reply to Charles D'Avenant, who went by the name of Tom Double), "a Daughter of the Church of England," and "Mr. Wotton." But her reticence on the title page was more for show than otherwise, and in truth she enjoyed teasing her audience about her identity. In the 1706 preface to *Some Reflections Upon Marriage* she reported with delight that a certain ingenious gentleman "had the Good-Nature to own these Reflections, so far as to affirm that he had the Original M.S. in his Closet." She enjoyed writing as a woman, making sure that her anomalous gender was not lost on her audience, with sarcastic references every once in a while to the usual antifemale clichés. As a respectable woman she could not sign her productions in the vulgar marketplace; but she had no aversion to anyone knowing who had written them.

Only three weeks after Anne's reign began, the Tories tested the water by proposing the first Occasional Conformity Bill in Parliament. It was a bill designed to exclude all but Anglicans from holding public office and as such promised to strengthen the hand of High Church Tories and redistribute electoral control of the boroughs. Many Tories thought of it as a means to recoup what they considered their rightful power after losing ground to Whig and Dissenter interests since 1689.[16] The rationale for such a measure was that since the High Church was a national church, with the sovereign at the head of both church and state, only the genuine adherents could have the country's best interests fully at heart.[17] The point was to exclude those Dissenters who had no scruples about taking communion in an Anglican church from time to time in order to qualify for a public office to which they may have felt well and truly called. The practice of occasional conformity, as this was called, had been institutionalized by William III's *Toleration Act* of 1689, and a great many Dissenters took advantage of this chink in the Anglican monolith.

Inevitably there was grumbling. How could one feel the necessity of an alternative church fervently enough to renounce the Church of England, but then be willing, on occasion, to take the sacraments in the latter for the sake of personal ambition? Either the religious differences between the Church of England and Dissenter sects mattered enough to forfeit political advantage, or they did not—in which case, why did these half-way Dissenters, these equivocators, feel the need to separate from the Church of England in the first place?

Many High Churchmen felt that the practice of occasional conformity weakened the national church and made a mockery of the holy rituals. This disapproval erupted in 1697 over the case of Sir Humphrey Edwin, lord mayor of London, who in a single Sunday attended services of both the Church of England and his own Presbyterian conventicle. Worse, Edwin had the effrontery to require that his attendant at the former, who carried his sword of state, follow him into the latter, bringing with him that symbol of his office. Sir Humphrey was condemned by Anglicans and Dissenters alike; controversy raged on both sides of the question.

Defoe published his first statement on the subject that year, a twenty-eight-page pamphlet called *An Enquiry into the Occasional Conformity of Dissenters in Cases of Preferment with a Preface to the Lord Mayor, Occasioned by his carrying the Sword to a Conventicle.* There he asserted that although the mayor was accused of forcing Mr. M. to carry the sword of state into Pinners-Hall, the law was after all forcing Sir Humphrey to attend St. Paul's against his will. Nevertheless, Defoe was not sympathetic to the cynical behavior of the conforming Presbyterian mayor. One could not dodge religion in that way, he wrote, and any who wanted to wield political power or who thought it their duty to serve had better either run the risk of attending only his own dissenting meetinghouse, "or openly and honestly Conform to the Church and neither be ashamed of his Honour, nor of his Profession."

Queen Anne attended the first parliamentary session of her new reign to listen to the debates about the bill to outlaw occasional conformity. Godolphin and Marlborough felt compelled to speak for the bill publicly, but they killed it behind the scenes by seeing to it that amendments were added which turned around the initially favorable vote in Commons. Twice more in the next year and a half this Tory bill was stalled by various tactics of the opposition until the friction over it made it a symbolic point of difference between the two parties, the nub of their enmity. Not until 1711, a year after Sacheverell was paraded triumphantly through the streets of London, the highest point of Tory power in the century, was the Occasional Conformity Bill finally passed into law. In its final version it carried all the original penalties, and by the time it passed, to add insult to injury, it stipulated that the offender—the secret conventicle attender—pay £40 bounty to whomever informed against him.

Already by 1702 and 1703 there was movement in this political direction, and many who favored stricter penalties for Dissenters listened attentively to the High Church bigotry of Sacheverell and Leslie. Those displaced by the breakup of James II's court and the crowning of the Dutch prince swelled the restive audience of high flyers in the pulpit and in the press. One measure of the popularity of these intemperate views was the alarm of Dissenters such as Defoe, whose parodic *The Shortest Way with the Dissenters* (1702) satirized the haranguing pamphlets of Sacheverell and Leslie among others, in the vein of Swift's later *Modest Proposal*. So extreme were some of the High Church writings, however, that Defoe's ironies were lost on his readers, who could not perceive much difference between the original and the satire—except for the crude suggestion that Dissenters be hung rather than merely fined. Readers have always had difficulty in discerning Defoe's irony, as Maximillian Novak points out in his analysis of this text, and modern critics have often felt that "Defoe got carried away, identified with his High Church Hot Head and created a work of fiction rather than irony."[18] In any case there was a great deal of publicity over Defoe's pamphlet, not least because it was swallowed whole by numbers of people who did not see its parodic intent. Some of the very High Churchmen whom it was ridiculing missed the edge in the tone and simply counted it as one on their side. Needless to say, when the author came to be known and his satiric intent clear beyond a shadow of a doubt, that initial acceptance was doubly infuriating. It was a real coup in the world of political pamphleteers.

"*No Gentlemen*, the Time of Mercy is past, your *Day of Grace is over*," intoned Defoe's high-flying Tory to his Whig enemies. "We have been huff'd and bully'd with your Act of Tolleration. . . . You have *Butcher'd* one King, *Depos'd* another King, and made a *mock King* of a Third; and yet you cou'd have the Face to expect to be employ'd and trusted by the Fourth." He argued that if only a new law could be passed to exterminate Dissenters rather than simply punishing them for occasional conformity and barring them from public office, it would be more effective and there would be less whining and complaining about it. If the "Gallows instead of the Counter, and the Galleys instead of the Fines were the Reward of going to a Conventicle . . . there wou'd not be so many Sufferers, the Spirit of Martyrdom is over."

For his libelous accuracy, Defoe was chastised by the ministry, fined two hundred marks (£133 33s.), and made to stand in the pillory on three separate occasions.[19] He subsequently wrote an "Explanation" of *The Shortest Way* to clear up all the public confusion as to its intent and meaning. He says there that "it seems Impossible to imagine it should pass for any thing but an Irony," although of course extremism of the sort he was condemning *did* exist, albeit in a more veiled form; he was simply "making other Peoples thoughts speak in his Words." But any reasonable person, he continued, could see how close to self-parody such intolerant attitudes already were: "'tis Nonsence to go round about, and tell us of the Crimes of the *Dissenters*, to prepare the World to believe they are not fit to live in a Humane Society, that they are Enemies to the Government, and Law. . . . *The shortest way*, and the soonest," he concludes, "wou'd be to tell us plainly that they wou'd have them all hang'd, Banish'd and Destroy'd."[20]

This was the atmosphere, and this the issue that initially drew Mary Astell into the line of fire. During the fall of 1703 she worked on *Moderation Truly Stated,* her first salvo in the Occasional Conformity controversy, and published it in December. This time she did not try to maintain her fashionably amateur status by insisting that she had tossed off these pages in an afternoon or two. *Moderation Truly Stated* is a careful, definitive reply to arguments for occasional conformity in the current pamphlet literature, discussed in the context of the larger questions about conscience, "moderation" (by which Astell meant indifference or apathy), and the relation between politics and religion—that which is Caesar's and that which is God's.

The immediate purpose of *Moderation Truly Stated* was to refute James Owen's *Moderation A Vertue* (1703), an eminently reasonable tract defending the practice of occasional conformity. Owen, a nonconforming minister, took a moderate line—more moderate than Defoe, for instance—and Astell probably chose to reply to him because he presented the most cogently stated arguments in favor of occasional conformity and was therefore the enemy to be taken most seriously. A Welsh Presbyterian minister, Owen was known for erudite clerical essays published in English and Welsh, on such subjects as baptism, ministerial duties, and so on. The restrained reasonableness of his *Moderation A Vertue* made it the logical target for opponents of all shades of opinion, and it is noteworthy that extremists from both camps—Defoe *and* Leslie—attacked it.

Owen began by arguing that occasional conformity was nothing new but had been practiced since ancient times, to the inestimable advantage and spiritual enrichment of the established church. John the

Baptist had been the first occasional conformist, said Owen, going to Jewish synagogues in Jerusalem three times a year on ritual feast days but otherwise holding his own services in the wilderness of Judea, at Jordan, and at Enon. It could be fairly said, observed Owen, that "Christianity had its first beginnings in *Occasional Conformity*."

He also defended the practice of occasional conformity against the obvious charge of hypocrisy—that Dissenting officials took communion in the Church of England solely for their personal advancement. Dissenters had always believed in variety of styles of worship, Owen argued. They continued to adhere to Dissenting congregations rather than to their parish churches, because they felt them to be purer and more disciplined than those of the Anglican church—particularly in matters such as censuring scandal or keeping the Sabbath strictly. But there was nothing that went seriously against the grain in communicating in the established church upon occasion. The areas of agreement were more significant than the areas of disagreement; and the practice of occasionally conforming generated a sense of an extended Christian community, which was a good thing. In short, he concluded, "*Occasional Conformity* is not a *late Invention of crafty men to get into Places* but the Effect of Christian and Catholic Principles, which the *Moderate Dissenters* professed long before the *Corporation and Test Acts* were made."

Mary Astell replied to Owen with characteristic thoroughness, power, and accuracy. In fact, *Moderation Truly Stated* seems a little out of place in the company of most of the other answers to Owen, with their slapdash composition or, in the case of Leslie's *The Wolf Stripp'd of His Shepherd's Clothing* (1704), their virulence. For one thing, Astell's *Moderation Truly Stated* is longer than these other texts. Leslie wrote eighty-three pages to answer Owen; Astell produced 185 pages of small print, densely annotated with references and lists of books for further reading. She marshaled and documented all the current arguments on both sides of the issue with impressive care. She obviously had a large library to work from. Indeed, one rumor of the 1740s—for which no evidence has been found—is that she left an extensive library to Magdalen College when she died.[21]

Astell begins her refutation with theological arguments from the Bible against occasional conformity. She cites example after example from the Old Testament of instances of toleration which proved dangerous in the long run to the "mother" religion. Judged as a moral issue—and assuming that the continued strength of the national church was necessary to maintain the moral standard of the culture—the matter was simple. "True Policy then requires nothing of us that is unreasonable or unjust, or contrary to Religion and its Interests," she wrote.

"For right Reason is Uniform, all of a piece, and if it is our Guide in Politicks, it won't lead us into measures inconsistent with its Dictates in other Cases. So that if Occasional Conformity is an Immoral Action, or prejudicial to Religion, consequently it is impolitick to allow it."[22] To be moderate in matters of religion, wrote Astell, was to be lukewarm. Since royal authority rested on divine right invested by the church, no zeal to her mind could be intemperate in such a cause. Her defense of the combined authority of church and monarch rested on a pure Augustan belief in the intrinsic spiritual qualities of Order:

> In a word, Order is a Sacred Thing, 'tis that Law which God prescribes Himself, and inviolably observes. Subordination is a necessary consequence of Order, for in a State of Ignorance and [De]Pravity such as ours is, there is not any thing that tends more to Confusion than Equality. It does not therefore become the gross of Mankind to set up for that which is best in their own conceit; but humbly to observe where GOD has Delegated his Power, and submit to it, *as unto the Lord and not to Man.*[23]

She accused the opposition of wanting to undermine this order for selfish reasons; anyone could see from their conduct that they were primarily interested in power and not in the good of the country. These were not men who could regulate themselves, much less a state. Their license was dangerous to themselves as well as to the larger community.

> To see a Man who pays no body, but feeds upon the sweat and tears of his poor Creditors, declare for Property! A Man who would have every one conform to his Magisterial Dictates, cabal for Liberty! He who violates the dearest Interests of his Neighbour, exclaim against Arbitrary Power! He who wrongs another's Honour, and robs him of what he values most, pretend to stickle for the Birthright and Privileges of his Countrymen! A Rake who transgresses all the Laws, become a Zealous Advocate in their Defence! A Knight of the Toast, a Champion for the Reformation against the Corruptions of the Church of *Rome*! To hear a *Socinian* argue for Articles of Faith, and a *Deist* for the Protestant Religion! Certainly *Democritus* never met with so Comical a Scene as this! It would indeed be extremely Diverting, were the Jest receiv'd as it ought to be; and did not the Credit that is given to this Pageant, by too many, render it of dangerous Consequence to their Country.[24]

She constructed for Owen an elaborate history lesson, drawn from a host of writers upon the Civil War, citing the proceedings of both Houses and particular speeches, letters, and sermons to show how dangerous it was to give Dissenters an inch, for they would always take a mile. Her reading was very up-to-date: she appeared to know every word of Clarendon by heart, only just published, 1702–04. She turned Calamy inside out, with his accounts of the sufferings of ejected nonconforming ministers at the Restoration, and discussed instead the way the Anglican clergy had been treated during the years of the Commonwealth. Her technique, as always, was to find the inconsistencies. She pointed out the passages in nonconformist books that promised no quarter to the Church of England; she enjoyed locating again and again in their own favorite writers diatribes which declaimed against toleration and pressed for uniformity. She listed the abuses the Dissenters perpetrated upon the Anglican clergy during the interregnum: how they were fined for using the Book of Common Prayer, how they were turned out of their livings with no support for their wives and children, how they were imprisoned and tormented by callous treatment, how their goods were plundered, and so on. Painstakingly she argued against allowing Dissenters into places of power, reading the case out of their own authors—Baxter, Edwards, Bastwick—with as much ease as out of the authors of the other side—Foulis, Young, Stillingfleet. She delighted in absurdities of expedient rationalization, and in uncovering beneath the latticework of an author's double purposes the proof of his real convictions.

The work exhibits the range of eighteenth-century rhetorical strategies, from sarcasm to exhortation, and from perfectly turned witticisms to logical step-by-step exposition. Nor does it focus narrowly on the Occasional Conformity debate, but refers these political realities of her own time to the observations of Tacitus and Machiavelli, Sir Thomas More and Milton—who, she remarked, was a better poet than a politician or divine. Quoting Dryden's translation of *The Aeneid*, she likened the Puritans at the outset of the Civil War to false Greeks bearing gifts, and the fall of London to the fall of Troy:

> What Diomede, nor Thetis greater son,
> A thousand ships, nor ten Years Siege had done,
> False Tears and Fawning Words the City won.

Moderation Truly Stated was a very effective piece of political pamphleteering. Its serious charges drew replies from Defoe, from Leslie, and from Owen himself. Tory leaders were at some pains to identify their mysterious ally. Dr. Hickes, the Saxonist and nonjuring bishop of Worcester, wrote to Dr. Charlett, master of University College, Oxford: "And you may now assure your self, that Mrs. Astell is the author of that other book against *Occasional Communion*, which we justly admired so much."[25]

In many ways, the long polemical essay was an ideal form for Mary Astell, well suited to the strengths of her prose style. Her strongly held opinions were convincing when delivered with the conversational informality possible in the pamphlet. Her sense of historical parallels, her moralizing, and her penchant for philosophical formulation worked well together and gave animation and variety to her reflections. Sympathetic Tory writers later in the century recognized her grasp of the issues and steady, irrefutable logic. William Parry, to whom George Ballard lent a copy in 1743, determined at once to buy one of his own, for he said that it put "the Character and Principles of the Dissenters in the truest Light" better than any book he had ever seen on the subject:

> I thank you very much for the perusal of Mrs. Astell's Moderation truly Stated: which book is a convincing Proof of her Strong Sense, great Genius, and excellent Capacities, and of her great Affection to the Church of England: It is written with so much Life and Spirit, that every Sentence has a peculiar Weight, and is so poignant as to stick an Arrow into her Adversary's Side. She has with a distinguished Judgement dissected and display'd the ambitious views and sinister Designs of the Dissenters, and discover'd what abominable Dissimulation & Hypocrisy & Self-Interest lies conceal'd under their Mask of superior Piety, and how averse they are to practice that Moderation which they seem to recommend. In short, she has fairly routed their Champion Dr. D'Avenant, traced him thro' all his Shufflings, and thrown his Arguments in his Face. It is in my Opinion an incomparable and valuable Book, and puts the Character and Principles of the Dissenters in the truest Light: and as it is the best of its kind, that I have yet mett with, (and I despair of a better) I propose to purchase one for my self.[26]

Everyone agreed that the liveliest part of Mrs. Astell's *Moderation Truly Stated* was the long "Prefatory Discourse to Dr. D'Avenant Concerning His late Essays on Peace and War." Thomas Rawlins, another of George Ballard's antiquarian friends, introduced for the first time to Astell's *oeuvre* in 1743, wrote:

> The Serious Advice to ye Ladies is a very ingenious Book for Ladies to peruse wherein they will meet with abundance of very good advice as also is The Reflexions Upon Marriage. She is very smart in her Treatise called A fair way with Dissenters wherein she expresses ym with a great deal of

Truth and Mirth but I never read anything attended with more wit and
ingenious Bantor than is contained in her Prefatory Discourse to Dr.
D'Avenant. One cannot help exercising one's risible faculty in the reading
of it.[27]

Charles D'Avenant, the man at whose expense the "risible faculty"
was so readily exercised, was a Tory pamphleteer who had, in obedience
to directives from Queen Anne's new bipartisan ministry, reversed himself and defended the principle of toleration that he had made his earlier
reputation in attacking. Isaac Kramnick, in *Bolingbroke and His Circle*,
cites him as the "first major Augustan writer to respond unfavorably"
to the entrepreneurial spirit of the new age—its disregard for tradition,
its infatuation with the new, its capitalist enterprises puffed up on
borrowed capital and paper credit—and to presage the Tory gloom of
Swift and Pope and Bolingbroke.[28] His earliest pamphlets described the
new sort of Whig politician as an obscure and hungry climber who
used the government to make his fortune, who manipulated trade and
even international policies to further his private interests, and who cared
nothing for the health of the state. At that early stage in his career he
had asseverated, as Astell often did, that government ought to be in
the hands of those whose birth and estates insured less self-interested
motives and put them above common temptations.

The eldest son of Sir William D'Avenant, poet laureate and play-
wright, D'Avenant wrote his satires in a form which demonstrated his
own considerable dramatic talent. *The True Picture of a Modern Whig*
(1701) is a dialogue between an opportunistic runaway apprentice named
Tom Double, who has cheated his way into government—"'Tis the
Principle of us Modern Whigs to get what we can, no matter how"—
and Mr. Whiglove, an old-fashioned Whig who cares about honesty,
the good of the country, and so on. To Whiglove's stammering objections to his tactics, Tom Double replies: "Prithee what's the Nation to
us, provided our Friends get into power and are in a Condition to
make us thrive?" He cites the name of Dr. D'Avenant on the last pages
of the booklet, as an enemy whom the more shameless Whigs have tried
to discredit with false stories of bribes and French influence, but who
is properly antagonistic towards France. Honest Mr. Whiglove queries:

But don't we hurt the Cause, by uttering these Notorious Falsehoods? I
was check'd very sharply not long ago by one of our own Side, a Man of
known Truth and Candor, for dispersing such a groundless and malicious
Slander. The Gentleman said, if he be brib'd he deserves his Bribes but
very ill, for in all his Writings, in his last especially, *Upon the Ballance of*

Power, he has declar'd himself no Friend to French Councils. The Scope
of his whole Book is for an immediate War, and his private Conversation
always concludes that way.

To which Tom Double replies:

I wish the Beams of the Room would fall and beat out his working Brains;
his indefatigable Industry had done us a World of Hurt. We must throw
what Dirt we can upon him. If we can prevail to have him Ill thought on,
'twill make his Writings have the less weight.

In addition to imagining the satisfying scenario of being feared by his
enemies for all the right reasons, D'Avenant here glosses his own moderate Tory position. He condemned the graft and corruption of the
"modern Whig," but not the party as a whole, and not the political
ideas of leveling or democracy.

There was a sequel to this little book, *Tom Double Return'd Out of
the Country* (1702), which gave more of the same. The insatiable upstart
Tom Double rises to power and drains the very coffers of the nation
to keep himself and his friends in luxuries and advancements. "I dispise
a sneaking Genius," he opines, referring to small-scale corruption, "that
is satisfy'd with moderate Wealth and Honours. Suppose a Gentleman
from Eight hundred Pound a Year, comes to have at least Five hundred
thousand Pound in his Pocket, and to be made an Earl, Is he to sit
quiet? No, let him endeavour to get a Million, and to be a Duke."
Needless to say, such polemics were very popular and there were a
number of attempts both to imitate D'Avenant's dialogues and to refute
them.

When Anne came to the throne, urging reconciliation between
Whig and Tory and trying herself to maintain a bipartisan ministry, she
commissioned D'Avenant, through Halifax, to write another popular,
but less polarized work, which would argue for unity at home. D'Avenant, who in addition to his "Tom Double" pamphlets had been the
author of several economic treatises criticizing Whig policies with respect to taxes and trade in the previous regime, was given two months
vacation from his new post as inspector-general of exports and imports
(which carried the considerable salary of £1,000 per annum) to write
this piece of propaganda for the government. The result, *Essays Upon
Peace at Home and War Abroad* (1704), is a curiously eviscerated, mealy-
mouthed book, repetitive and pretentious (he repeats himself in Latin
at every opportunity). Page after page, he equivocates and overqualifies
his statements until the effect is confusing and irritating. "Davenant's

book is come out this day," wrote Francis Atterbury to his Tory crony bishop Trelawny, "where he talks in a very different manner from what he hath done in all his other writings; and is all for moderation and healing. There is a chapter against the bill about occasional conformity; the argument of which is managed with that weakness that usually attends men who write against their honor and conscience."[29]

The essential points of *Essays Upon Peace and War* are that representatives in Parliament are not responsible to the people, their constituencies, but to the country as a whole; that Whig and Tory ought to unite to form a solid front to carry on the wars of Spanish succession abroad; that although the English constitutional monarchy and the Church of England are an effective and indissoluble combination, there is no reason to persecute those who choose to belong to another church— to curtail liberty of conscience, as he put it, never did any good. Furthermore, he argued, if the Toleration Act were maintained and the practice of occasional conformity were allowed to continue, it would eventually undermine the unity of the separate congregations, which derived strength from their isolation, for each separate member would be paying his private court to the state, and thus making his own terms.[30]

D'Avenant drew fire from all sides; Astell and other High Tories attacked him for betraying their cause, and the Whigs, who had never looked upon him as a friend, recognized in his description of the proper role of elected officials (i.e., to represent the interests not of any particular constituency but of the country as a whole) a desire to deprive the people of any direct say in their representative government. Thus Defoe criticized him for "depriving the People of all Power, but what is representative and giving the delegated power a superiority over the Power Delegating"; and Charles Leslie from the other side felt that D'Avenant had blamed the Stuart kings inordinately in his retelling of the history of dissent and the Civil War.

Mary Astell, who had just finished *Moderation Truly Stated* when D'Avenant's book came out, immediately added to it the detailed "Prefatory Discourse to Dr. D'Avenant" in which she demonstrated a familiarity with his previous works on economic policy. She signed her essay "Tom Single" to focus attention on D'Avenant's duplicity, and wrote a section of it as a dialogue in imitation of his own productions. The two epigraphs on her title page are "Out of thine own mouth will I judge thee, thou wicked Servant" (Luke 19:22) and "Women are strongest, but above all things Truth beareth away the Victory" (1 Esdras 3:12).

Mercilessly she traced the internal inconsistencies of D'Avenant's arguments and attacked the cynicism and expediency of his position.

"So great is our Author's Civility and Compassion," she mocked, "that he never seems to strike a blow in one Page, but he takes care to ward it in another." He was trying to please everybody, she said, and the brain could not endure so many turnings. She made sport of his wishy-washy statements about how to handle those who plotted to overthrow the government:

> But stay—I think I have found it: Bad Men are to go unpunish'd—not always—but for a while. They are to have Impunity, but not a total Impunity; there it is, and this nice Distinction has brought us off![31]

She showed his stupidity, his inconsistency, his lack of moral center. Her stance was that of a simple, plainspoken person who could not understand such fancy footwork. She quoted Boileau's first satire:

> Je suis rustique et fier, et j'ai l'ame grossiere.
> Je ne puis rien nommer, si ce n'est pas son Nom;
> J'appelle un Chat un Chat, et Rolet un Fripon.

She repeated her own grandmother's simple wisdom that to change society one had to begin with oneself—although "in a book so Rhetorical as yours," she teased, "it sounds a little Flat, and is neither set off with True nor False Eloquence."[32]

Because she was against "moderation," she reminded her readers that Tom Double had once remarked that since modern Whigs cared only for their personal power, once ousted from office they "were never known to forgive, and that this is the Weakness of those Fools they have so long contended with." She recommended more definitive action than D'Avenant's current line, which was to neither punish nor to forgive the seditious, but to somehow put them on their good behavior. Either punish enemies of the government if they deserved it, or else forgive them generously and mercifully, wrote Astell, "for by not forgiving them entirely, you keep up their Fears and do not gain their Love; and by not Punishing, you leave them a Power to Hurt you. . . ." D'Avenant's advice, neither one nor the other, did only "nourish Faction and keep us in endless Broils. Nor is this only my Opinion," she added, "for looking into *Machiavel* a little after I had wrote this, I found that Great Politician exactly of my Mind; in his Discourses on *Livy*."[33]

She did not understand why in one place D'Avenant claimed that the exercise of arbitrary power always caused revolt, while elsewhere he noted that although Henry VIII changed the religion of the nation, taxed his subjects heavily, and lived in unnecessary luxury, neither he—

nor Queen Elizabeth nor Queen Mary—forfeited their power by wielding it. She also reminded her readers that the tyranny of one's fellow subjects—of "popular demagogues"—was also an exercise of arbitrary power. She corrected him on matters of fact, from particulars in the history of the Civil War to the chronology of the ancient world. But inevitably their most fundamental difference was about the notion of the liberty of the people—to which Astell was opposed and about which D'Avenant was ambivalent. He had argued that the power of the "mob" was neutralized by its delegation to parliamentary representatives, but he granted that people were born with liberty to begin with, in the original state of nature.

Astell flatly refused that premise. People were not born free, she said; they were born into the structures of civilization: the family, the state, and the church. No infant could survive in a state of nature without the protection of these institutions, and no amount of theorizing could erase a person's dependencies upon and obligations to them. Quite rightly she blamed the chimera of a "state of nature" on Hobbes, and dismissed his construct with her usual sprightly wit.

> *I have hitherto thought, that according to* Moses, *we were all of* Adam's *Race, and that a State of Nature was a meer figment of* Hobbs's *Brain, or borrow'd at least from the Fable of* Cadmus, *or AEacus his Myrmidons, till you were pleas'd to inform me* "of that Equality wherein the Race of Men were plac'd in the free State of Nature." *How I lament my stars that it was not my good Fortune to Live in those Happy Days when Men sprung up like so many Mushrooms or* Terrae Filii, *without Father or Mother or any sort of dependency!*[34]

Astell's argument is of particular interest as an early critique of these seventeenth-century political theories by a feminist. She does not explicitly state the objections that modern feminists have posed to Hobbes— that he omitted the childrearing work that women do, and the maternal functions of nurturance, concern, guidance, and relating, from his portrait of human nature. But by gesturing towards the necessity of parents and the dependence of infants, she points the way. The unmitigated selfishness of Hobbes's notion of the human condition, and his assumption that expedience was the sole motive for the social contract, appalled her. "*And truly who can blame a Man who finds himself not at Ease, or so well as he would be, if he reassumes a Fundamental Right,*" she asked shrewdly, "*a Privilege of which no Man can divest himself, and so soon as he can get more Men of his Mind to make his Party strong enough, declares the* Contract broken."[35]

Her own image of nature, offered some years later in her response to Shaftesbury, was a maternal ideal, nature as generous—"the best sort of Gentlewoman." Wise and beneficent, Mother Nature could always be counted upon to further "General Good, or the Good of the Whole," with which "her own Private Good must needs be one and the same." Thus gold and jewels were hid in the earth, "to put them out of the reach of most people," whereas if they were "really Good, they wou'd not be such Rarities," but "our Indulgent Mother Nature wou'd have bestow'd them on all her Children, made them as Common and Universal as Earth and Air, Sun and Water."[36]

Elsewhere in these early political pamphlets, Astell's difference of gender asserts itself in images and examples, as when she pictures Religion as a plain, honest matron who almost gets trampled in the crowd.[37] In the "Prefatory Discourse to Dr. D'Avenant," right in the middle of the dialogue about whether or not it is hypocritical to take sacraments occasionally in the Church of England, there is a remarkable flight of fancy about women leaders, which goes on for six pages, in which Astell's feminism bubbles up almost involuntarily.

It begins when the gentleman who deplores the practice of occasional conformity remarks that his opponents, the Dissenters, count in their number many women as well as working folk; they have in their ranks "not a few of the Female Sex, more Sea-Faring Men, likewise very many Tradesmen, or Retailers, Artificers, Manufacturers and Day-Labourers, and in these Multitudes their chief strength consists."[38] But their women, he continued, were of the flighty, thoughtless, and sexually active sort: "*the Young and the Handsom, the Witty and the Gay, the Intriguing and Politick Ladies are all on the Factious Side.*" These were to be distinguished from the other sort—"*the Old and the Ugly, the Praying and the Women of Thought*"—Astell's sort, who took the Tory view of the debate. Astell's speaker then goes into an extraordinary fantasy about how if only a woman put herself at the head of the Dissenter multitudes, "what a formidable Insurrection would it make!" She spins example after example of strong women who commanded armies and did feats of derring-do. It is as if Astell could allow herself to imagine rebelliousness only in the ranks of Dissenter women, but that once imagined, she was carried away by her enthusiasm for women's power.

Then, as if all this talk had actually conjured her up, a woman steps forward into the dialogue and berates the two male spokesmen for their bad manners, "*since in a Lady's Reign, and even in Books that you Dedicate to her Majesty* [as was D'Avenant's *Essays on Peace and War*], *you take upon yourself to tell the World that* in this Kingdom no more Skill, no more Policies are requisite, than what may be comprehended by a

Woman. *As if there were any Skill, and Policy that a Woman's Under-standing could not reach!*"[39] This female intruder lectures them at some length about Anne's superior wisdom, and advises them to follow her lead in the matter of occasional conformity—after which she exits, leaving them openmouthed.

The entire section is almost surreal in its unexpectedness. It comes from nowhere, and erupts into little perorations about obscure heroines, like Valasca of Bohemia, who *"inspir'd her Women with a great Contempt of the Men, and a strong Resolution to throw off their Yoke,"* or Agrippina, wife of Germanicus, who drilled the Roman troops and stopped a mutiny. And then it all subsides again, just as abruptly, into conventional party polemics.

Owen answered all his detractors—Astell, Leslie (whose page-by-page refutation was more savage than anything Astell wrote), Sacheverell, and Defoe—at the same time in *Moderation Still a Vertue in Answer to Several Bitter Pamphlets: Especially Two Entituled "Occasional Conformity a most Unjustifiable Practice"* [Samuel Grascome] *and "The Wolf Stripp'd of his Shepherd's Clothing"* [Charles Leslie] (1704). It was not, as Astell noted in her subsequent reply, "so properly an *Answer* to the *Pamphlets* it pretends to reply to, as a second Edition of *Moderation A Vertue* with some Enlargements, neither answering the Arguments nor disproving the Matters of Fact, but waving the one and recriminating upon the other." Again the Presbyterian minister justified occasional conformity. Many gentlemen, he said, lived for half the year in the country and attended one church there, and lived the other half of the year in town where they attended another. There was nothing so unusual in that practice. He attacked Leslie as a Jacobite and accused him of being involved in secret conspiracies based in France. He condemned the practitioners of passive obedience as undermining the liberties of the people: "the Doctrine of Unlimited Passive Obedience and Absolute Non-Resistance tempted K. J. II to trample on Laws and Fundamental Constitution." Astell, he alleged, was a fanatic: "*Some of them violently oppose all* Moderation, *and confound it with* Lukewarmness in *the* Essentials *and* Vitals *of Religion; so the Verbose and Virulent Author of* Moderation *truly stated*." It is interesting to note that Owen did not know that the "Stater" was a woman, and refers to the author of Astell's pamphlet several times as "he."

Owen had also been attacked on his other flank by Defoe, who disapproved of Dissenters ever conforming for purely pragmatic reasons, as he wrote in *The Sincerity of the Dissenters Vindicated From the Scandal of Occasional Conformity with some Considerations on a late Book, Entitul'd, "Moderation a Vertue"* (1703). Owen had claimed that there were a great many honest Dissenters who could take the Anglican sacraments in perfectly good faith, without violating their consciences. Defoe replied that when Owen granted that conforming for a place was a scandalous practice, he had granted all the real ground of the dispute. For what other reason was there for a Dissenter to conform? or for a Churchman to object to it? Owen had put his finger on *the* objection to occasional conformity. If Dissenters left the Church of England because their consciences bade them to do so, there was no reason why they should ever return unless they made up their minds to rejoin the Anglican fold for good. Defoe was gentle with Owen, called him a man of honesty and discerning judgment, but he firmly insisted that occasional conformity was a breach of serious Dissent.

Meanwhile, another storm had been brewing over Defoe's earlier attack on the high flyers, *The Shortest Way With the Dissenters*. Charles Leslie, for one, had been stung by Defoe's burlesque and had responded with a twenty-eight-page pamphlet called *Reflections Upon a Late Scandalous and Malicious PAMPHLET entitul'd "The Shortest Way With the Dissenters"* (1703), to which he attached Defoe's offensive tract entire. He then further capitalized on the controversy by republishing both pamphlets again, with further remarks of his own, titling the whole *The New Association Part II* (1704). Leslie claimed that Defoe's tactics stirred up unease and suspicion and bred paranoia in Dissenters and moderate Churchmen who began to believe, contrary to all sense, that the Queen and Parliament intended their destruction. Defoe's satire had touched a nerve, for Leslie takes special pains in *The New Association Part II* to disassociate himself from the Jacobites, and to put as much distance as possible between his own views and those of Defoe's high-flyer gentleman speaker.

Defoe, irrepressible, fired back *More Short Ways With the Dissenters* in 1704, both as a gesture of defiance towards those who had attacked him for *The Shortest Way With the Dissenters*, and as a very real protest against the current High Church talk about closing down the Dissenting academies. He opened by asserting that he had been right all along; there *was* a plan to extirpate all the Dissenters, and the satirical exaggerations of *The Shortest Way With the Dissenters* had not been so far off after all:

> But Gentlemen, if what you Preach, Print or Say be in Earnest, if you would have us believe you, and give any heed to your Sermons, your Satyrs and Invectives, if your *Woolf Stript*, your *Associations*, your *Peace and Union* [Sir Humphrey Mackworth], be of any weight, then 'tis no Scandal to affirm that there is a barbarous Design on foot, in, and among some who

call themselves the Members of the Church of *England*, to Extirpate and Destroy the Dissenters, and to do every thing by them that is Equivalent to what has been call'd *the Shortest Way*, and consequently that Author was barbarously treated.[40]

If Dissenters were kept from educating their children in their own attitudes and opinions, these beliefs would end with their own generation, and "next to the Methods formerly propos'd in the Book so call'd, this is doubtless *the Shortest Way with the Dissenters*." Mr. Sacheverell still had not taken down his "Bloody Flag," he continued—referring to the shibboleth in Sacheverell's sermons, that one could not be a true son of the Church unless one lifted up the bloody flag against the Dissenters. In short, cried Defoe, the extreme High Churchmen were still breathing down their necks; Sacheverell *could* have written *The Shortest Way With the Dissenters* "tho' another was Punish'd for it."

He then went on to defend the Dissenting academies, which he said were often very good schools. He cited his own experience at the Dissenting academy of Mr. Charles Morton of Newington Green as an educational success. Antimonarchical principles were not taught there, he asserted, although Wesley (probably referring to John Wesley's father) and others pretended that they were as a reason for closing the schools down. He defied anyone to go through his school notes and find any sentiments subversive of the government or constitution of England—an offer that Astell later said she would like to take him up on if he could find his notes. These Dissenting schools were necessary, Defoe continued, because Dissenting youth were excluded from Cambridge and Oxford by required oaths designed for that purpose. That ought to have struck a responsive chord in Astell, given her own resentment at women being excluded from institutions of higher learning. Of course, Defoe added, Cambridge and Oxford would have to be cleaned up of drunkenness and lewdness before his clean-living Puritan sort would be comfortable there.

Ordinarily, *The Shortest Way With the Dissenters* would not have been taken seriously by Mary Astell. Defoe's assumption that nonconformists were purer than Anglicans would have irritated her, but as he, too, argued against occasional conformity, albeit from the other side, he was not, on the face of it, dangerous. Yet, in this case, there had been such a big public fuss over *The Shortest Way With the Dissenters*—both because it had been taken seriously at face value by some High Churchmen, and because Defoe had been arrested for it, that she could hardly ignore it. Then, too, it was her viewpoint—more or less—that was being satirized, which is why she advertised her reply as *A Fair*

Way With The Dissenters and Their Patrons Not Writ by Mr. L[esle]y, or any other Furious Jacobite, whether Clergyman or Layman; but by a very Moderate Person and Dutiful Subject to the Queen. Perhaps the writer in her responded to the exceptional verve and clarity of Defoe's prose. His enormous success as a pamphleteer is easy to understand when one reads his large-gestured, free-flowing prose in its Grub Street context. His speakers have stronger personalities than most of their fictional counterparts in other pamphlets. Astell begins her reply to Defoe on a different note than her other tracts, and explicitly remarks on his tone.

> Well! If Disputes in print and Disputes at *Billingsgate*, which, as they are manag'd, are equally scolding, he were to carry the day who rails loudest and longest; Wo be to the poor Church and its Friends, they could never shew their Faces or hold up their Heads against the everlasting Clamour of their Adversaries. For what Thunder may we expect from those *too violent Spirits*, which these meek and good Christians *do not deny* they have *among them.* . . .

The words "too violent Spirits" refer to Defoe's description of Sacheverell's preaching—"the Language only of one mad Priest" he called it "a *Fury* made up of a Complication of Malice, intollerable Pride, bigotted Zeal, and bloody Hellish Unchristian Principles."[41]

But if she began by showing that Defoe himself was not exactly a restrained, temperate writer, she also did not offer to mitigate Sacheverell's statements. She did not deny that Sacheverell had demanded that all Dissenters be destroyed—indeed, she made it clear that she too wished to destroy them—politically. Yes, "*Total Destruction of Dissenters as a Party* . . . is indeed our Design," she wrote, and ought to be the aim of all honest Christians who hate faction and believe in a strong, unified England. She defended Sacheverell's remarks as "modest and cool" (which they are not) and reminded "Mr. Short-Ways" that "it is his own and not Mr. S's Conclusion, that *Because they never showed us Quarter, therefore* We will revenge ourselves." She pretended to miss the irony of Defoe's assertion that Sacheverell was the real author of *The Shortest Way With the Dissenters*—that is, that Sacheverell's expressions were every bit as extreme as his own inventions. She wrote, "it is not true that Mr. *Sacheverel* is the *Real Author of the Shortest-way*, or else your Friend *Defoe* is a Plagiary; that Original of Honesty, Truth, and Ingenuity, being Printed among his *Handicrafts*, with his own *shining* Face in front of them."

She was shocked by the epithets Defoe applied to Sacheverell, who was after all a minister of the Church of England. She accused him of writing "with an *Heart full of Malice, through a Mouth full of Cursing and Bitterness,*" of disdainfully laying "*Drunkenness and Lewdness* to the charge of two Famous Universities, besides those more substantial Crimes of *Unjust and Unfair Terms and Imposed Oaths*, that is, Oaths to be true to the Government in Church and State, which if they were laid aside, the honest conscientious Dissenters, to get in two thousand of their Children, would *venture* the poor Babies *Morals*, in *relation* to the former *Trifles of Lewdness and Drunkenness.*"

She tried to discredit Defoe by mocking his grammatical mistakes, and delighted in pointing out his mix-ups in historical names and dates. She charges him with misreading Clarendon: "Bless me! what hideous Spectacles Prejudice and Prepossession are upon a Reader's nose! But when our Brother *Short-ways* has laid these aside, has wip'd his Eyes, and is willing to see clearly, I would then advise him to another Perusal of that excellent and useful History." Reluctant herself to go through all the arguments again, she recommends to the reader her own earlier work, *Moderation Truly Stated*, "where he may find such *unanswerable Proofs, from such Just Authorities, and Plain Matters of Fact* . . . as make it out beyond a Contradiction, that Dissenters are by Principle and Practice irreconcileable Enemies to our Government in Church and State, declar'd Opposers of Liberty of Conscience, when they themselves have the Power in their Hands."

While this reply to Defoe was at the printer's, Owen's *Moderation Still A Vertue* appeared. Astell hastened to defend her right flank in a postscript, dated and appended to *A Fair Way With the Dissenters and Their Patrons*. Owen had charged her *Moderation Truly Stated* with being "Verbose and Virulent"; if these adjectives were true, she wrote, and they might well be so, it was the fault of the tract she had been answering and none of her own.

> And it is very true that several Pages of it are *Verbose and Virulent*, for they are taken up in answering the Dissenters Arguments against Schism and Toleration in their own Words, and their Virulency against the Government in Church and State as by Law established. . . .
>
> I should be too verbose, did I reckon up all our Author's Mistakes and Disingenuities; he tells us that the *Stater* [i.e., Astell] *opposes all Moderation, and confounds it with Lukewarmness in the Essentials of Religion.* The next Page to that he quotes will shew him his Error, for there *Moderation* is made to consist in the *Proportioning our Esteem and Value of every thing to its real worth.*[42]

Having restated her definition of "moderation," Astell went on to draw a distinction between "Dissenters in conscience"—which she thought included most Dissenters, and for whom she had great compassion—and "Dissenters in faction" as she called them, who disturbed the peace and had designs on the government. "What moderation can they lay claim to?" she asked. "If *Non-Conformity* were only a Matter of Conscience, Dissenters might be brought off it by coming Occasionally to our Churches, and observing how much more edifying our Worship is than their own," she said sensibly. "But *Occasional-Conformity* is made an Engine to promote Secular Interests; and for the Reasons above, it Weakens and Undermines the Church, and keeps up our Divisions." She also noted that Owen had not refuted the evidence she had marshaled in *Moderation Truly Stated.* "To conclude, the Author ought either to disprove the Authorities cited out of their own Writers, or else to prove to us that the Modern Dissenters have deserted the Principles, and do not approve the Practices of their Fore-fathers. . . . But till this is done, he must allow us to make all the Provisions we can, that they may never any more Triumph in the Ruin of GOD's Church among us."[43]

At the same time as this debate with Defoe was being carried on, another public dialogue arose in which Mary Astell took part. It is probable that her bookseller Rich Wilkin prodded her to write this third political pamphlet. She had proved her political grasp of the issues and her satiric gift, and he was impressed by the rapidity with which she digested others' tracts and formulated her clear and determined opinions. This last controversy concerned a sermon preached by Dr. White Kennett on the fast day commemorating the martyrdom of Charles I. Over the years Charles I's day had increasingly fallen into disuse, especially under a Whig government and a Calvinist king. But in 1704, with a Stuart on the throne again, and the Occasional Conformity Bill before Parliament, the history of the schism was a particularly inflammable subject, and all eyes were on Dr. Kennett.

As Mary Astell was well aware, Dr. Kennett had sided with the Whigs during the internecine church struggles over Convocation.[44] An exceptionally learned medieval scholar, Kennett had put his talents at the service of Archbishop Tenison (who had been appointed by William III to replace nonjuring Archbishop William Sancroft) to establish Tenison's prerogative to forbid the Convocation of the lower clergy in Parliament and so forestall their power. His most serious opposition came from Atterbury, the organizer of the Convocation, Mary Astell's friend and neighbor.

Dr. Kennett, being a Whig, was not interested in repairing Tory losses or in discrediting the forces of Dissent. Indeed, in his January 31 sermon he treated the republican rebels of the Civil War gently, laying the causes of that conflagration to French intrigue, to fear of Catholicism, and to the general decay of values in the culture.[45] Nevertheless, many feared the potential popularity of the Stuart cause, and Kennett's sermon was attacked for too strongly idealizing the Christian leadership of James I and Charles I. Mary Astell jumped into the fray to defend him, and to second more vehemently his rather lukewarm sentiments about the piety of the "royal martyr." Nothing could have been more delicious to a controversialist like herself than this situation, one in which she could proclaim Puritan culpability for starting the war and warn the public about the present threat posed by the Dissenters to both the established church and to the state—all in the guise of merely corroborating the opinions of a noted theologian from the other party's camp.

Since the occasion for Astell's *An Impartial Enquiry Into the Causes of Rebellion and Civil War in This Kingdom: In an Examination of Dr. Kennett's Sermon Jan 31, 1703/4* (1704) was a commemoration of Charles I's execution, this sixty-four-page piece is more a royalist manifesto than her other political writings that year. In it she made clear that she thought the challenge to traditionally constituted authority was the most serious problem her society faced. The Whigs and the Dissenters were subversive elements against whom sufficiently strong measures had never been taken.

She thought the dangers of papism much overrated and in no way so serious a threat as Dissent. It has already been noted that she admired a number of French Catholic writers and thinkers—Pascal, Descartes, *les messieurs du Port-Royal*, Fénelon. But here she makes explicit her belief that the menace of popery was limited for the most part to some wrongheaded superstitions: "every Doctrine which is profess'd by the Church of *Rome*, is not Popish; GOD forbid it shou'd, for they receive the Holy Scripture and teach the Creeds. But that Superstructure of Hay and Stubble, those Doctrines of Men or Devils, which they have built upon this good Foundation, this is Popery." Dissenter doctrines on the other hand were intrinsically dangerous because deeply saturated with insurrectionist impulses. "*Presbytyrians* or *Whiggs*," she wrote, "or whatever you will call them . . . are all of the same Original, they act upon the same Principles and Motives and tend to the same End, to place the Supreme Power originally in the People, giving them a right . . . to put their *Thoughts* and *Fancies* in Execution."

Defoe answered this pamphlet as well. His *Moderation Maintain'd in Defence of a Compassionate Enquiry into the Causes of the Civil War &c. In a Sermon Preached the thirty-first of January at Aldgate-Church By White Kennett D.D.* (1704) was a continuation of the public discussion of Owen's *Moderation A Vertue*, as well as a reiteration of White Kennett's argument that the Civil War had not been caused by Dissenter cabals but by the widespread profanity of the age, the plays and theaters, nurseries of sin, swearing and profanity, drinking and licentiousness.

Rich Wilkin took care to advertise both *Moderation Truly Stated* and *An Impartial Enquiry Into the Causes of Rebellion and Civil War in This Kingdom* on the back page of *A Fair Way With the Dissenters and Their Patrons*. They cost two shillings apiece, expensive as these things went and twice or four times as much as the other pamphlets he printed, or indeed as most other pamphlets sold in London bookshops. Whether Astell or Wilkin set these prices to give them a kind of upper-class status, or because Astell needed the money, or because they knew that the audience for them would pay that much—or all three—the fact is that Astell's pamphlets were higher-priced than most.

1702, 1703, and 1704 were the years of Astell's greatest public reputation. She became a figure in London society. Her pamphlets were read widely and discussed. One writer included in his own Tory pamphlet of 1704 this praise for her:

> But tho' an Innundation of Faction, Libertinism, and Wickedness be broke in upon us, yet there do appear some few Generous Spirits, who endeavour to Stem the Tide, and express their Fear of God, and Sense of Religion. And truly I cannot forbear to take Notice of one, both for the singularity of the *Person*, and the *Undertaking*: It is a *Heroine*, if I am rightly inform'd, Mrs. A——l, who would Cure them of the *Evil* by Stroaking them with a *Soft and Gentle Hand*. The Treatise truly Answers the Title, *viz. A Fair Way with the Dissenters &c*, and therein she proves *That the Destruction of the Dissenters, as a Party, neither Hurts their Consciences, Persons, nor Estates*. . . . They who please to read it, will find it to be no *Paradox*, and that she hath maintain'd her Position not only with the Air of a Disputant, but the Spirit of a *Christian*.[46]

"Soft" and "gentle" are hardly appropriate adjectives for Astell's prose, although they were *de rigeur* for her sex. But he also notes her skill with paradox, the way "she hath maintain'd her Position not only with the Air of a Disputant, but the Spirit of a *Christian*."

Numbers of admirers came to visit her in her rooms on the second floor of a shared house in Chelsea. Sometimes, in order to better command her own leisure, she impersonated a servant—not hard to do in her simple sober dress—and threw open the second-storey window and called down to her visitors that "Mrs. Astell is not at home." She was enough of a celebrity so that when she wrote in 1706 to Henry Dodwell, the famous nonjuring professor of ancient history, to question the crit-ical point in his recent book *Case in View*, his reply praised her "excellent and ingenious writings," and he signed himself "A hearty honourer of your excellent Endowments, H. Dodwell."[47]

The exchange with Dodwell shows how deeply Astell identified with the nonjurors (those who refused to swear allegiance to William and Mary of Orange on the grounds that they still owed allegiance to James II), both with their loyalty to the Stuarts and with their perse-cution. For their principled recalcitrance, the nonjurors were deprived of their livings, fired from their university posts, and expelled from public office.[48] Among these people, Astell found many admirable ex-amples of those who had become "fools to y.ᵉ World," thus giving proof of their deeper wisdom.

Dodwell had been Camden Professor of Ancient History at Oxford, but as a nonjuror, had been expelled from his post in 1691. George Hickes wrote to Dr. Arthur Charlett of Oxford that year: "We are now in great concern for our poor fellow sufferers of the Universitys some of which will have nothing to subsist on, when they are turned out to the World, and I doubt Mr. Downes, and Mr. Dodwell have not very much."[49] Fortunately, Dodwell did not starve, but was supported by Mr. Francis Cherry, the nonjuring squire of Shottesbrooke, who main-tained a number of these political victims at his own expense.[50]

Astell's letter to Dodwell began by honoring him for the suffering he had undergone for the sake of his beliefs.

> S.ʳ
>
> That truely X.ᵗⁱᵃⁿ Temper, as well as eminent Learning that appears in all y.ʳ Writings; that great Charity & Love to Truth, w.ᶜʰ are w.ⁿ united y.ᵉ Signature of a real Christian, but w.ᶜʰ are of little worth w.ⁿ separated, makes me presume that you will pardon this Address, from one who tho' a Stranger to y.ʳ Person, Sincerely Honours you for y.ʳ Merit, & faithfull Sufferings for the Testimony of y.ʳ Conscience. . . .[51]

But she went on to disagree with what he had written in *Case in View*, a book about the schism in the church and the implications for the behavior of nonjuring clergy. Arguing from orthodox dogma, Astell pointed out what she saw as weak points in Dodwell's arguments. Like her first letter to Norris, this document is a set of closely reasoned questions prepared for a respected thinker, whose other work she knew well, to clear up the inconsistencies she detected.

The point at issue this time was that Dodwell had modified his earlier intractable stance towards the "juring" clergy—those who had recognized William and Mary as the head of the national church. By now an old man, Dodwell had decided that the schism which had meant so much to him in his younger days, and over which he had sacrificed his position and home, was no longer worth contesting. All but one of the original deprived bishops had died, a Stuart was again on the throne, and Dodwell thought the time had come to heal the schism in the church. In *Case in View* he suggested that when the last deprived bishop died (the bishop of Norwich), the remaining nonjurors declare the struggle over, and accept the jurisdiction of their present bishops, whatever their side in the schism. In other words, he recommended that allegiance be once again geographical rather than political.

Astell resisted even this capitulation, on the grounds that individual lay persons could not privately decide to suspend their allegiance to (nonjuring) bishops who had been illegally terminated—that is, who had not been canonically deprived by the true archbishop. Such doctrine gave ordinary people "too great a Latitude, sets us up as Judges of our Spiritual Fathers, giving us Liberty to withdraw our obedience before they are Canonically Deprived, wch is the very thing y.^{t} they who teach us mean to argue agst." Astell's arguments show a thorough familiarity with the theological ins and outs of the nonjuring position, and her letter is studded with references to precedents in the works of various conservative scholars. That she defended the absolute principle of authority with even more certainty than the unyielding Mr. Dodwell, is another index of her die-hard conservatism.

During these years, Astell could often be found in town, spending the afternoon reading in Rich Wilkin's bookshop amidst a row of other booksellers' shops in St. Paul's Churchyard. Wilkin's shop was a kind of headquarters for the High Church faction at that time. Many of the books on his own list were political, all of them High Tory. That was where Astell kept *au courant*, picking up and discussing the latest pamphlets with other writers and other browsers. Much of her political activity of this period was carried on from there. When she corresponded with other writers—like Dodwell or Hickes—she directed them to reply to her at the bookshop. In Wilkin's shop she first heard of John Walker's project to collect information about the sufferings of the Anglican clergy during the interregnum. Walker had been using Wilkin's place as a drop for the information about the treatment of the clergy that various friends and acquaintances were gathering for him.[52] Astell was there one day when Walker stopped in to get his mail, and Wilkin introduced them.

Walker originally began his project as a response to a book by Edmund Calamy, the respected nonconformist divine whose *The Life of Baxter* caused such a furor among the Anglican clergy when it came out in 1702. Richard Baxter had been a moderate Puritan, admired for his temperate theological writings by High and Low Churchmen alike. A chaplain in the parliamentary army, Baxter was known to have restrained his soldiers' zeal when it became violent or excessive, and always preached that the general principles of religion were more important than factionalism. For this reason he had favored the Restoration. Nevertheless, when he complained of the persecution of his Dissenting brethren under James II, he was tried, fined, and imprisoned by the implacable Lord Jeffreys. Calamy's book included a condensed version of Baxter's autobiographical *Narrative*, which he brought up to Baxter's death in 1691, and a summary of Baxter's *English Nonconformity Stated and Argued*. But it was Calamy's ninth chapter, his list of the casualties of the 1662 Act of Uniformity and his evidence of the sufferings of the nonconforming clergy under the Restoration, that made the Anglican churchmen itch for rebuttal, and John Walker set out to counter it with many proofs of the sufferings of the High Church under the Commonwealth.[53]

Many notable Tory divines helped Walker collect the materials for his history. Rich Wilkin may have engaged Mary Astell's aid, for he was one of the printers of Walker's book and was actively involved in the project from the start. Astell, who had kept up her Newcastle connections, agreed to inquire into persecutions of the Anglican clergy in the North during the years of the Commonwealth. She wrote to the current vicar of Newcastle on behalf of Walker, but he had little information to give her.[54]

Then Rich Wilkin himself turned up some documents regarding one Mr. Squire, a well-connected, popular minister who had been turned out of his house and pulpit in 1640 and imprisoned in Gresham College where he was made to sleep upon straw. Wilkin gave Astell these documents—a "life" of Mr. Squire written by Roger Ley, the petition Squire's parishioners presented to Parliament on his behalf, his own speech to Parliament, his deathbed statement of belief and other writings—in order that she might digest them and write out the complete story of Mr. Squire's misfortunes for Walker.

It was a story of the abuse of an upright gentleman at the hands of an unruly and uneducated mob, and it appealed to Astell on every level. Mr. Squire's persecution had begun when, at the outbreak of hostilities in the Civil War, he had preached loyalty to the monarch; an order was obtained from the House of Commons, enforced by the "ignorant rabble" of the place, that his sermon was to be supplemented with a lecture from a "New England man," and finally that he was to be replaced. Astell remarks that his reply to the charges brought against him showed the "Wisdom & Integrity of this excellent Man, & yᶜ Malice & Unreasonableness, yᶜ frivolous as well as unjust allegations of his Accusers, & may serve for an Instance how groundlessly yᶜ Orthodox Clergy were Persecuted." She went on to relate his cheerfulness in the face of his hardships, a sign of God's grace and the supports of true faith.[55]

Astell sent her contribution to Walker in 1706, and he included the account of Mr. Squire's persecutions in his *Sufferings of the Clergy* (1714). He was quick to tell his readers that Astell had been among his contributors, obviously expecting them to know of "the most ingenious Mrs. Astell; to whom I beg leave in this Place to pay my Thanks."

These political years were crucial for Astell. The pamphlet writing was a kind of political and literary apprenticeship for her, forcing her to formulate her views in relation to the other opinions arrayed before the public, and giving her a sense of agency in political matters. Her letter to Dodwell and her participation in Walker's project, two instances of political work undertaken as a private citizen (and there may well have been more for which we have no surviving evidence), both reveal a new ease and boldness in her style, reflecting how often by then she had addressed the public. The new preface that she wrote for the third edition of *Some Reflections Upon Marriage* in 1706 bears the earmarks of her pamphleteering and demonstrates the politicization of her thinking in the intervening six years. In this preface, which has about it the ring of the debating hall, she protests that she is not seditious—as indeed she is not. Expertly she turns to account the political position of her usual opponents, on this matter of marriage. She asks that liberals who did believe in republican government be conscious of the implications of this political position in regard to women, and face up to their inconsistency if they decried tyranny in civic matters but permitted it in private life.

Probably the most significant consequence for Astell of these years of pamphleteering was not to be found in these private acts of solidarity and conviction, however, but in her decision to write her own extended exposition of religion. She had read a great many treatises in preparing her rebuttals of 1704, had thought long and hard about the vexed questions of obedience and conscience in religion. Now she decided to formulate her own conclusions in their philosophical context. In particular, she wanted to answer the threat that Locke's new ideas posed to her brand of Christian Platonism.

Less than nine months after the publication of *A Fair Way With the Dissenters*, Wilkin brought out *The Christian Religion As Profess'd By a Daughter of the Church*. The sympathetic response of at least one reader of the next generation, William Parry, a fellow antiquarian and friend of George Ballard's, to this, Astell's *magnum opus*, was as follows:

> I cannot but esteem Mrs. Astell's Account of her Religion as an excellent Treatise; it is written with that Strength, Perspicuity, and Smoothness, with such Elegance of Diction, such refined Judgement, such an uncommon Spirit of true Christianity & Orthodoxy and supported with such clear, solid, full & convincing Arguments, that I have Scarcely ever read a Book with greater Delight and Satisfaction. In my Opinion, the Learned Authoress hath with great Dexterity and Success retorted Mr. Locke's Metaphysical Artillery against himself, confuted his whimsical Idea of *Thinking* Matter, and given him a genteel Foil. She has stripped him of his Disguise in personating a Clergyman, and yet writing like a Socinian; and has fairly shewn the Imperfections and erroneous Tenets contain'd in those Two Tracts of his, *The Reasonableness of Christianity* and *The Ladies Religion*: and has convinced me, that he had no honest Design in writing either of them . . . instead of promoting Christianity they tend rather to undermine and subvert the True Faith, and are derogatory to the Honour of our Saviour.[56]

Wilkin continued the Astell revival with a second edition of *Letters Concerning the Love of God* a few months after the publication of *The Christian Religion* in 1705. He had already reissued a second edition of *Some Reflections Upon Marriage* in 1703, and a fourth edition of *A Serious Proposal in Two Parts* in 1704. By 1705, with the publication of this new work on philosophy and religion, all four of Astell's major writings were in print (counting two parts of *A Serious Proposal* as one)—as well as two long topical pamphlets. She had become a significant force in the literary world of London; her contemporary reputation was assured. Her intelligence, her class and erudition, and her energy had brought her a long way from the desperate and starving young woman who had thrown herself upon Archbishop Sancroft's mercy so many long years before.

Throughout this narrative, I have referred to Astell's connection with Francis Atterbury, bishop of Rochester, the political and religious leader who defended the Tory cause and masterminded its strategies from the

Glorious Revolution until his exile from England in 1723. Astell followed Atterbury's career with great interest, both as a family friend and a political ally. On at least one occasion she ventured to advise him, with a self-confidence that astonished him.

In truth, Astell was better friends with Mrs. Catherine Atterbury, Atterbury's wife, than with the good bishop of Rochester, who had less use for the companionship of women than his good friend Jonathan Swift. Catherine Atterbury was fairly well-educated. She had grown up near Oxford, daughter of a cultured country parson, the Reverend Osborne, who was a coattail relative to the duke of Leeds. Their proximity to the university gave Reverend Osborne the opportunity of teaching French to the young gentlemen there. Catherine Osborne's marriage to Francis Atterbury was said to have been a love match; she was a great beauty, and also brought her husband a fortune of £7,000.[57]

The Atterburys' house in Chelsea was not large, but it had a pleasant garden and a view of the river. It was roomy enough for their servants and three growing children. Here Mrs. Atterbury kept a good table, as Swift found during his lonely year in Chelsea; he was grateful for her warm hospitality. Catherine Atterbury often managed things alone when Atterbury stayed in town, for he maintained his official lodgings at Bridewell near the Temple as a convenient pied-à-terre when business kept him overnight.[58]

Astell was an occasional guest at the Atterburys' house. It was but a short walk from her lodgings, and she enjoyed Catherine Atterbury's company as a practical, informed woman who understood the ins and outs of Tory politics. A letter from Lord Stanhope to Atterbury in December of 1706 refers to Mrs. Astell as that "female friend and witty companion of your wife's."[59]

From time to time Mrs. Astell would engage Francis Atterbury in conversation about the High Church cause, about which they were both extremely concerned and well informed. Atterbury is the probable author of one of the answers to D'Avenant's *Essays* for instance, published at the same time as Astell's "Prefatory Discourse."[60] They also saw eye to eye about the need to defend Sacheverell.

One of the elements of Atterbury's public life, as Astell was well aware, was the bishop's enmity towards Benjamin Hoadley, the leading spokesman for the Whig faction among the Anglican clergy. It was inevitable, given their politics and capabilities, that they should square off as leaders of rival factions within the church, and engage in hand-to-hand combat as it were, during the battles over liberty of conscience and authority. G. V. Bennett describes Benjamin Hoadley thus from the Tory perspective.

Francis
Atterbury,
bishop of
Rochester.
Portrait by
G. Kneller. By
permission of the
Governing Body,
Christ Church,
Oxford.

For a generation he teased and sneered at his opponents, and without a shadow of a doubt he was the most detested Anglican clergyman of his day. In no way could Hoadley be described as an attractive figure. He was diminutive in stature with a bulbous, unequally shaped face. An illness during his Cambridge days had left him so crippled that he could walk only with the aid of crutches and had to preach kneeling on a cushion. His mind was logical, his view of religion bare and prosaical, and he had made the whole apparatus of Locke's theory of government his own. That this courted deep unpopularity he was fully aware, and he observed without dismay that his style of preaching had emptied the pews of his London church. His sermons were practically never upon any topic of Christian faith and devotion: heavy, unadorned, remorseless, their one concern was to savage and demolish the Tory view of Church and State.[61]

In September of 1705, on the occasion of the election of the lord mayor of London, Hoadley preached a sermon in St. Paul's designed to antagonize the Tories by calling into question the interpretation of one of the standard biblical texts supporting the doctrine of nonresistance, Chapter 13 of St. Paul's *Epistle to the Romans*: "Let every soul be subject to the higher powers." Relentlessly Hoadley reversed the usual understanding of the passage. Any ruler, he argued, who acted in a manner contrary to virtue and the just deserts of his people, violated the injunction to "be subject to the higher powers" and thus forfeited his claim to obedience. Obedience was due only to those whose requirements were fair and just, and not to those whose demands were tyrannical.

The sermon was published later that year, with an extended section on the people's right to refuse to submit to rulers who were trying to rob them of liberty, property, and freedom of conscience. To comply with such tyranny—to practice passive obedience under such circumstances—said Hoadley in *The Measures of Submission to the Civil Magistrate* (1705), would appear to act more against the will of God than to mutiny against lawful authority. Given the current debates over punishment for the nonjurors and the rights and wrongs of the Occasional Conformity Bill, the publication of this sermon could only be perceived as an outrage and affront by the Tory clergy. Atterbury led the retaliatory attack, organizing the Lower House of Convocation to deliver a vote of censure against the sermon as a "scandal" and a "grave dishonour" to the church. He himself also preached a sermon against Hoadley's *Measures* in which he defended the doctrine of divinely ordained authority.

This was as far as things had gone when the Atterburys dined one night with Astell, and the issue of Hoadley's sermon and Atterbury's answer came up. She had followed the interchange with great interest and told Atterbury that he ought to print his sermon, since in this instance the church cause needed more publicity. But she thought that it ought to be fortified somewhat, for he had left himself open to counterattack in several places. Without revealing her motives she asked if she might read it more carefully, and he sent it over to her the next day.

Astell intended to give constructive suggestions for emendation. She had offered her services in all seriousness, as a comrade-in-arms, for was she not a seasoned veteran in political controversy by this time? Had she not read widely and thought deeply about these very questions? It is not clear what Atterbury expected, whether adulation or silence. But he was dumbfounded when she returned him his sermon with a sheet of corrections. He had not expected the effrontery of actual criticism. When he wrote about the incident to George Smalridge, bishop of Bristol, he characterized it as an attack upon him rather than as a set of constructive and neighborly suggestions.

Dr George —

I happen'd about a fortnight agoe to dine with Mrs Astell. She spoke to me of my Sermon & desired me to Print it: & after I had given her the proper answers, hinted to me that she should be glad of perusing it. I comply'd with her & sent her the Sermon the next day. Yesterday she return'd it with this sheet of Remarks, wch I cannot forbear communicating to you because I take 'em to be of an extraordinary Nature, considering that they came from the Pen of a Woman. Indeed one would not imagine that a Woman had written 'em. There is not an expression that carries the least Air of her Sex from the Begining to the End of it. She attacks me very home you see, & Artfully enough, under a Pretence of taking my Part against other Divines, who are in Hoadley's measure. Had she as much good Breeding as good sense, she would be perfect: but she had not the most decent manner of insinuating what she means, but is now or then a little offensive & shocking in her expressions; wch I wonder at because a Civil Turn of Words (even where the matter is not pleasing) is what her Sex is always Mistress of. She, I think, is wanting in it. But her Sensible & rational Way of Writing makes amends for that defect, *if indeed any Thing can make amends for it.* [Ballard's italics] I dread to engage her; so I only wrote a general civil Answer to her & leave the rest to an oral conference with her. Her way of solving the Difficulty about swearing to the Queen is somewhat singular.[62]

George Ballard, in writing about the incident forty years later, anxious to shield "this excellent Gentlewoman" from any accusation of unladylike vehemence ("Rough & unpolish'd" talk), conjectures that she gave her address a little more force than usual when speaking to Atterbury because she knew that "this warm Prelate" was unlikely to credit the intelligence of a woman's remarks. According to Ballard, Atterbury's conversation characteristically condescended to women, and as Astell had known him for many years and was well aware of these attitudes, "she might probably sharpen her Style designedly when she had that lucky opportunity of conversing with him. . . ." Ballard then embarked on a lengthier defense of her character, reconstructed from stories of people who had known her.[63]

If she was deficient in the little niceties & punctilios in the Arts of Address it's not at all to be wonder'd at by those who are acquainted with her retired & studious way of Life, for she was so wholly wrapt up in Philosophical, Metaphysical & Theological & indeed all kinds of Divine Speculations, that she had but small opportunities of making her self acquainted with the Worlds Theatre or any of it's Appendages: So that a Thinking

Person, or one that had had but a small share of candour or good nature wou'd readily & easily have made allowances upon this Score, & not have troubled the World with such uncharitable Exclamations, for so small a Transgression.

Ballard went on to remark that studious people commonly were not skilled in the social graces, although he had never before heard that particular charge laid to Mrs. Astell. Quite the contrary, he said, her writings on "Decency & Decorum" in *The Christian Religion* showed her to have given some thought to these matters, and she was always one to practice what she preached. "Her *Life & Doctrine* was exactly conformable," he wrote, "unspotted & all of a Piece." Certainly she had behaved with "good Breeding & equanimity of Temper" in her dispute with Mr. Locke, he went on, "but I think her famous Controversy with D.ʳ Davenant is a far more excellent proof what an exact Mistress she was of *Decency* & *Decorum*; for as the controversy was about Religion & the advantage of her Country, these were Topicks which (if any) wou'd admit of a warmth of Zeal somewhat extravagant, & yet I dare venture to challenge the most captious Reader to find me out one uncharitable Word or indecent expression. And perhaps, no Controversy of that kind was ever managed with more Temper, art, & Gentility."

Bishop Atterbury, on the other hand, was known for his acrimony and intemperate language. Given his high temper, wrote Ballard, "I need not wonder at the angry resentment which M.ʳˢ Astells sheet of remarks drew from him. His great Friend D.ʳ Smalridge used to complain that he was forced to carry water after him where ever he came to quench the Flames he had raised. I mention none of these things to reproach this Learned Prelate, but purely to shew the small Reason he had to upbraid M.ʳˢ Astell with a fault w.ᶜʰ he himself was so notoriously guilty of." Ballard went on to say that were he to use the same rule to censure Atterbury that Atterbury had used with Astell—that nothing could make amends for incivility—all of Atterbury's considerable attainments would have to be dismissed.

Ballard's reading of the incident seems a likely interpretation. Astell had learned to trust her judgment on political matters and in this instance neglected to sugar the pill that she administered to Atterbury. She did not try to "handle" him; she simply told him what she thought. She too had read the vitriolic *A Letter to the Reverend Dr. Francis Atterbury concerning Virtue and Vice* (1707) directed by Hoadley and his minions at Atterbury following the censure in Convocation. And she had some suggestions about how to deal with their accusations.[64]

In retrospect, it seems that Atterbury could have used some help in framing his reply; perhaps he should have followed Astell's advice. What happened next was that Atterbury chose the next Lord Mayor's Day as the symbolic occasion for a refutation of Hoadley's *Measures*, and arranged to preach a sermon from the same text Hoadley had used: "Let every soul be subject to the higher powers." Atterbury then arranged his rebuttal to be printed simultaneously in Latin and English and distributed publicly—where alas! it soon proved vulnerable to Hoadley's relentless logic. As G. V. Bennett has remarked: "Even one of Atterbury's friends had to admit that 'Hoadly has made most sad stuff of his late Latin [sermon], and what is most sad he has maul'd the Dean with his words.' "[65]

One last encounter deserves emphasis in this consideration of Astell's career in the reign of Queen Anne, both because it was her last public encounter of that era, and because it defines another aspect of her counter-Enlightenment thought. If she disputed Hobbes's conception of a "state of nature," if she denied Locke's assumption that one began in the world as a spiritual tabula rasa but somehow managed in the course of experience to inscribe that blank slate with immaterial thought, and if she objected to Defoe's assertion (after Locke) that the people had the right to choose their own rulers, then it ought to come as no surprise that on the question of a free marketplace of ideas, that bourgeois capitalist model for intellectual advancement, she disagreed fundamentally with Shaftesbury.

Anthony Ashley Cooper, third earl of Shaftesbury, author of *Characteristics of Men, Manners, Opinions, Times* (1711) and founder of the "moral sense" school of philosophy, was just the sort of deistical liberal thinker whom Mary Astell detested. She considered his thought weak and sentimental, and dangerous to the social order. But as he was a powerful writer and the most careful proponent of these emerging ideas, she felt compelled to reply to them. After a little urging from her friends—with whom, no doubt, she had amply aired her opinions of what she had read—she wrote her last book, *Bart'lemy Fair: or, An Enquiry After Wit* (1709), her answer to his *A Letter Concerning Enthusiasm* (1708), which later became the first treatise of *Characteristics*.

Originally a private letter addressed to Lord Somers, Shaftesbury's *A Letter Concerning Enthusiasm* was occasioned by the activity of a group of French Protestant enthusiasts known to us as "the French Prophets," who had come to England seeking toleration in 1706. By 1708 they had become enough of a public nuisance that there was talk of silencing them legally. Their movement had begun in Dauphiné, a few years after the revocation of the Edict of Nantes, when a sixteen-year-old shepherdess named Isabeau Vincent, who had already spoken and sung ecstatically in her sleep, was taken with fits, and prophesied the end of the persecution of the Huguenots. These symptoms of religious hysteria spread; people in Languedoc as well had visions and fell into trances. Many took the phenomena as omens that their trials were coming to an end, and determined to take up arms against their oppressors. They began to engage in a kind of guerilla warfare with royalist troops in the mountainous region on the border of Spain. And then in 1706 three of these Camisards, as they were called, came to England. Although they had an immediate audience of forty or fifty thousand Huguenots already living in London, they were also interested in publishing their views to a larger public, and began to spread the word of the coming apocalypse and the need for repentance.[66]

The English, in the throes of their own internal controversy about religious toleration, were not receptive to these enthusiasts. However much sympathy they deserved for being hounded from papist France, no one welcomed the example of these *inspirées*, with their seizures and mystical visions, not even the most zealous nonconformists. Disapproving tracts, broadsides, pamphlets against them began to appear.[67] Their grimaces and gyrations were denounced from many a pulpit as being demonically inspired, the result of inflamed imaginations, or the sheerest charlatanism:

> the Agitations of these pretended Prophets are only the Effects of a voluntary Habit, of which they are entirely Masters, though in their Fits they seem to be agitated by a Superior Cause. . . . But the Way in which they make the Spirit speak, is still more unworthy of him, which is by perpetual Hesitations, Childish Repetitions, unintelligible Stuff, gross Contradictions, manifest Lies, Conjectures turned into Predictions, already convicted of Falsehood by the Event; or some moral Precepts, which may be heard every day much better expressed, and have nothing new but the Grimaces, with which they are accompanied.[68]

Such was the context in which Shaftesbury wrote *A Letter Concerning Enthusiasm*, a generous-spirited bid for rational response to these enthusiasts. It was absurd, he said, to try to legislate in matters of religion any more than one should legislate the proper way to do mathematics or the standards for wit. Religious fervor, he said, was a kind of temporary insanity, a "Pannick"—like being in love—and until it passed, the person seized by it was not likely to hear any criticism. The best way to handle the distasteful excess and extravagance of the

French prophets was not by withdrawing the famed English liberty of
conscience, but by ridiculing them, exposing them to the laughter they
deserved. In the present instance, he continued, he had heard that a
puppet show about them had been mounted in Bartholomew Fair, that
yearly collection of open markets and sideshows which, in spite of
protests from the neighbors, mushroomed for two weeks every August
in the yard of the old priory of St. Bartholomew, Smithfield.[69] This
was by far the best way to treat such extreme ideas, he said. Truth
would always bear up under ridicule and the rest would simply drop
away. Provided the investigation was mannerly, he said, religion could
not be treated with "too much good Humor, or [examined] with too
much Freedom & Familiarity." To legislate against the French prophets
would elevate them to the status of martyrs. It was more effective simply
to subject them to this "Bart'lemy Fair method," and to dismiss them.
With mock sympathy, he pretended to pity their fate:

> But how barbarous & more than heathenishly cruel are we tolerating
> English Men! For not contented to deny these Prophesying Enthusiasts
> the Honor of a Persecution, we have deliver'd 'em over to the cruellest
> Contempt in the World. I am told they are at this time the subject of a
> choice Droll or Puppet-Show at Bart'lemy-Fair. There doubtless their strange
> Voices and involuntary Agitations are admirably well acted, by the Motion
> of Wires, and the Inspiration of Pipes.

Why, if the Jews had but the idea to put on puppet-shows about Jesus,
he went on, "I am apt to think they wou'd have done our Religion
more harm, than by all their other ways of Severity."
  Astell was appalled by these attitudes. She believed in a very personal God, an Authority to be reckoned with and treated with utmost
respect; Shaftesbury wrote about religion conceptually, as a set of propositions to be bandied about in the free marketplace of ideas. Everything
she had ever written assumed that religious belief could be—ought to
be—founded on a series of strictly logical propositions, beginning with
recognizing the centrality of human reason. And here was Shaftesbury
saying that religion was a "Pannick," founded on overheated, superstitious feeling, and that Christianity might have been blighted in the bud
had it been subjected to ridicule in its early days. She certainly did not
approve of the French prophets, but she did not think religion a fit
subject for ridicule under any circumstances:

> For until this Blessed Age of *Liberty*! which has made us so much Wiser
> than our Fathers, and that Men of Wit, found it turn to their Account to

be thought Men of Business; it was never thought a Service to the Public to expose the Establish'd Religion, no not when it was ever so false and ridiculous in it self, to the Contempt of the People.[70]

Astell did not know exactly who had written *A Letter Concerning Enthusiasm*, although she knew it was someone of an aristocratic, educated, Whiggish stamp, someone connected to the Kit-Kat Club. Those were its sentiments, and she had heard that the *Letter* had originally been addressed to Lord Somers, a prominent Kit-Kat member. This club "consisted of the principal noblemen and gentlemen who opposed the arbitrary measures of James II, and conduced to bring about the Revolution."[71] It was an eating and drinking club, taking its name from a favorite pie-man, Christopher Cat, who operated at the sign of the Cat and Fiddle on Shire Lane. There the Kit-Kat Club celebrated King William's anniversary each year with great *bonhomie*, and discussed matters of state. Addison was a member, and Steele could often be found there. Bishop Hoadley was a frequent visitor. It was, in short, a Whig inner sanctum, where like-minded liberal thinkers came together to talk and drink. A contemporary wag celebrated them this way:

> I am the founder of your loved Kit-Kat,
> A club that gave direction to the State:
> 'Twas there we first instructed all our youth
> To talk profane, and laugh at sacred truth:
> We taught them how to boast, and rhyme,
> and bite,
> To sleep away the day, and drink away
> the night.[72]

Mary Astell opened her *Bart'lemy Fair: Or, An Enquiry After Wit*, with a dedication addressed "to the most Illustrious Society of the Kit-Cats," which accused members of this club of living in wanton indulgence, beating their creditors, seducing virtuous women, and wasting a lot of money. "Can anything be more ridiculous, than that the Fool shou'd have Money enough to throw away upon every Extravagancy, whilst the Ingenious is crampt for want of it in his generous Undertakings for the Good of Mankind!" asked impecunious and ingenious Mrs. Astell. These men were all deists and Socinians, libertines and malicious wits, she said. And as for the *Letter* itself, she quoted Boileau, as translated by Dryden and Sir William Sloane:

> . . . for in our scribling times
> No fool can want a sot to praise his rhymes:
> The flattest work has ever, in the court,
> Met with some zealous ASS for its support:
> And in all times a forward, scribling fop
> Has found some greater fool to cry him up.
>
> Canto I, *Art of Poetry*

At first Astell actually thought Steele might have written *A Letter Concerning Enthusiasm*. She also suspected Swift as one of his "Prompters," Swift being at that time a Whig like his patron, Sir William Temple.[73] This is undoubtedly why Astell chose "Mr. Wotton" as her pseudonym for this work, because Wotton was famous for having opposed Sir William Temple on the question of the relative merits of modern and ancient authors, a debate immortalized by Swift in his mock epic *The Battle of the Books* (1704).[74] What also endeared Wotton to Astell was his belief in women's education. She was fond of quoting from his *Reflections Upon Ancient and Modern Learning* (1694) to the effect that a century earlier, Greek and Latin had been modish acquirements for women, "and *Plato* and *Aristotle* untranslated, were frequent ornaments of their Closets."[75]

But although Astell was at first mistaken about Swift or Steele's connection with *A Letter Concerning Enthusiasm*, she knew the sort to whom she was speaking: someone bold and confident, very much in the spirit of the new way of ideas, hailing liberty, scornful of the restraints of the past, optimistic about the natural order which would be laid bare when the encrustations of custom and superstition were scoured away. "The *Letter*, in a word," said Astell, "is a very *Drawcansir* of a Book. It *cuts and slashes* all that Men have hitherto accounted Sacred; is so *fierce a Hero*, as to *fright* the *Good Christian*."[76]

Astell was quite right in recognizing a serious adversary in the writer of *A Letter Concerning Enthusiasm*. Shaftesbury's thinking had been molded by Locke, who had been retained by the first earl of Shaftesbury for that purpose, to supervise the education of the heir apparent. Shaftesbury held the optimistic view of mankind subscribed to by forward-thinking natural philosophers of his day, that human beings left to their own devices would gradually find their way to the Good. With an attitude that found its best representation later in the century in Rousseau, Shaftesbury believed that the problem lay in repression, in external pressures that distorted the natural process. People were by nature sensible, rational beings, and if they were not manipulated, sooner or later they would arrive at the truth of any matter.

Mary Astell was disturbed by the lack of attention to any kind of self-discipline in such a formulation; "in our Father's Days, excessive and unrestrain'd Liberty might perhaps be call'd Licentiousness," she reproved. She was aware that her point of view was old-fashioned, and that *A Letter Concerning Enthusiasm* had been very well received by urbane Londoners: "it is cry'd up as a *Non-Pariello* for Language, Thought, and all that—'Tis industriously spread in the nation; put, by way of ABC, into the hands of every young Fellow, who begins to speak great swelling Words. . . . And sent, by way of Mission, into Foreign Parts." Nevertheless, these newfangled notions held by the young Whig Lords—not to mention the way they conducted themselves—were a betrayal of the ideas she had been raised on.

> Our Antient *English* Peerage were of another strain; they were not more remarkable for their Loyalty to their Prince, than their Piety to their GOD. They subdu'd themselves, as well as their Enemies. Their Health was not consum'd in Debauchery, nor were their Estates squander'd in Vanity, Gaming and luxury; but Genrously bestow'd in Charity, Hospitality and Liberality. Real Merit only obtain'd their Friendship; and whatever a Man's Outward Circumstances might be, if his Mind was great enough to emulate and follow, much more if it was able to set a Pattern of the most Generous, Virtuous and Noble Actions, he was duly qualify'd for their Esteem and Kindness. . . . They despis'd a Man who wou'd forsake his own Reason, and blindly follow other Men's; who wou'd violate his Conscience to make his Fortune or save his Estate; and who had either no Principles, or such as wou'd conform to every Fashion.[77]

Astell's image of a mythologized English patriarchy shows her basically feudal impulse when registering the changes she witnessed in her society. How could "men of wit" or "men of business" compare with such idealized integrity? Their "freedom" was really a kind of ignominious enslavement to the senses, to the material world, whereas the dignity and restraint of the forefathers had been true liberty. She thought it a bad trade to exchange established institutions, faith, and stability for a Whig notion of "liberty."

Astell argued cogently, if longwindedly, for this point of view. To begin with, wit was not the same thing as reason. Locke himself had said that it lay "quite on the other side of Judgment." Did the author of the *Letter* think it possible to laugh war out of existence? Should magistrates lead the disputants who stood before them to a Smithfield booth to soothe their passions and divert their anger? Ridicule was hardly an infallible test of truth. If a man was told that his house was on fire, it was probably not the wisest course for him to ridicule the statement and the speaker. Columbus would never have reached America if Isabella and Ferdinand had subjected his initial proposal to the "Bart'lemy Fair method."

"Good manners" had nothing to do with it either. Should murder or theft be sanctioned if the crime were committed in a mannerly fashion? How could this sophisticated new generation be expected to be able to talk sense about religion, when they had never had any real experience of its precepts or assumptions? It was like hearing a man "Born under the Line, who had never been out of his own Climate, had not convers'd but with his own Countrymen, discourse of the Snows and Frosts in *Greenland*."[78]

As for herself, she was familiar with both territories, and knew how to argue for the existence of God against such as these who subscribed to the new sort of rationalism. If there were no God, she asked, how did the world come into existence? It cannot have existed eternally— "Mathematics as well as Divinity, have discover'd too many Absurdities in the Supposition." No one who had seriously considered the descriptions of matter offered by the new science could dispense easily with the notion of a causal Intelligence. "Shew us then, some New and Better way of Accounting for our own Being, and the Origin of the World, if you reject that of an Infinitely Perfect and Self-Existing Mind, the Maker and Governor of all Things."[79]

The heart of Astell's critique lay in rejecting Shaftesbury's assumption that all ideas had an equal chance of being recognized and adopted in his "free" marketplace of ideas. As she well knew, no one was ever unencumbered by previous commitments, pressures, and preexisting *idées fixes*, as Shaftesbury's model posited. No one was ever as free as Shaftesbury's line of reasoning required humans to be in order to judge the truth for themselves. For one thing, "marketplace" thinking was not possible so long as power relations among people were unequal. Rank, property, titles, would have to be abolished before all ideas could be approached with utter neutrality. She understood very well that the "Bart'lemy Fair method" could only work in the most ideal circumstances—circumstances that had never yet obtained in the real world:

> Were *Matters ballanc'd*, were no other *Force* us'd but that of *Wit and Raillery*, *Reason* wou'd have *fair play*, Mankind wou'd *flourish*. *Wonderful* wou'd be *the Harmony and Temper* arising from *all these Contrarieties*, they wou'd make up that *right Humor*, which the Letter *contends* for, as going more than half way toward *Thinking rightly* of every thing. And Men *being mildly treated, and let alone*, they wou'd never Rage to that degree, as to

occasion *Blood-shed, Wars, Persecutions, and Devastations in the World*; which proceed from nothing else but their being put out of Humor, by not being permitted to do what they Will.[80]

She mocked Shaftesbury's optimism, his vision of potential harmony and good humor, reminding her readers of the *"Blood-shed, Wars, Persecutions, and Devastations in the World,"* much as Voltaire would do later in that burlesque of the best of all possible worlds, *Candide*. Astell fully understood the pull of such utopian belief in "the natural"—as she understood the appeal of empiricism, of democracy, and of the cultural relativism that these new ideas implied. But she braced herself to resist that pull, because she saw that what was to be sacrificed was a belief in absolute authority, the cornerstone of an ethical system, and—to her mind—the only means to lasting civil peace.

We do not know at this distance how the public responded to *Bart'lemy Fair*. Presumably there was a small, select circle of religious Tories who consistently read and appreciated her work. It seems unlikely that the opposition saw her—a single, middle-aged woman of no family or fortune—as a serious threat to their new liberal philosophy; so rarely did anyone seriously question the new values of material success, wit and style, sophisticated cynicism, and an internationalism born of extended commerce, that Astell's points must have seemed hopelessly antiquated.

Within a matter of months, Astell found herself satirized twice in *The Tatler*. The first time was in number 32, where she was portrayed as the leader of a set of ladies of quality who some years before "gave out that Virginity was to be their State of Life during this mortal Condition, and therefore resolved to join their Fortunes, and erect a Nunnery. . . . *Madonella*, a Lady who had writ a fine Book concerning the recluse Life [was] the Projectrix of the Foundation." Mr. Tatler—whether Steele or Swift is a matter of dispute—then told an anecdote in which a shrewd rake, who wanted to worm his way into her school to get at the young women, is able to dupe Madonella because her mind is so fixed upon airy abstractions that she does not understand the realities of the world. So earnest is she in her crusading intellectualism and piety, that she fails to recognize the ulterior motives of the young man. He pretends to have come to speak to her about her writings, and she falls for his ruse, replying, absolutely deadpan: "If what I have said could have contributed to raise any thoughts in you that may make for the advancement of intellectual and divine Conversation, I should think myself extremely happy." It is as if she were always so busy looking above the heads of her interlocutors to some vision of her own that she missed the expressions on their faces.

Three months later, a second installment in *The Tatler* reported that Madonella "who, as 'twas thought, had long since taken her Flight towards the Aetherial Mansions, still walks, it seems, in the Regions of Mortality," and characterized her educational philosophy as a desire "to imprint true Idea's of Things on the tender Souls of those of her Sex" so that they might "arrive at such a Pitch of Perfection, as to be above the Laws of Matter and Motion; Laws which are considerably enforced by the Principles usually imbibed in Nurseries and Boarding Schools. To remedy this Evil," continued the speaker mockingly, "she has laid the Scheme of a College for young Damsels; where, instead of Scissors, Needles, and Samplers; Pens, Compasses, Quadrants, Books, Manuscripts, Greek, Latin, and Hebrew, are to take up their whole Time. Only on Holidays the Students will, for moderate Exercise, be allowed to divert themselves with the Use of some of the lightest and most voluble Weapons; and proper Care will be taken to give them at least a superficial Tincture of the Antient and Modern Amazonian Tactics." Astell shared the honors of this second *Tatler* column with two other women of her age who had the effrontery to wield the pen: Mrs. Manley ("the Writer of *Memoirs from the Mediterranean*, who, by the Help of some artificial Poisons conveyed by Smells, has within these few weeks brought many Persons of both Sexes to an untimely Fate") and Mrs. Elstob ("who is now publishing Two of the choicest *Saxon* Novels, which are said to have been in [as] great Repute with the Ladies of Queen *Emma's* Court")—two utterly opposite and unlike figures, but for their common gender and propensity to "scribble."

If Swift was the author of these columns, and it probably was he, we must remember how little use he had for the theoretical or abstract. He disapproved of all schemes which separated the intellectual and academic from the rest of life. The quadrants and compasses of Madonella's school foreshadow the absurd proclivities of the Laputans in Book III of *Gulliver's Travels* (1726), even if Madonella herself was a stock character, the "learned woman," presented to the public with increasing frequency ever since Molière's *Les Précieuses* (1659). But this was also the image of herself that Astell projected, never doubting for a minute that life could be lived according to Platonic principles, or that great overriding ideas could dissolve the complexities of material circumstances.

This is what Swift—or Steele—could not swallow. Mr. Tatler doubted the central premise of *A Serious Proposal Part II*: that there are "true Idea's of Things" which can be deduced by reason and taught in the abstract. He was impatient with theory that took leave of reality; the Laputans constructed an ill-fitting suit for Gulliver with their quadrants, rules, and compasses. Moreover, Swift's attitude towards women was extremely complicated, a combination of sneering condescension towards their intellectual ambitions, with a real appreciation of their common sense and practical intelligence.[81] It is not surprising that he was especially allergic to Astell's combination of Platonism and feminism. This much is clear: from his opening gambit with its double entendre to the neologism "projectrix," Mr. Tatler did not take Astell or her proposal seriously for a minute.

Astell was sure that these columns were reprisals for *Bart'lemy Fair*, and that Shaftesbury, smarting over the attack on his *Letter*, had set Steele upon her.[82] She was willing to forgive Steele his part in the satire, as she said, because in satirizing her old-fashioned idea of virtue he was writing against the grain; and in other columns he condemned "his friends," these modern empirically minded types. Besides, she explained wryly, he plagiarized from her in his *The Ladies Library* (1714), and that after all was the highest form of flattery.

> The Tatler tells a Tale very agreeably, when he pleases, but he has Scatter'd none of his Attic Salt on this. One cannot help pitying him to see how he writes against the Grain, and labours under the Task his noble Benefactors impos'd. The harmless Satyr does not bite; and tho' it shew'd its Teeth against the *Proposal to the Ladies*, our honest *Compilator* has made an honourable Amends to the Author, (I know not what he has to the Book-Seller) by transcribing above an hundred Pages in to his *Ladies Library*, *verbatim*; except in a few Places, which if the Reader takes the Trouble to compare, perhaps he will not find improv'd. He has also made Satisfaction to Religion, in several Papers, particularly in Tatler III. where he treats his Friends with proper, but coarser Language, than the *Enquirer* [i.e., Astell] thought fit to use.[83]

Her only complaint about Steele's lampoons was that he unnecessarily dragged in her friends, Lady Elizabeth Hastings and her three half-sisters Lady Anne, Lady Frances, and Lady Catherine, none of whom had had anything to do with the plan behind *A Serious Proposal*. "But tho' the Enquirer [i.e., Astell] had offended the Tatler, and his great Friends, on whom he so liberally bestows his Panegyrics, by turning their Ridicule very justly upon themselves; what had any of her Acquaintance done to provoke him? Who does he point at? For she knows of none who ever attempted to erect a Nunnery, or declar'd, That Virginity was to be their State of Life." Did the *Tatler* mean these ladies—"three or four Noble Orphans who chose to live (in Town as well as Country) with a Gentleman and his Wife, their Relations"—to be two of the "nuns" so ridiculed? If so, he should be informed that "this was long before the Enquirer had the Honour of their Acquaintance."[84]

Astell's response to Shaftesbury in 1709 was the last new thing that she wrote for a public audience. She reissued it with a new preface in 1722 because the birth of Prince Charles in 1721 had renewed Jacobite hopes on the Continent (and Walpole had renewed his campaign against them) with what results we have seen. By 1710 she was developing a cataract which made it more difficult for her to do so much close work. But she probably also stopped writing and publishing because she recognized that the weight of history was against her. Her last two works had not sold well; she was being lampooned in the public papers as a peculiar old maid. She had probably overstayed her welcome in the world of letters. It was time to leave the acts of public vigilance to others.

She also stopped writing because in 1709 she opened a charity school for the daughters of outpensioners of the Royal Hospital; and it would have been unseemly to remain in public controversy after that. Since 1694 she had been actively proselytizing for female education. Now it seemed there was a chance to do something practical about it. A number of the wealthy women with whom she had developed intimate friendships in the last few years were willing to contribute substantially to help open a school in Chelsea under the auspices of the Royal Hospital. They wanted to engage her as headmistress. Perhaps the time had come once again to change the focus of her life.

Chapter Eight
The Company She Keeps

Now I am loath to abandon all Thoughts of Friendship, both because it is one of the brightest Vertues, and because I have the noblest Designs in it. Fain wou'd I rescue my Sex, or at least as many of them as come within my little Sphere, from that Meanness of Spirit into which the Generality of 'em are sunk. . . .

    Mary Astell to John Norris, All Saints Eve, 1693

As I am dear madam finishing this most long letter I receive a fresh instance of my endless obligations from my most valuable Betty Hastings of the thing I most love of all eatables a most fine pot of char which I long for and did not know where to get I know it will give yr Lsp much pleasure to tell you this truth as it gave me to receive it from your kind and obliging hands to be beyond my expressions. . . .

    Lady Catherine Jones to Lady Elizabeth Hastings, April 4, 1738

The Chelsea school was Astell's project from idea to execution, and not surprisingly, it entirely occupied her attention in its early years. To begin with, she had to convince a number of wealthy Chelsea citizens to subsidize it, including the governor and the lieutenant governor of the Chelsea Royal Hospital, where it was to be housed. She helped to plan it, ordering linen and smocks and spelling books, deciding on a curriculum, and she helped to keep it financially afloat by arranging for the annual charity sermon and collecting the annual pledge from its regular subscribers. These new duties, as well as the unwelcome satirical notices in the press, account for Astell's withdrawal from the public world which was, in any case, only marginally appropriate to her as a gentlewoman.

The Chelsea school has long been the central thing noted about Astell in histories of women's education and rights.[1] It is a good symbol to memorialize her, for it was the visible sign of her cherished belief in women's education, as well as being utterly characteristic of London social reform in this period. It also involved three of her closest friends, women who were her patrons and associates the rest of her life.

Soon after the establishment of the Society for the Propagation of Christian Knowledge in 1699, that organization began to agitate throughout London and the rest of England for the Christian education of the parish poor. These charity schools—privately endowed by people of quality in each neighborhood but coordinated and staffed by the SPCK—became the rage of English social reformers from all walks of life. The idea was to save the souls of poor young innocents in an era of atheism and fashionable skepticism. More to the point, the schools were meant to rescue, clean up, and discipline a potential labor force from hundreds of orphans and children of indigent or not-so-indigent lowlifes of the city, children who swarmed the streets of London committing acts of petty thievery to keep alive, or who constituted a present and potential drain on the coffers of their country parishes.[2] The charity schools taught basic literacy to these children, and then placed them in service or in apprenticeships. The function of the schools was not to educate the children to rise above their station as "hewers of wood and drawers of water," nor to fit them for an elaborate life of the mind. They were clothed in plain but decent uniforms, taught to pray and sing in unison, and instructed in the Christian virtues—including gratitude, obedience, and a horror of pilfering from their employers.[3] An example of a typical prayer from the period, with which the girls in a Sheffield charity school began their day is: "Make me dutiful and obedient to my benefactors, and charitable to my enemies. Make me temperate and chaste, meek and patient, true in all my dealings and content and industrious in my station."[4]

The people who contributed to the maintenance of these schools were largely middle-class donors who pledged themselves for a yearly subscription of a few pounds apiece and who took great satisfaction in such an effortless opportunity for benevolent action. As M. G. Jones pointed out in her splendid book on the charity-school movement, the eighteenth century was a philanthropic time par excellence, and some form of charity work was essential to the self-images of large numbers of people who fancied themselves benevolent Christians.[5] For such as these, the parades through the streets of London of hundreds of plainly dressed charity children with their scrubbed faces was a particularly gratifying spectacle. The public catechizing of these children or the exhibiting of several schools' worth in a large church singing hymns of gratitude together in chorus (solos were discouraged), many of which were composed especially for the occasion, were dramatic events which drew thousands of spectators. On the public day of thanksgiving for the Peace of Utrecht in 1713, four thousand charity children were stood on risers in the Strand, six hundred feet long and eight rows deep, "in full View of both Houses of Parliament," after which they marched in procession to St. Paul's and sang hymns for three hours to the inestimable satisfaction of all spectators, which included some dazzled "Foreigners who never had beheld such a glorious Sight."[6]

M. G. Jones emphasizes in particular the new class of benefactors who were given a chance to do something for the needy with the organization of these charity schools, and states that "the success of the voluntary societies was closely bound up with what contemporaries term the joint-stock method of finance."[7] In other words, large numbers of middle-income people, by pooling their gratuities, together sponsored these schools, much as people financed prints or books collectively by subscribing to them in advance. Steele extolled them in *Spectator* no. 294 as "the greatest instances of public spirit the age has produced," and urged his readers to contribute the price of one-half yard of the silk for a petticoat "towards cloathing, feeding and instructing an innocent helpless creature" in one of these schools. Local citizens (often following the lead of a noblewoman or a resident squire) were organized by their parish minister to contribute regularly a small sum to support a district charity school. The SPCK sponsored these schools, and encouraged them with advice, direction, books, and SPCK-approved teachers; but final decisions about running these schools remained with the local benefactors.

The participation of large numbers of women in planning and managing these schools was also revolutionary, inasmuch as it was the first time that women, on such a scale, were involved in the work of the church. Not only did they contribute to these worthy causes out of their pin money, but they organized special anniversary sermons to raise contributions for them, and held special lotteries, concerts, and other fund-raising benefits for them. Together with their local churchmen, they made curricular suggestions, collected books, and corresponded with the SPCK about the management of the charity schools. Women's participation may have been a significant factor in the astonishing growth of the charity-school movement—all the more astonishing because it was only the beginning of widespread elementary education

Figures of charity boy and charity girl at Bishopsgate Ward charity school, London. From M. G. Jones, The Charity School Movement *(Cambridge University Press, 1938).*

in England. Between May 1699 when the SPCK was founded and 1704, fifty-four charity schools were set up in thirty-two parishes in London and Westminster alone. A total of £2,164, contributed by myriad hands, created the auspices under which two thousand children were taught to read, write, say their catechism, and knit and sew. (Boys were taught to do simple sums rather than needlework.) By 1729 there were 132 schools in London, and the SPCK claimed that 5,225 charity children had been educated within their walls.[8]

By 1733, some twenty thousand children in England had been served by the charity schools. Of these, 15,761 had been placed in decent employment in the community by school administrators: 7,139 boys were apprenticed (the overwhelming majority of these to Thames watermen and fishermen) and 3,366 were "put to service"; 1,383 charity girls were apprenticed (to sempstresses and mantuamakers) and 3,873 "put to service" as maids, cooks, housekeepers, and the like. Apprenticeship was more of a drain on the coffers of a school than putting them "to service" or otherwise placing them, because the school was expected to pay the apprentice fee, which ran anywhere from 30s. to £5. It appears to have been easier to find servant positions for girls, and more frequently necessary to apprentice boys to skilled laborers or tradesmen in order to insure their future employment, for it was harder to place boys in service.[9]

The charity-school movement spread through England, Wales, and Ireland. Astell's native Newcastle was an especially receptive locale, possibly because of the presence there of the Royal Grammar School and the prior belief in the value of education, and possibly because of the large royalist population, which was the single most active political element in the charity-school movement.

N. Ellison, the minister of St. John's Newcastle,—the man to whom Mary Astell wrote in 1714 for instances of mistreated Church of England ministers for Walker's *Sufferings of the Clergy*—was involved in several of the five charity schools which served over three hundred of Newcastle's poor children.[10] By 1712, St. John's parish (in which Astell had been born) had a charity school which served forty-four poor children. Endowed by a legacy of £100, support to this school was supplemented by £37 5s. 2d. in subscriptions, and (in 1712), by £18 2s. 7d. taken at the annual charity sermon. The master of the school was provided with a house and a salary of £20 per annum, which was a little better than many a country curate could count on. N. Ellison, in correspondence with Henry Newman, the secretary of the SPCK, reported that there were a number of pitmen's children in the school, and that coal fitters as well as others concerned in the colliery made voluntary contributions to it.[11]

The rise of elementary-school education in England also created a new profession for the hundreds of men and women who taught in them. The SPCK acted much as an employment agency, locating for school after school as they mushroomed, teachers who met their standards of academic accomplishment and piety. Both schoolmistresses and schoolmasters were required to be members of the Church of England, to have taken communion once a month for some years, with grounding in the Bible and theological works; they were also to be twenty-five years of age, of sober life and conversation, and able to write a good hand. Men were expected to understand arithmetic, and women to be able to teach knitting and "plane work" or plain sewing.[12] No teacher was recommended for a post who was not known personally to at least one member of the Society. As they were expected to do this work fulltime (from seven to eleven and one to five in the summer and from eight to twelve and one to four in the winter), these men and women had to be paid in a manner that made it possible for them to devote themselves to it.

Particularly for women, this meant a new and excellent opportunity for independent employment. Schoolmistresses could make up to £25 a year, and frequently were provided with a rent-free house as well. Schoolmasters usually averaged about £30 per annum. Mrs. Mary Harbin, for example, the first mistress of the girls' school in the parish of St. Martin's-in-the-Field, was a single woman of forty, who had read to her credit, besides the Bible, the religious writings of Drs. Taylor, Scots, Horneck, and Sherlock. She could also write a very good hand and do knitting and "plane work." She was appointed mistress at a salary of £24 a year "with the conveniency of a lodging," and required to report to the trustees of the school on the third Thursday of every month, on the conduct of her pupils.[13]

For the organizers, trustees, and supporters of the charity schools, the commitment to the Christian education of poor children was often an all-consuming religious and political cause. M. G. Jones holds up Robert Nelson, Jacobite, nonjuror, and High Churchman, as an example of the energy and enthusiasm common among these social reformers. From SPCK records, Jones made this tally: "He corresponded with fellow enthusiasts for charity school instruction in York, Beverley, Oxford, Cirencester, Leicester, Tring and Bray; he was manager of St. Andrew's parish charity school, Holborn; he was responsible for the schools attached to St. George's Chapel, Windsor; he drafted the printed forms used in the establishment of the schools; he compiled a catechism for the children, drawn from *The Whole Duty of Man* [designed for children and called *The Whole Duty of a Christian*]; he busied himself in finding teachers for St. Anne's school, Soho, and for the charity schools at Bath; and to his organizing powers fell the duty of arranging the anniversary meetings of the London charity schools."[14]

Nelson's politics were not unusual among those involved in the early charity-school movement. Increasingly, the High Tory wing of the church came to be associated with these institutions, in that teachers chosen often had Jacobite sympathies and the charity sermons were often used to expatiate upon High Tory politics. By 1710, Low Churchmen were withdrawing their subscriptions.[15] Things came to a head following the Jacobite outbursts of 1715, when charity students demonstrated for "High Church and Ormonde," and some were seen wearing the Pretender's colors. Archbishop Wake, a Hanoverian appointment, translated to Canterbury that year, censured the use of religious societies for fomenting sedition and rebellion and asked the SPCK "to restrict its membership to persons who were well affected to the King and his Government, and to refuse to assist the country schools unless the masters and mistresses were equally well affected."[16] Mary Harbin's employers fired her that year, reluctantly, after sixteen years of service, because she could not find it in her heart to require her girls to pray each day for King George.[17]

Not every school enforced this rule, however, and the SPCK continued to ignore the numbers of teachers on their rolls with Jacobite leanings. In 1723, following the Layer incident and the Atterbury trial, there was another campaign to purge disaffected, Jacobite-sympathizing teachers.[18] This time the charge had the full attention of Walpole and Townshend, and the active support of Dr. Edmund Gibson, bishop of London, longtime supporter of the charity schools and one of the earliest members of the SPCK. On November 14, 1724, Gibson called together all the teachers of the London charity schools and reminded them of their duties to the Church of England and to the constitutional monarchy. He sternly warned that disaffection would not be tolerated any longer, and directed that henceforth students were to pray for the royal family and for the Protestant succession in both the morning and the evening, and that any sign of disrespect for the Hanoverian line was to be publicly punished. The SPCK sent out copies of this discourse to every charity school in England.[19]

Astell's school was begun in 1709, at the outset of the movement, and was meant to handle thirty poor girls at Chelsea. "It was founded," wrote Astell in a memorandum to the SPCK in 1712, "by a Lady of Great Quality & Greater Merit [Lady Elizabeth Hastings of Ledston, Yorkshire] whose Charity, as in this Instance, is not confin'd to ye Places to wch she has Relation, but is as extensive as her Power and Opportunity of doing Good. She subscrib'd five Guineas Apr. 5 1709, and her Example had so good an Influence on Several Ladys & others in the Parish, and many out of it, t! their Subscriptions together with ye Rever^d ye Rector, the Governor, Lieutenant Governor, & others, of Chelsea College, amounting to about 50£ the School was open'd June 6 1709."[20]

The children were instructed in the doctrine and discipline of the Church of England, and taught to read, write, cast accounts, knit, mark, and do plain work. The £50 was evenly divided between buying clothes for the girls and paying the schoolmistress £25 per annum for salary, rent, and coals. "This Charity is cheifly design'd for ye Children of Pensioners & Out Pensioners belonging to Chelsea College," Astell added, "who are not able to provide for y^m."

Since the school opened, her report continued, one girl had been "bound Apprentice, and several of ye rest are ready for Service or other Employment, as soon as it can be found for y^m." Twelve had been confirmed and were ready to take communion, as soon as Dr. King, the rector of the parish, was ready to admit them. Once a year a collection taken in Chelsea church was laid out in buying paper and pens to teach them to write, and in "Books & other Contingencies." The final sentence of the report explains the system of governance for the school: "The School is Govern'd by Seven Trustees chosen out of ye Ladys & other Gentlewomen who are Subscribers; & is always to be under ye Direction of Women."

Astell's school fulfilled her desire to do something for other women—the ambition she had confided to Norris—both for those who administered it and those who attended it. The school was run sensibly; no rhapsodies there about Christian love and the need to bend one's thought always to God. The Chelsea charity girls, daughters of Chelsea Hospital veterans, were expected to be in the classroom from nine to twelve in the morning and from one to five in the afternoon, and to apply themselves to spelling, reading, and writing. Each day upon arriving they recited the Lord's Prayer, the Belief, and a prayer from the communion service for their benefactors. They were catechized every Thursday and Saturday and attended church twice on Sunday. Each year they were given one gown, two shifts, two pairs of shoes and stockings, and other necessaries; if they applied themselves, they were also given copies of the New Testament or Dilworth's Spelling Book.[21]

Despite the classes offered in the Bible and on religion, the main business of the school was not devotional. Girls were there to become literate and to learn how to take care of themselves, not to spend their time in meditation and prayer. The regimen was similar to that of other charity schools of the day, except that the girls did not have to spend their time in part-sewing or other remunerative labors often required to support the institution, and none lived there. The school was wholly maintained by the philanthropic ladies in Astell's circle.

It opened in borrowed rooms on the premises of the Royal Hospital, that large, square, handsomely proportioned brick building designed by Christopher Wren—where it continued until 1862. It was located "behind the Barber's Shop, first in that part of the artificers' Yard long since demolished, and later in what are now the Chief Clerk's kitchen premises, where the mistress lived in an attic over the schoolroom."[22] Although Astell actively campaigned from at least 1719 for the land and construction costs to build a separate establishment, the charity school never did get its own building, for those negotiations were stalled by the stock market crash of 1720, and then ground to a halt, as Lady Catherine Jones lamented, when "the worthy Mrs. Astell" died.[23]

Astell's interest in the daughters of outpensioners was reasonable enough for anyone living in Chelsea. The Chelsea girls were charity cases of a special sort; their fathers' service to the country made them a kind of national responsibility. These men, if they lived outside the Royal Hospital, were given meals, uniforms, and five pence a day to live on—hardly a sufficient sum to support any family they might have had, and certainly not enough to send any children to school.[24]

The Royal Hospital, built to house and serve these veterans, dominated Chelsea both visually and geographically. The largest building in town, it sat at the entrance of the road into London, solid and graceful; everyone traveling to or from the city passed by it. Its high, wide structure embodied the simplicity, regularity, and perfectly proportioned dignity for which Wren's buildings are famous. Tradition has it that Charles II's mistress, the actress Nell Gwynn, first urged him to build the Royal Hospital as a residence for the growing number of veterans of England's many foreign wars. To this day, soberly dressed elderly men stroll about the Chelsea streets in their heavy navy-blue wool uniforms with brass buttons and brightly colored ribbon decorations. In Mary Astell's day, too, they were much in evidence, patrols of able-bodied pensioners protecting citizens from robbers on the bridge to London, and watching over the older and weaker pensioners as they made their way to the Royal Hospital to collect their little allowance.[25]

The Royal Hospital at Chelsea. Engraving by T. Bowles. Yale Center for British Art, Paul Mellon Collection.

The SPCK archive contains letters about the charity school from the minister of Chelsea church, among other things reminding the society that the pupils in the school belonged as much to St. Margaret's parish and St. Martin-in-the-Field's parish as to his, since all but five or six of the girls were daughters of outpensioners who lived some distance from the Royal Hospital. He wanted it noted that he contributed to the school personally, and that he permitted a charity sermon to be preached in his church, which favor he wished the ministers at St. Margaret's and St. Martin-in-the-Field's would extend likewise. In 1715 he noted of the school that "Mrs. Astel has the cheif care of it, and it is now in a flourishing condition."[26]

The Chelsea school had a fair success in placing its students: of the 135 who attended, 7 were apprenticed and 97 "put to service." Even when a new schoolmistress was appointed in 1724, a Mrs. Cosgrove, and Astell moved to Mannor Street (this was the year Dr. Gibson declaimed against Jacobitism and stipulated public swearing of loyalty oaths and praying for the house of Hanover), Astell's concern for the welfare of the school did not cease. She continued to hold meetings of the trustees, to search for a suitable parcel of land, and to organize efforts towards raising a separate building for the school.[27]

That Astell should have been an organizer of a charity school in Chelsea during this period of their rapid proliferation is hardly surprising. But her stipulation that the school was "always to be under y^c Direction of Women," is unusual. It tells us how she assumed the world worked—and also that there was a local community of women to sustain the instruction.

As we have observed, Chelsea was very much a female enclave when Astell settled there. Besides the boarding-school students who lived there, a tax record of 1694 shows that one-fifth of the assessed population in Chelsea were single women, paying taxes for property in their own names. Far enough from the city for respectable seclusion but readily accessible by boat or coach, by the 1690s Chelsea was a rich suburb with its own protected society. Among the noblewomen who made their homes there were Charles II's neglected queen, Catherine of Braganza, the duchess of Ormonde, the countess of Radnor, the duchess of Hamilton, the duchess of Mazarin, and Lady Elizabeth Montague, to whom Mary Astell inscribed a 1694 edition of *A Serious Proposal To The Ladies*.[28] (When his lordship died, Lady Elizabeth continued to inhabit alone what the Reverend Dr. King, rector of the Chelsea church, described as "a House of large conveniencies and Noble Apartments."[29] This family had been among the most important in Chelsea from an earlier period, with the right to graze their cattle on the Chelsea common.) Lady Mary Wortley Montagu's aunt, Gertrude Pierrepont Cheyne, second wife of Lord Cheyne, also lived in Chelsea and the young Lady Mary often stayed there as a girl, where she may have first glimpsed the celebrated Mrs. Astell. An advertised entertainment at the Royal Hospital in 1702 gives the genteel and woman-centered atmosphere of the neighborhood:

> In Honour of the Queens Coronation; The Ladies Consort of Musick; by Subscription of several Ladies of Quality (by permission) at the Royal College of Chelsea, on Monday the 25th of the present May, . . . The Hall to be well illuminated; the said Consort to begin at exactly five a Clock, and to hold 3 full hours. Each Ticket 5s. Notice that the Moon will shine, the Tide serve, and a Guard placed from the College to St. James's Park, for the safe return of the Ladies.[30]

The other women involved in the Chelsea school were Astell's closest associates, her oldest friends in London and her main sources of emotional and financial support over the years—Lady Catherine Jones, Lady Elizabeth Hastings, Lady Ann Coventry, and Elizabeth Hutcheson. Like her they were known for their old-fashioned piety, their charity, and their homing instinct in thought and conversation for devout topics. All three were single ladies, although Lady Ann Coventry had been married for fifteen years to Thomas, the second earl of Coventry, a man much older than herself, whose death left her a wealthy widow.[31] Like Astell, Lady Betty Hastings (as her friends called her) and Lady Catherine Jones never married.

A closer look at these women, who were the real center of Astell's network of support and patronage, reveals an interesting pattern. Although knowledge of a woman's friends may not always be an infallible source of information about her, Astell was so passionate about the subject of friendship and so identified with other women, that her choice of friends can hardly be thought to be irrelevant to her character. She also valued and maintained numbers of friendships with women other than these three; she encouraged less experienced writers like Lady Mary Chudleigh, Elizabeth Elstob, and Lady Mary Wortley Montagu, and she never omitted to commend herself to the wives of the men with whom she corresponded.

Lady Ann, Lady Betty, and Lady Catherine, unlike Mary Astell, had impressive pedigrees and large, independent incomes. But like her, each chose to live in retirement from the court and the world of fashion, a withdrawal all the more striking because of the positions in society to which they were otherwise entitled by wealth and birth. Lady Ann

Coventry, for example, seems to have spent the greater part of her life alone. She was a widow for fifty-three years, her husband having died in 1710. Her only son died in 1712, at nine years old, while he was away at Eton. In the spring of 1728, she boasted to a favorite niece in Devonshire that she had not lain one night away from Snitfield, her country house, for over three and a half years.[32]

Each of these women maintained a web of connections with many women—including the relatives of their personal servants—and each manifested an impulse to support, encourage, and educate other women in a variety of ways, whether by teaching servants how to read, interesting herself in the schooling of a favorite niece, giving money to poorer women, or taking in homeless widows and spinsters. It is not surprising that they responded to Astell's picture of an orderly, disciplined life in a community of religious and intellectual women, for each within her own circumstances yearned for such an arrangement. Lady Betty Hastings in particular harbored an early ambition to found just such a celibate "Religious, Regular, well ordered family" as Astell recommended in her *Serious Proposal*.[33] (Some think she—rather than Queen Anne—may have been the "great lady" who, according to Elizabeth Elstob, was ready to finance Astell's scheme for a women's college with £10,000 but was dissuaded from it by Bishop Burnet.)[34]

They were all, relatively speaking, bookish women—highly literate, voracious readers—by no means a common phenomenon in that era. Lady Ann, countess of Coventry, had an extraordinary library by any standards. Not another woman's library in the period could match its scope and seriousness, for few had both her money and inclination. She herself published a slender volume of religious thoughts in 1707—*Meditations and Reflexions Moral and Divine*—through her husband's agent.[35] They all admired Astell's eloquence, learning, and familiarity with the world of scholarship. They were proud of her as an author. They all believed in education for women and applauded her as an exemplar of their faith.

Lady Elizabeth Hastings, active all her life in the charity school movement, operated a very innovative girls' charity school on her estate at Ledsham for years. She also sent several poor scholars to Oxford every year, and maintained a fund for the widows of vicars at Ledsham. We have seen that she was the prime mover in Astell's school. She was also a good friend of Robert Nelson and a partner in many of his activities. With Bishop Wilson of the Isle of Man she operated thirteen charity schools in his district alone and filled them with pupils by fining parents one shilling who did not send their children to them. Lady Ann, countess of Coventry, sponsored a charity school in Badminton,

Gloucestershire.[36] Lady Catherine Jones, besides being a trustee and subscriber to the Chelsea charity school, contributed to a number in Wales through the SPCK and left a bequest in her will to the chaplain of Chelsea College "or to the chaplain or chaplains who shall succeed him upon trust to lay out and apply the same in buying good Religious Books for the Infirmary of Chelsea Hospital."[37] Jonathan Swift, writing to her in 1729 to ask for a small annuity to repair and maintain a family monument in St. Patrick's Cathedral (which request she readily complied with), noted that "although I am a stranger to your Ladyship's person, yet I have heard much of your piety and good works."[38]

Like Astell, all these women had reputations for quiet cheerfulness, devotion to learning and to good works. They were often described as "saintly." All three had lively minds. Each was known for her independence, her piety, and her beneficence. They exerted more power in the world than most women did. We do not know whether they came to know Mary Astell because of the books she had written or because she settled in their neighborhood. Astell explicitly says she did not come to know Lady Elizabeth Hastings until after 1705, but in that year Lady Betty made a gift of an elegant calf-bound presentation copy of the second edition of *Some Reflections Upon Marriage*—which suggests a serious respect for the views and admiration for the book. Lady Ann owned Astell's *Letters Concerning the Love of God* as early as 1696.[39]

Lady Catherine and Lady Ann already had houses in Chelsea when Astell moved there, although Lady Ann spent most of the year at her country estate. But Lady Catherine Jones lived with her father, the earl of Ranelagh, at that time, on his Chelsea estate bordering the grounds of the Royal Hospital. By 1695 Astell was well enough acquainted with Lady Catherine to insist to Norris that they dedicate the *Letters Concerning the Love of God* to her. They probably met at the Chelsea church, for Astell declared of Lady Catherine in the preface to that book, that every time she prayed by her, and had occasion to observe her public worship, she fancied herself "in the Neighborhood of Seraphick Flames!"

Describing Astell's friends in order of acquaintance, it makes sense to begin with Lady Catherine Jones, who was the first and probably the most important of Astell's lifelong connections. She was neither so philanthropically inclined as Lady Betty Hastings nor so learned and widely read as Lady Ann Coventry—indeed she spelled worse than either of them, and Astell apologizes to her for the "hard words" in *The Christian Religion*, ostensibly written as a letter addressed to her. But she was Astell's oldest and steadiest friend, a neighbor in Chelsea for over three decades; in Astell's declining years, she prevailed upon her friend to move into her house on Jew's Row (later Queen's Road

East) and submit to the care and comfort of her household.⁴⁰ After Astell died there in 1731, Lady Catherine packed up and went for a visit to Ireland, where she had been born—as if she did not want to stay in Chelsea once her old friend who had shared the place with her so long was dead.

We know more about Lady Catherine's father, a colorful and prodigal peer of Ireland, than we do about her; indeed her piety and generosity could be viewed as a kind of reaction to his extravagant worldliness. A favorite at the English court, he was, despite continued scandals about mismanagement of funds, appointed and reappointed paymaster general of the army.⁴¹ He built a handsome brick house in Chelsea on twenty-three acres of land which he leased from the Royal Hospital for a token payment of £5 per annum for ninety-nine years. He was a man of extravagance and taste. No expense was spared in finishing his house, the rooms "wainscoted with Norway oak, and all the chimnies adorned with carvings. . . ." His grounds were no less elaborately finished, the greenhouses and stables embellished with festoons and urns, and seven acres of gardens laid out elegantly with shaded walks, shrubs and trees, painted seats, and beautiful flower borders and paths whose turnings opened into the larger vistas of the walks of the Royal Hospital itself. After Ranelagh's death this estate—with significant additions like the Rotunda—became the very pleasure grounds of London, resort of the fashionable people of the city.⁴²

He died in difficulty, having galloped through his fortune and finally been discharged from his government office. Swift wrote to a friend in 1712: "Lord Ranelagh died on Sunday morning: he was very poor & needy & could hardly support himself for want of a pension which used to be paid to him, & which his friends Sollicited as a thing of perfect charity—He died *Hard* as the term of art is here, to express the woeful state of men who discover no religion at their death."⁴³

Little is recorded of Lady Catherine's mother, who predeceased him. Of their three daughters, Lady Elizabeth married the earl of Kildare, and Lady Margaret Lord Coningsby of the kingdom of Ireland; their dowries were supplied by Ranelagh's Irish estates.⁴⁴ Only Lady Catherine never married, "despising the Temptations of Birth and Beauty," as Astell put it. Ranelagh made this maiden daughter his executrix, and it took honest Lady Catherine a number of years to settle his tangled affairs properly. Despite contrary advice from her two brothers-in-law, who were reluctant to pay the debts of the profligate Ranelagh, Lady Catherine sold off a certain amount of furniture and plate from the Royal Hospital estate and disposed of the houses at Cranbourne and St. James, to pay back all that her father owed.⁴⁵ In 1716 she herself moved to a less expensive house on Jew's Row, where she lived a relatively simple existence. She probably rented out Ranelagh House occasionally over the next fifteen years; the Royal Hospital does not appear to have reclaimed the property until 1730.[46] She managed her property to advantage, or inherited money from her mother's line, or both; for when she died in 1740, she was worth well over £10,000.[47]

During her lifetime Lady Catherine spent her income as befitted one of Mary Astell's friends—supporting charity schools for girls, one in Chelsea and one in Ireland, giving money to be distributed to Chelsea's poor, and contributing to the relief of private cases of hardship. The will she left is a model of modesty and generosity. She asks to be buried near her father's grave in the Henry VII chapel in Westminster, but stipulates that it be done "late in the night without any show or distinction." She wanted no attendants or pallbearers but her servants; her honest old coachman was to drive her to the grave. She also remembered her servants financially in her will and a great many women, "close friends" and "old acquaintances" she calls them, most of them spinsters and widows. One gets the impression of a network of women friends whom she looked after, some of them neighbors, some living elsewhere in the city.

It must have been through Lady Catherine that Mary Astell met both Lady Elizabeth Hastings and Lady Ann, countess of Coventry—each destined in her own way to become a disciple of Astell's. These women exemplify the element in society that Astell was identified with; furthermore, in the similarities of their characters, styles, and concerns, we can read something of the qualities of our elusive subject. It can never be the whole story, but one can infer a certain amount about a person from knowing the company she keeps.

Lady Ann, the countess of Coventry, was an extremely cultivated woman, the third daughter of Henry, first duke of Beaufort, one of England's richest noblemen in the middle of the seventeenth century. Her sister Mary married the future duke of Ormonde. Henrietta married first Lord O'Brien and then the duke of Suffolk. Lady Ann herself married Thomas, the second earl of Coventry, who apparently admired his wife's literary bent, for he arranged to have her *Meditations and Reflexions Moral and Divine* published.[48]

The name of Beaufort is a highly esteemed one in England, and the estates of this family in the time we are speaking of, constitute in themselves a little chapter in great English houses. Lady Ann's estate was Snitfield in Warwickshire; her brother, Sir Arthur Somerset, had the country seat of Posten, near Bath; one sister lived in Beaufort House, Chelsea; and the other at Badminton, in Chippenham.

When Astell moved there, Chelsea had no larger or handsomer house and grounds than Beaufort House. It fronted on the Thames, more than 250 feet in length, with a long, stately, tree-lined entrance from the river, two spacious courtyards, and sixteen acres laid out in back in the choicest fruit trees and walled gardens. It was supplied with running water—both the outhouses and the main houses—and the road from the stables led straight into King's Road, the way to London. Dr. John King, minister of the Chelsea church at this time and a local

Beaufort House by the Thames in Chelsea. Engraving by Kip. From M. and C. H. B. Quennell, A History of Everyday Things in England, vol. 2 (London: B. T. Batsford, 1924).

historian, claimed that Beaufort House stood on the site of Sir Thomas More's house, although he acknowledged that there were a number of other contenders for that honor.[49] A slight rise gave a view of the Thames from one direction and all of London from the other. The duke of Beaufort had bought the house for £5,000 in 1682 from the countess of Bristol and repaired and refurbished it at great expense.[50] After he died, his duchess dowager had lived there as a widow, enjoying the quiet and the good air until her death in 1712. Her daughters visited her frequently—Lady Ann included—and the Chelsea parish register reveals a number of family weddings held at this grand old place.

The family of the duke of Beaufort also held the estate of Badminton, in Gloucestershire, which Lady Ann's sister Henrietta inherited. To this day it stands, maintained in part by the National Trust, family portraits by Kneller and Lely and Reynolds still hanging on the walls, Grinling Gibbons' carvings in the magnificent dining room, and two views of the estate in oils, commissioned from Canaletto in 1748, stationed in the great drawing room. The scale of the rooms is palatial, the carved and inlaid furniture opulent, and the servants' quarters extensive. The ponds and woods were stocked with game; the libraries contained a full and choice selection of volumes.

Badminton had two thousand acres when Lady Ann grew up there as a girl; her father bred horses and dogs as well as managing it as a farm. Two hundred servants and workers lived in the household, and when a meal was laid out, they sat down to eat at nine tables, the seating arranged by rank within the staff. The duchess herself, Ann's mother,

inspected every detail of the household in a daily tour of its myriad apartments and departments. Soap and candles were made on the premises. The salt was ground there, after being dried in the sun on the leads of the mansion, and that in sufficient quantity to make all the liquor consumed at the Duke's table.

The day in this vast household began with breakfast in the duchess' gallery that opened into the gardens. Then a stag was hunted on horses provided by the duke, or guests walked admiringly round the gardens, or through the parks to look at the various kinds of deer. Twice a day the bell rang for prayers, at half past eleven in the morning and at six o'clock in the evening, when the chaplain officiated in the neighboring ducal church. The duchess and her gentlewomen occupied the evening with pastimes in one of the galleries, mainly embroidery and fine needlework for use on beds at home.

The duke farmed a large area of the estate. His wife and daughters were employed in many tasks of domestic utility, and necessities of every kind both for the farm and the mansion were made at home, as indeed they had been for centuries in such great establishments, and in very much smaller ones. The number of families that lived in such rural splendour was very limited, but they set a pattern to those on a more restricted scale.[51]

Beside making useful things, Lady Ann undoubtedly spent her girlhood days in the country much as her niece did in the next generation, as she reported to her aunt:

> The mornings I constantly imploy at my drawing writing or work a small part with a Book and ye whole afternoon in reading (except tea time) and ye Evening at my Stitching while read to by Mr Grevil My Spinett tis impossible to touch till I can have a Person to set it in order. Y^e weather

Painting of the north front of Badminton by Canaletto, 1748. Reproduced by kind permission of the Duke of Beaufort. Photograph: Royal Academy of Art.

Lady Ann Somerset (later Countess of Coventry). Portrait by G. Kneller, c. 1678–80. Photograph: Courtauld Institute of Art.

and Country are excessive melancholy but y^c being constantly imploy'd amuses me very tolerably. . . .[52]

More than Catherine Jones, Lady Betty, and certainly Astell, Lady Ann participated in the life of the *beau monde* when young; she "came out," she had suitors, and she married. Even in soberer years, she teased the serious-minded Astell for always thinking on "ye Grave."[53] In addition to her collection of histories and sermons, and the lugubrious volumes of morality found on the bookshelves of all of Astell's friends, Lady Ann also owned a number of plays, romances, and novels—as compared, for example, with Lady Betty, who once remarked that she had only once read a novel, and had always regretted it.

Lady Ann's sister was the duchess of Ormonde, about whom there is more fully recorded information since she had held a public position at court, as Lady of the Bedchamber to Queen Anne.[54] The duchess settled in the house at Chelsea where her mother had been living, when her husband the duke of Ormonde went abroad to live in 1715, exiled by George I for his Jacobite politics. Her brother, second duke of Beaufort, founded the Loyal Brotherhood in 1709, a Tory drinking club. She was a fashionable but not a frivolous woman, this duchess of Ormonde. She had a reputation for liking to play cards too much, but as her biographer writes: "Cards being at that Time, as well as now [1735] the fashionable Amusement of the Fair, it was impossible for the Duchess, whose house was continually filled with the best Company in the Kingdom, to do otherwise than comply with the Inclinations of her Visitors in that Diversion."[55] Lady Ann sometimes stayed with her sister Ormonde during the winter season when she came to London, a few blocks away from Mary Astell's little house, and she and Astell renewed their friendship on these visits. And when pious Lady Ann returned to Snitfield, the elegant duchess of Ormonde took more than a neighborly interest in good Mrs. Astell, inviting her to dine and putting her carriage at her disposal to save her the three-and-a-half-mile walk into town.[56]

Roughly Mary Astell's age, the duchess of Ormonde had two daughters—nieces to Lady Ann—Lady Mary, who married Lord Ashburnham and Lady Elizabeth Butler, who stayed single. The latter eventually became another of Astell's friends, and in later years it was "Betty Butler" who passed along news of the family to Astell, had her to dine, or visited her. It must have been pleasant for Astell to have her own connection in that newer generation.[57]

Although Lady Ann was in many ways unlike her sister—less public, less caught up in the social whirl—she and her sister Ormonde shared a family literary interest. The duchess of Ormonde was one of Dryden's patrons and is said to have been so pleased at his dedication to her of his translation of Chaucer's *Palamon and Arcite* in his *Fables Ancient and Modern* (1700) that she gave him £500. This dedication is a charming poem of Dryden's own composition, more charming in some ways than his version of *Palamon and Arcite*. It compliments the duchess gracefully in Chaucerian terms, comparing the situations of Lord Ormonde and herself to those of Palamon and Emily—with William III as Theseus, about to send Palamon to Thebes (Ireland) to guide the government there. He praises the duchess's beauty and her lord's skill in combat—their preeminence in love and arms—in keeping with the themes of medieval romance.[58]

No doubt through Lady Ormonde Astell met Elizabeth Hutcheson, the friend to whom she entrusted her financial arrangements for the charity school, and whom she designated her executrix upon her death. Archibald Hutcheson, this woman's second husband, was the duke of

Lady Mary Somerset (later Duchess of Ormonde). Portrait by M. Dahl. Photograph: Courtauld Institute of Art.

Ormonde's man of business in London during his years of exile, and a regular in the Ormonde Chelsea establishment.

Elizabeth Hutcheson's first husband had been Robert Stewart, a wealthy plantation and slave owner in the Leeward Islands.[59] Stewart had also had a hand in the colonial government of the West Indies, as the registrar in chancery, and clerk of the crown in Barbados, for which he was paid £400 or £500 per annum out of the profits of the bank there. He appears to have returned to England in 1709 or thereabouts, bringing a letter from "the most Considerable Proprietors of Barbadoes" entreating support of a petition to the House of Commons to regularize the slave trade. African trading had to be consolidated, these colonials thought, in order to ensure the importation of a sufficient number of slaves, else "we shall not be in a condition to support our Plantations." Free competition among the slavers had driven up prices and they wanted the government to step in and organize a monopoly on the slave trade. "The late high price for negroes has risen from no other cause but the liberty given to separate traders," they wrote.[60]

Robert Stewart died in 1714, whether in London or Barbadoes is not clear. Many years later his widow married Hutcheson, whom she may have met when he was commissioner of the Leeward Islands. A lawyer and economist, M.P. for Hastings from 1713 to 1727, Archibald Hutcheson was that combination of worldliness and piety, of partisan politics and Christian idealism, that keeps cropping up in all of Astell's connections. A man of unquestioned probity, he was trusted by both

Whigs and Tories, but his conservative fiscal policies and personal sympathy for many of the Jacobites edged him increasingly into the Tory camp. He defended Atterbury warmly in 1722 and cared for the duke of Ormonde's affairs both privately and publicly with real devotion. In 1724 Lord Orrery wrote to the Pretender: "Mr. Hutcheson is a very honest man, and to be depended upon. I think he is a good friend of yours, but he is of a peculiar turn, and will serve the cause in his own way."[61]

One wonders if Astell realized that Elizabeth Hutcheson had owned slaves, and what she thought of it—she who cared so keenly about the injustice done to women. Such inconsistency pains a modern conscience, but it passed without notice in the class-bound milieu in which Astell lived. Many aristocrats in Astell's day owed their luxuries—their carriages and imported lace—to the brisk slave trade between Africa and the Caribbean, which they accepted unconsciously as a fact of life.

Elizabeth conformed to the pattern of the rest of Astell's friends—wealthy, pious, studious, chaste. Other shared affinities are suggested by the fact that after Archibald Hutcheson died, his widow Elizabeth went to live with Hester Gibbon—aunt to the historian—and William Law, the nonjuring author of *A Serious Call* (1728). Together these three lived in a religious household à trois, contributing to many charities, opening first a school for poor girls and then one for poor boys. A biographer of Law remarks that as Miss Gibbon had about £700 a year, and Mrs. Hutcheson £2,000 a year, "none of which, it is believed, was retained or allowed to accumulate," and as "the expenditure within the house was remarkably frugal, great must have been the disbursement without."[62]

Their regimen was regular and pious: "Law rose at 5 a.m. and began the day with private prayer and study; but the characteristic feature of his regime was that the day was punctuated by periods of household prayer at three-hour intervals—at 9 a.m., at noon, at 3 p.m." He concluded the day, as one might expect, "with an examination of conscience, which he likens to the way in which a business man makes up his accounts every night."[63] On Wednesdays and Fridays, after the morning service, they took an airing, Hester Gibbon and William Law on horseback, and Mrs. Hutcheson in the carriage. The same chronicler reports: "On the day of the annual audit of the charities founded by Mrs. Hutcheson and himself [Law], it was their custom to entertain the trustees at dinner, after which Miss Gibbon played on the organ."[64] Of all Astell's friends only Elizabeth Hutcheson actually managed to realize in practice the communal, religious, and socially useful life that Astell had argued for in her first book.

Politically, all these friends of Astell's were High Tory, even Jacobite. There is some evidence that Lady Ann may also have been a Catholic, although reluctant to register as such. Catholics in England at that time were required to take the oaths of allegiance and supremacy when they reached the age of eighteen, and if they refused, were forbidden— among other things—the inheriting or purchasing of land. The penalties on recusants also included not being able to live within ten miles of London, not being permitted to hold public office or employment, nor to bear arms, nor even to travel more than five miles from their homes without permission, under pain of forfeiting all their goods. A married woman forfeited two-thirds of her jointure or dower if she did not take the oaths, and was disabled from being executrix to her husband.⁶⁵

While her husband was alive Lady Ann was protected from the consequences of any personal reservations about taking the oaths. But as Sir Thomas was dying, she wrote something in alarm to George Hooper, bishop of Bath and Wells, which elicited from him a soothing and reassuring letter to the effect that "no one will ever surmise any change in your Ladyship's Principles either of Religion or Loyalty." He also assured her, as he wrote, that "I know your Ladyship is in a continual preparation for that Better [World]: and sufficiently despises all the changeable thoughts and mistakes of this troubled and trouble-som World."⁶⁶

The abjuration oath was a particularly offensive requirement of the house of Hanover. Many English subjects, not all of them Catholic, with no treasonable intentions towards the government, were perfectly prepared to swear allegiance to George I and promise never to conspire against him but balked at this oath which stated that the son of James II had no right to the Crown, that the Protestant succession was the only true succession, and moreover that the oath itself had been taken "heartily, freely, and willingly." This final clause required an obvious act of perjury for any Catholic. Lady Ann felt keenly the conflict between prudence and conscience in this matter, and among her papers, pre-served at Badminton, is a letter from another woman with whom she apparently discussed her dilemma—Cassandra Willoughby Brydges, duchess of Chandos. Lady Ann had asked the duchess what her own mother was going to do about the oath, and received this reply:

> I can't answer yᵗ part of yʳ Laᵖˢ Letter wᶜʰ relates to my Mother, who is
> very uneasie in her mind, & as yet undetermin'd what to doe in relation

to y.ᵉ Oaths, she had resolved to have made over her joynture to my Brother, & have taken a yearly Allowance from him instead of it, but my Broᵗ has writ her word that yᵗ is not to be done wᵗʰ any safety to hirself, & therefore has desired her not to think of it, but advised her to Read Hidgens Book upon yᵉ Oaths, to yᵉ Governmᵗ, who was long a non-juror himself, & after wrote his thought upon yᵗ Subject, wᶜʰ book I doubt is pretty Scarce because I could not meet wᵗʰ it wⁿ I was last in Town.

Cassandra Chandos then went on to retail sympathetically the story of a friend of hers in a similar dilemma.

> A neighbor of mine has been in very great distress upon this Account, who had long Suffer'd in her own affairs rather yⁿ take yᵉ Oaths, but now she has taken upon herself yᵉ Care of a very much burthened Estate for yᵉ benefit of a Nephew & Neece who are Orphans, & must be Ruined if she should now Suffer their Estate to fall into other hands, or else to be Register'd, wᶜʰ were hardly possible in regard to yᵉ very great intricacy of their affairs[.] [T]his has made her a very Diligent Searcher of yᵉ Scripture, & some Texts she has found wᶜʰ give her great Satisfaction, & made her almost resolve to Comply wᵗʰ what is so very necessary for her to doe. . . .

The duchess added that she felt very sorry "for all those Pious People who wish well to yᵉ Governmᵗ, but at yᵉ same time can't bring yᵐˢelves to be willing to Swear to all those hard words at yᵉ end of yᵉ Abjuration Oath."

She advised Lady Ann not to expect that Parliament would drop the act requiring the oath in the next session as she had hoped, and warned her that the only present safety for those who did not swear was to register as recusants "and wᵗ inconveniency may arise from thence, . . . wⁿ they shall be thus marked out from yᵉ rest of yᵉ Kingdom, must be left to everyone to form what judgmᵗ they please upon." She hoped Lady Ann would see her way clear to some course of self-protection. "In yˢ great affair I hope yᵗ Laᵖˢ own reason will give you such Satisfaction as may make you perfectly easie, without yᵉ trouble of Registering, & what may be a benefit to you will always be wished by . . . Cassandra Chandos."

Cassandra, duchess of Chandos, is a further example of the serious, competent, intellectual women associated with Astell and her friends. As a young woman she had chosen not to marry, but to live with her bachelor brother on their paternal estate at Wollaton and to share with him the business of managing it. Together they rebuilt and replanted it, and Cassandra gained considerable experience, which she later put to use refurbishing the estate of the man she married.

From all accounts Cassandra Willoughby was better educated than most women of her time—she read better, spelled better, and wrote a better hand. She shared with her brother the standard intellectual pursuits of eighteenth-century country gentlemen. When they went to London, for instance, instead of the usual plays or balls, their excursions were rather to see the scientific instruments of Mr. Flamstead, the astronomer royal at Greenwich, or Mr. Charlton's collection of natural curiosities—later purchased by Sir Hans Sloane.[67]

Her brother married when she was forty-three, which changed her status in the household. Soon after, she made a prudent match with her first cousin, James Brydges, whom she had known all her life. Brydges had made a fortune (£600,000), as paymaster during the War of the Spanish Succession, profiteering on army clothing contracts. They were married in 1713 at the Royal Hospital in Chelsea, and then they removed to Cannons, the estate that Brydges inherited from his first wife, to rebuild it together.[68] Cassandra's experience from Wollaton was invaluable for this work, although Cannons was on a much grander scale. Defoe refers to it in his *Tour Through the Whole Island* (1725) as possibly the most splendid estate in England, with such a beautiful situation, a house "so Lofty, so Majestic the Appearance of it, that a Pen can but ill describe it, the Pencil not much better."[69] The land around the house was terraced and decorated; there were "ornamental waters—canals and basins—fish stews, wildernesses, grass plats, fruit and vegetable gardens, a physic garden groves and walks lay further out. The pleasure gardens were a walled area of 83 acres . . . peopled by storks and whistling ducks, mock-birds and macaws, Virginia deer, flamingos, eagles and other birds.[70] Many thought Pope meant to ridicule this estate as "Timon's Villa" in his *Epistle to Lord Burlington* (1731). Pope protested—to Chandos's satisfaction—that he had not modelled his description on Cannons or on Chandos: "I never imagined the least application of what I said of Timon could be made to the Duke of Chandos, than whom there is scarce a more blameless, worthy, and generous beneficent character among all our nobility."[71]

The duke and duchess of Chandos continued to live at Cannons even after losing their fortune when the South Sea Bubble burst. Chandos spent the rest of his life trying to recoup his money as easily as he had made it the first time, speculating in a number of schemes in the new world of business. In 1721, for example, he entered into the Royal African Company, dreaming of riches from gold mines and the slave trade. Cassandra Chandos, in her letter to Lady Ann Coventry, lamented

Lady Elizabeth Hastings. Portrait attributed to G. Kneller. By permission of G. H. H. Wheler.

her husband's anxiety over a gold mine in Africa, and thought that his health was too dear a price with which to purchase "y.ᵉ mine."[72]

Astell's friend and patron Lady Elizabeth Hastings, the third of her highborn friends to collaborate with her on the Chelsea school, was a woman of wealth, imagination, and scope. Pious like the others, and wealthy, she bought up as many advowsons (the right to confer a clerical living) as she could in the vicinity of Ledston, so that she could reward worthy ministers of the church, and choose the best shepherd for the flocks she considered to be under her care.[73] Answering to Fanny Price's idealization in *Mansfield Park* of domestic religious life in the great English country estates of the seventeenth century ("There is something in a chapel and chaplain so much in character with a great house, with one's ideas of what such a household should be! A whole family assembling regularly for the purpose of prayer, is fine!"), Lady Elizabeth could have belonged to another age, with her benevolent "paternalism" and sense of obligation for the spiritual welfare of those who worked for her.

She ran her household like a religious establishment; everyone was assembled four times a day to join in prayer and Bible reading, servants and guests alike. One or another of the clergymen constantly in attendance would conduct these short services, either visiting eminences like Richard Lucas, prebend of Westminster, or Thomas Wilson, bishop of Sodor and Man, or one of her own vicars from Thorp Arch, Ledsham, or Collingham. Ralph Thoresby, the Leeds antiquarian, describes the scene in his diary, for he was summoned from time to time by Lady Betty to Ledston to help her read ancient family documents. On August 10, 1711, he wrote:

> Rode to Ledstone Hall, got in time for prayers; was extremely pleased with the most agreeable conversation of the most pious and excellent Lady Elizabeth Hastings, who showed me some curious books, delicate pictures and fine needlework but her exemplary piety and charity is above all.

In the following years he was many times a visitor of Ledston Hall. On October 19, 1720, he reports getting there "in time for prayers; after dinner, with my Lady perusing some ancient Court-rolls and Charters that her Ladyship wanted to understand more fully, which took up the whole time from afternoon prayers till supper, and after till bedtime; had family prayers, with a chapter, and Burkitt's Annotations or Paraphrase."[74]

Lady Elizabeth was the daughter of Theophilus, the seventh earl of Huntingdon, a man whose unwavering loyalty to James and to the Stuart succession caused him to be excluded from the benefits of King William's Act of Indemnity of 1690, and landed him in the Tower for a short while in 1692. It seems that the deposed James II summoned a number of English peers to Mary of Modena's lying-in, and when the letters were intercepted, Lady Betty's father was arrested and imprisoned with several others. The news must have upset Lady Betty. Only ten years old at the time, she had lost her mother four years earlier on the occasion of another political disturbance—when a riot on the night of "the Cry of the Irish" caused her to miscarry and hemorrhage.[75] Lady Betty remembered being put out of a parlor window that night, into the next-door garden of Lord Leicester. When her father was sent to prison, her older brother George wrote to her from university, to reassure her that their father would soon be released.

One gets the sense of too much long-distance comforting in Lady Betty's life. She was a poor little rich girl. The family coach was pulled by six stallions and their servants wore livery, but she was unhappy at home, and never comfortable with the woman her father took as a second wife. She was extremely fond of her brother George, her only full sibling, but he was hardly ever home—first away at school and then off leading his regiment in the Low Countries under the duke of Marlborough. In 1700 George sued their father for his maternal inheritance, and eighteen-year-old Lady Betty tried to mediate between them. These painful procedures were put to an end by Theophilus's death in 1701. Then her beloved brother George died suddenly a few months after returning from the wars, in 1705.[76] The next year her maternal grandmother, of whom she was very fond, also passed away. At twenty-four Lady Betty was alone in the world with no living kin, which is why Mary Astell refers to her as a "noble orphan."

Perhaps this deprivation explains why Lady Betty spent her life in nurturing and protecting others—as if she were always deeply aware of a general neediness in the world, an insufficiency which she continually tried to rectify. She cared for her half-sisters with truly maternal devotion and invited them to live with her at Ledston when she moved there. As her biographer writes:

> She loved to have her relations with her at her table and enjoying her hospitality. She would seek out the less fortunate branches of her family and place them in better circumstances, aiding them both by alms and by her influence. Wherever possible she discovered the benefactions of remote ancestors, and made them of more extensive use and service by her own added munificence. She was particularly solicitous as to the welfare of the sick and the poor, she not only constantly visited such as she discovered in their own homes, but to such as were able she gave a position in her own house or grounds, and fed and clothed a very large number of those unable to do so for themselves.[77]

She came to be known far and wide as a woman of unfailing generosity and was continually solicited by people for a wide variety of causes. She spent over £1500 annually in charitable causes.[78]

What was remarkable about Lady Betty was not merely the charitable impulse, but how effectively she administered her estate in order to serve charity. Her will and trust deed are masterpieces of detail and care. For example, she left money for a brass plate to be mounted in each of her churches, with instructions about polishing it regularly to remind the incumbent clergyman "That he content himself [not only] with an orderly and regular discharge of his duty . . . but from a true fervency of spirit and Christian zeal for the salvation of his people and his own, add to the obligation required of him . . .[and] enforce his preaching upon the minds of men by holiness of Life and the strength and power of his own."[79] She stipulated that no clergyman could hold more than one of her livings at a time, because she disapproved of clergymen who were responsible to so many as to be of use to none. She considered herself the guiding spirit of both her servants and her tenants, and when she was dying only the strictest injunction from her physician kept her from summoning the entire village for final instruction.[80]

She devoted her life to good works, many of which survive today, thanks to her far-sighted arrangements. In 1913 and again in 1955, her trust deed was brought up to date in accordance with her instructions. Fixed yearly payments are still being made to the schools in the diocese of Sodor and Man, to the trustees of Chelsea Hospital, to the managers of the Pontefract school, to the vicars of Ledsham, Thorp Arch, Collingham, Aberford, Wike, Melbourne (Derbyshire), and How in Norfolk, as well as the schools of Ledsham, Thorp Arch, and Collingham, with the residue directed to children in the parishes of Ledsham, Thorp Arch, Collingham, Wike, Shadwell, and Burton Salmon. She left money for the communion wine for Ledsham, Thorp Arch, Collingham, Thorner, Mirfield, Aberford, and How; for beautifying six churches in these villages; for assisting poor vicars or retired clergymen and their dependents in the counties of Yorkshire, Westmoreland, Cumberland, and Northumberland; for maintaining and repairing almshouses in Ledsham and Stoke Poges; and improving the vicarages in Ledsham, Thorp Arch, Collingham, and How. One of her trusts still supports several scholars at Queen's College, Oxford, although they do not all come from Yorkshire schools as they once did. It is a remarkable list of benefactions, both for the number of lives and institutions it touches, and for its long-range effectiveness.[81]

She was a woman of extraordinary imagination and executive ability, a throwback to one of the great abbesses or feudal landowners of medieval times. The schools she set up on her estates and the benefactions she decreed in her will have all operated smoothly into this century; the Yorkshire law office that handled her affairs 250 years ago is still carrying out her trusts. She understood how to design her programs with enough elasticity so that changing land values could reshape the circumstances but never cancel the initial intentions of her will.

She attended to the largest and the smallest details of running her establishment. The grounds of her estate were laid out innovatively under the direction of the architect Charles Bridgeman; the Ledston estate had one of the earliest ha-ha's to be found in England. She was very interested in forestry, and insisted that the tenants of her farms at Compton plant and protect every year three oaks, three elms, and three ash trees. No detail of her domain was overlooked or delegated, from the manuring of the field and the legal arrangements with neighboring farmers about the cutting of reeds, to the "table maps" she prepared for the refreshments set out for laborers at harvest time, showing where exactly on the table each dish and jug was to be set.[82]

She improved, planted, stocked, and irrigated her lands so sagaciously that her estates prospered, and she lived very well indeed out there in the country; we have the menus for some elegant luncheons she arranged from the produce of her own domains.[83] She probably inherited her character and learned some of her skill in management from her maternal grandmother. This woman had been first married to Sir John Lewys of the East India Company; when he died she had married Sir Denzil Onslow, M.P. from Pyrford, Surrey. Lady Betty was close to her grandmother—had stayed with her occasionally as a girl—and had draped her London house in deep mourning when she died in 1706. John Evelyn visited the household of Sir Denzil Onslow in 1681 and notes its remarkable economy in the same way people later spoke of Lady Betty's establishment:

> I was invited to Mr. *Denzil Onslows* at his seate at *Purford*, where was much company, & such an extraordinary feast, as I had hardly ever seene at any Country Gent: table in my whole life; but what made it more remarkeable was, that there was not any thing, save what his Estate about it did afford.[84]

If her skill in management descended to Lady Betty matrilineally, her fortune came that route as well. Before he died, her brother George took care to insure her future independence by settling her grandmother's entire estate upon her (albeit with the proviso that if she tried to claim any part of their father's estate that he had inherited she would forfeit the Lewys money). She thought of her money as her grandmother's fortune, deriving ultimately from her first husband, Lewys the merchant, who had accumulated it in his years of trading in East India. She stipulated that her scholarships for poor students at Queen's College be earmarked for those who expressly wanted to preach "the Gospel in the East," "since the Estate I enjoy was gained by trading hither." Recognizing that something was owed these countries, she thought that by sending missionaries where her grandfather had skimmed off his enormous profits she would set the balance straight and pay back where he had taken away.[85]

As early as 1714 Lady Betty gave money on a regular basis to Mary Astell. Some of it Astell simply collected to redistribute to her own charitable enterprises. But the Hastings family tradition has it that Lady Betty supported Mary Astell generously to her very last days, and Ballard says that she gave her as much as fourscore guineas at a time, "well knowing that she did not abound in riches."[86] Undoubtedly some of the money was intended for Mary Astell's own impoverished purse.

There are records in Lady Betty's bank account of a draft of £8.1.6 to Mary Astell in 1714, £33 in 1718, £25 in 1720, and so on—until the last entries in August 1730, which amounted to £55. 15. 00.[87] These records give us a clue as to how Mary Astell survived in London all those years, without family, without property, and without much, if any, inherited wealth. Her bookseller Rich Wilkin may have paid her a little something from time to time; he probably commissioned her pamphlets of 1704. But she must have depended mainly on her wealthy women friends to maintain her in her simple way of life.

It must be understood that Astell was not just one more charity case for Lady Betty. Lady Betty's relation to her was more that of a patron than of a benefactor. She had been twelve years old when Mary Astell's *A Serious Proposal* swept London—a book which called powerfully to the independence, self-respect, and seriousness of other women, and which must have been a heady experience for the motherless girl. Everything the older woman believed in—her political convictions, her insistence on the centrality of education to religion, her preference for a life of retirement and study, and her desire for community with other women—all of this was hearkened to and treasured up by the younger, and enacted as fully in her own life as possible.

Like Astell, Lady Betty never married, though her wealth and position attracted many suitors. Among the family papers are many letters of proposal, tied up with a blue ribbon. What she wanted instead was to provide a home for her half-sisters, and to create with them a family. She wrote to one of them: "You know that having Religious, Regular, well ordered family has been one of the things my heart has most desired, and the many disappointments I have met in this way, has not, and I think never will, prevent my endeavouring of it, as I really look upon it to be my duty for the order of a family if I mistake not has an influence on the minds' and consequently on the better part of the several members of it."[88]

Mary Astell's influence on Lady Betty is nowhere clearer than in her charitable arrangements for education. In addition to her scholarships and charity schools, she encouraged servants on all her estates to attend school, especially in the winter when the days were short and the weather bad. "It is to be hoped," she wrote, that "even housekeepers if so unhappy as not to have been taught in their youth will not be ashamed to go for their instruction and that those who have been more happy will contrive to give their servants time to go in the school hours if they have neglected learning in their youth and are then desirous of Christian knowledge." To Mary Astell's Chelsea charity school she contributed an initial £200 and left behind instructions that three of her vicars—Ledsham, Thorp Arch, and Collingham—were to pay ten guineas out of their yearly rents to help maintain it. Always aware of the difference time would make, Lady Betty put in a clause stating that this ten guineas should increase at the same rate that rents increased.[89]

Her own favorite project, on which she lavished much loving care, was the Ledsham school which boarded and educated twenty poor orphan girls. She tried to think through every aspect of the establishment, to fence it legally against indifferent and dishonest trustees, or untrained and incompetent teachers. To begin with, she included the extraordinary stipulation that whoever was hired as schoolmistress, had to show "a genius for teaching and instructing the Children." She was to be at least twenty-five years old, single or widowed, and without children. Her salary was to be £10 per annum, and if she held the position for fifteen years and behaved well, she was entitled to that amount annually for life, provided she did not marry. There was also to be a maidservant, at least twenty-seven years old. Household arrangements were specified in detail: £82 per annum was to be spent replacing worn linen, utensils, furniture—as well as for glassing the windows, buying seed and plants, and hiring a handyman to take care of the garden and the courtyard, to keep the house and outbuildings clean, and to fence the pasture ground of the crofts adjoining the schoolhouse. She provided separate money for books, paper, quills, ink, medicines for the girls when sick, and notebooks for the accounts of the school. There was £10 a year to make chests for the girls to keep their clothes in, and money was set aside for spinning the jersey for their dresses. Two girls were to be clothed yearly at May Day. The pewter was to be changed every ten years, four dishes and twelve plates, it "being designed rather for ye girls to learn to clean than to use." The vicars of Ledsham, Thorp Arch, and Collingham were to visit the school every year in the third week of July to "examine the girls on their learning and knowledge of the Christian Religion, and their morals, behavior, and conduct." Each girl upon leaving the school was presented with copies of the New Testament, *The Whole Duty of Man, The Sac-*

rament of the Lord's Supper explained by Edmund, lord bishop of London, Bishop Ken's *Exposition on the Church Catechism* (Thomas Ken was the most famous of the nonjuring bishops), Bate's *Short Exposition*, and *The Country Parson's Advice To His Parishioners*.

The best known of Astell's friends, Lady Betty put into effect what would have been merely altruistic impulses in anyone else. These qualities, no less than her idealism, appealed immensely to Mary Astell. One could actually do something in concert with such a powerful friend. The literary women in whose company Astell had inevitably found herself when she first came to London had no such power in the world but were as ineffectual as she. Elizabeth Elstob could not collect enough advance subscriptions to publish her own Anglo-Saxon translations; the poet Elizabeth Thomas was reduced for subsistence to dealing in scandalous materials, and satirized for it by Pope in *The Dunciad* as "Corinna." Without influence or money these women could hardly help themselves, let alone help Astell realize her dream of independence.

The friends and patrons of Astell's maturity, on the other hand, with their sisters and cousins, constituted the top layer of London's highly stratified society. They knew one another before they made her acquaintance, although she and her charity school eventually became a focus of their relationships with one another. They moved in the same social circle; their families knew one another from court, even though all three of these ladies shunned it themselves. They met at philanthropic activities like charity raffles, benefit balls, and lotteries. In addition to gossip about mutual acquaintances, their letters to one another often included requests for contributions to their latest cases of charity. Each had a reputation for piety and good works; each was considered an "ornament to her sex."

Obviously, Astell was not born to the wealth or class of these women, but she had educated herself to an unusual degree, and her articulate presence, her gracious manners, and her conservative political and religious opinions qualified her—as they would have qualified any woman—for entrée into this aristocratic circle. By the time her writing became known, Astell was acquainted with her wealthy neighbors and they had decided to take her under their collective wing. Each had a particular commitment to women and focused her charitable activities to some extent on doing something for others of her sex. Astell became for them a cause, and they wrote to one another of "good and great Mrs. Astell," "worthy Mrs. Astell," "eloquent Mrs. Astell," the "celebrated and ingenious Mrs. Astell." One feels especially in the letters between Lady Catherine and Lady Betty how they shared Mary Astell, how their admiration of her was a bond between them.[90]

There is some indication that Astell set about cultivating these women for their patronage. If true, it displays prudence on her part. A contemporary letter, collected in one of Edmund Curll's less-than-trustworthy miscellanies, gives the distinct impression that our impoverished gentlewoman carefully improved her contacts with these great and philanthropic ladies at the expense of older friends who had less to offer. The letter—if authentic—was written by Elizabeth Thomas, who felt herself snubbed by the new and "haughty carriage" of their mutual friend, and pressed Lady Chudleigh for a reason for it. Her "Ladyship's own thought were, that she was so much sollicited by Women of the greatest Quality and Fortune, that she had not Time enough to repay all their Kindnesses with her Conversation." Although that was perhaps the case, continued Elizabeth Thomas snidely, "and she who has no *certain Substance*, may be allowed to improve a Friendship with those *that have*," nevertheless "methinks she might forbid the Addresses of her insignificant Admirer with a little more Decency, in Gratitude to her true Friend, *Mr. Norris*, who gave the Acquaintance."[91]

The polite and flattering tone of Astell's letters to these "Women of the greatest Quality and Fortune" is not inconsistent with the suggestion that she took a particular interest in those who could help her improve her fortune. It is the respectful tone of one fully cognizant of her proper social distance from the elite circle of aristocrats with whom she identified and chose to associate. It must also be borne in mind that given Astell's attitudes towards class, she probably genuinely considered these women good and pure *because* they were wellborn. She believed that class often reflected worth, and that people of rank had nobler and more generous dispositions than the rest of poor drab humanity. That was one reason she thought that poor gentlewomen, trained in her women's college and freed from a petty and demeaning preoccupation with getting a living, would make the best tutors for the children of persons of quality. Such pupils could be "instructed in lesser matters by meaner persons . . . but the forming of their minds shall be the particular care of those of their own Rank; who cannot have a more pleasant and useful employment than to exercise and encrease their own knowledge, by instilling it into these young ones." "Mercenary people," she went on severely, "having often but short view of things themselves, [and] low and sordid Spirits . . . are not like to form a generous temper in the minds of the Educated. Doubtless 'twas well consider'd of him, who wou'd not trust the breeding of his Son to a Slave, because no thing great or excellent could be expected from a person of that condition." Envy and lack of charity, she wrote, were less likely to be found "amongst persons whose Dispositions as well as their Births are to be

Generous."⁹² Such attitudes could only have been flattering to her high-born friends.

Yet there is no doubt of the sincerity of her feelings for these ladies. With Lady Ann, for instance, although careful never to trespass the boundaries of class, she nevertheless made sure that the countess recognized the honest admiration and affection behind her elaborate compliments. "I will not pretend to be more a Philosopher than really I am & therefore cannot deny being extremely affected wᵗʰ every thing relating to yᵒʳ Lᵃᵖ," she wrote when she learned that one side of Lady Ann's face had swelled up painfully. She could not be a stoic when Lady Ann was in pain. "Yoʳ Marcus Antonious I know reproaches me for what he calls 'depending on Foreign supports, & beg[g]ing our Happiness of another.' But since he so frequently inculcates what might be thought Ill manners in a Meaner Person to observe, 'Yᵗ we are all of one Nature & Family; yᵗ our Minds are nearly related as being extracted from yᵉ Deity' "—she could claim her right by nature, if not by blood, to care about Lady Ann's well-being. Affirming her intimacy with Lady Ann at the same time as she acknowledged their class differences, she ended with a characteristic paradox: "Were I to wish for any thing in this World, it shou'd be to be agreeable to Yoʳ Lᵃᵖ. But then You wou'd have less occasion of exercising Yoʳ Patience & Charity towards . . . M Astell."⁹³

In other letters she told Lady Ann the news of the town or sent her small gifts to amuse her in the country. "This little Book wᶜʰ now waits on You in Obedience to Yoʳ Lᵃᵖˢ Comands, has bin a Favorite of mine this 20 years," she wrote in one. In another she apologized for not sending up a basket of orange blossoms from Lady Catherine's garden as soon as she had promised, but explained that although the weeder woman told her she might have some, when she went to get them, the gardener told her "there were not 20 buds on all yᵉ Trees."⁹⁴ She asked Lady Ann for a copy of a ballad and a political declaration that she had missed when they first came out; she promised to return her book of prophecies promptly.

There is an old-fashioned letter of condolence in which she first lectures Lady Ann about how "a Happy Death" is the chief blessing of life and how inappropriate it is to "Condole yᵉ Departure of a Noble Person who after an Honourable Life & yᵉ doing much Good in her Generation, is gather'd to her Fathers in a full Age like as a Shock of Corn in it's Season"—and then asks for a private interview to express her sympathy. "Allow me only to remind yoʳ Lᵃᵖ how grievous it is to me to be at any time debar'd Yoʳ Presence," she wrote. "I do not need yᵉ fear of lossing you from this place to heighten my Impatience," she continued, referring to Lady Ann's imminent return to Snitfield. "I make no doubt yo.r Justice will distinguish between those who waite on Yo.r L.ap out of Ceremony, & her who begs Leave, out of y.e Sincerest Esteem & Affection," she added.[95]

It must also be urged to mitigate Elizabeth Thomas's charge of opportunism, that Astell used her interest with her powerful friends to benefit others. "Lady Jekyll . . . has often complain'd of her Ill Fortune at Yo.r L.aps door," she wrote to Lady Ann, telling her that she planned to accompany that unfortunate lady the next time. In another she pleads for "an amiable Lady at Chelsea," who also desired admittance, and assures Lady Ann of the woman's excellent character. "The misfortune is, she neither speaks English nor French, & cannot Converse w.thout an Interpreter," wrote Astell, giving us a glimpse of her own neighborly charity. "I dare not presume so much on my own skill in dumb signs as to pretend to be a faithful one, tho I fancy, use has a little acquainted me w.th her meaning." Meeting Elizabeth Elstob one day in Chelsea and learning that her bookseller was not promoting speedy publication of Elstob's translation of Saxon homilies "because they don't find their own account in it," she subscribed to Elstob's production for Lady Ann and sent to Snitfield the receipt for the first payment.[96]

Largely due to her connections with these aristocratic women Astell enjoyed her irreproachable respectability, in spite of being a writer, in the high society of her day. We tend to think of the female wit as a phenomenon of the world of later eighteenth-century London, represented by women like Lady Mary Wortley Montagu, Mrs. Vesey, Elizabeth Montagu, Elizabeth Carter, Mrs. Delany, and the other bluestockings. Yet Astell virtually created the role. Elizabeth Elstob's learning might have qualified her as an early bluestocking, but her social position was too marginal. Even without the pedigree of Lady Mary Wortley Montagu or the wealth that allowed her young friend such *éclat*, Astell's aristocratic support group conferred upon her all the social power that her own origins lacked. With connections like these, it did not matter how many books she had written for money, nor how odd and unadorned a gown she wore. Their status canceled her peculiarity, and what emerged was the possibility of a learned lady who mixed with the best society, who was literary without being ridiculous or eccentric (whatever succeeding generations have made of the bluestockings), whose opinions were respected, and whose bons mots were repeated with relish throughout the fashionable world. What the twentieth-century historian Myra Reynolds said of Lady Mary Wortley Montagu is more truly said of Mary Astell: "She was not the first woman of letters to be eulogized, but she was the first woman, not in fiction or drama, whose writings every one wished to read."[97] Her works circulated widely among the intelligentsia; she had a reputation even among those who only "wished" to read her. She became a model whom younger women wished to emulate, and in that sense at least she was the mother of the next generation of learned women that history has come to call the bluestockings.

A number of links between Astell and these later bluestockings substantiate the claim that they were carrying forward a tradition she began. Sarah Chapone, Mrs. Delany, and Mrs. Dewes, central to the circle of the English "blues," helped to rescue Elizabeth Elstob from poverty and obscurity in 1736 and to set her up in a comfortable sinecure as governess of the duchess of Portland's children.[98] From Elstob they learned more about Astell, who had been her comrade in London, and who had died only a few years earlier. They bought and read her books with the greatest interest.

Lady Ann, who lived well past the middle of the century, was another link to this next generation. Her kindly and meditative asceticism made her a figure of considerable admiration to them, just as Astell had been for her an exemplar. "There is something in the mild lady so refined and delicate that she looks as if she were in the *millennium state*, part of the earthly mortal state had gone off, and somewhat of the angelic *already* bestowed on her!" wrote Mrs. Delany to her sister Mrs. Dewes in 1750, after a visit to Snitfield. She continued:

> This reflection leads me to consider if it were not possible for old age to arrive at that sort of perfection, by throwing by all the mere trifling concerns of this life, contracting our wants, and fixing our thoughts on the one thing necessary above all others to make us endure this life and lift us for another. I don't mean by this to give up the innocent amusements of life, or to endeavour at extinguishing, or even lessening, our affections; *one* is necessary to keep up good humour and to make us agreeable to our acquaintance; and without affections, or with lukewarm ones, what wretches should we be! what should we do for society, and how weary should we soon grow of ourselves! But the condition of mind I wish to arrive at is to enjoy all blessings thankfully, to consider every disappointment as a merciful correction, and under great and heavy afflictions to submit with entire humiliation.[99]

Lady Mary Wortley Montagu herself forms still another link between Astell and the bluestockings, although her character had a greater admixture of Augustan sophistication than the strict piety and philanthropic interests of Astell's older friends. Astell admired Lady Mary at the same time as she despaired of her salvation. One suspects that she was attracted to her very unconventionality, her liveliness of mind and frank appetitiveness, although as we have seen, Astell disapproved of Lady Mary's flirtatiousness and warned her of its dangers. Nevertheless, when she dreamed of Lady Mary drowning in the sea of folly, her dream-response was to jump in after her. She took pleasure in Lady Mary's triumphs in the world of gallantry, proud that everyone was a little in love with her, and perhaps a little in love with her herself. Lady Mary's versifying inspired her, and she wrote a poem to "The Fair Clarinda" (Lady Mary's literary name), celebrating Lady Mary's prowess in both wit and love, like a combination of Venus and Minerva:

Lady Mary Wortley Montagu. Portrait by Carolus De Rusca, 1739. By permission of the Government Picture Collection.

> The Antients thought no single Goddess fit
> To Reign at once, o'er Beauty and o'er Wit.
> Each was a sep'rate Claim till now we find
> Those diff'rent Talents in Clarinda joyn'd.

She flatters Lady Mary in smooth couplets, and sets the stage "at the Park, the Court, the Play" where "All eyes" regard Lady Mary "with unusual fire,/ One sex with envy burns, the one with soft desire." Such lines are dictated by convention, reminiscent of scores of panegyrics on beautiful women. But the second half of the poem, depicting Lady Mary at home, retired from "Public Show and noise" and engaged in the typical employments of her class, is more remarkable. To read in the elevated diction of heroic couplets, without deflating irony, of a woman drawing, singing, writing, sewing, and cutting intricate paper patterns of flowers or trees, produces a curious effect. Pope without his satire, writing affectionately about women, might have penned these lines.

> But when retired from Public Show and noise,
> In silent works her fancy she employs
> A smiling train of Arts around her stand
> And court improvement from her curious hand,
> She there bright Patroness o'er all presides,
> And with like skill the Pen and Needle guides
> With *this*, we see gay silkend Landskips wrought
> With *that*, the Landskips of a Beauteous thought
> Whether in artful strains her Voice she moves,
> Or cuts resembling Flowers, or Paper Groves.
> Her notes transport the Ear with soft delight
> Her Flow'rs and Groves transport the ravish'd sight
> Which ev'n to Nature's Wonders we prefer,
> All but that Wonder Nature form'd in Her![100]

It is praise offered with a light touch, meant to please and to show the author's skill, written by one who wished Lady Mary would stay at home more, drawing landscapes rather than breaking hearts.

They did not come to know one another well, Lady Mary Wortley Montagu and Mary Astell, until 1715 or so, when the younger woman was already married, and Astell had for some years been retired from public life. Lady Mary had long known of Astell, of course, for she had been a public figure while Lady Mary was growing up. Chances are that the girl even knew the celebrated Mrs. Astell by sight, and that she had been pointed out to her on the street or introduced to her in one drawing room or another. (If they did not originally meet in Chelsea, then they met through their common connections in Newcastle. Lady Mary's husband, Edward Wortley, owned a number of coal mines in the environs of Newcastle, and his partner, George Bowes, belonged to an old Northumberland family.)[101]

At fifteen Lady Mary had been captivated by Astell's earnest intellectuality and the notion of a "Protestant Monastery." According to a letter written in 1709, she was educating herself by then, reading dictionaries and grammars: "I am trying whether it be possible to learn without a master," she wrote to her friend Ann Wortley.[102] Uncertain of her progress, she wrote to Gilbert Burnet, as Astell had written to John Norris, to ask his aid and benediction for her scholarly pursuits. She sent him her translation of Epictetus' *Enchiridion*, so that he might check it for errors, as well as discuss the ideas with her. "My Lord," she wrote, "Your hours are so well employ'd, I hardly dare offer you this Triffle to look over but . . . You have allready forgiven me greater Impertinencies, and condescended yet farther in giving me Instructions."[103] He did correct it very carefully, according to Halsband, but only the first half.

Later in life she advised her daughter Lady Bute to educate her girls, for she said it would render them happy in retirement. Her opinions on women's education remind one of Astell's views: "I think it the highest Injustice to be debarr'd the Entertainment of my Closet, and that the same Studies which raise the character of a Man should hurt that of a Woman. We are educated in the grossest ignorance, and no art omitted to stiffle our natural reason."[104] Again and again she counsels Lady Bute to permit her girls to develop their minds, not for the sake of a new society, but for themselves. "If your Daughters are inclin'd to Love reading, do not check their Inclination by hindering them of the diverting part . . . but teach them not to expect or desire any Applause from it. Let their Brothers shine, let them content themselves with makeing their lives easier by it."[105] As she told their mother, she saw these granddaughters of hers as "a sort of Lay Nuns" in their inclinations. She imagined them growing up to be women of the sort Astell had been when she wrote her *Serious Proposal*, temperamentally more suited to quiet intellectual life than to the life of fashion and society.

Whether or not Astell's books made as deep an impression on Lady Mary's early thought as I am conjecturing, when Astell came to know her later in life, she found Lady Mary to be a woman with tastes and attitudes remarkably like her own on matters of class, gender, and literary sensibility. She recognized in Lady Mary a lively mind and set of passions, which, if not as steadfastly dedicated to the spiritual life as her own, were nonetheless to be cherished as unusual in a woman. There was a great deal of truth in what Lady Louisa Stuart, Lady Mary Wortley Montagu's granddaughter, said of their relationship—that Mary Astell "felt for Lady Mary Wortley that fond partiality which old people of ardent tempers sometimes entertain for a rising genius in her own line. Literature had been hers; and she triumphed in Lady Mary's talents as proofs of what it was her first wish to demonstrate, namely, the mental equality of the sexes. . . ."[106]

According to Lady Louisa Stuart, Astell wrote a poem about friendship for Lady Mary, transcribed in Lady Mary's hand in one of her scrapbooks, among papers and letters dated before 1730. But a difficulty about provenance arises, for this same poem was printed anonymously in 1743 in the *Gentleman's Magazine* with the substitution of "To men and angels only giv'n" for "To Wortley and to angels giv'n", and two new last verses, neither of which invokes the "*sister*-souls" of Lady Mary's copy. It has also been attributed to the sixteen-year-old Samuel Johnson.[107] Astell could have written it; there is nothing in it that she did not believe or publicly proclaim, from the celebration of same-sex friendship as a species of emotion free from the destructive fire of lust— a virtuous union in which "*sister*-souls together join"—to the tender sentiments about Lady Mary herself.

> Friendship! peculiar gift of Heav'n,
> The noble mind's delight and pride,
> To Wortley and to angels giv'n,
> To all the lower world denied:
>
> While Love, unknown among the blest,
> Parent of rage and hot desire,
> The human and the savage breast
> Inflames alike, with equal fire.
>
> With bright but oft destructive gleam
> Alike o'er all his lightnings fly;
> Thy lambent glories only beam
> Around the fav'rites of the sky!
>
> Thy gentle flow of guiltless joys
> On fools and villains ne'er descend:

In vain for thee the monarch sighs
Who hugs a flatt'rer for a friend.

When virtues, kindred virtues meet,
And *sister*-souls together join,
Thy pleasures, lasting as they're sweet,
Are all transporting, all divine.

In 1766, four years after Lady Mary Wortley Montagu's death, the *Gentleman's Magazine* published a poem that may have been Lady Mary's reply to these verses of Astell's: "To Clio, occasioned by her verses on Friendship By Lady Mary W. M." The description of Clio—so different from others of her sex, living in her calm retreat, so prudent and gracious, studious and sweet—accords with what we know of Astell; and the phrase "scorning what the world calls great" echoes from several of her poems and essays. Moreover, Lady Mary's wish that "Clio" might find a friend worthy of her own great and giving soul, to live with in "studious leisure" and "Join in each wish, and warming into love,/ Approach the raptures of the blest above," is what Astell wished most of all for herself, and what Lady Mary must have fervently hoped she would find—especially as she found herself incapable of fulfilling that expectation personally.

While, *Clio*, pondering o'er thy lines I roll,
Dwell on each thought, and meditate thy soul,
Methinks I view thee in some calm retreat,
Far from all guilt, distraction and deceit;
Thence pitying view the thoughtless fair and gay,
Who whirl their lives in giddiness away.
Then greatly scorning what the world calls great,
Contemn the proud, their tumults, power and state,
And deem it thence, inglorious to defend
For ought below, but virtue and a friend.
How com'st thou fram'd, so different from thy sex
Whom trifles ravish, and whom trifles vex?
Capricious things, all flutter, whim and show,
And light and varying as the winds that blow.
To candour, sense, to love, to friendship blind.
To flatterers, fools, and coxcombs only kind!
Say whence those hints, those bright ideas came,
That warm thy breast with friendship's holy flame,
That close thy heart against the joys of youth,

And ope thy mind to all the rays of truth,
That with such sweetness and such grace unite,
The gay, the prudent, virtuous, and polite.
As heaven inspires thy sentiment divine,
May heaven vouchsafe a friendship worthy thine:
A friendship, plac'd where ease and fragrance reign,
Where nature sways us, and no laws restrain.
Where studious leisure, prospects unconfin'd,
And heavenly musing, lifts the aspiring mind,
There with thy friend, may years on years be spent,
In blooming health, and ever gay, content;
There blend your cares with soft assuasive arts,
There sooth the passions, there unfold your hearts;
Join in each wish, and warming into love,
Approach the raptures of the blest above.[108]

When Lady Mary returned from her travels in Turkey, where her husband had been an ambassador in 1717 and 1718, she told Astell about her "Turkish Embassy Letters," a travel-memoir of her experiences in those years, written in the form of letters but based on a journal she had kept. Astell, always interested in the work of other women, and particularly Lady Mary's, asked to see the composition, and borrowed the bound manuscript. She judged it a fine piece of work, and tried to convince Lady Mary to print it. "I once had the Vanity to hope I might acquaint the Public that it ow'd this invaluable Treasure to my Importunitys," she wrote.[109] She even offered to write a preface to it, to lend her prestige as a respected woman writer to the project. But although Lady Mary may have originally intended it for publication, she decided not to publish the "Turkish Letters" while she was alive, despite Astell's arguments that women ought to participate more in public discourse. Her family thought it déclassé and immodest "to print."[110] Astell extracted a promise to have the manuscript published posthumously—and Lady Mary did make the proper arrangements for this—and she then wrote a preface after all, copied into blank pages at the back of Lady Mary's notebook, a preface clearly intended for the eyes of future generations. "If these Letters appear hereafter, when I am in my Grave," she wrote, "let *this* attend them in testimony to Posterity, that among her Contemporarys *one Woman*, at least, was just to her Merit."[111]

This preface illuminates the relationship between these two women in a number of ways. Astell obviously identified with Lady Mary's accomplishments as a woman and considered her an ally in her efforts

A fanciful engraving of Lady Mary Wortley Montagu in Turkish garb. From Frank B. Goodrich, World-Famous Women *(1891).*

to convince London society of women's intellectual potential. "I confess I am malicious enough to desire that the World shou'd see to how much better purpose the LADYS Travel then their LORDS," wrote spritely Astell. She also knew that Lady Mary shared her convictions about women's education and the prejudice against their minds, so that there was poetic justice in her appreciation of Lady Mary's "easy gracefulness and lovely Simplicity." She saw Lady Mary as a sort of spiritual daughter, an inheritor, another like herself who lived among aristocrats, who championed other women, and who could write about the society she observed with humor and penetration. In this letter to posterity she urged others to share her pride of gender, and not to envy or grudge the writer her superior gifts. "Let the Men malign one another, if they think fit, and strive to pul down Merit when they cannot equal it. . . . Rather let us freely own the Superiority of this Sublime Genius as I do in the sincerity of my Soul, pleas'd that a *Woman* Triumphs, and proud to follow in her Train."[112]

The implicit comparisons in these phrases—"when they cannot equal it," "freely own the Superiority of this Sublime Genius," or "proud to follow in her Train"—these competitive wordings show us that at the same time that Astell was urging her future audience to uproot all envy from their bosoms, she herself might have been wrestling with some such feelings. Perhaps for the first time since she had come to London there was now another woman of real learning and wit on the scene, one equally welcome in the best houses, one whose bons mots were repeated as choice gossip. But Astell stifled whatever jealousy these perceptions engendered with a sisterly appreciation of Lady Mary's talents: "*Charm'd into Love of what* obscures *my Fame*," she wrote. Four times in two pages she repeats the metaphoric gesture of laying her laurels at Lady Mary's feet—until one begins to recognize that this is no mere rhetorical flourish.

The "Turkish Letters" were to establish Lady Mary's reputation as a writer, and Astell's preface, which she insisted on writing, was for her a kind of public naming of Lady Mary as her successor, the next in line for the position of female wit which she had created. The verse with which she opens the preface is quite explicit about all of this: her admiration, the rivalry, and the passing on of her crown to the new reigning wit.

> Let the *Male-Authors* with an envious eye
> Praise coldly, that they may the more decry:
> *Women* (at least I speak the Sense of some)
> This little Spirit of Rivalship o'recome.
> I read with Transport, and with Joy I greet
> A Genius so Sublime and so Complete,
> And gladly lay my Laurels at her Feet.

Astell recognized in Lady Mary a mind equal to her own, with an eloquence and a literacy equally out of place in the world in which they found themselves. Astell's solution, of course, was to retreat from the world as much as possible. Lady Mary's, on the other hand, was to flout it and carry on bravely. They must have spent some of their time together in earnest argument, these two women, differing as they did on the question of sexuality and all other attachments to the physical world.

Astell's friendships remind us to locate her in a world of women's activities—of teas and lotteries and herbal remedies, of embroidery and gossip about the latest matches—as well as in the context of those who debated the Occasional Conformity Bill or read Clarendon's *History*. In her correspondence with her friends, she is more consistently intellectual than they, but with the same set of acquaintances and many shared interests. One finds her admiring an extraordinary flowerpot made of shells by the duchess of Ormonde. Or sifting the "prints" to tell her interlocutor what was in them that day. She and Lady Ann and Lady Betty sent one another books and curiosities: "I am sorry the Packet miscarried," she wrote, for in it "there were 3 Ballads, & Dame Britton, unless it went in a former Packet. This is a favorite of mine, I take it to be Priors by y.ᵉ manner." In another she enclosed a coin with the explanation "The Caesars head is an Antique of M.ʳˢ Methuens where I at present am."¹¹³ She kept Lady Ann apprised of the health of their mutual friend Mrs. Methuen, with the confident medical misinformation of her age: "thro a great aversion to y.ᵉ Gout in her Feet, she has for some weeks endur'd y.ᵉ torture of it in her Bowels & Lungs, rather than drive it out, as her Mediciens infallibly do, when ever she will be persuaded to take y.ᵐ." And she reported on the ups and downs of her own failing eyesight: "I find so much advantage by M.ʳ Fountain's Medicines y.ᵗ I believe I must be his Patient all my Life. This seems but an odd Comendation, but I shall be content if his Skil supplys y.ᵗ degree of sight w.ᶜʰ Age & Infirmitys deprive me of."¹¹⁴

She obviously felt called upon to educate these friends of hers. She was always recommending books for them to read, or paraphrasing classic authors in her remarks to them, or instructing them in the philosophical basis of their duties as Christians. She passed on her favorite tracts ("a more particular & Authentic account of ye Scots Persecution") or interesting new finds: "I hope very soon to wait on Yo.ʳ L.ᵃᵖ w.ᵗʰ y.ᵉ Chefs Book, & an Antidiluvian Billet Doux," she wrote Lady Ann cheerily.¹¹⁵ When they were in the country she procured for them India paper, perfumed snuff, and medicines. She noted the latest parliamentary returns. She tried out on them her observations, such as that the present degeneracy in morals had to do with the flourishing condition of the church, and that the spirit and temper of the primitive Christians, as deduced from the Gospels, grew out of the total commitment required of them, since "in y.ᵉ first Ages one cou'd not be a Xian w.ᵗʰ out giving up all their Expectations in this World to their Hopes in another; we think to reconcile both, & tho S.ᵗ Paul might think it necessary to admonish y.ᵉ Roman Converts not to be confirm'd to the World, w.ᶜʰ was at y.ᵗ time Heathen, it wou'd be Ill Manners in us not to conform to such as bear y.ᵉ name of Xtian."¹¹⁶

Perhaps most significant of all, she had disagreeable bouts of self-disgust and despair about the world which found their only outlet in long, self-consciously cerebral letters to these understanding friends.

It is a Melancholy consideration y.ᵗ those Excell.ᵗ Facultys our Maker adorns us w.ᵗʰ & y.ᵉ Talents He comits to our Trust are either Carelessly neglected or shamefully abus'd. Reason the Prerogative of our Nature is often set up as an Idol by y.^m who profess to value & cultivate it, & oppos'd to Revelation Whilst others for fear of this make little or no use of it where it ought to be cheifly imploy'd. That incessant desire of Happiness our Maker impress'd on our Minds to draw us to Himself in whom alone we can find complete Felicity, puts us on a variety of Vain pursuits after y.^t wch cannot satisfy. Our Love of Grandeur wch shou'd raise our Souls to a vigorous endeavour after what is truly perfective of our Nature, spends it self on Glitter & Show & all ye Follys of Ambition. Our Natural propensity to Society & desire to be agreeable to those we converse w.th insted of giving occasion to ye exercise of all Social Vertue & distinguishing Human Societys from Heros of Brutes, becomes a Snare & Temptation, whilst our Horror of Sin wears off w.ⁿ we see it a comon Practise, & our liking to ye Person reconciles us in some measure to ye Vice. At best it is an intolerable waste of Time y.^t precious Treasure, & we come together for ye worse & not for the better. It seems to us Pride or Folly to oppose a torrent, & set our own Private Judgm.^t in opposition to ye Many: Or if we have Courage for this we either really grow morose & self-conceited, or else pass for such. W.ⁿ we go on in ye beaten road, we remain insipid & good for nothing; & if we venture to step out of it, we become Suspected, are clog'd w.th reserve & censure, are taken for Monsters fit only to be star'd at & avoided. Our Vertues ruin us w.th ye World perhaps oftener than our vices And tho ye Supports of Religion are in y.^mselves sufficient to overcome all difficultys, yet we some times fail in ye use of y.^m thro natural Infirmity, w.ⁿ we are forc'd to contend w.th ye malice & opposition of ye Bad, & to stand forlorn w.th out ye assistance & encouragem.^t of ye Good. Yo.^r L.^{ap} who takes so much pleasure in relieving ye Temporal wants of those who are in need, I dare say will not find less in removing more dangerous & deplorable Distresses. Doing good to ye Mind is ye Noblest Charity, it is a Universal Benefit wch none are too great or too little to give or to receive. It is what one needs not be asham'd to Beg, especially from so dear & skilful a hand as Yo.^r L.^{ap's} none of whose Prescriptions can fail of Success, at least on her who wou'd esteem y.^m as ye highest Obligation & who is

> Dearest Madam,
> Most Obediently & Faithfully
> whatever you will please to have
> her be
> M Astell

They saved her letters, impressed by the seriousness of her thought and the excellence of her expression.

Nor did she always preach at them. As we have seen, she admired as well as admonished Lady Mary Wortley Montagu, and she supported and encouraged Elizabeth Elstob in her work. She borrowed Lady Ann's books and entertained the visitors in Lady Catherine's drawing room. She conferred with Lady Betty about the Chelsea charity school, as well as Lady Betty's other educational ventures. As the years went by, she relaxed into her community; the initial stiffness born of her consciousness of class difference and obligation melted into affection for those who became in time simply old friends. She could chatter; she could be playful: "I thought myself very unlucky in runing full upon Mrs Grevile's coach by my Garden Wall & yet neither knowing ye Lady nor her Equipage," she wrote in the summer of 1718. "But I hope ye fragrancy of Mrs Methuen's Honey Suckles will bring her the same way next Year, y^t I may be more fortunate; unless I take a Journey to Spain, w^n we have Conquer'd it, to cure my hoarseness, & thence pursue our Conquests to ye Indies to grow Rich, wch will make me Tall & young & handsom & every thing y^t is agreeable; for according to Boileau Quiconque est Riche a tout. . . ."[117]

They were a remarkable group of women, this circle around Astell—pious and philanthropic as the great ladies of a bygone time, and intellectual and studious as the bluestockings three decades later. Mrs. Delany's sentiments and phrases in later life inspired by Lady Ann's saintliness—"contracting our wants," and "fixing our thoughts on the one thing necessary above all others to make us endure this life and fit us for another," and considering "every disappointment as a merciful correction"—sound very much like Astell. They could all be said to be part of a women's tradition which was both intellectual and religious, resting on a base of Christian Platonism which made the best of powerlessness and which, in eschewing the physical, may have protected its adherents from the very real vulnerability of female sexuality.[118] As a women's tradition, it can be distinguished from its male counterpart, the religious sentiments of John Norris or William Law or Robert Nelson, in that it was more concerned with living out Christian idealism than with defining it theologically, more concerned with subduing the flesh and elevating the spirit than in arguing details of belief. It was a more absolutist religious ideology because it had less to do with church politics and protecting livings than with cultivating the inner state of the soul, in the way of the French quietists whom Astell read, by meditation and a private, contemplative life.

Profoundly influenced by Astell's romantic ideal of friendship, these women also took seriously their responsibility for one another's spiritual and physical welfare. They recognized their best traits in each other and took strength from their shared commitments. Their lives were enriched by Mary Astell, nor could she have survived as she did without them. Theirs was a Protestant nunnery without walls or vows, a community without a charter, one which developed over the years a sense of strongly shared purpose and, "if it be not too familiar a word" (as Astell wrote to Lady Ann), love.

Chapter Nine

Private Life in Chelsea

This Happy spot is likewise blest by Nature with a peculiar kind
soil which produceth nine or ten rare Physical plants not found
elsewhere in England, and the Apothecaries' Garden here lying
upon the Thames Side is a clear instance of the opinion the learned
Botanists of their Society had of the aptitude of the Soil for the
nourishment of the most curious Plants.

> J. Bowack, *The Antiquities of Middlesex*, 1705–6

As much of the former part of her life had been spent in writing
for the propagating and improvement of learning, religion and virtue; so the remaining part of it was chiefly employed in the practise
of those religious duties, which she had so earnestly and patheti-
cally recommended to others. . . .

> George Ballard, "Mary Astell," in *Memoirs of Several Ladies of
> Great Britain*, 1752

After the first decade of the eighteenth century, Mary Astell lived less as a public figure, although the distinction between public and private was a permeable one, in a city where almost all the intelligentsia knew one another, at least by sight. Each one knew the habits of the others and their families, what they habitually wore and what they paid their servants, with an intimacy not approached by the disclosures of our modern staged television interviews. Indeed, most of those Astell addressed in print were her Chelsea neighbors at one time or another. To Lady Catherine Jones, she dedicated her volume of letters with Norris and later addressed her philosophical manifesto, *The Christian Religion*. The duchess of Mazarin, who inspired *Some Reflections Upon Marriage*, lived in a square brick house just two blocks from Mary Astell's house on Paradise Row. Swift and Steele both dwelt in Chelsea too—Swift for three months in 1711, across the way from Francis and Catherine Atterbury, and Steele for several years in a little house on the Thames, which he used as an occasional retreat from town.[1] Shaftesbury, too, maintained a house in Chelsea from about 1698 to 1710. He could not stay in the city because he was asthmatic, and the smoke and fog of London were intolerable. So whenever business or politics obliged him to come to the capital, he stayed in the salubrious environs of Chelsea.[2]

Narcissus Luttrell, who bought Shaftesbury's house in 1710, wrote: "This estate is Sometimes within ye reach of London Smoke, for when ye wind sitts Easterly, wth a gentle breeze will bring ye Smoke of London & you may Smell it on ye top of ye Sunhouse."[3] Dr. John King, who came to the Chelsea church as rector in 1694, remarked proudly on the dry soil and healthy air of Chelsea, adding, "no village in the neighborhood of London contributes more to the ease or recovery of Ptysical, Astmatical & Consumptive Persons, or is more resorted to for that purpose than Chelsey."[4] Here in Shaftesbury's Chelsea house, Locke wrote part of his *Essay* and Addison several numbers of *The Spectator*.

Financially secure at last, Mary Astell moved into her own house in 1712, after living in rented lodgings since the early 1690s. It is possible that she was actually hired outright as schoolmistress of the Chelsea school, and that the house was one of the perquisites of the job. It is also possible that Lady Betty Hastings and Lady Catherine Jones arranged it for her. Assessed in her name at only £10 on the Chelsea tax records, it was an extremely modest little house, among the smallest in the village.

It would have been a two-story red brick house, narrow and vertical, with two rooms on each floor: the kitchen and dining room on the first floor and a parlor and sleeping chamber up a narrow flight of steps. By that time fear of fire in London had led to the outlawing of decorative carved and painted wooden eaves and cornices which jutted out into view from the streets in earlier times. Since larger panes of glass could now be manufactured, the old transomed and mullioned casements were giving way to sash windows such as the Dutch used. So Mary Astell's house would have had that plainer, squarer Georgian look, with recessed woodwork and simple cornices of brick or stone.[5]

It stood at the bottom of what was then called Paradise Row (now Royal Hospital Road) with the countess of Radnor's large house to the right on Robinson's Lane proper, and the White Swan Tavern to the left, standing between her and the river. The tavern's dock and wharf extended onto the water. Across the way lay the Apothecary's garden, and from the window on the second story she could see the pattern of its rows, or Mr. Petiver walking about inspecting his plants. She had a little garden to the side of her house, with a stone wall around it to provide some privacy from the street. On the other side of the wall lay the house and garden of Elizabeth Methuen, an elderly gentlewoman, widow of the English ambassador to Portugal, Astell's nearest neighbor and friend. The sweet honeysuckle from Mrs. Methuen's yard crept over Astell's garden wall every summer, spreading its lovely fragrance.

It was a fine little house for her simple life. She probably employed a servant to help with the cleaning, shopping, gardening, washing. From Paradise Row she was within easy reach of people she was fond of: the Atterburys, the duchess of Ormonde, Lady Ann when she was in town, Mrs. Methuen, Lady Catherine, and Mr. and Mrs. William Green, who owned much of the open land that she passed to the north and west when she walked into town. She was lucky to find such society close at hand, for she kept no carriage, and it was expensive—from six pence to a shilling—to hire a coach to drive just one way into town.[6]

That price for a coach ride—or a boat ride—into the city was as much as a laborer might earn for a whole day's work; Mary Astell could rarely afford such luxuries. Judging from the records that survive of her bank account, Astell had about £85 or £90 a year—somewhat more than a skilled artisan earned although considerably less than the allowances of the noblewomen of her acquaintance.[7] Lady Mary Wortley Montagu's "pin money" was to have been £500 a year if she had married

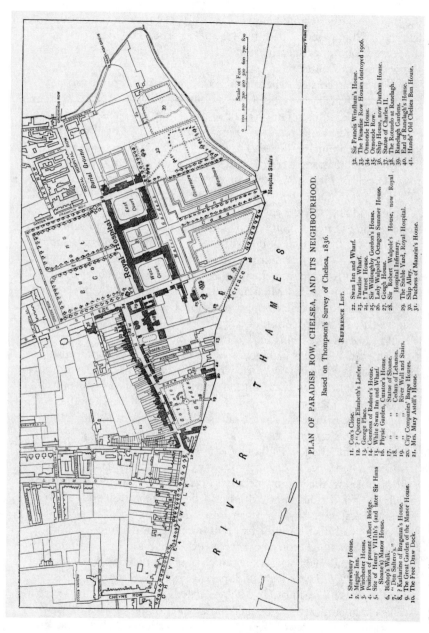

PLAN OF PARADISE ROW, CHELSEA, AND ITS NEIGHBOURHOOD.

Based on Thompson's Survey of Chelsea, 1836.

REFERENCE LIST.

1. Shrewsbury House.
2. Magpie Inn.
3. Winchester House.
4. Position of present Albert Bridge.
5. Site of Henry VIIIth's (and later Sir Hans Sloane's) Manor House.
6. Bishop's Walk.
7. "Don Saltero's."
8. ? Katharine of Braganza's House.
9. The Great Garden of the Manor House.
10. The Free Draw Dock.
11. Cox's Close.
12. ? "Queen Elizabeth's Larder."
13. George Place.
14. Countess of Radnor's House.
15. White Swan Inn and Wharf.
16. Physic Garden, Curator's House.
17. "   "   Statue of Sloane.
18. "   "   Cedars of Lebanon.
19. "   "   River Wall and Stairs.
20. City Companies' Barge Houses.
21. Mrs. Mary Astell's House.
22. Swan Inn and Wharf.
23. Paradise Wharf.
24. ? Turret House.
25. Sir Willoughby Gordon's House.
26. Lady Walpole's Octagon Summer House.
27. Gough House.
28. Sir Robert Walpole's House, now Royal Hospital Infirmary.
29. The Stable Yard, Royal Hospital.
30. Ship Alley.
31. Duchess of Mazarin's House.
32. Sir Francis Windham's House.
33. The Paradise Row Houses destroyed 1906.
34. Ormonde House.
35. Ship House, now Durham House.
36. Ormonde Row.
37. Statue of Charles II.
38. The Rotundo at Ranelagh.
39. Ranelagh Gardens.
40. Earl of Ranelagh's House.
41. Hand's Old Chelsea Bun House.

Mary Astell's neighborhood in Chelsea as it was in the mid-eighteenth century. From Reginald Blunt, Paradise Row (London: Macmillan, 1906).

285

the man her father wanted her to marry.[8] At the time of the South Sea fiasco, Astell apparently had, or was given, an extra £100 to invest in stock, and had hopes in early August 1720 of realizing £1,000. So clearly she was not destitute.

It is not recorded where this moderate income came from. As mistress of the charity school she might have earned £30 a year in addition to her house. This was almost certainly supplemented by her wealthy friends. The recorded bank drafts from Lady Betty alone amounted to about £20 or £30 a year.[9]

For one of modest needs, this was certainly enough to be comfortable. Samuel Johnson, it will be remembered, claimed in the middle of the century that a gentleman could do quite nicely on £30 a year.[10] Simple food and services such as laundry were quite cheap. In 1710 the same shilling that paid for a carriage ride into London could buy two pounds of butter, or four pounds of cheese, or three pounds of candles, or four pounds of veal or mutton, or a bushel and a half of coal. Medical advice was a luxury item: a doctor's visit might be as much as a guinea. Astell frequently visited Mr. Fountain and took his medicines for her failing eyes in the course of these years in Chelsea, an indication of the relative ease of her circumstances.[11]

Produce of the fields and fish from the Thames were cheap in Chelsea. Much of the produce sold in London—asparagus, turnips, carrots, beans, and peas—was grown here. Many kinds of fish were also taken at Chelsea, for the London markets and for private tables— salmon, trout, pike, carp, perch, chub, smelts, gudgeon, flounder, eels, and lampreys. Sturgeon, the "royal fish," was also occasionally caught; the lord mayor claimed those, and sent them on to the king. Already in Astell's time, the local inhabitants noticed that there were fewer fish than there had once been in those waters, and passed laws about the size of holes in the fishing nets, so none of them would take in the small fry.[12] Sir Richard Steele thought Chelsea the perfect spot to breed fish and obtained a royal patent to set up a commercial fishpond, and to stock it with fish brought from all over the kingdom.

Astell abstained from meat frequently—certainly more often than her fellow Londoners, who ate so much of it that they shocked a visiting Frenchman. "*The Diet of the* Londoners, *consists chiefly of Bread and Meat*, which they use instead of *Herbs*," he wrote home to a friend; "whereas we have a great deal of Cabbage, and but a little bit of Meat, they will have Monstrous pieces of Beef; I think they call 'em Rumps, and Buttocks, with a few Carrets, that stand at a distance as if they were fright'd; nay I have seen a thing they call a Sir-Loin, without any Herbs at all, so immense, that a *French Footman* could scarce set it upon the Table."[13]

The meat markets appalled him, where "there was a Thousand times too much of it to be good, the sight of such a Quantity was enough to surfeit one. I verily believe in my Conscience there were more Oxen than Cabbages, and more Leggs of Mutton, than Heads of Garlick in the Market. What Barbarous Soups then must these poor People Eat!" He swore that with the chines of beef he saw reserved for one man, "together with Cabbage, Turnips, and other Roots, Herbs, and Onions proportionable," he could make enough soup for the "Parliament of Paris." Furthermore, these peculiar English liked their meat fresh and did not understand the pleasures of meat that had been allowed to go high. "I saw but one Fowl in the Market that was fit to be Eaten," he said wistfully, "its Smell was delicious, and its Colour of a Beautiful Green; I desired my Friend to ask the Price, but the Poulterer told him it was sold to a *French* Merchant."[14]

Mary Astell's biggest expense, given her moderate habits of eating and drinking, would have been clothing. Groceries could be generously supplied for £15 a year, and the annual poor tax on her house was 6s. 8d. But cloth was very expensive, and where there was any taste for finery such as imported lace, silver or gold thread, ribbons, or the like, prices advanced very sharply. That was why Moll Flanders had such an eye for pieces of silk and packets of lace. The cheapest, coarsest garb for a woman—of the quality a parish purchased to clothe the poor—cost about £11. An account of disbursement of poor-tax money in Sprowston, Norfolk, in 1719, includes this item: "Paid for clading of the widow Bernard with a gown, petecoat, bodice, hose, shoes, apron, and stomacher, £10. 18s. 6d."[15] Such charity dress as this would have been hardly appropriate for Mary Astell, given the circles she traveled in.

Lady Selina, the wife of Theophilus, ninth earl of Huntingdon— Lady Betty's half brother—wore the following gown to a London ball: "her petticoat was black velvet embroidered with chenille, the pattern a *large stone vase* filled with *ramping flowers* that spread almost over a breadth of the petticoat from the bottom to the top; between each vase of flowers was a pattern of gold shells, and foliage embossed and most heavily rich; the gown was white satin embroidered also with chenille mixt with gold ornaments, *no vases* on the sleeve, but *two or three on the tail.*" Mrs. Delany, at the same ball, thought it far too much. "[I]t was a most laboured piece of finery, the pattern much properer for a stucco staircase than the apparel of a lady,—a mere shadow that tottered under every step she took under the load."[16] Such a costume must have cost upwards of £100. A simpler mantua and petticoat of French brocade without all that embroidery might have cost £78. Silk hose were 13 shillings a pair, and shoes and clogs—those protective overshoes which one strapped on awkwardly in bad weather—were at least £1 a pair. Hoops and stays cost several pounds; caps and aprons were a few shillings each if they had no edging of costly lace, and a great deal more if they had, lace being about 20 shillings a yard. An indoor cap, made of Brussels lace, could cost as much as £40.[17] Mary Astell surely did not indulge in the excesses of Lady Selina, but her prose shows an understanding of the allure of choosing, matching, and arranging. And it must be remembered that to "dress" at that time, meant to decide about the colors, the weight and sheen of the various fabrics used, the mix of solid and patterned cloth, the use of ribbon and other trim—in short, to design an original dress—each time one replaced one's gown. Her clothes would have cost her £20 a year if she habited herself from top to bottom in a plain but respectable style every third year or so. Chances are she spent more like £50 or £60 a year on dress and linen.

She would have had other expenses as well—books and paper, for one thing. These could run as cheap as a few pennies to a shilling for the latest pamphlets; but older books, classics—especially with good calf bindings—often were as high as 15 shillings or even a pound. She also had to lay out a certain amount every year in paper and pens, and she had elegant taste in both. For letter-writing, she chose a high quality, smooth, cream-colored gilt-edged stationery.

Another hidden expense with highborn friends such as hers would have been the tips required for servants in the great houses at which she so often called. A person of quality in her era was expected to give a shilling or two to the footman who waited on her, and a crown (five shillings) or more each to the porter and the butler. A story was told of a poor peer of Ireland who lived upon a small pension from Queen Anne, and could not afford to attend the duke of Ormonde as frequently as he was invited to do so. When pressed for the reason for repeatedly refusing Ormonde's hospitality, the man honestly confessed that he could not afford it. Said he, " 'if your Grace will put a guinea into my hands as often as you are pleased to invite me to dine, I will not decline the honour of waiting on you.' This was done; and my Lord was afterwards a frequent guest in St. James's Square."[18] It took strength of character, as well as smallness of purse, to disappoint the expectations of servants in such houses, who considered such emoluments their due from all visitors, regardless of their financial circumstances.

When she went into town, Mary Astell usually walked, an hour and a half each way, unless someone put a carriage at her disposal. Swift thought Chelsea too far from the center of London when he lived there. He found the distance a terrible nuisance, and rode half the time.

Characteristically, he grudged the money spent in coach fare more than the time he spent walking.[19]

Increasingly, Astell's activities centered in Chelsea. The local minister, whom she saw every day, was an important figure in her life. Dr. Littleton had the living when she first moved to Chelsea, but he died in 1694 and was succeeded by Dr. John King. The barns, houses, and paling of the parsonage were miserably out of repair when Dr. King came to claim them, yet he could not recover the cost of their restoration because Dr. Littleton had died insolvent, leaving even his widow, who had brought him a large fortune, "in mean circumstances & an Object of Compassion."[20] The living was worth about £150 a year, but Dr. Littleton had apparently taken his tithes in turnips and carrots, the crops in which the surrounding fields were planted. Mrs. Littleton's neighbors and friends took up a collection for her, and kind young Dr. King freely gave her the current half year's income.

When Dr. King did take over the affairs of the parsonage and the living, he proved a more orderly manager than his predecessor: he assessed his lands, straightened out his rents, sued some of his tenants, and made do quite nicely. He was the rector of the Chelsea church for the rest of Astell's lifetime, dying the year after she died.

Dr. King must have developed a relationship with Mrs. Astell, who came to his church every day to pray and meditate, the most faithful of his flock. He was himself an intellectual man and an amateur antiquarian. His history of Chelsea has always been an important source for that period.[21]

Altogether, Dr. King's parish had an intellectual tone to it. When Astell arrived in the 1690s, there were already numbers of boarding schools, and new ones opened every decade or so. Chelsea was the logical place for Elizabeth Elstob to try to establish her school for young ladies, although she did not start with enough capital, and failed in six months.[22] The Reverend Mr. Rothery started a school for young gentlemen in the next street over, to qualify them for business. It was known as the "Turret House" because of the cupola-topped hexagonal tower in the center of its balconied roof. He collected £25 per annum for live-in students and £15 for day students.[23] Lady Catherine and Mary Astell must have known him, for Lady Catherine designated Mr. Rothery in her will to choose "good books" for the infirmary of Chelsea college. According to the 1947 report of the Chelsea Society, Mr. Rothery went wrong somewhere along the way and by 1759 had become "insolvent and lost in drink."

The Atterburys had lived in Chelsea since the early 1690s, first in one of the narrow town-houses facing the river between the Chelsea church and Lawrence Street, where they were fined £6 for not repairing their river wall. In 1704 they moved to a somewhat larger house on the east side of Danvers Street, with a garden that extended back 113 feet. Addison lived in the extreme southwest corner in 1708; Swift came to Chelsea for part of 1711; Steele took a house in 1716. Writers, critics, statesmen, and men of science all lived in Chelsea. Thomas Shadwell, the poet laureate, died there in 1692.[24] The earl of Shaftesbury had a house in Chelsea until 1710.[25] Dr. Arbuthnot, who was chief physician to Queen Anne while she reigned, lived in Chelsea.[26] The eminent London merchant Sir Richard Gough lived there, rich from the India and China trade.[27] Sir Isaac Newton stayed there from November 1709 to September 1710, while correcting and amplifying his *Principia* for a

Chelsea Church. By permission of the Royal Borough of Kensington and Chelsea Libraries and Art Service.

new edition.²⁸ It was a community in which news of politics and the court, the latest books and scientific discoveries, went the rounds quickly. All through this period Don Saltero kept a famous coffeehouse in Chelsea that was the meeting place for the local literati. It is mentioned in letters as early as 1695, and the antiquarian Bowack describes it in 1705 as if it had been a fixture for years:

> What we mean by the Pleasures of the City here, is the good Conversation for which this Place is at Present noted, the many Honourable Worthy Inhabitants, being not more remarkable for their Titles, Estates, Employments, or Abilities, than for their Extraordinary Civility, and Condescention, and their kind and facetious Tempers, living in perfect Amity among themselves, and have a general meeting every Day at a Coffee-house near the Church, well known for the pretty Collection of Rarities in Nature and Art, some of which are very curious.²⁹

Benjamin Franklin mentions it as a famous landmark in 1724 during a trip in England.³⁰ Steele describes the place with the relish of a recent excursion in an entertaining anecdote for the readers of *The Tatler*.

> Being of a very spare and hective constitution, I am forced to make frequent journeys of a mile or two for fresh air; and indeed by this last, which was no further convinced of the necessity of travelling to know the world. For as it is usual with young voyagers, as soon as they land upon a shore, to begin their accounts of the nature of the people, their soil, their government, their inclinations, and their passions, so really I fancied I could give you an immediate description of this village, from the Five Fields, where the robbers lie in wait, to the coffee-house where the *literati* sit in council. . . . When I came into the coffee-house, I had not time to salute the company, before my eye was diverted by ten thousand gimcracks round the room and on the ceiling. When my first astonishment was over, comes to me a sage of a thin and meagre countenance; which aspect made me doubt, whether reading or fretting had made it so philosophic: but I very soon perceived him to be of that sect which the ancients call Gingivistae, in our language, tooth-drawers. I immediately had a respect for the man; for these practical philosophers go upon a very rational hypothesis, not to cure, but take away the part affected. My love of mankind made me very benevolent to Mr. Salter, for such is the name of this eminent barber and antiquary.³¹

Don Saltero was a neighbor of Mary Astell's, and lived in Chelsea as long as she. He had been Sir Hans Sloane's servant for a number of years and had traveled with him, whence he came by his collection of curiosities. In the room of his establishment, he displayed them in cases, suspended from the ceiling, tucked into ledges. He would expatiate upon this amazing assortment, the various petrified objects, corals, crystals, shells, animals preserved in bottles, stuffed birds and fish, Chinese manuscripts, butterflies, medals, models, firearms, portraits, prints, and so on.[32]

Astell of course would not have been found in this company; women of her class did not pass the time in public places. But she must have

Don Saltero's coffee house, 1723, with the signatures of some regular customers.

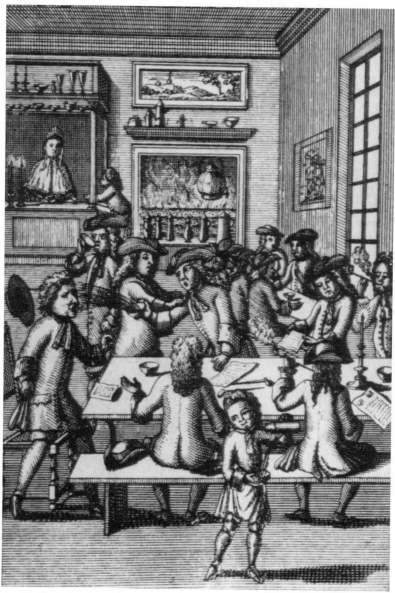

A coffee house in the reign of Queen Anne. From M. and C. H. B. Quennell, A History of Everyday Things in England, vol. 2 (London: B. T. Batsford, 1924).

seen Don Saltero's curiosities. One wonders what she thought about the conversation of the literati at Saltero's establishment, and whether she felt drawn to it, excluded from it, or thought of it at all.

Chelsea combined the advantages of urban life with the space and fresh air of the country. Beautiful houses with tended grounds were set back from the lanes and roads of this suburban "village of the palaces." It must have been delightful to stroll down the road along the Thames, and watch the watermen hand out passengers onto the piers, or the barges float lazily on the river. And there were public gardens as well. After Lady Catherine sold her father's house, Ranelagh gardens merged with the grounds of the Royal Hospital. Astell must have also walked in the physic garden, with its profusion of delicately flowering herbs in the spring, where she might have met Jonathan Swift during his months in Chelsea. When James Petiver took over as demonstrator and supervisor of the Apothecary's garden in 1709, he added the attractions of his conversation to the place. A dedicated and learned botanist, and a fellow of the Royal Society, it was probably he who introduced Astell to Sir Hans Sloane, with whom she later had some business dealings. Indeed, the large and valuable collection of natural history that Petiver gathered over the years that he ran the garden at Chelsea eventually went to Sir Hans Sloane, and thus formed the core of the collection of the British Museum.[33]

Next door to Astell's house on the river side was the White Swan Tavern, another Chelsea landmark. Pepys reports going there as early as 1666, on an afternoon's outing from London,[34] and it was a favorite holiday destination all through the first part of the eighteenth century. It is unlikely that Mary Astell frequented it, but she might well have sent her maid across the way from time to time for a pint of small beer or a bit of roasted meat. It was probably a great convenience to live next door to a tavern in those days, even with its boisterousness, for they sold cooked food at all times of night and day and did their own brewing.

The White Swan Tavern also figured every year in Doggett's boat race, a special London event, a rowing contest from the old Swan near London Bridge, to the White Swan at Chelsea. It was instituted in 1715 by Thomas Doggett, an Irish actor and a fervent Whig, on the occasion of George I's accession to the throne. The contestants were six young watermen who had just finished their apprenticeships, in which most of them had been placed by charity schools around the city. The winner was given a waterman's orange coat and a silver badge with the Hanoverian horse on it.

The race for Doggett's coat and badge, finishing at the Swan Inn. From a drawing by Rowlandson. Reproduced by courtesy of the Trustees of the British Museum.

Doggett's race was an enormous success and became an annual event. On the first of August gawkers gathered all along the Thames to watch the six boats vying for the lead down the river, the six young watermen bending furiously to their oars.[35] A large crowd probably collected at the White Swan, common people lounging and talking, eating and drinking, some of them friends of the contestants, waiting for the finish. Astell's little house was inundated with the overflow from the Swan on those days, and she probably closed her shutters against the hubbub, the shouting voices and the cries of street sellers shrilling their wares.

Her days were of a piece. She read, walked to church along the river, meditated, wrote letters, and had an occasional visitor. In addition to the charity school, Astell tried to organize another intellectual project for herself and her friends to work on collectively. It was to be a compendium of natural philosophy written for women: a schematic laying out of what could be known with certainty about philosophic truth, religious belief, and the natural world. She divided up the textbook-to-be into "such Branches as she thought Proper" and assigned to each woman a different branch to cover. She herself intended to "undertake the remaining part of the work." Whether she really intended to compile

295

a set of developed philosophical formulations, or simply wished to set her friends upon the contemplation of serious questions, there is no way of knowing. But to her great disappointment, she could not enroll any of them to work seriously on the project, and it is uncertain how much progress on it she made by herself.[36]

She owned a pet parrot, perhaps a gift from an admirer, whose antics created hilarity in the household and often entertained her guests.[37] She might have occasionally treated herself to a frosted bun at Chelsea's famous bun house. "Rrrrare Chelsea buns," wrote Swift to his Stella, imitating the call.[38] They cost a penny apiece—the same price as a more substantial loaf of wheaten bread. Swift complained that the one he bought was stale.

She was invited by her friends and neighbors to the usual entertainments: teas, card parties, lotteries, musicales, and dinners. The duchess of Ormonde had a reputation for enjoying cards, a popular pastime among women of her class. Mary Astell must have joined in sometimes; so regular was her friendly attendance upon the duchess, that she could not have avoided playing after dinner, especially if the duchess, recognizing the state of her guest's finances, staked her to play.[39] Astell probably knew how to play basset and ombre, and given her pleasure in matching wits with adversaries, she might have enjoyed an occasional game in which the aim was to outmaneuver the other. She was not averse to the idea of gambling; like the wealthy women she associated with she bought lottery tickets for charity raffles and, as we shall see, even dabbled in South Sea stock.

A distant cousin, John Astell, a coal merchant from Newcastle, dropped in from time to time. He was appointed comptroller of the coal yard at the Royal Hospital in the spring of 1716. His job was to contract for coal and candles used by the pensioners, most of which supplies came from Newcastle. For this he was provided with "a pretty little lodging fit indeed only for a single man," meals, coal, and candles according to his needs, and £30 per annum. He was appointed by Robert Mann—"Mʳ Walpole's worthy Woollen Draper," Astell had called him sneeringly—the London merchant who had received a £1,000 bribe out of an Army forage contract while Walpole was secretary of war. Cited for corruption by the Tory majority in the House of Commons in 1712 for this lapse during his term, Walpole nevertheless appointed Robert Mann deputy treasurer when he became commissioner of the treasury. As Robert Mann described John Astell's position: "'tis to a man that will be here and mind his business a good £100 a year."[40]

John Astell probably supplied his elderly kinswoman with coal and candles. It would be interesting to know if Astell thought anything was wrong with the way John Astell conducted his business, or if she just assumed that graft went with the territory. She was undoubtedly pleased when he sent over his man with a sack of coals for her, and was happy enough to have her cousin John occasionally to tea. Their relations may have become strained in 1722 after the Layer trial, when Robert Mann harassed Astell as part of the campaign against Jacobitism.

The Royal Hospital was also the home of Christiana Davis (later Welch and also Jones). Its only female pensioner and a well-known figure in Chelsea, this "fatt jolly woman" was admitted in November 1717 after having served in the army for years disguised as a man. Distinguished for her courage and discovered only when wounded at Ramillies, Christiana Davis had continued to live among the soldiers for a while, married to one of them, cooking for the officers, pitching her own tent, and traveling with her troop. She had joined the army originally in search of her first husband, whom she did find but who was subsequently killed in battle. In 1712, widowed for a second time, she applied to the duke of Ormonde for passage to England, which he provided with his customary generosity. When she arrived, several notable persons advised her to petition Queen Anne for a permanent provision. The audience was granted, and when Queen Anne perceived that Mrs. Davis was pregnant again she gave her £50 to defray the cost of her lying-in, in addition to the sum of one shilling a day for life and the privileges of the Royal Hospital, which munificence was continued by George I. It was said that in addition to receiving her pension, Christiana Davis was supported by persons of quality in the neighborhood.[41]

Concerts were given regularly at the Royal Hospital, and there were even entertainments—music and fireworks—provided by boats on the river. One of the most memorable of these occurred in July 1717, when the king and his court got up an outing to Chelsea which was to culminate in a dinner provided by Lady Catherine Jones. It was planned as a concert on the water, followed by a midnight supper at Ranelagh House. Lady Catherine opened up her father's ornate house and had it aired and cleaned to receive the royal party which came by boat from Whitehall. Astell may have been among those who dined with the king that night. Even if she was not among the guests, the details of His Majesty's manners and dress furnished her acquaintances with matter enough for gossip and speculation for many weeks.

Baron Kilmanseck had arranged the occasion as a treat for George I, who had suggested a subscription concert on the Thames to substitute for the subscription masquerades he had so enjoyed through the winter season. At eight o'clock in the evening the king and his party—the Duchess of Bolton, Countess Godolphin, Madam de Kilmanseck, Mrs.

Mary Astell's neighborhood as seen from the Thames. From Reginald Blunt, Paradise Row *(London: Macmillan, 1906).*

de Vere, and the Earl of Orkney, the Gentleman of the Bedchamber in Waiting—clambered aboard the royal barge, which was docked next to another barge which carried the fifty concert musicians, with their trumpets, horns, oboes, bassoons, German and French flutes, violins, and basses. It was a soft summer night, and the clear notes of the instruments tuning wafted over the water.[42]

As described by a number of spectators, the river was covered with boats and barges of all descriptions that night, floating expectantly with their cargoes of fine lords and ladies. It looked as if the fashionable people of London had engaged every possible craft that plied a more sober business in the daytime. The glitter of silks and satins, and the sparkle of jewels and the flare of torches must have been a singular and spectacular sight out on the river in the darkening night.

The tide was running towards Chelsea, and the boats, released from their moorings, began slowly to move without having to be rowed. As they gathered speed and rounded past Lambeth Palace, the orchestra began to play the symphony that Handel had composed especially for the occasion—his famous *Water Music*. The performance lasted an hour, and so delighted the king that when the last strains had died away, he gave orders for the entire piece to be played again from the beginning.

The king and his party landed at Chelsea after midnight. Lady Catherine greeted them with a staff of servants, and conducted them to a "choice supper" in the earl of Ranelagh's dining room. The repast was not finished until 3:00 A.M., at which point they straggled back to their barge. Orders were given to row for St. James. A third time King George asked that the orchestra play the lovely *Water Music*, this time drowsing as they played.

The village of Chelsea expanded rapidly in the first quarter of the eighteenth century. While Astell lived there, it grew from a small sprinkling of noble estates into a thriving township. Bowack described it in 1705 as follows:

> The greatest part of the buildings lie stretch'd along by the Thames side, and (with the Royal Hospital) at some distance make a pleasant Prospect. The Body of the Town is near the Church, from whence come Two Rows of Buildings, a considerable Way toward the North, call'd Church-lane, toward the West likewise are Buildings on both sides of the way to the Duke of Beauforts, and beyond there are scatter'd Houses and good Seats. At the East End of the Town runs a Street up from the Thames as far as the Royal Hospital [Paradise Row], and beyond it a Row of Houses a considerable way towards London. This Town was ever much resorted to by Persons of good Fashion.[43]

Of the three hundred houses or so that he estimated, most—two hundred and seventy anyway—had been built in recent memory. Chelsea was becoming less and less rural. The fields were beginning to develop well-worn paths and some of them turned into public roads. Slowly its character changed from that of a suburb into that of a small but bustling town.

The dispute of 1719 over the so-called "King's Road" (it had been called the "Queen's Road" under Anne) helps to date the sequence of urban development in Chelsea. In that year George I tried to reassert his traditional sovereign's right to the road, as a royal prerogative, but there was a great outcry because by that time it had become a general thoroughfare. Originally Charles II had widened it from a footpath which gave farmers access to their fields, and lined it with gravel so that his coach might pass more easily to Hampton Court. It had been a road for royalty in the days of the Restoration, and appreciated by the aristocrats who inhabited the "village of the palaces." (It was the only direct access to Beaufort House, for instance.) Subsequent monarchs—James II, William III, and Anne—had maintained the road.[44] But the public that used it grew and became more heterogeneous than the original population, which was little more than an extension of the

court. And so when George closed it for repairs in 1719, and then kept
it closed for three months, an inquest was held, after which it was
reopened as a public road.[45]
The records of the Chelsea Common tell a similar tale of property
once claimed by feudal privilege, turned to use in the second decade
of the eighteenth century by burgeoning business interests. When Dr.
King first came to Chelsea in 1694, these acres had long been divided
up among the most "Ancient Houses Farmes & Cottages" for the purposes of pasturing household cows. Traditionally these houses had hired
a cowherd collectively, one who tended all the animals in the daytime,
and then drove them home to their various owners at night. Each family
had a strictly specified number of cows and heifers they could graze on
the common. But as these families died or moved away and sold their
estates, their grazing rights reverted to the township. Fewer and fewer
cows were to be seen in the old spot. In 1721, the common was leased
by a company which had obtained a patent for manufacturing raw silk,
and it was planted with mulberry trees.[46]

Although Ballard's account of this period of Astell's life emphasizes her
hermit-like asceticism in the midst of the frivolous gaiety of the *beau
monde*, her letters between 1714 and 1724 do not reflect a studious withdrawal from the world. They come from the pen of one living in the
thick of things, brimming over with opinions about the news in the
"prints," and always able to report on the latest stories going the rounds.
The judgment and wit of her comments remind one of Swift or Steele
or the later Horace Walpole:

> This Age of Wonders in w.ch Truth is y.e greatest rarity, has produced
> a Speaking Dog. He is a Native of y.t Country y.t is so famous for Brightness
> & Ingenuity. He pronounces y.e French Alphabet distinctly, tells what y.e
> Ladys drink for breakfast, & answers all y.e Questions his Master asks. I
> have not yet heard him but a Lady y.t has, gave this account Yesterday,
> when I had y.e honor to dine at her Grace of Ormonde's who is very well
> & Courageous as ever, (Tho rob'd since her Grace came to Chelsea, as tis
> like yo.r L.ap has heard) & hard at work on a beautiful Flower Pot.
> The Dog's Master has it seems found y.e Art of playing on his Windpipe
> as on a Flute, & makes it articulate w.t sounds as he pleases.[47]

She kept up with the latest broadsides, essays, books, and pamphlets.
"Has yo.r L.ap seen y.e *Dedication to a Great Man, concerning Dedications*"?
she asked Lady Ann in December 1718. It was a satire generally thought
to be by Swift, and its sales depended primarily upon that understand-

ing. "There are two Notable Inscriptions" in it, she added, for "statues to be erected a thousand years hence to George-y^c-twentieth."[48] As it turned out, the attribution of this pamphlet irritated Swift immensely, for he thought it "as empty, dry, and servile a composition as I remember at any time to have read. But above all, there is one Circumstance which maketh it impossible for me to have been Author" of it, he added, namely the panegyric on King George, "of whose character and person I am utterly ignorant, nor ever had once the curiosity to enquire into either."[49]

Astell also kept remarkably well informed about current events for one who was supposed to be such a recluse. She noted when Benjamin Hoadley, bishop of Bangor, was translated to the see of Herefordshire, a Tory stronghold not likely to appreciate their new bishop's political or ecclesiastical latitudinarianism.[50] In another letter she reported indignantly: "We are grown so religious y^t Toland has produc'd another Gospel (of Barnabas as he calls it), wch is in a fair way to supercede ye 4 old ones, to ye great Edification & enlargem^t of ye Protestant Church, Jews & Mahometans having it seems as good a Title to Xtianity as ye best of us."[51]

She followed political news with the keenest interest: "The Pretender, (you understand me M^d) grows more & more contemptible, even among his own Party. He lives in his Borrow'd Palace, his Urbino as another Tiberius in Capra."[52] Her analogy displays her bias: the Jacobites of the day were impatient with James for not acting with more boldness and courage. Tiberius had been a legitimate and effective emperor; but his last years were said to have been spent in debilitating dissipation. "As for our pious Protestant Court at Kensington, ye Gates are shut & double Guards are kept ag^t the Wicked," she continued, referring to the Hanover king's fear of a Jacobite uprising, a fear which proved still to have some basis in the weeks that followed, during which hostility to his regime erupted in the defacing of his public portrait in Dublin and the public declaration of a certain Robert Harrison who cried out in the streets: "King James the Third for ever! God damn all his Foes! Who dare oppose King James the Third?"[53] Meanwhile, Astell wrote, "the Devout Mr Munster & young Ulrick, go every Sunday to ye Swedish Church in ye City." The connection between these two thoughts—the double guards on George's palace and the behavior of the Swedish prince—is explained by the widespread hope among Jacobites at that time, that Sweden would intervene to help the Pretender's loyal followers oust George and return the rightful king to the throne of England. Papers outlining such a plan had been discovered in the possession of the Swedish minister the year before.[54] The train

*Sir Hans Sloane.
Portrait by Stephen
Slaughter, 1736. By
permission of the
National Portrait
Gallery.*

of association in Astell's mind reveals her interest in and sympathy with
the plan.

Like many another citizen of the Enlightenment, Astell's imagination was also stirred by news of scientific discoveries and reports of
unusual natural phenomena. "I suppose yor L$^{.p}$ has seen y^e Acc^{ts} in y^e
Prints from several parts of Engl. & elsewhere, concerning y^e Meteor,"
she wrote when Halley's comet was seen streaking across the sky. "Dr.
Halley computes it to be 81 Miles above y^e Earth," she added, "but
others think it must be more, considering at w^t distant places it was
seen almost at ye same time."[55] She sent Lady Ann a bit of the stone
"wch makes ye Cloth y^t is clean'd by Burning"—by which she meant
asbestos—"in wch ye Ancients us'd to preserve ye Ashes of their Dead."[56]

Another time she wrote: "I find in y.ᵉ Evening Post y.ᵗ a Globe of Fire (y.ᵉ same day we saw one here) fell on y.ᵉ City of Ronsen about 3 in y.ᵉ Afternoon & burnt 510 houses & 12 Persons."⁵⁷

She and her friends arranged an afternoon to visit Sir Hans Sloane's collection of natural curiosities. Like the rest of her educated contemporaries, she was convinced that classification was the first step towards understanding natural phenomena. At a later date she wrote to Sloane offering to show him a mysterious specimen that she had already told him about, an object which appeared to be neither animal nor mineral.⁵⁸ She asked if she might bring some friends with her when she came, for Lady Betty's half brother Theophilus, Lord Huntingdon, and his wife, Lady Selina, had expressed a great curiosity in seeing Sir Hans's famous collection.

Astell never stopped reading widely and seriously. Her letters contain references to Homer, Virgil, Hippocrates, Marcus Aurelius, Machiavelli, Milton, Sallust, Pascal, and Fénelon. She sent Lady Ann some Latin verses that she thought apposite, and a book on the subject of generosity which she had treasured for many years, but which "seems not to have fallen in wᵗʰ y.ᵉ goust of y.ᵉ Age." It was a book written after her own heart as she described it, emphasizing what she always liked to have corroborated—that "Friendship of this World is enmity wᵗʰ God," and that "whilst they Live, the just & Upright will be laugh'd to scorn." It apparently also preached that people had to learn to "govern yᵐ.ˢelves by Right Reason, & not by Example, or y.ᵉ receiv'd Maxims & Fashions of the Age," and that it required "all y.ᵗ Firmness of Mind they possess, to get above Vulgar Prejudices, to make an estimate of yᵐ.ˢelves & others by their intrinsic Value, & not by y.ᵉ measures y.ᵗ are comonly taken."⁵⁹ She remarked with characteristic class consciousness, that this book she so prized had been written by a "Meaner Person" than she had supposed him to be, his subject—Generosity—"being properly y.ᵉ Vertue of yᵉ Great, tho as he handsomely proves, not unsuitable to y.ᵉ lowest Rank of Rational Creatures."

She read the duke of Buckingham's *Works*, beginning with the second volume which had "made y.ᵉ most noise." For a man so praised by the wits of his generation for literary talent, she wrote, neither his thoughts nor his style warranted such a reputation. The sole exception, she thought, was his account of the Revolution, which was admirably written "after y.ᵉ manner of my favorite Sallust, & has no fault y.ᵗ I perceive, except y.ᵗ it is left unfinish'd." She also considered his *Memoirs* to be well written and remarked "he seems to be fittest for Ruination & Argumᵗ." But his essays and witty remarks were flat to her taste.⁶⁰

Astell was interested in Buckingham's views on religious toleration and in his firsthand acount of the politics of the Restoration period. It is worth noting that she was not disturbed by his licentious conduct, or by the scandal of the duel in which he killed his mistress's husband, the duke of Shrewsbury, as a proper lady of a later age would have been. Her contemporaries, Dryden and Pope, focused on nothing else in writing about him, and stressed his lack of moral purpose and quicksilver inconstancy.[61] But Astell did not judge him for his political machinations or his reputation for gallantry, but for his ideas and his prose—both of which she found disappointing.

As she passed fifty, Astell was incapacitated by several long bouts of illness so painful and so irremediable that she several times wished to die. The summer of 1718 she was laid up with a fever and an inflamed throat, unable to leave her house for two months. Indeed, she thought her "glass" had "run out." To her friends who inquired anxiously after her health she intoned gloomily: "Is it kind Dear M.ᵈ to wish a weary Traveller a longer Journey? W.ⁿ one is past y.ᵉ Meridian of Life, yᵉ Grave is the only Bed of Repose. Methinks every one shou'd be of Spencers Mind, y.ᵗ

> Peace after War,
> Port after Stormy Seas,
> Ease after Pain,
> Death after toilsom Life does greatly please."[62]

Agues and aches of every sort plagued her during 1718 and 1719, and more than once she hoped fervently for the end to her troubles. Once she excused a long silence by explaining that she had "a sort of fever & S. Anthonys fire on my face, so y.ᵗ my eyes were shut up & I was incapable of writing."[63] Her failing vision was another problem, too, although there were occasional reprieves—as when her doctor prescribed some new medicine that seemed to help, or another time when she thought her cataract was growing thinner by itself. "We ought indeed to be Content & Courageous in our Port till yᵉ Great Coṁander calls us off," she wrote, calling attention simultaneously to her misery and to her stoicism. "But surely there is sufficient Reason to be extremely Thankful w.ⁿ He is pleas'd to discharge us from our Welfare." Those with families or estates to dispose of might have reason to linger in the world, she continued; but she had no business with the world nor it with her: "we were never so endear'd as to be loth to Part."[64]

In 1719, she gave up her little house in Chelsea and moved south
for the season to the village of Burwash in Sussex. She had always loved
the country, and as Chelsea grew more and more crowded, had envied
her wealthy friends their country retreats—the "pure Air, ye Beauty &
Simplicity of ye Country"—although she realized that one might have
also said "in times of yore, ye Innocency & Simplicity, ye Quiet &
Retirement,—but by ye happy Improvements of ye Age, these are almost
as much banish'd from ye Country as from Towns & Courts."⁶⁵ Nonetheless, as the London season drew on each year she longed for a place
to retire to. She congratulated Lady Ann upon possessing "those serene
& unmingled Delights wch Noble Minds enjoy when they are got loose
from the Town to Converse wth y^m.selves & a few of their own Character.
This being ye Season y^t ye Flys buz most in it ye time of Noise & Clutter
and consequently of least enjoym^t to a reasonable Mind. I do not wonder
at Yo^r L^aps Winter Journey."⁶⁶

After a year of ill health, she was doubtless advised that a change
of scene would do her good. The generosity of friends made it possible.
Her journey to Sussex may also have signalled the winding down of
her active participation in the charity school.

When she returned to London, Astell took up lodgings on one of
the newer streets that had opened up in the northern part of Chelsea,
next to a public house called "The Blew Fluke." She moved onto what
was then New Bond Street (now Cale Street), probably where it in-
tersects with Astell Street, the only landmark in Chelsea today that bears
her name. She may have taken up residence on New Bond Street in
anticipation of a change in her circumstances, as this was the time that
the South Sea mania was infecting everyone with wild optimism. Astell,
like the rest of the nation, expected to make her fortune in this miracle
of modern finance, although one assumes her sense of irony about the
enterprise was not shared by all. "I wish we were as diligent in making
sure of a Treasure y^t faileth not, for wch every body may be Adventurers
& obtain it wth less Anxiety & Pains than is daily bestow'd on uncertain
Riches," she wrote at the height of the frenzy.⁶⁷

The South Sea Company had been chartered in 1711 to help defray
the cost of the War of the Spanish Succession. In return for trade
privileges, the company was to absorb and pay off a sizeable proportion
of the national debt which had been accruing at an alarming rate since
the beginning of the war in 1703. People who had invested in the
government, who had lent their capital to the country's war effort by
buying annuities that gave a fixed, relatively safe rate of return, were
encouraged to convert these annuities to South Sea stock; and South
Sea stock was also issued to those wishing to purchase government

securities. The company had been granted an exclusive monopoly on trade in the South Pacific and in South America from the Orinoco River to the southernmost tip of Tierra del Fuego—a mercantile privilege whose financial possibilities were vastly overrated, fed by stories of pirates with their Spanish gold taken from the fabulous Spanish-American colonies.[68] Older tales of Elizabethan sea rovers plundering Spanish galleons filled with treasure were remembered and refurbished. Robinson Crusoe's pursuit of riches in Brazilian sugar and tobacco and in the slave trade, shows the association in the popular imagination of easy wealth with commerce in plantations in South America.

On the face of it, there was nothing shady about this debt-conversion proposal. It was standard fiscal procedure to incorporate portions of the public debt with the stock of flourishing companies. But Spain had no intention of sharing its trade monopoly in South America with the English, and had driven a hard bargain in the 1713 Treaty of Utrecht (the settlement of the war with France and Spain), which considerably weakened the South Sea Company's hand. Subsequent mismanagement of the stock by the dishonest and grasping directors of the company led to the disaster known to the world as the South Sea Bubble, England's first great stock market crash.[69]

In 1719, the government renegotiated the arrangements with the South Sea Company on so large a scale that the real value of the South Sea stock would not sustain it. Parliament passed a bill providing that irredeemable government annuities be converted into South Sea stock, and there was talk of the company assuming the entire national debt. Too much rested on speculative faith in the potential of the South Sea trade, the profits of which were far from what the directors pretended. If the stock or annuities were called in, the genuine assets of the company could not pay them off. Meanwhile, the directors of the company manipulated the value of the stock in order to encourage the general public to buy, and urged annuitants to exchange their sureties from the government for overvalued South Sea stock.[70]

In the months that preceded the final denouement of this national drama, the price of South Sea stock climbed to absurd levels, and a wave of speculative frenzy swept England. Many smaller "bubbles" or "get-rich" schemes were floated in this atmosphere of fantastic optimism. Some were remarkably practical and modern, like the company that promised its investors a handsome profit on pressing oil from radish and sunflower seeds. Others were less so, like the company that proposed to extract butter from beechnuts or those which sought to convert salt water to fresh, cure venereal disease, or insure marriages against divorce. As some of these smaller bubbles burst, there was a run on the South Sea Company to furnish cash to pay these lesser debts. And when the South Sea Company was unable to fulfill its obligations to stockholders who wanted to sell, a general panic ensued which drove down the price of South Sea stock disastrously fast.⁷¹

In spite of her protestations that no one could attend to the business of the mortal world and at the same time try to live out Christian ideals, Mary Astell—with the rest of London—watched enthralled as the South Sea stock climbed higher and higher. Rated at 128 in January of 1720, by the middle of February it had reached 184. Astell wrote to Lady Ann that "Every body here who has a Pound takes care not to bury it in a Napkin" and that even those in the first ranks of society were turning stockjobbers. "I wish we were as diligent in improving our Talents y.ᵉ right way," she added predictably, while at the same time observing— a little wistfully—"He y.ᵗ is Rich multiplys his Riches; & he y.ᵗ has little, may content himself w.ᵗʰ y.ᵗ little, for he has nothing to encrease." Many were the murmurers, she said, who complained not about any actual loss they suffered, but "for y.ᵉ imaginary loss of what they *might* have gain'd."⁷²

In March, when the stock began to climb, Astell permitted herself to wish that she had some money invested in it. "Last night South Sea was 320, & they say it will soon be 1000 or 1500," she said, giving the details which imprinted themselves on her imagination as vividly as on everybody else's. "I wish y.ᵉ poor Girls of Chelsea's money had bin in it, we might y.ⁿ have immediately begun to build," she added, referring to the capital still needed to finance the new building for the charity school. "This new way of Multiplying Gold & Silver takes up every bodys thoughts & Conversation," she continued, observing that women as well as men were making fortunes. Again she noted that many were the complaints—not for the loss of anything real but for what people might have gained if they could have foreseen what was going to happen. "I cannot say it is a busy time w.ᵗʰ Me, who have no Talent to improve, whilst y.ᵉ Rich are adding heap to heap in y.ᵉ English Mississipi," she wrote, unable to suppress a sigh for her own lost opportunities.⁷³

At some level, Astell knew that the South Sea project was too good to be true, and that it was bound to turn to ashes. Even as she wrote her letter, the spectacular rise in South Sea stock to 320, which she had noted enviously, was caused in part by the transferral into the London market of foreign money from Paris, by smarter speculators who had just lost their confidence in John Law's Mississippi scheme. This venture, a pattern for the South Sea Company, was a similar attempt to redeem the national debt in France by tying it to the fabulous prospects for rich settlements in the newly acquired Louisiana territory. As the bottom dropped out of the Mississippi scheme four months before the South Sea Bubble burst, it ought to have frightened English investors.[74] But no one was willing to give up the dream of easy riches until it was too late. As one historian writes about it:

> The mischief affected all classes. Landlords sold their ancestral estates; clergymen, philosophers, professors, dissenting ministers, men of fashion, poor widows as well as the usual speculators on the 'Change, flung all their possessions into the new stock.[75]

Astell could obviously draw her own conclusions from the fiasco in France, and she wrote to Lady Ann: "I hope yo.r L.aP was early in it, for since y.e greatest part of y.e Nation are to be ruin'd to enrich a Few, I can't but wish y.t y.e money may fall into those generous hands who will most freely coṁunicate it to such as want."[76] But by August, when South Sea stock had reached a staggering 900, we find that even she was swept into the mania. "I know not how Prosperity might turn my head," she wrote happily, "but God be thanked I am not like to come w.th.in y.e danger, £1000 or 1500 being y.e most I am like to make w.ch at a time y.t Printers, Upholsterers, etc. make their 100,000 will appear but in a sorry figure."[77]

Astell may have been among the government annuitants who permitted the government to convert their annuities into South Sea stock in 1719. Or she may have put the money for the "poor Chelsea Girls" into South Sea stock, although her friend Archibald Hutcheson, Ormonde's agent, warned her against investing in what he gauged was a scurrilous company.[78] Her South Sea investment may also have represented a private, independent purchase on her part. However she came by her shares, it is clear that the possibility they carried with them of financial ease was, after a lifetime of privation and dependency, irresistible to her.

As we have seen, she returned from Burwash to take up new lodgings on New Bond Street in 1720; and the tone of her letters during this hopeful time was cheerier than she had ever sounded. She was gay as a girl as she predicted modest riches for herself. In one letter, she tells about going to the Herald's office, on a lark, to look up the Astell coat of arms, which she knew existed somewhere, as an act of fellowship and gratitude for William Astell, the president of the South Sea Company, a man who shared the same last name with her—and presumably the same coat of arms—although they had no traceable kinship.

I have not for a long time bin so diverted as I was at y.ͤ Herald's Office, whither Curiosity carried me; & I thought it but reasonable y.ͭ since my Name-sake helps me to Money, I shou'd help him to a Pedagree tho he does not value it. The Heralds seem to me very Ingenious in bestowing upon our new L.ᵈˢ & Gentry Arms suitable to their remarkable Names & Noble Atcheivem.ͭˢ The noble L.ᵈ Cadogen in his Quartered Coat (for he has some alliance to a Cottage in Wales) has a Lion y.ͭ very Soldier-like, looks behind him, w.ᶜʰ they told me was in token of Vigilence; his tongue is Blew, I thought it shou'd have bin Gold or Silver. The B.ᴾ of Bangor [Hoadley] too has his quarterly Coat, w.ᵗʰ a Pelican; a Globe & Dove w.ᵗʰ an Olive branch for his Crest, & y.ͤ Motto *Veritus* & *Patria*, Truth & his Country. One reason he assigns in his Petition for Arms is his Grandfather's being Chaplain to General Monk & very instrumental in y.ͤ Restoration. I was so diverted w.ᵗʰ these & many more New Men's fresh & clean, y.ͭ I almost forget my dusty Great Great &c Unkle Harry, who about 400 years ago had an Augmentation given him for taking Don Diego Valdera Prisoner. But w.ͭ does it signify & for 400 years hence, y.ͤ Cups & y.ͤ Saws, y.ͤ Implem.ͭˢ of their Trades, & Puns upon their Names, will be more considerable, if they learn but y.ͭ Art, w.ᶜʰ y.ͤ other wanted, to tack their Estates to their Arms.⁷⁹

The relaxation of snobbish class consciousness indicates the state of her mind at this time. Although she is careful to explain that her own coat of arms goes back four hundred years, she is not really contemptuous of the *arrivistes* Cadogan or Hoadley. Happy that the South Sea Company was about to provide a tidy sum to go with her "Unkle Harry's" ancient claim to a title, she was willing to live and let live.

At the same time, she recognized that the fixation on money—her own as well as others'—was unhealthy. "The Love of Money seems to extinguish y.ͤ Love of Fame," she wrote to a friend in the country. Even the Muses address the "Ocean of Riches, it is become their Helicon. And we hear no more of Lady Mary Wortley's Wit, but of her Bargains."⁸⁰ Dreams of wealth were preempting all higher ambition. She recognized that the emerging culture of capitalism was crass, that it perverted literary value and ignored tradition. Nevertheless, she was not immune to the attraction of profiting from it, and even appreciated the fact that gender did not automatically bar her from participating in it.

If she really hoped to make her fortune in the South Sea speculation, she was doomed to disappointment. Only a week after her happy letter to Lady Ann about how prosperity was not turning her head, and how her £1,000 would be "a sorry figure" next to the enormous fortune others expected to make, the bottom fell out of the South Sea market, and Mary Astell, along with thousands of others, was forced to give up once and for all her dreams of affluence.

She may have also lost the £300 she had collected for the charity school, for as it came in she had put it "to interest" in a government fund for building churches, and the fund had been applied to a lottery when the work on churches came to a halt. Parliament converted £135,000 worth of lottery annuities to stock in 1719, and thus Astell's charity school savings may have been among those lost or devalued when the bubble burst.[81]

She does not mention building again after her letter to Sir Hans Sloane of July 1720, in which she advised him that there was some question about the title to the land he was offering her for the school. He had offered her a site on the edge of the great garden of Lord Cheyne's manor house—where Lady Mary Wortley Montagu's aunt had used to live—on what was then Pound Street (now Flood Street). It turned out that Mr. Green, the owner of the abutting property, had objections to building on that site and suggested another place. "I shou'd be glad of an uncontested Spot. y.t might please every body," Astell had written Sloane.[82] But there was no more talk about building after that, and the project seems to have been postponed indefinitely.

Astell did not dwell on her disappointment. She was fifty-four years old by the time the South Sea Bubble burst, and the habit of disappointment was deeply rooted in her soul. Only once did she mention the South Sea Company—when John Law, the Scotsman who masterminded the French Mississippi scheme, was smuggled across into England at the time that the public clamor against him in Paris became too fearsome.[83] Her passing reference to the bubble is casual and wittily detached, and without bitterness.

> It is very certain y.t M.r J:Law came to England in S. J. Norris's Fleet; since he can hardly make y.e Nation poorer, it is to be hoped he will make it Richer. Were not y.e Life of y.e Gay and Busy World at all times a sort of Southsea Scheme they might be happy at less expence & trouble than it cost to render y.m.selves miserable. Happy are they who are got safe ashore; but they wou'd be yet Happier cou'd they help those to Land who are lost upon y.e Ocean.[84]

She seems to have survived the bursting of the bubble well enough, and to have landed "safe ashore."

In 1722 she opened a bank account in Lady Betty's bank, having learned something about where to put extra capital "to interest." The amounts of money she withdrew from this account would suggest that she continued to live well, if not royally. She bought South Sea bonds again—undoubtedly on the advice of Lady Betty's banker, Harry Hoare. The government had taken over the enterprise, and the stock had subsided into a perfectly safe blue-chip stock, dependable for 5 percent a year interest. Over the next four years she invested £400 in South Sea bonds, until in 1725 she was making about £12 annually in interest.

It seems she moved again, for in 1724 she writes from Mannor Street. The lodgings in New Bond Street proved too expensive after all. Or perhaps she was obliged to change residences when Walpole's men harassed her in the aftermath of the Layer trial.

Her friendships were more important than ever throughout her changing circumstances. She kept in almost daily contact with Mrs. Methuen, who had lived "by the Swan" since 1707, her first neighbor on Paradise Row. Older than Astell and in ill health, she had come to depend on her, and Astell made a point of looking in on her even when she no longer lived next door. "Poor M.ʳˢ Methuen can hardly find her way in her own Chamber," she wrote to Lady Ann in 1720.[85] Many and varied were the bottles of drops and prescriptions for cures that Astell conveyed from Mrs. Methuen to Lady Ann or from Lady Ann to Mrs. Methuen. The latter had a reputation among their friends for her medical lore, and prepared nostrums for most of them. Astell had perfect faith in Mrs. Methuen's skill and was sure that nothing would improve the older woman's failing health so much as her own medicines. She herself always drank down Mrs. Methuen's mixtures unhesitatingly.

In Mrs. Methuen's last days, she stayed close at hand. Apparently, she was with her at the end. As she wrote to their mutual friend:

> Poor M.ʳˢ Methuen laid down y.ᵉ Burden of Mortality last Thursday ab.ᵗ noon. She had an Apoplectic fit y.ᵉ Week before, but after 24 hours sleep was perfectly brought to her Understanding by a Blister. It continued w.ᵗʰ her to y.ᵉ last, & she died w.ᵗʰout Agony, tho Mortify'd in several places. I lament my own loss & y.ᵗ of many to whom she did good, but know not how to regret her deliverance from w.ᵗ was not so much Life as a continual dying. . . .[86]

For years Astell had described life as a burden and death as a deliverance, but now that her old friends were dying she felt less fierce about it. Everything was changing around her. She no longer lived in her own charming little house on Paradise Row, but in the second set of rented rooms in as many years. Her old political comrades-in-arms were all but gone: Robert Nelson, Dr. Hickes, Henry Dodwell, Bishop Smalridge had died. The days of Tory preeminence were surely past, and that smooth pragmatist Walpole held the reins of power securely. Her publisher Rich Wilkin was failing; another bookseller put out the second edition of *Bart'lemy Fair: or, Enquiry After Wit*. Catherine Atterbury was dead after a long illness; Francis Atterbury was in exile. Elizabeth Elstob had vanished into thin air.

To be sure, there were some younger people who showed her certain attentions: Elizabeth Hutcheson, Lady Betty Butler, Lady Mary Grevile, Lady Mary Wortley Montagu. Lady Catherine, of course, was as great a comfort as ever. Ever since the Layer trial, when she heard that Robert Mann's deputies were sniffing about Mrs. Astell, following her to church, asking her questions, she had been pressing her old friend to come and live with her in her house on Jew's Row. Now some important corner had been turned, and Mary Astell was beginning to feel like a holdover from another age.

Chapter Ten

The Final Chapter

And altho' from the very flower of her age, she lived and conversed with the *Beau Monde*, amidst all the gaity, pomp, and pag-
eantry of the great city; yet she well knew how to resist and shun
those insinuating snares; and wisely guarded against all these temptations and evils; and in the midst of it, led a holy, pure, and even
angelical life.

> George Ballard, "Mary Astell," in *Memoirs of Several Ladies of*
> *Great Britain*, 1752

She had made a vast progress in the spiritual life for the last two
or three years she lived.

> Lady Elizabeth Hastings, in a letter to Bishop Wilson upon the
> death of Mary Astell, 1731

It was a great relief to Mary Astell to accept Lady Catherine Jones's offer to join her establishment on Jew's Row.[1] At sixty, she welcomed the daily companionship of her old friend and the release from anxiety over money matters that these new arrangements promised. Her room was comfortable, and the quality of life in Lady Catherine's household cushioned her own severe habits. Her health revived and her spirits lifted. She resumed her daily visits to the Chelsea church. She arranged with William Parker, who had taken over Wilkin's stock, to republish her most popular books.[2] And she began to walk all the way into the heart of the city every Sunday to hear the new minister that everyone was talking about, young Zachary Pearce, who preached at St. Martin's-in-the-Fields.

It takes an hour and a half each way to walk from Chelsea to Trafalgar Square today in slacks and low-heeled shoes, and the walk is much what it was in Astell's day. But women's footgear was less comfortable in the eighteenth century.[3] And in tribute to her energy, one also wants to point out the other feminine impediments that Mary Astell had to contend with—in the way of at least a small whalebone hoop, a gown which swept the ground and a long mantle over it, and yards and yards of starched, ruffled petticoats.[4]

Past the Royal Hospital, over "Bloody Bridge," through fields and past farm nurseries she marched into London, a slight, straight figure in dark clothes. As she passed Buckingham House on Birdcage Walk, she could see the exotic water fowl in the artificial pond at the other end of St. James Park, and glimpse the strollers on the Mall, in ruffles and broadhoop skirts, making their way as she did towards St. Martin's-in-the-Fields. Down St. Martin's Road into what has become Trafalgar Square she walked, the streets quiet but for other churchgoers, dressed in their finery, moving sedately towards their destination, nodding and greeting one another along the way. Many powerful people lived in this parish and attended Zachary Pearce's sermons, including the royal family, Mr. Pulteney, Mr. and Mrs. Clayton (later Lord and Lady Sundon), and other members of the court.

Pearce's term of preaching was in November and December, so that Mary Astell had to brave the sleet and rain of the inclement winter season on these weekly excursions. The clogs or pattens she wore over her shoes slowed her down considerably, and the overflow from the

Inside St. Martin-in-the-Fields. Engraving by T. Bowles. Yale Center for British Art, Paul Mellon Collection.

kennels—the ditches that ran on either side of the road to collect rainwater and debris—and the splashing from passing coach wheels and striding chairmen would have soaked the bottom of her full skirts.[5] She must have been pretty bedraggled most Sundays in December by the time she got to St. Martin's-in-the Fields, and very glad to enter its high, wide portals.

The church was designed like a temple, a rectangle with a deep portico and columns in front. Indeed, Dr. Pearce had written an essay on "The Origin and Progress of Temples" on the occasion of its opening. The steeple with its peal of twelve bells reached even higher than the spire on St. Nicholas cathedral in Newcastle. Inside, the elliptical ceiling was decorated with baroque fretwork, and the elaborate pulpit was carved by Grinling Gibbons. The organ, a gift from George I, was thought to be an exceptionally fine instrument, and was occasionally played by the great Handel, to Astell's probable delight.[6]

We do not know whose pew Astell shared, or if she sat in an upper gallery. She positioned herself as close to the front as possible, because Zachary Pearce's voice was notoriously feeble and could not be heard all the way back. She went to hear his sound good sense, his eminently

rational sermons deeply infused with classical learning. A High Churchman but no polemicist, he never forgot that his parish included the
royal family and other members of the Hanoverian court. Indeed, Walpole chose Pearce as the man to write the apology to the alarmed clergy
of the Church of England when Bishop Atterbury was charged with
treason and imprisoned for his Jacobite activities. To some fearful ears,
the rumblings around the nation in response to the news of Atterbury's
arrest began to sound like the prelude to another Sacheverell trial, and
the ministry cast about desperately for some way to calm the rising
High Church hysteria.

Into this highly charged and politicized atmosphere, Pearce issued
his honorable and conscientious *A Letter to the Clergy of the Church of
England: On occasion of the Commitment of the Right Reverend the Lord
Bishop of Rochester to the Tower of London* (1722). He assured the men
of the cloth that Atterbury was being treated with the respect and
reverence due his station. What was under investigation, he explained,
was the treasonable activity of the man, as distinct and separable from
his sacred office, his possible designs "to subvert our Constitution,
and place upon our Imperial Throne one grown up under the very
Wing of the Papal See." As a man of God, Pearce said, Atterbury was
enjoined by his office "to promote the Peace of Mankind, and to
preach the Doctrines of Obedience to the Higher Powers in being";
he was culpable if he had chosen instead to promote strife and blood-
shed. Besides, he added, "we are all bound by the most solemn Oaths
of Allegiance and Abjuration . . . and now that this Gordian Knot is
fasten'd on our Consciences, which no Art or Time can loose, nothing
but Violence and Wickedness can cut, how must we appear to the
World, how black, how detestable, if we act contrary to this sacred
Engagement!"

Whether Astell disapproved at the time of Pearce's apology, or
thought it necessary to preserve the peace, the issue had cooled five
years later when she went to hear his sermons. In any case, Pearce was
more a literary man than a political animal. A philological scholar equally
at home defending Milton from Bentley's heavy-handed *Emendations*
or the miracles in Hebrew and Greek scripture from Thomas Woolston's
rationalistic dismissal, he was considered one of the most learned men
of his day.[7] When Samuel Johnson was working on his great *Dictionary*,
the only assistance he received, according to Boswell, "was a paper
containing twenty etymologies, sent to him by . . . Dr. Pearce."[8] Pearce
also encouraged Sir Isaac Newton to publish his *Chronology of Ancient
Kingdoms*, a project thirty years in the making, discussed often between
the two friends.[9]

Pearce was known to be a man particularly sympathetic to women. Celebrated for his devotion to his wife of more than fifty years, he enjoyed the confidence of several powerful women at court, as well as a number of more modest gentlewomen. Every year the Society for the Propagation of the Gospel in Foreign Lands (an organization closely tied to the SPCK), of which he was an active member, noted that several anonymous gentlewomen donated money to the organization through the agency of Dr. Pearce. When he died, the largest benefaction in his will was £5,000 to support a college of twenty clergymen's widows in Bromley, Kent, a little community of women that was in danger of bankruptcy because of its inadequate endowment.[10]

That Mary Astell was able to gratify her desire at sixty-three and sixty-four to attend the sermons of this up-and-coming clergyman about whom there was so much admiring talk, although she had no carriage and would hire no chair, is testimony equally to the liveliness of her mind, the firmness of her will, and the vigor of her body. She could not suspect how ill she was soon to be.

It began as a painful lump in one of her breasts. As Ballard tells the story, Astell dressed and managed the cancer by herself in utmost secrecy, until she plainly saw that the breast would have to be cut off. The tumor must have grown large and painful for her to decide to take such extreme measures. That it required dressing means that there was an ulceration of the skin or a sore that would not heal. This suggests such an advanced invasion of the tumor that it is likely the cancer had metastasized by the time Astell sought an operation. In Mary Astell's day, the victims of breast cancer rarely survived more than three years after the onset of symptoms, and in this case it is probable that she died of the disease rather than the primitive means used to stem it.[11]

The causes of such a cancer, as they were understood by the most advanced surgeons of the mid-eighteenth century, were an overindulgence in lard and pork meats, or the application of "acrimonious or caustic Medicines" to the breast. It was also believed that "Grief and Trouble of Mind are very apt to create a cancerous Disposition of Body." At least one book of surgery noted: "It is observable that old maids and even married Women that do not breed, are very subject to Cancers in the Breast; this generally happens to them when they are turned of forty Years of Age, at the time when the menstrual or haemorrhoidal Discharge begins to decrease or disappear."[12]

For Astell, the sore that would not heal was at first just one more trial in a difficult life—one more painful irritation that mortal flesh had to suffer before she could go to her eternal rest. Nonetheless, when the lump became unendurable she sought a cure at the hands of a surgeon named Dr. Johnson and asked him to perform a mastectomy, hoping that it would relieve her suffering and prolong her life.

Dr. Johnson was a Scottish-trained physician with considerable skill in surgically removing tumors, and was increasingly well-known as a specialist in women's breast cancers.[13] He was attached to the court of Queen Caroline when Astell first approached him and asked him to examine her. At that time his reputation was growing, and women troubled by pains and lumps in the breast came to consult him from all over England. He is likely the original of the special surgeon from the queen's household in Maria Edgeworth's *Belinda* (1801), who comes from the palace to operate on Lady Delacour's putative breast cancer. It was said that Dr. Johnson, who was also a clergyman, operated successfully on Charlotte Clayton, one of the maids of honor, and that she was so grateful that she had used her influence with Queen Caroline, then princess of Wales, to have him appointed her domestic chaplain.[14] To all who knew the story, Charlotte Clayton was happy proof of Dr. Johnson's skill, as she went about her active life. She could be seen hale and hearty every Sunday at St. Martin's-in-the-Fields, for instance, for she too was a great admirer of Zachary Pearce. Pearce makes it clear in his autobiography that he owed his initial introduction at court to Charlotte Clayton's favor.[15]

There is some evidence that Queen Caroline feared breast cancer, and for that reason found Dr. Johnson's attendance comforting. Indeed, Sir Robert Walpole conjectured that Charlotte Clayton gained her ascendancy over the queen because she was privy to some secret of ill health that her majesty suffered. He guessed this aloud to his son Horace once after a conversation in which the queen questioned him obsessively about the physical causes for the recent death of Lady Walpole, his wife.[16]

There were not many medical personnel who were thought to be expert in women's diseases at that time. Women usually treated breast cancers and other gynecological disorders privately among themselves. Two home remedies for breast cancer recommended among Astell's friends, for example, were Lady Stapleton's recipe for a potion made of warts sliced off a horse's foreleg and boiled in white wine, and a plaster recommended by a Mrs. W., to be applied externally, made of mutton suet, beeswax, and flaxseed. But a number of women of Astell's acquaintance trusted Dr. Johnson, and they advised one another to see him for any "pain or cancerish complaint in the breast."

Mary Greene, for one, a Chelsea neighbor to Astell and Lady Catherine, told Lady Betty that she had once gone to see Dr. Johnson when she had been alarmed by a pain in her shoulder and breast, a pain accompanied by a swelling and lump in her arm. First she had sent to Sir Hans Sloane who told her to be bled, prescribed a gentle physick, and ordered her to take wood lice both morning and night. Then a friend of hers who was having a wen cut out by Dr. Johnson persuaded her to also ask his opinion of her soreness and the lump. He told her that she had merely strained herself, probably by lifting something, and advised her not to trouble herself any more about it. "I can't but have a good opinion of Dr. Johnson's judgment and honesty," concluded Mrs. Greene, "because he would not tamper with me, nor order me so much as a diet drink, whereby he might have got more than a guinea by me."[17]

When the time came, Astell went to see the Reverend Dr. Johnson. It is conceivable that by then she had met Charlotte Clayton, for Lady Mary Wortley Montagu had been a maid of honor with her at court. When Mary Astell saw that Dr. Johnson knew of no other way to cure her ulcerated breast, she entreated him "to take it off in the most private manner imaginable." She was very secretive about the operation, and brought only one person to attend her. In her modesty, she even objected to the presence of those others whom Dr. Johnson deemed necessary to assist at the surgery. With great dignity, she is supposed to have accepted the suffering and pain that she was about to undergo. As Ballard reported the scene: "she refused to have her hands held, and did not discover the least timidity or impatience, but went through the operation without the least struggling or resistance or even so much as giving a groan or a sigh."[18]

In the early nineteenth century, Fanny Burney underwent a similar operation, which took twenty minutes. Astell's sangfroid is remarkable in view of Burney's description of the "dreadful steel" plunging into the breast, cutting through veins, arteries, flesh, and nerves, after which she endured the excruciating experience of feeling and *hearing* the flesh scraped from the breastbone, atom by atom, all without the benefit of anaesthesia.[19]

After the breast was removed, the standard medical practice of the day was to sprinkle onto the wound a large quantity of scraped lint, or even fine-powdered plaster of paris. The patient's chest was then wrapped with thick compresses. It was not until the end of the century that the great surgeon Henry Fearon showed that the operation was much more successful when a sizeable flap of skin was preserved to cover the wound, as opposed to the old way, "in which the whole breast was frequently swept off with too little regard to the sufferings of the patients and none at all to the preservation of skin."[20]

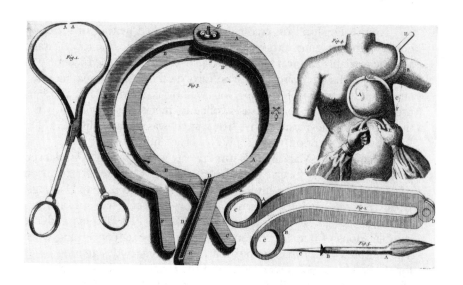

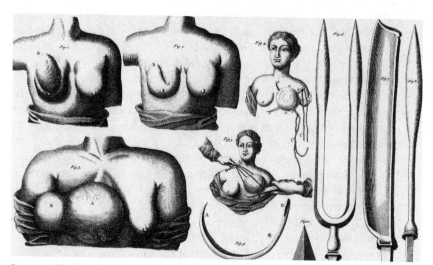

Images of breast cancers and surgical instruments used in their removal, from Laurence Heister, A General System of Surgery, *1743. By permission of the Countway Library, Harvard University.*

322
Chapter Ten

To give Dr. Johnson credit, Mary Astell died neither of infection nor of hemorrhaging, although the conditions were none too sanitary, and the available surgical techniques fairly crude. It is true that she was never well again afterwards, and was "carried off in less than two months" after the operation "of a dropsy or swelling tympany."[21] But it seems probable that her abdomen was swollen by metastases, and that by the time she had the mastectomy, her system was already diseased. Dr. Johnson's intervention was simply too little and too late.

We know that Mary Astell's surgery was considered successful, even though she did not survive long, because some years later Dr. Johnson was called in to perform a similar operation on Lady Elizabeth Hastings. Great care was used in selecting a surgeon—the case had national importance because of the scale of Lady Betty's benefactions and the complications of new legislation, just passed in 1736, concerning wills. The Statute of Mortmain stipulated that any legacy designating lands for charitable purposes was nullified if the testator died less than a year after registering the will. This meant that Lady Betty had to live for a full year after making up her will, if her final wishes were to be carried out. She had not thought to draw up a will until she detected the first signs of cancer, and then it progressed so rapidly and became so painful, that even given the uncertain prognosis of surgery, it began to seem that she would not live long without making the attempt.

The Reverend Dr. Johnson himself was impressed with the seriousness of the case and explained to his brother-in-law after it was over that it had not only been a matter of "saving a life which has done so much honour to Religion in general," but a matter of protecting the "thousands" who were "supported by her great and extensive charities. If her Ladyship had miscarried, all this must have fallen to the ground, by reason of the Statute of Mortmain . . . but, I bless God, I have been the happy instrument of completing the cure."[22]

Lady Betty did not live much longer than the time required of her by law—only eight days past the limit of Mortmain. Still, she survived her operation the better part of a year while Astell lived only little more than a month after hers. Undoubtedly there were many differences in their cases—their physical stamina, the virulence of their tumors, and the overall treatment that each received. Nevertheless, one cannot avoid the impression that in the final chapter Lady Betty clung stubbornly and willfully to life whereas Astell as eagerly welcomed death once the end was finally in sight.

In Lady Mary Wortley Montagu's family, the anecdote was told for generations of how Astell used her coming death to try one more time to pressure Lady Mary into mending her worldly ways. It was in the middle of one of those pious perorations with which Astell regularly edified Lady Mary that she decided to tell the younger woman that her own reckoning was close at hand. Breaking off her somewhat scolding tone abruptly and gazing keenly at her friend for some moments, she said: "My days are numbered. I am old; that you know; but now I tell you in confidence, I have a mortal disease which must soon bring me to the grave. I go hence, I humbly trust in Christ, to a state of happiness; and if departed spirits be permitted to re-visit those whom they have loved on earth, remember I make you a solemn promise that mine shall appear to you, and confirm the truth of all I have been saying."[23]

Mary Astell had all her life spoken of death as a blessing, a release from the burdens of the flesh into an ecstatic realization of spiritual perfection. And indeed when her time came she seemed to welcome it. She had her coffin brought into her room weeks before she actually died. Impatient with the slowness of the process, she also cut herself off from the world two full days before death came, and lay there expectantly, neither eating nor drinking and permitting no one to attend her. As Ballard reports it: "finding the time of her dissolution drawing nigh, she ordered her coffin and shroud to be made and brought to her bedside and there to remain in her view as a constant memento to her of her approaching fate, that her mind might not deviate or stray one moment from GOD, its most proper object. Her thoughts were now so entirely fixed upon GOD and eternity, that for some days before her death she earnestly desired that no company might be permitted to come to her, refusing at that time to see even her old and dear friend the Lady Catherine Jones, purely because she would not be disturbed in the last moments of her divine contemplations. She departed this life about the eleventh day of May, in the year 1731, and was buried at Chelsea the 14th day of the same month."[24]

When Lady Betty recounted the story to Bishop Wilson of the Isle of Man, she reported the additional detail that Lady Catherine had been moved by the eloquence of Astell's final leave-taking: "The great and good Mrs. Astell died at Chelsea the 9th of this month; she was five days actually a-dying. Lady Catherine Jones was with her two days before her death; she then begged to see no more of her old acquaintance and friends, having done with the world, and made her peace with God; and what she had then to do was to bear her pains with patience, cheerfulness, and entire resignation to the Divine will. Lady Catherine adds that she believes her words were turned into as perfect an exercise of those virtues as ever mortality arrived at."[25]

So ended an exemplary life with an exemplary, if impatiently awaited, death. The newspapers carried a few notices, but as Mary Astell was no longer in the public eye, they made little of the story. *The Daily Journal* of May 29, 1731, carried the longest obituary:

A few Days ago died at Chelsea, in an advanced Age, a Gentlewoman very much admired for several ingenious Pieces, with which she had favour'd the Publick, in the Cause of Religion and Virtue. Her Correspondence with the famous Mr. Norris of Bemerton, on the celebrated Subject of the *Love of God*, gain'd her no small Applause: And whoever reads her *Reflexions on Marriage* (a new Edition of which, with Alterations and Additions, she lately publish'd) her Book intitled *Proposal to the Ldies*, that intitled, The Christian Religion as professed by a Daughter of the Church of England, together with her other Pieces, will observe in them the Traces of an elevated Mind, display'd in an excellent Manner of Reasoning, and a Turn of Genius above what is usual in her own Sex, and not unworthy of the most distinguish'd Writers of the other.

But the flurry of publicity quickly passed. Dr. John King buried her in the Chelsea churchyard on May 14. It was a simple ceremony; Lady Catherine Jones and a few servants attended.

She had lived sixty-five years—a riper age than either parent had attained—time, as she so often observed, although the most precious of treasures, being distributed without regard to wealth or status. She had done more with her life than almost any other woman of her time, if the measure of achievement is ideas formulated or books published, or an independent example set before the public.

She was forgotten almost immediately, with a rapidity which is surprising, even granted her own frequent observation that history tended to record the exploits of men and to ignore those of women. Her reputation barely survived her. By the end of the decade those who had known her best were themselves dying, Lady Betty in 1739 and Lady Catherine in 1740. The last sale of her books in 1743 was meant to dispose of surplus stock from the unsold printing of 1730.[26] The advertisement, which listed *Some Reflections Upon Marriage*, *A Serious Proposal* Parts I and II, and *The Christian Religion* "by the late Mrs. Astell," was proof not of Astell's renewed reputation, but of the optimism of a bookseller old enough to remember her earlier popularity. In the 1740s, when George Ballard was seeking information for his book about the learned women of England, his antiquarian colleagues had never heard of Mary Astell.

Ballard began collecting facts about Mary Astell's life and work as early as 1736, as part of his great antiquarian project, *Memoirs of Several Ladies of Great Britain Who Have Been Celebrated for their Writings or Skill in the Learned Languages, Arts, and Sciences* (1752). A dressmaker by trade and an amateur historian and numismatist, he conceived of this encyclopedic enterprise, which took him fifteen years to complete, after making the acquaintance of Elizabeth Elstob. Once a famous scholar, but reduced by the time Ballard met her to teaching in a dames' school, Elizabeth Elstob was living in nearby Evesham under the name of Frances Smith when Ballard first learned of her whereabouts. The shock of finding such a celebrated Anglo-Saxon scholar in these reduced circumstances, and the realization that her fate was by no means atypical, resolved Ballard to compose a book which he hoped would dispel the prejudice in his society against learned ladies.[27] He would inform the world about the many learned women of England's past; he would write a series of biographical sketches about them and prove by example that women were as capable of improvement by education as men, and that given the opportunity they became great linguists, philologists, poets, theologians, statesmen, and scholars.

Astell was one of the first women George Ballard interested himself in, probably because Elstob had spoken about her to him. Ballard exerted himself to find out everything he could about Mary Astell and her works. He put his friends to work on the task, a network of trained antiquarians whose sources and knowledge would be impossible to duplicate today, and whose political and religious leanings predisposed them to appreciate this rare woman to whom Ballard introduced them.

He encouraged Elstob to remember what Astell was like; she told him one story about the writer and her pet parrot that made him roar with laughter.[28] But he never passed along the anecdote, deeming it beneath the scholarly dignity of his project. He only retained and printed such evidence as contributed to his argument that women were as educable and intellectually capable as men. Indeed, our picture of Astell's high-mindedness, her one-sided seriousness, the only eighteenth-century image of her available to a modern historian, may be in part an artifact of Ballard's vision of learned ladies and his decisions about detail and emphasis.[29]

In addition to Elstob, Ballard may have also gleaned some information about Astell from Lady Ann, countess of Coventry, who lived long enough to subscribe to his book. He seems not to have made contact with Lady Mary Wortley Montagu, however, who in any case lived out of the country most of the time Ballard's book was in progress. Lady Mary is not even on the list of his subscribers.

Astell's example confirmed Ballard's observation that the "many ingenious women of this nation, who were really possess'd of a great share of learning and have, no doubt, in their time been famous for it, are not only unknown to the publick in general, but have been passed by in silence by our greatest biographers."[30] Had it not been for Ballard, Astell too would have disappeared in silence; fortunately, his book was meant to remedy the public amnesia as well as to lament it. He collected the known facts about her before they were hopelessly dispersed.

To Ballard, the most important things about Mary Astell were that she wrote learned books, and that she would have been more famous for them if she had been a man. In our day she has become significant for other reasons. She was the first English feminist fully conscious of the political implications of her position on gender; her arguments and rhetorical strategies have been with us ever since. Her lasting contribution was the articulation of a set of ideas premised on the Enlightenment assumption that it was a rational universe, and that God distributed the powers of reasoning more or less equally—and certainly without regard to gender. Robert Halsband calls her "the founder of the feminist movement."[31] Moira Ferguson differentiates her from the other, earlier polemicists in the English "querelle des femmes" by specifying that she was the first to argue for women's equality in a sustained and systematic way.[32] Behind both these remarks is an awareness of a radically innovative woman-centered consciousness in Astell, a sensibility which rarely ignored, and never disguised, gender. The way she insisted on her speaking self as a female self, her primary loyalty to other women, the reasoning behind her separatist impulses—these make her life and thought of interest to modern feminist thinkers.

In *Reinventing Womanhood*, Carolyn Heilbrun describes how a young woman of the Klementi, an Albanian tribe, must give up her gender identification if she refuses, for whatever reason, to marry the man her parents have picked out for her. She must steadfastly and at length state her resolution, and then she must swear an oath before twelve witnesses that she will never marry at all. After this, she "ranked as a man, might, and often did, wear men's attire, eat with the men (which no other woman did), smoke with them and carry weapons; such women were known as 'Albanian virgins' and worked as herdsmen of sheep and goats."[33] Such a system leaves no ambiguity about the purpose of a woman's life. If she does not marry she forfeits her identity as a female and henceforth lives, and is considered in the eyes of society, another sort of man.

Mary Astell had no interest in being counted as a man or in living like one. Indeed, her mixture of styles is what is so odd about her, what made her unique among her (male) contemporaries. Her comfortable affection for other women and their gossip about court fashion in combination with her relentless arguments about the Occasional Conformity Bill; the way she passed along recipes for medicinal potions one day and carefully interpreted results of parliamentary elections the next—these make her unlike any other intellectual of her time. She rejected marriage, not because she did not want to be a woman, but because she thought that the institution limited a woman's agency and volition more than was good for her. It should be possible to retain one's primary identity as a woman but to live outside of marriage, she argued; her *A Serious Proposal* suggests one feasible way to manage it economically.

Nor did Astell come to feminism by way of narcissism. She never thought of herself as a special case, better than most women and as good as any man. She thought that women in general were not sufficiently valued in the culture, and that as a population they were every bit as intelligent, as good, as kind, as men. She only contended for her laurels, as she so often said, to lay them at the feet of "ye Ladies."

She took it as one of the central tasks of her life to spread this conviction of agency to other women. It pained her to see women value themselves only as they were desired by men, while so much of the male world treated them with barely veiled contempt. She appealed to women to cultivate their "higher" natures that they might become more fully human. "Do not neglect that particle of Divinity within you," she wrote. "A desire to advance and perfect its Being is planted by GOD in all Rational Natures." Her exhortations often have a modern ring: "Let us learn to pride our selves in something more excellent than the invention of a Fashion: And not entertain such a degrading thought of our own *worth*, as to imagin that our Souls were given us only for the service of our Bodies, and that the best improvement we can make of these is to attract the eyes of men."[34]

Astell was also a philosophical idealist, and this intellectual position simultaneously reinforced and disarmed her feminism. She assumed that the point of developing one's higher nature and cultivating one's "particle of Divinity" was to achieve spiritual transcendence—not a surprising strategy in a society which denied and thwarted every impulse for personal advancement and which held out little hope for social change. With almost stoic detachment she wrote:

> From this sacred Mountain where the world will be plac'd at our feet, at such a distance from us, that the steams of its corruptions shall not obscure our eyesight; we shall have a right prospect of it, and clearly discern that

all its Allurements, all those Gaities and Pageantries which at present we admire so much, are no better than insignificant Toys, which have no value but what our perverse Opinion imposes on them.[35]

She assumed that the only way for a woman to maintain and live up to a serious ambition was to invert the usual terms of worldly achievement, and to replace the ordinary goals of power and wealth with the more abstract—but, as she would have said, more lasting—goods of a disciplined mind and spirit.

From Christian Platonism she took the terms for redefining the aims of life, the virtues to be striven for in lieu of the ephemeral rewards of a corrupt world. Descartes' radical skepticism provided the rationale for discarding the current materialistic ethos and positing an inverted system of values. The meditative introspection that Descartes described, inching forward on the basis of clear and distinct ideas, provided her with a much needed method for analysis. The Cartesian assumption that rationality is natural and does not have to be taught, and that it is more or less equally distributed in the population, licensed her to take her own mind seriously.

But where many had learned an intellectual discipline from Descartes or a new orientation to reality from the Platonists, few actually tried to put these precepts into practice, to live as if truth lay in ideas and essences. Hume, for instance, writes winningly about how the hubbub of a tavern was a necessary restorative when he wandered too long in the morbidly self-reflecting and contradictory mazes of his thought.[36] Astell, on the other hand, wanted nothing to separate her own practices from those philosophies she admired. With too literal a sense of her duty, and against her own rather passionate nature, she tried to follow the Christian injunction to eschew the pleasures of this life, to be a fool to this world, in preparation for the next. The personal cost of channeling her own immense ambition into pious self-abnegation is suggested by the rigid obstinacy with which she denied the importance of material reality, as if it were a lesson she had to teach herself again and again.

Astell's philosophical idealism was also the source of her originality, for it enabled her to set aside the customary hierarchy of values in English society. She insisted on testing the truth of her experience, starting from scratch, accepting nothing on faith. Her novel observations about the position of women in the culture and their demeaned status in marriage were part and parcel of her generalized refusal to accept anything as true or right, without subjecting it to radical doubt. To her, "He for God only, she for God in him" was not a clear and distinct idea. Again and again she exhorted her readers to think for themselves and to contemplate the meaning of their lives with minds cleared of mystifying preconceptions.

Astell began the modern dialogue in print about the power relations between the sexes. Novelists from Defoe to Richardson drew upon her example and her writings for their portraits of independent womanhood.[37] For intellectuals like Lady Mary Chudleigh and Lady Mary Wortley Montagu or the later bluestockings, she was an important model whose acomplishments helped them to imagine their own potential. Her influence can be traced in the novels of Jane Austen, Charlotte Brontë, and Virginia Woolf, in their efforts to present heroines with sufficient spiritual and psychological strength to hold their own in a patriarchal society. George Gissing's heroine Rhoda Nunn in *The Odd Women*, who lives in Chelsea and is convinced that marriage cripples women psychologically, and that the only alternative is for single women to live together and provide support for one another, owes much to Astell.

She was the first thinker to question the benefits of marriage in the bourgeois era, when the possibility of individual choice and marrying for love were thought to improve the institution so immeasurably beyond the arranged marriages of the past. In a period which witnessed the serious contraction of possibilities for women within society, when the anonymity of the nunnery, the autonomy of the manor, or even a range of independent professions such as midwifery and silk throwing, were no longer available as respectable roles for women, hers was the only protest that marriage ought not be the only solution to a woman's life. In a period when urban life increasingly excluded women from the public world and the adaptive English increasingly saw the entire sex more and more as meant exclusively for domestic life, Mary Astell's was the only voice that asked seriously, from a female point of view, if marriage were really a woman's only and greatest good.[38] As gender and marital status began to be more central to the definition of a woman than any other attribute—be it her brains, her productivity, her class, or her piety—Astell urged other women to resist such definition. They had to learn again how to live for themselves, to understand their own needs and purposes and not to allow definition of their lives from outside. She warned that the tyranny of men in marriage could destroy all moral agency. Her proud spirit shuddered at submitting to an inferior mind or a less delicate sense of virtue.

She was the first woman to live alone publicly without forfeiting her respectability. It was unusual for a single woman of marriageable age to live alone before that time. In that sense she was the first of that modern breed, "the new woman," a forerunner of the species of energetic, independent women who dominate the stage in the plays of Shaw or Ibsen. After her it became more common to opt for single self-sufficiency. It was easier for Elizabeth Carter to live alone and write (or for Hannah More or Hester Mulso or Mary Wollstonecraft) because Mary Astell had done so.

Astell's immediate successor in English letters is less easily ascertained. Lady Mary Wortley Montagu is the obvious candidate, although, as we have seen, her sense of class debarred her from taking any strenuous part in public debate. Today, with the publication of her letters and the many retellings of anecdotes that display her wit, Lady Mary is sometimes counted among the Augustan intelligentsia, although always as an unofficial member.

No other woman writer picked up where Astell left off. No other tried self-consciously and publicly to live up to the dignity of her nature and to do something with her life for posterity to remember her by. By 1710, the feminist impulse that Astell had fanned into being with the publication of her own books was dying back into embers again. The series of feminist texts that had been initiated by *A Serious Proposal* stopped coming from the presses. Women's place in society ceased, for a while, to be a regular topic in the popular media. This is one of the reasons, of course, that Astell herself was forgotten so quickly. Such authors as Eliza Haywood, Jane Barker, and Mary Davys, who were writing romantic novels in the 1720s, 1730s, and 1740s, did not concern themselves much with conscious polemics about sexual politics. Roxana, the independent heroine to whom Defoe gave Astell's language and sentiments about marriage, came to a bad end, as everyone knows. Not until 1739 would feminism again appear in England with the Sophia pamphlets and Mary Collier's *The Woman's Labour: an epistle to Mr. Stephen Duck: in answer to his late poem, called "The Thresher's Labour"* (1739), followed by Richardson's novels and Ballard's *Memoirs*.[39]

But if Astell had no direct disciples, she had many readers among the women of her generation. The memory of her person and the meaning of her life did not die with her, but went underground. The intellectually minded women who read her kept her memory alive for several decades. Whatever the reason for the inactivity of feminists in the years after Astell—whether backlash or general prosperity—her ideas about marriage and education and her pride of gender were carried by word of mouth into the next generation. Lady Ann Coventry and Lady Mary Wortley Montagu told anecdotes about her among the bluestockings; Elizabeth Elstob spoke frequently to George Ballard about her; and Sarah Chapone praised her writings to her good friend Samuel Richardson. Inventing a new tradition as they spoke, they talked of Mary Astell and circulated their own copies of her books among their friends.

Astell would be an anomalous figure to find leading any radical movement. A High Churchwoman and a Tory pamphleteer, her defense of the existing political forms was absolute. She seems somewhat out of place in the company of those usually associated with the growth of egalitarian ideas in England—at one end of the chronology with the Diggers and Ranters and other communal sects in the time of the Commonwealth, and at the other end with the circle of English free-thinkers who sympathized with the French Revolution, a group which included Godwin, Wollstonecraft, Priestley, and Hays.

Feminism in the late seventeenth century seems to have had a different genesis. Rather than developing as a natural extension of the concept of political equality, it seems to have been an outgrowth of philosophical premises resting on an experiential base. Astell's indignation at the injustice of forbidden education and advancement, and her sympathy for women subjected to tyrannical marriage, led her to write and publish her books of protest. The personal became for Astell, as they say, political.

In terms of conventional politics she was conservative. Her writings are often mistaken by modern historians for those of Thomas Wagstaffe or other minor Tory writers. She lent her voice to the High Church chorus when crowds were demonstrating in the streets for "Sacheverell and the Church forever"; she opened a charity school under the auspices of the SPCK when that conservative organization was sponsoring schools in every county and scores of them in London, to educate the laboring masses for their places in the social pyramid. She sympathized with the Jacobites in 1715 and in 1722, the years of their greatest momentum. In other words, she rode the crest of whatever was the current Tory enthusiasm, whether the issue was occasional conformity—the schism in the church—or the defense of divine right and the commemoration of the death of the royal martyr, Charles I. She certainly did not ground her feminism in a larger analysis of social inequity based on class, labor, or property.

Her thinking on the "woman question" was not derived from the political theorizing that developed in the aftermath of the Civil War, although she was undoubtedly affected by those events and that atmosphere. Revolutionary thought never occurs at times of deepest darkness, just as revolutionary leaders are never among the most downtrodden. It takes some gleam of hope through a crack in the existing system to encourage radical perceptions and radical acts. Many orthodoxies were shattered in England in the course of the seventeenth century, and each contributed to the instability of the whole. Not only Astell's feminism but her conservatism too reflects the uncertainties of the rapidly changing world into which she was born.

The key to Astell's radicalism is radical doubt, not radical politics. She was liberated by philosophy, the terms and methods of which obviously helped her to rationalize the disappointments of her life. The "new way of ideas" with its emphasis on a naively empirical rational introspection encouraged her to look hard at her own experience. The philosophers of the seventeenth century taught her to take her own vantage point as a thinking woman as the perfectly appropriate starting place from which to analyze the world—indeed, as the only possible starting place. Once there, given the force of her character, it was only a small step to wanting to convince others of the validity of her perceptions.

She was a pioneer, a thinker, and a writer, living alone in London at the turn of the century, with the temerity to publish her ideas. In doing so, she left for scholars a record of the responses of an intelligent, literate, self-respecting woman in the reign of Queen Anne. She inspired many women of her time to take themselves seriously as rational creatures. And she left for other women the example of her independent life, her uncompromising stands, her pleasure in what was finally a defiant intelligence, and her abiding love for others of her own sex.

Appendixes

Appendix A

Inventory of Peter Astell's Worldly Goods, Newcastle, 1678

An Inventory of all and Singular the goods & Chattells and Creditts, wch late were and did belong unto Peter Astell^{late} of the Towne and County of Newcastle upon Tine Gentleman deceased, Taken and apprized the tenth day of December Anno regni regis Caroli Secdi Augt et tricisimo primo Anno 'p Dni¹ 1679.

Inp^{es} In the Hall Twelve Trim worke chaires, One long Seate, One thrumworke² Cushion, Two Spanish:Tables, Two green Cloth:Carpets, One Suite of hangings, One pair brasse End Irons, Two Window Curtaines, One long Curtainerod, One large looking glasse, One Clock, One fire-shovill, One porr³ & One pair of Tongs . . . . £ 9 19s 10d

In the Parlour Eight Russia Leather Chairs, One Spanish Table, One little side Table, Two green:Carpets, One Curtaine rod, two Window Curtains, One hanging Shelfe, Two mapps, One Picture, One porr, One fireshovill & tongs three Cushions . . . . £ 4 1s 4d

In the Hall Chamber One Large bedstead, One quilted:matresse, One ffether bed and bolster One pair of pillows, two little pillows, Two pair of blanketts, One

---

1. per Domini. The regnal years of Charles II are reckoned from January 30, 1649, the date of the execution of Charles I. Thus 1679 was considered the thirtieth year of the reign of Charles II.
2. tufted.
3. poker.

rugg, One Suite of green curtaines and head peece, One
little table & Cloth, One Case of drawers, Seaven
low:chaires two curtaine rods four Window curtaines, one
skreene, One looking-glasse, three pictures, One pair of
end Irons One porr, one fireshovill & Tongs . . . . . . £ 13 3s 4d

In the Parlour Chamber, One large bedstead One quilted
Mattrisse, One fether bed and bolster, Two pillows, One
pair of blanketts, One Suite of Curtaines and head peece,
Six low chaires, One Case of drawers, One pair of Stands
and Table, One looking glasse One pair tongs &
fireshovill One curtaine rod, and two window
Curtaines . . . . £ 10 6s 8d

In the Nursery One high bedstead & Curtaines One
Matrisse, One fether bed & bolster, One pair of blanketts,
One Coverlid One rugg, Two pillowes One presse, One
Trundle bed, One Matresse, One fether bed and bolster
One pair of blanketts & rugg One case of drawers three
chaire and One little Table. . . . . £ 5 10s

In the Garett Chamber, One bedstead, One Matresse, One
fetherbed & bolster, One pair of blanketts, Three
Coverlids One little Chest, One Table, Six Stooles and
One skreene . . . . £ 3

In the Kitching Eighteen large Pewter dishes, Two dozen
and one half dozen of pewter plates, four sawsers four
pair of Candlesticks, three Pewter basons, One Pewter
Cullender,[4] Two large flaggons One pint pott two pewter
pye plates, Tenn dozen of bottles, One latten[5] Cullender,
two dish Covers, one pasty pann, Two pair of Snuffers
and two snuffing dishes, one dridyingbox one
extinguisher, One saveall,[6] four Chyna dishes, nine plates,
One Salt.seller, One trencher[7] case, four dozen trench[es]
One Wodden:morter & pestell and Scummer, Two brasse

4. collander.
5. a mixed yellow metal predominating in brass.
6. a contrivance, like a spike on a plate, for burning candle-ends down to the end.
7. flat wooden or earthenware plate for everyday use.

morters & pestells, Two pye peales,[8] Two pye boards,
Two roleing pinns, One paire of brasse tongs and
fireshovill, four Wooden bowles, two Trays One brasse
warming pan, one Copper Chaffindish, One brasse
scummer, Six brasse panns, two brasse potts One
Stewpan, two spitts, one pair of racks and one Chopping
knife . . . . £ 20 18s

One paire of beefe forks and Whymze,[9] Two brand Irons,
One Iron potlid two box Irons & Standard[10] One dozen
of Skewers, One Chaffindish, One latten dripping pann,
One little brandiron,[11] One fire shovill tongs and porr,
Two recking crooks,[12] Two Tables One Cawell,[13] One
Candle box, One Salt kitt, Three Croquetts, two chaires,
One Lanthorne, One pair of Searcirs,[14] One greate pepper
box mustard pott, and three White Earthen Chamber
potts . . . . £ 1 3s 4d

In the Brewhouse Masking [Mashing] Tubb, Wort tubb[15]
gile fatt,[16] Skummer, Stirrer and Sieve, One Sia[17] three
collers four hogsheads One Rhenish Wine caske two paire
of Gantrees[18] 17s

Twenty paire of Sheets, One pair of Spreading sheets
twelve paire of pillowbers,[19] Six pair little pillowb^cs twelve
dresser cloths, twelve dozen napkins Eighteen long table
cloths, three dozen of Towells Six pair of course sheets,
three dozen ordinary napkins Six ordinary Tablecloths,
One dozen Kitching Towells . . . . £ 30

8. pounding or mashing implement.
9. platter.
10. tall candlestick.
11. basket.
12. browning or glazing iron.
13. coal recks; rakes for coal and ashes.
14. scissors.
15. Wort is the infusion of malt or other grain which then ferments and becomes
   beer.
16. vat holding a gill.
17. from the Hebrew "seah," a dry measure equal to a bushel and a half.
18. four-footed wooden stand for barrels.
19. pillowcases.

Plate One large Silver Kann & One leste[20] Two Silver
plates, One large Salt and three Lester,[21] one Cawdle
cupp,[22] One Tumbler, One dozen of Spoones, two little
spoones three porreng[es] and one Taster . . . .   £ 41

One pair of Tosting Irons 15s

One Suite of Wrought Curtaines One wroughtbed and
Tenn wrought Chaire Covers . . . .   £   5   6s   8d

One Eighth part of a Shipp called the hercules of
Yarmouth . . . .   £ 23

One Sixteenth part of the Shipp called the Mary and
Katherine, Bartholomew Kirkhouse being Master . . . .   £ 60

One Eight part of M[r] John Emmersons Buss . . . . . .   £ 26

One Two and thirtieth part of the Shipp whereof Mr.
John Rudstone is Master . . . .   £ 30

One Two and thirtieth part of the Shipp whereof Leonard
Vaughn is Master . . . .   £ 15

The Books of the deceased[23] . . . .   £   5

Money received w[ch] [was] due to the deceased at the time of
his death . . . .   £ 170   17s   6d

The purse & apparrell of the deceased . . . .   £ 50

Summa.   £ 535   18s   8d

Robert Henderson ⎫
Tho: Potts   ⎬ Apprizers
Bartholomew: Kirkhouse ⎭

---

20. i.e. one smaller one.
21. i.e. three smaller ones.
22. cup for drinking a posset: warm, spiced, gruel mixed with wine or ale.
23. This did not represent many books; perhaps a Bible and three or four others.

Appendix B

Book Collections of the Countess of Coventry

A Catalogue of Books belonging to the Right Honble The Lady Ann Countess of Coventre taken July the 10th 1702

Folio

A Large Bible B^d Red Turkey
  Leather.
The History of the Bible in 2 Parts.
Le: Grands Body of Philosophy.
Westly's life of Christ.
Evelyn's Sylva.
Cowly's works.
Pearson on the Creed.
A Book of Cyphers.
A Book of Heraldry.
The works by the Author of the
  whole Duty of Man.
Miege's French Dictionary.
Cambridge concordance.
Caves Lives of the Apostles.
Caves Lives of the Primitive fathers.
A Blank book for Receipts
A Book of Cutts

Plucknett's works in 4 Parts.
Cambdens Britañia.
A Large Coñon Prayer book B^d
  Red Turkey Leather.
A Large Bible with guilt leaves B^d
  blew Turkey Leather.
Craig of Succession.
Sherlocks practical Christian.
Dr Taylors Holy Living and Dying.
Reform'd Devotion.
Inetts Devout Christian.
Patrick's heartsease.
Du = Moulin of Contentment.
The Daily office for the Sick.
2 Bibles.
3 Testaments wth the Common
  Prayer.
1 Small Common Prayer book.

These listings of her books, apparently drawn up by Lady Ann herself and found in the muniment room at Badminton, have been transcribed as exactly as possible. I reproduce them here as an aid to scholars who have long wished to know what books might be in the library of an intellectual and independent woman of the day—one who could afford to buy what pleased her.

3 Books w.ᵗʰ Locks.
The Countess of Mortons Daily exercise.
Tonkins Christian Religion in 2 Parts.
Scots Discourse in 2 Parts.
Scots Christians Life in 5 Parts.
Weeks preparation in 2 Parts, 1 Vol:
12 Parts of The Newyears gift, in 4 Parts.
Kettlewell of death.
Chronologicall Tables.
Chelliers Meditations.
Taylors abstract of the Bible.
Wakes principles of the Christian Religion.
Le = du = Pin's Life of Christ.
Sparks Devotion.
Parable of the Pilgrim.
Book of Receipts.
Seneca's Morals.
Sherlock upon Death.
Sherlock of Judgment
Tillotson's Sermons.
Divine addresses by Arwaker.
Method to Private devotion.
L.ᵈ Capell's contemplations.
French Catechism translated.
Whole Duty of a Comunicant.
Bishop Andrew's Devotion.
Hornick's best exercise.
Snake in the Grass.
Combers Epitomy.
Dispensary.
Staynoe of Salvation.
Goodman's Penitent.
5 Volumes of Plays.
Compleat Gardiner.
Norris's Miscellanies.
Erasmus.
Gordens Geographicall gramer. 99.
Evening conference.

Garden of Eden.
Herberts Poems.
Art of drawing.
Countess of Kents Manuall.
Instructions for officers of the Month.
Ovids Metamorphosis.
Temple of Death.
Lady's Letters.
Queens Closet.
Epictetus.
Pechy's herball.
Loveday's Letters.
Contempt of the World.
Art of Prudence.
Ovids Epistles.
Berkly's Argonies.
L.ᵈ Hattons Psalter.
Bishop Duppa's Devotions.
Terence's Comedys.
Dorrington's Journall.
Caves Primitive Christian.
Quevedos Visions.
An Essay of Queen Mary.
Gordens geographicall grammer: 93.
Quarles Emblems.
Pain de L'ame.
Modern Novells.
Advice to a Daughter.
Thomas a Kempis.
Jou d'arm.
Conversationes Novelles.
The gallantries of Versailes.
Harvy's Physitian.
Turkish Spie the 7.ᵗʰ and 8.ᵗʰ Vol:
De L'Educationes des Princes.
Norris's Letters.
Ogilby's Virgill.
Vanity of Arts.
Letters by M.ʳˢ Manly.
Consolation.
Les Plaintes de Protestans.

Le Monde.
Instructions Pour un Jeune
    Seigneur:
Histoire des Oracles.
Conseil Spirituel.
The Count de Soissons.
Semaine Sainte et Priere.
La vie de Gaspard de Coligny.
Les Anecdotes de Florence.
Le etat de L'Europ in 3 Vol:
French Esop.
Evenemens Historiques Choisis.

Le 'tat de la France, in 2 Parts.
Instruction pour une Jeune
    Princesse.
Secrets de Mery.
Portrait des Foiblesses Humaines.
L'Eglise Romaine.
Browns Letters in 2 Parts.
Pellyng of Holyness.
Glanvill's invitation to the
    Sacrament.
Ray's Wisdom of God.
Salmon's family Dictionary.

Jones of Opium.
Dr Moor's exposition of the
    Apocalyps.
Dr Moor's exposition of the
    prophecy of Daniel.
Burnett's Life of Sr Mathew Hale.
Jenks's Devotions.
Walkers vertuous woman found.
Bip Patrick's Xtian Sacrafice.
The triumphs of grace.
Tullies Officies.
Hornocks exercise of Prayer.
Patrick's advice to a friend.
Justification evangelicall. Sr Charles
    Woosely.
Dorringtons family devotions.
King Charles the first's book

} *Had from Edston*

The Christians Pattern by Dr
    Stanhope.
Sr Augustine's meditations.
The Vertuous womans meditations
    and prayers.
Remarks in ye grand Tour of France
    and Italy.
Chudleigh's Poems.
Limborchs Body of Divinity 2 Voll:
The Solitary Gardiner.
Instructions for the education of a
    Daughter.

Lord Clarendon's History 6 Voll:
The Adventures of Catullus.
Colonel Parson's Chronologicall
    Tables.
Arabian Tales. 2d
Herberts Memoirs.
The adventures of Telemachus 2 Voll:
Sr Philip Warwick's Memoirs.
Officium Eucharisticum.
Kalendarium Hortense.
Hale's Contemplations.
Fleetwood's Relative dutys.

A Catalogue of Books Belonging To The Right hon^ble the Lady Anne Coventrye

1. The lives of ye Primitive Fathers   P[plain]   By Dr Cave
2. The lives of the Apostles   Plane[plain]   D. Cave
3. 1st part An Enquiry after happyness.   Guilt [gilt]   Mr Lucas
4. 2^d part An Enquiry after happyness.   G[gilt]   Mr Lucas
5. The Penitent Pardon'd   G   D. Goodman
6. A Discourse upon Death   G   D. Sherlock
7. A Discourse of future judgment   G   D. Sherlock
8. Consolations.   G   M. Drelincourt
9. Emanuel.   G   M.^r Le Noir
10. Evening Conference   G   D. Goodman
11. An introduction to a Devout life   B. Sales
12. Devout Christian   G   D. Patrick
13. Reform'd Devotion   G
14. Holy Devotions   G   B. Andrews
15. Bible   G
16. Common Prayer Book   G
17. Paix de l'ame   G   M. Moulin
18. Devine Addresses   G   translated by Mr Arwaker
19. Sacred Poems   G   Mr Herbert
20. Helps to Devotion   G   B. Duppa
21. Contemplations Devine & Morral   G   Ld Capel
22. 1st part Newyears gift   G
23. 2^d part Newyears gift   G
24. 1st 2^d p^t Whole Duty of Man   G & P
25. La Liturgie   G
26. Comon Prayer ye Best Companion   G
27. 1st part Weeks preparation   G
28. 2^d part Weeks preparation   G
29. Whole Duty of a Communicant.   G   B. Gauden
30. Daily Exercise of y^e   G   Count of Morton
31. Christians Pattern   G   Tho: of Kempis
32. Thresor de prieres   G
33. Silva   G   Mr Evelyn
34. Virgil translated by   G   Oogilby
35. 4 Volumns of Comedy's   G
36. 2 Volumns of Tragedys   G
37. Vissions of Hell by   G   Dom Quevedo
38. La vie de Coligny   G
39. Fables D'Esop avec des reflexions Morales   G   T. Baudoin

40. ────────────────────────────

41. Anecdotes de Florence   G   M. Varillas
42. L'education des princes   G   M. Varillas
43. plaintes des protestans   G
44. Kalendarium hortense   G   Mr Evelyn
45. garden of Eden   G   Sr Hugh Plat
46. The flower garden bound with ye garden of Eden   G   W. Hughes
47. Recueil de Curiosites   G   M. Demery
48. Morale du monde   G   M Scudry
49. Conversations Novel   G   M. de Scudry
50. Instruction pour une jeune princesse   G   en Chetardye
51. Foiblesses humaines   G
52. Histoire des oracles   G
53. Applications histoireques   P [plain]   Ld Bartlet
54. Turkish Spie 5 volumnes   P
55. French gardener   P   translated by Mr Evelin
56. Guide to Eternity   P   translated by Sr Roger L'estrange
57. History of women by   P   John Sherly
58. Prophesies   P   M Nostradamus
59. Emblems   G   quarles
60. Mathematicall recreation   P   W. Oughtned
61. Butlers Ghost   P   Mr Durfey
62. Poems   P   Mr Waller
63. Aesopian Fables translated by   P   Mr Ayres
64. Art of contentment   P
65. paraphrase upon Devine poems by   P   Mr Sandys
66. primitive Christianity   P   D. Cave
67. 21 Sermons by   P   Mr. Holsworth
68. a collection of private devotion   P   B. of Durham
69. Sermon by   Samuel Crooke
70. Books of drawings
71. Flora   P   Mr Rea
72. Dodona's grove   P   by J. H. Esq.
73. A vertous wife   C [comedy]   Mr Tho: Durfey
74. English Fryar   C [comedy]   Mr Crown
75. Belphegor   T.C. [tragic comedy]   Mr Wilson
76. The princess of Cleve   Mr Lee
77. Mock Tempest   C   Mr Durfey
78. London Cuckolds   C   Mr Ravenscroft
79. forc'd Marriage   Trag: C   Mrs Behne
80. juliana   Trag: C   Mr Crowne
81. ye prophetes   an opera   Mr Beaument

82. ye Scowers   C Mr Shadwell
83. Love for money Mr Durfey
84. Treacherous Brothers   T [tragedy] Mr Powell
85. ye sophy   T [tragedy] Sr John Denham
86. Irene   T Mr Swinhoe
87. Witt for money
88. a Sermon   B. of Worcester
89. ye Accomplish't Ladys delight   P [plain]   T.P.
90. London dispensatory   P Mr Culpeper
90. English physition   P Mr Culpeper
91. The Queens Clossett   G [gilt]   W. M.
92. Countess of Kents Clossett   G
93. Queen-Like Clossett Mrs Woolly
94. instructions for ye officers of ye month   G Mr Rose
95. whole Body of Cookery   P Mr Rabisha
96. Modern Curiosities   P
97. ————————————————————————————
98. Bussy D'ambois   T [tragedy] Mr Durfey
99. Don Sebastion   T Mr Drayden
100. Love in a Tub   C [comedy] Sr George Etheridge
102. ye Mistakes   a Tra C [a tragic comedy] Mr Harris
103. ye Lankishere Witches   C
104. ye Libertine   Trag. Mr Shadwell
105. Cleomenes   T Mr Drayden
106. Instructions pour un jeune Seigneur.   Chetardye
107. Manuscrips one book of braids, 2 sermons Mr Crofts His: of ye favourits of france
108. Two large, & one little Book of Receipts Bound
109. paper Book of Receipts
110. paper Book of Gardening
111. parable of ye Pilgrim   G Dr Patrick
112. Letters   G Mr Loveday
113. Way To gett wealth   G Mr Markham
114. Art of Prudence   G
115. New London dispensatory   G   Salmon
116. Turkish Spy Vol: 7th G
117. Turkish Spy Vol: 8th G
118. Count Tekeli a Novel   G
119. Advice To A daughter   G
120. Hattens Salter   G
121. Holy living & dying Dr Taylour
122. Family physician   G Dr Harvey
123. Compleat Herbal   G   Peckey

124. Erasmus translated   G   S^r R LeStrange
125. Epistles   G   Ovid
126. Best Excercise   G   Horneck
127. practical Christian   G   Dr Sherlock

Discours Of Providence   P   Dr Sherlock
The lives of all ye Princes of Or: P   Brown
Zaide   P   Segrave
Life of Theodotious   P   Fra: Maning
Life Of Ld Rochester   P   Dr Burnett
Memmoirs   P   Dr de Rochefoucault
Honnor Redivivus   P   Matt Barber
Tour of France   P
His: of Father la Chaise   P

Books in my closett at Crombe

1. The life of Theodosius.
2. The Whole duty of Man in 2 parts.
3. The Common prayerbook ye best companion.
4. A Manual of Prayers for Winchester school.
5. The Duty's of ye Closet.
6. A collection of Devotions.
7. The Christians daily sacrifice.
8. The Weeks preparation in 2 parts.
9. A guide to Eternity.
10. The Godly Man's companion.
11. History of King William ye 3^d.
12. The Unreasonableness of separation.
13. The Vertuous woman's meditations and Prayers.

Bennett's Paraphrase upon ye comon prayer.
The works of Josephus Epitomiz'd.
South's sermons in 3 Voll:
Young's sermons in 2 Voll:
Taylor's contemplations.

Contemplations morall & divine ye 2^d part
The life of James Bonnell Esqr
Dorrington's reform'd Devotions.
A Letter to a Deist.
Meditation on ye holy Eucharist-Manuscp^t
The Winchester Manuall.
Ellis's defence of ye 39 Articles.
Instructions For ye education of a daughter.
Plutarch's Morals Voll: 2^d
Dr Hornock's Sermons Voll: 1st
The Characters of ye manners of ye Age.
The history of ye Storm.
An explanation of ye Church Catechism
An Historicall Geography of ye new Testam^t
Collyer's Essays in 2 Voll.
The necessity & advantage of Publick prayer by Dr Beveridge
A large bible printed at Cambridge 1638
The history of england 2 Voll:

The lives of yᵉ Princes of Orange.
The life of Theodosius yᵉ great.
The Character of Q Elizabeth.

A compleat history of Europe in 8
Volls.
The life of the French King.

A Catalogue of Books and Papers brought from the Vicarage House.

A Sermon preached at Bromsgrove
by D.ʳ Talbott Dean of
Worcester in yᵉ year 1695.
The confession of John Shorn
relatoing to the Murther of
Tho: Thynn Esq.ʳ
Articles agreed upon in Convocation
in yᵉ year 1562.
The Foundations of yᵉ Universities.
King Williams Letter to yᵉ Bishop of
London.
A Treatise of Wind.
A sermon preached at Warwick
assizes by D.ʳ Willes.
An abstract of Acts of Parliament for
granting dutys upon Marriages
&c:
Moderation of Vertue 1703.
Christianity restored by Jos: Perkins.
The true Character of a Church man
1703.
An Account of yᵉ Fleet and Land
forces concerned in the Victory
at Vigo 1703.
King Williams affection for the
Church of England.
A letter from King James to the
Arch Bishops in yᵉ year 1685.

S.ʳ Ben: Rudyards speech concerning
Bishops &c:
Courtly Masquing Basse.
The History of Guy of Warwick.
An Elegie on King Charles the first.
A Sermon preached before King W:
and Queen M. by Edward
Bishop of Worcester, 1690.
A Discourse of Bees.
A Treatise concerning Patrons and
Patronage. M. S.
Easter Dues belonging to Snitfield.
A Terrier of yᶜ: Vicars Lands in the
Rushes
The Vertues of Sal Sobitivum by D.ʳ
Packe.
Domiduca Oxonionsis 1662.
Descriptio Colebrande
Convocationis.
Couciones Duce, per Henricum
Wilkinsoun.
Britannia rediviva.
Plutarchi Charonei deliberorum
ivestitutione.
Γρηγοριου Ναζανζηνου
τουϑεολογῶ λογος.
[The Works of Gregory Nazianzen]

A Catalogue of Plain Bound Books Belonging to the R.ᵗ Honᵇˡᵉ the Lady Ann, Countess of Coventry, 1704

Cassandra.
Clelia.
S.ʳ Philip Sydnies Arcadia.
M.ʳ Draybons works.

English adventures.
The amours of the Sultana of Barbary
The amours of Madam and the
Count de Guiche

The Ephesian and Ciñarian Matrons.
Diana Dutchess of Mantua.
Phyloxypes

The History of Europe in 5 Vol. to
 yᵉ year 1705
Dʳ Burnett's Theory of the Earth.
Dodona's Grove.
Mʳ Oldhams works.
The Life of King James the 2ᵈ.
The Athenian Oracle 2 Voll:
The History of the Storm.
Mathematicall recreations.
The Scoffer Scope.
Culpepper's London Dispensatory.
Poems by Mʳ Waller.
Actions upon yᵉ Case of Slander.

The Rehearsall transgressed.
Dʳ Chamberlains present State of
 England 1676.
A new help to discourse.
History of women.
Cynthia a Novell.
Brittains Glory.
English Liberties.
History of Tetzer.
The art of Painting by Smith.
Nostradamus.
The flower Garden.
The art of angling.
Arts masterpiece.
Applications Historiques.
Help to English History:
The accomplished Ladies delight.

Books from Edston

Clark's lives.
Charron of wisdome.
Glanvill's essays.
Bible edit: 1603.
Glanvill's witches.
Stillingfleets 2ᵈ vindication of the
 protestant grounds of religion.
Senaults use of the passions.
Contemplations Morall and Divine.
BP: Taylor's contemplations.
Englands black Tribunal.
Capell of Tentations.
Dʳ Hornocks 1ˢᵗ voll: of sermons.
Plutarchs moralls 2ᵈ voll:
Arwakers duty of self observation.
Crofts's wise Steward.
Stillingfleets letter to a deist.
Relliquia woltoniana.
Sandy's Cardinal vertues.
The reasonableness of Christian
 Religion.
Saundersons 8 cases of conscience.
Treatise of contentment.

The 3ᵈ pᵗ of the Bible in 24?
The present State of London 1661:
Plays By Mʳˢ Behn 2 voll:
The Court and Country Cook.
The Character of Queen Elizabeth.
L'Histoire Comique de Francion.
A tale of a Tub.
A Prospect of yᵉ State of Ireland.
Virgil Travestie.
Present state of Moroccoe.
The art of war.
History of father LaChase.
Conversations on several subjects.
Love letters.
The Soldiers guide.
The Turkish Spie 6 voll:
The exact dealer.
The young Clarks guide.
The French gardiner.
England's happyness improved.
Cent excellentes Nouvelles.
Observations on the Statutes of
 King Charles the 2ᵈ

The adventure of 4 Hours.
Miscellaneous works Duke of Buck:
&c:
Broom's Plays.
Salmon's Polygraphice 2 voll:
Arts improvement.
Caesars coméntaries.
M! Youngs Sermons 2 voll:
The vally of vision
The Ladys dictionary.
Divine Poems by Sands.
Cullpepper's English Phisitian
enlarged.
Whole body of Cookery.
Virgil Travestie.
Discourse of the Bath.
Fortune in her witts.
Wonders of yᵉ Peake.
Defense of the 39 Articles.
Preparation to yᵉ Sacrament Manus.
The cure of Diseases in infants.
Maison Rustique.
A Book of Heraldry 2 voll:
Memoires of the Court of France.
Memoires of the Duke de la
Rochefoucault.
The Sovereighn power of
Parliaments.
A manuall of Prayers.
Book of Receipts in Manuscript.
A Large Book of Mappes.

Blackmore on Job.
A Large Book of Prints.
A guide to eternity.
Hicks's reformed devotion.
D! Sydenham's works.
Boverig's Catechism.
The Spanish Decameron.
An Historical Geneol: and Poet:
Dictionary
The coñon prayer book yᵉ best
companion.
The English Dictionary or a
compleat explanation of words
&c:
M! Bonnell's Life.
A Thousand Notable things.
The way to gett Wealth.
Collyers Essays 3 Voll:
Dorrington's Devotions in 4 Vol:
from M! Mariets study.
Browns Religio medici.
Ditto Vulgar errours.
Josephus Epitomized.
The Queens Closett opened.
George a Green.
The Hanover Succession by Elkanah
Settle.
Fears and dangers fairly displaide by
yᵉ same Author.
Browns enquiries.

Books

M! Baron's Sermons.
M! Cook's Sermon:
M! Kimberleys Sermon.
A Collection for the improvement of
Husbandry and trade in 11 Voll:
By M! Houghton.
Haagen Swendsen's tryall.
Mʳˢ Killigrews Poems.
A Collection of Songs By M! Abell.

A Consolatory Poem to the Lᵈ Cutts.
Blackhead and Youngs conspiracy
against the Bishop of Rochester
The gentlemans Journal for Aprill 1694.
The Bishop of Worcester's Sermon.
An answer to King James's
Declaration 1693.
M! Collyers diswasive from the play
house

A Hymn to victory.
Mr. Atterbury's Sermon on My Lady Cutts.
Mr. Kimberleys Sermon att Warwick
A defence of the Scots settlement.
The Dean of St. Pauls sermon on the Death of Queen Mary.
An answer to King James's last declaration.
Artificiall versyfiing
Mr. Stephen's Sermon.
Mr. Adams's Sermon.
The Paris relation of ye. battle of London July 1693.
Mr. Provosts Sermon on my Lady Cutts.
A Discourse of Persecution.
Dr. Sherlocks Sermon on ye. Queen.
The new association.
The sentiments of the most excellent Painters.
The Tryalls of Charnock &c:
Tables of Multiplication &c:
Songs in Don Quixiott.
Tryall of Sr. William Poskins.
A Poem on Badminton.
Proceedings of the house of Lords upon the Bill of Divorce.
The Tryall of my Ld. Mohun.
The Tryall of the occasionall bill.
A Sermon by Dr. Manningham.
The reformation of manners.
Sr. Edmund Bury Godfry's funeral sermon by Dr. Floyd.
A reply to an answer of King James's Declaration.
The Judgment of Paris. Mr. Congr.
Dr. Langfords Sermon on ye. 30th. Jan:
An impartiall account of ye. ffleet.
Sr. Wm. Daws's Sermon at Sarford.
The present State of Europe 1692.
Bishop of Oxfords sermon before ye. Queen 92.
A form of Prayer for a fast 1703/4
A funerall Oration on the late King James.
Bleinheim A Poem.
An Elegy on Queen Mary by Mr. Gould.
An elegy on Queen Mary by Mr. Congreve.
An Elegy on Queen Mary by Mr. Stepney.
Rules of devout behaviour in the time of divine service in the church of England.
Quatrains du Seigneur de Pybrac.
The Bill for the relief and Settlemt. of ye. Poor.
The Dyet of Poland with a Key in Manuspt.
An Ode for the thanksgiving day by Mr. Walsh.
A Sermon on Sr. Frances Russell by Mr. Brooke.
Dr. Stanhope's thanksgiving sermon June the 27th. 1706
Dr. Burnet's Thanksgiving Sermon Dec. 31st. 1706.
Mr. Smallbrook's Sermon preached at Oxford June the 9th 1706.
An Answer to my Lord Brillhaven's Speech.
The Ld. Brillhaven's Speech.
Mr. Seton's Speech in the Scotch Parl: on ye. first Article of the Union.
A Convincing reply to the Lord Brillhaven's Speech.
The Bishop Of Oxford's Thanksgiving sermon for the Union.
Dr. Chandler's Thanksgiving sermon for the Union.
Mr. Bean's Sermon Preach'd before the University of Oxford on the same occasion.
The Humble address of the Lords to

the Queen on Monday 22.^{d} March
1707.

Mr Fieldings Tryal.

Mr Traps Assize Sermon Preach'd at
Oxford March the 4th 1707.

Dr Trimnoll's Sermon preach'd before

the house of Com̃ons Jan: the
14.th 1707/8.

The Bishop of Lincoln's sermon
preach'd before ye house of Lords
on the 30th of January 1707.

A Catalogue of Plays both bound and unbound belonging to the R.^{t} Honble the Lady Ann Countess of Coventry 1704:

Co.^{r} }
The Country wife.
The Plain Dealer.
Love in a Wood.
Gent: Dancing Master.
} Bound—Mr Wycherley.

Cō }
The Rover or the banih'd Cavaliers;
    in 2 p.^{ts}
The Dutch Lover.

Trag: }
Abdelazer; or the Moors revenge.
The Young King or ye Mistake.
The Round heads or the good old cause.
The Citty Heiress, or Sr Timothy Treatall.
The Town Fop, or Sr Timothy Tawdrey.
The False Count, or a new way to play an
    old Game.
The Lucky chance, or an Aldermans
    bargain.
Forced marriage, or the Jealous
    Bridegroom.

Co.^{r} }
Sr Patient Fancy.
The Widdow ranter, or the history of
    Bacon in Virginia.——————
The feign'd Curtizans, or a nights Intrigue.
The Emporour of the Moon.
The Amorous Prince.

} Bound in 2
Volumes
By Mrs Behn.

Co.^{r} }
The Ambitious Statesman.
The Citty Heiress.
The Mulberry Garden.
The London Cuckolds.
Gloriana.
The Mall.
The Joviall Crew.
} Bound—Mr Crowne.

Trg:	The Rivall Queens. The Duke of Guise. The maids Tragedy. Pastor Fido.	Bound—Mr Lee.
Com:	The Humorists. Epsome Wells.	Bound—Mr Shadwell.
Cõ:	The way of the World. The double dealer.	By Mr Congreve.
Co:	She wou'd and she wou'd not. Loves last shift or ye Fool in fashion.	By Mr Cibber.
Cõ:	The fatal marriage, or ye innocent adultery. The maids last prayer, or any rather than fail.	By Mr Southern.
Cõ:	The Scowerers. The Volunteers or ye Stock Jobbers. The True Widdow.	By Mr Shadwell.
Cõ:	Love for mony or the boarding Schoole. The Richmond Heiress. Madam Fickle, or the witty false one. The Campaignors.	By M.^r D'urfey.
Cõ: Trag:	The Kind Keeper or Mr Limberham. Sr Martin Marr: all. Don Sebastion K: of Portugall.	By Mr Dryden.
Co:	The Twin Rivals. The inconstant, or the way to win him	By Mr Farquhar.
Trag: Com:	The Treacherous brothers. A very good Wife.	By Mr Powell.
Com:	Citty Politiques. The Country Witt.	By Mr Crowne.
Cõ:	The Modish husband. The Ladies visiting day. The reformed wife.	By ————

TrgCō: } A Duke and no Duke.
The ingratitude of a Comon:wealth.   } By Mr Tate.
The History of King Lear - - -

Abramule, or Love and Empire.

Cyrus the Great, or the Tragedy of Love.

The Rape or ye Innocent imposters.

Trag. } The Tragedy of the unhappy fair Irene.
The Sophy.

Neglected Vertue or the unhappy
    conquerour.

Tamerlane ye Great.

Ibrahim ye 13.th Emperour of ye Turks.

The wit of a woman.

All for ye bette. or ye Infallible cure.

The Country Wake.

Marry or do worse.

Com: } The humorous Lieutenant, or ye generous
    Enemies.

The Mock Marriage.

Guzman.

The false friend.

The Sham Lawyer, or ye lucky extravagant.

Sawney the Scott, or ye taming the Shrew.

The wary widdow or S.^r noisy Parrat.

The Cornish Comedy.

The Lost Lover, or the Jealous husband.

The wild Gallant.

The Impostor Defeated, or a trick to
    Cheat ye Devile.

The Relapse, or Vertue in Danger.

The Oxford Act.

As you find it.

Loves contrivances, or Le Medecin Malgre
    Lui.

Com: } The Gentleman Cully.
The Beau's duel, or a Souldier for the
    Ladies.
The Rehearsal.

The pretenders, or ye town Un mask't.

Grief A-la-mode.

The Mock Tempest, or the enchanted
    Castle.
The Canterbury Guests, or a bargain
    broken.
The Loving Enemies.
The Princess of Cleve.

Trag:Cō: } Belphegor, or ye marriage of ye Devil.
King Henry ye 4th wth ye humours of S^r
    John Faulstaff.

Oper: } The world in ye Moon.

The Careless Husband.
The Amorous Miser.
Love the Leveller.
The Tender Husband.
Gibraltar.
The Stage Coach.
The fair Example.
The Confederacy.
Liberty asserted.
The Royall Merchant or beggars bush—
    Com̄:
The Royall Subject or the faithfull
    Generall.
Ulysses—Trag:
The Lawyers fortune or Love in a hollow
    tree. Com̄:
The Basset table. Com̄:
The Northern Las—Com̄:
Hampstead heath. Com̄:
The way of the World. Com̄:
The recruiting officer.
The Amorous Widdow or the wanton
    wife. Co$^?$
The Platonick Lady—Co$^?$
The double Gallant or the sick Lady's
    cure—Com$^?$
Venice preserv'd or a Plott discovered—
    Trg^{dy}
The Humorists—Com$^?$

The abdicated Prince or y⁰ adventures of 4
years—Tra:Com:
The Maid the Mistress—Com⁰
Irene or y⁰ fair Greek—Trag:
The Beaux Stratagem—Com⁰
The English Frier or y⁰ town Sparks—
Com⁰
The Loyall subject or y⁰ faithfull generall.

Appendix C
Mary Astell's Letters, 1693–1730

[I   *To John Norris of Bemerton, 9/21/1693*]

Sir,

Though some morose Gentlemen wou'd perhaps remit me to the Distaff or the Kitchin, or at least to the Glass and the Needle, the proper Employments as they fancy of a Womans Life; yet expecting better things from the more Equitable and ingenious Mr. *Norris*, who is not so narrow-Soul'd as to confine Learning to his own Sex, or to envy it in ours, I presume to beg his Attention a little to the Impertinencies of a Womans Pen. And indeed Sir, there is some reason why I, though a Stranger, should Address to you for the Resolution of my Doubts and Information of my Judgment, since you have increased my Natural Thirst for Truth, and set me up for a *Virtuoso*. For though I can't pretend to a Multitude of Books, Variety of Languages, the Advantages of Academical Education, or any Helps but what my own Curiosity affords; yet, *Thinking* is a Stock that no Rational Creature can want, if they know but how to use it; and this, as you have taught me, with Purity and Prayer, (which I wish were as much practis'd as they are easie to practise) is the way and method to true Knowledge. But setting Preface and Apology aside, the occasion of giving you this trouble is this:

Reading the other day the Third Volume of your excellent Discourses, as I do every thing you Write with great Pleasure and no less Advantage; yet taking the liberty that I use with other Books, (and yours or no bodies will bear it) to raise all the Objections that ever I can, and to make them undergo the severest Test my Thoughts can put 'em to before they pass for currant, a difficulty arose which without your assistance I know not how to solve.

Methinks there is all the reason in the World to conclude, *That* GOD *is the only efficient Cause of all our Sensations*; and you have made it as clear as the Day; and it is equally clear from the Letter of the Commandment, *That*

GOD *is not only the Principal, but the* sole Object *of our Love*: But the reason you assign for it, namely, *Because he is the only efficient Cause of our Pleasure,* seems not equally clear. For if we must Love nothing but what is Lovely, and nothing is Lovely but what is our Good, and nothing is our Good but what does us Good, and nothing does us Good but what causes Pleasure in us; may we not by the same way of arguing say, That that which Causes Pain in us does not do us Good, (for nothing you say does us Good but what Causes Pleasure) and therefore can't be our Good, and if not our Good then not Lovely, and consequently not the proper, much less the only Object of our Love? Again, if the Author of our Pleasure be upon that account the only Object of our Love, then by the same reason the Author of our Pain can't be the Object of our Love; and if both these Sensations be produced by the same Cause, then that Cause is at once the Object of our Love, and of our Aversion; for it is as natural to avoid and fly from Pain, as it is to follow and pursue Pleasure?

So that if these Principles, *viz. That* GOD *is the Efficient Cause of our Sensations,* (Pain as well as Pleasure) *and that he is the only Object of our Love,* be firm and true, as I believe they are; it will then follow, either that the being the Cause of our Pleasure is not the true and proper Reason why that Cause should be the Object of our Love, (for the Author of our Pain has as good a Title to our Love as the Author of our Pleasure;) Or else, if nothing be the Object of our Love but what does us Good, then something else does us Good besides what causes Pleasure? Or to speak more properly, the Cause of all our Sensations, Pain as well as Pleasure being the only Object of our Love, and nothing being Lovely but what does us Good, consequently, that which Causes Pain does us Good as well as that which Causes Pleasure; and therefore it can't be true, That nothing does us Good but what Causes Pleasure.

Perhaps I have express'd my self but crudely, yet I am persuaded I've said enough for one of your Quickness to find out either the strength or weakness of this Objection. I shall not therefore trouble you any further, but to beg Pardon for this, and to wish you all imaginable Happiness, (if it be not absurd to wish Felicity to one who already possesses a Virtuous, Large and Contemplative Soul, and a quiet convenient Retirement, which is indeed all the Happiness that can be had on this side Heaven) and to subscribe my self

Honoured Sir,

Your great Admirer

and most humble Servant.

London, St. Matthew's day, 1693. [*Sept. 21, 1693*]

[II   *To Henry Dodwell, 3/11/1706*]

Chelsea March y^e 11th. 170 $\frac{5}{6}$

S^r

That truely X^tian Temper, as well as eminent learning that appears in all
y^r Writings; that great Charity & Love to Truth, wch are w^n united y^e Signa-
ture of a real Christian, but wch are of little worth w^n seperated, makes me
presume that you will pardon this Address, from one who tho' a Stranger to
y^r Person, sincerely Honours you for y^r Merit, & faithfull Sufferings for the
Testimony of y^r Conscience & who makes it in pursuance of y^r Pacific Design in *y^r Case in View*, by the readings of wch I received much Pleasure &
information.

Let it then be humbly offered to y^r Consideration, whether all the constant & real members of the Church of England, if they mean to approve
themselves as such, are not oblig'd to present Communion wth the Actual
Possessors of the English Sees, & that by ye Principles of *ye Cyprianick Age*,
& of *the Case in View*; Excepting only those who reside in the Diocese of
Norwich, whose Obedience is due to their Deprived Father 'till he discharge
them from it?

For since the Bishop is the *Principle of Unity* to his own particular
Church & Head of all Christians living wth in his district; so that they who
are not wth the Bishop are not in the Church, Disobedience to GOD'S B^ps
being the occasion of Heresy's & Schisms, since there can be but one B^p in a
District, so y^t he *who is alone in Possession, is for this Reason presum'd to be
design'd by God himselfe for y^t Office*; (as is learnedly proved in *ye Case in
View*;) Since *Foreigners* must not *intermedle* in another B^ps *Jurisdiction* w^n the
Faith is not in danger, (Ibid) & *Foreigners* being opposed to *Incumbent*
(p. 46) it seems to me y^t all B^ps are Foreigners in another B^ps District, unless
the Metropolitan at most; since Subjects cannot be discharg'd of the Duty
owing to their Spiritual Father, otherwise than by his Death, Cession, or Canonical Deprivation, & lastly since it was the Practice of the Primitive
Church, and Cyprianic Age in Cases of Heresy or Schism, for ye Metropolitan or ye Neighbouring B^ps to whom it belong'd to provide a Pastor for the
Flock, to Excommunicate ye Heretical or Schismatical B^p and to chuse another in his place, as appears by St Cyprian's Letter to P. Stephen concerning
Marcian B^p of Arles: Therefore there being now no Rival B^p but in ye Diocese of Norwich, so that ye present Possessors are & must be the only Right-
full B^ps, each in his Respective Diocese, and the *only Principle of Unity*, no
other B^p whatsoever having any Right to medle there, as being but a Foreigner; and our late excellent Metropolitan, and his Deprived Collegues who

were ye only Persons who cou'd pretend to a Power of Discharging us from our Obedience to y^e *Actual Possessors* and of Substituting others in their Districts, (considering the Church as under Persecution, and therefore to provide for its own Subsistence without ye intervention of ye Magistrate) not having done it, whereby we may reasonably conclude y^t they did not think it necessary; and further, *Scism from ye Catholic Church being Consequent to Schism from ye local B^p. of the place, & fundamentally grounded on it*; (Case in View p. 301) it must needs follow, y^t unless the People in ye several Districts (Norwich only excepted be united to the present Actual Possessors as their B^p. & Head they can be united to none; and consequently it is as necessary for them to live in Communion wth him, as it is for them to be united to none; and consequently it is as necessary for them to live in Communion wth him, as it is for them to be United to their true Pastor, in order to Communion with ye Catholic Church & with X^t his head. N.B. Constantine found the "Church in possession of Dioceses, & all the Christians of his time in possession of that opinion, that their living in a particular Diocese made them oblig'd in Conscience to pay their Duty to that particular B^p who had the Right to that Diocese. Case in View. p. 600."

To this there is but one Objection that I can find, & that is w^t some call the *Contagion*, or to use the words of the Case in View p. 2, "It is thought necessary to abstain from ye Communion not only of ye Rival B^{ps}. Themselves who are the principal Schismaticks, but of all others who have made themselves *accessory* to ye Schism by any sacred Communion wth those Rivals." For, 1st. We adhere to out present Diocesans for the same reason why we adhered to our Deprived Fathers in their respective Districts (viz) because having been once Lawfull B^{ps}. they have not been regularly or Canonically Deprived.

2dly We have no other *Principle of Unity*: so that we must either be as Sheep without a Pastor, wch were to unchurch us; or else we must be United to that one Deprived Father, who has not yet Renounc'd his Title, but this cannot be in Foreign Districts. For shou'd he intermedle in another occupied Jurisdiction agreeing wth him in ye same Faith, he cou'd not be excus'd from Schism by the Catholic Principles of ye Cyprianic Age. (Case p. 42)

3dly. Our present Metropolitans being Rightfully so, ye B^{ps} & Clergy in their respective Provinces are oblig'd by Oath to Canonical Obedience. W^{ch} Oath how far it may affect ye Depriv'd Clergy I shall not now enquire.

4^{thly} If I rightly apprehend ye Case p. 50. & 57., it makes the danger & guilt of Contagion to consist in being gain'd over to the opinions of ye infected Party. Whence I gather, y^t possibly our present Diocesans may not approve a Rival B^p tho they do not reject him from their Communion: or supposing y^t they don't disapprove ye Schism, their Subjects may however live in Union w:ᵗʰ them without Contagion; for this yᵉ *Case in View* not only grants but even proves w:ᵗʰ respect to the Doctrine of yᵉ *Independency of the Church on yᵉ State* Sec. 11, 12. Neither are their Subjects proper Judges of their Action; for we may not judge God & X.ᵗ nor make ourselves B.ᵖˢ of B.ᵖˢ to their own Master they stand or Fall. For, 5ᵗˡʸ In my poor Opinion, besides all other ill Consequences of this Doctrine of Contagion, and yᵉ hazards & endless Scruples to which it exposes Ignorant & well meaning Persons; it leaves yᵉ People too great a Latitude, sets us up as Judges of our Spiritual Fathers, giving us Liberty to withdraw our Obedience before they are Canonically Deprived, w:ᶜʰ is the very thing y.ᵗ they who teach us mean to argue ag.ˢᵗ

Lastly, it seems to me that we have the most unexceptionable Precedent of quiet Submission even to Disputable Titles without Danger of being infected w.ᵗʰ yᵉ usurpers Guilt, or partaking in their Sins, & that is yᵉ Example of our most Holy Lord, who did not refuse Communion w.ᵗʰ yᵉ Jewish Church tho' the Succession of the Priesthood (entail'd by God himselfe) was shamefully broken.

These hints, on w:ᶜʰ I might easily have enlarged, and w:ᶜʰ are but inartificially [inartfully] put together; I submit Sir to y.ʳ candid consideration. Not doubting y.ᵗ a person of y.ʳ great Sagacity and blessed Peacemaking Temper will improve them all that may be, in order to yᵉ happy Re Union of which you appear so desirous, and w:ᶜʰ is so heartily wish'd by all who pray for the Peace of Jerusalē, and by none more than by her who is S.ʳ y.ʳ faithfull Serv.ᵗ in all yᵉ offices of Xⁱᵃⁿ Charity. M. Astell

P.S. if you think me worthy of an Answer, be pleas'd to direct to be left at Mr. Wilkins at yᵉ Kingshead in S.ᵗ Pauls Church yard.

[III   *To John Walker, 8/22/1706*]

Rev.ᵈ Sir,

The following account is taken out of a M.S. I have now in my hands, entitul'd *Somew.ᵗ observ'd in y.ᵉ Life of y.ᵗ Good Man M.ʳ John Squire, vicar of yᵉ Parish of S.ᵗ Leonards Shoreditch in yᵉ County of Middle Sex. By Roger Ley M.A. J.C.C.* who tells us, y.ᵗ M.ʳ Squire was Son to Adam Squire D.D. & Master of Baliol Coll. Oxon; & Grandson to D.ʳ John Aylmer Bp. of London, by M.ʳˢ Judith Aylmer his Mother, "who understood y.ᵉ Greek & Latin Tongues, & was a good Physician, grounded in y.ᵉ Theory as well as expert in y.ᵉ Practise." He was born (as I collect) about y.ᵉ year 1587; Educated in Jesus College Cambridge, where M.ʳ Ley was acquainted w.ᵗʰ him 7 years, & was afterwards his Curate at Shoreditch for almost 30 years. To w.ᶜʰ place M.ʳ Squire being presented by his Uncle D.ʳ Aylmer ArchDeacon of London, left yᵉ University after they had testify'd their esteem of him by offering to double his Income in order to keep him, where he was a much desir'd Preacher, & remarkable for his extraordinary diligence in his Study & w.ᵗʰ his Pupils. Nor was he less esteem'd by his New Parishioners, who in yᵉ time he was their Pastor, & during his Troubles, gave him all possible marks of their affection & esteem.

The Parish being large, yᵉ Coṁunicants whose Names were taken (according to yᵉ Rubric) every Easter, somew.ᵗ exceeding 3000, his Income was doubl'd, & by yᵉ generous Contributions of his People, to w.ᶜʰ he added out of his own Purse £ 100. he was enabled to build a New Vicarage house. He spent his time in Private in Study, in Public in composing differences, & assisting a yᵉ Public Meetings for yᵉ coṁon good, having yᵉ felicity to please several Partys, & to unite yᵉ formerly jangling Vestrys, nothing of moment passing wᵗʰ.out him, & his w.ᵈ often going for an Oracle; Visiting yᵉ Sick, Providing for yᵉ Poor, instructing on all occasions. Tho he had a Family to provide for, this did not hinder him from "being given to Hospitality, free to his Friends & Parishioners to yᵉ utmost, but to yᵉ Poor he was a Steward & Father, whom he some way or other provided for, his Character obtaining many voluntary gifts in yᵉ City. His way was to Preach to yᵐ on yᵉ day he had warn'd yᵐ to come & receive his Charitable Collections, & as he did not spare yᵉ Rich in due Reproofs upon occasion; so at yᵉ time he laid open yᵉ faults of yᵉ Poor, instructing & releiving at once their Souls & Bodys.

His Charity in yᵉ Plague time was incomparable; in yᵗ great sickness in 1625 tho he retir'd w.ᵗʰ his Family to Mitcham, yet he did not neglect his Pastoral Duty, but came to Town to observe yᵉ weekly fast as long as it held, & to perform Divine Services on yᵉ Lᵈˢ day. And besides, soliciting his Rich Parishioners, by Letter, to relieve yᵉ afflicted, he obtain'd considerable Sums of Money for yᵉ Sick & Needy in their pressing wants.

In his Pulpit his Auditors found him full of Edification & delight so yᵗ they were transported w.ᵗʰ his Preaching, w.ᶜʰ was Constant, & to w.ᶜʰ he added yᵉ Necessary work of Catechising, sometimes 20 Youths on a Lᵈˢ day answering to his Instructions to yᵉ great comfort of his People & admiration of Strangers. As he was a "*Preacher* so was he likewise a constant *Practiser*, of Obedience, an Observer of Order, a lover of decency in yᵉ Church, & a Zealous Defender of yᵉ Service book, w.ᶜʰ he did often reade in yᵉ Congregation, & *constantly* w.ⁿ he himself did not Preach; as also Privately in his Family." So yᵗ by his Instructions & Example, & yᵉ tractableness of his People, they were brought to a Reverᵗ & Orderly behavior in GOD's House, none but a few of yᵉ meaner sort, & these very ignorant & shallow, stumbling at yᵉ Ceremonys of yᵉ Church, & whose miscarriages in other particulars betray'd their weakness.

Wⁿ yᵉ troubles began by yᵉ Scot's Rebellion agᵗ their Sovereign, & Invasion of England, w.ᶜʰ was but too forward to follow their bad example, Mᵗ

Squire magnanimously became yᵉ Champion of Allegiance, proving in his Sermons "yᵗ they were Rebells, exhorting his Auditors to give yᵉ King Relief & Assistance." For this he was call'd Incendiary, & an order obtain'd from yᵉ House of Comons to set up a weekly Lecture in his Church. But ye Faction being weak in so orderly a Parish, yᵉ honest Part Met, & outvoting yᵉ other, chose their Vicar for Lecturer, & if he shou'd fail his Curate. To wᶜʰ yᵉ Ringleader of yᵉ Factions taking exceptions sᵈ *I detest agᵗ it*, & being call'd on to repeat his wᵈˢ did it in yᵉ same absurd Manner, provoking yᵉ Laughter of those who heard him. However, this ignorant Rabble supported by yᵉ Men at Westminster, by using plain force brought in a New England Man at last to Preach on yᵉ Lᵈˢ day in yᵉ Afternoon. And Mʳ Squire was displac'd, first not suffer'd to perform his office by Imprisonment, & yⁿ Sequester'd yᵉ Sequestration being so contriv'd as to rob him of yᵉ fruit of his last years labour. It being yᵉ Custom in yᵗ Parish, yᵗ he who had possession before yᵉ 25 Mar. shou'd enjoy yᵉ years Profit, they sequestered Mr. Squire yᵉ day before.

The Parish did all they cou'd to keep their Apostolical & much beloved Minister, & in order thereto drew up yᵉ following Petition.

To yᵉ Rᵗ Honᵇˡᵉ Lᵈˢ of yᵉ higher house of Parlᵗ

The humble Petition of yᵉ Inhabitants of yᵉ Parish of Shoreditch Shewing, yᵗ whereas Mʳ Squire of yᵉ Parish of Shoreditch having about 30 years bin very painful in discharging his Cure, by his constant Preaching twice every Sunday; as also by his Catechising of yᵉ Youth of yᵉ Parish, & in his Sermons continually beating down Popery; & in his Catechising instructing yᵉ Youth wᵗʰ Argumᵗˢ agᵗ yᵉ Papists. As also hath not in yᵉ great Sickness forsaken his Flock, but hath procur'd yᵉ Charity of many for yᵉ relief of yᵉ Poor, in yᵉ time of extremity, & hath liv'd blameless, & done much good in yᵉ Parish.

We therefore his Parishioners do humbly pray, yᵗ he may continue wᵗʰ us, for otherwise he & his Children may be ruin'd, he having little means to subsist; & we his Parishioners shall have a great loss.

This Petition was subscrib'd by Sʳ Alex. Sᵗ Johns Brother to yᵉ Earl of Bollingbroke, Mʳ Squire's dear Friend, & the other parishioners of Note. It was also resolv'd yᵗ a Multitude shou'd have Presented it, according to yᵉ yⁿ Fashion; but yᵉ purpose was chang'd, least wᵗ was encourag'd in others shou'd be censur'd in yᵐ as tumultuous. I do not find yᵗ he had any Redress by this Petition; on yᵉ contrary, his Adversarys coyn'd Articles agᵗ him & were so violent as to cause yᵐ to be Printed before they were prov'd, & to be cry'd & sold in yᵉ Streets. To these he printed a Sufficient Answer, & their Complaint was brought before yᵉ Comittee, where Miles Corbet was Chairman, & yᵉ harsh wᵈˢ & looks did forestall wᵗ wou'd ensue. "Alderman Penington vented a Relation upon Trust, of his having disturb'd a Company of GOD's Serv:ts at their Devotions." The truth of wch was thus: Some disaffected Persons holding a Conventicle in Spittle Fields, ye strangeness of ye thing in those parts made ye Ordinary People & Boys gather about ye house, & some of ym threw stones & brake ye Windows so yt ye Assembly was interrupted; but Mr. Squire clear'd himself of being present, or of knowing anything of ye matter.

I do not find ye Articles exhibited agt him, but they will in good measure appear by his Answers deliver'd Feb. 18, 1640. wch because it shews in some measure ye Principles & Practises, ye Wisdom & Integrity of this excellent Man, & ye Malice & Unreasonableness, ye frivolous as well as unjust allegations of his Accusers, & may serve for an Instance how groundlessly ye Orthodox Clergy were Persecuted, I will transcribe as follows.

"May it please this Honble Assembly,

Both ye Petitioners & Witnesses are incompetent etc. see ye Appendix

——— ——— ——— ——— ——— ———

After he had made this Answer, he told me, says our Author, "yt his Mind was much quieted, & it was his comfort seeing he was handled wth so much rigor, yt he shou'd die in ye Arms of his Parish yt flock'd wth him in Troops to Westminster to see ye Juce! [Judgment?] It being hardly discernable whether more Love or Grief did appear in their Countenances & Carriage. And tho his Meekness was try'd to ye utmost, tho he was baited by ye Comittee, slander'd by his Adversarys, & his Accusers not being sworn talk'd loosely, & being encourag'd grew high & confident; & after Edge hill Battel he was Imprison'd in Gresham College & loaded wth Injurys & abuses, yet ye Good Man possessed his Soul in Patience, bearing his Persecutions wth a compos'd Chearful & Undaunted Mind. The very morning after he had suffer'd so much before ye Comittee, he was not easily awakned some business requiring him being call'd up.

The Schismatics into whose Custody he & some others of his Fellow Sufferers were put at Gresham College, treated ym barbarously hardly admitting his Friends to come to him; & exacting unreasonable Arbitrary Fees, & the Prisoners not answer'd their demands were kept from their Ordinary Diet prepar'd at home; also from lodging upon Beds, wch ye Professors in Civility lent ym. So yt Mr. Squire & Mr. Swadlin did often lie upon Straw being pric'd [pricked] every way. And so it might have continued, but yt their Keepers for other abuses agt those who employ'd ym, were remov'd as base Fellows unfit for any Trust.

From Gresham College he was remov'd to London House, & thence to Newgate, & to avoid ye noisome Comon Prison he liv'd to his very great Charge in ye Press Yard; his long durance wasting his Estate & imparing his health, for he fell into a Dropsie. However he had ye Comfort of his Friends, to whom he Preach'd & Pray'd according to his own Mind, ye

Keeper giving way to it; being "accompany'd there wth Dr Some a Preben-dary of Windsor & Mr Swadlin thrown out of St Bottolps Algate, his Fellow Sufferers for Loyalty & ye Church." Finding a sore decay, Mr Squire wrot to Miles Corbet by whom he was Comitted, entreating a milder Confinem.^t, who after much importunity order'd ye Keeper to bring him to ye Comittee, where having attended a whole afternoon w.^th.out Accesse his Keeper went to Corbet, desiring to know w.^t course shou'd be taken wth his Prisoner who was brought thither by his Warrant. Corbet answer'd, Let him be hang'd— nor cou'd better Satisfaction be obtain'd. But notw.^th.standing this ill usuage, our Author going at night to hear ye events of this days Expectation, found Mr Squire at a friends house near Newgate where his Keeper had trusted him, & *never more Pleasant in his Life*: So great are ye Supports of GOD's Grace afforded to His Suffering Servants!

After this his Friend Mr Osbulston found a way to remove him to ye Kings bench, where he had better accomodations, & at last obtained his Dis-charge of Mr Knightly, who had ye oversight of ye Prisoners. Surety being given for his appearance, & a promise y.^t he wou'd not Act ag.^t ye Parl.^t Whereupon his Parishioners ye Night he was releas'd made above 20 Bone-fires to express their Joy.

Having for ye cure of his Dropsy & to see his Friends walk'd to Cam-brige & to Suffolk & Norfolk & being of opinion y.^t a Man cou'd not live w.^th.out offence in anothers house, he married happily, retir'd to Richmond in Surrey where he kept a Private School, Reading ye Liturgy & Catchising his Scholars & Family, & Preaching every other L.^ds day, till he fell into a Quar-tan Ague of wch he died, on St Simon & Jude's day 1653. At wch time, says my Author, "being at his house he put me upon reading any Service, & be-gan to Catechise but cou'd not hold out half ye time so he died full of De-vout & Xtian Resolution wth a quiet & well composed Mind; & was buried at St Leonards Shoreditch, by his first Wife who was buried 2.^d March, 1639."

A little before he died, Dr Mosson who was his Neighbour, "desir'd a Manifestation of his Judgm.^t concerning ye War & ye Kings Cause who suf-fer'd so much in defending ye Church & ye Kingdoms R.^t wch he gave as followeth.

"The Sum of y.^t voluntary Profession made by Mr John Squire late Vicar of Shoreditch. Upon his Death-bed A° 1653.

"Thro faith in ye Mediator X.^t Jesus he was no more affraid to look Death in ye face than me ye Minister who came to Visit him. That he had his Assur.^n of Eternal Life in gracious evidences of Divine Love thro X.^t.; only he must remember y.^t of ye Apostle, Let him y.^t stands take heed least he fall. Y.^t he had gone thro good Report & bad; he had suffer'd by scandalous Tongues & by violent hands, GOD forgive y.^m. but none of those things troubled him. His trouble was his Compassionate Sense of ye Churche's Suffering's.

"Y.t he had y.s Confidence in his Soul, y.t if he were to pass thro 4 Prisons, y.e Rack & death it self, he shou'd willingly (thru y.e power of X.t) constantly do it, in testimony to y.e Churche's & Royal Cause.

"Y.e he did abominate from his Soul y.e grand Imposture of y.e Covenant, & y.e Disloyal Acts of y.e late Assembly of Divines. And he did desire y.t M.r Marshall in particular (if opportunity were offer'd,) might receive this Intimation from a dying Man & Minister in perfect Mind & Memory, who was shortly to appear before y.e Supreme Judge; Y.t w.th.out Repentance of his disloyal Preaching & Printing, his last end wou'd be miserable.

"Y.t between y.e Papist on y.e one hand, & y.e Pres.t factions on y.e other, y.e Ch. of Engl. (he fear'd) wou'd be brought into so sad a distress, y.t by y.e Wiles & Subtiltys of y.e Popish Party prevailing a Persecution wou'd be rais'd in Engl.d

"After some Religious Comunications & Prayers, I departed from him, & before I had the opportunity of seeing him again he departed from us, & now sleeps in y.e L.d"

Hac anima vere & examino testatr Rob. Mosson in sac. Ministrae

Mr. Squire left behind him, besides w.t is mention'd in his Answer, several large Folios in M.S. entitul'd "An English Rhapsodie: Or y. Judgm.t of Particular Men concerning y. general Judgmt of GOD on England, Our Civil War. It was begun in Newgate May 12, 1643, & ended nigh Kings Bench May 14, 1646, is by way of a Dialogue, giving a large account of y.e Occasions of y.e Civil War, &c. according to y.e opinions of several Partys, & Persons whose word he recites. But having not perus'd it, I cannot give a further Character of it.

S.r if this account or any part of it may be serviceable to you in yo.r very Useful, Necessary & Generous Design, w.ch w.th so much Labour & Expence you so Strenuously carry on, for y.e Glory of GOD & y.e Service of His Church, & to do Justice to those Excell.t Martyrs & Confessors of whom y.e World was not worthy; it will be a great Satisfaction to her who is

R.d Sir,
Yo.r most humble Servant
M. Astell.

Chelsea Aug. 22.d. 1706.

P.S.

M.r Wilkin telling me y.t M.r Squire was one of y.e Ministers in Whites Century, it may not be amiss to give you an account of an Affliction befell him, w.ch tho it ended to his honor, yet possibly y.e false Accusers of those days might use it to his Discredit. And tho y.e Woman who Calumniated him confessed she aim'd at Maintenance, w.ch she often demanded & was as constantly deny'd; yet by y.e Support she found afterwards, it is not improbable y.t y.e Faction had a hand in it. The Story is thus; During y.e life of his first Wife, a Servant & no handsome woman, in a house in his Parish whether he did not often Resort, but who was known to him by sight, laid Claim to him for a Promise of Marriage. And being inform'd y.ᵗ a mere Promise was an empty pretence, she became so impudent as to affirm she had bin Married. But being urg'd to shew y.ᵉ Register for a Proof, had nothing to allege in her Justification. However continuing to keep a Clamor, & make a Challenge, & being no longer to be endur'd, she was put into Bridewell, & at y.ᵉ Public Sessions ask'd him & his true wife forgiveness on her Knees in y.ᵉ Open Court. After this becoming a Servant to one M.ʳˢ Jerom, a great Professor of Religion & follower of Sermons, & of Law-suits, by her Mds's encouragem.ᵗ y.ᵉ woman renued her Accusation in y.ᵉ foulest manner, both of y.ᵐ coming to his house & occasioning Tumults, & y.ᵉ woman being past all shame, presenting her self before him whilst he was preaching; yet neither in Public nor Private did he shew any sign of a disturbed Spirit. At last, no persuasions prevailing, he was forc'd to cõmence a Suit ag.ᵗ M.ʳˢ & Maid in y.ᵉ Star Chamber for a Conspiracy, where y.ᵉ Defend.ᵗˢ cou'd get no Counsel to Plead at y.ᵉ Trial, their Cause was so foul. Only an Answer of y.ᵉ M.ʳˢ's was Read Pen'd in Scripture Phrase, but little to y.ᵉ purpose. In short her abusing Scripture was sharply Censur'd by y.ᵉ L.ᵈ Keeper Bp Williams, & she was sentenc'd in a good Sum for Costs and Damages; y.ᵉ Servant being Order'd to make Confession of her fault & to be Whipp'd w.ᶜʰ was accordingly perform'd.

[*Rich Wilkin's note enclosed with the foregoing*]

S.ʳ

    I am heartily concern'd to hear of y.ʳ Illness, but hope these will find you perfectly recovered.

    I hope the Enclosed will not be unacceptable to you, they were transcribed from Papers I had from D.ʳ Payne's Widow who was Mr Squire's Daughter: M.ʳˢ A intreats you to Excuse her Blots and Interlinings for she could not Spare time to write them over fair. M.ʳ Bennet the Christ-Church Booksell.ʳ was buried last night & the Dean of Carlisle preach'd his Funeral Sermon. If you could by writing or otherwise make any Interest for me among the Christ-Church-Men before they are Engaged to another I should be very thankful and it should always be acknowledg'd as a particular favour by

        Dear S.ʳ
          Y.ʳ most obliged
            Humble Serv.ᵗ
              Richᵈ Wilkin

Aug: Ult:

1706

[IV   *To Lady Ann Coventry, Summer 1714*]

Dearest Madam

I am impatient to hear of my Lady Duchesses health, and hope her Graces Indisposition was not so great as to prevent Yo.ʳ Lᵃᵖˑˢ Journey to Kennington. It will be very obliging if You please to tell me how yᵉ Queen does? Yᵉ account I met wᵗʰ last night of Her M.ˢ Illness, being a great surprise since I heard nothing of it wⁿ. I was to wait on Yoʳ Lᵃᵖ It is Stupidity ' Ill-nature to be insensible of yᵉ Calamitys w.ᶜʰ Mortals are born to: But it is yᵉ want of a true Xian Temper yᵗ makes us droop & sink under yᵐ. They who duly consider yᵉ excellent Instruction we had in yᵉ Morning Service Yesterday (Ps. 146) will be as Happy at present as is consistent wᵗʰ frail mortality, & qualify'd for a Felicity hereafter wᵗʰ. out End or Interruption. Both wᶜʰ as they are ardently wish'd to Yoʳ Lᵃᵖ so the finding in you yᵉ Temper wᶜʰ cannot fail of obtaining yᵐ is an unspeakable Pleasure to

Dearest Madam

Yᵒʳ Lᵃᵖˑˢ

Most faithful and

devoted Servant

M Astell

[V   *To Lady Ann Coventry, probably June or July 1714*]

Dearest Madam,

Meeting wᵗʰ Mʳˢ Elstob at Chelsea I enquir'd whether Mʳ Clement has Subscrib'd to her Homilys for my Lady Duchess. She said she heard nothing of it, & yᵗ yᵉ Bookseller's don't forward yᵉ work because they don't find their own account in it. She goes in a little time to Oxfᵈ to put it to yᵉ Press, but I expect to see her next Monday, & have enclos'd a Receipt for Yoᵗ Lᵃᵖˑˢ first payment. The Queen has subscrib'd £100. There will be no difference in yᵉ Paper, except in yᵗ one wᶜʰ is for her Majᵗʸ My Lady Duchess if she lets us know her Pleasure before it goes to yᵉ Press, may have such another, but Mʳˢ Elstob cou'd not tell me how much it wou'd come to above yᵉ comon Subscription.

I can truly say, wᵗʰ all yᵉ Sincerity yᵗ becomes a Xtian, yᵗ it is yᵉ greatest Pleasure to Obey yoᵗ Lᵃᵖˑˢ Comands. And know not any thing yᵗ makes me more regret my insignificancy than yᵉ want of oppertunity to express this ardent desire of my heart. But Yoᵗ Lᵃᵖ has too much discernment not to distinguish yᵉ Honest & Faithful Heart, wᶜʰ in yᵉ eye of Heaven, yᵉ best Judge,

is y.ᵉ only valuable offering. Allow me then D.ˢᵗ M.ᵈ to be w.ᵗʰ y.ᵉ greatest
Respect

> Yoʳ L.ᵃᵖ'ˢ
>> Most Obed.ᵗ & devoted
>> humble Serv.ᵗ
>> M Astell

Saturday morning
I hope Yoʳ L.ᵃᵖ & my Lady
Duchess continue in good health.

[VI   *To Lady Ann Coventry, n.d.*]

Dearest Madam,

I beg leave to enquire after my Lady Duchesses Health for w.ᶜʰ, besides all other Reasons, I am extremely solicitous because it is so dear to Yo.ʳ L.ᵃᵖ And since I have this excuse to put myself in Yo.ʳ Thoughts, I can't resist y.ᵉ Temptation of continuing in so desireable a place to y.ᵉ end of my Paper. Tis like I may be Impertinent, as having nothing to say more than is known already. But tho Yo.ʳ L.ᵃᵖ'ˢ own Heart affords you much better Reflections, I am sure they can't proceed from a more sincere & cordial Affection. It was no small instance of our L.ᵈˢ Humility, y.ᵗ He in whom dwelt all y.ᵉ fullness of Wisdom & Knowledge, shou'd in His last Agony vouchsafe to receive Consolation from His Serv.ᵗ His Creature, who cou'd impart no Light or Strength but what he had receiv'd from this L.ᵈ of Angels; Whose Condescention doubtless was for our Example rather than His own Support; to excite y.ᵉ Members of His Body however different in Rank & Excellency, to mutual Good Offices, especially such as conduce to their Spiritual improvem.ᵗ w.ᶜʰ tho y.ᵉ Greatest are y.ᵉ Least regarded.

One wou'd think no Subject cou'd so properly enter into all Discourses & Company, as y.ᵗ w.ᶜʰ it wou'd be an affront to suppose any Person Ignorant of or Unconcern'd about. A subject truly Noble & highly entertaining, of y.ᵉ utmost Importance & suitable to all Capacitys, y.ᵉ most necessary & proper Business of every one, cannot sure be an Offence of ag.ᵗ Good Manners, if Good Manners be a Reasonable thing & not y.ᵉ mere caprice of y.ᵉ worst Judges.

I believe Yo.ʳ L.ᵃᵖ has often w.ᵗʰ Concern observ'd how very different y.ᵉ Lives of y.ᵉ Modern are from what we are told of y.ᵉ Primitive X.ᵗⁱᵃⁿˢ, & from what if we read y.ᵉ Scriptures we can't but discern to be y.ᵉ Spirit & Temper of y.ᵉ Gospel. Yet this is our Rule as well as it was theirs it proposes y.ᵉ same

Reward to both & encourages us wth ye same Motives & Assistance. Perhaps I might be thought no good Church Woman did I assign ye Degeneracy of Manners among Xtians to ye flourishing condition (as it is call'd) of ye Church. In ye first Ages one cou'd not be a Xtian wth out giving up all their Expectations in this World to their Hopes in another; we think to reconcile both, & tho St Paul might think it necessary to admonish ye Roman Converts not to be conform'd to the World, wch was at yt time Heathen, it wou'd be Ill Manners in us not to conform to such as bear ye Name of Xtian.

It is a Melancholy consideration yt those Excell! Facultys our Maker adorns us wth & ye Talents He comits to our Trust are either Carelessly neglected or shamefully abus'd. Reason the Prerogative of our Nature is often set up as an Idol by ym who profess to value & cultivate it, & oppos'd to Revelation Whilst others for fear of this make little or no use of it where it ought to be cheifly imploy'd. That incessant desire of Happiness our Maker impress'd on our Minds to draw us to Himself in whom alone we can find complete Felicity, puts us on a variety of Vain pursuits after yt wch cannot satisfy. Our Love of Grandeur wch shou'd raise our Souls to a vigorous endeavour after what is truly Perfective of our Nature, spends it self on Glitter & Show & all ye Follys of Ambition. Our Natural propensity to Society & desire to be agreeable to those we converse wth insted of giving occasion to ye exercise of all Social Vertue & distinguishing Human Societys from Heros of Brutes, becomes a Snare & Temptation, whilst our Horror of Sin wears off wn we see it a comon Practise, & our liking to ye Person reconciles us in some measure to ye Vice. At best it is an intolerable waste of Time yt precious Treasure, & we come together for ye worse & not for the better. It seems to us Pride or Folly to oppose a torrent, & set our own Private Judgmt in opposition to ye Many: Or if we have Courage for this we either really grow morose & self-conceited, or else pass for such. Wn we go on in ye beaten road, we remain insipid & good for nothing; & if we venture to step out of it, we become Suspected, are clog'd wth reserve & censure, are taken for Monsters fit only to be star'd at & avoided. Our Vertues ruin us wth ye World perhaps oftener than our vices. And tho ye Supports of Religion are in ymselves sufficient to overcome all difficultys, yet we some times fail in ye use of ym thro natural Infirmity, wn we are forc'd to contend wth ye malice & opposition of ye Bad, & to stand forlorn wth out ye assistance & encouragemt of ye Good. Yor Lap who takes so much pleasure in relieving ye Temporal wants of those who are in need, I dare say will not find less in removing more dangerous & deplorable Distresses. Doing good to ye Mind is ye Noblest Charity, it is a Universal Benefit wch none are too great or too little to give or to receive. It is what one needs not be asham'd to Beg, especially from so dear & skilful a hand as Yor Lap's none of whose Prescriptions can fail of Success, at least on her who wou'd esteem y.ᵐ as y.ᵉ highest Obligation & who is

        Dearest Madam,
           Most Obediently & Faithfully
             whatever you will please to have
               her be
                 M Astell

Tuesday morning

[VII   *To Lady Ann Coventry, 7/16/1714*]

Dearest Madam,

I shou'd not know what Apology to make for not sending y.ᵉ Orange Flowers I expected, were not Truth always y.ᵉ best. Other Excuses being indeed a most disobliging sort of Lye, as endeavouring to impose on our Good-Nature as well as our Understandings. The Truth then is y.ᵗ y.ᵉ Weeder Woman told me I might have some Flowers last Tuesday, but w.ⁿ I came to enquire of y.ᵉ Gard'ner he assur'd me there were not 20 buds on all y.ᵉ Trees. I shou'd have done my self y.ᵉ Honor to have waited on Yo.ʳ L.ᵃᵖ insted of this, had I bin able, & presume to send you y.ᵉ Spectators w.ᶜʰ may be more entertaining Company. I heard tother day y.ᵗ a Learned Critic is of Opinion y.ᵗ M.ʳ Steeles Papers are Injurious to Religion & Vertue, by discoursing of y.ᵐ in a ludicrous & superficial manner, representing some of y.ᵉ vilest Sins as Gallantrys, & rendring y.ᵗ y.ᵉ Obj.ᵗ of Raillery only, w.ᶜʰ ought to be detested. I make no doubt y.ᵗ Yo.ʳ L.ᵃᵖ has often observ'd y.ᵗ in his highest fits of Piety he talks more like a Man of y.ᵉ World than a Real Xtian. Two Characters so opposite, y.ᵗ he who endeavours to reconcile y.ᵐ only spoils y.ᵐ both. The Plausible Man having too little of Religion to do his business in y.ᵉ next World, & too much to succeed in this. Our Books of Morality & Piety are, I fear, not always free from y.ᵗ general Error too evident in our Conduct of not keeping our Right End in view. We rest in those things as our End, w.ᶜʰ shou'd only be Motives or Means to it; y.ᵉ reason why we are so inconsistent w.ᵗʰ ourselves. Whereas if GOD only were our End, as surely ought to be, our Principles & Practises wou'd be Uniform & all of a Piece, in w.ᶜʰ consists their greatest Beauty. We shou'd not y.ⁿ complain of *two Souls*; nor say y.ᵗ *Vertue & Vice are blended*; but conclude w.ᵗʰ a better Moralist, y.ᵗ whosoever keeps y.ᵉ Whole Law & yet Offends (wilfully) in One Point, is guilty of All, as transgressing ag.ᵗ y.ᵗ Principle of Love to GOD w.ᵗʰ out w.ᶜʰ all our Performances, how specious soever, are nothing worth. Y.ᵒʳ L.ᵃᵖ seems to have secur'd this great Point, by Resigning Y.ᵒʳ Will entirely to y.ᵉ Will of Heaven. And since GOD is pleas'd to require as y.ᵉ surest Evidence of our Love to Himself y.ᵗ we Love one another, I make no doubt of Yo.ʳ Favour, w.ᶜʰ is desir'd only for His sake & in conformity to His Will, by D.ˢᵗ M.ᵈ Yo.ʳ L.ᵃᵖ⁗ˢ ever Faithful, & as far as y.ᵗ Superior Obligation will allow,

Most Obedient & Devoted

humble Servant

M Astell

Friday July 16.ᵗʰ 1714

I hope yo.ʳ L.ᵃᵖ & my Lady

Duchess are well.

[VIII *To Lady Ann Coventry, 7/26/1714*]

Dearest Madam,

This little Book w.ᶜʰ now waits on You in Obedience to Yo.ʳ L.ᵃᵖ⁗ˢ Com̄ands, has bin a Favorite of mine this 20 years. I can't say it is more so since I was told y.ᵉ Author, tho doubtless a Discourse of this Nature, comes w.ᵗʰ a better Grace from y.ᵉ Pen of a Man of Quality than from y.ᵉ hand of a Meaner Person. Generosity being properly y.ᵉ Vertue of y.ᵉ Great, tho as he handsomly proves, not unsuitable to y.ᵉ lowest Rank of Rational Creatures. But I shall like it much better if it has y.ᵉ good fortune to receive Yo.ʳ L.ᵃᵖ⁗ˢ approbation. It seems not to have fallen in w.ᵗʰ y.ᵉ goust of y.ᵉ Age, y.ᵉ first Impression not having gone off in so many Years. Nor is this to be wonder'd at, since if our Authors description be just, the truly Generous are very inconsiderable as to their Number, tho for this among other Reasons, more valuable in y.ᵐˢelves. It is indeed essential to y.ᵉ Character of y.ᵉ Generous, y.ᵗ they govern y.ᵐˢelves by Right Reason, & not by Example, or y.ᵉ receiv'd Maxims & Fashions of the Age. And perhaps it requires all y.ᵗ Firmness of Mind they possess, to get above Vulgar Prejudices, to make an estimate of y.ᵐˢelves & others by their intrinsic Value, & not by y.ᵉ measures y.ᵗ are com̄only taken. For if we were not apt to be Conform'd to y.ᵉ⁻ World, we need not have bin so frequently caution'd ag.ᵗ it; so strictly forbid to follow a Multitude in doing evil; assur'd y.ᵗ y.ᵉ Friendship of this World is enmity w.ᵗʰ GOD; & whilst we are enjoyn'd to pursue every thing y.ᵗ is Praise-worthy & of Good Report, instructed y.ᵗ we must not expect even *this* Reward of it, till we are in possession of a greater. For tho y.ᵉ Memory of the Just shall be blessed, yet (as Job complains) whilst they Live, the Just & Upright will be laugh'd to scorn. But is not this Scorn & contempt a Real Honor, inasmuch as it was y.ᵉ com̄on Lot of all those Generous Persons who have gone before us, til Envy & Ill-nature were extinguish'd in their Graves? The Son of GOD Himself cou'd not escape it, for He was dispis'd & rejected of Men. Even y.ᵉ⁻ Wise Men of y.ᵉ Age, y.ᵉ Rulers & Teachers of y.ᵉ People who shou'd have known better, revil'd & rejected Him as a contemptible Person, or worse, an

Imposture, a Madman, one who had a Devil, &c. This is therefore to be submitted to, I had almost said Gloried in, by all who make a Right use of their Liberty, endeavouring to do always what is Best. It is a usage they must expect from those who are reproach'd by y.ᵉ lustre of their Vertues; but surely not from one another. For to discern & value Merit, is some pretence to it, such as may be claim'd w.ᵗʰout assuming, by her who must always acknowlege an unfeigned Veneration for Yᵒ.ʳ L.ᵃᵖ'ˢ & who is w.ᵗʰ y.ᵉ utmost Respect & tenderest Sentiments

Dearest Madam

Yo.ʳ most Faithful & most

Obed.ᵗ Servant

M Astell

Monday July 26.ᵗʰ 1714

[IX *To Lady Ann Coventry, 12/10/1714*]

Dearest Madam,

I was in hope of y.ᵉ Honor of waiting on Yᵒʳ L.ᵃᵖ but y.ᵉ weather not favouring me in y.ᵉ morning, I can no longer be satisfy'd w.ᵗʰout knowing how you do. M. Paschal, I own, argues so justly ag.ᵗ all attachment, y.ᵗ I begin to think y.ᵉ giving a check to our most innocent desires is no little Obligation. It being harder to keep y.ᵉ right measure in w.ᵗ is in it self Innocent & Laudable (this requiring exactness of Judgm.ᵗ Comand of ones Passions, & constant Watchfulness) than to avoid great & obvious Faults w.ᶜʰ are too glaring to escape our Observation, & always shocking to a well tempered Mind. And to confess to Yoʳ L.ᵃᵖ I find it much easier to Love all y.ᵉ World in general, even Enemys, than to avoid excess in y.ᵗ particular Affection w.ᶜʰ we owe to y.ᵉ Image of GOD in Minds truly Xtian.

It may indeed seem a contradiction to desire Yoʳ L.ᵃᵖ'ˢ good Opinion & yet make such frequent discoverys of my Infirmitys, w.ᶜʰ are apter to produce Contempt than Kindness; & so put a Book in Yᵒʳ hands w.ᶜʰ seems to condemn y.ᵗ degree of Affection I have so often & sincerely profess'd. But Yᵒʳ· L.ᵃᵖ will find by this, y.ᵗ I have no Design, if I had y.ᵉ Power, to lead you into any mistake, tho to my own advantage; my Sincerity, I hope will atone for my Infirmitys, & Y.ᵒʳ Humanity & Charity overlook those Faults w.ᶜʰ I am not altogether ignorant of nor unwilling to amend. I have therefore left y.ᵉ Margin of y.ᵉ Book w.ᵗʰout rubbing out w.ᵗ I noted for my own use, hoping it won't be seen by any but Yᵒʳ L.ᵃᵖ

There is indeed one expression of Love w.ᶜʰ is y.ᵉ only infallible proof of a valuable Affection & can never be excessive, & y.ᵗ is in S.ᵗ Paul's Language to his Dear Corinthians, (for whom he expresses such a tender and ardent Passion) the *Wishing* & Endeavouring *their Perfection*. Very contrary to y.ᵉ way

of y.ᵉ World, where concern for ones Health, Reputation or Fortune is reckon'd a Favour, but for our truest & greatest Interest an Affront. A Melancholy Observation! w.ᶜʰ y.ᵒʳ Lᵃᵖ I doubt not has often made whilst you act by
better Principles; & therefore tho I wou'd at all times pay You all y.ᵉ Honor
& Deference w.ᶜʰ is so justly due on all Accounts, I take it to be no mistake
in my Respect to pay the highest Honor to y.ᵉ highest Excellence, & to Esteem Yᵒʳ Lᵃᵖ infinitely more as a real, good Christian, than for all other pre-
eminencys of Nature & Fortune: And I Love You too well to beg Y.ᵒʳ Favour
further than as I endeavor to approve my self in all y.ᵉ ways of Xtian Duty.

> Dearest Madam,
> Yoʳ Lᵃᵖ'ˢ
> > Most faithful Obed.ᵗ &
> > devoted Serv.ᵗ
> > M Astell

Friday Dec. 10ᵗʰ. 1714.
I hope my Lady Duchess is well. If yoʳ
Lᵃᵖ cou'd spare y.ᵉ Declaration & Ballad I wou'd
soon & thankfully return y.ᵐ

[X   *To Lady Ann Coventry, n.d.*]

Dearest Madam,
   I am extremely oblig'd to Yo.ʳ Lᵃᵖ. for yo.ʳ kind Enquirys after my health,
w.ᶜʰ I bless GOD is better than I expected; but give me leave to say y.ᵗ nothing contributes more towards it than Yo.ʳ favourable remembrances of Yoʳ
Servant. I am heartily sorry I have not so good an account as I desire of Yoʳ
Lᵃᵖ'ˢ health, w.ᶜʰ you say nothing of, tho it is so valuable & so dear to me,
but yo.ʳ Serv.ᵗ tells me yo.ʳ cold continues.
   I stay at home to day expecting y.ᵉ Declaration, w.ᶜʰ. if it comes Yoʳ Lᵃᵖ.
shall have by y.ᵉ first opportunity. I wish I may be able to be y.ᵉ Messenger,
those short interrupted minutes I have y.ᵉ honor to be in Yᵒʳ Lᵃᵖ'ˢ presence,
being y.ᵉ greatest Pleasure (next to y.ᵗ w.ᶜʰ. nothing but our own folly can deprive us of) to

> Dearest Madam,
> Yoʳ Lᵃᵖ'ˢ
> > Most faithful Obed.ᵗ & devoted Serv.ᵗ
> > M Astell

Wednesday morning
Generosity is Yo.ʳ Lᵃᵖˢ Book,
for I have one of y.ʳˢ I will thankfully return y.ᵉ
Prophesys

[XI *To Lady Ann Coventry, 1/12/1715*]

Dearest Madam,
One who thinks a Happy Death the Cheif Blessing of Life, as y.ᵗ w.ᶜʰ puts an end to our Labour & Warfare, & secures our Reward; shou'd w.ᵗʰ an ill grace Condole y.ᵉ Departure of a Noble Person who after an Honourable Life & y.ᵉ doing much Good in her Generation, is gather'd to her Fathers in a full Age, like as a Shock of Corn in it's Season. Nor wou'd it be less Impertin.ᵗ to talk of Resignation to a Lady who is the brightest Example of it in y.ᵉ severest Trials. Allow me only to remind yo.ʳ L.ᵃᵖ how grievous it is to me to be at any time debar'd Yo.ʳ Presence. I do not need y.ᵉ fear of lossing you from this place to heighten my Impatience. And I make no doubt yo.ʳ Justice will distinguish between those who waite on Yo.ʳ L.ᵃᵖ out of Ceremony, & her who begs Leave, out of y.ᵉ Sincerest Esteem & Affection; nor tye her down among y.ᵉ Croud to Formalitys whom you have bin pleas'd to Honor w.ᵗʰ many endearing Assurances of Yo.ʳ Favour.
It is so highly & so justly valued, y.ᵗ she can omit no occasion of Improving it, who is w.ᵗʰ the greatest Veneration
Dearest Madam
Yo.ʳ L.ᵃᵖ's
Most faithful Obed.ᵗ &
devoted Serv.ᵗ
M Astell
Jan. 12.ᵗʰ 1714/5

[XII *To Lady Ann Coventry, n.d.*]

Dearest Madam
I will not pretend to be more a Philosopher than really I am & therefore cannot deny being extremely affected w.ᵗʰ every thing relating to yo.ʳ L.ᵃᵖ Yo.ʳ Marcus Antoninus I know reproaches me for what he calls "depending on Foreign supports, & beging our Happiness of another." But since he so frequently inculcates what might be thought Ill Manners in a Meaner Person to observe, "Y.ᵗ we are all of one Nature & Family; y.ᵗ our Minds are nearly related as being extracted from y.ᵉ Diety; & since a greater than Antoninus allows us y.ᵉ Honor of being Members of His Own Body, one shou'd methinks be a mere Block, a gangreen'd part, if when y.ᵉ Heart or Eye, y.ᵉ. Noblest & Dearest Part of y.ᵗ Body were indispos'd they cou'd remain Insensible. The Emperor says very truly "Y.ᵗ every ones Good Opinion is not worth y.ᵉ gaining, but their's only who live up to y.ᵉ Dignity of their Nature," & it is for this Reason I am so very solicitous to secure Yo.ʳ L.ᵃᵖ's scarce

knowing wch wou'd be most grievous to me, to Deserve yor Ill-Opinion or to fall under it wth.out Desert. I will not suppose either, because all y.^t can recommend one to a Lady of yor Vertue, is an Esteem & Love of y.^t Vertue & a sincere endeavor to Imitate it, wch is the unfeigned disposition of my heart. And since Yo.^r L^{aP}'s early Goodness towards me prevented even my expectation, & must ever be acknowleg'd wth ye utmost Thankfulness; since You were pleas'd to be so Condisending as to give me many assurances of Yo.^r Favour, & y.^t Yo.^r Character is ye highest Security; for acting by the Principles of Reason & Religion not by Caprice & ye way of ye World, You can neither be Inconstant nor Unjust; it wou'd be Ingratitude & Disrespect to Yo.^r L^{aP} as well as Stupidity, and Unkindness to my self, not to improve ye Blessing, & consequently not to feel an impatient desire to know how You do, & to take all opportunitys of waiting on You, wch is so necessary an effect of a Sincere Affection, y.^t ye one can't be disallow'd wth out forbidding ye other. Were I to wish for any thing in this World, it shou'd be to be agreeable to Yo.^r L^{aP} But then You wou'd have less occasion of exercising Yo.^r Patience & Charity towards

> Dearest Madam
> Yo.^r L.^{aP}
> Most faithful & devoted
> humble Servant
> M Astell

Wednesday five in ye morning.

I hope y^{or} L.^{aP} has slept better
to night than I have done, & y.^t the
swelling in yor Face is abated.

[XIII   *To Lady Ann Coventry, n.d.*]

Dearest Madam,
It is so uneasy to me to live so long as I have done of late, wthout seeing or Hearing from Yo.^r L.^{aP} y.^t I know yor Goodness will forgive my Impertinitys. In this time of Mortification it may seem unseasonable to desire w.^t is one of ye highest Pleasures. But it being also a time of Commemorating ye greatest Charity y.^t ever was or can be shewn, there is no better way of expressing our Thankfulness than by imitating y.^t Goodness. What I aim at is, y.^r being engag'd to be to morrow wth Lady Jekyll who has often complain'd of her Ill Fortune at Yo.^r L^{aps} door, I wou'd beg leave to try if we can

meet wth. better, wch no doubt will be very acceptable to both, but especially to

>> Dearest Madam
>> Yo^r L^ap's
>>> Ever Faithful Obed.
>>> humble Servt
>>> M Astell

Tuesday Apr. 12th

[XIV   *To Lady Ann Coventry, 8/29/1715*]

Dearest Madam,

Yo^r L^ap. may think me very Rude & Unthankful in taking no notice of either of y^e. Letters You were pleas'd to Honor me wth. but indeed I did not receive y^e. former till my last was sent, & this is y^e. first opportunity I had of making my Acknowledgem^ts. for y^t. of Saturday.

I am glad to hear y^t. my Lady Duchess of Ormonde enjoys her Health. A good Cause & a Good Conscience & y^t. Nobleness of Spirit wch. her Grace Inherits from so many Heroic Ancestors, render y^e. Injur'd abundantly more Great & Happy than those who have y^e. Power and Injustice to Injure y^m. And I so sincerely wish her Grace everything she likes, y^t. I cannot regret any part of the time Y^or. L^sp. spends in Her Company, how uneasy soever it be to me to be so long banish'd from Yo^r. Presence. But if I am not to have y^e. Satisfaction of seeing You D^st. M^d. till You are *Settled*, I am like to stay till y^t. happy time when we shall part no more; when we shall Understand, & be Understood, & it will be in no bodys power to misrepresent or mistake: For you are too good a Christian to Settle in a Strange Land; a Vale of Misery; where is nothing Fixt; no abiding City; no stediness even in our own Tempers & Inclinations, wch. are vary'd by a thousand Accidents; no certainty but in those Principles of Religion & Honor y^t. conduct Yo^r. Amiable Life, & by wch. if I do not mightily deceive my self, I am intirely govern'd when I assume y^e. Honor of being wth. an unfeigned Respect & unchangeable Passion,

>> Md.
>>> Yo^r. L^ap's
>>> Most faithful & most
>>>> Obed^t. humble Servt
>>>> M Astell

Chelsea Aug. 29th. 1715

376

Appendix C

[XV   *To Lady Ann Coventry, 11/10/1715*]

Dearest Madam,

I thankfully acknowlege ye honor of Y^or L^ap's Letter, & ye goodness exprest in it; am sorry to hear ye Duchess of Ormonde has any indisposition, & beg Y^or L^ap. will not give Yo^rself any trouble about ye Dialogue wch her Grace may keep as long as she pleases. I hope Y^or L^ap enjoys perfect Health; I need not wish you Happiness, it is inseperable from a truly Xian Mind, at least as much of it as Mortality will bear, & future Good requires. Here is an amiable Lady at Chelsea who desires as much as possible, ye honor of being admitted into Y^or L^aps Presence. The misfortune is, she neither speaks English nor French, & cannot Converse w^thout an Interpreter; I dare not presume so much on my own skill in dumb signs as to pretend to be a faithful one, tho I fancy, use has a little acquainted me wth her meaning; & much less can I give her any hopes of an Audience this four or five Moneths, unless her Merit prevails wth. y^or L^ap to admit us sooner. The Character y^t was given me of her is too long to be incerted in this paper, tho I am told it falls short of what she deserves. It begins,

From Heroes sprung, adorn'd wth every Grace,
Strength in Her Mind, & Beauty in her Face.
The Sweetest Nature, wth ye best Good-Sense;
The Serpent's Wisdom, Dovelike Innocence.
A Vertue Solid, Active of a Piece,
And ever in ye most becoming Dress.
In all Conditions equal & unmov'd; &

I humbly beg pardon for this freedom, & intrusion upon Yo^r L^ap's precious hours, but you will not wonder at ye Respect I pay her in regard to ye resemblance she bears to that Dearest Lady to whom I am wth unfeigned Esteem & Passion
an ever Faithful & most
Obed^t. humble Servt.
M Astell

Chelsea
Nov. 10th. 1715.

[XVI   *To Lady Ann Coventry, 9/4/1716*]

Dearest Madam,

I shou'd be very Impertinent did I pretend to offer Consolation to a Lady whose Resignation & Xian Fortitude is so Exemplary; & who upon all Occasions Acts according to those Principles w^ch· most of us only talk of, That GOD's Will is always Best: And y^t whom He Loves He Chastens. I only beg leave to Suffer w^th· Yo^r L^ap· & to be sensibly affected w^th· whatever Touches a Person so Dear & so highly Esteem'd, for if this be a Presumption I know not how to help it.

To lose what one Loves is indeed very grievous; but ye Wisdom & Goodness of Providence silences our Complaints, especially when it is by His Hand: For to Lose what one tenderly & justly Loves by other Means, is most afflicting, Anxiety in this Case seems Reasonable; whereas in y^e· other, what we Love is safe in GOD's keeping; it is not Lost, but Restor'd & Deposited to Advantage.

Were not y^e· Designs of Heaven infinitely out of our reach, it might seem strange y^t ye Young & ye Happy, ye Good & Usefull, they who to all appearance wou'd be great Blessings to y^e· World, are snatch'd out of it: Whilst those are left behind who grow a nuisance to y^m·selves & others, & therefore long for Death more than for hid Treasures, & wou'd be Glad if they cou'd find y^e· Grave, being little better than a Burden to y^e· Earth, & to ill Minds an Objection ag^t Providence.

Yo^r L^ap's Life & Health are so very valuable, y^t I cannot be satisfy'd till I know how You do; & cou'd wish it were not disagreeable to give me leave to waite on You, w^ch· is an Honor always desir'd, perhaps w^th· too much Impatience, by

Dearest Madam,
Yo^r Lap's
Ever faithful & most
Obed^t humble Servt
M Astell

Chelsea Sept. 4th. 1716
I hope my Lady Duchess of Ormonde
is well.

[XVII   *To Lady Ann Coventry, 6/20/1717*]

Dearest Madam,

I hope Yo^r L^ap & Mrs. Grevile are in good health at Tichfield, & had as pleasant a Journey as ye hot weather wou'd permit, & find as I heartily wish, all y^t Satisfaction w^ch· ye pure Air, ye Beauty & Sweetness of ye Country af-

ford; one might have said in times of yore, y.̣ᶜ Innocency & Simplicity, y.̣ᶜ
Quiet & Retirement,—but by y.̣ᶜ happy Improvements of y.̣ᶜ Age, these are
almost as much banish'd from yᵉ Country as from Towns & Courts.

When I went from Yoṛ Lᵃ.ᵖ to wait on Mʳˢ. Grevile, whose humble Servant I beg leave to be, I had not y.̣ᶜ good fortune to find her, so did not
perform my promise concerning y.̣ᶜ Indian Paper, being likewise disappointed
in sending it, by some accidents I will not trouble Yoṛ Lᵃ.ᵖ wᵗʰ. I had y.̣ᶜ
Honor of her Grace y.̣ᶜ Duchess of Ormonds Company at my Cell last week,
& of dining wᵗʰ. her this; Yoʳ Lᵃ.ᵖ will be pleas'd to hear her Grace is well, &
much Greater and Happier than her Persecutors. If yoʳ L.ᵃᵖ has any Coṁands
you will do me y.̣ᶜ Justice to believe I shall receive yᵐ̣ as an Honor, & obey
yᵐ̣ wᵗʰ. all y.̣ᵗ Sincerity & Diligence y.̣ᵗ becomes

> Yoʳ Lᵃ.ᵖ'ˢ
>
> Most obedient & ever
> faithful humble Servᵗ
> M Astell

Chelsea
June 20ᵗʰ. 1717

[XVIII   *To Lady Ann Coventry, 7/1/1717*]

Dearest Madam,

I make my humble & Thankful Acknowlegemᵗˢ. for y.̣ᶜ Honor of Yoʳ Lᵃ.ᵖ'ˢ
Letter, wᶜʰ. was upon all Accounts very obliging, it being a very great Pleasure to hear from yoṛ Lᵃ.ᵖ on any occasion, but more especially of what is to
yoṛ Satisfaction, & y.̣ᵗ you are so good as to enjoyn me to write, my letters
having nothing to recommend yᵐ̣ but y.̣ᶜ Sincerity of y.̣ᶜ Writer: A strange
sort of Quality, wᶜʰ. every body seeks, & few care to find; tho rather than be
sensible of our want of it, we become y.̣ᶜ Dupes of oʳ own hearts. I congratulate Yoʳ Lᵃ.ᵖ y.̣ᵗ y.̣ᶜ World will suffer you to spend Yoṛ Time so well, & according to Yoʳ own desire; for tho it be y.̣ᶜ most valuable Treasure, most People
think we are oblig'd to yᵐ̣ for taking it off our hands, so y.̣ᵗ we scarce know
y.̣ᶜ use of it till it is gone, insensibly gone! Our Inclinations, Sentiments &
Taste go wᵗʰ. it, Truth only, & y.̣ᶜ Maxims deduc'd from it, remain fixt &
unchangeable, a foundation sufficient to support what ever is built upon yᵐ̣

I have not seen my Lady Duchess of Ormonde since Thursday night, y.̣ᵗ
her Grace did me y.̣ᶜ honor to carry me to Town after Dinner & bring me
back again. I am very happy in so obliging a Neighbour, but yet in spite of
Self-Love shou'd rejoyce exceedingly to see her Grace remove to Richmond
or Sᵗ. James's. I have perfum'd Yoʳ Lᵃ.ᵖˢ Snuff, & reminded Lady Cath. Jones

of her debt of a Basket of Orange Flowers, wch she remembred, & promis'd to discharge; by sending y.^m to Yo.^r L.^{ap's} house. I beg leave to express my Respect & humble Service to Mrs. Grevile; & y.^t I may always be allow'd to own myself, what I must ever be,

Madam

Yo.^r L.^{ap's}

Most faithful & most

Obed.^t humble Servant

M Astell

Chelsea

July 1.st 1717

[XIX   *To Lady Ann Coventry, n.d.*]

Dearest Madam,

It seems to me so long since I had ye Honor to See or Hear of Yo.^r L.^{ap} y.^t I hope you will forgive this Importunity, & allow me to remind You of one from whose Thoughts You are never absent, a necessary consequence of y.^t Esteem & Passion wch is due to Yo.^r Merit, & wch tho Severe quite forgot wou'd be as lasting. I will not trouble You w.th those unavoidable hindrances y.^t have impos'd on me the penance of not attempting all this while to waite on Yo.^r L.^{ap} Colin will in some measure tell You how heavily ye time has past. Tho had he felt w.^t he complains of, I fancy he cou'd hardly have told his Tale w.th such agreeable vanity. So much are real Sentiments too great for W.^{ds} to express y.^m I can only say, y.^t it is not possible any longer to forbear beging to know how Yo.^r L.^{ap} does; & y.^t till she deserves ye contrary, You will be pleas'd to continue Your Favour, so highly valued by,

Dearest Madam,

Yo.^r L.^{ap's}

Ever Faithful &

devoted Servant

M Astell

Monday morning

[XX   *To Lady Ann Coventry, 6/7/1718*]

Dearest Madam,

I had ye honor of yor L.^{ap's} Letter on Tuesday afternoon & will not defer my Acknowlegem.^{ts} since your Comands are so indulgent as to enjoyn me w.^t is at all times most agreeable. Mrs Methuen is yor L.^{ap's} most Obed.^t Servant, it is a great pleasure to us both to hear of yor good health, but y^t it might be perfectly establish'd, she wishes yor L^{ap} for a few days at least, had taken yor Drops, to free you entirely from y^e bad effects of y^e Ill air of y^e Town. It being much easier to prevent, or to cure an Evil in the beginning than to Conquer it w^n it has got ground. And Yo^r L$^{ap's}$ health is of so much consequence to all yor Friends & Servants y^t at least in kindness to y^m I hope you will be persuaded to take care of it.

This Age of Wonders in wch Truth is y^e greatest rarity, has produc'd a Speaking Dog. He is a Native of y^t Country y^t is so famous for Brightness & Ingenuity. He pronounces ye French Alphabet distinctly, tells what ye Ladys drink for breakfast, & answers all ye Questions his Master asks. I have not yet heard him but a Lady y^t has, gave this account Yesterday, when I had ye honor to dine at her Grace of Ormonde's who is very well & Courageous as ever, (Tho rob'd since her Grace came to Chelsea, as tis like yor L^{ap} has heard) & hard at work on a beautiful Flower Pot.

The Dog's Master has it seems found ye Art of playing on his Windpipe as on a Flute, & makes it articulate w^t sounds he pleases. We are grown so religious y^t Toland has produc'd another Gospel (of Barnabas as he calls it) wch is in a fair way to supercede ye 4 old ones, to ye great Edification & enlargem^t of ye Protestant Church, Jews & Mahometans having it seems as good a Title to Xtianity as ye best of us. There being no reason to deny ye Grand Signior a Mosque for ye Service of ye good Musselmen in Town if he thinks fit to ask it. The Pretender, (you understand me M^d) grows more & more Contemptible, even among his own Party. He lives in his Borrow'd Palace, his Urbino as another Tiberius in Capra. As for our pious Protestant Court at Kensington, ye Gates are shut & double Guards are kept ag^t the Wicked. The Devout M^d Munster & young Ulrick, go every Sunday to y^e Swedish Church in y^e City.

I beg pardon for making my Acknowlegem^{ts} to my Ld Arthur Somerset under yor L^{aps} Cover, & hope you will always do me y^e Justice to believe y^t it is y^e greatest pleasure to me to approve myself in w^t I can

> Dearest Madam,
>> Y^{or} L$^{ap's}$
>>> Most Obed^t & ever
>>>> faithful humble Servt
>>>>> M Astell

Chelsea
June 7th 1718
I hope yor L^{ap} will hear y^t Mrs Grevile who set out yesterday, has got safe to Tichfield, & y^t her fears from Change of air will prove Groundless. Mrs M. will have a packet this post.

[XXI   *To Lady Ann Coventry, 7/19/1718*]

Dearest Madam,

I did myself y.ᵉ Honor to Acknowlege y.ᵉ first & only Letter I receiv'd
from Yo.ʳ L.ᵃᵖ since you went to Posen, together w.ᵗʰ my L.ᵈ Arthur Somer-
setts, in a very few days after I receiv'd y.ᵐ & by y.ᵉ same Post sent y.ᵉ Latin
Verses, & several others w.ᶜʰ I hope yo.ʳ L.ᵃᵖ receiv'd from M.ʳˢ· Mary to whom
I send another by this Post. I had long ago renew'd my enquirys after yo.ʳ
L.ᵃᵖ'ˢ Health, but that being on y.ᵉ point of a long Journey whence there is no
return, I was not in a capacity to do it. But I had time enough to perfume y.ᵉ
Snuff w.ᶜʰ attends yo.ʳ L.ᵃᵖ'ˢ Orders.

I make no doubt but yo.ʳ L.ᵃᵖ & yo.ʳ Noble Relations, whose most humble Serv.ᵗ I am, enjoy those Pleasures Y.ᵗ arise from Innocence & Beneficence,
from a Right Use of y.ᵉ Present World, & y.ᵉ Glorious Hopes of Happiness
w.ᵗʰout alloy in a better; w.ᶜʰ is most heartily wish'd you, (for w.ᵗ can one
wish y.ᵗ is equivalent?) by

>Dearest Madam,
>>Yo.ʳ L.ᵃᵖ'ˢ
>>>Most obed.ᵗ & ever
>>>faithful humble Serv.ᵗ
>>>M Astell

Chelsea
July 19, 1718

[XXII   *To Lady Ann Coventry, 8/5/1718(?)*]

Dearest Madam,

I am glad to find by y.ᵉ Letter Yo.ʳ L.ᵃᵖ honor'd me w.ᵗʰ last week y.ᵗ my
Packets went safe. And tho it is always a great Satisfaction to hear from Yo.ʳ
L.ᵃᵖ & no little mortification w.ⁿ I do not, I must always submit to Yo.ʳ Pleasure & be thankful for w.ᵗ you grant, w.ᵗʰout complaining of w.ᵗ you think fit
to deny. My Health is of too little importance to trouble Yo.ʳ L.ᵃᵖ w.ᵗʰ a word
concerning it, did not yo.ʳ Comands excuse y.ᵉ Impertinence. I thank GOD I
got to y.ᵉ Chappel last Sunday, w.ᶜʰ is more than I've bin able to do almost
this two moneths. My D.ʳ is Yo.ʳ L.ᵃᵖˢ most Obedient humble Servant &
makes Constant enquirys after yo.ʳ Health.

I have not yet bin able to wait on y.ᵉ Duchess of Ormond, but I heard
by Lady Betty Butler yesterday y.ᵗ her Grace is well & y.ᵉ Snuff is sent according to yo.ʳ L.ᵃᵖˢ orders. From whom I am sorry to differ in any thing, but is
it kind Dear M.ᵈ to wish a weary Traveller a longer Journey? W.ⁿ one is past

y.ᵉ Meridian of Life, yᵉ Grave is the only Bed of Repose. Methinks every one shou'd be of Spencers Mind, y.ᵗ

Peace after War, Port after Stormy Seas,

Ease after Pain, Death after toilsom Life does greatly please.

We ought indeed to be Content & Courageous in our Port till y.ᵉ Great Comander calls us off. But surely there is sufficient Reason to be extremely Thankful w.ⁿ He is pleas'd to discharge us from our Warfare, & so much y.ᵉ more as it is sooner over. For what Good can we do when we are Dead to all Rational purposes & only capable of patching up a little Mouldring Clay by being troublesom to all about us? They who have Relations to take care of, & Estates to dispose of, may have Business in y.ᵉ World to retain y.ᵐ GOD be thanked, I have none w.ᵗʰ it, nor it w.ᵗʰ me: we were never so endear'd as to be loth to Part. I do not so much as understand it's Language, & shou'd therefore be a silly Poltron were I not glad to quit this Foreign & no very hospitable shore. A Land where is nothing Real, nothing Satisfying; where all is Contradiction. Where we Condole when we shou'd Congratulate, & Envy what deserves our Pity. Where Love & Hatred spring up from Roots y.ᵗ in Reason ought to produce their Contrarys. I am a Contradiction even in this Letter, whose Business shou'd be to endeavour to be agreeable to Yo.ʳ L.ᵃᵖ whereas I have all along pursued my own Inclinations fond of yᵉ Grave every since I cou'd discern between Good & Evil—But I am sure I follow y.ᵐ when I profess my self w.ᵗʰ y.ᵉ greatest Respect & Sincerity,

Dearest Madam

Yoʳ Lᵃᵖˢ

Most faithful & most

Obed.ᵗ humble Servᵗ

M Astell

Chelsea

Aug 5.ᵗʰ

I beg leave to be an

Obedᵗ Servant to my L.ᵈ &

Lady Somersett.

[XXIII   *To Lady Ann Coventry, 9/9/1718*]

Dearest Madam,

I desire to make my most humble Acknowlegem.^{ts} for ye Honor of yor Letter, & ye obliging Concern express'd in it. I shou'd think my life not alto-gather Unuseful cou'd it be of any Consideration w.th Yo.^r L.^{ap} I find so much advantage by Mr Fountains Medicines y.^t I believe I must be his Patient all my Life. This seems but an odd Comendation, but I shall be content if his Skil supplys y.^t degree of sight wch Age & Infirmitys deprive me of. M.^{rs} Me-thuen receiv'd yor L.^{aps} kind remembrance w.th great Respect & Thankfulness, desiring to make her humble Complim.^{ts} & tho she hopes yor L.^{ap} is in a good State of health, she begs y.^t upon any little Cold or disorder you wou'd take a dose of ye drops. It being much ye best to Oppose ye Beginings, ac-cording to a famous Apothegme of Hippocrates ye Father of Physicians. I am sorry it is not in my power to prevail w.th her to take ye good advice she gives, for thro a great aversion to ye Gout in her Feet, she has for some weeks endur'd ye torture of it in her Bowels & Lungs &, rather than drive it out, as her Medicines infallibly do, when ever she will be persuaded to take y.^m

I am very sorry to find ye Duchess of Ormonds health so uncertain, but her Grace was pretty well on Friday last when I had ye Honor to dine w.th her, who is a most obliging Neighbor, & yet I can't help wishing her Grace at Richmond next Sumer & not at Chelsea.

Yo.^r L.^{ap} is doubtless very happy in ye Good Company at Posten, to whom I beg leave to be a most Obedient Servt I thought myself very un-lucky in runing full upon Mrs Greviles Coach by my Garden Wall & yet nei-ther knowing ye Lady nor her Equipage; But I hope ye fragrancy of Mrs Methuen's Honey Suckles will bring her the same way next Year, y.^t I may be more fortunate; unless I take a Journey to Spain, w.ⁿ we have Conquer'd it, to cure my hoarseness, & thence pursue our Conquests to ye Indies to grow Rich, wch will make me Tall & young & handsom & every thing y.^t is agree-able; for according to Boileau Quiconque est Riche a tout & You see M.^d I do not always think on ye Grave; But I am always w.th great Respect

Yo.^r L.^{ap's}

Most faithful & most Obed.^t humble

Servt

M Astell

Chelsea

Sept. 9th 1718

I shall have a packet for M.^{rs}
Mary in a Post or two.

384

Appendix C

[XXIV   *To Lady Ann Coventry, n.d.*]

Dearest Madam,

I am extremely oblig'd to Yo.ʳ L.ᵃᵖ for yᵉ Justice you do me whenever you are pleas'd to remember, yᵗ nothing, except yoʳ dear Presence, can be a greater Satisfaction to me than yᵉ honor of a Letter; more especially when I find by it yᵗ Yo.ʳ Indisposition is gone. May Yo.ʳ L.ᵃᵖ be always Well & Happy, as I have reason to hope You will, since both depend so much on a good Constitution of Body & Mind; & may you ever find a Pleasure in accepting of the ardent good wishes & yᵗ Sincere Respect & Affection yᵗ is humbly paid you by

Dearest M.ᵈ

Yoʳ L.ᵃᵖ's

Most faithful &

devoted Serv.ᵗ

M Astell

Wednesday morning

If I am not sick as I have bin this day or two, I hope very soon to wait on Yo.ʳ L.ᵃᵖ wᵗʰ yᵉ Chefs Book, & an Antidiluvian Billet Doux.

[XXV   *To Lady Ann Coventry, 12/6/1718*]

Dearest Madam,

I was much rejoyc'd to hear from Yoʳ L.ᵃᵖ it being a long time since I had yᵗ honor. I have a Book of many Sheets wᵗʰ a more particular & Authentic account of yᵉ Scots Persecution, wᶜʰ wᵗʰ other things I design'd to send to Marleborough Street if I had yoʳ L.ᵃᵖ's Orders, wᵗʰout wᶜʰ I know not how they may be receiv'd from me. D.ʳ Sharp has bin at the Bath &c to collect for his distressed Brethren, I know not whether he went so far as Hereford.

M.ʳˢ Methuen is extremely sensible of yoʳ L.ᵃᵖ's Favour & desires the acceptance of her most humble Thanks & Service. She is yet in the Confines of Life & Death, & tis hard to judge to wᶜʰ of yᵐ she must proceed.

I have not bin able above once to wait on yᵉ Duchess of Ormonde since she left Chelsea, but I hear to day yᵗ her Grace who has bin ill is now pretty well. I hope my L.ᵈ & Lady Somersett will always believe me to be their most Obedient Serv.ᵗ

Time no doubt is precious above all other Treasures, tis yᵉ only thing yᵗ Providence seems chary in distributing, as not allowing to yᵉ Greatest, any more than to yᵉ Least, above a Moment at once. So much depends upon yᵗ Moment it cannot be too much valued, & my Glass is so far run out, yᵗ I ought doubtless to make yᵉ most of yᵉ small remainder. Yet I can never reckon it a lose of Time to express my Esteem & Gratitude to those I justly

Honor, & (if it be not too familiar a word) Love, & very particularly to yor L^{ap} to whom I beg leave to be always

A most Thankful, Obedient
& Faithful hum: Servt
M Astell

Chelsea
Dec. 6. 1718.

Has yor L^{ap} seen "*ye Dedication to a Great Man, concerning Dedications*? tis publickly sold & thought to be Dr Swifts. There are two Notable Inscriptions for 2 statues to be erected a thousand years hence to George-y^{e}-twentieth.

[XXVI *To Lady Ann Coventry, 1/6/1719*]

Dearest Madam,

On Saturday last I sent a Parcel to Marleborough Street according to Yo^{r} L$^{ap's}$ Order. I am glad to find by y^{t} Elegant & Xtian Speech in it, wch I suppose you have heard of, y^{t} there are so many honest Folks at Hereford, y^{t} y^{e} good Ld Coningsby can find but 3 Men to his Mind in y^{t} City.

Yo^{r} L^{ap} according to your wonted goodness is extremely obliging in yor kind Enquirys. I thank GOD Mrs Methuen is somewhat better. Wth great Thankfulness she makes her Acknowlegem^{ts} & begs yor L^{ap} will always permit her to be yor most Obedient Servt She is always solicitous for yor L$^{ap's}$ health, wch we hope you enjoy. I find nothing does her so much good as her own Medicines. And wou'd she have bin prevail'd on at first to have taken a sufficient quantity to drive out y^{e} Gout, in all probability her distemper might have bin much more easily conquer'd. I am much at a Stay & unless I deceive myself ye Cataract growes thiner.

I am much concern'd at my Lady Duchess of Ormondes ill State of Health; ye bad ways & weather have depriv'd me of ye Honor of waiting on her Grace, but I heard last Saturday y^{t} she was pretty well. I beg leave to be my L^{d} & Lady Somersets most Obedient Servt & hope yor L^{ap} will always do me ye Justice to believe y^{t} I am always truly Sensible of, & thankfull for y^{e} Honor you are pleas'd to do me in letting me hear from you, & y^{e} oftner you condescend to allow it me y^{e} greater is y^{e} Satisfaction being I am in y^{e} Sincerity of my heart & wth y^{e} utmost Respect,

Dearest Madam,
Yo^{r} L$^{ap's}$
Most Obedient &
most faithful humble
Servant M Astell

Epiphany
1718/9

[XXVII   *To Lady Ann Coventry, 4/10/1719*]

Dearest Madam,

I am extremely oblig'd to Yo.ʳ L.ᵃᵖ for yoʳ kind wishes & yᵉ honor of yoʳ last, wᶜʰ had bin sooner acknowleg'd had I bin able to write. But yᵉ Ague day is quite lost, & yᵉ intermediate, a very heavy one. The Caesars head is an Antique of Mʳˢ Methuens where I at present am. She makes her most thankful acknowlegemᵗˢ for yoʳ L.ᵃᵖˢ obliging remembrances of her & is wᵗʰ great Respect yoʳ Obed.ᵗ Serv.ᵗ I suppose yoʳ L.ᵃᵖ has seen yᵉ Acc.ᵗˢ in yᵉ Prints from several parts of Engl. & elsewhere, concerning yᵉ Meteor. D.ʳ Halley computes it to be 81 Miles above yᵉ Earth. But others think it must be more, considering at wᵗ distant places it was seen, almost at yᵉ same time. I find in yᵉ Evening Post yᵗ a Globe of Fire (yᵉ same day we saw one here) fell on yᵉ city of Ronsen about 3 in yᵉ Afternoon & burnt 510 houses & 12 Persons. I am sorry the Packet miscarried, there were 3 Ballads, & Dame Britton, unless it went in a former Packet. This is a favorite of mine, I take it to be Priors by yᵉ manner. If your L.ᵃᵖ pleases I will send yᵐ to try their Fortune another time. I had lately a Letter from M.ʳ Norris full of Grateful Acknowlegemᵗˢ to his generous Benefactors. He has taken Orders & is quiting yᵉ University in expectation of a Curacy under some grave Divine. This puts him to some extraordinary Charge, & he wou'd fain pay off all demands before he leaves yᵉ University. He owns his Benefactors have bin Charitable & Generous beyond Expectation; & if they please to Crown their own work by assisting him once more, he will be no further troublesom.

Yoʳ L.ᵃᵖˢ goodness will pardon this dull scrawl: I find an Ague makes one a perfect Job. But in all tempers & at all times, I shall be wᵗʰ yᵉ greatest Respect & Deference

Dearest Madam

Yoʳ Lᵃᵖˢ

Most faithful & most

Obed.ᵗ humble Serv.ᵗ

M Astell

I beg leave to be my L.ᵈ &
Lady Somersett's most Obed.ᵗ
Serv.ᵗ

Apr. 10ᵗʰ 1719

[XXVIII   *To Lady Ann Coventry, 5/11/1719(?)*]

Dearest Madam,

    Tho it be a long time since I did myself this Honor, I hope I have not lost y.ᵉ Permission; the greatest of my Respect, & prefering Yoʳ L.ᵃᵖˢ Pleasure before my own, being y.ᵉ reason why I forbore my Importunities. For my heart will always feel the most Respectful & Tenderest Sentiments when it Thinks of Yoʳ L.ᵃᵖ since the Effects cannot Cease whilst y.ᵉ Cause remains; And I make no doubt y.ᵗ Vertue to w.ᶜʰ alone I paid my Homage, will shine more & more unto a Perfect day. I beg leave to acquaint Yoʳ L.ᵃᵖ y.ᵗ there will be a Charity Sermon for yo.ʳ poor Chelsea Girls Preach'd by M.ʳ Smalridge Bp. of Bristol next Sunday, at y.ᵉ Chappel in Spring Garden near y.ᵉ Mews: And also, y.ᵗ I have at Yoʳ L.ᵃᵖ'ˢ Service a Couple of Shels taken out of Jacob's Well; & a bit of y.ᵗ Stone w.ᶜʰ makes y.ᵉ Cloth y.ᵗ is clean'd by Burning, in w.ᶜʰ y.ᵉ Ancients us'd to preserve y.ᵉ Ashes of their Dead. I have so ill success at Yo.ʳ L.ᵃᵖ'ˢ Door, & now so little oppertunity to attempt it, y.ᵗ I dispair of y.ᵉ Happiness of Seeing Yoʳ L.ᵃᵖ, since y.ᵉ time draws on apace y.ᵗ y.ᵉ most desireable as well as more indifferent Objects will be equally remov'd from

        Yor L.ᵃᵖ'ˢ

           Ever Faithful & most
             Obed.ᵗ humble Serv.ᵗ
               M Astell

Chelsea May 11ᵗʰ

I hope my Lady Duchess of Ormonde & Lady Mary O'Brian are well being much their L.ᵃᵖˢ humble Serv.ᵗ

[XXIX   *To Lady Ann Coventry, 10/27/1719*]

Dearest Madam,

    I thankfully acknowlege y.ᵉ Honor of yo.ʳ L.ᵃᵖ'ˢ obliging Letter w.ᶜʰ I receiv'd yesterday, & hasten, in obedience to Yo.ʳ Comands to let you know y.ᵗ I am still in Town, & perhaps shall be so all y.ᵉ Winter, there being 20 Miles from Tunbridge to Burwash, w.ᶜʰ now y.ᵉ season for y.ᵉ Waters is done, I can't get over but on Horseback or in a Wagon: And shou'd be very sorry not to have y.ᵉ Pleasure of seeing yo.ʳ L.ᵃᵖ before I go, since y.ᵉ difficulty of y.ᵉ Journey, besides all other Reasons, will keep me from thinking of a Return to Town. And I shou'd be glad to see y.ᵉ School at Chelsea built & settled, but we have as yet got but £300 towards it (w.ᶜʰ I am going to put to Interest) & want two more. It was put to Interest upon y.ᵉ fund for y.ᵉ Churches, (as it came in) but this is not a time it seems for building Churches, a full stop being put to y.t Work, & y.e Fund apply'd to y.e Lottery. I have little expectation of a Prize, tho I have a Ticket w.ch Mrs. Pitt gave me, still in y.e Wheel.

Lady Betty Butler has had y.e Small Pox she fell ill y.e begining of this Moneth, & has already bin twice out Airing. I am affraid I was accessory to her illness, my Lady having had y.e goodness y.e day before to set w.th y.e Window open to give me Air. But I thank GOD it is so well over, they being y.e best sort, & her L.aP. happily deceiv'd by Mrs. Sharp till out of danger. Her Grace of Ormonde is expected next Friday, & I hope in a good State of Health. I never saw her Grace so dispirited or look so ill as y.e day before she went, y.t she did us y.e Honor to come to Chelsea. Those y.t come from y.e Bath say, her Grace looks now extremely well & healthy. Poor Mrs. Methuen who has always a gratefull sense of yo.r L.aps favours has by a preparation of Guiacum after her own way (it doing her no good but hurt as y.e D.rs prescrib'd it) got y.e better of her Gout, her great complaint now is her eyes on w.ch it spent it's malice, & w.ch are indeed very bad. M.r Pitt gives me leave to have Letters under his Cover as Member of Parl.t, if your L.aP. pleases to use this way, it will surely come safe. And I shall distinguish it from his if it be superscrib'd by y.e same hand w.ch y.e last & seal'd w.th y.e same Seal, or y.e little Cupid w.th his *Mauger tous je passe*. The same direction will be y.e best when I go to Burwash in Sussex. For y.e Letters must pass thro London, & M.r Pitt will be so good as to forward & frank y.m when I am gone. But I hope before y.t time to have y.e further Honor of Hearing from & Writing to Yo.r L.aP. being w.th y.e greatest Respect, & sincerest Passion

Dearest M.d

Yo.r L.aps

Most faithful & most

Obed.t humble Serv.t

M Astell

Oct.27.th 1719

I beg my humblest Service
to my L.d & Lady Somerset

[XXX   *To Lady Ann Coventry, 1/8/1720 (?)*]

Dear Madam,

I had y.ᵉ honor of yo.ʳ L.ᵃᵖ'ˢ Letter of Dec.ʳ but nothing worth writing occuring since, perhaps insted of asking pardon for not acknowleging it sooner, I ought to do it for troubling yo.ʳ L.ᵃᵖ so soon. I have bin reading y.ᵉ late A. Bp. of Cambrays Letters, w.ᶜʰ make me very sick of my own. He has left a Noble Model in y.ˢ as in other things, but y.ᵉ World is too much y.ᵉ World to follow it. Good manners, falsely so call'd, & a mean Complaisance to y.ᵉ follys & vices of y.ᵉ Age, has quite banish'd y.ᵗ Noble Simplicity w.ᶜʰ he so admirably describes & w.ᶜʰ is indeed y.ᵉ Ground, & y.ᵉ Perfection of all y.ᵗ is Great, Good & Agreeable. It consists in a perfect disengagem.ᵗ from ourselves, as well as from y.ᵉ World, & a concern to approve ourselves to GOD only. It differs from Sincerity & very much excells it. The Sincere do indeed say nothing but w.ᵗ they Think; nor wou'd pass for any thing but w.ᵗ they Are. But they are always studying y.ᵐˢelves, composing their Words & Thoughts, reflecting on y.ᵐˢelves thro fear they have done too little or too much, & therefore are not Simple. They are neither easy w.ᵗʰ others nor others w.ᵗʰ y.ᵐ There is nothing free & natural in their Conversation. They are always as it were setting y.ᵐˢelves in the Glass, & are too full of y.ᵐˢelves to be lik'd either by GOD or Man. Nothing is so contrary to Divine Simplicity as Worldly Wisdom, w.ᶜʰ wou'd do every thing itself, & trust nothing to GOD, is always admiring it's own Works, & ordering y.ᵐ for it's own Glory. But he y.ᵗ wou'd be Simple, must become a fool to y.ᵉ World, w.ᶜʰ is in reality to be truly Wise. I am affraid y.ᵉ good A. Bp. did not meet w.ᵗʰ many Proselytes to this Doctrine in his own Country, nor is it like to be much relish'd here. Men will be Men, y.ᵗ is, Weak, Vain, Inconstant, Unjust, False & Presumptuous. They will follow their own Ways, Inclinations & Customs, & we must be Content, for we cannot new Model y.ᵐ

I wish yo.ʳ L.ᵃᵖ all Happiness, in this World & y.ᵉ Next, & to yo.ʳ Noble Relations whose most obed.ᵗ Serv.ᵗ I have y.ᵉ honor to be. I am sorry M.ʳˢ Price has no better health, since she makes a very good use of it. But every one has their Cross, w.ᶜʰ is design'd to lead y.ᵐ to Happiness. I hope yo.ʳ L.ᵃᵖ enjoys yo.ʳ Health, & am w.ᵗʰ great Respect & Deference

Dear M.ᵈ Yo.ʳ L.ᵃᵖˢ

Most Obed.ᵗ humble Serv.ᵗ

M Astell

Jan. 8.ᵗʰ

A. Bp. of Cambrays Letters. These are the letters of Fénelon, first published in Paris in 1718. Although Astell could not read Malebranche in the original in 1693, when Norris suggested him to her, she seems to have mastered the language by this time.

[XXXI   *To Lady Ann Coventry, 2/25/1720 (?)*]

Dearest Madam,

Tis so long since I had ye honor of hearing from Yo^r L^{ap} y^t I can't help reminding you of one who often thinks of yor L^{ap} wth a very high Esteem & Solicitude for yor health & all y^t is desireable; I had done it long since, but y^t I was affraid of being too impertin^t having no entertainm^t Yo^r L^{ap's} in ye Country is so much beyond any thing one hears of in Town, y^t if we did not love you heartily, & share in ye Happiness you enjoy, we shou'd be tempted to envy you. Every body here who has a Pound, takes care not to bury it in a Napkin. The Great as well as ye Rich turn Stock-jobbers. I wish we were as diligent in improving our Talents ye right way. He y^t is Rich multiplys his Riches; & he y^t has little, may content himself wth y^t little, for he has nothing to encrease. One meets wth few y^t are Thankful but many murmurers, not so much for losing what they actually Had, as for ye imaginary loss of what they *might* have gain'd.

I had ye Honor to wait on ye Duchess of Ormond yesterday, & to hear from Mrs Grevil to day, & am glad to find both Familys so well. I hope her Grace who has hitherto confin'd herself to her own Apartment will find ye benefit of Air & Exercise w^n she goes to her House in Paradise Row; I know not whether I made my Lady Betty Hastings Complem^t to yor L^{ap} in my last. She is still adding one good Work to another. Poor Mrs Methuen can hardly find her way in her own Chamber, but whenever I see her, expresses her Esteem of Yo^r L^{ap} & rejoyces to hear of yor health. I pray GOD continue it, ye benefit you receive by ye good air of Posten is ye only Consolation for yor Absence to

Dearest Madam

Y^{or} L^{ap's}

Most faithful &

most Obed^t humble Servt

M Astell

Feb. 25th

I beg my most humble Service
to my L^d & Lady
Somerset.

[XXXII   *To Lady Ann Coventry, 3/26/1720*]

Dearest Madam,

The Honor of Yo^r L^{ap's} most obliging Letter requir'd a speedier Acknowlegem^t but I had rather depend on yor Goodness for pardon, than make a lame excuse. I cannot say it is a busy time wth Me, who have no

Talent to improve, whilst y.ᶜ Rich are adding heap to heap in y.ᶜ English Mis-
sisipi. I hope yo.ʳ L.ᵃᵖ was early in it, for since y.ᶜ greatest part of yᶜ Nation
are to be ruin'd to enrich a Few, I can't but wish yᵗ y.ᶜ money may fall into
those generous hands who will most freely comunicate it to such as want.
Even y.ᶜ Ladys as well as y.ᶜ Lᵈˢ turn Stock-Jobbers, & have got y.ᶜ Cash out
of y.ᶜ Citizens hands. As yet there are not many Real Losers, tho abundance
of Complaints, not for y.ᶜ loss of what they were possess'd of, but of what
they might have gain'd had they forseen what wou'd happen. I wish we were
as diligent in making sure of a Treasure y.ᵗ faileth not, for wᶜʰ every body
may be Adventurers & obtain it wᵗʰ less Anxiety & Pains than is daily bestow'd on uncertain Riches. So purblind are we as not to look beyond y.ᶜ
Present Trifles, tho they bear no proportion to yᵉ future everlasting Treasure.
I meet wᵗʰ none of those Papers I us'd to send Yoʳ L.ᵃᵖ This new way of
Multiplying Gold & Silver takes up every bodys thoughts & Conversation.
Last night South Sea was 320, & they say it will soon be 1000 or 1500. I
wish yᵉ poor Girls of Chelsea's money had bin in it, we might y.ⁿ have ime-
diately begun to build. However, I hope it may be done this Sumer, &
wou'd fain beg Yo.ʳ L.ᵃᵖ to be a Trustee, wᵗʰ Lady Betty Hastings (who gives
£100 towards y.ᶜ building, & whose Complements I am to return to yo.ʳ L.ᵃᵖ
in y.ᶜ most engaging manner) & Lady Cath. Jones &c. I hope Baron Price
will be another, & give us his Charitable Advice as to y.ᶜ Writings whereby
M.ʳ Green must convey y.ᶜ Ground he gives to build upon.

 I had yᵉ honor to wait on her Grace of Ormond this Week, who looks
well, but has bin abroad but once, & y.ⁿ got Cold. I have a Letter from Paris
of y.ᶜ date of this New Style, wᶜʰ says yᵉ Duke is very well at Madrid, & in as
much Honor & Esteem wᵗʰ yᵉ New Ministry there as he was wᵗʰ y.ᶜ old; And
yᵗ y.ᶜ Lady at Rome is 4 moneths gone. I have tyr'd yoʳ Lᵃᵖ wᵗʰ this tedious
scrawl. And must comfort my self in yo.ʳ L.ᵃᵖ'ˢ absence wᵗʰ y.ᶜ Health & Satisfaction you enjoy. For our Affection falls very short if we do not prefer yᵉ
Happiness of those we Esteem & Love before our own; I cannot then re-
pine, so long as yo.ʳ L.ᵃᵖ is Pleas'd, being I am wᵗʰout reserve
   Dearest Madam
    Yoʳ Lᵃᵖˢ
     Most faithful & most
      Obed.ᵗ humble Servᵗ
       M Astell
Mar. 26ᵗʰ 1720

I beg my most humble Services to
my L.ᵈ & Lady Somerset

[XXXIII   *To Sir Hans Sloane, 7/2/1720*]

Sir,

You will please to remember, y.^t when You allow'd me ye most [. . .]able entertainm.^t of seeing y.^r valuable Collections in company of some honor^ble Ladys, they [. . .]ended ye Charity School at Chelsea & you were so good as to offer a piece of ye ground, wch offer, as I hear by M.^r & Mrs Green, you lately renew'd. I make no doubt S.^r but you are able to make good yor Title, but we are [. . .] & I find, upon Inquiry, it is disputed. Besides, ye building by ye Road wou'd [. . .]k up Mr Green's ground, & be more prejudicial to him than in y.^t place wch Wm Green offers. I shou'd be glad of an uncontested Spot. y.^t might please every body, & to receive yor directions. [. . .]Season is pretty far advanc'd, & there are many strong reasons for Building, wch I hope will excuse this trouble from

> Sir,
> > Yo.^r most humble Servt
> > > M Astell

From my Lodging
in New Bond Street
next door to ye Blew
[Fl]uke. July. 2. 1720

I beg my humble Service
to my Lady Sloane

[XXXIV   *To Lady Ann Coventry, 8/12/1720*]

Dearest Madam,
I am always sensible of Yo.^r L.^ap's Goodness & Kind Wishes towards me, & thankful for y.^m I know not how Prosperity might turn my head, as it doth most other Peoples, but GOD be thanked I am not like to come w.^thin ye danger, £1000 or 1500 being ye most I am like to make wch at a time y.^t Printers, Upholsterers, &c. make their 100,000 will appear but in a sorry figure. The Love of Money seems to extinguish ye Love of Fame, ye Muses address to the Ocean of Riches, it is become their Helicon. And we hear no more of Lady Mary Wortley's Wit, but of her Bargains. I have not for a long time bin so diverted as I was at ye Herald's Office, whither Curiosity carried me; & I thought it but reasonable y.^t since my Name-sake helps me to Money, I shou'd help him to a Pedagree tho he does not value it. The Heralds seem to me very Ingenious in bestowing upon our new L.^ds & Gentry,

Arms suitable to their remarkable Names & Noble Atcheivem.^{ts} The noble Ld Cadogan in his Quartered Coat (for he has some alliance to a Cottage in Wales) has a Lion y.^{t} very Soldier-like, looks behind him, wch they told me was in token of Vigilence; his tongue is Blew, I thought it shou'd have bin Gold or Silver. The B^p of Banger too has his quarterly Coat, wth a Bleeding Pelican; a Globe & Dove wth an Olive branch for his Crest, & ye Motto *Veritus* & *Patria*, Truth & his Country. One reason he assigns in his Petition for Arms is his Grandfather's being Chaplain to General Monck & very instrumental in ye Restoration. I was so diverted wth these & many more New Men's fresh & clean, y.^{t} I almost forget my dusty Great Great &c. Unkle Harry, who about 400 years ago had an Augmentation given him for taking Don Diego Valdera Prisoner. But w.^{t} does it signify & for 400 years hence, y.^{e} Cups & y.^{e} Saws, y.^{e} Implem.^{ts} of their Trades, & Puns upon their Names, will be more considerable, if they learn but y.^{t} Art, wch y.^{e} other wanted, to tack their Estates to their Arms.

I obey'd yor L$^{ap's}$ Comands to Mrs Coventry, whose Complim.^{ts} I am to return in y^e best & most respectful Manner, I beg mine to my L^d & Lady Somerset, Mrs Grevile & Mrs Price, who is I suppose at Posten. I live in expectation of y^e happiness of Waiting on Yo.^{r} L^{ap} in Town, wch makes all Inconveniency easy to her who is wth y.^{e} greatest Respect

    Dearest M^d

    Yo.^{r} L$^{ap's}$

     Most obedient &

     faithful humble Servt

     M Astell

Aug 12th 1720

[XXXV *To Lady Ann Coventry, n.d.*]

Dearest Madam,

  This is y.^{e} third Letter I have writ since I had y.^{e} Honor to receive one, wch being contrary to yor wonted Goodness, makes me persuade my self y.^{t} some have miscarried thro my misfortune. For I can never suppose y.^{t} Yo.^{r} L.^{ap} who is so humane & good to y.^{e} worst of Mortals, can be unkind to one who loves you as her own Soul. And tho it shou'd happen otherwise I cannot reckon it a faulty Importunity since I have both y.^{e} Principles of Xtianity & Yo.^{r} L$^{ap's}$ Merit to justify me, whilst I pursue you wth an Affection wch being founded on y.^{t} Merit must last as long as it does. No Dst M^d You are too valuable to be lost by mere froideur: And as I am not Conscious of having given any Cause to repent of Yo.^{r} Favours, I can't believe y.^{t} yor L.^{ap} will change w.thout Cause. For ye Esteem of my heart has always kept pace w.th or indeed exceeded, ye highest expressions, & however grievous it is neither to See nor Hear from a Lady so deservedly dear to me, I will impute it to any thing rather than want of goodness in Yo.^r L.^{ap} towards

Your ever Faithful &

most Obed.^t Servt

M Astell

Chelsea

St. Matthew's day

[*September 21*]

[XXXVI *To Lady Ann Coventry, n.d.*]

Dearest Madam,

It is impertinent to trouble Yo.^r L.^{ap} w.th my Complaints, but this is certain y.^t nothing but absolute necessity of some kind or other can hinder me from paying y.^t agreeable devoir of waiting on Yo.^r L.^{ap} To whose Goodness I am highly oblig'd for this last Favour, & to whom I have so much to say, y.^t I wish to Converse as Angels do by Intuition, in wch I hope there wou'd be no danger. For what ever Opinion the World may form of Yo.^r Servant, I shou'd be glad y.^t Yo.^r L.^{ap} cou'd see my heart w.th all it's faults, since you cou'd not but entertain some kind Sentiment towards it when you observ'd Yo.^r Power, & y.^t unalterable disposition it has to be,

Dearest M.^d

Yo.^r L.^{ap's}

Most faithful &

devoted Servt

M Astell

Monday night

[XXXVII *To Lady Ann Coventry, 10/24/1721*]

Dear Madam,

I wou'd not trouble Yo.^r L.^{ap} w.th a Letter till I cou'd suppose you were recover'd of ye fatigue of Yo.^r Journey & in possession of those serene & unmingled Delights wch Noble Minds enjoy when they are got loose from the Town to Converse w.th y.^mselves & a few of their own Character. This being ye Season y.^t ye Flys buz most in it ye time of Noise & Clutter and consequently of least enjoym.^t to a reasonable Mind, I do not at all wonder at Yo.^r L.^{ap's} Winter Journey, but congratulate my L.^d & Lady Somerset upon it, being their most obedient Servant, & I hope I may also do it upon his L^{Ps} perfect Recovery. By what I hear of Yo^r Herefordshire Neighbors, they are not like to be pleas'd wth their new Bp. nor he to trust himself among y^m It is very certain y^t M^r J:Law came to England in S.J. Norris's Fleet; since he can hardly make ye Nation poorer, it is to be hoped he will make it Richer. Were not ye Life of ye Gay & Busy World at all times a sort of Southsea Scheme they might be happy at less expence & trouble than it costs to render y^{m}selves miserable. Happy are they who are got safe ashore; but they wou'd be yet Happier cou'd they help those to Land who are lost upon y^e Ocean. Yo^r L^{ap} delights in good Works of all kinds, & when a spare minute is found from better Employm^t I flatter myself you will be so Charitable as to bestow it upon

                 Dear Madam
                   Yo^r L$^{ap's}$
                       Most faithful & most
                       Obed^t humble Servt
                       M Astell

Chelsea. Mannor Street
Oct. 24.th 1721

[XXXVIII   *To Lady Ann Coventry, 11/24/1722*]

Dear Madam,

    I humbly thank yor L^{ap} for y^e honor of yor Letter, & am glad to hear mine was acceptable & came safe wthout ye prying eyes of ye Vigilant Ministers. All ye talk now is about Mr Layer's Trial who was found Guilty Thursday morning about 3—for so long ye Trial held. The Witnesses ag^t him were fully prov'd infamous, no Jury wou'd have taken their evidence, but his own Confession before ye Council, wch exactly agreed w^t all they swore, did his business. It was indeed more particular than ye Evidence in some things, wch one wou'd have thought he cou'd not have mention'd wthout a design to turn Evidence. For instance, he said L. N. & Grey stood Godfather to his Child representing ye Pretender KNOWINGLY. He had told ye Council much more than his Accusers cou'd urge ag^t him. As y^t he was at Rome, y^t he ask'd a Letter of Credit, but y^t it was not granted &c. The Scheme found among his Papers he also own'd there. And yet he told his Friends before his Trial y^t he had made no Confession y^t cou'd hurt him. In a w^d a Gentleman of ye Law who stay'd out ye whole Trial & from whom I had this account thinks it is hard to determine, whether there is more Folly, Madness, or Knavery in y^t Confession. His Council insisted to have y^t Confession brought into Court wch was a point of Law, but ye Judges over-rul'd it; &

insted thereof took Mr. De la Fay & M.ʳ Stanians Oaths. They alleging yᵗ to bring in yᵉ minutes of yᵉ Council book was to discover yᵉ Secrets of yᵉ Governmᵗ, & the names of those he had accus'd. The Declaration from *Lucca* is another matter of Discourse. The Chevalier's Friends disown it; it is in yᵉ hands of none but yᵉ Governmᵗ There was no Mob, or Rout at yᵉ Burning of it, according to yᵉ Accᵗ yᵉ Sherif gives his Friends, tho yᵉ News Papers make a lying Story. It seems it denys yᵗ there is any present design on foot. So yᵗ as a Gentleman well observ'd, either the Plot, or yᵉ Declaration is an Imposture.

M.ʳˢ Methuen continues as she was, & is always Yoʳ L.ᵃᵖˢ most humble Serv.ᵗ I hope Posten agrees wᵗʰ yoᵗ health, & am sorry to hear my L.ᵈ Arthur Somerset enjoys his no better, being his L.ᵖˢ & my Lady Somerset's, & wᵗʰ great Respect

M.ᵈ Yoᵗ L.ᵃᵖ'ˢ

Most Obedient

humble Serv.ᵗ

M Astell

Nov. 24.ᵗʰ

1722

[XXXIX   *To Lady Ann Coventry, 3/7/1723*]

Dear Madam,

This morning I had yᵉ honor of yoᵗ L.ᵃᵖ'ˢ obliging Letter; but, as ill news flys apace, had heard of my L.ᵈ & Lady Somerset's good fortune to our disadvantage. I am their most Obedient Servant, & wish their Satisfaction in every other thing. I was wᵗʰ yᵉ Duchess of Ormonde yᵗ Evening when yoᵗ L.ᵃᵖ'ˢ Letter brought yᵉ like tydings, her Grace allowing me yᵗ honor pretty often whilst she is at Chelsea whose air agrees extremely well wᵗʰ her Grace. I wish it did so wᵗʰ yoᵗ L.ᵃᵖ tho perhaps this wou'd not be much to my advantage, yᵉ folks in fashion being so ill-natur'd in this Neighborhood, yᵗ I think I must quit it, since they will not allow me to go to yᵉ Chappel quietly. M.ʳ Walpole's worthy Woollen Draper (Robin Mann) now M.ʳ Justice of Peace, thinking fit to take upon him Ecclesiastical Jurisdiction, & my Acquaintance, except yᵉ good Duchess, being affraid of me, convey yᵐˢelves from me. A persecution I am not concern'd at for my own sake, since I shall always account it an honor & happiness to suffer for a good Conscience.

There are Two Protests about printing Layer Trial, wᶜʰ but for yᵐ had never appear'd & was printed at 14 Presses in 4 days as yᵉ Bookseller owns. There is to my knowledge a very great lie in it, about yᵉ Xtning, but it is too long to insert yᵉ story here. There is likewise a long Protest abᵗ yᵉ Mutiny Bill, all wᶜʰ yoʳ L.ᵃᵖ had had e're this, if they were Printed, but my eyes wont allow me to copy y.^m & w.^n they will be Printed I know not, a Poor Man who was before a Prisoner in ye Fleet being found guilty, & his Sentence cruelly defer'd till next Term, whereby he will lie in Prison 4 Moneths & his Wife & two Children as well as himself starve in ye mean time, only for selling 5 or 6 Books to get y.^m bread.

I am now reading ye D. of Buckinghams Works, begining wth ye 2.^d Volume (ye Prose) wch has made ye most noise & if I may presume to pass my Judgm.^t on a Man so great among ye Wits, as well as ye Nobility, neither his thoughts nor his Style in ye general seem to answer his Character. Excepting his Account of ye Revolution wch is admirably wrot after ye manner of my favorite Sallust, & has no fault y.^t I perceive, except y.^t it is left unfinish'd. His Memoirs are also very well wrot, he seems to be fittest for Ruination & Argum.^t But his Essays & peices of Wit fall flat; tho perhaps this may only be my want of Tast.

The Report of ye Plot is to be printed, but it appears very ridiculous to all who are not concern'd to promote it; & has inrag'd ye L.^ds whose Names are mention'd upon base hear say, so y.^t they mean to require in Parl.^t ample Satisfaction from ye Ministry for so great an Injury. Many of those among ye Burford (a cramp name for Ld Orrery) Club, not so much as having ever seen one another. I heartily wish yor L.^ap's health & happiness & all those delights, wch ye Country & Retirement, alone afford, being wth great Respect & Simple Affection,

> Dear Madam
> Yo.^r L.^ap's
>
> Most Obed.^t & faithful
> humble Servt
> M Astell

Chelsea
Mar.7.th 1722/3

[XL   *To Lady Ann Coventry, 7/6/1723*]

Dear Madam,

Your L.^ap may justly wonder y.^t I have not in all this time acknowleg'd yor obliging Letter. The Truth is, for ye Truth is always best, I stay'd at first to give yor Note to Mr Johnson, but ye Lady at whose house I saw him, having buried her Husband, I have not yet bin able to meet wth him. I have since had a sort of fever & S. Antonys fire on my face, so y.^t my eyes were shut up & I was incapable of writing, having but just got clear of it.

Poor Mrs Methuen laid down ye Burden of Mortality last Thursday ab.^t noon. She had an Apoplectic fit ye Week before, but after 24 hours sleep was perfectly brought to her Understanding by a Blister. It continued wth her to y.ᵉ last, & she died w.ᵗʰout Agony, tho Mortify'd in several places. I lament my own loss & y.ᵗ of many to whom she did good, but know not how to regret her deliverance from w.ᵗ was not so much Life, as a continual dying. Miserable to all outward appearance but happy & desirable in a Religious Sense, because whom GOD Love's He chastens most severely, & even scourges every Child y.ᵗ is dearest to Him. They are indeed most to be pitied, whose eyes swell w.ᵗʰ fatness & who do even w.ᵗ they list, who corrupt others &c of w.ᶜʰ we have great & flagrant Instances.

I hope yo.ʳ L.ᵃᵖ enjoys your health, & all y.ᵉ Good Company now at Posten whose most humble Serv.ᵗ I am. Beging yo.ʳ L.ᵃᵖ to believe me w.ᵗʰ y.ᵉ greatest Respect & Thankfulness for all yo.ʳ Favour,

> Dear M.ᵈ
> Yo.ʳ L.ᵃᵖ's
> Most Obed.ᵗ humble Serv.ᵗ
> M Astell

Chelsea
July 6.ᵗʰ1723

[XLI   *To Sir Hans Sloane, 4/25/1724*]

> Mannor Street
> Apr. 25.ᵗʰ 1724

When I had y.ᵉ good Fortune to meet you at M.ʳˢ Green's, you were so [. . .]s to give me leave to waite on you w.ᵗʰ a small Curiosity. I know not to w.ᵗ its kin, Mineral, or Animal you will [. . .] it, but I know it is akin to both. My L.ᵈ Huntingdon & y.ᵉ Ladys his [sisters?] are desirous to see yo.ʳ noble Repository. Will you be pleas'd Sir, to name a day w.ᶜʰ will not be inconvenient, & permit me to waite w.ᵗʰ y.ᵉ Ladys thither, w.ᶜʰ will be a great favour

> Yo.ʳ most humble Serv.ᵗ
> M Astell

I may go out of Town very soon

[XLII   *To Lady Ann Coventry, n.d.*]

Dearest Madam,
I know not what Fate there is in Marriage, but I find a most agreeable & irresistable Fate in my Concern & Respect for Yo.ʳ L.ᵃᵖ & therefore beg You'l Excuse y.ᵉ trouble of this Enquiry how you do? I hope Yo.ʳ L.ᵃᵖ got no Cold

yesterday, & y.ᵗ y.ᵉ Head Ach you complain'd of is gone w.ᵗʰ out being attended w.ᵗʰ a Cold. I shou'd grow Impertinent did I give way to a thousand
Thoughts y.ᵗ croud upon me. But Yo.ʳ L.ᵃᵖ knows my heart perfectly well, &
y.ᵗ words cannot sufficiently express w.ᵗʰ how much ardor & faithfulness
I am

> Dearest Madam,
> Yo.ʳ L.ᵃᵖ's
> > Obedient & devoted
> > humble Servant
> > M Astell

Friday morning.

I shou'd be glad to hear
y.ᵗ my Lady Duchess &
M.ʳˢ Price are well

[XLIII   *To Lady Betty Hastings, 9/4/1730*]

RECEIVED of the Lady Betty Hastings by the hands of the Rt Hon
the Lady Catherine Jones a bill on Mr Hoare for £50 which sum is in part
of the £200 promised by Lady Betty Hastings towards building a charity
school for the teaching and instructing of the children of poor soldiers belonging to Chelsea Hospital provided at the time the building is begun £200
more is raised by benefactions towards the use of the building and if the said
£200 cannot be raised or secured for the use of the school in the compass of
two years from the date of this I promise for myself my heirs and executors
to return the bill above mentioned to the said lady her heirs and executors as
witness my hand,

> M. Astell

This letter is copied from *Hastings Wheler Family Letters*, 2 vols. (Wakefield: Privately
Printed By The West Yorkshire Printing Co. Limited, 1935), 2:87. The editor, George
Hastings Wheler, appears to have regularized the spelling, which I reproduce here.
Grateful thanks are due his son, G. H. H. Wheler of Otterden Place, Kent, for provid-
ing me with this volume of his family's correspondence.

Appendix D

Rawlinson Manuscript of Mary Astell's Poetry, 1689

A
COLLECTION OF POEMS
humbly
presented and Dedicated
TO
the most Reverend Father in
GOD
WILLIAM
By Divine Providence
Lord Archbishop of *H*
CANTERBURY &c
1689.

May it please your Grace

Next to the committing of a Crime, the doing of that which stands in need of an Apology, has ever been most disagreeable to me. But since we cannot command our own circumstances, and are therefore sometimes inforced to do, not as we would but as we can; this, tho it will not excuse us in the commission of an evil may be allowed to Apologize for a less proper and less becoming Action. Of which sort your Grace may justly reckon, this my repented boldness and importunity, as I must needs confess it in a person of my sex, and meaness, to intrude into so venerable a presence, w.th nothing else to recommend me but a few trifles, which even themselves stand in need of an excuse. It is not without pain and reluctancy, that I break from my beloved obscurity, (which is so agreeable to my temper and proper for my sex) to expose to so judicious a Censure, those mean productions which a little reading, a small experience, and smaller fancy, has made shift to bring forth; and yet I may say as David did in another case, is there not a Cause? not to mention what your Grace dos not love to hear, but what I must always remember with Honour and Veneration, that real worth (and not only external Greatness) which is the true motive to veneration and esteem: Permit me to say, that the Condiscention and Candor, with which your Grace was pleased to receive a poor unknown, who hath no place to fly unto and none that careth for her Soul, when even my Kinsfolk had failed, and my familiar Friends had forgotten me; this my Lord, hath emboldened me to make an humble tender of another offering, which tho but of Goats hair and Badger skins, is the best I have to give, and therefore I hope may not be altogether unacceptable.

May your Grace be pleased to receive it with your wonted Charity and Goodness, and pass a favourable censure upon the failures of a Womans pen, who would very thankfully be informed of her errours and amend them; and permit me with all Humility to profess myself.

>My Lord,
>>Your Graces
>>>Most humble, thankfull
>>>and obedient Servant
>>>M A.

made June 28
1683

The Invitation

I

Come Muse, and leave those wings that soar
  No further than an Earthly flight,
Let us the GOD of Heav'n implore,
  And tune our Notes AEtherial height;
Heav'n thy Parnassus be, thence learn thy Song,
Thy Saviour's side shall be thy Helicon.

II

Hark how he calls, come unto me
  All that are laden and opprest,
My service is true Libertie,
  My bosom an Eternal Rest,
With open arms he begs of thee to come,
Make hast my Soul, leave all & thither run.

III

Wipe thy blind eyes dark'ned with tears,
   From all but Penitentiall ones,
Harbour only Religious Fears,
   And for thy Sins keep all thy Groans;
Then he who never lets us sigh in vain,
Will turn to brightest Joy thy Greif & pain.

IV

Teach ev'ry word to chant his Praise,
   And ev'ry verse to sing his Love,
His Crown of thorns shall be thy bays,
   His Cross shall be thy shady Grove,
Which will at last be to a Kingdom blown,
And thy sharp bays will sprout into a Crown.

Jan. 7. 168⅞   In emulation of M.ͬ Cowleys Poem
             call'd the Motto page I.

I

What shall I do? not to be Rich or Great,
   Not to be courted and admir'd,
   With Beauty blest, or Wit inspir'd,
Alas! these merit not my care and sweat,
   These cannot my Ambition please,
My high born Soul shall never stoop to these;
But something I would be thats truly great
In 'ts self, and not by vulgar estimate.

II

If this low World were always to remain,
   If th' old Philosophers were in the right,
   Who wou'd not then, with all their might
Study and strive to get themselves a name?
   Who wou'd in soft repose lie down,
Or value ease like being ever known?
But since Fames trumpet has so short a breath,
Shall we be fond of that w.ᶜʰ must submit to Death?

III

Nature permits not me the common way,
By serving Court, or State, to gain
That so much valu'd trifle, Fame;
Nor do I covet in Wits Realm to sway:
But O ye bright illustrious few,
What shall I do to be like some of you?
Whom this misjudging World dos underprize,
Yet are most dear in Heav'ns all-righteous eyes!

IV

How shall I be a Peter or a Paul?
That to the Turk and Infidel,
I might the joyfull tydings tell,
And spare no labour to convert them all:
But ah my Sex denies me this,
And Marys Priviledge I cannot wish,
Yet hark I hear my dearest Saviour say,
They are more blessed who his Word obey.

V

Up then my sluggard Soul, Labour and Pray,
For if with Love enflam'd thou be,
Thy JESUS will be born in thee,
And by thy ardent Prayers, thou can'st make way,
For their Conversion whom thou may'st not teach,
Yet by a good Example always Preach:
And tho I want a Persecuting Fire,
I'le be at lest a Martyr in desire.

Enemies

I

Mar: 18.1683   I Love you whom the World calls Enemies
You are my Vertues exercise,
The usefull Furnace to refine
My dross, the Oil that maks my Armour shine.

II

Nay you're the best of men because you are
The truest Friends, tho this appear
A Paradox to them who seem,
The only men of Wit & of esteem;

III

Who measure Friendship by the Rule of Power,
And love him best who has most store;
Who prostitute that sacred Name,
Unto the partners of their sin and shame.

IV

Yet if the merits of a Friend be weigh'd,
His worth in a just balance laid,
Light Flattery will blow away,
And just reproof will all the rest out-weigh.

V

But a Friend's loving eyes are sometimes blind,
And will not any blemish find,
Or if a secret ulcer they espie,
They'l sooner Balsom then sharp Wine apply.

VI

Kind Monitors you tell me of my faults,
Your spurs correct & mend my halts,
With cleansing Physick purge my mind,
That no crude humours may remain behind.

VII

Meekness wou'd lose her vast inheritance
If you were not the evidence;
You bring to light our Charitie,
Without you we shou'd but half Christians be.

VIII

Best Benefactors! let Earths Children pray
For those who give them loads of Clay,
Who puff their bubbles, I'le for you
Implore, & think it God-like so to do.

Mar 30.1684   ***Ambition***

I

What's this that with such vigour fills my brest?
  Like the first mover finds no rest,
  And with it's force dos all things draw,
Makes all submit to its imperial Law!
Sure 'tis a spark 'bove what Prometheus stole,
  Kindled by a heav'nly coal,
  Their sophistry I can controul,
Who falsely say that women have no Soul.

II

Vile Greatness! I disdain to bow to thee,
  Thou art below ev'n lowly me,
  I wou'd no Fame, no Titles have,
And no more Land than what will make a grave.
I scorn to weep for Worlds, may I but reign
  And Empire o're my self obtain,
  In Caesars throne I'de not sit down,
Nor wou'd I stoop for Alexanders Crown.

III

Let me obscured be, & never known
  Or pointed at about the Town,
  Short winded Fame shall not transmit
My name, that the next Age may censure it:
If I write sense no matter what they say,
  Whither they call it dull, or pay
  A rev'rence such as Virgil claims,
Their breath's infectious, I have higher aims.

IV

Mean spirited men! that bait at Honour, Praise,
  A wreath of Laurel or of Baies,
  How short's their Immortality!
But Oh a Crown of Glory ne're will die!
This I'me Ambitious of, no pains will spare
  To have a higher Mansion there,
  Where all are Kings, here let me be,
Great O my GOD, Great in Humilitie.

Sept. 8.1684   *Solitude*

I

x the wish   Now I with gen'rous ˣCowley see,
p.22   This trifling World & I shall ne're agree.
Nature in business me no share affords,
And I no business find in empty words:
I dare not all the morning spend
To dress my body, & not lend
A minuit to my Soul, nor can think fit,
To sell the Jewel for the Cabinet.

II

My unpolish'd converse Ladies fly,
'Twill make you dull, I have no railery,
I cannot learn the fashionable art,
To laugh at Sin, and censure true desert.
Alas I no experience have,
With my weak eyes to make a slave,
Nor am I practis'd in that am'rous flame,
Which has so long usurpt Loves sacred name.

III

No satisfaction can I find
In balls and revelling, my thinking mind,
Can't reconcile 'em with a mournfull Spirit,
Nor with the solid comfort they'l inherit
Who here love sorrow; Complement
I am as guiltless of as paint,
No fucus for my mind or face I use,
Nor am acquainted with the modern Muse.

IV

O happy Solitude, may I
My time with thee, & some good books employ!
No idle visits rob me of an hour,
No impertinents those precious drops devour.
Thus blest, I shall while here below
Antedate Heav'n, did Monarchs know
What 'tis with GOD, & Cherubims to dwell,
With Charles they'd leave their Empires for a Cell.

Death

I

It was a glorious and a chearfull day,
When Nature in it's Primitive beauty lay,
Fresh & new fall'n from the all powerfull word,
  Of it's most bounteous Lord;
'Twas all a Paradise, no poys'nous weed
  Sprung up, no hurtfull beast did breed,
  No Gold was seen, that seed of hate,
  Of Murther, Villany, Debate;
The Vine did chear but not intoxicate:
The harmless Elements did not then conspire
Against their Makers Vice-Roy, he might dwell
Secure, nor Man, nor Beast knew to rebell;
  Water cou'd quench not drown, and fire
   Mild as the Morning Sun,
  Knew how to warm but not to burn:
   No bustling Winds did roar,
  Nor foaming Seas assault the Shore,
  Innocent Nature ment no ill,
Nor Milk, nor Wine, nor Figs knew how to kill;
Mirth had no sting, nor Laughter carried Death,
No ecstasies of Joy did stop the breath;
There no Oppressors were, nor mournfull cry
To drown the universal melody;
  The strong did not devour the weak,
None did the sacred laws of Nature break;
But ev'ry Species his due Praises sung,
From whose enlivening word all the Creation sprung.

II

Thrice happy Man had nothing else to do,
But the most gratefull business to persue,
To Love and Praise that GOD who made him Be,
  On purpose to enjoy felicitie.
But what can keep that wretched man from ill,
Who will be mis'rable because he Will?
What can that lawless Appetite suffice,
Who longs for nothing but what Heav'n denies?
  Is't possible that he shou'd happy be,

Who less esteems the World than one forbidden Tree?
But sure unjustly we cry out of this,
'Twas great and brave, he did not do amiss,
Or if he did why do we foolishly
    Strive his folly to out-vie?
And with far less excuse repeat his fault!
When none else can our Happiness assault,
    And Satans self can but entice,
Unable to compell us to a vice;
Like Adam valiently we shut our eyes,
    And our own hands in fetters ties,
We like stout Champions throw our Arms away,
Quarrel with him that wou'd our ruin stay;
Fear nothing more than not to be o'recome,
And above all desire to be undone!

III

    Besotted Man! not one full day
    Wou'd he the easy Law obey,
He wou'd be Great, & to it takes the ready way,
    And throws himself below
The meanest beast, that at his feet did lately bow!
    (For tell me did you never know
    The way to Greatness yet?
How he that can for that mean thing be fit,
Must first to ev'ry sordid art submit?)
Vain man! he wou'd be Wise, he fain wou'd know
    Which is the ready way to Woe,
He wants to know the blessing he has lost,
What a prodigious price his folly cost!
And to be sure of Immortality,
He next resolves to eat the fruit and Die!
'Tis done: now too late he must confess,
All he has gain'd is only Nakedness,
    Did he for this Felicity forsake?
But such a purchase Sinners always make!
Methinks I see the Sun abscond his beams,
As lights go out when hurtfull shades appear,
Roses grow pale, & Lions shake for fear,
Nature inverted now dos all things fill
    With discord, Barrenness, and ill,

And monst'rous Sin her cursed offspring teams,
Polluted Earth groans deep, and wanteth breath
To bear the heavy load of Sin and Death.

IV

Turn, turn, my Muse, turn from this dismal story,
And lift thy eyes up to the King of Glory;
The second Adam who too clim'd the Tree,
Yet not to lose, but gain Felicitie.
      He wip'd Deaths clammy face,
      Deck'd it with beauteous grace,
   And made it now a blessed thing,
Left us the Honey, took himself the sting.
'Tis now no more an Infelicity,
Since Christ himself did once vouchsafe to Die;
But a short passage to eternal Joy,
   A happy period to our misery.
Wish'd by th' afflicted, to the good man dear,
    Which only Wicked men need fear.
When the false dress that we have put it in,
The pomp of Fun'rals, & the sting of sin,
Are done away, Death is an easy thing.
   Natures best Gift, the end of strife,
Preferable in all before this mortal life:
    For there the wicked sin no more,
    Nor add new reck'nings to their score;
The Mighty and the mean togather sleep,
   None at uneasy distance keep;
    For all are equal in the Grave,
The Poor no want, Rich no satiety can have.
Nay, we by Death a Priviledge obtain
Which the best man alive can hardly gain;
No catterpillars in the Grave are bred,
Not Envy's self will prey upon the Dead;
None but the very dregs of malice will,
Disturb the sacred Dead with speaking ill.

V

O happy Death! 'tis thou that sets us free
From our insulting passion's Tyrannie.
    Falsely we call thee blind, since we
    Thro' thee a blest cessation find,

From those false senses which did truly blind,
And errours that impos'd upon our mind.
    We're Slaves and bondmen all,
      By our vile Bodies kept in thral,
Till Death dos kindly all our bands untie,
We then begin to live when we are said to Die.
Best refuge Death! No Persecuting arm
When we are fled to thee can do us harm;
Thou final period of a Tyrants lust
    Like China dishes in the Dust,
    The bodies of the Righteous lie,
To be refin'd for Immortalitie:
Who wou'd not trust thee faithfull grave?
    Since with such int'rest he shall have
      His body back again,
      Free fom sin & free from stain,
What we in weakness and dishonour sow,
Shall up again in strength and glory grow.

             VI
Let them be fond of life, and loath to Die,
Who value Time, before Eternity;
Short sighted men! who can this poor abode
Prefer before the presence of their GOD.
    O Life how bitter wouldst thou be,
      How unacceptable to me,
With how much pain shou'd I retain this breath,
Did I not know 'tis a short way to Death.
'Tis a short way that all have gone before,
And all that come behind must traverse o're;
For ev'n those few whom the last trump shall call,
When they perhaps are in the Camp, or Court,
    Or in the Shop, or in the Hall,
    Minding their business or their sport;
These must be chang'd e're they come to bliss,
And Death it self is nothing more than this:
'Tis but a change what we a dying call,
Which from our Birth till our last sand be run,
Is imperceptibly a coming on.

VII

Who would not wish to have his Happiness
    Secur'd from all disturbances;
But dos he think that Pow'r or Riches can,
    Make him a firmly happy man?
Alas tis only Death that can do this!
How do we see the Wealthy, and the Great,
    Thrown from their gay and tow'ring seat,
    How oft do they survive their bliss!
On such a Pinacle they cannot stand,
Till Death dos gently take them by the hand.
For he's the man has most felicity,
Who dos not drink, but tast th' enchanting Cup,
And when his Fortune's at the height gives up,
Wisely withdrawing in due time to Die.
    Yet Lord with what a wondrous care,
Do we behold men building houses here!
Purchasing Titles, laying Land to Land,
As if secure from Deaths well-aiming hand!
    And by a lying Elegy,
Think to procure an Immortality;
    Death laughs at all their Pride,
And dos their busy Idleness deride,
Wonders that all this while they should neglect,
The only way all their desires t'effect;
The certain way an endless Life to gain,
And victory over Death himself obtain

VIII

How happy wou'd it be for ev'ry one,
    To mind no other business but his own!
That proper nat'ral work which GOD design'd,
When he endow'd us with a reasonable mind:
'Twas his intent we shou'd our selves employ,
    This mind to tend and cultivate,
And in this time of tryal to prepare,
    For that most blest and perfect state,
In which he has deposited that Joy,
    Which we in vain do seek for here;
    As wisely might we sow

Wheat in the sea, and look for harvest there,
  Or cast our hooks into the air,
  Or in the fire inquire for snow,
  As seek for Happiness on Earth,
'Tis not of this World's growth, 'tis of another birth.
    But if we never look on high,
If we on things below our time employ,
And here set up our rest, & here expect our Joy,
No wonder if we be affraid to die.
  Oh Death how dost thou make him grieve,
Who dos at rest in his Possessions live!
    With what surprize,
  Dost thou on that poor mortal seize,
Who look'd on thee as some far distant thing,
And fancied many years 'twixt Death and him!

        IX
Happy is he that can with Pleasure say,
  I'me not affraid to Die to day.
  Who by oft thinking on this King
  Of terrours, makes it none to him.
  He fears no danger, dreads no pain,
  A Tyrants threatenings doth disdain;
Knows that his malice can no further go,
Than to the Grave, & do what Time e're long must do.
  Or Death, or Sleep's to him the same,
Life is his trouble, Death his hope and gain;
Tho he may suffer here he knows he shall hereafter reign.
Ah Blessed Lord! might I be such an one,
I'de envy none that sets upon a throne.
From being such an one what hinders me,
If I but use becoming Industrie:
GOD's grace is still the same, & we might rise
    Unto the Primitive excellencies,
Wou'd we revive that zeal by which they went,
And not with lower measures be content.
Youth and good hours I will not idly lose,
  But make of them a proper use;
That ev'n this poor mean I may welcome make
That Death which makes y.ᵉ Great ones fear & quake.
    For O my GOD to me,

Or life or Death indifferent shall be,
May I live just so long as pleaseth Thee.
This only grant, that while I live I may
    Lay up for that expensive day,
    Lest, if I now neglect to hear
Those calls, and those kind invitations Thou
Vouchsafes to me, and lose this happy NOW,
    A sad and dismal time shou'd come,
    When thou my GOD wilt shut thine ear;
'Twill be too late to Live when Life is done,
Nor must a Christians warfare be begun,
At that late hour when he shou'd bring his Trophies home.

Judgment

I

'Tis said: the sacred word is past,
And the long look'd for day is come at last.
        The party colour'd Day,
Compos'd of Mirth & Sadness, Joy & Tears,
    On this side Hope, on that side fears,
Justice and Mercy both themselves display.
    The dreadfull Flame is kindled now,
    Which must refine all things below,
Stay and you'l see a Phoenix from the ashes grow.
        But try first if you can sustain
        The terrors, and th' amazing noise,
        The Thunder of th' Almighty's voice;
        Can you behold th' aspiring flame?
        Which mounts and crackles as it goes,
And swallows ev'rything that dare oppose.
When all beneath, above, & round about you's fire,
        Tell me where will you retire?
        Have you erected in your brest,
        A cool and shady place of rest,
        Dos a good Conscience florish there?
        Then happy man what can you fear!
Hark, hark, I hear the dreadfull Trumpet call,
                Come away all;
                Make hast and rise,

This is the reck'ning day the grand Assize:
'Tis vain to plead excuses now,
None of the Lawyers quirks will do,
And they who always liv'd in subtilty,
Must now as naked be as you and I.

II

S. Matth.
24.30

Behold, in Heav'n the glorious sign,
No more scandal, now 'tis all divine.
The dazling Throne's already plac'd,
And Saints and Angels to the Triumph hast.
But above all, with greedy eyes behold
The Judge himself, see how he shines,
Not with so mean a thing as Gold,
Or luster borrowed from the sparkling Mines;
But with his own refulgent beams,
Which like new worlds of light about him streams,
And circle round the sacred Companie,
Who in this glorious dress,
Like Stars shine round the Son of Righteousness.
What pomp of Language can suffice to shew,
The mightly splendor of this solemn day!
Too weak's my pen, my fancy much too low,
In lively colours to display,
The wonders that about it throng,
Too great, too many, for a mortal's song!
'Tis well we then shall be
Refin'd Mortality,
Such luster is too bright for humane eye:
The Sun himself amaz'd at such a sight,

St. Matth.
20.29

Flies to put out his sham'd & now unusefull light.

III

Summon th'Assembly, let the Books be spread,
Call the Living and the Dead.
See, some bright Souls already flown above,
Drawn by the powerfullest attractive Love.
But who are these that tarry here?
The guilty sure, for guilt is always dog'd with fear.
Poor Souls where woud you fly!

The Mountains cannot vail you from that eye
Which saw thro all those little arts you us'd,
To hide your sins in dark obscurity,
'Twas your own selves you cheated and abus'd,
He knows it all and you in vain deny.
What were you doing all this while?
'Tis now too late to go and purchase Oil.
You who so long in dust have lain,
As you decended there so must you rise again.

IV

Come ye beloved of the Father near,
Since JESUS is your Judge why shou'd you fear?
JESUS, who has himself been cloth'd with flesh,
Knows the infirmities of such a dress,
And pitties them; he will not be severe,
With those who tho but weak, were yet sincere.
Tis time your Innocence shou'd be
Rescu'd from their obloquy,
Whom your just Lives did secretly upbraid,
By shewing what they shou'd have done:
You who cou'd never be affraid
To act as Vertue bid, in the worst times,
Come forth and let 'em see,
That Vertue is the only Policie:
Alas their Subterfuges now are gone,
And all their little arts are useless grown!
We have no Laurels here for prosp'rous Crimes.
Now Providence her Vindication makes,
And laughs at all those poor mistakes
Fond men were guilty of, when they apply'd,
Her approbation to the prosp'rous side.

V

Ye sacred Tribe come to the highest seat,
Tho' some ill men dispis'd you GOD thinks meet,
That all shou'd know the highest Honour's giv'n,
To those whose business was to people Heav'n.
Ye glorious Twelve who led the way,

And to us all reveal'd the blessed Day,
Mount to your Thrones, & let your Successors,
    Who follow'd you, ascend to theirs:
    Such as Great Athanasius was,
Who like a mighty bulwark stopt the tide,
When all men else did with the current slide;
    The well-back'd error cou'd not pass
With him, who measur'd Truth not by the Vote,
    But by that sacred rule, which shall
Stand firm when mens weak reas'nings w.th their intrest fall.
    Old fashion'd man! who strait made Coat,
Fitted himself but not the times, for he
Prefer'd dispised Truth, before applauded Noveltie.

VI

See, how those generous souls who never cou'd,
For Wordly int'rest part with Vertues greater good,
    Amongst the Confessors and Martyrs stand;
    Bright Souls, they Eagle like did rise,
    Above the sight of vulgar Eyes,
And now their Enemies shall do 'em right,
Now Vertue stands in its just proper light.
These are the men you sinners us'd to brand,
With names of humourous and obstinate;
    Vain men how idly did you prate!
Just so we see Dogs barking at the Moon,
    Cou'd we their Language understand,
We certainly shou'd hear what names they call,
    How in their Cynick Rhetorick bawl,
And say she shines too late or shines too soon;
    When all the fault is only this,
    Above and out of reach she is.
    And ye too O ye shining Stars!
Ye Champions with your honourable scars,
    Ye men of Paradox, to whom
    Prisons did palaces become.
Cou'd you in beds of flame more pleasure find,
Than in a bed of Roses dipt in dew?
Alas they're not so sweet, they're not so fair as you,
Had you not suffer'd you had never shin'd.
He that can for a radient crown be fit,
    Must by the Cross arrive at it:

Labour and Sufferings are the way to rest,
And he most Triumphs who can conquer best.

VII

And ye Thebean Legion, tho ye cou'd
    Have sav'd or dearly sold your blood,
Were no vain prodigals to let it tamely fall,
When Heav'n did loudly for your passive Valour call.
    (Passive Obedience always due
      To GOD, and his Vicegerents too!)
        'Tis easy to serve heav'n
With that which costs us nought, but he that can
Conquer by suffering, is the valient man.
'Tis Passive Valour which the difference makes,
    By it the true distinction's giv'n,
    Between the fury of a Beast,
And Courage of a Man, whose gen'rous breast,
    Unprejudic'd with weak mistakes,
Full of right notions, tells him the best blood
    Runs in his noble veins, who wou'd
Rather than do one evil suffer all,
And ne're plead Natures Laws when Heav'n dos call.
    Mahomets followers may
    With Sword and Pistol make their way,
JESUS the Prince of Peace, did never mean,
His Christians shou'd with other arms be seen,
Than Prayers & tears, dispised Prayers and Tears,
Which cannot stop the Jealousies and Fears,
Of those short sighted men, who never knew,
What they with Faith and Patience joyn'd can do.

VIII

Ye heav'nly Lillies, humane Angels, ye
Who out of choice and not necessitie,
    Let the World drop and from it stole,
To offer up your selves entire and whole,
A Virgin body with a Virgin Soul
To your dear Spouse; you were all Heav'n before,
    And now can be but little more;
Prayer was your food, and Praises your delight,
No sow'er moroseness drew you from the sight
Of Mortals, but a noble Pride to be
    Always in Heav'nly Companie:

Here's a peculiar Coronet for you,
This JESUS your dear Spouse declares your due.
   See Joseph comes, clad all in White,
   And with him those fair Sons of Light,
   Who for the Beatifick sight
Preserv'd their eyes, they knew the subtile art,
   That Beauty has to gain a heart,
How he that parlies is half overcome,
And he that gives consent is whole undone.
And ye too temp'rate Souls, who kept your tast
   For Pleasures that can never wast,
   The most delicious dish is here,
Feed on, satiety you need not fear,
That Righteousness you hungred for is now your Chear.

IX

Here Abr'am Father of the faithful stands,
   And by him all those num'rous bands,
Those who look'd up to Heav'n to find their way,
   Whom Golden Apples cou'd not stay,
   Nor terrors turn from the right course;
   Nor all the various snares betray,
   Which with united policy and force,
The Devil, world, & flesh before 'em lay.
The World shall laugh at you no more,
   For making Heav'n your place of store,
Who has an int'rest there can ne're be poor.
Faith without Works is dead, but here you may
See those wise Souls, who knew the certain way
To keep that wealth which has so fleet a wing,
Was not by hoarding but distributing:
They knew that JESUS the best debtor was,
He'd give 'em Crowns for pebbles, Gold for Brass,
What to the poor they gave for JESU's sake,
As done unto himself they knew he'd take.
   What's of those mighty sums become,
Which were laid out in sin and vanity?
   Now is the Worldings trafick done,
And Charity takes all the usury!

X

Come worthy Souls, come and that Praise receive,
Which you wou'd ne're accept when men did give.
    Proud Humble men, who wou'd not be
Pleas'd with the praises of mortalitie.
Was it or Pride, or Modesty in you,
Who wou'd be prais'd by all and not a few?
Durst not your Fame to mens short tongues expose,
Lest whilst you got their Praise you should a greater lose.
No longer shall your Piety be hid,
Nor all those Verteous acts which you in private did:
JESUS the best Panegyrist shall raise
    His glorious voice to give you Praise;
You who contentedly cou'd suffer shame,
Of loss, or, any thing for his dear Name,
Who suffer'd with him once now with him reign.
You blessings to Mankind, while they
In Publick sin'd, you did in private pray,
    And GODs avenging hand delay.
Come now and Judge those base ingratefull men,
Who did your good with injuries repay,
    They were the only Persons then,
But you're the Wise and they the fools to day:
Their Hopes and Joys like dust away are driv'n,
But yours can never fail for they are fixt in Heav'n.

XI

What are those Souls which now like Diamonds shine?
    Diamonds we know thro anvils pass,
Polish'd by that wch breaks the counterfeiting Glass,
And these by suffering came to be divine.
Job leads 'em on, the Prince of Patience he,
    Arm'd with his tough Integritie,
    The only coat of Mail, that can
Against all hurtfull ill's defend a man.
See how behind 'em they in triumph bring,
    Harmless and without a sting,
    Poverty, pain, disgrace and all
What you mistaken men afflictions call.
    Bring forth the bottles of their tears,
    Those pearly drops which grace their Crown,

And let the number of their sighs be known,
   A plaudit give for ev'ry one.
   But who is this that next appears?
   'Tis Moses sure, and with him all
Those noble souls who tho they had a gall,
Temper'd it so, that they could never be
Provok'd beyond the rules of decencie.
   Who dos not mix with dross that Ore
Was giv'n him pure dos well, but he that can
Tho cumbred with the frailties of a man,
   Live like a God dos somewhat more.
   Ye who are still to learn, come see
Who 'tis receives a true indignitie;
     Not he that can pass by,
But he that doth resent an injury.

XII

   O what a noble sight is here,
   Now all the Saints of Heav'n appear!
Those who made GOD their Joy, their Hope, & Fear.
     Here stands the Innocent;
     And there the Penitent,
Who with a double diligence repay,
What they had lost of Vertues day.
   See here the Faithfull, and the Just,
Men who were only fit to trade with Heav'n,
Their way so strait, their purposes so ev'n.
     And here are they,
Who could in greatest exigencies trust
That GOD to bring 'em out, who led 'em in;
Tho he a while might turn his face away,
   They knew e're long it would be day,
And nothing fear'd but the dark night of sin.
   Blest men who always had their will,
For unto GOD's theirs was resigned still:
   Heav'n was before hand in their brest,
   So peacefull, sweet and much at rest,
For there Content had built her Halcyon nest.

XIII

Come, O thou sweet and lovely grace,
Which shine's so bright in JESU's face;
 Charity, which must be
The sole possessor of Eternitie.
All other Vertues do to thee give place,
Their race is finish'd and their work is done,
Come Queen of Graces mount the Throne alone.
 All ye that hope to have a share
 In Heav'nly Joys, look in your brest,
 And see if Charity be there,
 If her you want, tho all the rest
Of her dear Sisters seem to shine in you,
  Alas they will not do,
They're counterfeit they cannot pass the test.
Hasten apace, come ev'ry lovely Soul
 Whose Vertue was intire and whole;
You who did always live as Reason bid,
 GODs Laws observ'd in all you did;
Not one beloved lust was in your bosoms hid.
Souls all perfum'd with Heav'ns best Frankinsence,
Flaming with Love, and with Obedience:
 Your stations take while to the bar,
GODs enemies and yours assembled are.

XIV

Set forth the Proud, the high and mighty man,
He'd take it ill shou'd he not lead the Van.
 Tall and mighty tho he be,
 He's not to big great Judge for thee.
Job 36.19 Not all his pow'r and int'rest can withstand
Thy just decree, nor pluck him from thy hand.
 Look up my eyes, what do I see
This is a Pigmy, sure, it is not he!
 Ah can the Grave contract men so!
Dos he himself the fatal less'ning know?
For all men else did know it long before;
Now all external pomp is gone how poor,
 How very mean a thing is he,
 Who has no solid bravery,
And wants that shining Gem Humility.
 Where is the Pomp and the Parade?

Will none of all his Vassals own him now,
Those who did lately at his footstool bow?
    So soon doth wordly Greatness fade!
Like a bird in the air 'tis fled and gone,
    And not its smallest footsteps known.
Had he courageously preserv'd the poor,
Rescu'd the Fatherless from the Oppressors power;
If in an impious age he bravely wou'd,
Discourage Vice and cherish ev'ry good:
    If his high station serv'd to raise
    Vertue to deserved praise,
And set disfigur'd worth in a due light,
Fit to attract the dimmist and most vulgar sight:
        He shou'd have been
A truly great and celebrated thing.
If to enjoy ye World he us'd his Greatness, & his Power,
His Portion's paid, & he can justly ask no more.

                        XV
To him the angry and the wrathful bring,
    For Pride and Wrath are near a kin;
They're folly both, and so is ev'ry sin.
Let him look yonder up to Heav'n, and see
If that mild region can with him agree:
None there but meek and peacefull Spirits dwell,
    But he is set on fire of Hell.
Where is the sweetness of revenges now?
    Alas 'tis sour and bitter grown!
He was revenged of himself alone,
And must the sad effect of Heav'ns just Vengeance know!
Can he expect GOD shou'd his mighty debt acquit,
Who never wou'd his Brothers pence remit?
Let Mammons Son his audits now bring in,
And say how has his wealth expended been;
So much in Vanity, so much in sin,
So much laid up for his young spend-thrift Heir,
For the true use of wealth not the lest share!
Strange folly this! that he who gave it all
    Shou'd long by his receivers call,
    For some smal quit-rent, and still be
    Refus'd with surly crueltie.
    Can a small Legacy at Death,
    Which Custom, Fear, and parting breath

Extort from you, out of that num'rous heap,
   Which fain you would but cannot keep,
      A compensation make,
For all that wealth you did unjustly take,
And more unjustly keep; what can you say
To all those Widdows tears, those Orphans cries,
Which you beheld with such regardless eyes,
(How your full bags against ye plead to day!)
      In vain do you for mercy sue,
You who were deaf to them, your Judge is deaf to you.

XVI

   With blushing face and down cast eyes,
Here comes mistaken Pleasures Votaries.
A shapless mass of filth and ugliness,
In their own folly clad and not in Natures dress.
Not the lest footstep dos in them appear
     Of Heav'ns Imperial Character:
     The sacred Image of their GOD
     Is quite defac'd, and his abode
     Usurpt by ev'ry shameless thing,
Things whose enjoyment's pain, and end a sting.
For tell me, you who spend your days
Pleasure to hunt thro all her various ways,
    When ye the Phantome do embrace,
And nearly stare upon her painted face,
    Where is the joy she promis'd you?
And all the mighty things she'd for her Lovers do?
Hope has devour'd already the best part,
Frustrate desire converts to pain and smart;
And in the place of long expected joy,
Starts up pale loathing and satiety.
Unthinking men! why did you chuse the night,
To act those sins which were unfit for view?
    How came it that ye never knew,
They'd one day be reveal'd in all mens sight?
    Wou'd sinners take advice from me,
I'de have'em sin where GODs eye cannot see,
'Tis folly sure to shun a mortals eye,
Unless they cou'd from GOD their Judge, & Wittness fly.

XVII

Ye modern sinners come,
And hear your final doom:
Ye who so oft have call'd on GOD,
Not to implore his mercy but
        To dare his Rod;
Ye, who so oft your bloody tongues have put
Into these wounds, not to suck balsom thence,
        But spider like, to add
    The deeper die to your offence;
            Say quickly what you plead,
Bring forth the mighty purchase of your sin,
    The harvest it has brought you in,
That airy nothing, that inconstant thing,
Fashion! which ev'ry fop can blow away,
Fashion! the Mushrome of a short liv'd day.
Tho ev'ry sinners purchases are small,
They some few trifles get, but you lose all.
    Nor shall ye scape, ye who so ready were
        Your Neighbours frailties to declare;
With spitefull glasses, made his Mote to seem
Of greater Magnitude than your own beam.
        Fine modish art, that doth sustain
        Many a wither'd sinking fame,
And often spoil it's neighbours purer Name.
        'Tis a mean worth that doth recoil
            Behind a skreen,
        When shining Vertues must be seen,
And dares not shew it self without a foil.
Such sordid arts are wholy useless here,
They make your ugliness the more appear;
Who were so hard to others, now must be
Judg'd with a great and just severitie.

XVIII

The num'rous stock of Fools togather set,
        Who Indian like, trafick'd away
        Their Gold and Pearls, for Glass and Jet,
Yet these alas are greater fools than they,
        (No real difference we see,
Between those things the World affords us here,
'Tis fancy only makes'em cheap or dear,
        But what comparison can be

Between a point of Time and vast Eternitie?)
    No other Wittnesses we need,
Besides the Conscience of an evil deed;
Open their guilty hearts, that they may be
Expos'd in all their vile deformitie.
    No secret word tho whisper'd in the ear,
Nor thought tho dark as Night but must appear,
And their much blacker sins be publish'd here.
Why do you droop, and hide your face away?
Ye who with brazen front the other day,
Cou'd laugh at Heav'n, and this great day defy
    Say, is Religion still a forgery?
    What can your topping courage dread?
Is it the sight of Spirits makes ye affraid?
Your raillery pall'd, and Wit quite out of door,
    What not one argument in store?
Those Characters were in your bosom write,
    Which ye blur'd o're with drink and noise,
Or with bold foreheads, and pretended Wit
Sought to evade, have now assum'd a voice;
    They tell you plainly, he that can
Violate Reason, and himself unman,
Pretended Monster! who such pains did take
To be worse than the Devil, must now with Devils pertake.

S. Jam. 2r19

XIX

Unhappy men! can ye behold his face
Now as a Judge, whom ye would never hear,
    When with a sweet and winning Grace,
With all the holy art that could endear,
He pray'd ye sick and wounded to him come,
    Ye Prodigals invited home;
That nothing might be wanting to your good,
Offer'd the precious balsom of his blood,
Did for you all Omnipotence cou'd do,
    Spur'd on by pitty and by Love,
Long bare your follies, waited your return,
Ev'n then when you did at his favours spurn.
Behold the Rocks do at his presence move,
They hear his voice, and hearing do obey,
But you were more obdurate far than they.
Not Mercies call, nor Judgments louder noise,

The Spirits whisper, nor the Preachers voice,
Not Conscience daily checks, nor what is more
Your Saviours bloody wounds, and sacred gore,
Cou'd work upon and charm your deafned ear,
     For what persuasions can
     Reclaim that wretched man,
  Who is resolv'd he will not hear?
And do you think they Judge will hear you now?
You who did still persist in your offence,
  Till deaths approaches forc'd you to
  A weak and feigned Penitence:
Alas the Gate of Mercy's shut long since.
He that dos hope for Heav'n, with time and care
    Must for that sacred place prepare,
'Tis not a dying wish will blow him there.

XX
  Bring them all here who durst prophane
By their Unchristian Lives, Christ's sacred Name:
Heathens and Jews have more excuse than they,
Who knew their Masters will but would not it obey.

S.Luc.
13.26,27

  'Tis not enough, that they have been
Heard in his House, and at his Table seen,
  'Tis not enough their brests are clear
  From many a Crime, if harbour'd there
They kept a darling Vice tho ne're so small,
One unrepented sin will ruin all.
Where are the men that half their Journey went?
And so they did no evil, were content
To do no good, as if Omissions were
But venial sins, and faults we need not fear:
These in some Limbus are most fit to dwell,
Cou'd there a medium be 'twixt Heav'n and Hell.
Christ knows you not ye Hypocriticall,
    Who did your selves the godly call;
    And to Religious zeal pretends,
Not for GODs glory, but your own base ends;
And wou'd your little politick juggles have,
As if his arm were short and cou'd not save:
Stick to'em still, there's no Meanders here,
Who hopes for Heav'n an even course must steer,
And not submit with ev'ry wind to veer.

XXI

Say sinners say, how was your Time employ'd?
  In serving Avarice and Pride;
In following vain impertinence and toys;
In idle greifs, and in more foolish joys;
Ambitious projects, Quarrelling and strife;
What nothing left for the true end of Life?
Ye murmure so at Heav'ns decree and grutch,
  As if Time had too fleet a wing;
Ye throw't away on ev'ry trifling thing,
  As if ye thought it were to much!
  Ah senseless men what wou'd you have,
Rest in the World and musick in the Grave?
  Ye'd all your Life time sow to sin,
  And look the harvest shou'd bring in
  The fruits of Peace, and Righteousness.
  So may the Husbandman go dress
His hedge of Thorns and Briers, and while he digs
  Think they'l convert to Vines and Figs.
  The World and Devil had your prime,
And Sin, and Vanity, your Wealth and Time,
What then remains for him who gave you all?
Some rotten bones, faint purposes, and dying call!
  Go to your Prince and offer these,
And try if they a mortal man will please.
Not sin it self will be with them content,
  When they approach'd away it went;
You left not sin for sin relinquish'd you,
You minded Heav'n when you nought else cou'd do.
Shou'd GOD for you dispence with his whole Law,
You might be blest, till then your plea withdraw.
The Judge regards no Priviledge, no Decree,
As were your works, so shall your Sentence be.

XXII

'Twou'd be an endless task to speak of all,
  Whom this al-seeing Judge will call.
Not from the highest who once fill'd a Throne,
To him who late did on a dunghill grone,
Shall any scape, but the just sentence shall
  Indefinitely pass on all.
Bow down your heads with rev'rence lend an ear,
  Some with Hope, and some with Fear,

JESUS is now declaring who shall be
Made or undone, to all Eternitie.

S. Matth.
25.34,&c

You blessed Souls who on the right hand stand,
You who did ne're dispute your Lords command,
But with a chearfull and obedient will
  Chose the good, and left the ill:

S. Matth.
25.21.

Who did not idly let your talents lie,
  Made it your business, and your Joy,
  To trafick for Eternity.
The storm is o're and all the danger past,
And an eternal calm is come at last.
  That seed of grace in you was sown,
Is now sprung up to Glory and a Crown;
  Here take it from my hand, and be
  Sharers in my Felicitie,

S. Luc. 12.32.

'Tis my good pleasure you shou'd reign with me.

XXIII

And ye Apostate spirits, who began
To sin so early and to ruin man;
Say what temptation can excuse your crime,
  Or what pretence can make it less?
Ye were not cumber'd with a load of flesh,
  And in the infancy of Time
  Wanted a precedent to sin,
But wanted no restraints to keep you in.
  (O most deplorable are they
Who 'gainst the greatest Priviledges disobey!
And want a Saviours blood to wash their guilt away!)
Go then accursed Spirits, who have been

S. Jude 6.

  So many years in Custody,
Who in the never failing chains did lie,
Of GOD's almighty Pow'r, and your own sin.

S. Matth.
25.41.

That dreadfull place below was made for you,
But ah unhappy man wou'd have it too!
Unhappy man! for whom kind Heav'n design'd,
  A place where ev'ry glory shin'd,
Ah can there be such charms in endless woe,
That man shou'd seize upon't whither Heav'n will or no!

XXIV

Depart ye Cursed, from my presence fly,
And when from me, ye part from ev'ry Joy.
But if your sensual eyes the sight will bear,
First look to Heav'n and see what Joy is there,
A Joy which one day might have been your share.
    Look on these Saints with glory clad,
You the same right, the same advantage had,
The same free will to chuse, and 'tis but fit
Hell shou'd be their's, who have made choice of it.
The loss of Heav'ns but half your Punishment,
                Go wretches go,
To endless and uninterrupted woe:
        Tis GODs command and go you must,
Your guilty Consciences confess it Just;
And all this bright assembly joyn with me,
To pass the irreversible Decree.
Methinks I see the hopeless wretches mourn,
        With Anger, Rage, and Envy burn.
Not all the stock fancy can furnish, is
Able to fit out Metaphors for this.
Bad men and Devils with fruitless fury see,
Those Saints they once dispis'd their Judges be,
And this adds weight unto their miserie.
The wicked into Hell fall tumbling down,
The Righteous they ascend unto a Throne;
These go to endless Life, and endless day,
The other to a never dying Death are sent away.

1 Cor. 6.2. (beside "And all this bright assembly joyn with me,")

S. Matth. 25.46. (beside "The wicked into Hell fall tumbling down,")

Heaven

I

In a poor simple Girl 'tis a bold flight,
    To aim at such a glorious height,
And with weak eyes to gaze on brightest light.
Forbear fond wretch, it is enough for you
        To do as other women do,
        To dress and talk and make a shew.
        Or if you needs will dabling be
            In Poetry,

The theater will furnish you with theams,
Go spend your life in Pleasures golden dreams;
But never study Heav'n if you would be
Or blest with Wealth, or grac'd with Dignitie.
Go ask the world, and it will let you know
　　The proper time to think on Heav'n,
When age and Sickness makes unfit for things below,
And you may quickly make long reckonings ev'n,
With one short Penitential sigh or two.
*Why? cannot you sufficient matter find
On Earth, to exercise a busy mind?
See how the man that wou'd be counted Wise,
With many a toilsom care, and waking eyes,
　　Lades himself with shining clay,
And finds enough to think, to do and say.
　　Look how the gay, the busy one,
　　That loves to buz about a Throne,
Is follow'd and carest, who wou'd not be
Such an admired thing as he!
Poor foolish men! will ye no further go,
　　Can ye with trifles be content?
Trifles that for your portion ne're were ment!
　　Then e'en take up with things below.
　　But none of these my Genius please,
　　Alas we were not born for these,
They're not our business they're but our disease.
No, to its native place my Soul aspires,
　　And something more than Earth desires,
Heav'n only can it's vast Ambition fill,
And Heav'n alone must exercise my mind and quill.

II
Tell me ye Sons of Honour, were ye born
　　Joyfull Heirs unto a Throne,
Wou'd not your busy thoughts be always there,
And your approaching Greatness antidate?
Wou'd you not wish to be no longer Heir,
But full possessors of the long'd for state?
Wou'd not your minds disdain all meaner things,
And you in fancy be already Kings?
Tell me ye Worldly wise, were ye to take
　　A voyage to the East or West,

*These lines added in a later version of the poem.

Whereby your o're grown fortunes might be more encreased,
Would you not carefull preparations make?
Wou'd you not see your Vessel firmly made,
And all things rightly fitted for your trade?
Lay up your store since if it here neglected be,
Hereafter you too late the errour see.
Wou'd you not arm, and watch against a foe?
    And all the Rocks and dangers know?
    Learn the Language of the place,
    The secret arts of commerce trace;
    And see that all accounts were clear,
Wou'd you leave your estates unsettled here?
And yet when all your pains and care are done,
How soon's the Kingdom lost! how soon the Riches gone!
Ah simple men! can you cut out your business here,
Dos Heav'n not need, or not deserve your care?

III

Help me my Muse, thou who are unconfin'd,
And with no luggage of a body joyn'd,
    Untie those chains that hold
    My heav'n born Soul imprison'd here,
    Raise it above the seventh Sphere;
Thou who dost Natures secret mysteries unfold,
    A second nature art,
And from wild fancies Chaos can'st impart
    New Creatures of thine own,
    To natures self unknown.
Now summon all those glittering things,
    Which so enchant the hearts of Kings,
Those which make dareing men out brave the Sea,
    And with the Sun joint Travellers be.
    That make him thro all danger run,
    Nor stop at any wickedness,
    But thro the Sacred flood,
Of his dear Sovereign, or his Countrys blood,
    Wade to greatness.
Alas! when all is said thou hast not done,
    Or rather not begun,
    Tho ev'ry Letter were a Sun,
    And ev'ry word a Firmament;
    For what large word can we invent,
T'express that glory, which can never be
So much as comprehended by mortalitie.

IV

How I admire thy Wisdom gracious Lord,
Which dos in this and all thy ways appear!
Thou wilt not a clear sight of Heav'n afford,
Lest none shou'd be content to tarry here:
     And yet so much thou lets us know,
As may exalt our minds above all things below.
       For how can he
An object worth his admiration see,
Who with a stedy eye looks up to thee?
     Can he for shame repine,
     Who one day hopes to be divine?
What discontent can e're disturb that brest,
Whom GOD by a wise discipline prepares
     For everlasting rest?
He lives secure and free from anxious cares,
Looks thro the threatning Cloud with chearful eye,
Sees the short passage to Eternal Joy,
And with secure and undisturb'd repose,
So Heav'n be his, cares not if all besides he want or lose.

V

Methinks I feel my self already rise
Above these transitory Vanities;
     Those chains and fetters here below,
Made up of seeming joy, and real woe:
Rais'd with the hopes dear Heav'n that I may be,
Tho most unfit for this world, fit for thee.
Those bug-bear words I now no longer fear,
     Of unsuccessfull and unfortunate,
Nor Hope nor fear can ever reach me there,
Too big's the Joy, and too secure the state.
In vain mistaken World dost thou assay
To stop my course to Heav'n, I'le force a way
     Thro all thy little rubs and Thorns,
And live secure and calm amidst thy Storms.
While Heav'n's the happy purchase of my pain,
     Toil's a Pleasure, loss a Gain;
     I feel no want while it's in view,
And in the hopes of Heav'n can all things do_____
Stop, stop my Muse, for if I higher fly,
My Soul will breathe out in the ecstasie,
E're it is fit for Immortalitie.
     Ah blessed Place when shall I be,
     Admitted to a sight of thee?

When shall these mouldring Cords asunder break,
When shall I in thee dwell not of thee speak?
If hopes of Heav'n can such refreshment give,
Lord what do they enjoy who in it Live!

VI

To know what they enjoy, would be
A kind of Heav'n ev'n here below;
Poor we that toil in life's hard drudgerie,
Pick up scraps of knowledge here and there,
While the blest Souls above do all things know;
All things worthy to be known,
And what's not so is better let alone
They know no pain, Satiety, or care,
None of those things that make us sigh and weep,
Sorrows at a due distance keep,
Where shou'd they rest, whence shou'd they grow,
Since you thrice happy souls can never know,
Sin the Original of all our woe?
Nature which now concealed lies,
And from the most refin'd inquirer flies,
Shall here discover all her mysteries.
And Providence, tho one wou'd think,
That sometimes she can fall asleep,
While her reproachers do her favours keep,
And she at Prosp'rous villanies appears to wink:
Will teach us all her secret ways,
Unveil her beauty, and extort our Praise.
Shew us with what a curious art,
She manageth and brings about,
The hearts of Kings, and the unconstant rout,
Can misery to Happiness convert.
And by her prudent management,
Make good appear, where evil was the sole intent.
Shew us sweet fruit reer'd from a bitter ground,
How wickedness dos wickedness confound.

VII

The pain of asking shall have here no place,
No fear of disappointment or disgrace.
No stormy passion can approach thy gate,
O most refin'd and happy state!
Nor shame in thee admittance find,

That greatest pain to an ingenious mind.
The Soul and body shall not disagree,
But both contribute to felicitie,
    That shall holy be and wise;
    This bless'd with new abilities,
With Glory, vigour, immortality.
Here all are full yet with enlarg'd capacity,
Desire and have a new encrease of Joy.
Their Crowns set fast, no bold usurpers arm
    Can reach their heads, or do'em harm.
Not such poor Crowns as Princes strive for here,
    Made up of Crosses, lin'd with care;
But Crowns that are with glorious Vertues bright,
Bright with their own and not a borrow'd light.
            None shall repine
Because another dos with greater luster shine,
But all in love and Praise togather joyne.
Blest Harmony where Angels bear a part,
And ev'ry note's breath'd from a loving heart!
Our Musick's discord when compar'd with thee,
For only Love can make true Melodie.

VIII
And here Love dos in its full Zenith shine,
    A Love all pure and all Divine,
Purg'd from that dross, which foolish men wou'd throw
    Upon it here below.
No misconstructions can this Love destroy,
Each Saint is happy in his Neighbors joy.
    To Love in vain we need not fear.
For all are Jonathans and Davids here.
Were there no other Happiness than this,
Vast were the joy, and infinite the bliss,
For all that's pleasant is where FRIENDSHIP is.
Friendship thou Epitome of all that's good,
O that thou wert more practis'd & more understood!
    Art thou already gone above,
Or hast thou left some sparks of the below?
            Ah let me know,
Since thou reigns in my brest thou sacred Love,
            Why shou'd it be,
Friendship shou'd only be forbid to me?

IX

How dost thou flag, how do thy pinions tire,
Poor Muse as thou ascends higher and higher.
Eternity's too big too fathomless for thee,
And yet those Joys shall all eternal be;
Tho one rich minuit of such joy as this,
Worth an Eternity of this Worlds pleasure is.
　　　　　　O for an Angels tongue,
　　　That what remains be rightly sung!
And yet a Seraphim woul'd be struck dumb!
Forgive me Heav'n, forgive this infamy,
While I wou'd Praise I but disparage thee.
Vision of Peace! Region of endless bliss!
Where ev'ry Saint has all his heart can wish,
And Happyness in it's perfection is!
What bold Pindarique strains can further go?
　　　What Metaphors suffice to shew?
　　　That unexpressible delight,
　　　Flows from the beatifick sight.
　　　Enough, enough and come not ne're
This abyss, only say the GOD is there;
This said all other words are dull and flat,
For ev'ry joy thou comprehends in that.
Here JESUS lives, and here the rapt'rous sight,
Of him who dwells in unapproached light
Shall be unveil'd, here we shall see, and be,
I know not what_____
O alsufficient GOD we shall be full of Thee.

Hell

I

With a short line, and scanty wit,
Shall I assay the bottomless and dreadfull pit!
At such a task Nature recoils, and flies,
For who can think of endless miseries,
Without Convulsion fits and melting eyes!
Horror and trembling seize upon my pen,
　　　How shall I trace the darksom den!
　　　　Or a discription make,
　　　Of the sulphry burning Lake!

Since all my pains and all my care must be,
That I this place may never know or see,
Oh wretched they that do experience thee?
    What an Almighty power can do
To make and bless we have already known;
    And sure to punish he can too,
    As great and mighty things perform.
    Cast in the black ingredients there,
    Folly, Ingratitude, and shame,
Self-ruin, Anger, Madness, Sorrow, Fear,
Most biting anguish, and regret, Dispair,
Past Pleasures ne're to be recall'd again,
    And an ever present pain,
With secret horrors we want words to name;
A gnawing Envy, and a warm desire,
Ne're to be satisfied and ne're remove;
And all these blown into a raging Fire,
By slighted mercy, and abused Love.
    Who can with endless burnings dwell
And who cou'd sin shou'd he but often think of Hell?

             II
Ah sinfull men, cannot the present ill,
    The Nemesis and sure revenge,
Th' inseperable shadow that attends
        On ev'ry sin,
    Lay some restraints and keep you in?
    Can nothing stop a headstrong will?
That ne're regards whither it's folly tends.
Fool-hardy will of man, that dare withstand
Ev'n GOD himself, and slight ev'n his command;
With it's poor one 'gainst Heav'nly Legions run,
And to it's own distruction overcome.
Stop, stop the furious course a while, and see
    Who will the final losers be.
Look on the sting which ev'ry painted vice
Conceals, when it to ruin wou'd intice.
    What shall a sugar'd bait go down,
    Ev'n when the fallacy is known!
        Think when enjoyments past,
          How sin will be

Seen in her natural deformitie,
But above all think what will come at last!
Whom Death cannot persuade, nor Heav'n invite,
   Them Hell and Judgment must affright,
   Out of the broad and beaten way,
   Where in the midst of danger they
      Securely play.
Ye have your choice of Life and Death, than why
O inconsid'rate men why will ye Die,
And be the cause of your own misery?
For ev'n that GOD who ev'ry thing can do,
Can't force us to be blest whither we will or no.

III

Ye dainty Sinners, who e're while
Wash'd your delicious steps in Oil,
   Whose tenderness cou'd hardly bear,
   The smallest breathings of the air,
   Must now for rougher things prepare.
Racks are faint Metaphors, to tell
The strange distorting pains prepar'd in Hell.
   We talk of Fire, because 'tis here
To us most terrible, and most severe;
But Racks and Fire, and all the witty ways,
That Tyrants can invent to end our days,
   Or make 'em mis'rable, wou'd be
A Paradise O Hell compar'd with thee!
How equitable Lord are all thy ways,
   How they contribute to thy praise!
While ev'ry sinners punishment's a fit
Discription of the sin that caused it.
Dives who roll'd in plenteous Luxery,
Must now in starving want for ever lie,
Not one cool drop to mitigate his pain,
Not one refreshing breath to fan his flame.

IV

Ah can that curious ear,
Which to the Harp and Viol us'd to dance,
   Endure to hear
Those groans, and murmures, and that howling noise,
   Worse than the Evening Wolves hoarse voice.

Good breeding's all lost here and complaisance,
Will those incarnate Devils who tempted ye,
To whom more than to GOD ye paid civilitie,
    Will their society asswage?
    No 'twill encrease your pain and rage.
Do ye 'gainst Theives and Murthers shut your doors
Who wou'd but rob you of some fleeting thing,
    A Life that cannot long be yours,
And Riches that's already on the wing;
And shall the instruments of Satan be
    Suffer'd, and invited too,
    Foolish men to ruin you,
Not for a time but unto all Eternitie?
For ever, O for ever, is the sting!
A finite greif's not worth the mentioning.
For where sweet Hope can find the smallest place
    To enter in, with her bright face
She clears up sorrows, and restores the light,
Tho they were black as the Egyptian night.
But not the smallest glimpse of Hope, can be
Forsaken place! suffer'd to shine in thee.
    When thy duration has been more,
    More years if we may count by years,
    Than there are sands upon the shore,
    Or Grass piles on the earth, or Stars,
In the bright firmament, alas the sum
Compar'd t'Eternity, dos just to nothing come.

V

Surely I hear one of these caitifs roar,
    And his unhappy case deplore.
Hearken gay sinner to the mighty truth,
    These words will one day fit thy mouth.
Ah senseless wretch where have I brought my self!
What have I pluck'd upon my wretched head?
With the fond Love of Honour, Pleasure, Pelf,
Which now like treach'rous Friends are from me fled
    Now when in greatest need I stand,
    Like reeds of Egypt pierce my hand.

I cannot, no I cannot enter Heav'n,
Shou'd GOD vouchsafe t'unlock it's gate for me,
I who am nothing but impuritie,
With that most holy place can ne're agree.
Alas none of my brutish pleasures can
Live in that Air, or florish in that soil,
    Not all my crying, tears, and toil,
Can retransform this beast into a man.
    Repentance now is out of date,
And like the foolish Virgins comes too late;
Repent I shall for ever, but in vain,
Since 'tis not Love makes me repent, but fear and pain.

VI

    Come ye Companions of my choice,
My tempters once, and my tormentors now,
(Curs'd I who cou'd dispise a Saviours voice
    To hear and follow you!)
Come spitefull Devils, and let your malice be
    In a full tide pour'd out on me.
This greedy mouth, and these lascivious eyes,
    This tongue innur'd to blasphemies,
These ears which cou'd the needy's prayer withstand,
    This bloody and rapacious hand;
    Let 'em their sev'ral torments know,
    For that's the lest of all my woe;
Me on yon lake of Brimstone throw,
    Break me in pieces on yon shelf,
    Oh come and save me from my self!
    Bodily pains are soft and kind,
    Compar'd with anguish of the mind!
    What shall I do! where shall I rest?
    How shall I fly from my own brest?
For there the gnawing worm has made her nest!

VII

    Why dos reflection follow me?
And what have I to do with memory,
    Since I must never tast again of Joy?

These my most exquisite tormenters be.
I who ne're us'd to think must think at last,
Now all the benefit of thinking's past.
I saw, alas I saw, the endless bliss,
For which so often fruitlessly I wish:
  With rage and envy I beheld,
Those who the happy thrones have fill'd.
  What have I lost? and Oh for what?
A Crown, a Kingdom, Glory, Happiness
  And all Eternall too, for that
    Which worse than nothing is,
O stupid folly brutish madness this!
Rise blushes rise to cover such a shame,
Till your high colour rival with my flame:
And ev'ry Passion in my bosom move,
Come take your full revenge on wretched me,
Fear and dispair I feel with all their train,
Anger and Grief already kindled be,
  But I alas can never Hope nor Love:
  For Heav'nly Joys I have no gust,
Nor can away with Hell, and yet I must.
Ah my dear Pleasures whither do ye stray?
Alas they laugh at me and fly away,
Only their raging thirst dos ever with me stay.

VIII

  What shall I say? what shall I sing?
No more no more of such a dismal thing!
Whose ev'ry breathing's pain, and thought a sting!
  Yet e're we leave this horrid pit,
Let's try what good we can extract from it.
For them 'tis bootless to lament and mone,
Who to this Tophet are already gone,
But something for the Living may be done.
With restless toil, and an unwearied zeal,
  Strike the dull sinner till he feel;
  Such wounds will always do him good,
  And let out the Lethargick blood.
Cruelly civil they who let him die,
Rather than break the rules of decency,
  And Friendship's choicest Law dispise,

To truckle to unworthy flatteries:
'Tis not enough mistaken civil men,
To free you from this vice, that you disdain
    With praiseing Sin your tongues to stain,
    That dastard spirit which can refrain
From speaking Truth, plain tho unpleasant when
    He hath a Power, and oppertunity,
Is guilty of a negative flattery.
All ye that know the value of a Soul,
And what a price it cost to make it whole,
    How much was paid to ransom it,
    From Hell and make't for Heaven fit;
In season, and out of it beat his ear,
    Till importunity force him to hear,
And tho unwilling, make his prospect dwell,
Over a roaring and devouring Hell.
As those above all others suffer shall,
Who caus'd their Neighbour in this pit to fall;
So shall a double joy to him be giv'n,
Who brings his Brother with himself to Heav'n.

Vertue

I

    Go dispicable Vertue go,
      And seek some other World,
Go live with them whom we have rob'd of Gold,
      Since thou art far too mean and low,
For this refined age, perhaps the dull
The sottish Indian, may admit of thee,
      But we are full
Of sparkling wits, who know thy poverty,
And see thro thy home-spun simplicity.
      Some sixteen hundred years ago,
When men did only practick notions know,
And infant Christianity began
With its mirac'lous force t'impose on man:
Vertue perhaps, like some new thing might be
Admir'd and follow'd, for it's noveltie.
But we by their dear bought experience find,
      That Vertue's nothing but a name,

Which neither can protect from loss nor pain,
    A name by cunning men design'd,
To lay restraints on the best part of Humane-kind.

2

Go, Verteous fop and leave the World to us,
    'Twas never sure design'd for thee;
    A mind so nice and scrupulous,
Can never rise to wealth or dignity.
Alas poor man! he cannot one thing say,
    And act a quite contrary way!
No gain goes down with him, but what must be
First measur'd in the scales of equity
He cannot swallow Oaths, and Perjury,
His squeamish stomach hardly can digest a lie.
Nor can with evil means good ends persue,
Nor lawfull things with ill intention do.
Religion that unfashionable thing,
    Too firm and closely sets on him,
He thinks it still the same, and knows not how
Wisely to make it to his int'rest bow.
Dull Soul that never our great secret hit,
    Who for a Cloak make use of it,
    (None better villanies to hide)
    And then 'tis quickly thrown aside,
When our designs it can no longer fit.

3

Why do I thus idly my time employ?
Since others seek preferment why shou'd I,
For some weak scruples slip the oppertunity?
He that will nothing do but what is best,
May properly be said to live in jest.
    He that will for Preferment stay,
Till he come to it by a reg'lar way,
    May with the blinded Jews,
Vainly himself for evermore amuse,
With expectation of the ever absent day.
    But he that never boggles at a vice,
    Obtains his purpose in a trice;
    And what great hurt is done?
Only a Verteous simipleton out-run.
    If he to Heav'n has been a debter,

He hopes here after to do better;
Tho much of his too-morrows may be past,
Yet this hereafter sure will come at last;
      And when it comes O then,
A little matter sets all right again,
A Lord forgive me wipes away the shame and sin.

4

But one thought more before I venture out.
    Let me but solve one little doubt:
Will Vertue always under hatches lie?
And Vice for ever have impunity?
See which bids fairest for Eternity.
Ah now I find Vertue's the only good;
They who forsake her never understood
      Her safety and felicity,
Let me with Vertue live, and with her die.
I cou'd have richer bargains offer'd me,
As the World thinks, but now I plainly see,
There's nothing glorious or rich but thee!
      Enough thou hast to charm us here,
      Enough to bear our charges on the way,
But ah what hast thou at the great rewarding day!
And I'me content to have all laid up there.
Content said I, nay rather let me say,
      For this I'le study, strive and pray;
And to the World this last farewell I give,
Henceforth my only bus'ness shall be how to live.

The Complaint

I

    What dost thou mean my GOD, (said I,
Once in a sad and melancholy fit,)
      Why dost thou so severely try
        Thy Servant, as if yet
I had not been explor'd sufficiently.
    So much to stretch will break the wire,
What Gold can always strugle with the fire?
And Lord what mortal in thy sight can stand,
If all his ways be too exactly scan'd?

2

If I ask wealth, it is to be
Thy Steward only, not to make it mine.
    And when I wou'd have dignitie,
        'Tis that it might be thine,
And Vertues light to more advantage shine.
        'Tis my design when Wit I crave,
That thou both use and principal shou'd have.
For well I know that these no blessings be,
If as from thee they came, so they ascend not up to thee.

3

Yet without these I can be pleas'd,
When thou remember's me how oft they are.
    A spur to Vice, and Vertues snare,
        Strong Souls have been diseas'd,
By coming fresh into infected air.
        Who wou'd a cup of Poyson take,
That of his Antidote he might trial make?
All are not fit the Ordeal to endure,
Conquest is brave, but Peace is most secure.

4

But yet methinks 'tis somewhat hard,
My mind being to the lowest measure fit,
    Content with wages, begs not a reward,
        Thou shou'dst contract it yet,
And I of necessaries be debar'd.
        Long have I liv'd on hope, but will
A Hope that's always baulk'd continue still?
Is't not a sign the flood dos still remain,
When my poor Dove comes empty home again?

5

Lord thou didst give thy only Son
To die for me, and can I doubt thy Love?
    In his dear name thou bids me come,
        And yet no Prayers will move!
Friendless and helpless, I'me exposed here,
        As if thou took'st of me no care.
My equitable suit canst thou deny,
Since all I ask is oppertunity,
To serve my GOD and trafick for Eternity?

6

Fondly I thus complain'd, when lo
A beamling shot from Heav'n upon me shin'd;
In a right medium did the objects show,
And my dull thoughts refin'd.
Then I remembred who did undergo
Far worse for me, why shou'd I mone,
Since 'tis my daily Prayer, GODs will be done?
Ah simple Soul cou'dst thou his Wisdom see,
Thou wou'dst not sad, but pleas'd and joyfull be,
Dos not thy GOD know best what's good for thee?

Affliction

1

I know not what Affliction means,
The Play is still the same, tho diverse scenes
Divert our eyes, now a fair Tower,
And then a melancholy Bower.
I find I can both eat and drink,
And sleep and breathe, and move, and read, and think
The Sun shines on me, flow'ers their odor yeild,
If not in mine yet in my neighbours feild.

2

I hear the Airs Musitians sing,
And see the various Beauties of the Spring;
When I wou'd something glorious see,
Then up to Heav'n I lift my eye,
There I behold the richest Canopy,
Spread over such a mean dispised thing as me.
And in my cloths I warmth and cleaness find,
Tho mean, they're fitted to my body and mind.

3

I can have liberty to Pray,
And to examine when I go astray;
And may employ my time to gain
A Treasure which no Tyrannie,
Nor theives, nor fire can pluck from me,
A Treasure which for ever, will remain.
And when I wou'd pleasant and merry be,
It is but thinking what my GOD has done for me.

4

I fear not to obtain my ends,
While GOD and a good Conscience are my Friends;
    Nor need a Patron, if with Heav'n
    I can preserve my reck'nings ev'n.
And to secure me from all hurtfull ill,
My GOD his Angells sends to guard me still.
Then tell me O ye happy, rich and brave,
What blessings have ye which I cannot have?

5

Is it because your Fathers were
Noble and rich, and you are born their Heir?
    Is it because you're serv'd in state,
    With cringes and obsequious shews,
    And have more than ye know to use,
That you are blest and I unfortunate?
Tell me where dos the mighty diff'rence lie,
Where will it be when both of us must die?

6

'Tis ev'n in this, I can resign
With ease this poor afflicted Soul of mine,
    I who no sweet possessions have,
    And no fine toys t'seduce my heart,
    Can from this world with Joy & triumph part,
And go as to my bed so to my Grave;
No care to get wealth did disturb me there,
No fear to loss it will persue me here.

7

Easy and short my reck'nings are,
When I am call'd to the last dreadfull bar,
    And your's a great and mighty sum;
    'Tis all you must expect, 'tis all your share;
    I who have had the bitter here,
May humbly hope for some good things to come.
Oh poor rich man how will you wish to be,
Such a dispis'd afflicted thing as me!

8

Then welcome O ye happy things,
Ye blessings commonly too good for Kings!
But he that doth converse with you,
Will quickly great and Kingly grow,
Or nothing else can make him so,
When your instructions fail nothing will do.
'Tis you that are of all Preferments cheif,
Since JESUS was himself the King of Grief.

9

Welcome again, by you I learn
To value what's most worthy our concern,
I might have always been a fool,
And Happiness have measur'd then,
In the false ballances of men,
Had I not been inform'd in your best school;
That true felicity is never joyn'd
Unto the World, but to a Verteous mind.

10

Affliction! O 'tis but a name,
Mistaken men devise to hide their shame.
When they complain and find no ease,
Because their fortune dos not please,
Unwillingly they own the fact,
Since weak and childishly they act,
'Tis my Affliction makes me so they cry,
Heav'n must be blam'd for their absurdity.

11

But surely Heav'n all pure and good,
Could it's most righteous ways be understood,
By our weak reasonings, dos not love
To please it self in our calamity,
Our pains are more it's greif than joy;
All GOD design's thereby's to try and prove,
Whither we will at last our int'rest know,
And by short suff'rings scape a never ceasing woe.

12

Lord how unhappy shou'd I be,
Could want or plenty sep'rate me from thee!
   'Tis all a case whither I starve,
   Or whither drown for Death's the same
   In both, and diff'renc'd only by a name.
If any Passion rule I'me sure to serve,
Nor is that servitude of greatest ease,
Where Pride and impotence are the disease.

13

Well, if I keep from discontent,
And can be pleas'd with all that Heav'n has sent,
   If self-love do not choak my mind,
   But wholesome Vertues florish there,
   Am to my self a Friend, what need I care
   Shou'd fortune be or curst or kind.
If GOD think fit in me to exercise
His Graces, shou'd not I the favour prize?
GOD's will I'me sure is holy, just and wise.

14

Happy are they whose quiet mind,
To GODs disposal freely is resign'd:
   Secure and much at ease they live,
   (Since for 'em such a Friend dos chuse,
   Who cannot be deceiv'd, nor will impose,)
And gladly what so e're he sends receive.
The heaviest yoke dos very easy sit,
When we with Patience can submit to it.

15

Nay if I knew that heav'n were pleas'd,
That I shou'd be defamed, poor, diseas'd,
   I'de run to meet the welcome state,
   With greater triumph greater joy,
Than the Proud Macedonian boy,
From flatt'ring men heard his prodigious fate:
Nor wou'd I change my dunghil for his Throne,
Tho all the Worlds he wept for were his own.

16

Great Job how much we'rt thou above
That vapour, who was call'd the Son of Jove,
    Such as his Father such was he,
    But thy strong Vertue like a Rock,
    Heroickly endur'd the shock
Of winds and waves, thy naked Vertue we
More eligible find, of more renown,
Than all the tinsel glories of a crown.

The Thanksgiving

1

Hence you complaining thoughts away,
    I have no time to sigh and grieve;
The little while allotted me to live,
    Is much too short a time to pay
Those Praises, and Thanksgivings I shou'd give,
    And am indebted to my GOD,
    Both for his staff, and for his rod,
    Both for his Physick, and his food,
And those severest ways whereby he dos me good.

2

Begin and count the mighty sum,
    Begin betimes for whilst I sing,
Each minuit a new blessing home doth bring,
    Say quickly what thy GOD has done,
How free his mercies flow, how quick they spring,
    Hast, they'l be numberless e're-long,
    To num'rous for a finite song;
    Already I beneath 'em fall,
For why Arithmetick's too short to count 'em all.

3

Wast not enough my GOD that thou
    Didst give me being, and infuse
A reasonable Soul, fit to refuse,
    The evil and the good to chuse;

And made me capable t'enjoy and know
    Thee the Supreme and only good,
    But when my stubborn will withstood
    It's own felicity, and went astray,
Thou by wise discipline recalls me to thy way.

4
    What am I Lord, ah what am I?
    That of me thou shou'dst take such care,
And for my sake thy one dear Son not spare!
    Dost thou behold me with a Friendly eye,
Vile me, on whom the world dos look awry?
    Then I'le no more the world regard,
    Value it's loss, nor care for it's reward,
    Thou kindly has withdrawn from me
All other things, that I might only Love & think on thee.

I
Awake my Lute, daughters of Musick come,
    To Allalujah's tune my tongue,
My heart already hath the Canticle begun:
And leaps for Joy, because it's business is
    In a better world than this.
Blessed be GOD and evermore extoll'd,
Who wou'd not let me fetter'd be with Gold:
Nor to a dang'rous World expose weak me,
    By giving oppertunitie
For ev'ry sin, which wanton appetite
    Too easily can entertain,
    Nor needs temptations to invite;
    Did we but know the secret bane,
The perdue poyson, hidden aconite,
    Which Riches do infold,
Not all its charms, nor all its shining would
    Persuade us to the Love of Gold.
Happy am I who out of danger sit,
Can see and pitty them who wade thro it;
Need take no thought my treasure to dispose,
What I ne're had I cannot fear to lose:
Nor am concern'd what I must wear or buy,
To shew my plenty and my vanity.

II

From my secure and humble seat,
I view the ruins of the Great.
And dare look back on my expired days,
To my low state there needs no shameful ways.
    O how uneasy shou'd I be,
If tied to Custom and formalitie,
Those necessary evils of the Great,
Which bind their hands, and manacle their feet.
Nor Beauty, Parts, nor Portion me expose
My most beloved Liberty to lose.
And thanks to Heav'n my time is all my own,
    I when I please can be alone;
Nor Company, nor Courtship steal away
    That treasure they can ne're repay.
    No Flatterers, no Sycophants,
        My dwelling haunts,
Nor am I troubl'd with impertinents.
Nor busy days, nor sleepless nights infest
My Quiet mind, nor interrupt my rest.
My Honour stand's not on such a ticklish term
That ev'ry puff of air can do it harm.
But these are blessings I had never known,
Had I been great, or seated near a Throne.
My GOD, forever blessed be thy name!
That I'me no darling in the list of Fame.
While the large spreading Cedars of the wood,
    Are by their eminence expos'd to storms,
I who beneath their observation stood,
    Am undisturb'd with such alarms.
None will at me their sharp detractions throw,
Or strive to make me less who am already low.

III

I thank thee Lord that I am Friendless too,
    Tho that alas be hard to do!
    Tho I have wearied Heav'n with Prayers,
    And fill'd it's bottles with my tears.
Tho I always propos'd the noblest end,
    Thy glory in a Friend.
And never any earthly thing requir'd,
    But this thats better part divine,

And for that reason was so much desir'd;
    Yet humbly I submit,
    To that most perfect will of thine,
And thank thee cause thou hast denied me it.
    Thrice blessed be thy Jealousie,
        Which would not part
        With one smal corner of my heart,
        But has engross'd it all to Thee!
Thou wouldst not let me ease my burthens here,
        Which none on Earth cou'd bear,
        Nor in anothers troubles share;
        O sweet exchange thy Joys are mine,
        And thou hast made my sorrows thine.
        Now absence will not break my heart,
        JESUS and I can never part,
        By night, or day, by Land or sea,
His right hand shades, his left hands under me
        Nor shall I need to shed a tear,
Because my Friend is dead or I must leave her here.

IV

If I can thank for this, what cannot I
Receive with chearful mind, and perfect joy!
No want so sharply doth affect the heart,
No loss nor sickness causeth such a smart,
No racks nor tortures so severely rend,
As the unkindness of a darling Friend.
Yet ev'n this bitter pil has done me good,
Without it I had hardly understood,
        The baseness which attends
        On ev'ry sin, because it is
Ingratitude and black perfidiousness,
        To thee my GOD the best of Friends.
        Thus by th' assistance of thy grace,
Joyn'd with a lively Faith, and honest mind,
In most untastefull things I pleasure find,
And beauty in the darkest sorrows face.
        The eater brings forth meat, the strong affords
Like Sampson's Lion sweetness to thy Servants boards.
Who has the true Elixir, may impart
Pleasure to all he touches, and convert
The most unlikely greif to Happiness.

Vertue this true Elixir is,
'Tis only Vertue this can do,
And with this choicest Priviledge invest,
Can make us truly happy now,
And afterwards for ever blest.

The end.

To
The most Reverend,
his Grace the Lord
Archbishop of
Canturbury

These humbly
present

Since Praise is nauseous to a modest ear,
No more in Panegyricks I'le appear.
I cannot praise the bad, & to the Good
Praise is a Language hardly understood;
May I but pardon have for what is past,
And that mistaken fault shall be the last.
Foolishly I forgot that they will lest
Endure to hear Praise, who deserve it best.
Henceforth in silence I'le admire the brave,
They shall less Praise more imitation have;
Tho I was apt to think, Vertue might be
Where e're 'twas seen Prais'd without flattery.
To his great Name I'le raise my humble Muse
Him, who the meanest off'ring won't refuse,
If it be offer'd with an honest mind,
A mind that labours to be more refin'd,
Tho't be not wholy from its errours freed,
But like the smoaking flax & bruised reed.
Him! unto whom alone all Praise is due,
And all that can be said too little to!
JESUS shall be the burthen of my Song,
Whom I can never Love & Praise too long:
Oh! that his Name by some Celestial art

Were graven in my head, & tongue, & heart,
That I might always of him think & speak,
And never any of his Precepts break;
To what a great and real dignity,
Wou'd that advance ev'n dispicable me!
How mean & how unworthy dos appear,
All the gay things that people dote on here!
Fame, Honour, Riches, all beneath us fall
And merit not our care since he dispis'd them all.
　　　　But whither do I run? I only ment
To let your Grace discern by whats here sent
That your good Councel was not thrown away,
And while to it I my Obedience pay,
May you be pleas'd to pardon this address
Forgive the errours of my homely Verse,
For tho it never did from Vertue stray,
Yet you have shewn a nearer & a better way.

Appendix E
Lady Elizabeth Hastings' Luncheon Menus and Table Maps

September 11, 1728 (for Lady Ramsden)*

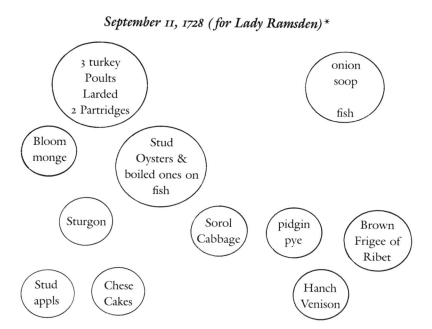

*I obtained these documents from G. H. H. Wheler from his private collection at Otterden, Kent.

Sept. 9, 1728 (for Mrs. Sewell and Miss Bright)

White soop Rem^d
with stude salmon

chicken & tongue   sorol cabbeg
in slices
calves head

Rabbits   calves foot pie

gravey soop
hanch venson

Turkey Poults   Spanish puffs
Creem all Brill   chese cake   Sturg on
Pickl'd Pidgeon
Stude apples   sallery (i.e. celery)   cheez
2 leveritts

Sept. 30, 1728 (for Lady Stafford)

Almond Soop
Boiled Pike

Batter'd rabbit   calves foot pye

sallid

Breast of vele   Dobed goes   sorol cabbeg
ragout

salid

tonng & chicken   sheeps—ragood

grave soop

Salmond Troots

Lady Elizabeth Hastings' Luncheon Menus and Table Maps

Pheasant-partridges

pease   Bloomange

Ragout of Rabbets, venison

Stude Oysters   Fride souls (i.e. soles)

Sturgeon

Damson Torte   Jansey

Turkey poults

Desert the same day

Jelley and Lemmon creme

Peaches   Stude Frute   Nectrins

Almond Butter Biskits

Wett Sweetmeats   Dry Sweet   Wet Ditte
Meets

Biskits   cream

nectrins   stude fruit   peaches

creemes   creems

Jelly & Lemmon Creems

Lady Elizabeth Hastings' Ledston menus Jan. 2, 1728:

plum porrige

fish

Brawn   mince pyes

Hanch Venison

Ham   Roast Goos

mince pyes   Brawn

plum porrige

turkey à chine

1 more hen (moor-hen) & paririges

chese (cheese) cakes   Bloommange

Scallup Oysters   Staragon (Sturgeon?)

Brill creem

capon

Aug. 26, 1728 (for Lady Lewysham)

Garvey soop

Lobsters

Rabbet   Chicken & Tongue

Piggin pye

Duck Ragood   Cabbeg

Hanch Venson

Phesents

Creem allabrile   beens

Sturgeon

peas   torte

Turkey Poults

Appendix F

Bibliographical Checklist of Mary Astell's Works

1a. A Serious Proposal To the Ladies, For the Advancement of their true and greatest Interest. By a Lover of Her Sex. London, Printed for R. Wilkin at the King's Head in St. Paul's Church-Yard, 1694.

> Union Library Catalog of Pennsylvania, Philadelphia, Pennsylvania
> Mount Holyoke College, South Hadley, Massachusetts
> University of California at Los Angeles, William Andrews Clark
>   Library, Los Angeles, California
> New York State Library, Albany, New York
> Alabama State University, Montgomery, Alabama
> University of Colorado at Denver, Denver, Colorado
> Cleveland State University, Cleveland, Ohio
> Pennsylvania State University, University Park, Pennsylvania
> Virginia State Library, Richmond, Virginia
> University of Texas, Austin, Texas
> Yale University, Beinecke Library, New Haven, Connecticut
> Princeton University, Princeton, New Jersey
> Graduate Theological Union, San Anselmo, California

1b. A Serious Proposal To The Ladies, For The Advancement of their True and Greatest Interest. By a Lover of her Sex. The Second Edition Corrected. London, Printed for R. Wilkin, at the King's Head in St. Paul's Church-Yard, 1695.*

> Columbia University, New York, New York
> University of Minnesota, Minneapolis, Minnesota

The number system for this check-list is based on J. E. Norton's bibliographical study of Mary Astell, "Some Uncollected Authors, XXVII: Mary Astell, 1666–1731," *The Book Collector* 10 (Spring 1961), 58–65.
*Titles marked with an asterisk are available from University Microfilms International, Ann Arbor, Michigan 48106.

Honnold Library, Claremont, California
Bryn Mawr College Library, Bryn Mawr, Pennsylvania (microfilm)
Henry E. Huntington Library, San Marino, California
New York Public Library, New York, New York

1c. A Serious Proposal To The Ladies, For The Advancement of their True
and Greatest Interest, Part I. By a Lover of her Sex. The Third Edition
Corrected. London, Printed by T.W. for R. Wilkin, at the King's-Head
in St. Paul's Church-Yard, 1696.*

Henry E. Huntington Library, San Marino, California
Stanford University, Stanford, California
Princeton University, Princeton, New Jersey

1d. A Serious Proposal To The Ladies, For The Advancement of their True
and Greatest Interest, Part I. By a Lover of her Sex. The Fourth Edition.
London: Printed by J.R. for R. Wilkin, at the King's Head in St. Paul's
Church-Yard, MDCCI.
[Parts I and II are issued together in this edition. In 1970 Source Book
Press published another edition of *A Serious Proposal* Parts I and II,
based on this 1701 text.]

Folger Shakespeare Library, Washington, D.C.
University of Cincinnati, Cincinnati, Ohio
Rice University, Fondren Library, Houston, Texas

1e. A Serious Proposal To The Ladies, Part II. Wherein a Method is offer'd
for the Improvement of their Minds. London: Printed for Richard
Wilkin at the King's Head in St. Paul's Church-yard, 1697.*

Henry E. Huntington Library, San Marino, California
University of California at Los Angeles, William Andrews Clark
Memorial Library, Los Angeles, California
Boston Public Library, Boston, Massachusetts
Stanford University, Stanford, California
Princeton University, Princeton, New Jersey

1f. A Serious Proposal To The Ladies, For The Advancement of their True
and Greatest Interest, In Two Parts. By a Lover of her Sex. London:
Printed for Richard Wilkin at the King's-Head in St. Paul's Church-Yard,
1697.

Vassar College, Poughkeepsie, New York

University of California at Los Angeles, William Andrews Clark
  Memorial Library, Los Angeles, California
Folger Shakespeare Library, Washington, D.C.
Union Theological Seminary, New York, New York
Newberry Library, Chicago, Illinois
Boston Public Library, Boston, Massachusetts
University of Chicago, John Crerar Library, Chicago, Illinois
University of Michigan, Ann Arbor, Michigan
Yale University, Beinecke Library, New Haven, Connecticut
Harvard University, Cambridge, Massachusetts
University of Texas, Austin, Texas
Union Theological Seminary, McAlpin Collection, New York, New
  York
New York State Library, Albany, New York
University of Cincinnati, Cincinnati, Ohio
Smith College, Northampton, Massachusetts

2a. Letters Concerning the Love of God, Between the Author of the Proposal to the Ladies And Mr. John Norris: Wherein his late Discourse,
shewing That it ought to be intire and exclusive of all other Loves, is
further cleared and justified. Published By J. Norris, M.A. Rector of Bemerton near Sarum. London, Printed for Samuel Manship at the Ship
near the Royal Exchange in Cornhil, and Richard Wilkin at the King's
Head in St. Paul's Church-Yard, 1695.

Whittier College, Whittier, California
University of Cincinnati, Cincinnati, Ohio
University of Texas, Austin, Texas
Newberry Library, Chicago, Illinois
Yale University, Beinecke Library, New Haven, Connecticut
University of Minnesota, Minneapolis, Minnesota
Henry E. Huntington Library, San Marino, California
University of California at Los Angeles, William Andrews Clark
  Memorial Library, Los Angeles, California
University of Wisconsin, Madison, Wisconsin
Stanford University, Stanford, California
University of California at Berkeley, Berkeley, California
University of North Carolina, Chapel Hill, North Carolina
Northwestern University, Evanston, Illinois

2b. Letters Concerning the Love of God, Between the Author of the Proposal to the Ladies And Mr. John Norris: Wherein his late Discourse,

shewing, That it ought to be intire and exclusive of all other Loves, is further Cleared and Justified. Published By J. Norris, M.A. Rector of Bemerton near Sarum. The Second Edition, Corrected by the Authors, with some few Things added. London: Printed for Samuel Manship at the Ship near the Royal Exchange in Cornhil, and Richard Wilkin at the King's Head in St. Paul's Church-Yard, 1705.

> University of California at Los Angeles, William Andrews Clark
>   Memorial Library, Los Angeles, California
> Henry E. Huntington Library, San Marino, California
> Bethany and Northern Baptist Theological Seminaries Library, Oak
>   Brook, Illinois
> University of Illinois, Urbana, Illinois
> Memphis State University, Memphis, Tennessee
> Massachusetts Historical Society, Boston, Massachusetts
> Case Western Reserve University, Cleveland, Ohio
> University of Chicago, Chicago, Illinois
> Athenaeum, Boston, Massachusetts
> New York Public Library, New York, New York
> Brown University, Providence, Rhode Island
> University of Wisconsin, Madison, Wisconsin

2c. Letters Concerning the Love of God, Between the Author of the Proposal to the Ladies And Mr. John Norris: Wherein his late Discourse, shewing, That it ought to be intire and exclusive of all other Loves, is further Cleared and Justified. Published by J. Norris, M.A., late Rector of Bemerton near Sarum. The Third Edition, Corrected by the Authors, with some few Things added. London: Printed for Edmund Parker at the Bible and Crown over against the New Church in Lombard-Street. 1730.

> Yale University, Beinecke Library, New Haven, Connecticut

3a. Some Reflections Upon Marriage, Occasion'd by the Duke & Dutchess of Mazarine's Case; which is also consider'd. London: Printed for John Nutt near Stationers-Hall, 1700.

> Yale University, Beinecke Library, New Haven, Connecticut
> Henry E. Huntington Library, San Marino, California
> University of California at Los Angeles, William Andrews Clark
>   Memorial Library, Los Angeles, California
> Alabama State University, Montgomery, Alabama
> University of Colorado at Denver, Denver, Colorado

Pennsylvania State University, University Park, Pennsylvania
Graduate Theological Union, San Anselmo, California

3b. Some Reflections Upon Marriage. The Second Edition. London:
Printed for R. Wilkin, at the King's Head in St. Paul's Church-Yard,
1703.

Newberry Library, Chicago, Illinois
Harvard University, Cambridge, Massachusetts
Stanford University, Stanford, California

3c. Reflections Upon Marriage. The Third Edition. To which is Added A
Preface, in Answer to some Objections. London: Printed for R. Wilkin,
at the King's Head in St. Paul's Church-Yard, 1706.

University of California at Los Angeles, William Andrews Clark
Memorial Library, Los Angeles, California
Harvard University, Cambridge, Massachusetts
Washington State University, Pullman, Washington
University of Texas, Austin, Texas
Yale University, Beinecke Library, New Haven, Connecticut
Princeton Theological Seminary, Princeton, New Jersey
Boston Athenaeum, Boston, Massachusetts
Honnold Library, Claremont, California
New York Public Library, New York, New York
Bryn Mawr College Library, Bryn Mawr, Pennsylvania (microfilm)

3d. Some Reflections Upon Marriage. With Additions. The Fourth Edition.
London: Printed for William Parker, at the King's Head in St. Paul's
Church-Yard. M.DCC.XXX.
[In 1970 Source Book Press published another edition of *Some Reflections
Upon Marriage*, based on this 1730 text.]

University of Illinois, Urbana, Illinois
Folger Shakespeare Library, Washington, D.C.
New York Public Library, New York, New York
Duke University, Durham, North Carolina
Harvard University, Cambridge, Massachusetts
Case Western Reserve University, Cleveland, Ohio
Athenaeum of Ohio, Cincinnati, Ohio
Rice University, Houston, Texas
University of Vermont, Burlington, Vermont
Columbia University, New York, New York

3e. Some Reflections Upon Marriage. With Additions. The Fifth Edition. Dublin: Printed by and for S. Hyde and E. Dobson, and for R. Gunne and R. Owen, Booksellers. M.DCC.XXX.

> Henry E. Huntington Library, San Marino, California
> University of Florida, Gainesville, Florida

4. Moderation truly Stated: Or, A Review Of A Late Pamphlet Entitul'd, Moderation a Vertue. With A Prefatory Discourse To D^r. D'Aveanant, Concerning His late Essays on Peace and War. London: Printed by J.L. for Rich. Wilkin, at the King's Head in St. Paul's Church-Yard. MDCCIV.

> University of Chicago, Chicago, Illinois
> Indiana University, Lilly Library, Bloomington, Indiana
> Harvard University, Cambridge, Massachusetts
> United States Library of Congress, Washington, D.C.
> Folger Shakespeare Library, Washington, D.C.
> New York Public Library, New York, New York
> Union Theological Seminary, New York, New York
> University of Texas, Austin, Texas
> Yale University, Divinity School, New Haven, Connecticut
> Boston Public Library, Boston, Massachusetts
> Columbia University, New York, New York

5. A Fair Way With The Dissenters And Their Patrons. Not Writ by Mr. L———y, or any other Furious Jacobite whether Clergyman or Layman; but by a very Moderate Person and Dutiful Subject to the Queen. London: Printed by E.P. for R. Wilkin, at the King's-Head, in St. Paul's Church-yard, 1704.

> McMaster University, Hamilton, Ontario, Canada
> Henry E. Huntington Library, San Marino, California
> Indiana University, Lilly Library, Bloomington, Indiana
> Harvard University, Cambridge, Massachusetts
> University of Minnesota, Minneapolis, Minnesota
> Folger Shakespeare Library, Washington, D.C.
> Boston Public Library, Boston, Massachusetts

6. An Impartial Enquiry Into The Causes of Rebellion and Civil War In This Kingdom: In an Examination of Dr. Kennett's Sermon, Jan. 31. 1703/ 4. And Vindication of the Royal Martyr. London: Printed by E.P. for R. Wilkin at the King's Head in St. Paul's Church-Yard, 1704.

Henry E. Huntington Library, San Marino, California
Folger Shakespeare Library, Washington, D.C.
University of Indiana, Lilly Library, Bloomington, Indiana
Harvard University, Cambridge, Massachusetts
Union Theological Seminary, New York, New York
University of Texas, Austin, Texas
California State Library, Sacramento, California
Princeton University, Princeton, New Jersey
Yale University, Beinecke Library, New Haven, Connecticut
New York Public Library, New York, New York
University of Nebraska, Lincoln, Nebraska

7a. The Christian Religion, As Profess'd by a Daughter Of The Church of England. London: Printed by S.H. for R. Wilkin at the King's-Head in St. Paul's Church-Yard, 1705.

University of Toronto, Toronto, Ontario, Canada
Trinity College, Hartford, Connecticut
Folger Shakespeare Library, Washington, D.C.
Newberry Library, Chicago, Illinois
University of Texas, Austin, Texas
General Theological Seminary of the Protestant Episcopal Church, New York, New York
University of Pennsylvania, Philadelphia, Pennsylvania
University of Minnesota, Minneapolis, Minnesota

7b. The Christian Religion, As Profess'd by a Daughter of the Church of England. London: Printed by W.B. for R. Wilkin at the King's-Head in St. Paul's Church-Yard. 1717.

Trinity College, Hartford, Connecticut
University of the South, Sewanee, Tennessee
University of California at Los Angeles, William Andrews Clark Memorial Library, Los Angeles, California

7c. The Christian Religion, As Profess'd by a Daughter of the Church of England Containing Proper Directions for the due Behaviour of Women in every Station of Life. With a few cursory Remarks on Archbishop Til lotson's Doctrine of the Satisfaction of Christ, &c. The Third Edition. London: Printed for W. Parker, at the King's-Head in St. Paul's Church Yard. M.DCC.XXX.

Yale University, Divinity School, New Haven, Connecticut

8a. Bart'lemy Fair: Or, An Enquiry after Wit; In which due Respect is had
to a Letter Concerning Enthusiasm, To my Lord***. By Mr. Wotton.
London: Printed for R. Wilkin, at the King's Head in St. Paul's Church-
Yard, 1709.

> University of California at Los Angeles, William Andrews Clark
>   Memorial Library, Los Angeles, California
> Henry E. Huntington Library, San Marino, California
> United States Library of Congress, Washington, D.C.
> University of Chicago, Chicago, Illinois
> Harvard University, Cambridge, Massachusetts
> University of Oregon, Eugene, Oregon
> University of Texas, Austin, Texas
> Oakland University, Rochester, Michigan
> University of Illinois at Urbana-Champaign, Illinois
> Yale University, Beinecke Library, New Haven, Connecticut
> Boston Public Library, Boston, Massachusetts
> Brown University, Providence, Rhode Island
> Stanford University, Stanford, California

8b. An Enquiry After Wit: Wherein the Trifling Arguing and Impious Raillery of the Late Earl of Shaftsbury, In his Letter concerning Enthusiasm,
and other Profane Writers, Are fully Answer'd, and justly Exposed. The
Second Edition. London: Printed for John Bateman at the Hat and Star
in St. Paul's Church-Yard. MDCCXXII.

> University of Texas, Austin, Texas
> Washington University, St. Louis, Missouri
> University of North Carolina, Chapel Hill, North Carolina

Manuscript Sources

Additional MSS	British Library, London
Additional 19ᶜ	University Library, Cambridge, England
Ballard MSS	Bodleian Library, Oxford
Beaufort MSS	Badminton, Gloucestershire
Calendar of State Papers for America and the West Indies	Public Record Office at Kew, London
Carew Pole MSS	Cornwall County Record Office
Chelsea Poor Rate Ledgers	Chelsea Library, Manresa Road, London
De Ros MSS	Public Record Office of Northern Ireland, Belfast
Diary of the Chelsea Charity School	Property of the Royal Hospital of Chelsea in the keeping of the chaplain
Harrowby MSS	Sandon Hall, Staffordshire
Hostman Minute Book	Tyne and Wear Record Office
Dr. John King's MS History of Chelsea	Chelsea Library, Manresa Road, London
Minute Book of the Common Council 1652–1722	Tyne and Wear Record Office
Osborn Collection	Beinecke Library, Yale University
Rawlinson MSS (including MSS Rawl. Lett. and MSS Rawl. Poet)	Bodleian Library, Oxford
St. John's parish register, Newcastle	Newcastle Public Library
St. Nicholas's parish register, Newcastle	Newcastle Public Library
Sloane MSS	British Library, London

Society for the Propagation of
Christian Knowledge archive

Stowe MSS

John Walker MSS

Trinity Church, Marylebone St.,
London

British Library, London

Bodleian Library, Oxford

Full Titles of Mary Astell's Published Works with the Abbreviations Used Here

1694	*A Serious Proposal To the Ladies For the Advancement of their true and greatest Interest. By a Lover of Her Sex.*	*A Serious Proposal*
1695	*Letters Concerning the Love of God, Between the Author of the Proposal to the Ladies and Mr. John Norris.*	*Letters Concerning the Love of God*
1697	*A Serious Proposal to the Ladies Part II Wherein A Method is offer'd for the Improvement of their Minds.*	*A Serious Proposal Part II*
1700	*Some Reflections Upon Marriage, Occasion'd by the Duke & Duchess of Mazarine's Case; which is also consider'd.*	*Some Reflections Upon Marriage*
1706	*Reflections Upon Marriage. The Third Edition. To which is Added a Preface, in Answer to some Objections.*	*Some Reflections Upon Marriage* 1706 edition
1704	*Moderation truly Stated: Or, A Review of a Late Pamphlet Entitul'd Moderation a Vertue. With a Prefatory Discourse to Dr. D'Aveanant, Concerning His late Essays on Peace and War.*	*Moderation Truly Stated*
1704	*A Fair Way with the Dissenters and Their Patrons. Not Writ by Mr. L——y, or any other Furious Jacobite whether Clergyman or Layman; but by a very Moderate Person and Dutiful Subject to the Queen.*	*A Fair Way with Dissenters*
1704	*An Impartial Enquiry into the Causes of Rebellion and Civil War in this Kingdom: In an Examination of Dr. Kennett's Sermon Jan. 31, 1703/4. And Vindication of the Royal Martyr.*	*An Impartial Enquiry into the Causes of Rebellion*

470

Full Titles of Mary Astell's Published Works with the Abbreviations Used Here

1705	*The Christian Religion, As Profess'd by a Daughter of the Church of England.*	*The Christian Religion*
1709	*Bart'lemy Fair: Or, An Enquiry after Wit; In which due Respect is had to a Letter Concerning Enthusiasm, To my Lord ***. By Mr. Wotton.*	*Bart'lemy Fair*

Notes

Chapter One: The Rediscovery of a Woman's Voice

1. Mary Astell, *Some Reflections Upon Marriage*, 88.

2. A selection of classics of early scholarship on learned women and women writers and the conditions that shaped their lives would have to include: Paul Bunyan Anderson, "Mistress Delariviere Manley's Biography," *Modern Philology* 33 (1935–36): 261–78; Margaret Ashdown, "Elizabeth Elstob, the Learned Saxonist," *Modern Language Review* 20 (1925): 126–46; Rae Blanchard, "Richard Steele and the Status of Women," *Studies in Philology* 26 (1929): 325–55; Alice Clark, *Working Life of Women in the Seventeenth Century* (London: G. Routledge & Sons, 1919); *Autobiography and Correspondence of Mary Granville, Mrs. Delany*, ed. Lady Llanover, 1st series, 3 vols. (London: R. Bentley, 1861), and 2d series, 3 vols. (London: R. Bentley, 1862); Jean Gagen, *The New Woman: Her Emergence in English Drama, 1600–1730* (New York: Twayne, 1954); Dorothy Gardiner, *English Girlhood at School; A Study of Women's Education through Twelve Centuries* (London: Oxford University Press, 1929); Robert Halsband, *The Life of Mary Wortley Montagu* (Oxford: Clarendon Press, 1956); Robert Halsband, ed., *The Complete Letters of Lady Mary Wortley Montagu*, 3 vols. (Oxford: Clarendon Press, 1965–67); Joyce Mary Horner, *The English Women Novelists and Their Connection with the Feminist Movement (1688–1792)*, Smith College Studies in Modern Languages, vol. 11, nos. 1–3 (Northampton, Mass., 1929–30); A. R. Humphreys, "The 'Rights of Woman' in the Age of Reason," *Modern Language Review* 41 (1946): 256–69; William H. McBurney, "Mrs. Penelope Aubin and the Early Eighteenth-Century English Novel," *Huntington Library Quarterly* 20 (1957): 245–67; Bridget MacCarthy, *Women Writers, Their Contribution to the English Novel, 1621–1744* (Cork, Ireland: Cork University Press, 1947); William McKee, *Elizabeth Inchbald, Novelist* (Washington: Catholic University of America, 1935); Gwendolyn B. Needham, "Mary de la Riviere Manley, Tory Defender," *Huntington Library Quarterly* 12 (1958–59): 253–88; I. B. O'Malley, *Women in Subjection* (London: Duckworth, 1933); *Thraliana: The Diary of Mrs. Hester Lynch Thrale (Later Mrs. Piozzi), 1776–1809*, ed. Katherine C. Balderston, 2 vols. (Oxford: Clarendon Press, 1942); Myra Reynolds, *The Learned Lady in England, 1650–1760* (Boston: Houghton Mifflin, 1920); Philip Webster Souers, *The Match-*

less Ori~da, Harvard Studies in English, 5 (Cambridge: Harvard University Press, 1931); Bertha Monica Stearns, "Early English Periodicals for Ladies (1700–1760)," *PMLA* 48 (1933): 38–60; Doris Mary Stenton, *The English Woman in History* (London and New York: Allen and Unwin, 1957); James R. Sutherland, "The Progress of an Error: Mrs. Centlivre and the Biographers," *Review of English Studies* 18 (1942): 167–82; A. H. Upham, "English Femmes Savantes at the End of the Seventeenth Century," *Journal of English and German Philology* 12 (1913): 262–76; Robert Palfrey Utter and Gwendolyn Needham, *Pamela's Daughters* (New York: Macmillan, 1936); Ada Wallas, *Before the Bluestockings* (London: G. Allen & Unwin, 1929).

3. Examples of such contributions in social and intellectual history which take seriously the point of view of women are: Joan Kelly, "Did Women have a Renaissance?" as well as other essays in *Becoming Visible: A History of European Women*, ed. Renate Bridenthal and Claudia Koonz (Boston: Houghton Mifflin, 1977); Irene Q. Brown, "Domesticity, Feminism, and Friendship: Female Aristocratic Culture and Marriage in England, 1660–1760," *Journal of Family History* 7 (1982): 406–24; Phyllis Mack, "Women as Prophets during the English Civil War," *The Origins of Anglo-American Radicalism*, ed. Margaret Jacob and James Jacob (London and Boston: George Allen & Unwin, 1984): 214–31; Natalie Z. Davis, "Women's History in Transition: The European Case," *Feminist Studies* 3 (1976): 83–103; Margaret George, "From Good Wife to Mistress: The Transformation of the Female in Bourgeois Culture," *Science & Society* 37 (1973): 152–77; John Rankine Goody, Joan Thirsk, and E. P. Thompson, eds., *Family and Inheritance: Rural Society in Western Europe* (New York and Cambridge: Cambridge University Press, 1976); Janelle Greenberg, "The Legal Status of English Women in Early Eighteenth-Century Law and Equity," *Studies in Eighteenth-Century Culture* 4 (1975): 171–81; Patricia Higgins, "The Reactions of Women, with Special Reference to Women Petitioners," in *Politics, Religion, and the English Revolution, 1640–1649*, ed. Brian Manning (London: Edward Arnold, 1973); Christopher Hill, "Base Impudent Kisses," in *The World Turned Upside Down: Radical Ideas During the English Revolution* (New York: Viking Press, 1972), 247–60; *Liberating Women's History: Theoretical and Critical Essays*, ed. Berenice A. Carroll (Urbana: University of Illinois Press, 1976); John Loftis, ed., *The Memoirs of Anne, Lady Halkett, and Ann, Lady Fanshawe* (Oxford: Clarendon Press, 1979); Carolyn Lougee, *Le Paradis des Femmes: Women Salons, and Social Stratification in Seventeenth-Century France* (Princeton, N.J.: Princeton University Press, 1976); Neil McKendrick, "Home Demand and Economic Growth: A New View of the Role of Women and Children in the Industrial Revolution," in *Historical Perspectives: Studies in English Thought and Society, in Honour of J. H. Plumb*, ed. Neil McKendrick, 152–210 (London: Europa, 1974); Carolyn Merchant, *The Death of Nature: Women, Ecology, and the Scientific Revolution* (San Francisco: Harper and Row, 1980); Keith Thomas, "Women and the Civil War Sects," *Past and Present* 13 (1958): 42–62; Roger Thompson, *Women in Stuart England and America* (London: Routledge and Kegan Paul, 1974); Louise Tilley and Joan Scott, *Women,*

Work, and Family (New York: Holt, Rinehart and Winston, 1978); Michael A. Seidel, "Poulain de la Barre's *The Woman As Good As the Man*," *Journal of the History of Ideas* 35 (1974): 499–508.

4. See the special issues of *Women's Studies* edited by Sandra Gilbert and Susan Gubar on women writers, 7, nos. 1 and 2 (1980). See also (and this is by no means an exhaustive list): J. R. Brink, ed., *Female Scholars: A Tradition of Learned Women before 1800* (Montreal: Eden Press, 1980); Nancy Cotton, *Women Playwrights in England, c. 1363–1750* (Lewisberg: Bucknell University Press, 1980); Natalie Zemon Davis, "Gender and Genre: Women as Historical Writers, 1400–1820," in *Beyond Their Sex: Learned Women of the European Past*, ed. Patricia H. Labalme, 153–82 (New York: New York University Press, 1980); Sandra G. Gilbert and Susan Gubar, eds., *Shakespeare's Sisters: Feminist Essays on Women Poets* (Bloomington: University of Indiana Press, 1979); Fidelis Morgan, *The Female Wits* (London: Virago Press, 1981); Roger Lonsdale, ed., *The New Oxford Book of Eighteenth-Century Verse* (Oxford and New York: Oxford University Press, 1984); Sandra G. Gilbert and Susan Gubar, eds., *The Norton Anthology of Literature by Women* (New York and London: W. W. Norton, 1985), esp. pp. 58–187. A new journal, *Tulsa Studies in Women's Literature*, devotes its space exclusively to the study of literature written by women. At the 1984 National Women's Studies Association conference held at Douglass College, Rutgers University, Jeslyn Medoff chaired a panel on "Seventeenth-Century British Women Writers" including papers by Susan Hastings on Anne Wharton, Melinda Sansone on Jane and Elizabeth Cavendish (Brackley), and Jeslyn Medoff on Jane Barker.

5. Roger Thompson's *Women in Stuart England and America*, mentioned above, brings together much of the demographic work on women. See also Peter Laslett, *Family Life and Illicit Love in Earlier Generations* (New York: Cambridge University Press, 1977), and David Cressy, "Literacy in Seventeenth-Century England: More Evidence," *Journal of Interdisciplinary History* 8 (1977): 141–50, and more recently his *Literacy and Social Order: Reading the Writing in Tudor and Stuart England* (Cambridge: Cambridge University Press, 1980). In a more popular vein, see Antonia Fraser, *The Weaker Vessel: Women's Lot in Seventeenth-Century England* (New York: Knopf, 1984).

6. Hilda L. Smith's *Reason's Disciples: Seventeenth-Century English Feminists* (Urbana: University of Illinois Press, 1982) and Moira Ferguson's *First Feminists* (Bloomington: Indiana University Press and Old Westbury: The Feminist Press, 1985) are the best of these. Also recently published is Katherine Rogers', *Feminism in Eighteenth-Century England* (Urbana: University of Illinois Press, 1982).

7. Some recent biographical treatments of eighteenth-century women which are feminist or notably empathetic with feminism: Angeline Goreau, *Reconstructing Aphra: A Social Biography of Aphra Behn* (New York: The Dial Press, 1980); Edith Larson, "Early Eighteenth-Century English Women Writers: Their Lives, Fiction, and Letters" (Ph.D. diss., Brandeis University, 1980); Mary Nash, *The Provoked Wife: The Life and Times of Susannah Cibber* (Boston: Little, Brown, 1977). Carolyn Heilbrun has remarked recently on the spate of women's

biographies written since 1970. See "Discovering the Lost Lives of Women," *New York Times Book Review*, June 24, 1984.

Two excellent dissertations on these contemporaries of Astell's are Sarah Huff Collins, "Elizabeth Elstob: A Biography" (Ph.D. diss., Indiana University, 1970); and Dolores D. C. Duff, "Materials towards a Biography of Mary Delariviere Manley" (Ph.D. diss., Indiana University, 1974).

8. Mary Astell, *The Christian Religion*, 113.

9. Germaine Greer also remarks on what she calls the "Woman of Genius Syndrome" in the case of the nineteenth-century writer L. E. L., implying that there are female psychological paradigms that accompany writing in women that we have not yet even begun to explore. "The Tulsa Center for the Study of Women's Literature: What We Are Doing and Why We Are Doing It," *Tulsa Studies in Women's Literature* 1 (1982): 5–26.

10. Astell was *not* a democratic thinker, and Jerome Nadelhaft is simply wrong in his recent article ("Englishwoman's Sexual Civil War, 1650–1740," *Journal of the History of Ideas* 43, no. 4 [October-December 1982]: 555–79) disputing, in n. 70, Joan Kinnaird's contention that Astell was a royalist. Nadelhaft does not understand Astell's use of irony in the passages he cites, an irony directed at the political liberals of her day who unquestioningly backed absolute authority in the home but not in the state. Kinnaird's article, "Mary Astell and the Conservative Contribution to English Feminism" (*The Journal of British Studies* 19, no. 1 [Fall 1979]: 53–75), is an excellent treatment of Astell's political thought. See also Regina Janes' "Mary, Mary, Quite Contrary, or Mary Astell and Mary Wollstonecraft Compared," *Studies in Eighteenth-Century Culture*, ed. Ronald Rosbottom, 5 (1976): 121–39. For a discussion of the relation between Astell's monarchist politics and her sexual politics, see chap. 6 below.

11. Mary Astell, *The Christian Religion*, 292.

12. Mary Astell, *The Christian Religion*, 49.

13. Mary Astell, *Bart'lemy Fair*, 116.

14. Ibid., 117–18.

15. Katherine Philips fled to the country and took to her bed, stricken, when an unauthorized edition of her poems was pirated and printed in 1662. She refused to come to London, lamenting to her friend Dorothy Osborne Temple: "I must never show my face there or among any reasonable people again." Quoted in Myra Reynolds, *The Learned Lady in England*, 58. Aphra Behn was stigmatized as "loose" because she was unmarried and wrote for the theater. Margaret Cavendish, the duchess of Newcastle, was considered crazy for writing and publishing so many books. Dorothy Osborne remarked: "Sure, the poor woman is a little distracted, she could never be so ridiculous else as to venture at writing books." *The Love Letters of Dorothy Osborne to Sir William Temple, 1652–1654*, ed. Edward Abbott Parry (New York: Dodd, Mead, 1901), 103. Margaret Cavendish clearly stated that her motive for writing was the wish for immortal fame. "Since all Heroick Actions, Publick Employments, as well Civil as Military, and Eloquent Pleadings, are deni'd my Sex in this Age," she wrote, "I may be excused for writing so much." Preface to *Nature's Pictures*

Drawn by Fancies Pencil to the Life (London, 1656). She published thirteen books between 1653 and 1668—poetry, drama, fiction, treatises on science and natural philosophy, fictional letters, orations, biography and autobiography. For a thorough summary of the duchess's career, as well as an analysis of her relation to fame and immortality, see Jean Gagen's excellent "Honor and Fame in the Works of the Duchess of Newcastle," *Studies in Philology* 56 (1965): 519–38.

16. Bathsua Makin, *An Essay To Revive the Antient Education of Gentlewomen* (1673), the Augustan Reprint Society Series, no. 202 (Los Angeles: William Andrews Clark Memorial Library, 1980), 4. For a fine article about Makin, see Mitzi Myers, "Domesticating Minerva: Bathsua Makin's 'Curious' Argument for Women's Education," *Studies in Eighteenth-Century Culture*, ed. O. M. Brack, 14 (1985): 173–92.

17. Thomas Clarkson, *Memoirs of the Private and Public Life of William Penn*, 2 vols. (London: Longmans, 1813), 1: 196–97. For more information about this fascinating woman, see Una Birch, *Anna Van Schurman: Artist, Scholar, Saint* (New York: Longmans, 1909).

18. Mary Astell, *A Serious Proposal*, 26.

19. For a fuller discussion of their impact in England, see below, chap. 3.

20. *The Journal of British Studies* 19 (1979): 53–75.

21. Hilda Smith, *Reason's Disciples*, 4–5.

22. Moira Ferguson, ed., *First Feminists*, p. 27.

23. Mary Astell, *A Serious Proposal II*, 4.

24. *The Complete Letters of Lady Mary Wortley Montagu*, ed. Robert Halsband, 1: 467.

25. Mary Astell, *Some Reflections Upon Marriage*, 55–56.

26. *The Letters and Works of Lady Mary Wortley Montagu*, ed. Lord Wharncliffe, 3 vols. (London: Richard Bentley, 1837), 1: 49–50.

27. Mary Astell, *Some Reflections Upon Marriage*, 23.

28. Mary Astell, *A Serious Proposal*, 21.

29. Mary Astell, *The Christian Religion*, 345–46.

30. Mary Astell, *Some Reflections Upon Marriage*, 1706 edition, 3.

31. George Ballard, *Memoirs of Several Ladies of Great Britain Who Have Been Celebrated For Their Writings or Skill in the Learned Languages, Arts and Sciences* (Oxford: W. Jackson, 1752), 445–60.

32. Mary Astell, *The Christian Religion*, 293.

33. See above, n. 20.

Chapter Two: The Coal of Newcastle

1. Astell's family was what W. A. Speck calls "pseudo-gentry," or gentlemen without estates. See W. A. Speck, *Stability and Strife in England, 1714–1760* (Cambridge, Mass.: Harvard University Press, 1979), 37. See the Visitation of Northumberland, 1666, recorded by W. P. Hedley, *Northumberland Families* (Newcastle-upon-Tyne, 1968), 9.

2. See app. C, Letter XXXV (August 12, 1720). The Astell coat of arms was a lion passant guardant or, between an orle of cross crosslets or.

3. *Extracts from the Records of the Company of Hostmen of Newcastle-upon-Tyne*, edited and introduced by F. W. Dendy, Publication of the Surtees Society, vol. 105 (1901): xiii-xiv. This volume, a collection of primary documents from the Newcastle archives, is an invaluable source of information on the coal trade. For the best full-scale treatment of the industry, see J. U. Nef, *The Rise of the British Coal Industry*, 2 vols. (1932; rpt., Freeport, N.Y.: Books for Libraries Press, 1976).

4. F. W. Dendy, ed., *Records of the Company of Hostmen*, 21–22.

5. For the names of these ships, and an inventory of all the rest of Peter Astell's possessions in 1678, see app. A.

6. See Paul M. Sweezy, *Monopoly and Competition in the English Coal Trade* (Cambridge, Mass.: Harvard University Press, 1938).

7. Ralph Gardiner (Gardner), *England's Grievance Discovered in Relation to the Coal Trade* (London, 1655), 22–23. Every chaldron of coal mined and loaded in Newcastle, was taxed. There were twenty-one bolls in a chaldron, a boll being the amount of coal a man could carry with his two hands, in a large bowl or barrow. Ten chaldrons made twenty-one tons. See F. W. Dendy, ed., *Records of the Company of Hostmen*, 39n, 44n.

8. William Jennison was the first governor of the Hostmen and the first mayor of Newcastle; William Jackson acted both as clerk for the town and clerk for the Hostmen. F. W. Dendy, ed., *Records of the Company of Hostmen*, 265.

9. Ibid., xl-xli.

10. Ibid., 43, 51, 63, 67, 72.

11. Edward Hughes, *North Country Life in the Eighteenth Century* (London: Oxford University Press, 1952), 152–56, 45.

12. Ibid. , 11. Edward Wortley, Lady Mary Wortley Montagu's husband, was one of those who used new mining methods and made a fortune in Northumberland coal. Ibid., 163.

13. For example, the keelmen who transported coal on the river originally contracted and combined with the Hostmen or independent fitters to set the price on coal bought from mine owners. But such was the new power of the coal owners in the early eighteenth century that they regulated the activities of the keelmen, and bound them to work for them in advance of the season. Defoe wrote an article about the oppressed Newcastle keelmen in 1711. Edward Hughes, *North Country Life*, 173.

14. Ibid., 118.

15. Ibid., 46.

16. *Records of the Committees for Compounding, etc., with Delinquent Royalists in Durham and Northumberland during the Civil War: 1643–1660*, edited and introduced by Richard Welford, Publication of the Surtees Society, vol. 3 (1905): xiv.

17. Ibid., 188.

18. *Extracts from Newcastle-Upon-Tyne Council Minute Books, 1639–1656*, Publication of the Newcastle Upon Tyne Records Committee, vol. 1 (Newcastle, 1920), December 19, 1645.

19. "Clerke Austell" appears in the records of the Company of Hostmen on January 4, 1646/7. See F. W. Dendy, ed., *Records of the Company of Hostmen*, 248.

20. *Extracts from Newcastle-Upon-Tyne Council Minute Books, 1639–1656*, vol. 1, August 20, 1655.

21. Edward Hughes, *North Country Life*, xvi.

22. Ralph Gardiner, *England's Grievance Discovered*, 86.

23. Ibid., 61–62.

24. Roger Howell, Jr., *Newcastle-upon-Tyne and the Puritan Revolution* (Oxford: Oxford University Press, 1967), 300–301.

25. Ibid., 302.

26. Ralph Gardiner, *England's Grievance Discovered*, 111.

27. Ibid., 70.

28. Ibid., 88.

29. Roger Howell, Jr., *Newcastle-upon-Tyne and the Puritan Revolution*, 304.

30. See Ralph Gardiner, *England's Grievance Discovered*, Plate III, 117. Reproduced here in chap. 2, p. 38.

31. See the list of Newcastle mayors in John Baillie, *An Impartial History of The Town and County of Newcastle upon Tyne* (Newcastle, 1801), 604.

32. F. W. Dendy, ed., *Records of the Company of Hostmen*, 105–6, 248–49; *Hostman Minute Book*, 1655–1741, Tyne and Wear Record Office, Acc. 248/1C and 248/2.

33. F. W. Dendy, ed., *Records of the Company of Hostmen*, 105–6.

34. The Newcastle hearth records for 1666 place Peter Astell in the Nevill Tower Ward and assess his property higher than that of most others in Newcastle. These records are in the Public Record Office, London. Westgate Street, which ran up to Nevill Tower, where St. John's still stands—the Astell family church—was described by John Baillie as "long the residence of the most opulent inhabitants" of Newcastle, in *An Impartial History of the Town and County of Newcastle upon Tyne*, 257.

35. For the complete inventory of Mary Astell's family's house in 1678, when her father died, see app. A.

36. *The English Catholic Nonjurors of 1715*, ed. Edgar E. Estcourt and J. O. Payne (New York: Catholic Publication Society, 1885), 180 (see George Errington), 334 (see Peter Blenkinsopp).

37. Celia Fiennes, *Through England on a Side Saddle in the Time of William and Mary* (London, 1888), 176.

38. *The Life of Ambrose Barnes* (Newcastle, 1828), 4n.

39. R. J. Charleton, *A History of Newcastle-on-Tyne* (London, 189?), 68.

40. Celia Fiennes, *Through England on a Side Saddle*, 175.

41. *An Impartial Enquiry into the Causes of Rebellion and Civil War* (London: R. Wilkin, 1704), 6.

42. John Norris's wife is supposed to have made this remark in a letter to Elizabeth Thomas. *Pylades and Corinna: or Memoirs of the Lives, Amours, and Writings of Richard Gwinnett, Esq. and Mrs. Elizabeth Thomas*, 2 vols. (London: E. Curll, 1732), 1: 104. One of Curll's collections, this book is considered unreliable; still, the sentence about Astell has the ring of truth to it.

43. John Brand, *History and Antiquities of the Town and County of Newcastle-upon-Tyne*, 2 vols. (London: B. White 1789), 2: 86–88.

44. Celia Fiennes, *Through England on a Side Saddle*, 177–78.

45. Richard Welford, *Men of Mark 'Twixt Tine and Tweed*, 3 vols. (Newcastle, 1895), 1: 23.

46. Celia Fiennes, *Through England on a Side Saddle*, 177.

47. M. A. Richardson, *Reprints of Rare Tracts*, 7 vols. (Newcastle, 1843–49), 3: 90.

48. Ibid., 3: 118.

49. Christina Hole, *The English Housewife in the Seventeenth Century* (London: Chatto & Windus, 1953), 168.

50. M. A. Richardson, *Reprints of Rare Tracts*, 3: 64ff., 108.

51. Ibid., 3: 72, 74.

52. Thomas E. Warner, *An Annotated Bibliography of Woodwind Instruction Books 1600–1830*, Detroit Studies in Music Bibliography, no. 11 (Detroit: Information Coordinators, 1967), 1–4.

53. Elstob's letter dated March 7, 1736, confesses to these homely accomplishments. Ballard MSS 43:17. She was born in Newcastle in 1683, and could not have known Mary Astell there, but met her later in London. That both these remarkable, scholarly women came from Newcastle suggests an unusually intellectual atmosphere in that city—perhaps a function of the Royal Grammar School.

54. These elaborate processes began with sprouting the malt or whatever grain was used, and then grinding it and mashing it with boiling water. The liquid "wort" was drawn off into copper pans where hops were added and the whole transferred to a working-vat to ferment with yeast. For March beer, peas, wheat, and oats were mixed with the malt before brewing. Small beer—which is what Astell drank—was the second brewing from the mash after the strong liquor had been poured off. They made ale similarly, except that oak leaves and branches were put in before adding the hops. Christina Hole, *The English Housewife in the Seventeenth Century*, 109.

55. John Baillie, *An Impartial History of the Town and County of Newcastle upon Tyne*, 294.

56. John Brand, *History and Antiquities of the Town and County of Newcastle-upon-Tyne*, 2:90.

57. Ralph Astell, *Vota, Non Bella* "New-Castle's Heartie Gratulation to her Sacred Soveraign King Charles the Second; On His Now-Glorious Restauration To His Birthright-Power" (Gateshead, 1660), 12. St. George in this poem is the Tory general George Monck (duke of Albemarle), hero of Northumberland, whose military strength and sage diplomacy helped set Charles II on the throne.

58. C. A. Patrides, ed., *The Cambridge Platonists* (Cambridge, Mass.: Harvard University Press, 1970), 1, 138 n.42.

59. Blaise Pascal, *Pensées*, trans. W. F. Trotter (New York: E. P. Dutton, 1958), 23, #77.

60. C. A. Patrides, ed., *The Cambridge Platonists*, 10.

61. Ibid., 17.

62. Ibid., 32, 221.

63. Mary Astell, *Letters Concerning the Love of God*, 26.

64. C. A. Patrides, ed., *The Cambridge Platonists*, 14.

65. Letter dated January 4, 1746. Stowe MSS 753:61–62.

66. Common Council Book of Newcastle on Tyne, January 18, 1674, f. 136.

67. These figures, which corroborate those of David Cressy (see n. 5, chap. 1), are calculated on the basis of signatures in court records. According to Sara Mendelson, female literacy cannot be judged only by an ability to write, for "it was a widespread practice to teach girls to read but not to write." See her "Stuart Women's Diaries" in *Women in English Society 1500–1800*, ed. Mary Prior (London: Methuen, 1985), esp. 182–83. There was a strong tradition of philanthropic endowment of educational establishments in the North of England. This fact, combined with the Protestant emphasis on reading scripture, and a tradition of later marriages and therefore fewer children, yielded a population more given to literacy than historians have traditionally recognized. Especially for those involved in commercial growth, as the Astells were, literacy rose steeply in the later seventeenth century. See R. A. Houston, "The Development of Literacy: Northern England 1640–1750," *Economic History Review*, 2d ser. 35, no. 2 (May 1982): 199–216.

68. R. J. Charleton, *A History of Newcastle*, 105–6.

Chapter Three: The Self-Respect of a Reasoning Creature

1. Christina Hole, *The English Housewife in the Seventeenth Century* (London: Chatto & Windus, 1953), 223ff.

2. The Hostmen Minute Book, Acc. 248/2 fol. 323. His father, William Astell, earned forty shillings as bailiff for the manor of Wickham, another forty shillings as clerk to the bailiff of Gateshead, and £6 13s. 4d. as clerk to the coroners of Newcastle (plus the fees customarily taken in those positions). See *Extracts from the Records of the Company of Hostmen of Newcastle-upon-Tyne*, edited and introduced by F. W. Dendy, Publication of the Surtees Society, vol. 105 (1901): 249–50; Minute Book of the Common Council 1656–1722, fols. 15, 16.

3. For the inventory of Peter Astell's possessions, see app. A.

4. John Baillie, *An Impartial History of the Town and County of Newcastle upon Tyne* (Newcastle, 1801), 494; Edward Hughes, *North Country Life in the Eighteenth Century* (London: Oxford University Press, 1952), 44.

5. The Reverend John Hodgson claims to have seen a letter dated Bellister 7, May 1667, from "George Blenkynsopp" to his "loving nephew Mr. Peter Astell." *The History of Northumberland*, 7 vols. (Newcastle, 1820–58), 3: 349. On October 26, 1665, George Errington posted a bond of marriage for Peter Astell, gent., and Mary Errington, sp., according to the St. John's parish records. Among the Durham Probate Records on deposit at the University of Durham is an entry listed under Peter Astell, 1678, for a bond for tuition (meaning guardianship rather than formal education) which no longer survives, for his two children, both legally considered underage (twelve years old or less).

6. Edward Hughes, *North Country Life in the Eighteenth Century*, 46.

7. The Hostman Minute Book, Tyne and Wear Record Office, Acc. 248/2 fols. 340, 359.

8. The Hostman Minute Book, Acc. 248/47: "and to old Mrs. Astell the company ordered £3 6s. 8d. paid annually, during the companies pleasure." See also F. W. Dendy, ed., *Records of the Company of Hostmen*, 251.

9. The Hostman Minute Book, Acc. 248/2: fol. 350.

10. According to the St. John's parish register, Mary Astell's mother was buried on April 18, 1695. Her aunt, also registered as Mrs. Mary Astell, was buried October 10, 1684. For the Astell family tree, as recorded in the heraldic visitation of 1666, see E. MacKenzie, *A Descriptive and Historical Account of Newcastle-on-Tyne*, 2 vols. (Newcastle, 1827), 1: 347–48.

11. The Hostman Minute Book, Acc. 248/2: fols. 365, 372, 381, 388, 401.

12. It cost about £160 a year to keep a law student at the Middle Temple. Edward Hughes, *North Country Life in the Eighteenth Century*, 82.

13. Ibid., 78–79.

14. According to demographers, this was the average age of menstruation for women in the seventeenth century, and it is conceivable that—given her circumstances—this sign of her procreativity was unwelcome to her at this time. For statistics on the average age of menstruation, see Peter Laslett, *The World We Have Lost* (New York: Charles Scribner's Sons, 1965), 82–84.

15. For this entire poem, "Enemies," see p. ooo, app. D. See also "The Invitation," "Solitude," and "Death." The central idea of this poem, that one should love one's enemies because they are more truthful about one's faults than friends (a sentiment she expressed often), can be found in the writings of the Cambridge Platonists, especially in Benjamin Whichcote's aphorism no. 755: "If I have not a Friend, God send me an Enemy: that I may hear of my *Faults*. To be admonished of an Enemy is *next* to having a friend."

16. When her grandfather, William Astell, died in 1658, his will went through the probate court of Canterbury although he was buried in Newcastle; this indicates that there were holdings in London.

17. John Sykes, *Local Records*, 2 vols. (Newcastle, 1865), 1: 132; Edward Hughes, *North Country Life in the Eighteenth Century*, 391. The announcement in the *Newcastle Courant* of October 1712, for the Edinburgh-London express was as follows: "Edinburgh, Berwick, Newcastle, Durham, and London stage-coach begins on Monday the 13th October, 1712. All that desire to pass from

Edinbro' to London, or from London to Edinbro', or any place on that road, let them repair to Mr. John Baillie's, at the Coach and Horses, at the Head of the Cannongate, Edinbro', every other Saturday, or to the Black Swan, in Holborn, every other Monday at both of which places they may be received in a Stage-Coach, which performs the whole journey in thirteen days without any stoppage (if God permit), having eighty able horses to perform the whole stage. Each passenger 20 lbs. weight, and all above to pay 6*d.* per pound. The coach sets off at six in the morning. Performed by Henry Harrison, Nich. Speighl, Robt. Garbe, Rich. Croft." By 1754, it took six days to travel from Newcastle to London. Roger Hart, *English Life in the Eighteenth Century* (New York: Putnam, 1970), 51.

18. Reverend John King's MSS history of Chelsea, deposited in the Chelsea Public Library, 153.

19. J. Bowack, *The Antiquities of Middlesex*, 2 vols. (London, 1705–6), 1: 13.

20. Mary Astell, *The Christian Religion*, 348.

21. Irvin Ehrenpreis, *Swift the Man, His Works, and the Age*, 3 vols. (London: Methuen, 1962–84), 1: 126–31. For an example of a poem acknowledging Archbishop Sancroft's kindness, see Rawlinson MSS 100:80.

22. Undated letter in MS Rawlinson Letters 59:89.

23. MS Rawlinson Poet 154:51. For my two published notices of these poems see "A Seventeenth-Century Feminist Poet," *Times Literary Supplement*, 29 August 1982, p. 911, and "Mary Astell's Poetry," *Tulsa Studies in Women's Literature* 1 (1982): 201–2.

24. See "This Day Published" in *The London Evening Post*, March 29, 1730. Also Terry Belanger, "Booksellers' Sales of Copyright/Aspects of the London Book Trade: 1718–1768" (Ph.D. diss., Columbia University, 1970), 16, 205–6.

25. John Dunton, *Life and Errors* (London, 1705), 314.

26. Auction catalogue of William Parker's stock dated March 1749 in the John Johnson Collection of the Bodleian Library, Oxford.

27. Mary Astell, *Some Reflections Upon Marriage*, 1706 edition, preface, 22.

28. For a fuller discussion of the implications of Cartesianism for the liberation of women, see my "Radical Doubt and the Liberation of Women," *Eighteenth-Century Studies* 18, no. 4 (Summer 1985), 472–94. These ideas are also discussed in Joan Kinnaird, *Mary Astell and the Conservative Contribution to English Feminism*, and Hilda Smith, *Reason's Disciples*.

29. Behn's remarks are appended to Fontenelle's text in *An Essay on Translated Prose*. The complete 1700 edition is in the Houghton Library at Harvard: Bernard Le Bovier de Fontenelle, *The Theory or System of Several New Inhabited Worlds Lately Discover'd and Pleasantly Describ'd, in Five Nights Conversation with Madam the Marchioness of* * * * * (London, 1700).

30. Keith Thomas, "Women and the Civil War Sects," *Past and Present* 13 (April 1958): 42–62.

31. The period of *les précieuses* culminated in the takeover by the Fronde, that uneasy coalition of aristocrats and parliamentarians who opposed the absolute power of the monarch.

For women's participation in the French Revolution, see Darlene Levy, Harriet Branson Applewhite, and Mary Durham Johnson, *Women in Revolutionary Paris, 1789–95* (Illinois University Press: Urbana, 1979).

32. For a fine discussion of the discrepancy between the development and enunciation of individualism in the seventeenth century and the rights of women in that period, see Susan Moller Okin, "Women and the Making of the Sentimental Family," in *Philosophy and Public Affairs* 11, no. 1 (Winter 1982): 65–88. One piece of evidence of the new interest in "the woman question" in the 1690s was the reissuing of Joseph Swetnam's *The Arraignment of Lewd, Idle, Forward, and Unconstant Women* (1615), a much reprinted misogynist satire which had originally called forth Ester Sowerman's defense of women, *Ester hath hang'd Haman; or, An Answere to a lewd Pamphlet, entituled, The Arraignment of Women* (1617). Swetnam's satire went through fourteen editions soon after its initial publication in 1615, and was revived along with the responses to it, in the flurry of feminist controversy of the 1690s.

Hilda Smith notes in *Reason's Disciples*, 15, that this "turn-of-the-century feminism was to fade when faced with eighteenth-century values that embraced sentimentality and feeling rather than reason."

33. For the contradictions in her thought, and her counter-Enlightenment tendencies, see my "Mary Astell's Response to the Enlightenment," in the special issue on Women and the Enlightenment of *Women in History*, 9 (Spring 1984): 13–40.

34. Marie Louise Stock, "Poullain [sic] de La Barre: "A Seventeenth-Century Feminist" (Ph.D. diss., Columbia University, 1961), 169–82. Two other excellent articles that connect Poulain de la Barre's work to English feminism of the 1690s are Joan Kinnaird's "Mary Astell and the Conservative Contribution to English Feminism" and Michael Seidel, "Poulain de la Barre's *The Woman As Good As the Man*," *Journal of the History of Ideas* 35, no. 3 (July-September 1974): 499–508. Hilda Smith also cites his influence in *Reason's Disciples*, 116–17, as does Moira Ferguson, *First Feminists*, 266–67. The French debate about *De l'égalité des deux sexes* (1673) is documented in Rae Blanchard, "Richard Steele and the Status of Women," esp. 328–30.

35. Mary Astell, *The Christian Religion*, 9.

36. The French edition of 1690 of *De l'égalité des deux sexes* rather than the earlier English translation of 1677 apparently had most influence across the channel. It caused quite a stir in Paris, and in 1692 and 1693 parts of it were exported to London by a French Huguenot named Pierre Motteux. Astell might have read these translations of Poulain de la Barre in the *Gentleman's Journal* or the *Ladies Journal*. She was living in London at the time, attracting attention as that curiosity "a learned woman," engaged in a learned correspondence with Norris, and already concerned with the ignorance and lassitude in which the generality of her sex seemed to be caught.

37. These correspondences, and that of Norris with Lady Mary Chudleigh, Elizabeth Thomas, and Lady Damaris Masham; both Locke and Stillingfleet with Elizabeth Berkeley Burnet; and John Evelyn with Margaret Blagge Go-

dolphin, etc. are discussed more fully in my "Radical Doubt and the Liberation of Women."

38. Mary Astell and John Norris, *Letters Concerning the Love of God*, 1–2.

39. Ibid., 3.

40. John Norris, *An Account of Reason and Faith: In Relation to the Mysteries of Christianity* (1697), as cited in Gerald R. Cragg, ed., *The Cambridge Platonists* (New York: Oxford University Press, 1968), 152.

41. Mary Astell, *A Serious Proposal Part II*, 82–83.

42. Malebranche's exposition of his idealist philosophy can be found in *Entretiens sur la Métaphysique* (1687). His earlier work, *Recherche de la Vérité* (1674–78) is really more a method and an exposition of psychology. Two excellent recent secondary sources on Malebranche's philosophy are Charles J. McCracken, *Malebranche and English Philosophy* (Oxford: Oxford University Press, 1983), and Beatrice K. Rome, *The Philosophy of Malebranche* (Chicago: Henry Regnery, 1963), the latter with an excellent bibliography. For Malebranche's influence on John Norris, see Flora Isabel MacKinnon, "The Philosophy of John Norris of Bemerton," *The Philosophical Monographs* 1, no. 2 (October 1910), and John Hoyles, *The Waning of the Renaissance, 1640–1740* (The Hague: Martinus Nijhoff, 1971). For Norris's relation to the Cambridge Platonists, see Frederick J. Powicke's *A Dissertation on John Norris of Bemerton* (London: George Philip and Son, 1894) and *The Cambridge Platonists* (Cambridge, Mass.: Harvard University Press, 1926). For an introduction to the continuities and variations among the Cambridge Platonists as a philosophical movement, see John H. Muirhead, *The Platonic Tradition in Anglo-Saxon Philosophy* (New York: Macmillan, 1931); Ernst Cassirer, *The Platonic Renaissance in England*, trans. James P. Pettegrove (New York: Thomas Nelson and Sons, 1953); and the selected bibliography in C. A. Patrides, ed., *The Cambridge Platonists* (Cambridge, Mass.: Harvard University Press, 1969).

43. Mary Astell and John Norris, *Letters Concerning the Love of God*, 134, 101.

44. Ibid., 149. She subsequently taught herself French.

45. Nicholas Malebranche, *Recherche de la Vérité*, bk. 2, pt. 2, chap. 1, in *Oeuvres de Malebranche* (Paris: Charpentier, 1853), 171–76. I am indebted to G. S. Rousseau for calling this passage to my attention.

46. Mary Astell and John Norris, *Letter Concerning the Love of God*, 278–82.

47. See "Remarks Upon Some of Mr. Norris' Books, etc." (1693), in *The Works of John Locke*, 10 vols. (London, 1812), 10: 249.

48. John Norris's Preface to *Letters Concerning the Love of God*.

49. Mary Astell, *A Serious Proposal Part II*, 233.

50. Mary Astell, *A Serious Proposal*, 79–81.

51. Mary Astell, *A Serious Proposal Part II*, 286–87.

52. Mary Astell, *A Serious Proposal*, 34–35.

53. Mary Astell, *A Serious Proposal Part II*, 287–88.

54. Mary Astell and John Norris, *Letters Concerning the Love of God*, 78.

55. Ibid., 146–47.

56. Ibid., 52.

57. Ibid., 101.

58. Mary Astell, *A Serious Proposal*, 85.

59. Mary Astell, *A Serious Proposal Part II*, 21–22.

60. I reproduce here Norris's entire letter to Elizabeth Thomas to demonstrate his views on education.

Madam,

Since we are rational Creatures, whose greatest Happiness consists in the perfect Contemplation of Truth and Love of Good, I think it concerns us most to apply our Thoughts to those Things that tend to the Improvement of our Reason, and to the Regulation of our Manners. The former as our best Learning, and the latter as our best Wisdom. As for what the World calls Learning, which consists rather in the Furniture of the Memory, and Force of the Imagination (such as Knowledge of Matters of Fact, History, Languages, great Reading, etc.) than in any clear intellectual Sight of Things, though I do not exclude, yet I would not much commend it, as not understanding the great Value of it, or how it contributes to the Accomplishment of a reasonable Soul, whose greatest Learning must needs lie in the most perfect Habit of Thinking, and whose best Study must consequently be that, which best serves to give her that Perfection. In Order to which, the first Thing you should regularly do, is to apply yourself to *Geometry* (in which I am glad to hear you have had some little Initiation) as being the Foundation of the rest, and that which will qualify and prepare your Mind for the Contemplation of any Truth, and for the profitable reading of any Books. Among which the first I would commend to you, is *L'Art de Penser*, both for the Value of the Book, and the Subject it treats of, which is *Logic*. The next that I would have you *read*, shall I say, or *study*, as that which lays the *Foundation* of all *Science*, and will best conduct and methodize your Thoughts, is *Malebranche's Recherche de la Vérité*. This, I say, I would commend next, but that in Order to your reading him with Pleasure or Advantage, it is absolutely necessary you should understand the *Cartesian* Philosophy, whereof *Malebranche* is a Superstructure and Improvement. *Descartes* therefore you must next undertake (after some Competency in the Principles of common *Geometry*) beginning at his *Metaphysical Meditations*, thence proceeding to his *Principles*, and after that as you please in the rest of his Works. When you understand *Descartes* thoroughly, read One or Two of the best *Cartesians*, such as *Robault* and *Regis*, and by that time, and truly not well sooner, you will be fit to undertake *Malebranche*, whom when you have made your own, you will be able to direct your self in all your farther Progress. Only there are a few Books, which I would put into your Hands, some for *Science*, some for *Entertainment*, and some for *Practice*. I shall only mention them, leaving you to range them under their distinct respective Heads as you come to read them. A late *French* Treatise of the *Knowledge of One's Self*, in four Volumes, a most excellent Book. Poiret's *Cogitationes Rationales*, and his *L'Oeconomie Divine*, a great and noble System. The *Port Royal's* Morality of the New Testament. The *Moral Essays* of Monsieur *Nicole*. Dr. *More's Ethics*, his

Immortality of the Soul, his *Mystery of Godliness*, and his *Philosophical Poems*. Burnet's *Theory*. Dr. Nichols's *Conference with a Theist*. *Wilkins* of *Natural Religions*. Dr. *Allestree's Sermons*, not so much for their Exactness, as for the Natural Flame of Wit, and Spirit of Devotion that shines in them. Dr. Scot's *Christian Life*. The *Country Parson's Advice to his Parishioners*, a plain, but very good Book, written with great Judgment and Consideration. *Mr. Locke of Understanding*, is a Book you should read, and may with great Advantage; but I would not have you read it yet, and when you do; it must be with *due Caution* and *Circumspection*. I might be more large, but I consider your Capacity, and am loth to charge you with too much at once. These, I think, may serve for the present, and for some of them, there will be a Necessity of a Language or two, *Latin* is more difficult, and *French* will now answer all, which therefore I would have you learn out of Hand. It is the most commanding, and therefore most useful Language at present, and *Malebranche* alone will abundantly reward all the Pains you shall take in it, which need not be great neither, if omitting the tedious Way of learning the *Grammar*, you only read over twice or thrice the *Particles*, next the *Verbs*, and then proceed to go over the *Dialogues*, and after that any plain Book with a Translation, by which Way you may be Mistress of *French* so far, as to read a Book by the Help of a Dictionary, in a Month's time. I speak upon Experience, and would have you try. And so I pray God to bless and prosper your Studies, and to make you Wise here, and Happy hereafter.

    I *am*, Madam,
      Your sincere Friend,
        and very humble Servant,
        J. Norris
Bemerton, July 12

Richard Gwinnett and Elizabeth Thomas, *The Honourable Lovers or Pylades and Corinna*, 2: 202–5.

61. Antoine Arnauld, *The Art of Thinking*, trans. with introduction by James Dickoff and Patricia James (Indianapolis: Bobbs-Merrill, 1964), Note on the Translation, lx.

62. Ibid., lv. The words are quoted from Charles Perrault, *Antoine Arnauld, Doctor of the Sorbonne* (1696).

63. Antoine Arnauld, *The Art of Thinking*, 7.

64. Mary Astell, *A Serious Proposal Part II*, 26–27.

65. Ibid., 132.

66. Astell suggested that her readers peruse the section on "particles" in Locke's *Essay*, bk. 3.

67. These steps were: (1) define the questions and the terms, (2) weed out all issues which are not directly connected to the matter under consideration, (3) proceed in an orderly fashion, (4) examine every aspect of the subject and subdivide the question into as many parts as is necessary for perfect understanding, (5) judge no farther than you perceive, taking nothing for truth that has not been proved.

68. The Port Royal Grammar and the Port Royal Logic were the first theoretical statements about language and thought to embody what Noam Chomsky has called a "Cartesian" approach to linguistics, an understanding of language as reflective of some basic human cognitive structures. Chomsky, of course, sees the Port Royal movement as a forerunner of his own brand of linguistics. This school first assumed a universal, underlying structure to the human mind, and recognized that all minds are created more or less equal, since language use and creative capability are a "common human endowment." This premise—that every human being had the same basic intellectual equipment—corroborated Mary Astell's instinct about the matter, and led her to the formulated Port Royal rules for rigorous thought. See Noam Chomsky, *Cartesian Linguistics* (New York and London: Harper & Row, 1966), 29.

69. Mary Astell, *A Serious Proposal Part II*, 106–7.

70. Mary Astell, *A Serious Proposal*, 109–10.

71. Ibid., 110.

72. Ibid., 49–51.

73. Mary Astell, *A Serious Proposal Part II*, 86.

74. Ibid., 199–200.

75. For the relationship between John Locke and Damaris Masham, see Sheryl O'Donnell, "Mr. Locke and the Ladies," *Studies in Eighteenth-Century Culture* 8 (1978): 151–64; and " 'My Idea in Your Mind': John Locke and Damaris Cudworth Masham," in *Mothering the Mind*, ed. Ruth Perry and Martine Brownley (New York: Holmes & Meier, 1984); and George Ballard, *Memoirs of Several Ladies of Great Britain* (Oxford, 1752), 379–89.

76. Damaris Masham, *Discourse Concerning the Love of God*, 27. Although Lady Masham never cites Astell's name or refers to the fact that her other adversary is a woman, both of Masham's books—*A Discourse Concerning the Love of God* in 1696 and *Occasional Thoughts in Reference to a Vertuous or Christian Life* in 1705—were written in response to books of Astell's.

77. Mary Astell, *The Christian Religion*, 82.

78. Ibid., 138.

79. Ibid., 131–36.

80. Damaris Masham, *Discourse Concerning the Love of God*, 54.

81. Mary Astell, *The Christian Religion*, 146.

82. Ibid., 130–31. She refers, of course, to bk. 2, chap. 8, pars. 13, 14, 15, and 16 in Locke's *Essay Concerning Human Understanding*.

83. Mary Astell, *The Christian Religion*, 140.

84. Ibid., 148–49.

85. John Locke, *The Reasonableness of Christianity* (London, 1695), 287–88.

86. Mary Astell, *The Christian Religion*, 295.

87. John Locke, *The Reasonableness of Christianity*, 279.

88. Ibid., 302.

89. Mary Astell, *The Christian Religion*, 399–400.

90. Ibid., 402–3.

91. Ibid., 135. For a fuller exposition of this doctrine and Astell's political beliefs, see below, chap. 7.

92. Ibid., 134.

93. Ibid., 68. John Redwood's *Reason, Ridicule, and Religion* (Cambridge, Mass.: Harvard University Press, 1976) chronicles the widespread fear of atheism in Astell's period, the contemporary view of the threat to Christianity posed by Locke, Newton, Shaftesbury, et al., and the desire to protect "the church in danger." Without knowing anything about Astell, Redwood cites a number of her anonymous works as typical of the political and religious resistance to the "new way of ideas." See, e.g., pp. 20 and 183.

94. John Locke, *An Essay Concerning Human Understanding*, 5th ed. (London: George Routledge and Sons, n.d.), 458n.

95. Mary Astell, *The Christian Religion*, 256–60.

96. Ibid., 261. Margaret Wilson has also observed that Locke's notion of superadded properties in the correspondence with Stillingfleet is a creative departure from the principles of the *Essay*. Margaret D. Wilson, "Superadded Properties: The Limits of Mechanism in Locke," *American Philosophical Quarterly* 16 (April 1979): 143–50. I am indebted to Edwin W. McCann for this reference.

97. Damaris Masham, *Occasional Thoughts in Reference to a Vertuous or a Christian Life* (London, 1705), 199.

Chapter Four: *A Serious Proposal to the Ladies*

1. The anonymous "Mary Astell: A Seventeenth-Century Advocate for Women," *Westminster Review* 149 (April 1898): 440–49 refers to Mary Astell as a feminist forerunner; a review of Charlotte Perkins [Gilman] in the *Englishwoman's Review* (October 16, 1899) compares Astell at the close of the seventeenth century to Wollstonecraft at the close of the eighteenth century, and to Perkins [Gilman] at the close of the nineteenth century.

2. Letter from Lady C. Schomberg to Lady Elizabeth Hastings, July 13, 1706, reprinted in *Hastings Wheler Family Letters*, 2 vols. (Wakefield: privately printed, 1929 and 1935), 2: 18.

3. John Evelyn, *Numismata, or, a Discourse Concerning Medals* (London, 1697), 265.

4. See John Dunton, *The Life and Errors of John Dunton*, 2 vols. (London: J. Nichols, Son, and Bentley, 1818), 1: 293; *The Athenian Oracle*, 3d ed. (London, 1728), 1: 382.

5. *The Challenge, Sent by a Young Lady to Sir Thomas . . . or, The Female Warr* (London, 1697), 53.

6. *Ralph Thoresby*, ed. Rev. Joseph Hunter, 2 vols. (London: Henry Colburn and Richard Bentley, 1830), 2: 161. On Richard Steele's borrowing from Astell, see below, chap. 7, n. 83.

7. Richard Gwinnett and Elizabeth Thomas, *The Honourable Lovers or Pylades and Corinna*, 2d ed., 2 vols. (London: E. Curll, 1736), 1: 95.

8. Terry Eagleton speaks of Richardson's novels as "feminizing" the cultural discourse of eighteenth-century England. *The Rape of Clarissa* (Minneapolis: University of Minnesota Press, 1982), 13–17.

Sarah Chapone, a member of the circle of mid-century "bluestockings" and a friend of Richardson's, admired Astell and owned a number of her books. When advising George Ballard about his sketch of Mary Astell, Sarah Chapone recommended (and lent him) her book of Astell's correspondence with Norris— *Letters Concerning the Love of God*—which she considered Astell's most sublime work. See letter to George Ballard dated March 12, 1742, Ballard MSS 43:132.

For Sir Charles Grandison's exposition of the "Protestant nunnery scheme" in Richardson's novel, see Samuel Richardson, *The History of Sir Charles Grandison* (1753–54), ed. Jocelyn Harris, 3 vols. (Oxford: Oxford University Press, 1972), 2: 355–56. Professor Harris's excellent paper "Samuel Richardson, Mary Astell, and the Protestant Nunnery," presented at the April 1979 American Society for Eighteenth-Century Studies meetings in Atlanta, Georgia, argues that the plan was derived from Mary Astell's *A Serious Proposal*. See also A. H. Upham, "A Parallel for Richardson's *Clarissa*," *Modern Language Notes* 28 (1913): 103–5.

9. See, for example, the letter from Hickes to Dr. Charlett dated December 9, 1704, Ballard MSS 62:85. Chapter 7 contains a more detailed discussion of Astell's position on the Occasional Conformity controversy.

10. John Walker, *An Attempt Towards Recovering an Account of the Numbers and Suffering of the Clergy of the Church of England* (London, 1714), pt. 2, p. 177a. A letter from James Yonge to John Walker attributes to Astell still another pamphlet in 1704 entitled *Remarks on Part of Calamys Book*, but I have not been able to locate a copy. Yonge writes: "Among Astell's writings of party, there is one called Remarks on part of Calamys book, and I find In her '*Moderation truly stated*' she falls close on him several times." Letter dated June 25 [no year]. John Walker MSS c.2:46.

11. Mary Astell, *A Serious Proposal*, 11, 7–8.

12. Mary Astell, *A Serious Proposal II*, 214–15. Tony Tanner's Introduction to the Penguin edition of *Mansfield Park* stresses Fanny's old-fashioned values, and the way they recall the England of an earlier time.

13. Mary Astell, *A Serious Proposal*, 14–15; *A Serious Proposal Part II*, 103.

14. Mary Astell, *A Serious Proposal II*, 35–36; *The Christian Religion*, 36. The Introduction to *A Serious Proposal Part II* is probably the most vivid, sustained, and concentrated example of "consciousness-raising" in Astell's works. Her task there is to convince her female readers that they are capable of learning to think rigorously and should apply themselves to that end.

15. Myra Reynolds, *The Learned Lady in England, 1650–1760*, 1–4; C. S. Bremner, *Education of Girls and Women in Great Britain* (London, 1897), 5; Eileen Power, *Medieval Women*, ed. M. M. Postan (Cambridge: Cambridge University Press, 1975), 81. Thomas Rawlins notes that Laura Bassi, in May 1732,

was given a Doctor of Philosophy degree with the usual formality in an Italian university after being "very strictly examined in several points of Philosophy to which she answered with such uncommon learning that she won universal applause." He mentions a similar case in France a hundred years earlier. Letter dated November 14, 1741, Ballard MSS 41:198. Queen Isabella of Spain included in her retinue a female professor of rhetoric from the University of Salamanca.

16. Myra Reynolds, *The Learned Lady in England 1650–1760*, 5–6. Among the treatises encouraged by Catherine were Dr. Lynacre's *Rudiments of Grammar* and Juan Luis Vives's *De Ratione Studii* and *De Institutione Faeminae Christiannae* (published in 1540 in Richard Hyrde's translation as *The Instruction of A Christian Woman*). See Foster Watson, *Vives and The Renascence Education of Women* (London: Longmans, Green, 1912), 11.

17. Quoted in Myra Reynolds, *The Learned Lady in England, 1650–1760*, 292–93. According to the figures reported by David Cressy, 82 percent of the women in the Norwich and London dioceses between 1660 and 1700 were illiterate, i.e. unable to sign their names. Using court depositions as his evidence—a method which may have its own bias—he writes: "By the 1690s female illiteracy in London had been reduced to 52 percent ± 6 percent, while it lingered around 80 percent in the provinces." The comparable figure for men, roughly, was 30 percent illiteracy. "Literacy in Seventeenth-Century England: More Evidence," *Journal of Interdisciplinary History* 8 (Summer 1977): 141–50. See also n. 67, chap. 2. For comprehensive treatments of the subject of women's education in England, see Dorothy Gardiner, *English Girlhood at School; A Study of Women's Education Through Twelve Centuries* (London: Oxford University Press, 1929), and Josephine Kamm, *Hope Deferred* (London: Methuen, 1965). There are also good chapters on women's education during this period in Jean Gagen, *The New Woman: Her Emergence in English Drama, 1600–1730* (New York, 1954) and in Roger Thompson, *Women in Stuart England and America* (London: Routledge, Kegan Paul, 1974).

18. Historical Manuscript Commission, *Hastings MSS*, 4 vols. 1928–34, 228/225; *Hastings Wheler Family Letters*, 1: 24.

19. Ibid., 1: 46.

20. Thomas More's daughters had been renowned for their learning; he had engaged tutors to teach all of them Latin, Greek, music, philosophy, astronomy, and mathematics. Margaret, his beloved eldest daughter, was famed for her Greek and Latin translations and compositions, her grasp of classical philosophy, and her sound and steady judgment. And there is the story of Margaret Griggs, an orphaned kinswoman sharing the blessings of this household, who one day when Sir Thomas felt flushed by the curious and uncomfortable sensation of being simultaneously too hot and too cold, was able to diagnose his illness and show him the apposite passage in Galen. Erasmus, who knew the family well, had been so impressed by these young women that he wrote a treatise defending women's education, *The Abbot and The Learned Women*.

Music was one of the accomplishments thought suitable for young ladies in the late seventeenth century, and though D'Urfey paints Josiah Priest's school as a cultural wasteland, Purcell was a friend of the headmaster, and in 1689 composed his opera *Dido and Aeneas* for the girls to perform for friends and family on visiting day. Randall Davies, *The Greatest House at Chelsey* (London: John Lane, 1914), 90–93; Josephine Kamm, *Hope Deferred*, 73. For the details of life and education of More's oldest daughter, Margaret, see E. E. Reynolds, *Margaret Roper* (New York: P. J. Kennedy & Sons, 1960).

21. Hilda Smith, *Reason's Disciples* (Urbana, Ill.: University of Illinois Press, 1982), 23. See also Lawrence Stone, ed. *The University in Society*, 2 vols. (Princeton, N.J.: Princeton University Press, 1974), 1: 19, 21–46. For a discussion of the scale of growth and the shifts in social distribution of education in England between 1560 and 1640—with cultural effects well into the 1690s—see Lawrence Stone's "The Educational Revolution in England, 1560–1640," *Past and Present* (July 1964), 41–81.

22. This point is made in Hilda Smith, *Reason's Disciples*, xi. See also Ruth Perry, *Women, Letters, and The Novel* (New York: AMS Press, 1980), esp. chap. 2, and Alice Clark, *Working Life of Women in the Seventeenth Century* (1919; reprint ed., London, 1968).

23. Mary Astell, *A Serious Proposal*, 159–61.

24. Although bibliographers still occasionally attribute this book to Mary Astell, she did not write it. See Florence M. Smith, *Mary Astell* (New York: Columbia University Press, 1916), app. 2, 173–82.

25. Judith Drake wrote with energy on behalf of her sex, and in this, if not in the content of her argument, she was a disciple of Astell's. She seems not to have written again after her *Essay in Defense of the Female Sex*. She apparently practiced medicine, possibly learned from or with her brother James Drake, who was a doctor. (His verse eulogy of her appears at the front of her book.) In 1723 she was summoned before Sir Hans Sloane to defend herself from charges of medical malpractice. In that exchange she claimed that she had been practicing for years and had prescribed medicines often enough before, and that her accuser had only raised a clamor when she asked for payment, when she was so "Extravagantly blind as to value my due above his Friendship." J. Drake to Sir Hans Sloane, Add. MSS 4047:38. *A Farther Essay Relating To The Female Sex* (1696) does not come from the same hand. It is a translation of Madame de Pringy's *Les differens caractères des femmes du siècle . . . Contenant six caractères et six perfection* (1694) according to Rae Blanchard, "Richard Steele and the Status of Women," *Studies in Philology* 27 (1929): 325–55.

26. Sir Charles Chudleigh succeeded to his father's title in 1691. For the anagram and other information about Lady Chudleigh I am indebted to Joanna Lipking, who discussed Astell's influence on Lady Chudleigh in a paper at the Modern Language Association meetings in December 1978. Here is the text of *To Almystrea* in full:

To Almystrea

1.

Permit Marissa in an artless Lay
    To speak her Wonder, and her Thanks repay:
Her creeping Muse can ne'er like yours ascend;
She has not Strength for such a towring Flight.
Your Wit, her humble Fancy do's transcend;
She can but gaze at your exalted Height:
Yet she believ'd it better to expose
        Her Failures, than ungrateful prove;
        And rather chose
To shew a want of Sense, than want of Love:
But taught by you, she may at length improve,
And imitate those Virtues she admires.
Your bright Example leaves a Tract Divine,
She sees a beamy Brightness in each Line,
And with ambitious Warmth aspires,
Attracted by the Glory of your Name,
To follow you in all the lofty Roads of Fame.

2.

Merit like yours, can no Resistance find,
But like a Deluge overwhelms the Mind;
        Gives full Possession of each Part,
Subdues the Soul, and captivates the Heart.
Let those whom Wealth, or Interest unite,
        Whom Avarice, or Kindred sway
        Who in the Dregs of Life delight;
And ev'ry Dictate of their Sense obey,
Learn here to love at a sublimer Rate,
To wish for nothing but exchange of Thoughts,
        For intellectual Joys,
        And Pleasures more refin'd
Than Earth can give, or Fancy can create.
Let our vain Sex be fond of glitt'ring Toys,
Of pompous Titles, and affected Noise,
Let envious Men by barb'rous Custom led
        Descant on Faults,
        And in Detraction find
Delights unknown to a brave gen'rous Mind,
While we resolve a nobler Path to tread,
        And from Tyrannick Custom free,

> View the dark Mansions of the mighty Dead,
> And all their close Recesses see;
> Then from those awful Shades retire,
> And take a Tour above,
> And there, the shining Scenes admire,
> Th' Opera of eternal Love;
> View the Machines, on the bright Actors gaze,
> Then in a holy Transport, blest Amaze,
> To the great Author our Devotion raise,
> And let our Wonder terminate in Praise.

27. Another pamphlet which defended women from Mr. Sprint's peremptory precepts, *The Female Advocate* (1700), was dedicated to "Mrs. W—ley" by Eugenia, "a Lady of Quality." Subtitled "A Plea for the just Liberty of the Tender Sex, and particularly of Married Women," it acknowledged Astell's influence explicitly and implicitly: "In a word, Ladies, I would recommend to your Thoughts something that is great and noble, viz. to furnish your Minds with true Knowledg, that (as an Ingenious Lady tells us) you may know something more than a well-chosen Petticoat, or a fashionable Commode. Learning becomes us as well as the Men. Several of the French Ladies, and with us the late incomparable Mrs. Baynard, and the Lady that is Mr. Norris's Correspondent, and many more, are Witnesses of this."

"Eugenia" must have also read Astell's *Some Reflections Upon Marriage* when she wrote *The Female Advocate* because she borrows Astell's comparison between passive obedience in marriage and passive obedience in the state, although with the difference that, as a Williamite, she does not think either can be enjoined as a moral duty.

28. *The Complete Letters of Lady Mary Wortley Montagu*, ed. Robert Halsband, 3 vols. (Oxford: Clarendon Press, 1965–67) "To Lady Bute," October 20, 1755, 3: 97; "To Lady Bute," March 6, 1753, 3: 25.

29. Some years later she sent a translation of Epictetus to Bishop Gilbert Burnet with a letter that was both an excuse and a justification for being a learned woman. Her phrases are very reminiscent of Astell's *A Serious Proposal* in their economy and pungency. "My Sex is usually forbid studys of this Nature," she wrote, "and Folly reckon'd so much our proper Sphere, we are sooner pardon'd any excesses of that, than the least pretentions to reading or good Sense . . . 'tis looked upon as in a degree Criminal to improve our Reason, or fancy we have any. . . . We are taught to place all our Art in adorning our Outward Forms, . . . while our Minds are entirely neglected, and by disuse of Reflections, fill'd with nothing but the Trifling objects our Eyes are daily entertain'd with." Certain of Astell's arguments also found their way into this letter to Bishop Burnet, including the one that education made women less vulnerable to men's sophistry because it made it harder (in Lady Mary's words) "for any Man of Sense, that finds it either his Interest or his Pleasure, to corrupt

them." "To Gilbert Burnet," July 20, 1710, ibid., 1: 43. The information about Lady Mary's early zeal for learning comes from the biography by Robert Halsband, *The Life of Lady Mary Wortley Montagu* (Oxford: Clarendon Press, 1956), 5–7.

30. *The Nonsense of Common-Sense 1737–1738* by Lady Mary Wortley Montagu, ed. and with an introduction and notes by Robert Halsband (Evanston: Northwestern University Press, 1947).

31. Although her uncle thought "one Tongue was enough for a woman," it was a matter of dispute in the first place because his wife, Elstob's aunt, was encouraging her to learn French. See Preface "To Mrs. Elstob" of Elizabeth Elstob's translation of *An Essay Upon Glory* (1708). For more information on Elizabeth Elstob's life, see Caroline A. White, "Elizabeth Elstob, The Saxonist," *Sharpe's London Magazine*, vol. 50, n.s. vol. 35 (1869): 180–90, 243–47, 304–10; vol. 51, n.s. vol. 36 (1869–70): 26–32, 95–99, 147–52, 190–95, 251–54; and Sarah Huff Collins, "Elizabeth Elstob: A Biography" (Ph.D. diss., Indiana University, 1970). For additional information in a briefer treatment, see Mary Elizabeth Green, "Elizabeth Elstob: The Saxon Nymph," *Female Scholars: A Tradition of Learned Women Before 1800*, ed. J. R. Brink (Montreal: Eden Press, 1980); Ruth Perry, "George Ballard's Biographies of Learned Ladies," *Biography in the Eighteenth Century*, ed. J. D. Browning (New York: Garland, 1980), esp. 104–11. For discussions of Elstob's work as a linguist, see Virginia Walcott Beauchamp, "Pioneer Linguist: Elizabeth Elstob (1683–1756)," *University of Michigan Papers in Women's Studies* 1, no. 3 (October 1974); and S. F. D. Hughes, "Mrs. Elstob's Defense of Antiquarian Learning in her *Rudiments of Grammar for the English-Saxon Tongue* (1715)," *Harvard Library Bulletin* 27, no. 1 (April 1979). For a good explanation of the political biases behind the Elstobs' scholarship see Michael Murphy, "The Elstobs, Scholars of Old English and Anglican Apologists," *The Durham University Journal* 58 (June 1966): 131–38. Elizabeth Elstob's *An Apology For The Study of Northern Antiquities* (1715), which was prefixed to her Anglo-Saxon grammar, has been reprinted by the Augustan Reprint Society as no. 61 (Los Angeles: William Andrews Clark Memorial Library, 1956).

32. *Tatler* no. 32, June 23, 1709.

33. Elizabeth Thomas, *Poems on Several Occasions* (London, 1722), p. 218. The entire poem is as follows:

> **To Almystrea on her Divine Works**
> Hail happy *Virgin*! of celestial Race,
> Adorn'd with *Wisdom*! and repleat with *Grace*!
> By *Contemplation* you ascend above,
> And fill your Breast with true *seraphic* Love.
> And when you from that sacred *Mount* descend,
> You give us Rules our Morals to amend:
> Those *pious Maxims* you your self apply,
> And make the Universe your *Family*.

No more, Oh *Spain*! thy Saint *Teresa* boast,
Here's one out-shines her on the *British* Coast;

Directs as well, and regulates her Love,
But in that Sphere, with greater Force doth move.
Whose Soul like hers! view'd its *Almighty End*!
And to that *Center*, all its Motions tend:
Like her! the glorious Monuments doth raise,
Beyond *male Envy*! or a *female Praise*!

Too long! indeed, has been our Sex decryed
And ridicul'd by Men's *malignant Pride*;
Who fearing of a just Return forbore,
And made it criminal to teach us more.
That *Women* had no *Souls*, was their Pretence,
And *Women's* Spelling past for *Women's* Sense
When you, most generous *Heroine*! stood forth,
And show'd your Sex's *Aptitude* and *Worth*.
Were it no more! yet you bright *Maid* alone,
Might for a World of *Vanity* Atone!
Redeem the coming Age! and set us free!
From the false Brand of *Incapacity*.

34. In the nineteenth century, Robert Southey advanced an identical "Protestant nunnery" scheme in 1824 in a work of social criticism called *Colloquies on Society*. He, too, thought that the estates and dowries of a few wealthy women might maintain educational establishments, and provide gentlewomen who had fallen on hard times a place to live and a community in which to function. Tennyson's *The Princess* (1847) portrays a young noblewoman who becomes an ardent feminist, and retires with a band of her friends to start a women's university. No men are to be admitted to this ideal community, although as with most male fantasies about all-female institutions, men soon infiltrate—in this case disguised as women—and the plan founders on the ensuing romantic complications. Gilbert and Sullivan's *Princess Ida*, following Tennyson's poem, but mocking the women separatists even more unsympathetically, is an interesting attenuation of Mary Astell's original plan.

35. *A Serious Proposal*, 10.
36. Ibid., 20.
37. Ibid., 41.
38. Ibid., 44.
39. Ibid., 97–8.
40. Ibid., 139.
41. See n. 15, chap. 1.

42. *The Diary of Samuel Pepys,* ed. Robert Latham and William Matthews, 11 vols. (Berkeley and Los Angeles: University of California Press, 1970–83), 8: 243.

43. *Home-Life of English Ladies in the Seventeenth Century,* by the author of "Magdalen Stafford" (London: Bell and Doldy, 1860), 78–79.

Mrs. Evelyn wrote thus to her son's tutor:

> Women were not borne to reade authors, and censure the learned, to compare lives and judge of virtues, to give rules of morality, and sacrifice to the Muses. We are willing to acknowledge all time borrowed from family duties misspent; the care of children's education, observing a husband's commands, assisting the sick, relieving the poore, and being serviceable to our friends, are of sufficient weight to employ the most improved capacities amongst us. If sometimes it happens by accident that one of a thousand aspires a little higher, her fate commonly exposes her to wonder, but adds little to esteeme.

Quoted in Myra Reynolds, *The Learned Lady in England, 1650–1760,* 142.

44. Margaret Cavendish, *A True Relation of the Birth, Breeding, and Life of Margaret Cavendish* (1656), reprinted in *The Lives of William Cavendishe, Duke of Newcastle, and of his wife Margaret, Duchess of Newcastle,* ed. Mark Antony Lower (London: John Russell Smith, 1872), 304.

45. Ibid., 297.

46. Ibid., 307. See n. 15, chap. 1.

47. Katherine Philips, *Poems* (London, 1667). The only full-length treatment of Mrs. Philips is still Philip Webster Souers, *The Matchless Orinda,* Harvard Studies in English, 5 (Cambridge: Harvard University Press, 1931). See also Edmund Gosse, "The Matchless Orinda," in *Seventeenth-Century Studies* (London: William Heinemann, 1914), 229–58; W. G. Hiscock, "Friendship: Francis Finch's Discourse and the Circle of Matchless Orinda," *Review of English Studies* 15 (1939): 466–68.

48. *The Diary of John Evelyn,* ed. E. S. deBeer (London: Oxford University Press, 1959), 802–3.

49. Hannah Woolley wrote several cookbooks and guides to household management, among them *The Ladies Directory* (1662) and *The Queen-like Closet, or A rich Cabinet stored with all manner of rare Receipts for preserving, Candying, and Cookery* (1670). She also wrote *New and excellent experiments and secrets in the art of angling* (1675). The text most interesting as a precursor of late seventeenth-century feminism is *The Gentlewoman's Companion; or a Guide to the Female Sex, with Letters and Discourses Upon All Occasions* (London, 1673), in which she rails against the lack of provision for women's education. In the Introduction she writes: "Vain man is apt to think we were meerly intended for the Worlds propagation, and to keep its humane inhabitants sweet and clean; but by their leaves, had we the same Literature, he would find our brains as fruitful as our bodies. Hence I am induced to believe, we are debar'd from

the Knowledge of humane learning lest our pregnant Wits should rival the towring conceits of our insulting Lords and Masters."

50. Robert Gould's *Love Given O're: or A Satyr Against the Pride, Lust, and Inconstancy, &c. of Women* (1682) and Sarah Fige's answer to it, *The Female Advocate* (1687), together with Richard Ames' *The Folly of Love* (1691) are bound together with an essay about satires on women by Felicity Nussbaum, as publication no. 180 of the Augustan Reprint Society (Los Angeles: William Andrews Clark Library, 1976). Jeslyn Medoff has written about Sarah Fyge Egerton: "New Light on Sarah Fyge (Field, Egerton)," *Tulsa Studies* 1 (Fall 1982), 155–176.

51. There are a number of pamphlets on women and marriage in Anthony à Wood's collection in the Bodleian Library, including a treatise on the excellence of marriage and an apology to women "against the Calumnies of the Men" called *The Batchelor's Directory; or The Maid's Defence* (1694), and *The Triumph of Female Wit or The Emulation* (1683) collated with the responses to it.

52. In her own day, Catherine Trotter was satirized, along with two other women writers—[Mary] Delariviere Manley and Mrs. Pix—in a play called *The Female Wits: or, The Triumvirate of Poets At Rehearsal*, which was first printed in 1697 and reissued in 1704 under the initials "Mr. W. M." after a successful run at the Drury Theater.

53. Edmund Gosse also wrote about this woman writer: *Catherine Trotter, The Precursor of the Bluestockings* (London, 1916). Another account is appended to her posthumously collected writings, *Works, theological, moral, dramatic and poetical with an account of the life of the author by Thomas Birch*, 2 vols. (London, 1751). Her exchange with John Locke is included in this collection.

54. See Myra Reynolds's editorial introduction to *The Poems of Anne, Countess of Winchilsea* (Chicago: The University of Chicago Press, 1903). Other sources on this woman's life and work are: Reuben A. Brower, "Lady Winchilsea and the Poetic Tradition of the Seventeenth Century," *Studies in Philology* 42 (1945): 61–80; Edmund Gosse, "Lady Winchilsea's Poems," in *Gossip in a Library* (New York: John W. Lovell, 1891), 121–32; Elizabeth Hampsten, "Poems by Anne Finch" and "Petticoat Authors: 1660–1720," *Women's Studies* 7, nos. 1–2 (1980): 5–21 and 21–39; Ann Longknife, "A Preface to an Edition of the Works of Anne Finch, Countess of Winchilsea" (Ph.D. diss., University of Houston, 1978).

55. Phoebe Clinket appears in a play written together by Pope, Gay, and Arbuthnot called *Three Hours After Marriage* (1717). With the publication of the final, expanded version of *The Rape of the Lock* that year, the countess of Winchilsea opened a poetic duel with Pope, ostensibly because of the way his poem treated women. Her final poem in this match, forgiving but with an edge to it, is recorded at the end of George Ballard's biographical sketch of her in *Memoirs of Several Ladies* (297–99):

> Disarm'd with so genteel an air,
>   The contest I give o'er;
> Yet Alexander have a care,

And shock the sex no more.
We rule the world our life's whole race,
        Men but assume that right;
First slaves to ev'ry tempting face,
        Then martyrs to our spite.
You of one Orpheus sure have read,
        Who would like you have writ
Had he in London town been bred,
        And polish'd to his wit;
But he poor soul thought all was well,
        And great should be his fame,
When he had left his wife in hell,
        And birds and beasts could tame.
Yet venturing then with scoffing rhimes
        The women to incense,
Resenting heroines of those times
        Soon punish'd his offence.
And as the Hebrus roll'd his scull,
        And harp besmear'd with blood,
They clashing as the waves grew full
        Still harmoniz'd the flood.
But you our follies gently treat,
        And spin so fine a thread,
You need not fear his aukward fate,
        The lock won't cost the head.
Our admiration you command
        For all that's gone before;
What next we look for at your hand
        Can only raise it more.
Yet sooth the ladies I advise
        (As me to pride has wrought,)
We're born to wit, but to be wise
        By admonitions taught.

56. Anne Dacier, daughter of the esteemed classicist Le Febvre, was trained by him. She was one of the foremost classicists of her day, and was commissioned by the government to translate Anacreon, Sappho, Terence, Plautus, Aristophanes. Pope leaned heavily on her *Iliad* when he made his own translation. She married a fellow scholar who had also studied with her father, who shared her passion for classical texts.

57. Robert Burton, *Anatomy of Melancholy* (1621), 3.2.5.3.

58. Barkdale was master of a free school in Hereford and later of a private school at Hawling in the Cotswolds.

59. Quoted in Myra Reynolds, *The Learned Lady in England 1650–1760*, 290–91.

60. Dr. Hickes mentions Dorothy Grahme in the Preface to his *Thesaurus* (1705), and includes Susanna Hopton's letters in *Controversial Letters* (1710). He referred to Catherine Bovey as "the Christian Hypatia" in the Preface to his *Thesaurus*. In 1687 he translated Fénelon's treatise on the education of daughters, *Traité de l'education des filles*, which was popular enough to warrant reissuing in 1707, with new editions in 1708 and in 1713. He appended a recommended reading list for young ladies to the 1707 edition, which included several books by Mary Astell: "She [i.e. the young lady to be educated] ought not likewise to be unacquainted with *A Serious Proposal to the Ladies . . . in Two Parts*; nor with *The Christian Religion as Profess'd by a Daughter of the Church of England*: These Two being written by one of her own Sex, may probably serve to make a deeper Impression upon her, and will be both Instructive and Delightful."

In 1712, we find a letter from Dr. Hickes to Dr. Charlett, master of University College, Oxford, recommending Elizabeth Elstob to his patronage: "the Publication of the MSS. she hath brought (the most correct I ever saw or read) will be of great advantage to the Church of England against the Papists, for the honour of our Predecessors the English Saxon Clergy; especially of the Episcopal Order, and the credit of our Country, to which Mrs. Elstob will be counted abroad, as great an ornament in her way, as Madam Dacier is to France." December 23, 1712, Ballard MSS 62:81. For more of the story of the circle of High Church antiquarians who followed Mrs. Elstob's fortunes and tried to help her, see my essay "George Ballard's Biographies of Learned Ladies."

61. Dr. Smalridge was dean of Carlisle and Christ Church and then bishop of Bristol. Just before he died, Mary Astell noted in a letter to a friend that he had preached the annual sermon to raise money for her Chelsea charity school. See app. C, Letter XXVIII (May 11, 1719?).

62. Two contemporary works championing women were *Dialogue Concerning Women, being a Defense of the Sex* (1691) by William Walsh, addressed to "Eugenia" (possibly Sarah Fyge), and *A Present for the Ladies, being an Historical Vindication of the Female Sex* (1692) by Nahum Tate. Tate's text is primarily a list of remarkable women, of the sort that John Evelyn published a few years later in *Numismata* (1697). Neither Walsh nor Tate explored new ground in these works, and Walsh's in particular has a tone of condescending gallantry.

Chapter Five: The Veil of Chastity

1. For an excellent treatment of this theme, on which I rely heavily, see Maren-Sofie Røstvig, *The Happy Man: Studies in the Metamorphosis of a Classical Ideal*, 2 vols. (Oslo: Akademisk Forlag, 1954).
2. J. Bowack, *The Antiquities of Middlesex*, 2 vols. (London, 1705–6), 1: 13.
3. Mary Astell, *A Serious Proposal*, 94–95.
4. Ibid., 93.

5. Mary Astell, *A Serious Proposal Part II*, 203.

6. Mary Astell, *A Serious Proposal*, 43.

7. Blaise Pascal, *Pensées*, intro. T. S. Eliot (New York: E. P. Dutton, 1958), 60.

8. Fénelon was a member of a French mystical sect known as the "quietists," to which he had been converted by Madame Guyon, a religieuse of St. Cyr. Madame Guyon was an apostle in this small but international sect of Catholics who were reacting against the excessive legalism of the church and who had been inspired by the sixteenth-century Spanish mystic St. Theresa. The quietists preached that a devout soul ought to cultivate a kind of adoring passivity, until he or she had attained the state of "a feather blown about by the winds of grace."

After his conversion, Fénelon preached quietist ideas even in the face of the intense disapproval of Louis XIV. The Sun King by this time was guided in his religious choices by Madame de Maintenon, whose judgment in turn was determined by the prevailing religious orthodoxy, and who did not feel safe straying as far from the accepted forms as the quietists strayed. The royal pair ordered Fénelon to renounce Madame Guyon and her quietist teachings; but he held firm. And so they banished him to his own diocese for the rest of his life, he who had enjoyed such favor. Only once in the last eighteen years of his life was he allowed to break this exile.

9. See app. C, Letter XXX (January 8, 1720 [?]). This is the strain in Fénelon's thought which appealed greatly to Astell when she read his *Letters*, published after his death, in 1718. For a fuller understanding of Fénelon's relation to the church and the court, see *Fénelon Letters of Love and Counsel*, selected and translated by John McEwen, with an essay, "Reflections on the Character and Genius of Fénelon," by Thomas Merton (New York: Harcourt, Brace & World, 1964). For a full treatment of his attitudes on women's education, see H. C. Barnard, *Fénelon on Education* (Cambridge: Cambridge University Press, 1966).

10. See app. C, Letter XXX (January 8, 1720 [?]).

11. Mary Astell, *A Serious Proposal Part II*, 106. Astell recognized that passions and sensation were "design'd in the Order of Nature for the good of the Body," and that one could not willfully control them. The involuntary responses of the organism were meant to preserve, protect, perpetuate the species, as she understood it; indeed, in a healthy person, "whose Taste is not vitiated," the appetites could be trusted to lead one to the physically salubrious. But since the world of fashion was not conducive to a healthy regimen, and since the impressionable soul could no more prevent movements of desire than it could "stop the Circulation of the Blood" or "hinder Digestion," the best that one could do was keep out of harm's way.

12. Mary Astell, *A Serious Proposal*, 55–56.

13. Røstvig finds in Cowley's poems "the most lucid exposition and the warmest defence of the retired country life in the seventeenth century." Maren-Sofie Røstvig, *The Happy Man*, 1: 10.

14. George Ballard's volume of biographies gives sketch after sketch of such women, living unexceptionable, responsible lives, giving and collecting bounteous charity to church and to schools for the poor, insisting on the religious instruction of everyone in the household, carrying on regular and disciplined private devotions. Lady Halkett allotted to her devotions every day the hours from five to seven in the morning, one to two in the afternoon, six to seven and nine to ten in the evening. She wrote twenty-one volumes for her own edification, with never a thought to release them to the world. Anne, countess of Pembroke, retired to her oratory three times a day to pray. Susanna Hopton, another earnest daughter of the Church of England, retired five times a day for religious worship and wrote a book of devotions. And that model of perfection, Margaret Blagge Godolphin, Evelyn's closest friend and *fille d'alliance*, passed part of every day in religious meditation and study: communing with her soul, writing resumés of sermons, compiling psalms and scripture for suitable occasions, annotating learned authors, and writing letters to the divine to whom she confided her spiritual struggles. For an excellent and moving essay about these forms of thought and introspection "in a century bewitched by theology" (as well as the sources of information about these women), see Harriet Sampson's Introduction to *The Life of Mrs. Godolphin* by John Evelyn (London: Oxford University Press, 1939).

15. These must be compared to the seventeenth-century biographies of men of the world who at some point decided to retire to the country. John Aubrey's friend Charles Howard, Isaac Walton, John Evelyn, and Sir William Temple all retired from active political life and turned their energies to fishing, study, and to experimental farming. Indeed, to this happy impulse we owe the Moor Park apricot, bred by Temple in his leisure.

16. Mr. Spectator refers to this fashion in no. 366, Wednesday, April 30, 1712.

17. Thomas Faulkner, *An Historical and Topographical Description of Chelsea and Its Environs*, 2 vols. (London: Nichols and Son, and Simpkin and Marshall, 1892), 2: 176.

18. Charles Hatton reported such an excursion to his father in 1690:

I have been to day at Chelsey garden and have made choice of 2 potts of ye passion-flower, and am very confident y^r Lo^{ppe} need not fear but they will thrive very well, they are soe lusty and stronge, and, if y^r garden[er] be carefull to lay y^m well, by this time 12 month you may have 20.

The Correspondence of The Family of Hatton, ed. Edward Mounde Thompson, 2 vols. (London: Printed for the Camden Society, 1878), 2: 147.

19. *The Diary of John Evelyn*, ed. E. S. de Beer (London: Oxford University Press, 1959), 819.

20. See app. C, Letter XXXVII (October 24, 1721).

21. Astell's *A Fair Way With Dissenters*, for example, attacks both Defoe's *The Shortest Way With Dissenters* (1702) and his *More Short Ways With the*

Dissenters (1704), and sneers at lewd and loud-mouthed "Mr. Short-Ways." See chap. 7 below for more detail.

22. Mary Astell, *A Serious Proposal,* 61–62.

23. Mary Astell, *A Serious Proposal,* 149–50.

24. Daniel Defoe, *An Essay Upon Projects* (London, 1697; rpt., Menston, England: The Scolar Press, 1969), 286–87.

25. Ibid., 282–84.

26. Ibid., 287.

27. See app. C, Letter XXXVII (October 24, 1721). It was the impress of their lives that made these books—each the author's first—so different. Defoe, a Whig dissenter, had already led a very adventurous life by the time he came to writing. One of the rebels who challenged James II in the uprising led by the duke of Monmouth, after their defeat he went to live in Spain for some years to escape reprisals. He returned to England just in time to join the army that welcomed William III to English soil and escorted him safely to London. By the time he wrote *An Essay upon Projects* (1697), he had ventured far enough in a risky business to go bankrupt—which explains his heartfelt harangue against the barbarous legal system which drove the debtor to despair and made him "perfectly incapable of anything but Starving." He had also gotten married; the value of a woman's school, he said, was that since "Men take Women for Companions," they ought to "educate them to be fit for it."

As for Mary Astell, raised to believe in the Stuarts and the Church of England, her ambition chastened by her experiences, the point of an establishment such as she proposed was to provide women with a place to live and the training to accomplish something noteworthy.

28. From Astell's arguments, one can infer what evidence was used in her day for the inferiority of women. Much of it came from scripture, and she has all the counterinstances by heart, all the wise women and heroines of the Old Testament. She also makes the point that the Bible was designed to teach people to become moralists and Christians—not philosophers—and that it was as inappropriate an authority on the question of female educability as it was on the debate between Copernicans and Ptolemeans. She explains God's remarks after the Fall as an augury rather than a command. She argues that although Adam was formed before Eve, it as little proves "her Natural Subjection to him as the Living Creatures, Fishes, Birds and Beasts being Form'd before them both, proves that Mankind must be subject to these Animals." Men were in ascendance only because they were stronger, she said, force being decisive in mankind's lapsed state. But physical strength did not imply superior moral or intellectual capacity since if "Strength of Mind goes along with Strength of Body," "'tis only for some odd Accidents which Philosophers have not yet thought worth while to enquire into, that the Sturdiest Porter is not the Wisest Man."

29. Lina Eckenstein, *Woman Under Monasticism* (London, 1896; rpt., New York: Russell & Russell, 1963), 365–405. Lina Eckenstein makes this observation about the power of the nunneries before and after the Normans invaded England:

It is worthy of attention that while all nunneries founded during Anglo-Saxon times were abbacies, those founded after the Conquest were generally priories. Sixty-four Benedictine nunneries date their foundation from after the Conquest, only three of which were abbacies. The Benedictine prioress was in many cases subject to an abbot; her authority varied with the conditions of her appointment, but in all cases she was below the abbess in rank. The explanation is to be sought in the system of feudal tenure. Women no longer held property, nunneries were founded and endowed by local barons or by abbots. Where power from the preceding period devolved on the woman in authority, she retained it; but where new appointments were made the current tendency was in favour of curtailing her power.

30. Ibid., 442.

31. Ibid., 432–57.

32. *Autobiography of Anne Murray, Lady Halkett*, ed. John Gough Nichols (Westminster: Camden Society, 1875), 13.

33. George Wheler, *A Protestant Monastery* (London, 1698), 17. Wheler's purpose in this book is to give a general defense of monastic life—its history, its purposes, its benefits. He cites Mary Astell's book at the end of his chapter 4: "Of Monasteries for Women: *See on this Subject*, A Serious Proposal, *Written by an ingenious Lady; and Proposal's of the same nature by the Reverend Mr. Stevens*".

34. Mary Astell, *A Serious Proposal*, 146–47.

35. George Ballard, *Memoirs of Several Ladies of Great Britain* (Oxford, 1752), 445. Ballard's informant in this matter was Elizabeth Elstob, who had known Astell in London, and who reported to him years later: "I don't remember that I ever heard Mrs. Astell mention the Good Lady's name you desire to know, but I very well remember, she told me, it was Bishop Burnet that prevented that good Design by diswading that Lady from encouraging it." Bodleian Library. Letter dated July 16, 1738. Ballard MSS 43:53.

36. R. J. Charleton, *A History of Newcastle-on-Tyne* (London, 189?), 169.

37. John Brand, *History and Antiquities of the Town and County of Newcastle-upon-Tyne*, 2 vols. (London, 1789), 1: 134.

38. Mary Oliver, *Mary Ward, 1585–1645* (New York: Sheed and Ward, 1959).

39. John Hacket, *Scrina Reserata: A Memorial Offer'd to the great Deservings of John Williams, D.D.* (London, 1693), pt. 2: 50. See also A. L. Maycock, *Nicholas Ferrar of Little Gidding* (London: SPCK, 1938; paper ed. 1963).

40. Mary Astell, *A Serious Proposal*, 18.

41. Mary Astell and John Norris, *Letters Concerning the Love of God* (London, 1695), 47–51. A commode was a high, wire-framed headdress. For a description, see chap. 10, n. 4. For Astell's final formulation of how God reaches humankind through "*sensible* Beauty," see chap. 3, p. 127.

42. Ibid., 75–77.

43. Note to Letter III, 2d ed. (1705).

44. Mary Astell, *A Serious Proposal*, 133, 139–40.

45. Mary Astell, *A Serious Proposal*, 135–36.

46. See "A Discourse of the Nature and Offices of Friendship In a Letter to the Most Ingenious and Excellent Mrs. Katherine Philips," in *The Whole Works of Jeremy Taylor*, 10 vols. (London: Longman, Green, Longman and Roberts, 1861), 1: 69–98. Philips established a "Society of Friendship" in 1651, complete with special romantic code names for the inner circle and a secret seal, to discuss poetry, religion, love, and friendship. Although some members of the club were men—Jeremy Taylor for one—Mrs. Philips's poetry was mainly devoted to celebrating friendships among the women. For thirteen years she addressed her most passionate verse to Ann Owen, or "Lucasia" as she was called.

47. See Nina Auerbach, *Communities of Women* (Cambridge: Harvard University Press, 1979), and Janet Todd, *Women's Friendship in Literature* (New York: Columbia University Press, 1980), and Lilian Faderman, *Surpassing the Love of Men* (New York: William Morrow, 1981).

48. The *locus classicus* for a discussion of love among women, is Caroll Smith-Rosenberg, "The Female World of Love and Ritual: Relations between Women in Nineteenth-Century America," *Signs* 1, no. 1 (August 1975): 1–29. See also Nancy Sahli, "Smashing: Women's Relationships Before the Fall," *Chrysalis* 8 (Summer 1979): 17–27; and Blanche Wiesen Cook, "Support Networks and Political Activism: Wald, Crystal Eastman, Emma Goldman," *Chrysalis* 3 (1977): 43–60.

49. Mary Astell, *A Serious Proposal*, 163–64.

50. Ibid., 161–62.

51. Ibid., 68.

52. Margaret Cavendish, "The Convent of Pleasure," in *Playes Never Before Printed* (London, 1668), 7.

53. For a more detailed exposition of the physical risks to women at this time and the appalling ignorance of women's physiology, see my article, "Mary Astell's Feminism: The Veil of Chastity," in *Studies in Eighteenth-Century Culture* 9 (1979): 25–43.

54. For a discussion of Astell's poem and a comparison to Lady Mary Wortley Montagu's poem on the same subject, see my "Mary Astell's Feminism: The Veil of Chastity." Here are the two poems; the first is Lady Mary Wortley Montagu's.

On the Death of Mrs. Bowes.

Hail happy bride! for thou art truly blest!
Three Months of Rapture crown'd with endless Rest!
Merit, like yours, was Heav'ns peculiar Care,
You lov'd,—yet trusted Happiness sincere:
To you the Sweets of Love were only shewn,
The Sure succeeding bitter dregs unknown:
You had not the fatal Change deplor'd,
The tender Lover, for the imperious Lord;
Nor felt the Pains that jealous Fondness brings,

Nor wept that Coldness from Possession springs.
Above your Sex distinguished in your Fate,
You trusted—yet experienced no Deceit.
Soft were the Hours, and wing'd with Pleasure flew,
No vain repentance gave a Sigh to you:
And if superior Bliss, Heav'n can bestow,
With Fellow Angels you enjoy it now.

On Mrs. Bowes Death

Blossom, Fragrant Spring, Bright Morn, adieu!
Virgins shall string their Harps, and mourn for you
Lost when the fatal Nuptial Knot was tie'd,
Your Sun declin'd, when you became a Bride.
A soul refin'd, like your's soar'd far above
The gross Amusements of low, Vulgar love.
Nor tempted by that Pois'nous Cup to stay
Tasting it scorn'd the draught and fled away.
Oh Cherubims and Seraph's Noblest string,
In Heavenly Raptures you're ordained to sing
The Immortal Spouse, in Bliss refin'd from Sense
Pure as your Mind, and Sweet as Innocence.

55. Harrowby MSS 255:55. I am grateful to Isobel Grundy for calling this fragment to my attention, and to Lord Harrowby for his generosity and co-operation in permitting me to use this document.

56. Others of her generation did, however. In 1705 Damaris Masham wrote that chastity was the duty of both sexes according to the Bible, but that "even with the aggravation of wronging another Man, and possibly a whole Family thereby, is ordinarily talk'd as lightly of, as if it was but a Peccadillo in a Young Man." The same crime in a woman, she continued indignantly, would "brand her with perpetual Infamy: The nearest Relations oftentimes are hardly brought to look upon her after such a dishonour done by her to their Family; whilst the Fault of her more guilty Brother finds but a moderate reproof from them." Damaris Masham, *Occasional Thoughts in Reference to a Vertuous or Christian Life* (London, 1705), 154.

57. Mary Astell, *The Christian Religion*, 219–20.

58. Mary Astell, *A Serious Proposal*, 64–67.

59. Mary Astell, *The Christian Religion*, 283.

60. Mary Astell, *A Serious Proposal Part II*, 247–48.

61. See app. C, Letter IX (December 10, 1714).

62. Quoted in J. W. Cross, *Life of George Eliot* (New York: Thomas Crowell, 1884), 20.

63. Mary Astell, *A Serious Proposal Part II*, 211–13.

64. Ibid., 206–7.

Chapter Six: A Monarch for Life

1. Gambling at cards, for money, was a favorite pastime of London's wealthier classes, enjoyed by men and women alike. For information about the duchess of Mazarin see Gérard Doscot, ed., *Mémoires D'Hortense et de Marie Mancini* (Paris: Mercure de France, 1965); Toivo David Rosvall, *The Mazarine Legacy* (New York: The Viking Press, 1969); Reginald Blunt, *Paradise Row* (London: Macmillan, 1906), 14–37; Grace and Philip Wharton, *The Wits and Beaux of Society* (New York: Harper & Brothers, 1861), 61–65.

2. George Ballard, *Memoirs of Several Ladies of Great Britain* (Oxford, 1752), 458–59.

3. See app. C, Letter XVII (June 20, 1717).

4. Reginald Blunt, *Paradise Row*, 26–27.

5. Grace and Philip Wharton, *The Wits and Beaux of Society*, 64.

6. Reginald Blunt, *Paradise Row*, 34.

7. *The Diary of John Evelyn*, ed. E. S. de Beer (London: Oxford University Press, 1959), 628–29.

8. *The Arguments of Monsieur Hérard for Monsieur Duke of Mazarin, Against Madam the Duchess of Mazarin, His Spouse* (London, 1699). Another document of this case, in Harvard's Houghton Library, is the fifty-six-page brief of the duke of Mazarin with the forty-six-page reply of the duchess, printed in Toulouse in 1689: "Plaideoyez touchant la demande faite par Monsieur Le Duc de Mazarin pour obliger Madame la Duchesse de Mazarin son Epouse de revenir avec luy, aprez une longue absence, & de quitter l'Angleterre ou elle est presentment."

9. *The Diary of John Evelyn*, 1036.

10. *Mémoires D'Hortense et de Marie Mancini*, 34.

11. Ibid., 33–39.

12. Grace and Philip Wharton, *The Wits and Beaux of Society*, 63.

13. *Mémoires D'Hortense et de Marie Mancini*, 211–12 n.33, 43–53.

14. Mary Astell, *Some Reflections Upon Marriage*, 5.

15. Ibid., 4–5.

16. Ibid., 4.

17. Ibid., 4.

18. Ibid., 46–7.

19. Samuel Richardson, *Clarissa*, 4 vols. (London: Dent, 1862), 1: 152.

20. Mary Astell, *Some Reflections Upon Marriage*, 13.

21. Ibid., 49.

22. Ibid., 36–37.

23. Ibid., 62.

24. Ibid., 35.

25. Ibid., 66–67.

26. Ibid., 15.

27. Ibid., 17.

28. Ibid., 6–7. Monsieur Hérard was the duke's advocate in the lawsuit.

29. Ibid., 23.

30. Ibid., 74–75.

31. Ibid., 65. For the section of Lord Halifax's instructions to his daughter that Astell quoted in the last edition of *Some Reflections Upon Marriage,* see *The Life and Letters of Sir George Savile,* ed. H. C. Foxcroft, 2 vols. (London: Longmans, Green, 1898), 2: 408–13.

32. William Congreve, *The Way of the World,* in *Restoration Plays,* ed. and intro. by Brice Harris (New York: Random House, 1953), 534.

33. See app. C, Letter VII (July 16, 1714).

34. John Redwood, *Reason, Ridicule and Religion: The Age of Enlightenment in England, 1660–1750* (Cambridge, Mass.: Harvard University Press, 1976), 48.

35. Ibid., 190.

36. Mary Astell, *Some Reflections Upon Marriage,* 93.

37. St. Nicholas parish register, Newcastle-upon-Tyne: January 14, 1703; October 1, 1704; January 2, 1710; October 16, 1712.

38. Mary Astell, 1706 Preface to *Some Reflections Upon Marriage,* 23.

39. For an understanding of the economic and intellectual forces at play during this period, see: Norman Sykes, *Church and State* (Cambridge: Cambridge University Press, 1935); A. L. Morton, *A People's History of England* (New York: International Publishers, 1938); G. H. Jones, *The Mainstream of Jacobitism* (Cambridge, Mass.: Harvard University Press, 1954); Keith Graham Feiling, *A History of the Tory Party* (Oxford: Clarendon Press, 1965); Lawrence Stone, *Crisis of the Aristocracy* (Oxford: Oxford University Press, 1967); J. H. Plumb, *The Growth of Political Stability in England, 1675–1725* (London: Macmillan, 1967); Geoffrey Holmes, *British Politics in the Age of Anne* (London: Macmillan, 1967); Isaac Kramnick, *Bolingbroke and His Circle* (Cambridge, Mass.: Harvard University Press, 1968); W. A. Speck, *Stability and Strife* (Cambridge, Mass.: Harvard University Press, 1974); J. G. A. Pocock, *The Machiavellian Moment* (Princeton: Princeton University Press, 1975); G. V. Bennett, *The Tory Crisis in Church and State, 1688–1730* (Oxford: Clarendon Press, 1975).

40. "Letter to Sir William Windham," *Lord Bolingbroke's Works,* 4 vols. (Philadelphia: Carey and Hart, 1841), 1: 115. John Carswell characterizes the attitudes of the two parties towards the Glorious Revolution this way: "For the Whig the Revolution meant pluralism and a limited monarchy; for the Tory it had been a painful necessity which had hazarded the due and proper relationships of society. When the Whig spoke of the Revolution he tended to speak of 'honesty,' meaning the frank recognition of the fact that Parliament had altered the succession to the Crown; and of 'liberty and property,' meaning that the sanctity of private property was the only effective guarantee of individual liberty. The Tory attitude was summed up in the slightly different phrase, 'religion and property.' The property factor, it will be noticed, is common to both; but the emphasis is very different. For the Whig the relevance of property is to connect self-interest and the stability of society; for the Tory it is to

symbolize habit and tradition as the guarantees of order." *From Revolution to Revolution: England 1688–1776* (New York: Charles Scribner's Sons, 1973), 40.

41. Linda Colley, *In Defiance of Oligarchy* (Cambridge: Cambridge University Press, 1982), Mary Goldie, "Tory Political Thought 1689–1714" (Ph.D. diss., Cambridge University, 1978), and J. G. A. Pocock, "Radical Criticisms of the Whig Order in the Age between Revolutions," in *The Origins of Anglo-American Radicalism* ed. Margaret Jacob and James Jacob (London and Boston: George Allen & Unwin, 1984), 33–59.

42. According to Colley, only thirty of all the M.P.'s elected to the five Parliaments of Anne's reign were Dissenters. Linda Colley, *In Defiance of Oligarchy*, 12, 4.

43. For a thorough discussion of the secularization of authority in this period, see Susan Staves, *Players' Scepters; Fictions of Authority in the Restoration* (Lincoln: University of Nebraska Press, 1979).

44. Doris Stenton, *The English Woman in History* (London: Allen and Unwin, 1975), 65.

45. Mary Astell, *Some Reflections Upon Marriage*, 29.

46. Ibid., 32–33.

47. Edward Hughes, *North Country Life in the Eighteenth Century* (London: Oxford University Press, 1952), 34.

48. Mary Astell, 1706 Preface to *Some Reflections Upon Marriage*, 9.

49. Mary Astell, Prefatory Discourse to *Moderation Truly Stated*, xxxviii.

50. Mary Astell, *Some Reflections Upon Marriage*, 39.

51. Susan Moller Okin, "Women and the Making of the Sentimental Family," *Philosophy and Public Affairs* 11, no. 1 (Winter 1982): 65–88.

52. Letter dated September 6, 1747. Ballard MSS 43:197.

53. Mary Astell, *Some Reflections Upon Marriage*, 93. This language is echoed by Defoe's Roxana in arguing against marriage with her Dutch merchant. See pp. 187–92 of David Blewett's edition (New York and Harmondsworth: Penguin Books, 1984).

54. Mary Astell, 1706 Preface to *Some Reflections Upon Marriage*, 5.

55. Beaufort MSS. This letter is dated March 31, 1713. Mary Grevile, Lady Ann's niece, was daughter of Lord Arthur Somerset and wife of the Hon. Algernon Grevile, son of Lord Brooke.

56. Mary Astell, *Some Reflections Upon Marriage*, 93.

57. Ibid., 9.

58. Ibid., 57.

59. Ibid., 88.

60. John Norris and Mary Astell, *Letters Concerning the Love of God*, Letter III, 45–46.

61. Mary Astell, *Some Reflections Upon Marriage*, 51.

62. John Baillie, *An Impartial History of The Town and County of Newcastle Upon Tyne* (Newcastle: Vint S. Anderson in the Side, 1801), 247.

63. I refer in particular to these three pamphlets: *Moderation Truly Stated: or, A Review of a Late Pamphlet Entitul'd Moderation a Virtue. With a Prefatory*

Discourse to Dr. D'Avenant, Concerning His late Essays on Peace and War. (December, 1703), 120 pp.; *An Impartial Enquiry into the Causes of Rebellion and Civil War in this Kingdom: In an Examination of Dr. Kennett's Sermon, Jan. 31, 1703/4.* (March, 1704), 64 pp.; *A Fair Way With The Dissenters and Their Patrons. Not Writ by Mr. L——y, or any other Furious Jacobite whether a Clergyman or a Layman; but by a very Moderate Person and Dutiful Subject to the Queen.* (June, 1704), 28 pp.

64. Mary Astell, *An Impartial Enquiry into the Causes of Rebellion*, 42. Her position on individual liberty is much like that espoused warmly by Oliver Goldsmith's speaker, Dr. Primrose, in *The Vicar of Wakefield*: "Now, Sir, for my own part, as I naturally hate the face of a tyrant, the farther off he is removed from me the better pleased am I. The generality of mankind also are of my way of thinking, and have unanimously created one king, whose election at once diminished the number of tyrants, and puts tyranny at the greatest distance from the greatest number of people. Now the great, who were tyrants themselves before the election of one tyrant, are naturally averse to a power raised over them, and whose weight must ever lean heaviest on the subordinate orders. It is the interest of the great, therefore, to diminish kingly power as much as possible; because, whatever they take from that is naturally restored to themselves; and all they have to do in the state is to undermine the single tyrant, by which they resume their primeval authority."

65. In addition to Clarendon's *History of the Rebellion*, Astell recommended the following sources to her readers to reinforce her view of the real causes of the Civil War, and her admiring characterization of Charles I: "*Mr. Foulis's History of our pretended Saints*, Sir *William Dugdale's Short View*, Dr. *Nalson*, or the Declaration and Papers that Pass'd on both sides; or even their own partial Writers, in some of which, even in *Will. Lilly's Monarchy or No Monarchy*, and in *John Cook's Appeal*, the same Cook that was their Solicitor against their Sovereign, he may find as great, or a greater Character of this excellent Prince, than the Doctor [i.e. White Kennett] gives him." Ibid., 37. The book by Henry Foulis (1638–69), according to the *Dictionary of National Biography*, was thought such a masterly treatment of Charles I's guiltlessness, that after the Restoration it was "chained to desks in public places and in some churches to be read by the vulgar."

66. Linda Colley, *In Defiance of Oligarchy*, 88.

67. Mary Astell, *An Impartial Enquiry into the Causes of Rebellion*, 33.

68. Ibid., 8.

69. Jonathan Swift, *Gulliver's Travels*, Book 2.

70. Bolingbroke's "Letter to Sir William Windham" in *Works*, 1: 115.

71. Quoted in G. V. Bennett, *The Tory Crisis in Church and State, 1688–1730*, 103. I have drawn heavily on Bennett's exposition of the Tory High Church position as it evolved in Mary Astell's time. It may be of interest that *The Whole Duty of Man*, that religious book which so clearly spells out the duties of obedience, was probably written by a woman—Lady Dorothy Pakington—

according to George Ballard. See George Ballard, *Memoirs of Several Ladies of Great Britain*, 316–36.

72. Mary Astell, *An Enquiry After Wit*, 36–7.

73. John Locke, chap. 19 of "An Essay Concerning the True Original, Extent and End of Civil Government" in *Works*.

74. Tobias Smollett, *The History of England From the Revolution in 1688, to the Death of George The Second* (Philadelphia: Thomas Davis, 1846), 318, 320.

75. See app. C, Letter XIV (August 29, 1715), and Letter XVII (June 20, 1717).

76. *The Jacobite Attempt of 1719*, ed. and intro. by William Kirk Dickson (Edinburgh University Press, 1895), 193–94, 199.

77. See app. C, Letter XXVI (Epiphany, 1718/19).

78. G. V. Bennett gives the context and gist of the speech made by Lord Coningsby in the course of which he compares Atterbury to Balaam the prophet. Atterbury replied that if Balaam had been reproved by his ass, he had been so served by Lord Coningsby. *The Tory Crisis in Church and State, 1688–1730*, 221.

79. See app. C, Letter XXXII (March 26, 1720).

80. See app. C, Letter XXIX (October 27, 1719).

81. See app. C, Letter XXXVIII (November 24, 1722).

82. R. W. Ketton-Cremer, *A Norfolk Gallery* (London: Faber and Faber, 1948), 136. For another account of Christopher Layer, see James Caulfield, *Portraits, Memoirs and Characters of Remarkable Persons*, 4 vols. (London: H. R. Young and T. H. Whiteley, 1819), 2: 110–20. For contemporary newspaper accounts, see *The British Journal*, November 24, 1722, and *The Weekly Journal* or *The British Gazetteer*, November 24, 1722.

83. G. V. Bennett, *The Tory Crisis in Church and State, 1688–1730*, 223–58.

84. See app. C, Letter XXXVIII (November 24, 1722). The "Letter of Credit" was the *carte blanche* which Layer was supposed to have obtained from the Pretender himself; the "Declaration from Lucca" was a statement from the Chevalier in support of the coup.

85. G. V. Bennett, *The Tory Crisis in Church and State, 1688–1730*, 265.

86. See app. C, Letter XXXIX (March 7, 1722/23).

Chapter Seven: In the Service of the Lord

1. Jane Lead, Eleanor Davies, and Joan Whitrowe were religious mystics and prophets. Katherine Chidley, Anne Docwra, and Elinor James wrote tracts about the relation between church and state; the first two were Dissenters and the latter a churchwoman. Elizabeth Burnet is an example of a contemporary of Astell's who published a devotional manual. For information on Jane Lead, see Catherine F. Smith, "Jane Lead: Mysticism and the Woman Cloathed with the Sun," in *Shakespeare's Sisters: Feminist Essays on Woman Poets*, ed. Sandra Gilbert and Susan Gubar (Bloomington: Indiana University Press, 1979), 3–18. Eleanor Davies, Katherine Chidley, and Elizabeth Burnet are discussed by George

Ballard in his *Memoirs of Several Ladies* (1752), and my recent edition also includes a selected bibliography of subsequent research on them (Detroit: Wayne State University Press, 1985). Joan Whitrowe and Anne Docwra are mentioned in a paper by Lois G. Schwoerer on "Women in Politics and Society: The Glorious Revolution" delivered at the Berkshire Conference on the History of Women, Smith College, Northampton, June 1984.

2. For information about women printers and booksellers, see Judith E. Gardner, "Women in the Book Trade, 1641–1700: A Preliminary Survey," *Gutenberg Jahrbuch* (1978), pp. 343–46 and Margaret Hunt, "Hawkers, Bawlers, and Mercuries: Women and the London Press in the Early Enlightenment," *Women in History*, no. 9 (Spring 1984), 41–68.

3. Elinor James, *Vindication of the Church of England* (London, 1687), 6. Lois Schwoerer estimates that prolific Elinor James published twenty-nine items between 1681 and 1699.

4. Her active support of James II and public resistance to the crowning of William III landed her briefly in Newgate in 1689.

5. John Nichols, *Literary Anecdotes of the Eighteenth Century*, 6 vols. (London: Nichols, Son, and Bentley, 1812), 1: 303.

6. Some of Mrs. James's publications were as follows: a broadside petition to James II to prevent popery in England headed *To the Kings Most Excellent Majesty* (1685); *Vindication of the Church of England* (1687); *An injur'd Prince Vindicated; or, A Scurrilous and Detracting Pamphlet Answered* (1688); *This Being Your Majesty's Birthday* (1689); *Mrs. Jame's* [sic] *Apology because of Unbelievers* (1694); a broadside petition about the East India Company headed *To The Right Honourable the House of Lords* (1701); *Mrs. James's Letter of Thanks to the Queen and both Houses of Parliament, for the Deliverance of Dr. Sacheverell* (1710).

7. John Nichols, *Literary Anecdotes of the Eighteenth Century*, 1: 306.

8. [Mary] Delariviere Manley took her political cues from her father, Sir Roger Manley, a staunch Cavalier soldier and scholar whose loyalty to Charles I cost him considerable money and property during the Civil War. She did not begin her career until Mrs. Astell had already published many of her celebrated tracts. Her *Secret Memoirs and Manners of Several Persons of Quality of Both Sexes, From the New Atalantis An Island in the Mediterranean* (1709) used to even better advantage the device first hit upon in *Queen Zarah and the Zarazians* (1705)—a satire on Sarah Churchill—that of exposing court life under the guise of describing a newly discovered kingdom. According to G. M. Trevelyan, *The New Atalantis* was enough of a serious threat to the ministry of 1709 so that there was an attempt to suppress it. G. M. Trevelyan, *England under Queen Anne: The Peace and the Protestant Succession*, 3 vols. (London: Longmans, Green, 1930–34), 3: 38.

Before he met her, Swift ridiculed Manley as a scandalmonger, as "the Writer of *Memoirs from the Mediterranean*, who, by the Help of some artificial Poisons conveyed by Smells, has within these few Weeks brought many Persons of both Sexes to an untimely Fate; and, what is more surprising, has, contrary to her Profession, with the same Odors, revived others who had long since been drowned in the Whirlpools of *Lethe*." See below, chap. 7, p. 229. But sometime during the winter of 1710–11, Swift actually came to meet Mrs. Manley and John Barber, and judging from the letters he sent back to Stella, he dined with them often and enjoyed their company. He came to appreciate Mrs. Manley's talents, and arranged for her to ghostwrite a pamphlet about the assassination attempt on Mr. Harley for the Tory ministry, because it needed to be handled delicately and because he thought it unwise to have his own name on it. *A True Narrative of what pass'd at the Examination of the Marquis de Guiscard . . . His stabbing Mr. Harley and other precedent and subsequent facts relating to the life of the said Guiscard*, a six-penny pamphlet, was a great success. During the next year Mrs. Manley collaborated on several pamphlets with Swift, and succeeded him as editor of *The Examiner*, a weekly, for five issues.

The two best sources on [Mary] Delariviere Manley are Gwendolyn B. Needham, "Mary de la Riviere Manley, Tory Defender," *Huntington Library Quarterly* 12 (May 1949): 253–88, and Dolores D. C. Duff, "Materials toward a Biography of Mary Delariviere Manley" (Ph.D. diss., Indiana University, 1974).

9. John Dunton, *The Life and Errors of John Dunton* (London, 1705), 334.

10. Gilburt Burnet, *History of His Own Times*, 4 vols. (London, 1818), 4: 227. The most thorough account to date of the Sacheverell affair is still Geoffrey Holmes, *The Trial of Doctor Sacheverell* (London: Eyre Methuen, 1973). G. V. Bennett gives an account of its meaning from the Tory vantage in *The Tory Crisis in Church and State, 1688–1730* (Oxford: Clarendon Press, 1975), 109–18. Linda Colley comments upon the trial from another perspective in *In Defiance of Oligarchy* (Cambridge: Cambridge University Press, 1982), 13.

11. G. V. Bennett, *The Tory Crisis*, cites the more usual figure of 40,000 copies sold, but Geoffrey Holmes states that more than twice that number were in circulation. *The Trial of Doctor Sacheverell*, 74–5.

Sacheverell's defense simultaneously reiterated the need for vigilant defense of the Church of England while at the same time denying a reactionary desire to obliterate the existing laws of indulgence towards Dissenters or to condemn the revolutionary settlement of 1688. The move to impeach Sacheverell in 1709–10 was a misguided one, for by that time in Queen Anne's reign, High Church sentiment was strong in England. There was great public support for Sacheverell, and when the verdict came in with a harmless token sentence—suspension of preaching for three years—there was rejoicing in the streets and shouts of "Sacheverell and the Church for ever!" When the three years of deprivation were up, Queen Anne herself conferred upon Sacheverell the wealthy rectory of St. Andrew's in Holborn.

12. Kathryn Kendall, "Queen Anne's England: A 'Golden Age' for English Women Playwrights," unpublished paper, April 1985.

13. Mary Astell, *The Christian Religion*, 143. The references to Queen Anne's possible patronage are above in chap. 5, p. 134 and n. 35.

14. Mary Astell, "A Prefatory Discourse to Dr. D'Avenant," in *Moderation Truly Stated*, lv.

15. Mary Astell, 1706 Preface to *Some Reflections Upon Marriage*, 3. Astell's staunch refusal of the concept of a "state of nature" may have been motivated, in part, by her resistance to the argument that women were "naturally" inferior.

16. See Geoffrey Holmes, *British Politics in the Age of Anne* (London: Macmillan, 1967); G. V. Bennett, *The Tory Crisis in Church and State, 1688–1730*; Henry Snyder, "The Defeat of the Occasional Conformity Bill and the Tack," *Bulletin of the Institute of Historical Research* 41 (1968): 172–92; George Every, *The High Church Party, 1688–1718* (London: SPCK, 1956); J. R. Jones, *Country and Court England, 1658–1714* (Cambridge: Harvard University Press, 1979); John Stoughton, *Religion in England under Queen Anne and the Georges*, 2 vols. (London: Hodder and Stoughton, 1878), I, chaps. 1–3. For a listing of the bishops who voted for or against the bill on December 14, 1703, see Norman Sykes, *Church and State in England in the Eighteenth century* (Cambridge: Cambridge University Press, 1935; repr., New York: Octagon Books, 1975), 35.

17. This same line of argument had produced the Test Act of 1673, which required of all persons holding any office, military or civil, that they take an oath of supremacy, abjure the doctrine of transubstantiation, and publicly receive the sacraments according to the rites of the Church of England. The Test Acts of 1673 and 1678 were designed to exclude James and any other Roman Catholic (and hence foreign, papist, and especially French) influence in the government.

18. See Maximillian E. Novak, "Defoe's Use of Irony," in *The Uses of Irony*, papers on Defoe and Swift read at a Clark Library seminar, April 2, 1966 (Los Angeles: William Andrews Clark Memorial Library, 1966), 21.

19. Ibid., 7–38.

20. This explanation originally appeared in *A Collection of the Writings of the Author of the True-Born English-man* (1703) along with the reprinted *An Enquiry into Occasional Conformity: Shewing that the Dissenters are no Way Concern'd in it* (1702), and *The Shortest Way with the Dissenters* (1702).

21. George Ballard recorded this in his manuscript copy of *Memoirs of Several Ladies of Great Britain* (Ballard MSS 74:329), but then crossed it out and did not publish it. I found no record of such a gift in the bequest book of Magdalen College, but then there are no women's names in it at all, and the gift may have been given through a male intermediary.

22. Mary Astell, *Moderation Truly Stated*, 28.

23. Ibid., 59.

24. Ibid., 107.

25. Letter dated December 9, 1704. Ballard MSS 62:85.

26. Letter dated March 12, 1743. Ballard MSS 40:161.

27. Letter dated February 19, 1743. Ballard MSS 41:229.

28. Isaac Kramnick, *Bolingbroke and His Circle* (Cambridge: Harvard University Press, 1968), 237–42. For an interesting analysis of the "intellectual scaffolding" of D'Avenant's thought, see J. G. A. Pocock, *The Machiavellian Moment* (Princeton: Princeton University Press, 1975), 437–38. An excellent short treat-

ment of D'Avenant can be found in D. Waddell, "Charles Davenant (1656–1714)—A Biographical Sketch," *Economic History Review*, 2d ser., vol. 11 (1958–59): 279–88.

29. *The Epistolary Correspondence, Visitation Charges, Speeches and Miscellanies of the Right Reverend Francis Atterbury*, ed. John Nichols, 4 vols. (London, 1783–84), 3: 135–36.

30. Charles D'Avenant, *Essays Upon Peace at Home and War Abroad* (London, 1704), 236.

31. Mary Astell, "A Prefatory Discourse to Dr. D'Avenant," in *Moderation Truly Stated*, xii.

32. Ibid., xxi.

33. Ibid., xiii.

34. Ibid., xxxv.

35. Ibid., xxxvi. Carole Pateman, in the Jefferson Memorial Lectures delivered at the University of California at Berkeley in February, 1985, makes a case for Astell's thought as an early instance of the feminist critique of the liberal political assumptions behind democracy. See also Susan Moller Okin, "Women and the Making of the Sentimental Family," *Philosophy and Public Affairs* 11, no. 1 (Winter 1982): 65–88.

36. Mary Astell, *Bart'lemy Fair*, 102–03.

37. Here is Astell's metaphorical passage:

> *Stand off now, and make Room for* Religion and Liberty of Conscience, *bring them in hand in hand! Alas Sir! Religion is left at the Door, she can't croud in, for Liberty of Conscience has got the Start of her. Liberty of Conscience is the Goodlier Person, uses a little Art, goes Finer, has the better Address and more plausible Eloquence. Religion is a Plain Honest Matron, and this as Times go is no great Recommendation. Room there for Dame Religion who has lost her Head Cloaths and is almost tore to pieces in the Croud. Help, help! let some good Christian run and intreat the* House of Commons *to send their Officers to make way for her!*

Mary Astell, "A Prefatory Discourse to Dr. D'Avenant," in *Moderation Truly Stated*, xli. It can be compared in its emotional loading to Charles Leslie's description of the church as a long-suffering mother, and the Dissenters as her rebellious children who pledge themselves to matricide. Charles Leslie, *The Wolf Stript of his Shepherd's Clothing* (London, 1704), 5.

38. Mary Astell, "A Prefatory Discourse to Dr. D'Avenant," xlix.

39. Ibid., lii. For Astell's reference, see Charles D'Avenant, *Essays Upon Peace at Home and War Abroad*, 364.

40. Daniel Defoe, *More Short Ways with the Dissenters* (London, 1704), 3.

41. Ibid., 18.

42. Mary Astell, "Postscript *Concerning* Moderation Still a Vertue," in *A Fair Way With The Dissenters*, 24.

43. Ibid., 26, 32.

44. For an account of this struggle, see G. V. Bennett's *The Tory Crisis in Church and State, 1688–1730,* 48–80.

45. White Kennett, *A Compassionate Enquiry into the Causes of the Civil War in a Sermon Preached in the Church of St. Botolph Aldgate, on January XXXI, 1703/4 the Day of Fast for the Martyrdom of King Charles the First* (London, 1704).

46. Page 59 of pamphlet bound with Wagstaffe's *The Case of Moderation,* etc., in the Boston Public Library collection.

47. Letter dated March 30, 1706. Rawlinson MSS D 198:101–14.

48. Dr. Hickes' declaration of 1696, stating his "unalterable adherence to the deprived Bishops being the true, lawfull, and canonical Pastors of their respective Dioceses," is preserved in the Bodleian. MS Eng. Hist. b. 2:117.

49. Letter dated October 15, 1691. Ballard MSS 62:60, 61, 65.

50. Dodwell was perhaps the most learned of all the nonjuring academics. Gibbon himself acknowledged that no one knew more about the history of the upper empire. But he harbored what seem to us incredible mixtures of knowledge and ignorance, as did many other learned men of his day. Locke, for example, instances mermaids as an example of mixed species in his *Essay on Human Understanding* (bk. 2, ch. 6, par. 12). Dodwell held peculiar ideas such as that the spinal marrow was the seat of sinfulness and that devils reached their human prey through this most susceptible part. Upon the body's decomposing, he believed that the spinal marrow turned into a serpent. Lord Macaulay, who, it must be remembered, was unsympathetic to the nonjuring position, doubted Dodwell's sanity. He suggested that the learned doctor had perused too many volumes in too many languages, and that he had "acquired more learning than his slender faculties were able to bear. The small intellectual spark which he possessed was put out by the fuel." *The History of England,* 5 vols. (Boston: Crosby and Nichols, 1862), 3: 365. Astell seems not to have been disconcerted by Dodwell's strange treatises. It was enough that he shared her religious and political bias. For further information on the Shottesbrooke nonjurors, as well as on others, see J. H. Overton, *The Nonjurors* (New York: Thomas Whittaker, 1903).

51. See app. C, Letter II (March 11, 1705/6).

52. Walker was asking Strype as early as 1704 to leave materials for *Sufferings of the Clergy* for him at Rich Wilkin's shop. See Mm 6.49:146 in the Cambridge University Library, England.

53. See G. B. Tatham, *Dr. John Walker and the Sufferings of the Clergy,* Cambridge Historical Essays, no. 20 (Cambridge: Cambridge University Press, 1911).

54. The response of the vicar of Newcastle, N. Ellison, survives in the Bodleian Library. Letter dated March 30, 1705. John Walker MSS c.3:14^r.

55. Letter dated August 22, 1706. John Walker MSS c.8: 198–200. See app. C, Letter III (1706, probably autumn).

56. Letter dated February 12, 1743. Ballard MSS 40:158.

57. H. C. Beeching, *Francis Atterbury* (London: Sir Isaac Pitman & Sons, 1909), 49–50.

58. G. V. Bennett, *The Tory Crisis in Church and State, 1688–1730*, 119.

59. *The Memoirs and Correspondence of Francis Atterbury, Bishop of Rochester*, ed. Robert Folkestone Williams, 2 vols. (London: W. H. Allen, 1869), 1: 170.

60. *The True Tom Double, or an account of Dr. D'Avenant* (1704) has been attributed to Atterbury, although G. V. Bennett does not list it among his works in the bibliography appended to *The Tory Crisis in Church and State*.

61. G. V. Bennett, *The Tory Crisis in Church and State, 1688–1730*, 105.

62. This letter is reproduced a number of places, among others in *The Epistolary Correspondence . . . of the Right Reverend Francis Atterbury*, ed. John Nichols, 1: 19–21.

63. Letter dated January 4, 1746. Stowe MSS 753:61–62. The excerpts which follow in the text are taken from this letter.

64. If I am right about the timing of this incident, then the conjectured date on Atterbury's letter to Smalridge ought to be 1708 rather than 1706.

65. G. V. Bennett, *The Tory Crisis in Church and State, 1688–1730*, 112. At this time Atterbury was still dean of Carlisle. He did not become bishop of Rochester until 1713.

66. Hillel Schwartz, *Knaves, Fools, Madmen, and That Subtile Effluvium* (Gainesville: University of Florida Press, 1978), 1–30.

67. Ibid., 21.

68. Quoted by Hillel Schwartz, ibid., p. 17.

69. Sybil Rosenfeld, *The Theatre of the London Fairs in the Eighteenth Century* (Cambridge: Cambridge University Press, 1960), 1–3.

70. Mary Astell, *Bart'lemy Fair* (London, 1709), 23.

71. James Caulfield, *Memoirs of the Celebrated Persons Composing the Kit-Cat Club* (London: Hurst, Robinson, and Company, 1821), 1.

72. John Timbs, *Clubs and Club Life in London* (London: Chatto & Windus, 1899), 53.

73. She makes this explicit allusion to Swift on pp. 82–83: "Their Prompters are indeed grown above the little Arts of those who write *Letters to Ladys*, who *creep into Houses*, and with their *Tales of a Tub*, lead captive silly Women. Silly, not through want of Natural Sense and Understanding, but by reason of their being *laden with Sin, and led away with divers Lusts*."

74. Although not printed until later, Swift's *The Battle of the Books* was written about 1697, according to the bookseller's preface, "when the famous Dispute was on Foot about *Antient and Modern Learning*. The *Controversy* took its Rise from an Essay of Sir *William Temple's* upon that Subject, which was answered by *W. Wotton*, B.D., with an Appendix by Dr. *Bentley*, endeavouring to destroy the Credit of *Aesop* and *Phalaris* for Authors, whom Sir *William Temple* had, in the Essay before-mentioned, highly commended."

75. Mary Astell, *A Serious Proposal*, 78–79.

76. Drawcansir is a character in George Villiers's play *The Rehearsal* (1671). See above, chap. 3, p. 73 for a discussion of it.

77. Mary Astell, *Bart'lemy Fair*, 83–84.

78. Ibid., 33.

79. Ibid., 115–16.
80. Ibid., 60.
81. For a discussion of whether Swift or Steele wrote *Tatler* nos. 32 and 63, both about "Madonella," see Herbert Davis, ed. *The Collected Works of Jonathan Swift*, 14 vols. (Oxford: Basil Blackwell, 1957–8), 2: xxix-xxx. An interesting analysis of Swift's attitudes towards women can also be found in Susan Gubar, "The Female Monster in Augustan Satire," *Signs* 3 (Winter 1977): 380–94, and in the comment on this article by Ellen Pollak, *Signs* 3 (Spring 1978): 729–32. See also, Ellen Pollak, *The Poetics of Sexual Myth* (Chicago: Chicago University Press, 1985). For Richard Steele's ambivalent attitudes towards the position of women in English society, see the classic article by Rae Blanchard, "Richard Steele and the Status of Women," *Studies in Philology* 26 (1929): 325–55. Swift assumed that the business of a woman's life was to catch and hold a husband, and he thought it ludicrous for her to take any other project of her own very seriously. See his "Letter To a Young Lady on Her Marriage" (1723) in *The Collected Works*, ed. Herbert Davis, 9: 83–94. See also his remarks "Of The Education of Ladies," written circa 1728.

There is a subject of controversy which I have frequently met with in mixt and select companies of both sexes, and sometimes only of men; whether it be prudent to chuse a wife, who hath good natural sense, some taste of wit and humour, sufficiently versed in her own natural language, able to read and to relish history, books of travels, moral or entertaining discourses, and be a tolerable judge of the beauties in poetry. This question is generally determined in the negative by the women themselves, but almost universally by the men. . . .

It is argued, That the great end of marriage is propagation: That, consequently, the principal business of a wife is to breed children, and to take care of them in their infancy; That the wife is to look to her family, watch over the servants, see that they do their work: That she be absent from her house as little as possible: That she is answerable for every thing amiss in the family: That she is to obey all the lawful commands of her husband; and visit, or be visited, by no persons whom he disapproves. That her whole business, if well performed, will take up most hours of the day: That the greater she is, and the more servants she keeps, her inspection must encrease accordingly. For, as a Family represents a kingdom, so the wife, who is her husband's first minister, must, under him, direct all the officers of state, even to the lowest; and report their behaviour to her husband, as the first minister doth to his prince. That such a station requires much time, and thought, and order; and, if well executed, leaves but little time for visits or diversions.

That a humour of reading books, excepting those of devotion or housewifery, is apt to turn a woman's brain. That plays, romances, novels, and love-poems, are only proper to instruct them how to carry on an intrigue. That all affectation of knowledge, beyond what is merely domestic, renders them vain, conceited, and pretending. That the natural levity of women wants ballast; and, when she once begins to think she knows more than others of her sex, she will begin to despise her husband, and grow fond of every coxcomb who pretends to any knowledge in books. That she will learn scholastic words; make herself ridiculous by pronouncing them wrong, and applying them absurdly in all companies. That, in the mean time, her household affairs, and the care of her children, will be wholely laid aside; her toilet will be crowded with all the under-wits, where the conversation will pass in criticising on the last play or poem that comes out, and she will be careful to remember all the remarks that were made, in order to retail them in the next visit, especially in company who know nothing of the matter. That she will have all the impertinence of a pedant, without the knowledge; and, for every new acquirement, will become so much the worse. . . .

The Collected Works, ed. Herbert Davis, 4: 225–27.

82. Steele explicitly denied writing *Tatler* no. 63 in a letter to Mrs. Manley. *The Correspondence of Richard Steele*, ed. Rae Blanchard (London: Oxford University Press, H. Milford, 1941), 29–30.

83. This is in the 1722 Preface to *Bart'lemy Fair*. A recent article analyzing Steele's "indebtedness" to Astell is Richard H. Dammers, "Richard Steele and *The Ladies Library*," *Philological Quarterly* 62 (1983), 530–36.

84. The gentleman in question was Sir Thomas Pope Blount, with whom Lady Betty and her sisters stayed occasionally at Fittenhanger. John Nichols, in his *Literary Anecdotes of the Eighteenth Century*, 6 vols. (London, 1812), notes that Astell gave Lady Blount several books and inscribed one in 1724. Vol. 4, p. 261.

Chapter Eight: The Company She Keeps

1. This school is usually mistakenly dated to 1729.

2. For a hair-raising description of the condition of pauper children in eighteenth-century England, see M. Dorothy George, "Parish Children and Poor Apprentices," chap. 5 in *London Life in the Eighteenth Century* (London: K. Paul, Trench, Trubner, 1925); M. G. Jones, *The Charity School Movement* (Cambridge: Cambridge University Press, 1938), 28–35; and Ruth K. McClure, *Coram's Children: The London Foundling Hospital in the Eighteenth Century* (New Haven: Yale University Press, 1981).

3. The clothing allowance for a charity boy in 1712 included the cost of materials for a broadcloth coat, a lined waistcoat of the same cloth, a pair of breeches, a knit cap, a shirt, a pair of woolen stockings, a pair of shoes and buckles, and a pair of knit or wash-leather gloves. The allowance for girls included the price of materials for a dress and petticoat, a shift, a cap, an apron, a leather bodice and stomacher, a pair of woolen stockings, a pair of shoes and buckles, a pair of pattens (i.e., platform shoes to wear in the rain), and a pair of knit or wash-leather gloves. M. G. Jones, *The Charity School Movement*, 376.

4. Ibid., 75.

5. Ibid.

6. John Ashton, *Social Life in the Reign of Queen Anne* (London: Chatto & Windus, 1911), 16. William Blake's poem, "Holy Thursday" recreates and comments on the scene:

> Twas on a Holy Thursday their innocent faces clean
> The children walking two & two in red & blue & green
> Grey headed beadles walkd before with wands as white as snow
> Till into the high dome of Pauls they like Thames waters flow
>
> O what a multitude they seemd these flowers of London town
> Seated in companies they sit with radiance all their own
> The hum of multitudes was there but multitudes of lambs
> Thousands of little boys & girls raising their innocent hands
>
> Now like a mighty wind they raise to heaven the voice of song
> Or like harmonious thunderings the seats of heaven among
> Beneath them sit the aged men wise guardians of the poor
> Then cherish pity, lest you drive an angel from your door

7. M. G. Jones, *The Charity School Movement*, 12.

8. Ibid., 57.

9. Ibid., 51–52. According to SPCK records, charity school pupils were apprenticed to butchers, bakers, chandlers (candlemakers), weavers, shoemakers, cheesemongers, barbers, joiners, tailors, carpenters, glovers, bricklayers, saddlers, coopers, dyers, clear-starchers, fan-makers, bookbinders, booksellers, wig-makers, linen-drapers, and makers of musical instruments.

10. Ibid., 69.

11. SPCK archive.

12. M. G. Jones, *The Charity School Movement*, 99.

13. Ibid., 107.

14. Ibid., 9.

15. Ibid., 112. Linda Colley corroborates this Tory influence in the charity schools. *In Defiance of Oligarchy* (Cambridge: Cambridge University Press, 1982), 99–100, 109, 117.

16. M. G. Jones, *The Charity School Movement*, 116–17.

17. Ibid., 107.

18. In 1723 Atterbury was tried and exiled for his Jacobite activities. The story of the trial is well told in G. V. Bennett's *The Tory Crisis in Church and State* (Oxford: Clarendon Press, 1975), 265–74.

19. M. G. Jones, *The Charity School Movement*, 128.

20. SPCK archive. Letter to Mr. Holiday dated June 11, 1712.

21. MS diary of the Chelsea charity school.

22. Captain C. G. T. Dean, *The Royal Hospital, Chelsea* (London: Hutch-

inson & Co., 1950), 195. Today the endowment for the school supports three pensioners' daughters at a boarding school.

23. *Hastings Wheler Family Letters*, Part 2 (Wakefield: Privately printed, 1935), 106.

24. Account books of the Royal Hospital, 1700–27.

25. Alfred Beaver, *Memorials of Old Chelsea: A New History of the Village of the Palaces* (London: Elliot Stock, 1892), 52.

26. There is a letter from Astell to Lady Ann Coventry from this period telling her that Bishop Smalridge was going to preach a charity sermon the next Sunday "for yo.ʳ poor Chelsea Girls" "at yᵉ Chappel in Spring Garden near yᵉ Mews." See app. C, Letter XXVIII.

27. In the Hastings Wheler letters, there is one from Lady Catherine Jones to Lady Betty Hastings at Ledston in 1732, after Astell had died, lamenting that "our poor school is still at a stand madam as to worthy Mrs. Astell's quick program of having a school house built because she wished it and all the trustees she left has never met so I do the best I can to keep it on foot as it was when she died. Our annual sermon is this month to be preached by Mr. Collier minister of Richmond." *Hastings Wheler Family Letters*, Part 2, 106.

The endowment of this school was substantial. Lady Catherine Jones left £400 to it in her will. The interest on a bond of £200 donated by Lady Elizabeth Hastings and Mary Astell and that of another bond of £200 from Lady Catherine Jones also supported the school. After Astell died, the bonds were assigned to Lady Catherine Jones by Archibald Hutcheson, in the right of his wife Elizabeth, executrix to Mrs. Astell. By 1759, after the death of Lady Catherine Jones, bank annuities for the school amounting to £933 17s. were administered by the countess of Coningsby, sister to Lady Catherine Jones, and in 1770 by her daughter, Lady Frances Coningsby. (MS diary of the Chelsea Charity School.)

The figures on the number of pupils who went through the Chelsea charity school are taken from the 1724 *Account of the Charity Schools*, a volume which was published annually by the SPCK. A full set of volumes can be consulted in the SPCK archive in London.

28. Lady Elizabeth Montague was the daughter of the earl of Down and the third wife of Robert Montague, the earl of Lindsey. It is more likely that the British Museum's copy of Astell's book of 1694 was meant for her than for Lady Mary Wortley Montagu, since Lady Mary did not add the surname Montagu until 1712.

The 1694 Chelsea tax record lists those who paid a surtax levied to finance the war in France. It is in the Corporation of London records at Guildhall. Fifty women in Chelsea—just less than one-fifth of the assessed population—paid taxes in their own names in this record.

Noteworthy inhabitants of Chelsea are mentioned in the following histories: Thomas Faulkner, *An Historical and Topographical Description of Chelsea and Its Environs*, 2 vols. (London: Nichols and Son, and Simpkin and Marshall,

1892); Alfred Beaver, *Memorials of Old Chelsea*; Reginald Blunt, *Paradise Row or A Broken Piece of Old Chelsea* (London: Macmillan, 1906).

29. Reverend John King's manuscript history of Chelsea, 154.

30. John Ashton, *Social Life in the Reign of Queen Anne*, 276.

31. He left her £2,600 of goods and chattel in addition to Snitfield, her jointure estate. Horatia Durant, *Henry First Duke of Beaufort and His Duchess, Mary* (Pontypool: Hughes & Son, 1973), 60ff.

32. Lady Ann, countess of Coventry, August 8, 1728, CVC/Z/22:6A. These papers are part of the Carew Pole muniments and are the property of Sir John Gawen Carew Pole, Bart., of Anthony House, Torpoint, Cornwall.

33. *Hastings Wheler Family Letters*, Part 2, fragment facing p. 1.

34. See above, chap. 5, p. 134.

35. A letter to Thomas, earl of Coventry, dated March 4, 1707, among the papers at Badminton, reports: "The Bookseller complys wth your comands in every particular, onely I took the liberty of altering one thing in the title page & instead of calling the author *a Gentlewoman of Some quality*, I put it *by a Private Gentlewoman*." The catalogues of Lady Ann's private libraries are included here as Appendix B.

36. M. G. Jones, *The Charity School Movement*, 64, 68.

37. See the SPCK book of letter extracts, letters dated November 16, 1738, and February 1739 to Mr. Griffith Jones. SPCK archive. The Minute Book on Charities to the SPCK reproduces the extract from Lady Catherine's will. (See below, n. 47.)

38. *The Correspondence of Jonathan Swift*, ed. Harold Williams, 5 vols. (Oxford: Clarendon Press, 1963–65), 3: 336.

39. Until recently there was no known copy of the second edition of *Some Reflections Upon Marriage*, but in 1979 Stanford University purchased the volume with Lady Elizabeth Hastings' inscription. The rare-book collection of the Wilson Library at the University of North Carolina at Chapel Hill owns the copy of *Letters Concerning the Love of God* given to "A. Coventrye" in 1696.

40. Letter from Thomas Birch dated May 22, 1743. Sloane MSS 4244:5.

41. For the charges and Ranelagh's response, see the Rawlinson MSS A/236/46.

42. Thomas Faulkner, *An Historical and Topographical Description of Chelsea and its Environs*, 2: 300.

43. Public Record Office of Northern Ireland, Belfast. Letter to Dr. King dated January 8, 1712, De Ros MSS D 638/142/11.

His character as a young man was given by Bishop Burnet, who granted him "great parts, and as great vices, he had a pleasantness in his conversation that took much with the king; and had a great dexterity in business." Gilbert Burnet, *History of His Own Time*, 2 vols. (London, 1724–34), 1: 373. Later, a contemporary wrote:

Richard Earl of Ranelagh, is a Peer of the kingdom of Ireland, of a great deal of wit, had originally no great estate, yet hath spent more money,

built more fine houses & laid out more on houshold furniture & gardening, than any other nobleman in England; he is a great epicure, & prodigious expensive; was Paymaster General all the last war, & is above a hundred thousand pound sterling in arrear, which several Parliaments have been calling him to account for, yet he escapes with the punishment only of losing his place, which the Queen took from him, and divided between Mr. Fox and Mr. Howe.

He is a bold man and very happy in Jests and Repartee and hath often turned the Humour of the House of Commons, when they have designed to have been very severe. He is very fat, black, and turned of sixty years old.

Public Record Office of Northern Ireland, Belfast. De Ros MSS D 638/142/9.

44. Public Record Office of Northern Ireland, Belfast. De Ros MSS D 638/105.

45. Swift refers to Cranbourne in the *Journal to Stella* as one of the finest places "for nature and plantations" that he ever saw. Jonathan Swift, *Journal to Stella*, ed. Harold Williams, 2 vols. (Oxford: Clarendon Press, 1948), 1: 363.

46. Alfred Beaver, *Memorials of Old Chelsea*, 293–97; Thomas Faulkner, *An Historical and Topographical Description of Chelsea and Its Environs*, 2:299–301.

47. Lady Catherine Jones died April 12, 1740; her will was proved May 13, 1740. See also the letter from Thomas Rawlins dated November 28, 1741. Ballard MSS 41:115.

48. See above, n. 35. For further proof of Lady Ann's authorship, see also the letter from Thomas Rawlins dated June 11, 1743, Ballard MSS 41:238.

49. Dr. John King's memorandum on the original location of Sir Thomas More's house in Chelsea was found and printed twenty-five years ago: "Sir Thomas More's House at Chelsea," *Notes and Queries*, 2d ser., 2, no. 43 (October 25, 1956): 324.

50. Alfred Beaver, *Memorials of Old Chelsea*, 138; Thomas Faulkner, *An Historical and Topographical Description of Chelsea and Its Environs*, 1:133n., 134.

51. Taken from an account of a visit to Badminton by Lord Guilford in 1680, reported in G. E. and K. R. Fussell, *The English Countrywoman: A Farmhouse Social History* (London: Andrew Melrose, 1953), 81.

52. Lady Ann Grevile, letter dated March 13, 1712/13, Beaufort MSS.

53. See app. C, Letter XXIII (September 9, 1718).

54. *The Correspondence of Sir James Clavering*, ed, and arr. by H. T. Dickinson, vol. 178 of Publications of the Surtees Society (Gateshead: Northumberland Press, 1967), 41n.

55. *A Short Memorial and Character of that Most Noble and Illustrious Princess, Mary Dutchess of Ormond*, in vol. 3 of Pope's *Literary Correspondence* (London: E. Curll, 1735), 24.

56. See app. C, Letter XVIII (July 1, 1717).

57. Thomas Faulkner, *An Historical and Topographical Description of Chelsea and Its Environs*, 2: 210. For references to Lady Betty Butler in Mary Astell's correspondence, see app. C, Letters XXII and XXIX.

58. *The Poems of John Dryden*, ed. James Kingsley, 4 vols. (Oxford: Oxford University Press, 1958), 4: 1459.

In the Preface to *Fables Ancient and Modern* (1700), one glimpses a wider circle of literary women connected with Dryden (and perhaps with the duchess of Ormonde). Dryden refers there to a lady of his acquaintance "who keeps a kind of Correspondence with some Authors of the Fair Sex in *France*," and who "has been informed by them, that *Mademoiselle de Scudéry* . . . is at this time translating Chaucer into modern French." One cannot help but wonder if Dryden's literary informant was known to the duchess of Ormonde—or to Mary Astell herself.

59. Additional MSS 18,683:6,11.

60. These facts can be found in the printed *Colonial Papers,* 1708:180; January 24, 1709:321; and in the *Calendar of State Papers for America and the West Indies,* 1709:892.iii; 1714:693.

61. Stuart MSS 74/58A; quoted in Romney Sedgwick, *House of Commons, 1715–1754,* 2 vols. (New York: Published for the History of Parliament Trust, Oxford University Press, 1970), 1: 163.

62. [Christopher Walton], *Notes and Materials for an adequate Biography of . . . William Law* (London: Privately printed, 1854), 425. This volume is in Dr. Williams's library in London. I am grateful to Dr. Patricia Craddock for calling it to my attention and for permitting me to see her notes.

63. M. T. Gibson, "Instructions For a Devout and Literate Layman," in *Medieval Learning and Literature: Essays Presented to Rev. Hunt,* ed. J. J. Alexander (Oxford: Clarendon Press, 1976), 419.

64. [Christopher Walton], *Notes and Materials for an adequate Biography of . . . William Law,* 501. Linda Colley uses William Law as an example of the modulation of High Tory religiousness into Quaker mysticism. *In Defiance of Oligarchy,* 113. In general, quietists and mystics have been egalitarian and receptive to women.

65. William Edward Hartpole Lecky, *A History of England in the Eighteenth Century,* 8 vols. (New York: D. Appleton, 1891), 1:298–317, passim.

66. Letter from George Hooper, bishop of Bath and Wells, dated December 31, 1709, Additional MS 32,096.

67. Cassandra Duchess of Chandos, *The Willoughby Family,* ed. A. C. Wood (Eton, Windsor: The Shakespeare Head Press, 1958), 125, 134–36. It is interesting that by living with bachelor brothers, as Cassandra Willoughby did from seventeen to forty-three, numbers of unmarried women were able to maintain respectable autonomy. Elizabeth Elstob is another notable example.

68. Mary Brydges, James Brydges' first wife, died at forty-four after fourteen years of marriage. In those fourteen years she gave birth nine times and had several miscarriages. Two children survived. C. H. Collins Baker and Muriel I. Baker, *The Life and Circumstances of James Brydges, First Duke of Chandos* (Oxford: Clarendon Press, 1949), 93. An earlier biography of Chandos, with some supplementary information, is John Robert Robinson, *The Princely Chandos* (London: Sampson Low, Marston, 1893).

69. Daniel Defoe, *Tour Through the Whole Island*, 3 vols. (London: 1724–27), 2: letter 3, 8–12.

70. C. H. Collins Baker and Muriel I. Baker, *The Life and Circumstances of James Brydges, First Duke of Chandos*, xvi.

71. Ibid., 432.

72. All Chandos's efforts were in vain, however, and he never made another fortune. When he died, the opinion of his contemporaries was that he was "sad dupe" and "a bubble to every project." Ibid., 364.

One of the formative influences on Cassandra Willoughby Chandos, according to her autobiographical account of her family, had been her aunt Lettice, Lady Wendy, sister to her father, a widow who lived many years alone on her own estate in seclusion from the world, "reviving in her family primitive Christianity" and religiously observing the feasts and fasts of the Church of England. She read aloud prayers to her assembled household several times a day, and invited the poorest women of the neighborhood to her table. This seventeenth-century aunt seems an even closer approximation to the style and sensibility of Astell's friends in her degree of autonomy, and in the philanthropy and piety that she habitually practiced. Cassandra Duchess of Chandos, *The Willoughby Family*, 96.

73. She bought the right of advowson of Thorp Arch in 1730 and that of Little Porringland, Norfolk, in 1734.

74. *The Diary of Ralph Thoresby*, ed. Rev. Joseph Hunter, 2 vols. (London: Henry Colborn and Richard Bentley, 1830), 2: 303. See also Thomas Barnard, *An Historical Character Relating to the holy and exemplary Life of the Right Honourable the Lady Elizabeth Hastings* (Leeds: Privately printed, 1742), 13.

75. For a full description of the events of this night see Thomas Babington Macaulay, *The History of England*, 5 vols. (Boston: Phillips, Sampson, and Company, 1858), 2: 437–39.

76. *Hastings Wheler Family Letters*, Part 1.

77. Charles Edward Medhurst, *The Life and Work of Lady Elizabeth Hastings* (Leeds: Richard Jackson, 1914), 62.

78. Ibid., 70. Lady Betty was eulogized in the *Tatler*, no. 42 (July 16, 1709) with this description:

> But these Ancients would be as much astonished to see in the same Age so illustrious a Pattern to all who love Things Praise-worthy, as the divine *Aspatia*. Methinks, I now see her walking in her Garden like our first Parent, with unaffected Charms, before Beauty had Spectators, and bearing celestial conscious Virtue in her Aspect. Her Countenance is the lively Picture of her Mind, which is the Seat of Honour, Truth, Compassion, Knowledge, and Innocence.
>
> In the Midst of the most ample Fortune, and Veneration of all that behold and know her, without the least Affectation, she consults Retirement, the Contemplation of her own Being, and that supreme Power which bestowed it. Without the Learning of Schools, or Knowledge of a long Course of Arguments, she goes on in a steady Course of uninterrupted

Piety and Virtue, and adds to the Severity and Privacy of the last Age all the Freedom and Ease of this. The Language and Mien of a Court she is possessed of in the highest Degree; but the Simplicity and humble Thoughts of a Cottage, are her more welcome Entertainments. *Aspatia* is a Female Philosopher, who does not only live up to the Resignation of the most retired Lives of the ancient Sages, but also to the Schemes and Plans which they thought beautiful, tho' inimitable. This Lady is the most exact Oeconomist, without appearing busie; the most strictly virtuous, without tasting the Praise of it; and shuns Applause with as much Industry, as others do Reproach. This Character is so particular, that it will very easily be fixed on her only, by all that know her: But I dare say, she will be the last that finds it out.

There has long been a tradition that Congreve, a cousin of Lady Betty's, wrote this eulogy. For some clarification of the dispute over authorship, see George A. Aitken, *The Life of Richard Steele*, 2 vols. (London: Wm. Isbister, 1889), 1: 251n.

79. Lady Betty's will can be found in an appendix to Thomas Barnard's *An Historical Character*, and also in Charles Edward Medhurst, *Life and Work of Lady Elizabeth Hastings*.

80. Charles Edward Medhurst, *Life and Work of Lady Elizabeth Hastings*, 68.

81. Beatrice Scott, "Lady Elizabeth Hastings," *Yorkshire Archaeological Journal* 55 (1983), 95–118.

82. Ledston Documents, Archives, Sheepscar Branch Library, Leeds, Yorkshire.

83. See Appendix E.

84. *The Diary of John Evelyn*, ed. E. S. DeBeer (London: Oxford University Press, 1959), 712.

85. Charles Edward Medhurst, *Life and Work of Lady Elizabeth Hastings*, 105.

86. George Ballard, *Memoirs of Several Ladies of Great Britain* (Oxford, 1752), 459.

87. The archives of Hoare's bank show the following drafts from Lady Elizabeth's account to Mary Astell:

May 22, 1714	8. 1. 6
May 4, 1718	21. 0. 0
September 10, 1718	12. 18. 6
September 13, 1720	25. 0. 0
August 3, 1721	5. 5. 0
April 21, 1722	5. 5. 0
August 5, 1723	5. 5. 0
March 25, 1724	31. 10. 0

August 4, 1730   15. 15. 0

August 25, 1730   50. 0. 0

88. *Hastings Wheler Family Letters*, Part 2, fragment facing p. 1.

89. These details are in her will.

90. See the *Hastings Wheler Family Letters*, Part 2.

91. Richard Gwinnett and Elizabeth Thomas, *The Honourable Lovers or, Pylades and Corinna*, 2 vols. (London: E. Curll, 1732), 2: 81.

92. Mary Astell, *A Serious Proposal*, 147–49, 98.

93. See app. C, Letter XII (n.d.).

94. See app. C, Letters VIII (July 26, 1714) and VII (July 16, 1714).

95. See app. C, Letter XI (January 12, 1715).

96. See app. C, Letters XIII (n.d.), XV (November 10, 1715), and V (June or July 1714). Elizabeth Elstob may have lived in Chelsea as early as 1716—just after her brother died. A letter from her in that year to the Reverend Mr. Wilkins—the librarian at Lambeth Palace—is superscribed from Chelsea. Historical Manuscript Commission, *Fairfax Correspondence*, Appendix to the Sixth Report, 5: 467.

97. Myra Reynolds, *The Learned Lady in England, 1650–1760*, 208.

98. There are references to this episode throughout the Ballard MSS. For a summary and references, see Ruth Perry, "George Ballard's Biographies of Learned Ladies," in *Biography in the Eighteenth Century*, ed. J. D. Browning (New York: Garland Publishing, 1980), especially 104–9.

99. *The Autobiography and Correspondence of Mary Granville, Mrs. Delany*, ed. Lady Llanover, 1st ser., 3 vols. (London: Richard Bentley, 1861), 3: 613.

100. Harrowby MSS 81:112–13. I am greatly indebted to Isobel Grundy for calling this poem to my attention, and to His Grace, Lord Harrowby, for permission to quote it.

101. See above, chap. 5, n. 54, for the contrasting poems written by Mary Astell and Lady Mary Wortley Montagu about George Bowes's young bride's death.

102. *The Complete Letters of Lady Mary Wortley Montagu*, ed. Robert Halsband, 3 vols. (Oxford: Clarendon Press, 1965), 1:6. Letter dated August 8, 1709.

103. Ibid., 1:43. Letter dated July 20, 1710. See chap. 4, n. 29.

104. Ibid., 3:40. Letter dated October 10, 1753.

105. Ibid., 2:449–50. Letter dated January 1750.

106. *The Letters and Works of Lady Mary Wortley Montagu*, ed. Lord Wharncliffe, 3 vols. (London: Richard Bentley, 1837), 1:50.

107. James Clifford, *Young Sam Johnson* (New York: McGraw-Hill, 1955), 78–79. The poem in its later avatar reads:

Friendship, peculiar boon of heav'n,
The noble mind's delight and pride,

To men and angels only giv'n,
To all the lower world deny'd.

While love, unknown among the blest,
Parent of thousand wild desires,
The savage and the human breast
Torments alike with raging fires;

With bright, but oft destructive, gleam,
Alike o'er all his lightnings fly;
Thy lambent glories only beam
Around the fav'rites of the sky.

Thy gentle flows of guiltless joys
On fools and villains ne'er descend;
In vain for thee the tyrant sighs,
And hugs a flatterer for a friend.

Directress of the brave and just,
O guide us through life's darksome way!
And let the tortures of mistrust
On selfish bosoms only prey.

Nor shall thine ardours cease to glow,
When souls to blissful climes remove;
What rais'd our virtue here below,
Shall aid our happiness above.

108. For a discussion of the uncertain provenance of this poem, see the note by Arthur Sherbo, "A 'Spurious' Poem by Lady Mary Wortley Montagu," and Isobel Grundy's reply in *Notes and Queries*, n.s. 27, no. 5 (October 1980): 407–10.

109. Mary Astell's Preface to the Embassy Letters, app. 3 of *The Complete Letters of Lady Mary Wortley Montagu*, 1: 466.

110. This is the reason Lady Mary's biographer offers. See Robert Halsband's introduction to *The Nonsense of Common Sense*, ed. and intro. Robert Halsband (Evanston: Northwestern University Press, 1947), xxviii.

111. Mary Astell's Preface to the Embassy Letters, app. 3 of *The Complete Letters of Lady Mary Wortley Montagu*, 1: 467.

112. Ibid.

113. See app. C, Letter XXVII (April 10, 1719).

114. See app. C, Letter XXIII (September 9, 1718).

115. See app. C, Letter XXIV (n.d.).

116. See app. C, Letter VI (n.d.).

117. See app. C, Letter XXIII (September 9, 1718).

118. *Les précieuses*, that seventeenth-century female Platonic cult in France, were in part motivated in their antimaterialistic fanaticism by a common self-protective need to guard against further pregnancies and miscarriages, according to Dorothy Anne Liot Backer, *Precious Women* (New York: Basic Books, 1974). The English bluestockings considered themselves to be direct descendants of these *salonistes* who met in the Hôtel de Ramboillet, as Hannah More's poem *Bas Bleu* (1786) makes clear.

Chapter Nine: Private Life in Chelsea

1. Thomas Faulkner, *An Historical and Topographical Description of Chelsea and Its Environs*, 2 vols. (London: Nichols and Son, and Simpkin and Marshall, 1892), 1:376; 2:155–57. It was dangerous to travel at night from Chelsea to London (or vice versa), through the empty fields and over "Bloody Bridge." This un-propitiously named passage had been a favorite ambush place for highwaymen and footpads since Queen Elizabeth's day. Local citizens of Astell's time appealed to the government again and again to assign larger patrols of pensioners from the Royal Hospital to protect those who had to use the roads regularly. And indeed, the books of the Royal Hospital record the rewards paid to pensioners who put attackers to flight. There is no evidence of Astell ever being attacked, but her friend the duchess of Ormonde was robbed on at least one occasion. Visitors from London were loath to return after dark. Swift wrote home to his Stella about walking back to Chelsea at midnight: "Lord Rivers conjured me not to walk so late; but I would, because I had no other way; but I had no money to lose." *Journal to Stella*, ed. Harold Williams, 2 vols. (Oxford: Clarendon Press, 1948), 1: 273. See also 1: 251, 261, 296, 309. Sir Richard Steele, in 1716, was afraid to pass through that territory at night. He wrote to his wife: "Mr. Fuller and I came hither to dine in the Air. But the maid has been so slow that We are benighted, and chuse to lye here rather than go this Road in the dark. I lye at [our] own house, and my Freind at a relations in the Town." *Sir Richard Steele's Epistolary Correspondence*, ed. Rae Blanchard (Oxford: Clarendon Press, 1941), 314. Letter dated February 14, 1715/16.

2. Chelsea Poor Rate Ledger, Chelsea Library.

3. Osborn MSS Collection (Beinecke Library). A small book owned by Narcissus Luttrell labelled "General matters relating to Chelsea house."

4. Reverend John King's manuscript history of Chelsea, deposited in the Manresa Road Chelsea Library, 152.

5. John Summerson, *Georgian London* (London: Pleiades Books, 1945), 50, 52, 63.

6. Jonathan Swift, *Journal to Stella*, 1: 252 and 2: 525.

7. This account was opened in 1722 and ran until 1731, when she died. I am grateful to R. McD. Winder and M. J. Kenney of Hoare's Bank for helping me to use the archives.

8. Robert Halsband, *The Life of Lady Mary Wortley Montagu* (Oxford: Clarendon Press, 1956), 23. This was to be the "pin-money" provision in the marriage contract with the Honourable Clotworthy Skeffington if Lady Mary had accepted his suit.

9. See above, chap. 8, n. 87.

10. Boswell's *Life of Johnson*, ed. George Birbeck Hill and revised and enlarged by L. F. Powell, 6 vols. (Oxford: Clarendon Press, 1934), 1: 103.

11. For a good manuscript source on London prices from 1711 to 1739, see the account book, Additional MSS. 42,675, British Library. A good secondary source on the cost of food in the days of Queen Anne is J. C. Drummond and Anne Wilbraham, *The Englishman's Food* (London: J. Cape, 1939), 205–28. Celia Fiennes's travelogue in 1695 gives the prices of food in the provinces. Celia Fiennes, *Through England on a Side Saddle in the Time of William and Mary* (London: Field & Tuer, 1888), 65. The relative expensiveness of medical care is pointed out in Edith Larson's "Early Eighteenth-Century English Women Writers" (Ph.D. diss., Brandeis University, 1980).

12. Thomas Faulkner, *An Historical and Topographical Description of Chelsea and Its Environs*, 1:18–30.

13. William King, *A Journey to London in the year 1698* originally in French, by M. Sorbiere, and newly translated into English (London, 1698), 29.

14. Ibid., 33.

15. Frederick William Fairholt, *Costume in England: A History of Dress*, 3d ed., 2 vols (London: G. Bell and Sons, 1885), 1:361.

16. *The Autobiography and Correspondence of Mary Granville, Mrs. Delany*, ed. Lady Llanover, 1st ser., 3 vols. (London: Richard Bentley, 1861), 3:28.

17. C. Willett Cunnington and Phillis Cunnington, *Handbook of English Costume in the Eighteenth Century* (London: Faber, 1957), 412, 413, 153, 173.

18. William King, *Political and Literary Anecdotes of His Own Times* (London: J. Murray, 1818), 52–53.

19. Jonathan Swift, *Journal to Stella*, ed. Harold Williams, 1: 251, 258–59, 270.

20. Reverend John King's manuscript history of Chelsea, 157.

21. See above, chap. 8, n. 49.

22. In the records of the Chelsea poor rates, deposited in the Chelsea Public Library, Elizabeth Elstob is listed as having a large house on Paradise Row, valued at £60, for the first half of 1718. In the second part of that year, the house was standing empty, and Elizabeth Elstob was not heard of again until George Ballard discovered her living in Evesham, Gloucestershire, in 1736. Elstob probably lived in Chelsea as early as 1716. See above, chap. 8, n. 96.

23. Reginald Blunt, *Paradise Row or A Broken Piece of Old Chelsea* (London: Macmillan, 1906), 175.

24. Thomas Faulkner, *An Historical and Topographical Description of Chelsea and Its Environs*, II: 54.

25. He sold it to Narcissus Luttrell. The complete inventory is in the Osborn Collection of the Beinecke Library, Yale University.

26. Thomas Faulkner, *An Historical and Topographical Description of Chelsea and Its Environs*, I: 159.

27. Ibid., 2:193.

28. Reginald Blunt, *Paradise Row or A Broken Piece of Old Chelsea*, 118–19.

29. J. Bowack, *The Antiquities of Middlesex*, 2 vols. (London, 1705–6), 1:13.

30. *The Autobiography of Benjamin Franklin*, ed. Max Farrand (Berkeley and Los Angeles: University of California Press, 1959), 60. His interest in curiosities also led Franklin to Sir Hans Sloane: "I had brought over a few curiosities, among which the principal was a purse made of the asbestos, which purified by fire. Sir Hans Sloane heard of it, came to see me, and invited me to his house in Bloomsbury Square, where he showed me all his curiosities and persuaded me to add that to the number, for which he paid me handsomely." Ibid., 54.

31. *Tatler*, no. 34.

32. Thomas Faulkner, *An Historical and Topographical Description of Chelsea and Its Environs*, 1:381–82.

33. Ibid., 2:177.

34. *The Diary of Samuel Pepys*, ed. Robert Latham and William Matthews, 11 vols. (Berkeley and Los Angeles: University of California Press, 1970–83), 7: 234.

35. Thomas Faulkner, *An Historical and Topographical Description of Chelsea and Its Environs*, 2:187–89.

36. Ballard MSS 74:328r. This information in the manuscript version of George Ballard's *Memoirs of Several Ladies of Great Britain* was omitted from the printed book.

37. Ballard MSS 43:31. Letter from Elizabeth Elstob to George Ballard dated December 24, 1736.

38. Jonathan Swift, *Journal to Stella*, ed. Harold Williams, 1: 259. Entry dated May 2, 1711.

39. T. S. Ashton notes in his fascinating book, *Economic Fluctuations in England, 1700–1800* (Oxford: Clarendon Press, 1959), that once a tax was levied on dice and playing cards (1711), the revenue from it constituted a measure of the degree of gambling in the population. Using this measure, he observes that gambling increased in 1715, the year of the Jacobite uprisings, and in 1720, when the South Sea Bubble burst. He conjectures that people turn to gambling and other superstitious behaviors at times of stress and social disorder. 178–79, 193.

40. Captain C. G. T. Dean, *The Royal Hospital Chelsea* (London: Hutchinson, 1950), 192–95. John Astell appears on the Royal Hospital account books between April 1 and June 30, 1716, as "Controler of the Coal," and is last mentioned at the end of 1729. In 1727 his quarter salary is entered as £7 10s.

41. Her third and final husband was also a pensioner of the Royal Hospital. Thomas Faulkner, *An Historical and Topographical Description of Chelsea and Its Environs*, 2:276. See also John Ashton, *Eighteenth Century Waifs* (London: Hurst and Blackett, 1887), 177–84.

42. The cost of hiring these musicians was £150. See Otto Erich Deutsch, *Handel, A Documentary Biography* (London: Adam & Charles Black, 1955), 76–79.

43. J. Bowack, *The Antiquities of Middlesex*, 1:13.

44. See volume II of *The Survey of London* (London, 1927), "The Parish of Chelsea," pt. 4, p. 6.

45. Thomas Faulkner, *An Historical and Topographical Description of Chelsea and Its Environs*, 1:43.

46. Reverend John King's manuscript history of Chelsea, 216; George Bryan, *Chelsea in the Olden & Present Times* (London: Published by the author, 1869), 71.

47. See app. C, Letter XX (June 7, 1718).

48. See app. C, Letter XXV (December 6, 1718).

49. *The Complete Works of Jonathan Swift*, ed. Herbert Davis, 14 vols. (Oxford: Clarendon Press, 1957), 9:27–28. Letter dated January 10, 1721.

50. See app. C, Letter XXXVII (October 24, 1721).

51. See app. C, Letter XX (June 7, 1718).

52. Ibid.

53. He was convicted on July 10, 1718, and made to stand in the pillory, fined twenty marks, and imprisoned for six months. Thomas Salmon, *The Chronological Historian*, 3d ed., 2 vols. (London, 1747), 2:84.

54. Ibid., 2:69–70. The treasonable papers of Count Gyllemberg, the Swedish minister to England, were printed and published by royal order on February 22, 1717.

55. See app. C, Letter XXVII (April 10, 1719).

56. See app. C, Letter XXVIII (May 11, 1719?).

57. See app. C, Letter XXVII (April 10, 1719).

58. See app. C, Letter XLI (April 25, 1724).

59. See app. C, Letter VIII (July 26, 1714).

60. See app. C, Letter XXXIX (March 7, 1723).

61. Dryden gave him the character of Zimri in *Absalom and Achitophel*:

> A man so various, that he seem'd to be
> Not one, but all mankind's epitome:
> Stiff in opinions, always in the wrong;
> Was everything by starts, and nothing long;
> But, in the course of one revolving moon,
> Was chymist, fiddler, statesman, and buffoon:
> Then all for women, painting, rhyming, drinking,
> Besides ten thousand freaks that died in thinking.

And Pope greatly exaggerated his sordid end in *To Bathurst*:

> In the worst inn's worst room, with mat half-hung,
> The floors of plaister, and the walls of dung,

On once a flock-bed, but repair'd with straw,
With tape-ty'd curtains, never meant to draw . . .
Great Villiers lies—alas! how chang'd from him,
That life of pleasure, and that soul of whim!

He died of a chill he caught hunting on his own estate.

62. See app. C, Letter XXII (August 5, 1718?).

63. See app. C, Letter XL (July 6, 1723).

64. See app. C, Letter XXII (August 5, 1718?).

65. See app. C, Letter XVII (June 20, 1717).

66. See app. C, Letter XXXVII (October 24, 1721).

67. See app. C, Letter XXXII (March 26, 1720).

68. My sources for the history of the South Sea Bubble are John Carswell, *The South Sea Bubble* (London: Cresset Press, 1960); Viscount Erleigh, *The South Sea Bubble* (London: Peter Davies, 1953); and John G. Sperling, *The South Sea Company* (Boston: Kress Library Series of Publications, 1962). Sperling's monograph is particularly useful, and includes an eighteenth-century bibliography on the subject.

69. The treaty of Utrecht permitted the Spanish colonial government in America to retain a number of fortified security ports, which meant that the South Sea Company could not protect their trade, however lucrative. These fortified ports gave Spain the power to coerce the English trade duties (such as the 28.5 percent of all profits from trade at annual fairs in Porto Bello, Cartagena, or Vera Cruz, claimed by the king of Spain), and to defy or protect English trade at will, regardless of any privileges the English Parliament might grant to an English company. The recompense to the English for these security ports was the Asiento, a Spanish slave-trading contract previously made with the French, guaranteeing the annual importation to the Spanish colonies of 4,800 "piezas de Indias," defined as black persons at least fifty-eight inches tall with no defects. But without any security ports, England relinquished the one provision which might have guaranteed them the successsful exploitation of the Asiento. In practice the slave trade lost money both because of the tariffs— the tribute to the king of Spain—and because the colonists would not pay for the human cargo in specie or bullion, but insisted on paying in "fruits of the country"—cacao, balsam, sugar, tobacco, and the like—or left large sums owing to the South Sea Company. See John G. Sperling, *The South Sea Company*, 14–21.

70. Ibid., 25–29.

71. Viscount Erleigh, *The South Sea Bubble*, 76–110.

72. See app. C, Letter XXXI (February 25, 1720).

73. See app. C, Letter XXXII (March 26, 1720).

74. John G. Sperling, *The South Sea Company*, 31. By March of 1720, it was clear that Law's Mississippi scheme was a disaster, and he sought refuge for his life in the Palais Royal.

75. William Edward Hartpole Lecky, *A History of England in the Eighteenth Century*, 8 vols. (New York: D. Appleton, 1891), 1:349.
76. See app. C, Letter XXXII (March 26, 1720).
77. See app. C, Letter XXXIV (August 12, 1720).
78. Archibald Hutcheson wrote a number of pamphlets warning against the government's financial involvement with the South Sea Company.
79. See app. C, Letter XXXIV (August 12, 1720).
80. Ibid.
81. John G. Sperling, *The South Sea Company*, 26.
82. See app. C, Letter XXXIII (July 2, 1720).
83. John Law had killed one "Beau Wilson" in a duel in Bloomsbury Square and was sentenced to death, which he escaped by fleeing the country. That was why he had to reenter England secretly and illegally. Viscount Erleigh, *The South Sea Bubble*, 43–44.
84. See app. C, Letter XXXVII (October 24, 1721).
85. See app. C, Letter XXXI (February 25, 1720).
86. See app. C, Letter XL (July 6, 1723).

Chapter Ten: The Final Chapter

1. According to Thomas Birch, Mary Astell "liv'd many Years at Chelsea with the Lady Catherine Jones." Sloane MS 4244:5.
2. William Parker was Wilkin's cousin. He reissued *A Serious Proposal Parts I and II* and a fourth edition of *Some Reflections Upon Marriage*. The changes in this fourth edition are slight, but since they are the only sample of public writing we have from this period of her life, and show the effects of age and experience, it is worth noting them.

To begin with, the dated references to the duchess of Mazarin are combed out. And the modish Italian phrases which were *de rigueur* for ladies of quality thirty years before are translated and abbreviated (see pp. 8, 44, and 66 of the 1700 edition). There is also a somewhat different focus in the sections added at the beginning and end of the 1730 edition, emphasizing more the evils of extramarital "gallantry" than of tyrannizing husbands. She had seen more of the fashionable world by that time, and had come to a different assessment of the dangers it held for women. Divorce apparently seems more of a possibility to Astell by 1730, too, for she remarks that "the laws of God and Man allow Divorces in certain cases." As she said at the end of the 1730 edition:

> When I made these Reflections, I was of Opinion, that the Case of married Women, in comparison of that of their Husbands, was not a little hard and unequal. But as the World now goes, I am apt to think, that a Husband is in no desirable Situation; his Honour is in his Wife's keeping, and what Man of Honour can be satisfied with the Conduct which the Licentiousness

of the Age not only permits, but would endeavour to authorize as a Part of good Breeding?

3. Swift wrote:

> By these embroidered high Heel Shoes
> She shall be caught as in a Noose;
> So well contriv'd her Toes to pinch,
> She'll not have Pow'r to stir an Inch.

These are lines 63–66 from "The Revolution at Market-Hill" (1730) in *Swift's Poetical Works*, ed. Herbert Davis (London: Oxford University Press, 1967), 449–52. Swift himself counted 5,748 steps into town from Chelsea—over two miles. Jonathan Swift, *Journal to Stella*, ed. Harold Williams, 2 vols. (Oxford: Clarendon Press, 1948), 1: 270.

4. Descriptions of women's dress from the time of William III can be found in Frederick William Fairholt, *Costume in England: A History of Dress*, 4th ed. 2 vols. (London: G. Bell & Sons, 1896), 1:349–59, 370–73; C. Willett Cunnington and Phillis Cunnington, *Handbook of English Costume in the Eighteenth Century*, describe women's dress between 1700 and 1750, pp. 106–79; and John Ashton gives the particulars of fashion in the reign of Queen Anne in *Social Life in the Reign of Queen Anne* (London: Chatto & Windus, 1911), 123–40. Although it is unlikely that Astell wore an enormous hoop any more than she indulged in the frippery of towering coiffures, patches on her face, fans or ribbons, powder or paint, she was class-conscious enough to want to be presentable, and the congregation of St. Martin's would have been dressed in the latest fashions.

Women who dressed their hair at all in Astell's day must have also found it hard to sleep, for, from the late seventeenth century until the end of Queen Anne's reign, the stylish coiffure was the tower—in which the front hair was frizzed or built up high on pads, as if to support an edifice of tiers of lace and ribbon perched on top of the head. These structures, made from the wire, cardboard, and padding sold by the "tire women" in booths and stalls along the Strand, rose to their greatest heights at the turn of the century when they could add as much as a foot to a woman's height. Towers, or commodes, were retrospectively ridiculed by Addison in *The Spectator*, no. 98, who objected to "Women who are taller than myself," and admired them "much more in their present Humiliation, which has reduced them to their natural Dimensions, than when they had extended their Persons, and lengthened themselves into formidable and gigantick Figures." The hair at the back of the head, behind the commode, was coiled in a bun, with the exception of a few artful curls left free at the nape of the neck, the "shining Ringlets" immortalized by Pope in *The Rape of the Lock*.

5. Jonathan Swift's *A Description of a City Shower*, which first appeared in *Tatler*, no. 238 (October 17, 1710), eloquently describes the hazards of walking in London during the rain.

6. The building was James Gibbs's widely acclaimed architectural triumph, rebuilt with much fanfare and costing the parishioners £33,000. Begun in 1721 and completed in 1726, each stage of the process was hailed as an important cultural event. A squib in *The Weekly Journal* of December 19, 1724, gives some sense of the civic excitement generated by the project:

> Last Monday was finish'd the Steeple of the new Church of St. Martin in the Fields, when the Vane, and other Ornaments of copper gilt were put upon it. The Steeple is 215 Foot high being a most beautiful Design, and an exquisite Piece of Workmanship; and the Church and Steeple are look'd upon to be the handsomest in England.

7. Zachary Pearce, *A Review of the Text of Milton's "Paradise Lost" in which the chief of Dr. Bentley's Emendations are considered* (1732). Pope refers to Bentley's *Emendations* (1731) in *The Dunciad*, bk. 4, ll. 211–14:

> Thy mighty Scholiast, whose unweary'd pains
> Made Horace dull, and humbled Milton's strains.
> Turn what they will to Verse, their toil is vain,
> Critics like me shall make it Prose again.

Bentley had "corrected" *Paradise Lost*, suggesting that the poem was published not as Milton intended it, but full of the inevitable errors of a blind author unable to check his own proof sheets.

His defense of Church of England doctrine can be found in *Miracles of Jesus Vindicated Containing Proofs of Jesus' Resurrection and Objections to it Answered* (1729) and *An Answer to the Letter to Dr. Waterland* (1731).

In his account of his life, he states that he organized a group of scholars who met at his house every week for years, to discuss learned and sacred subjects. He sugggested, as a group project, that each undertake to explain and illustrate one of St. Paul's epistles. His own translation and paraphrase of the First Epistle to the Corinthians was the first (and only) step in this project. See "The Life of the Author," prefixed to *A Commentary, with Notes, on the four Evangelists and the Acts of the Apostles*, 2 vols. (London, 1777), 1:xxxvi.

8. Boswell's *Life of Johnson*, ed. George Birbeck Hill and revised and enlarged by L. F. Powell, 6 vols. (Oxford: Clarendon Press, 1934), 1:292.

9. Zachary Pearce, "The Life of the Author," prefixed to *A Commentary, with Notes, on the four Evangelists*, 1:xliii-xliv.

10. Ibid., xxxii.

11. H. J. G. Bloom, W. W. Richardson, and E. J. Harries, "Natural History of Untreated Breast Cancer (1805–1933): Comparison of Untreated and Treated Cases according to Historical Grade of Malignancy," *British Medical Journal*

5299 (1962): 213. I am grateful to Dr. Peter Lang for bringing this article to my attention and for discussing the medical probabilities of Mary Astell's case with me.

12. Laurence Heister, *A General System of Surgery*, 2 vols. (London, 1743), 1:229.

13. In the annals of Durham, where he lived and practiced, numerous cases are recorded in which he acted with dispatch and skill. See the references to Dr. Johnson and his family in the diary of Thomas Gyll, 1748–78, in John Crawford Hodgson, ed., *Six North Country Diaries*, Publication of the Surtees Society, vol. 118 (Durham: Andrews, 1910), 191, 210–11.

14. William Hutchinson, *The History and Antiquities of the County Palatine of Durham*, 3 vols. (Newcastle, 1785), 2:208. Memorial inscriptions for Dr. Johnson and his family are printed in this work, 3:155. I wish to thank Margaret McCollum of the Department of Palaeography and Diplomatic at the University of Durham for these and other references to Dr. Johnson's career.

15. Zachary Pearce, "The Life of the Author," prefixed to *A Commentary, with Notes, on the four Evangelists*, 1:xliii-xliv. It was common knowledge that many appealed to Charlotte Clayton (later Lady Sundon) to intercede for them with Caroline. See Lewis Melville, *Maids of Honour* (London: Hutchinson, 1927), 122; and Katherine Thomson, *Memoirs of Viscountess Sundon*, 2 vols. (London: Henry Colburn, 1847), passim. The story is told of Lady Pomfret that she gave Charlotte Clayton diamond earrings worth £1,400 when her husband, Lord Pomfret, was made Master of the Horse. As Katherine Thomson recounts the anecdote, Mrs. Clayton wore them on one occasion when visiting the duchess of Marlborough. After she left, the duchess turned to another guest, Lady Mary Wortley Montagu, and exclaimed: "How can the woman have the impudence to go about in that bribe?" Lady Mary replied: "Madam, how can people know where the wine is to be sold, unless there is a sign hung out?" Katherine Thomson, *Memoirs of Viscountess Sundon*, 1:116.

16. Katherine Thomson, *Memoirs of Viscountess Sundon*, 1:26.

17. My thanks to G. H. H. Wheler, the present-day descendant of Lady Elizabeth Hastings, who copied out several letters for me from his private collection, including these from Mary Greene.

18. George Ballard, *Memoirs of Several Ladies of Great Britain* (Oxford, 1752), 459.

19. *The Journals and Letters of Fanny Burney* (Madame D'Arblay), ed. Joyce Hemlow, 10 vols. (Oxford: Clarendon Press, 1975), 6:550–631.

20. Laurence Heister, *A General System of Surgery*, 2:14; Henry Fearon, *A Treatise on Cancers, with a New and Successful Method of Operating, particularly in Cancers of the Breast and Testis*, 3d ed. (London: J. Johnson, 1790), Preface.

21. See Lady Elizabeth Hastings' letter to Bishop Wilson about Mary Astell's death, in John Keble, *The Life of Bishop Wilson*, 2 vols. (Oxford: Oxford University Press, 1863), 2:850.

22. John Nichols, *Illustrations of the Literary History of the Eighteenth Century*, 8 vols. (London, 1817–58), 1:478.

23. *The Letters and Works of Lady Mary Wortley Montagu*, ed. Lord Wharncliffe, 3 vols. (London: Richard Bentley, 1837), 1:52.

24. George Ballard, *Memoirs of Several Ladies of Great Britain*, 459–60.

25. John Keble, *The Life of Bishop Wilson*, 2:849–50.

26. See *The General Evening Post* of January 29, 1743.

27. This story is told in my article "George Ballard's Biographies of Learned Ladies" (see above, n. 31 of chap. 4) and in the Introduction to my edition of George Ballard's *Memoirs*, Wayne State University Press, 1985.

28. Elizabeth Elstob refers to this incident in a letter to Ballard. See above, n. 37 of chap. 9.

29. See my Introduction to the Wayne State University Press edition, 1985.

30. George Ballard, *Memoirs of Several Ladies of Great Britain*, 1752, Preface.

31. Robert Halsband, *The Life of Lady Mary Wortley Montagu* (Oxford: Clarendon Press, 1956), 117.

32. Moira Ferguson, *First Feminists* (Bloomington: Indiana University Press and Old Westbury, N.Y.: Feminist Press, 1985), 180.

33. Carolyn Heilbrun, *Reinventing Womanhood* (New York: W. W. Norton, 1979), 211.

34. Mary Astell, *A Serious Proposal To The Ladies*, 8, 32, 14.

35. Ibid., 128–29.

36. See the end of Book 1, "Of the Understanding," in David Hume, *A Treatise of Human Nature*, 3 vols. (London, 1739–40).

37. For Astell's influence on Richardson, see above, chap. 4, n. 8. Defoe had his Roxana argue that a woman who married was no better than "*an Upper-Servant*," which is Astell's phrase from *Some Reflections Upon Marriage*, and that the marriage contract made women slaves to their husbands. See the new edition of the original 1724 issue of Defoe's *Roxana*, ed. David Blewett (Middlesex, Eng.: Penguin, 1982), 187.

38. See chap. 2, "The Economic Status of Women," in my *Women, Letters, and the Novel* (New York: AMS Publishers, 1980).

39. For a discussion of later feminists such as Elizabeth Carter, Catherine Macauley, and Charlotte Charke, see the Introduction to Moira Ferguson's *First Feminists*.

Index

Royal Hospital of Chelsea, 240–41,
243, 246–47, 257, 297; and
Chelsea charity school, 231, 233,
239–40; and Ranelagh gardens,
246, 294
Rules for the Direction of the Mind
(René Descartes), 86
Rural retirement: Astell and, 127–28,
131, 305; political meaning of,
125; women and, 126–28

Sacheverell, Henry (clergyman), 183,
185–86, 191, 205–7, 216
St. John's Church, Newcastle, 33–34,
40, 46, 236
St. Martin's-in-the-Fields Church,
315–16
St. Nicholas Church, 40, 44, 53
Sallust, 303
Saltero, Don (Chelsea coffeehouse),
291–92, 294
Sancroft, William (archbishop of
Canterbury), 23, 66, 68–69, 101,
141, 208
Savile, George. *See* Halifax, first
marquis of
*Saxon Homily on the Birthday of St.
Gregory, A* (Elizabeth Elstob),
110
Schurman, Anna Van. *See* Van
Schurman, Anna
Scott, Sarah, 112
Scudéry, Madelaine de, 110, 118
Serious Call, A (William Law), 125,
254
Shadwell, Thomas, 142, 290
Shaftesbury, third earl of, 8, 179, 202,
221–31, 283, 290; Astell on, 221–
28; *Characteristics* (1711), 221;
Letter Concerning Enthusiasm
(1708), 179, 221–24
Sharp, John (archbishop of York),
101
Shortest Way with the Dissenters, The
(Daniel Defoe), 191–92, 204–5

*Sincerity of the Dissenters Vindicated
From the Scandal of Occasional
Conformity, The* (Daniel Defoe),
203
Sir Charles Grandison (Samuel
Richardson), 100
Slave trade, 8, 253–54, 257, 531 n. 69
Sloane, Sir Hans, 23, 291, 302, 320;
Astell negotiates land with, 310;
collection of curiosities of, 257,
294, 303, 529 n. 30
Smalridge, George (bishop of
Bristol), 119, 218–20, 312
Smith, Florence, 26
Smith, Frances. *See* Elstob, Elizabeth
Smith, Hilda, 17
Smith, John, 126
Snitfield, 247, 252
Society for the Propagation of
Christian Knowledge. *See* SPCK
Socinianism: Astell on, 194; in
Locke, 94, 187
Somers, Lord John, 186, 221, 224
Somerset, Lady Ann. *See* Coventry,
Lady Ann
Somerset, Sir Arthur, 247
Somerset, Lady Mary, 253
South Sea Bubble, 257, 286, 305–10;
Astell and, 305, 307–10
Southey, Robert, 494 n. 34
SPCK (Society for the Propagation
of Christian Knowledge), 233–
39, 242, 245, 318
Spectator, The 161
Spenser, Edmund, 48, 304
Sprint, John (minister), 107
Squire, Mr. (Astell's contribution to
Sufferings of the Clergy), 213–14
Steele, Sir Richard: Astell finds too
worldly, 161; on charity school
movement, 234; and Chelsea,
283, 286, 290–91, 527 n. 1;
plagiarized from Astell, 100;
satirized Astell, 229–30, 516
n. 81; Whig, 224–25